MERGER CONTROL IN IRELAND

An economic appraisal

Patrick Massey

OAK TREE PRESS

Published by Oak Tree Press, Cork T12 XY2N, Ireland.
www.oaktreepress.com / www.SuccessStore.com

A catalogue record for this book is available from the British Library.

ISBN 978-1-78119-648-9 Hardback
ISBN 978-1-78119-649-6 PDF
ISBN 978-1-78119-650-2 ePub

For EU product safety concerns, please contact Oak Tree Press at NSC Campus, Mahon, Cork T12 XY2N, Ireland or info@oaktreepress.com.

CONTENTS

TABLES

FIGURES

ABBREVIATIONS

1997MDN	EU Commission Market Definition Notice 1997
2024MDN	EU Commission Market Definition Notice 2024
ACCC	Australian Competition & Consumer Commission
ATPC	Australian Trade Practices Commission
AWG	Avonmore Waterford Group
B&C	Beamish & Crawford
BKA	*Bundeskartellamt*
C&D	construction and demolition (waste)
C&I	commercial and industrial (waste)
CA	Competition Authority
CAMG2002	Competition Authority *Merger Guidelines*, 2002
CAMG2013	Competition Authority *Merger Guidelines*, 2013
CCE	Chief Competition Economist (EU Commission)
CCPC	Competition & Consumer Protection Commission
CCPCMG2014	Competition & Consumer Protection Commission *Merger Guidelines*, 2014
CET	Chief Economist's team (EU Commission)
CIFSA (2008)	*Credit Institutions (Financial Support) Act, 2008*
CJEU	Court of Justice of the European Union (formerly the European Court of Justice)
CMB	common management and branding
CMRG	Competition & Mergers Review Group.
Co/Co	Company-owned/Company-operated (filling stations)

CR3	three-firm concentration ratio
CR4	four-firm concentration ratio
CSO	Central Statistics Office
DCC	Dublin City Council
Do/Do	Dealer-owned/Dealer-operated (filling stations)
ECJ	European Court of Justice
ECMR	*European Community Merger Regulation*
ECSCT	*European Coal & Steel Community Treaty*
EPA	Environmental Protection Agency
EPS	expanded polystyrene (insulation)
EUHMG	*EU Horizontal Merger Guidelines*
EUNHMG	*EU Non-Horizontal Merger Guidelines*
FAPL	Football Association Premier League
FCC	Fingal County Council
FRAND	fair, reasonable and non-discriminatory
FTA	Free to air (TV broadcast)
FTC	Fair Trade Commission
GAFAM	Google, Amazon, Facebook, Apple and Microsoft
GDA	Greater Dublin area
GUPPI	gross upward pricing pressure index
HHI	Herfindahl-Hirschman Index
IAG	International Consolidated Airlines Group S.A.
ICN	International Competition Network
ICPAC	International Competition Policy Advisory Committee
Impala	Independent Music Publishers & Labels Association
IPA	Isopropanol
IRS	Independent Radio Sales
IT	information technology
JV	joint venture
LBO	licensed betting office

LSE	London School of Economics
MDF	medium density fibreboard
MDN	*Market Definition Notice*
MES	manufacturing execution software (*Applied Materials/Brooks Software)*
MES	minimum efficient scale
MIPS	mobile instant payment services
MJG	MJ Gleeson Group
MoU	memorandum of understanding
MVNO	mobile virtual network operator
MVS	minimum viable scale
NAB	non-alcoholic beverage
NBFI	non-bank financial institution
NGFI	non-grain feed ingredients
NIM	net interest margin
NPCM	non-poultry cooked meats
NTA	National Transport Authority
NZCC	New Zealand Commerce Commission
ODTR	Office of the Director of Telecommunications Regulation
OECD	Organisation for Economic Cooperation & Development
OPL	on-premises laundry
OSB	oriented strand board
P2B	person-to-business (payments services)
P2P	peer-to-peer (payments services)
PCM	poultry cooked meats
PIR	polyisocyanurate (insulation)
POHPP	pharmacy-only human pharmaceutical product
PU	polyurethane (insulation)
R&D	research and development
RFI	Request for Information.

RPC	Restrictive Practices Commission
SDCC	South Dublin County Council
SEPA	Single European Payments Area
SIEC	substantial impediment to effective competition
SLC	substantial lessening of competition
SME	small/medium-sized enterprise
SMNP	simplified merger notification procedure
SSNIP	small significant non-transitory increase in price
TFEU	*Treaty for the Functioning of the European Union*
TSO	transmission system operator
UFBP	Ulster Farm By-Products
UKCAT	Competition Appeals Tribunal (UK)
UKCC	Competition Commission (UK)
UKCMA	Competition & Markets Authority (UK)
UKDBIS	Department for Business, Innovation & Skills (UK)
UKMG	UK *Merger Guidelines*
UKMMC	Monopolies & Mergers Commission (UK)
UKOFT	Office of Fair Trading (UK)
UPP	upward pricing pressure
URC	United Rugby Championship
USDoJ	United States Department of Justice
USFCC	United States Federal Communications Commission
USFTC	United States Federal Trade Commission
USHMG	United States *Horizontal Merger Guidelines* (various years)
USICC	United States Interstate Commerce Commission
USNHMG	United States *Non-Horizontal Merger Guidelines*
USSTB	United States Surface Transportation Board
WFI	Werden-Froeb Index

ACKNOWLEDGEMENTS

It is fair to say that when I was an undergraduate student in the late 1970s, competition was not a public policy priority in Ireland. The 1960s had witnessed a massive level of consolidation in Irish industry resulting in the creation of large dominant undertakings, reflecting a view that Ireland needed to develop "national champions" to compete in international markets. Many key economic sectors were the preserve of State monopolies. There were lengthy waiting lists for telephones and air travel, even to Britain, was an expensive luxury. The Government even attempted to introduce legislation to prohibit cheap air fares. One bright spot was the passage of Ireland's first merger control legislation, the *Mergers, Takeovers & Monopolies (Control) Act, 1978.* In this regard, Ireland was somewhat ahead of the curve as relatively few countries had merger control legislation at that time.

My interest in competition was initially sparked by Trinity's Sean Barrett, a tireless competition advocate, particularly in sectors such as transport. 1984 saw the launch of Ryanair, operating a single aircraft between Waterford and London-Gatwick. Working at DKM with Robbie Kelleher and Colm McCarthy during the 1980s, I was involved in several projects which highlighted regulatory restrictions on competition. I then spent two years working at the New Zealand Treasury, at a time when that country was undergoing major economic reforms, which further fuelled my interest in competition policy.

I served almost 12 years as a member of the Competition Authority and its predecessor, the Fair Trade Commission. This period saw the first steps toward the introduction of a modern competition law regime in Ireland. I certainly benefited from working with some excellent colleagues at the Authority. During that time, I also regularly attended meetings of the OECD Competition Law & Policy Committee and learned a lot through participating in its discussions. Since establishing Compecon in 2001, I have advised on numerous merger cases. For several years, I also lectured on a Master's programme on the economics of competition and regulation at Maynooth University where Gerry Boyle, as then head of the Economics Department, did sterling work promoting the programme and recruiting students. All of this has helped greatly in terms of writing this book.

The book has also benefitted from helpful comments by several individuals, and I am grateful for the time they took to read drafts and provide comments. I am particularly grateful to Moore McDowell, who I have worked both with and against on various occasions, and to John Considine, both of whom read the entire text. Special thanks are also due to John Meade and Oliver Budzinski who read and commented on various chapters.

Thanks also to Brian O'Kane for his meticulous editing and the rest of the team at Oak Tree Press for helping to bring this book to fruition. Although it has been 20 years since I previously worked with Brian, when I first approached him about this book, he was immediately enthusiastic.

Finally special thanks to my wife Anne for her patience and encouragement without which it would not have been possible.

PREFACE

When I originally contemplated this book, several years ago now, I envisaged it as a case book that would review key Irish merger cases. Despite my good intentions, however, I never seemed to find the time to progress it. However, when eventually I resolved to make a more determined effort to complete the project, the nature of the book had changed significantly compared to what I originally had in mind. The vast number of merger cases decided by the Competition Authority (CA) and its successor, the Competition & Consumer Protection Commission (CCPC), suggested that a more comprehensive work was required.

While the main scope of the book is to focus on merger control in Ireland, any assessment of the merger control regime has to consider the regime in a wider context. How does it compare with other countries? In particular, is the analytical approach consistent with best practice elsewhere?

In addition, not all Irish merger cases are decided by the CA/CCPC. The *EC Merger Regulation* (ECMR) grants exclusive competence to investigate mergers involving firms above a certain size to the EU Commission. In fairness, not that many Irish mergers come within the scope of the ECMR but those that do are likely to have significant implications for Irish consumers. The proposed *Ryanair/Aer Lingus* merger, for example, had implications for everyone in this country who travels abroad by plane, as well as for the nation's tourism industry and Irish business generally. Thus, any review of merger control in Ireland ought to recognise the importance of such cases.

Many mergers that fell below the ECMR thresholds were reviewed independently by both the Irish and UK competition authorities under their own domestic legislation. It is therefore worth comparing the approach and outcomes in such cases in both jurisdictions. It is also worth acknowledging that, following the EU prohibition of the *Ryanair/Aer Lingus* merger, it was the UK competition agencies rather than the CA/CCPC who took action to compel Ryanair to relinquish its significant minority shareholding in its rival on the grounds that it was anti-competitive. Any anti-competitive effects arising from this shareholding only affected British consumers wishing to travel to Ireland, whereas they affected virtually everyone in Ireland who travels abroad by air. One of the many effects of Brexit is that some mergers, which might previously have come within the scope of the ECMR, such as *Ryanair/Aer Lingus,* in future will have to be addressed at national level. Brexit also means that mergers coming within the scope of the ECMR will also be subject to review under UK merger legislation, raising the potential for the EU and UK to reach different conclusions.

I served as a member of the Competition Authority for 10 years and, for a short period before that, as a member of its predecessor, the Fair Trade Commission. Since establishing Compecon in 2001, I have acted as an expert economist advising on a large number of merger cases, including the only High Court Appeal of a CA merger decision. This book, however, is based on information contained in published CA/CCPC decisions and information that is otherwise in the public domain.

The *Competition Act, 2002,* heralded a major reform of merger control in Ireland by de-politicising merger decisions and transferring responsibility for them to an independent agency, something which the present author had long advocated for, even if some viewed it as empire building. There has been little detailed analysis of the operation of the merger control regime established under the 2002 Act. Such analysis is important. We need to know if the system is working and whether it can be improved. No merger regulator will get every decision right. However, it is important to review historic case outcomes, to identify potential errors and to learn from them in order to avoid repeating them in the future. Hopefully, this book can make some modest contribution in that regard.

Patrick Massey
April 2025

1: INTRODUCTION

Background

The *Competition Act, 2002,* heralded a radical overhaul of Ireland's merger control regime. Merger controls were first introduced in 1978 but the need for reform was highlighted in the *Report of the Competition & Mergers Review Group* (CMRG, 2000). The 2002 Act introduced three key changes to the merger control regime. First, it de-politicised the merger review process by transferring responsibility for decisions from Ministers to an independent regulatory agency. Second, it provided that mergers should be assessed solely on the basis of their impact on competition. Third, in doing so, it placed economics at the heart of Ireland's merger control regime (Massey, 2002). Although more than 20 years have passed since these radical changes were introduced, there has been relatively little analysis to date of their impact. This book seeks to address this by providing an economic appraisal of merger control in Ireland since 2002, based on an analysis of several hundred merger decisions over that period.

Mergers and takeovers are an essential element of a market economy. Mergers can occur for a variety of legitimate reasons. The economic case for merger controls is based, however, on a recognition that some mergers may increase market power, reduce competition, and enable firms to raise price and/or reduce output.

> *"The substitutability between mergers and cartels as alternative means of securing market power explains the strength of the American merger boom of 1899-1900 in comparison to the British. In the United States the anti-trust legislation of 1890 made cartel agreements more difficult and therefore encouraged mergers" (Wiedenfeld, 1927).*

Kwoka & White (2004) report that between 1887 and 1904 mergers created more than 60 monopoly or dominant firms in the US. Bergman *et al.* (2005) found that the stock market considered 75% of mergers prohibited under the *EC Merger Regulation* (ECMR)[1] to be anti-competitive, based on an analysis of share price movements following the announcement of those mergers.

Merger controls thus recognise that it may be preferable to prevent the acquisition of market power, because it can frequently prove difficult to control the exercise of such power once it has been acquired. Merger control has been described as the third element, along with laws prohibiting anti-competitive agreements and abuse of market power, in the modern triad which constitutes *"the universal model for competition laws around the world"* (Hawk, 2020, p.102).

Merger control is largely but not exclusively concerned with transactions which combine two previously independent firms under common control. Joint ventures may raise similar competition issues to those posed by mergers and the economic analysis of the effects of joint ventures is not hugely different to that of mergers (Motta, 2004). Minority shareholdings in competitors may also raise competition concerns because they can affect the parties' incentives to compete with one another and/or may be a mechanism to block attempted acquisitions by rivals.

Merger Control – A Brief History

The origins of modern competition law can be traced back to the passage of the US *Sherman Act* in 1890 (Hawk, 2020). While the Act contained no specific provisions in relation to mergers, in 1904 the Supreme Court ruled in *Northern Securities*[2] that mergers that created or strengthened a dominant position violated §2 of the *Sherman Act*.[3] The *Clayton Act* and the *Federal Trade Commission Act, 1914,* were introduced due to growing Congress concerns about the courts' subsequent narrow interpretation of the *Sherman Act* (Kovacic & Shapiro, 2000). §7 of the *Clayton Act* prohibited any company

1 *Regulation (EEC) No. 4064/89* of 21 December 1989 on the control of concentrations between undertakings. OJ 1989, L395/1.

2 *United States v. Northern Securities Co. et al.,* 193 US 197 (1904). In an earlier *Sherman Act* case the Court had permitted a series of mergers which enabled the Sugar Trust to acquire control of 98% of US sugar refining capacity, ruling that the trust's manufacturing operations did not constitute interstate commerce and were thus not subject to the provisions of the *Sherman Act*. *United States v. E.C. Knight Co.* 156 U.S. 1 (1895).

3 §2 of the *Sherman Act* prohibits *"monopolisation"* whereas Irish and EU competition and merger legislation refer to a dominant position.

from acquiring the stock of another *"where the effect of such acquisition may be to substantially lessen competition"*. An unintended loophole, however, meant that this prohibition only applied to the acquisition of stocks or shares in another company. Companies could circumvent the prohibition on anti-competitive mergers by acquiring another company's assets (Kwoka & White, 1999). Merger control suffered a further setback when the Supreme Court ruled in *Eastman Kodak*[4] that the US Federal Trade Commission (USFTC) did not have the power, under the *Clayton Act*, to order divestments in order to reverse anti-competitive acquisitions. This judgement proved to be a serious setback and held back merger enforcement by the USFTC until the late 1960s (Kovacic & Shapiro, 2000).

Concerns about growing industry concentration prompted Congress to enact the *Cellar-Kefauver Act* in 1950 (Hawk, 2020). This Act closed the loophole in relation to asset acquisitions in §7 of the *Clayton Act* and prohibited mergers where *"the effect of such acquisition may be to substantially lessen competition or tend to create a monopoly"*. This permitted the prohibition of mergers that fell short of establishing a dominant position and introduced what became known as the incipiency standard in merger control (Kovacic & Shapiro, 2000). The legislation resulted in mergers involving firms with combined market shares as low as 5% being declared illegal (see below). The *Hart-Scott-Rodino Act, 1976*, introduced a system of *ex ante* merger control (see **Chapter 4**) by requiring that mergers involving firms above a certain size had to be notified to the federal anti-trust agencies before they could be put into effect.

Until the latter half of the 20th century, few countries outside of the United States had merger control legislation. Canada first introduced merger legislation in 1910,[5] but despite several amendments the legislation proved largely ineffective due to a combination of a public interest test, a criminal burden of proof and provincial courts (Trebilcock & Iacobucci, 2002). The Courts ruled that a substantial lessening of competition did not constitute a public detriment (Green, 1993). The Government was required to prove the existence of a near monopoly in order to win a merger case. Not surprisingly, the Canadian Government never won a contested merger case prior to 1986, when Parliament enacted a new *Competition Act* that included specific merger control provisions (*ibid*).

---

4 *Federal Trade Commission v. Eastman Kodak Co.*, 274 US 619 (1927).

5 *Combines Investigation Act, 1910.*

In the UK, the *Monopolies & Mergers Act, 1965* brought mergers within the scope of matters which the Secretary of State could refer for investigation to the renamed Monopolies & Mergers Commission (UKMMC). The change followed increased calls for the introduction of merger controls, largely in response to an attempted takeover of Courtaulds by ICI (Scott, 2009). The UKMMC was required to advise the Secretary of State on whether a merger referred to it was likely to operate in the public interest. If a merger was found to be contrary to the public interest, it was then up to the Secretary of State to decide whether any action was required. According to Weir (1993), the UK legislation contained an in-built pro-merger bias, as the parties only needed to show that the merger was unlikely to be against the public interest.

West Germany, as it then was, decided against introducing merger controls when it introduced its competition legislation in 1957 (Weitbrecht, 2008). Merger control legislation was introduced in West Germany in 1973 and in France in 1977.

Merger Control in Ireland

Merger controls were first introduced in Ireland with the passage of the *Mergers, Takeovers & Monopolies (Control) Act, 1978*. Only three EU Member States – France, West Germany, and the UK – had legislation regulating mergers at that time.[6] The merger control regime introduced under the 1978 Act, however, suffered from several serious shortcomings (CMRG, 2000).[7] In particular, the regime lacked clarity and transparency (Massey & Daly, 2003; Massey, 2010).

The *Competition Act, 2002*, radically altered merger control in Ireland. The Act de-politicised merger control by transferring responsibility for merger review from the Minister for Enterprise, Trade & Employment to an independent agency, the Competition Authority (CA).[8] The 2002 Act also replaced the public interest test, first introduced in the 1978 Act and retained in subsequent amendments, by providing that mergers should be

---

6 Belke & Braun (1979) claim that France, West Germany and the UK were the only EU Member States with specific merger control laws at that time, overlooking Ireland's 1978 Act.

7 See **Chapter 2**.

8 In 2014 the CA merged with the National Consumer Agency to form the Competition & Consumer Protection Commission (CCPC).

assessed solely on the basis of their impact on competition.[9] In so doing, the 2002 Act placed economics at the centre of Ireland's merger control regime (Massey, 2002, 2010).

The switch to an economics-based approach to merger review in Ireland was in line with a wider international trend. While merger control in the United States can be traced back to the passage of the *Sherman Act* in 1890, economics played a relatively limited role over the following 80 years. The shift to a more economics-based approach to merger assessment in the United States began in the 1980s and gained momentum over the following two decades. Similarly, the 2004 reform of the ECMR, originally introduced in 1990, ushered in a more economics-based approach to merger analysis and the application of the EU Treaty rules on anti-competitive behaviour. Affeldt *et al.* (2019) describe mergers as the area of competition law where the largest consensus on best practice exists.

The *EC Merger Regulation*

The EU's competition rules were originally contained in Articles 85 and 86 of the *Treaty of Rome*, now Articles 101 and 102 of the *Treaty for the Functioning of the European Union* (TFEU). The Rome Treaty contained no specific provisions dealing with mergers, in contrast to its forerunner, the *European Coal & Steel Community Treaty* (ECSCT) (Whish, 2003). Weitbrecht (2008) attributes the lack of any merger control provisions in the *Treaty of Rome* to German influence. As previously noted, West Germany, which was in the process of enacting its own national competition legislation at the time the *Treaty of Rome* was being drafted, had concluded that there was no need to include any substantive merger control provisions in its legislation.

In the early 1960s, it was unclear whether Articles 85 and 86 applied to mergers (Massey & Daly, 2003). The Court of Justice of the European Union (CJEU)[10] ruled in *Continental Can*[11] that the acquisition by a dominant firm of most of the shares in a potential competitor, constituted an abuse of a dominant position and was therefore prohibited under Article 86, if it would substantially lessen competition. The EU Commission subsequently intervened informally in certain large merger cases and either prevented

9 §9(1)(a) of the 1978 Act provided that the Minister could prohibit a merger or permit it subject to conditions, following an investigation by the Examiner of Restrictive Practices, (The Examiner) *"if he thinks that the exigencies of the common good so warrant"*.

10 Previously known as the European Court of Justice (ECJ)

11 Case No. 6/72, *Europemballage & Continental Can v. Commission* [1973] ECR 215.

them or secured modifications, although it took no formal decisions in such cases (Korah, 2000).

In the summer of 1973, the EU Commission proposed a draft regulation that would have given it power to regulate mergers to the Council of Ministers. Despite repeated amendments, the draft made little progress (*ibid.*). In *Philip Morris*,[12] the CJEU appeared to extend merger control when it ruled that the acquisition of a minority shareholding in a competitor which led to the acquisition of control could infringe Article 85, if the acquisition restricted competition (*ibid.*). The Commission subsequently held that the acquisition by Gillette of an equity interest in a company that owned the competing *Wilkinson Sword* brand infringed Article 85 and ordered Gillette to dispose of its shareholding.[13]

The creation of the EU Single Market increased competition by removing barriers to trade between Member States (George & Jacquemin, 1992). The Single Market, however, also resulted in increased industry consolidation in the EU. This was due, in part, to the fact that, while the number of viable firms increases with market size, the rate of increase is proportionately less, i.e., a doubling in market size will result in a less than doubling in the number of viable undertakings, because prices are driven closer to marginal costs (Sutton, 1991). Mergers, however, also represented a means by which firms could seek to offset the competition increasing effects of the Single Market (George & Jacquemin, 1992). Consequently, an effective merger control regime was generally considered to be important for ensuring that the benefits of economic integration arising from the creation of the Single Market were maximised (Whish, 2003).

Ireland's EU Commissioner Peter Sutherland, who held the competition portfolio at the time, concluded that the Commission would never become the foremost institution for the enforcement of competition law in Europe if it lacked the capacity to control mergers. Following the *Philip Morris* judgement, Sutherland threatened to use Article 85 to control mergers (Weitbrecht, 2008). This prompted a response from the Council of Ministers and resulted in the introduction of the ECMR on 21 December 1989. The ECMR applies to mergers deemed to have a Community dimension. The EU Commission has exclusive competence to adjudicate on mergers that

---

12 Case Nos. 142 and 156/84 *BAT & Reynolds v. Commission* [1987] ECR 4487.

13 Case 93/252 - *Warner-Lambert/Gillette*, OJ [1993] L116/21, 12.5.1993.

come within the scope of the ECMR, and national competition law does not apply to such mergers.[14]

The ECMR originally defined a merger as having a Community dimension where:

i. The merging firms have a combined worldwide turnover greater than €5 billion; and
ii. At least two of the merging firms have an EU-wide turnover greater than €250 million.

This was expanded in 1997 by the addition of an alternative definition:

i. The merging firms have a combined worldwide turnover greater than €2.5 billion, and
ii. The merging firms have a combined turnover greater than €100 million in each of at least three Member States,
iii. With a turnover of more than €25 million for each of at least two of the firms involved in each of the three Member States included under (ii), and
iv. At least two or more participating firms have EU-wide turnover of more than €100 million.[15]

The ECMR does not apply if each of the firms achieves more than two-thirds of its EU-wide turnover within a single Member State.

Following the introduction of the ECMR, many EU Member States introduced their own merger control laws to regulate mergers that fell below the EU thresholds. Today, all EU Member States, with the exception of Luxembourg, have their own national merger control laws.[16]

Figure 1.1 provides information on the annual number of merger notifications under the ECMR since its introduction in 1990. The chart shows that the number of EU merger cases increased sharply from just 11 in 1990. There was a sharp fall in merger notifications post 2007, reflecting the financial crash. In the final quarter of 2008, the value of cancelled

---

14 This is in contrast to the position in the US where clearance of a merger by the Federal authorities does not pre-empt state enforcement under either State or Federal law (Kolasky, 2001). Merger review under the ECMR involves a two-stage process. In the initial stage, referred to as Phase 1, the Commission may either allow the merger to proceed or decide to launch a full investigation, which is referred to as Phase 2.

15 *Regulation (EC) No. 1310/97* of 30 June 1997.

16 https://www.ashurst.com/en/news-and-insights/legal-updates/quickguide-eu-merger-control/. Accessed 11.6.2021.

mergers was almost the same as the value of those completed (Reynolds *et al.*, 2011). Post-2012 numbers increased with 414 notifications in 2018. While there has been some levelling off in recent years, the number of merger notifications remains at historically high levels.

Figure 1.1: EU Merger Notifications by Year, 1990-2024

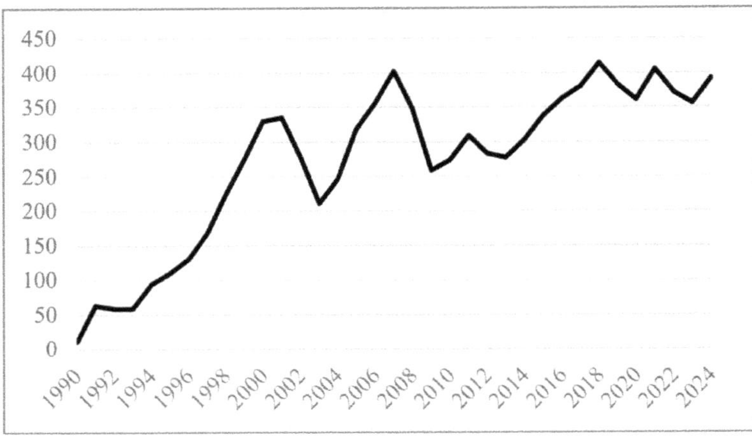

Source: https://competition-policy.ec.europa.eu/mergers/statistics_en. Accessed 19.1.2025.

Only a small number of mergers involving Irish firms satisfy the EU notification thresholds. Consequently, most Irish mergers come within the scope of domestic merger legislation. A question arose at the time of Ryanair's first attempt to acquire its Irish rival Aer Lingus as to whether the proposal came within the scope of the ECMR.[17] The combined worldwide turnover of the merging parties was more than €2.5 billion but less than €5 billion, while they each had an EU-wide turnover of more than €100 million. Whether the merger had a Community dimension depended upon whether Aer Lingus had an aggregate turnover of more than €100 million in at least three Member States and a turnover of more than €25 million in each of those States. The EU Commission argued that, in the case of return ticket bookings, revenues for the return flight leg should be allocated to the country from which the return flight departed, regardless of where the

---

17 *Ryanair* made three attempts to acquire *Aer Lingus*. The first was prohibited by the EU Commission (Case No. COMP/M.4439 – *Ryanair/Aer Lingus I*, 27.6.2007). The second was abandoned after it had been notified to the EU Commission when the Irish Government indicated that it would not support the bid. The third *Ryanair* bid was again blocked by the EU Commission (Case No. COMP/M.6663 – *Ryanair/Aer Lingus III*, 27.2.2013).

ticket booking was made. This had the effect of bringing Aer Lingus' revenue above the €25 million threshold in a third Member State – Spain[18] – and, on that basis, the proposed transaction was deemed to fall within the scope of the ECMR. Interestingly Ryanair had argued that the proposed transaction had a Community dimension, while Aer Lingus took the opposite view suggesting possible *"forum shopping"* by the parties.[19]

Following Brexit, certain mergers involving Irish and UK undertakings, which would previously have come within the scope of the ECMR, may be subject to review in both Ireland and the UK as the latter is no longer an EU Member State. Similarly, mergers which fall within the scope of the ECMR may also be subject to UK merger controls. The UK's Competition & Markets Authority (UKCMA) has taken an extremely expansive approach to merger control post-Brexit, which has been upheld by the Competition Appeals Tribunal (UKCAT).[20] In April 2023 UKCMA prohibited Microsoft's proposed acquisition of Activision Blizzard.[21] Following the UK decision the transaction was cleared, subject to remedies, by the EU Commission.[22] A revised transaction was subsequently cleared by the UKCMA subject to remedies.[23]

Article 4(4) of the ECMR provides that, prior to notifying a merger, the parties may make a reasoned submission to the EU Commission that the proposed transaction *"may significantly affect competition in a market within a Member State which presents all the characteristics of a distinct market and should*

---

18 Aer Lingus also exceeded the thresholds in Ireland and the UK.

19 *Ryanair/Aer Lingus I*, ¶s20 & 21. Although the transaction was found to have a Community dimension the competition issues identified by the EU Commission essentially related to air travel between Ireland and other EU Member States.

20 The UKCAT held that the UKCMA could exercise jurisdiction in cases where one of the parties had no sales in the UK in *Sabre/Farelogix* (Case No. ME/6806/19 – *Sabre/Farelogix*, 9.4.2020; UKCAT Case No. 1345/4/12/20 *Sabre Corporation v. Competition & Markets Authority*, 21.5.2020). The UKCMA argued that the target satisfied the share of supply requirement under UK merger legislation because an interlining arrangement meant that British Airways could use certain services provided by Farelogix to American Airlines. (UK legislation applies to mergers based on either the parties' overall turnover or their share of supply in a particular market.) The UKCMA also asserted jurisdiction in *Roche/Spark*, another case where the target had no UK sales (Case No. ME/6831/19 – *Roche/Spark*, 16.12.2019).

21 UKCMA, ME/6983/22 – *Microsoft/Activision Blizzard I*, 26.4.2023. The UKCMA's CEO later denied that it had blocked the transaction at the behest of the USFTC (*The Guardian*, 2023, May 16). Bon *et al.* (2021) confirm a post-Brexit increase in multi-jurisdictional merger cases being reviewed by the UKCMA.

22 EU Commission Case No. COMP/M.10646 – *Microsoft/Activision Blizzard*, 15.5.2023.

23 UKCMA ME/7068/23 – *Microsoft/Activision Blizzard II (ex. EEA Cloud Streaming Rights)*, 13.10.2023.

therefore be examined, in whole or in part, by that Member State". The EU Commission may refer such a proposed transaction to the relevant national competition authority, *"where it considers that such a distinct market exists, and that competition in that market may be significantly affected"* unless the latter disagrees.[24]

Article 9 of the ECMR provides that the EU Commission may refer a merger coming within the scope of the ECMR back to a national competition authority for decision following a request from such an authority, although such referrals are at the discretion of the Commission. The Commission referred the Irish elements of the 2008 *Heineken/Scottish & Newcastle*[25] case back to the CA for consideration. In Ireland, the transaction involved a merger between Heineken and Beamish & Crawford, two of the three brewers operating in the country at that time. A Member State competition authority may also refer a merger to the EU Commission under Article 22 of the ECMR and the CA/CCPC has done so on two occasions.[26] Article 22 was originally included because several Member States had no domestic merger control legislation at the time the ECMR was introduced. It was designed to ensure that anti-competitive mergers below the EU notification thresholds would not escape scrutiny due to the lack of national controls (Whish, 2003). In 2020 the EU Commission announced that national competition authorities could refer mergers to it, which fell below their own national merger notification thresholds as well as below the EU thresholds, but the CJEU subsequently ruled that the Commission had no jurisdiction to review mergers that were below national notification thresholds.[27]

The Role of Economics

Until the mid-1960s, the United States was effectively the only jurisdiction with an effective merger control regime. Although merger control in the US can be traced back to the 1904 Supreme Court judgement in *Northern Securities*, economics played a relatively limited role in US merger cases, prior to the 1980s. Schmalensee (1987) states that most economists would agree that the policy approach of the US anti-trust agencies and courts was

---

24 Cases referred to the CA/CCPC by the EU Commission under Article 4(4) include CA M/14/008 – *Fitzwilliam/Wittington Canada/Arnotts* 27.5.2014 and CCPC M/15/020 – *Topaz/Esso,* 15.10.2015.

25 EU Commission Case No. COMP/M.4999 – *Heineken/Scottish & Newcastle,* 3.4.2008.

26 CA M/03/004 – *General Electric/Agfa,* 14.4.2003 and CCPC M/21/XX – *Facebook/Kustomer.* The latter had no case number and the CCPC has not published the date of the referral decision.

27 Joined cases C-611/22 P and C-625/22 P *Illumina v. Commission,* ECLI:EU:C:2024:677. This approach was intended to address the issue of *"killer acquisitions"* particularly in areas such as IT and pharmaceuticals reflecting concerns that incumbents were acquiring start-ups which might in time become serious competitors (see **Chapter 8**).

hostile to mergers in the 1960s, while Williamson (2002) describes US anti-trust in the post-World War II era as populist. In the 1960s the US Supreme Court blocked mergers in cases where the merging parties had a combined market share of less than 8% in *Brown Shoe*[28] and *Von's Grocery*.[29] In a dissenting judgement in the latter case, Stewart, J. observed *"...the sole consistency that I can find is that in [merger] litigation under section 7, the Government always wins."* Such judgements are now widely considered unsound (Kauper, 2001). Ginsberg (2010, p.217) baldly stated *"[f]orty years ago the U.S. Supreme Court simply did not know what it was doing in anti-trust cases."* In similar vein, Kovacic & Shapiro (2000, p.51) observe:

> *"Most commentators today share Stewart's gloomy assessment of merger jurisprudence in the 1960s and view the Supreme Court's antipathy toward mergers and doubts about market forces as indefensible."*

Williamson (2002, p.5) describes Donald Turner's appointment as Assistant Attorney General for Antitrust as *"the beginning of what would turn out to be a vast reorientation of anti-trust in which more and better economic reasoning made progressive headway..."*. The idea of publishing merger guidelines had been mooted as far back as the late 1950s (Kaysen & Turner, 1959). The US Department of Justice (USDoJ) published its first *Horizontal Merger Guidelines* (USHMG1968) in 1968 with the express aim of informing *"the business community, the legal profession, and other interested groups and individuals with the standards currently being applied by the DOJ in determining whether to challenge corporate acquisitions and mergers"* (*ibid.*, p.1). While the *Guidelines* were intended to reduce uncertainty, according to Williamson (2002), when the original draft was circulated internally, career staff were relatively unenthusiastic because many of them viewed uncertainty as advantageous because it deterred mergers. The *Guidelines* also brought a halt to the progressive ratcheting down of what were regarded as acceptable levels of post-merger market shares.

Economics distinguishes between two types of mergers;

i. **Horizontal mergers:** Mergers between firms in the same market, *i.e.*, mergers between competitors.
ii. **Non-horizontal mergers:** Including vertical mergers, involving firms at different levels in the production/distribution chain, *e.g.*, a

---

28 *Brown Shoe Co. v. United States*, 370 US 294 (1962).

29 *United States v. Von's Grocery Company et al.*, 384 US 270 (1966).

merger between a firm and its suppliers or distributors, and conglomerate mergers between unrelated firms.

Competition problems tend to arise most frequently in the case of horizontal mergers as they involve a direct reduction in the number of competitors. In contrast non-horizontal mergers do not entail a direct loss of competition and may provide substantial scope for efficiencies. Vertical mergers may create competition concerns, however, if they foreclose rivals' access to essential inputs or customers. Conglomerate mergers are generally considered less likely to pose a threat to competition, although in a small number of cases they may do so.

USHMG1968 emphasised the importance of market structure, reflecting the prevailing views of economists, lawyers, and policy-makers at the time. Markets with a four-firm concentration ratio (CR4)[30] of more than 75% were defined as *"highly concentrated"* and the *Guidelines* provided that a horizontal merger between two firms each of which had a market share of 4% or more would *"ordinarily"* be challenged. The *Guidelines* further provided that such thresholds were conclusive except in *"certain exceptional circumstances"* (Kwoka, 2015). Williamson (2002) describes the thresholds as a compromise and notes that proposing higher market shares would have constituted an admission of error by the anti-trust agencies and the courts in earlier cases.

USHMG1982 were viewed as heralding a shift to a much more economics-based approach to merger analysis, described by Shapiro (2010, p.704), as *"a revolution"*.[31] They introduced the small significant non-transitory increase in price (SSNIP) test for defining markets (see **Chapter 6**). Baker (1997) observed that USHMG1982 highlighted factors facilitating collusion.[32] Shepherd *et al.* (2000, p.864) criticised the *Guidelines'* failure to address the issue of dominance, describing this as *"a puzzling deviation from sound economics"*. Ordover & Willig (1983) welcomed the new *Guidelines* as representing a significant improvement on USHMG1968 but identified important weaknesses with respect to potential entry, firm conduct, and vertical mergers. Shapiro (2010) acknowledges that USHMG1982 were limited in some respects due to their heavy emphasis on coordinated effects

---

30 The CR4 is the sum of the market shares of the four largest firms in a market. See **Chapter 7**.

31 Meese & Stafford (2017) report that an analysis of company stock price data indicates that the stock market regarded USHMG1982 as heralding a significant change in merger policy.

32 Based on an analysis of stock market responses to announcements of mergers and enforcement actions, Eckbo & Wier (1985) claimed that merger enforcement under USHMG1968 and, initially at least, under USHMG1982, targeted harmless mergers, a claim rejected by Schuman (1989).

but claims this was because they were written with relatively homogenous industrial products in mind. The *"leading firm proviso"*[33] was added in 1984 in order to address the issue of single firm dominance.

> *"Because the ease and profitability of collusion are of little relevance to the ability of a single dominant firm to exercise market power" (USHMG1984, §3.12).*

Unilateral effects theories of harm were added in USHMG1992. Unilateral effects recognise that horizontal mergers may enable firms to unilaterally raise prices post-merger, in circumstances where the merged entity could not be considered dominant. In particular, USHMG1992 recognised that, in differentiated product markets, closeness of competition between the merging parties' products affected the potential for post-merger price increases, although the central role of market shares in merger analysis was retained (Valetti & Zenger, 2021). Baker (1997) states that the development of unilateral effects theories was due to a combination of theoretical advances and the potential for greater empirical analysis due to the development of new analytical tools and data availability.[34] Despite this increasingly economics-based approach, Crandall & Winston (2003) argued that US merger policy was primarily undermining efficiency-enhancing mergers, rather than protecting competition. These claims were flatly rejected (see, for example, Baker, 2003; Kwoka, 2003; and Werden, 2003a).

USHMG2010 reduced the focus on market shares and placed closeness of substitution at the heart of unilateral effects-based analysis.

> *"The extent of direct competition between the products sold by the merging parties is central to the evaluation of unilateral price effects" (*ibid., *§6.1).*

USHMG2010 met with a mixed reaction with some welcoming them as representing a significant improvement (Hovenkamp, 2011), while others were critical (Simons & Coate, 2014).

Over time, economics has come to play a significant role in EU merger policy, even if it initially lagged behind the US. The Court of First Instance (now the EU General Court) was highly critical of the quality of the

---

33 This provided that *"the Department is likely to challenge the merger of any firm with a market share of at least one percent with the leading firm in the market, provided the leading firm has a market share that is at least 35 percent."* This provision was dropped in USHMG2010.

34 Similarly, Hosken *et al.* (2002) describe how the combination of increased data availability, reduced cost of computing power and an increased focus on unilateral effects resulted in remarkable developments in quantitative analysis of horizontal mergers.

Commission's economic analysis in a series of judgements overturning several Commission merger decisions around the turn of the century.[35] Motta (2004) argues that these judgements forced the Commission to fully reconsider its merger policy, in particular with respect to unilateral effects.[36] Valetti & Zenger (2021) support the view that these judgements initiated a shift to a more economics-based approach. Lyons (2008) suggests that, while the Court judgements in these cases hastened and sharpened reform of the ECMR, change was already underway. Duso *et al.* (2013) argue that the reform of the ECMR was not the result of these reversals. Weitbrecht (2008, p.85) suggests that the 2004 reform of the ECMR *"injected additional lifeblood into the use of economic analysis, including econometrics."* Neven (2006) reported that economic advice was referred to in about one third of Phase 2 EU merger cases with economists involved in the more important cases, *e.g.*, those involving new issues or large transactions.

Lyons (2008, p.52) described the Commission's merger regime as *"maturing nicely"* but cautions *"there is still work to be done and no room for complacency."* Duso *et al.* (2013) suggest that the overall results of the reforms have been mixed. Bergman *et al.* (2019) note that the likelihood of the Commission challenging a merger declined in unilateral effects cases but increased in coordinated effects cases post-reform. The number of early settlements increased following the reforms which Garrod & Lyons (2016) note is consistent with the reforms providing greater clarity. Affeldt *et al.* (2019) report that the EU Commission shifted from a structural to a more economics-based approach to evaluating mergers following the 2004 reform of the ECMR. Valetti & Zenger (2021) argue that USHMG2010, with their emphasis on economic methods, increased the shift, already underway, to a more economics-oriented approach at the EU Commission, noting that it increasingly applied a more quantitative approach.

> *"Economic analysis plays a central role in competition enforcement. Economics as a discipline provides a framework to think about the way in which each particular market operates and how competitive interactions take place. This framework further allows formulating the possible consequences of the practices under review, whether a merger, an agreement between firms, or single firm conduct" (DG Competition, 2011, November 17).*

---

[35] Case T-342/99, *Airtours v. Commission* (2002) ECR II 2585; Case T-310/01, *Schneider Electric v. Commission,* (2002) II ECR 4071; and Case T-5/02, *Tetra Laval v. Commission,* (2002) II ECR 4381.

[36] The EU Commission tends to use the term non-coordinated rather than unilateral effects.

Is Merger Control Too Lenient?

There has been considerable criticism that merger enforcement in both the EU and US has become too lenient (Duso *et al.*, 2024). Multiple authors have claimed that that merger policy in the US has become too lenient over the past 30 years. It is frequently claimed that this has resulted in higher prices, increased profit margins, a decline in research and innovation, a reduction in labour's share of income and reduced consumer welfare.

Coate *et al.* (1990) found that, in the past, pressure from Congress to block mergers was a statistically significant factor in USFTC decisions to challenge mergers. Adams & Brock (1994, p.236) argued that the 1980s witnessed *"an all out attack on structural anti-trust policy"*. They claim that the Reagan administration sought to effectively repeal the antimerger provisions of the *Clayton Act*, based on a belief that facilitating consolidation would enhance the ability of US business to compete internationally – a *"national champions"* argument. Lande (1994) suggested that the high success rate of the anti-trust agencies in merger cases up to the early 1990s indicated an overly conservative approach to challenging mergers. Lande (2001) notes that there was a significant decline in merger challenges under the Reagan administration.

Kauper (2001) acknowledges that criticisms that anti-trust was impeding the development of internationally competitive US firms led to significant reforms following strong political criticism of the USDoJ for challenging the *LTV/Republic Steel*[37] merger. Ironically, in light of the criticism that the case served as an example of how US anti-trust laws prevented the emergence of internationally competitive firms, the merged entity went bankrupt two years after the merger had been completed (Adams & Brock, 1994).

Baker & Shapiro (2008) also regarded US merger enforcement as overly lax, highlighting a much greater decline in enforcement activity by the USDoJ than by the USFTC.[38] Budzinski (2010) states that US agencies had a poor record in merger cases over the previous 20 years. Shapiro (2019) argues that the government's ability to win merger cases had been significantly reduced over the previous 25 years due to the approach adopted by the courts. The anti-trust agencies became more cautious about

---

37 *United States v. LTV Corp.*, 1984-2 Trade Cases (CCH) 66,133 (D.D.C.)

38 They cite the USDoJ failure to challenge the *Whirlpool/Maytag* merger as a highly visible example of under-enforcement.

challenging mergers as a result, while firms adjusted their approach to mergers in recognition of this.

> *"Remarkably, the treatment of proposed mergers under US anti-trust law has become much more lenient without Congress changing the substantive standard to be used for merger review and without any updated guidance from the Supreme Court, which has not heard a merger case since 1974. Rather, these changes have resulted from a dynamic involving the lower courts, the anti-trust agencies, anti-trust lawyers, and economists" (ibid., p.74).*

Weinberg (2008) reports that several US studies found that the majority of mergers over the previous 22 years which were examined resulted in post-merger price increases by the merging parties and their rivals. Philippon (2019, p.91) observes:

> *"What is undeniable, however, is that mergers have been allowed to proceed at an unprecedented pace, which has significantly contributed to a rise in concentration in the US."*[39]

The evidence indicates that the failure of the anti-trust agencies to successfully challenge mergers permitted a substantial increase in industry consolidation and led to higher prices and lower service quality in airlines and hospitals, for example. (Johnson *et al.*, 1989; Borenstein, 1990; Kim & Singal, 1993; Cooper, 2001; Moss & Mitchell, 2012; Berry *et al.*, 2019).[40] An analysis of over 14,000 mergers that occurred in various countries between 1981 and 1998 found that a majority appeared to be welfare-reducing (Gugler *et al.*, 2003). Baker (2003) cites evidence of US soft drinks mergers leading to price increases ranging from 3.5% to 12.8%. Ashenfelter *et al.* (2014, p.S78) state *"[t]he empirical evidence that mergers can cause economically significant increases in price is overwhelming"*. Kwoka (2015, p.158) concluded that most US mergers *"result in competitive harm, usually in the form of higher prices"*.

---

39 This is disputed by Macher & Mayo (2021) who state that the likelihood of merger challenges by the US anti-trust agencies increased over the period from 1979 to 2017.

40 A study of five post-2000 US domestic airline mergers, however, found evidence of post-merger quality improvements, measured on the basis of on-time performance, which were not driven by price changes (Prince & Simon, 2017). Brot *et al.* (2024) report that, out of more than 1,000 US hospital mergers between 2002 and 2020, 20% could have been predicted to lessen competition using USFTC standard screening tools. The USFTC took enforcement action in only 13 cases. They also state that between 2010 and 2015 predictably anti-competitive mergers resulted in price increases of more than 5%.

Following the *T-Mobile/Sprint* merger, US wireless mobile phone charges increased, having steadily declined for the previous decade (Stucke, 2023).[41]

Shapiro (2019) states that there is clear evidence that profits of US companies have risen in recent decades, indicating increased market power. Empirical research indicates that aggregate mark-ups in the US remained fairly stable between 1955 and 1980 but increased steadily thereafter from 21% in 1980 to 61% in 2016. This increase in markups coincided with an increase in profitability, indicating a rise in market power (De Loecker *et al.*, 2020). Shapiro (2019) cites increased industry concentration and rising price-cost margins and profits as evidence that US merger enforcement had been overly lenient over the previous 25 years. Berry *et al.* (2019) while stating that further research is required, observe that *"higher mark-ups imply a world that may require increased anti-trust vigilance"*. It is estimated that higher prices and lower wages due to a lack of competition was costing the median US household $5,000 *per annum* (US White House, 2021, July 9).

There is considerable evidence, therefore, that increased industrial concentration in the US has resulted in increased prices and profit margins, a decline in labour's share of income and led to reduced investment and innovation. Jean *et al.* (2019) note that before 2000, US markets were more competitive than those in the EU with lower prices and margins. Since the turn of the century this trend has reversed with a sharp increase in US profit margins. Philippon (2019) reaches similar conclusions.

Shapiro & Shelanski (2021) suggest that USHMG2010 signalled a tougher approach to merger control. They point out that changes introduced in USHMG2010 have influenced court judgments, while the anti-trust agencies' success rate in challenging merger before the courts increased from 62% in the decade up to 2010 to 79% over the following 10 years. The Biden administration issued an executive order to promote competition, calling on the Federal anti-trust agencies *"to enforce the anti-trust laws vigorously"* (Stucke, 2023). Shapiro (2024) notes that USHMG2023 ostensibly seek to further tighten US merger control but expresses concerns that they may have the unintended opposite effect. Salinger (2024) also stated that a tightening of merger control was justified to counter the fact

41 The merger was challenged by a group of US states. While acknowledging that that the states had established a *prima facie* case, the judge nevertheless ruled in favour of the merging parties based on claimed efficiencies and a divestment of some assets (Shapiro, C., 2024). (*State of New York v. Deutsche Telecom*, 439 F. Supp 3d 179 (2020)).

that enforcement had allowed increased market concentration in a number of areas but, nonetheless, criticised aspects of the new *Guidelines*.

There have also been calls for a tougher application of anti-trust laws and a stricter application of merger controls to large firms in the US, not on economic grounds, but on the basis that large corporations wield excessive political influence. It is argued that one of the original aims of the *Sherman Act* was to prevent the accretion of political power by large corporations (Lamoreaux, 2019; Khan, 2017 & 2019). Clearly such arguments fall outside the arena of economics.

There is evidence that EU merger policy may also have become too lenient. Neven & Röller (2002) suggested that the Commission blocked too few mergers, while Levy (2010) reported a decline in EU merger challenges in the five years after the 2004 reform of the ECMR. Bergman *et al.* (2019), however, note that the likelihood of mergers being challenged was higher in the EU than in the US over the 1993-2004 period, although they find that EU merger policy became more lenient post-2004. Budzinski (2010) claims that the Commission performed spectacular U-turns in several merger cases, allowing them to pass unchallenged, having earlier issued strong statements of objections referring to severe competition concerns.[42] Duso *et al.* (2013) also conclude that the EU blocks too few mergers. Kotzeva *et al.* (2019) also note that there have been calls for tighter EU merger controls. Affeldt *et al.* (2021, p.27) describe the EU Commission as *"possibly the strictest"* competition authority in the world, although they also suggest that a more restrictive approach to mergers is required. Lancieri & Valetti (2024) have argued that mergers above a certain size should be presumed to be anti-competitive unless the parties can prove that merger-specific efficiencies will be shared with consumers and produce tangible welfare gains.

The EU Commission has also been subject to criticism and political pressure to adopt a more lenient approach to merger control, particularly since its 2019 decision to prohibit the proposed *Siemens/Alstom*[43] merger on the grounds that it would reduce competition on the EU market. Shortly before this decision, 19 Member States called for changes to the competition rules in order to foster *"European Champions"* (Valero, 2019, January 9). Within a fortnight of the decision, the French and German governments issued a joint call for a change in EU industrial policy involving, *inter alia*, a

---

42 He cites as examples Case Nos. COMP/M.3216 – *Oracle/PeopleSoft*, 26.10.2024; COMP/M.3333 – *Sony/BMG*, 3.10.2007; and COMP/M.5440 – *Lufthansa/Austrian Airlines*, 28.8.2009.

43 Case No. COMP/M.8677 – *Siemens/Alstom*, 6.2.2019.

wider appreciation of global competition issues and adapting current merger *Guidelines* accordingly (Kotzeva *et al.*, 2019). Geroski & Jacquemin (1985) observe that industrial policies aimed at promoting national champions in various EU Member States during the 1960s and 1970s failed. Jean *et al.* (2019) reject claims that EU competition policy is overly strict and is hindering the achievement of strategic objectives. Massey & McDowell (2021) also argue against calls for an easing of EU merger control.

Concerns have also emerged in recent years regarding the ability of large firms to acquire entrants in order to eliminate potential competition, so-called "killer acquisitions" (Cunningham *et al.*, 2021). In 2020, the EU Competition Commissioner, Margrethe Vestager, announced that the Commission would accept referrals by Member State competition agencies of mergers below national and EU notification thresholds that had significant anti-competitive potential in pharmaceutical and digital markets under Article 22 of the ECMR in an attempt to tackle this problem (Karlinger *et al.*, 2020).[44]

The Objective of this Book

As previously stated, the objective of this book is to provide an economic appraisal of merger control in Ireland since 2002. Aguzzoni *et al.* (2016) emphasise the importance of reviewing merger case outcomes in order to identify whether there is scope to improve the effectiveness of decision-making. The absence of any systematic evaluation of merger cases handicaps efforts to improve merger policy (Kwoka, 2015). Stöhr (2024) points out that analysing merger cases and identifying potential errors is crucial for improving merger decisions.

From an economics perspective, an assessment of the effectiveness of the merger control regime needs to consider, in particular, whether it:

- Leads to correct decisions, preventing anti-competitive mergers while permitting mergers that are not anti-competitive;
- Provides an effective deterrent to anti-competitive mergers;
- Deals with harmless mergers speedily while also minimising regulatory costs for business;
- Delivers positive benefits for consumers.

---

44 As previously noted, the CJEU ruled that the Commission did not have the power to review such mergers. The issue of killer acquisitions is considered further in **Chapter 3**.

The objective of merger control is to prevent mergers that are likely to prove anti-competitive. Consequently, any assessment of a merger control regime needs to consider whether it is effective in preventing such mergers outright or subjecting them to remedies which eliminate the risk of anti-competitive effects. It is equally important, however, that merger controls should not prevent mergers which are efficiency-enhancing and pose no threat to competition.

Merger control is subject to two types of error. A false positive, also referred to as a Type I, error arises when an innocuous merger is incorrectly found to be anti-competitive. A false negative, Type II error, occurs when an anti-competitive merger goes undetected. Both types of errors will have negative effects on consumers and the wider economy. A failure to prohibit or modify anti-competitive mergers is likely to result in higher prices to consumers, poorer quality goods and services and have a negative effect on innovation. Prohibiting innocuous mergers will also have harmful effects as it will deny consumers and producers the benefits resulting from increased efficiency. The task for competition agencies is to minimise losses from such errors (Morris & Mosteller, 1991). We are therefore interested in identifying potential Type I and Type II errors. An assessment of individual merger decisions needs to ask whether the decision's analysis is consistent with relevant economic theory and the available evidence in the specific case.

An effective merger control regime should also deter anti-competitive mergers because, if firms expect that such mergers will not be permitted, they are less likely to attempt them. If, however, the merger control regime is ineffective at detecting anti-competitive mergers, it is unlikely to provide an effective deterrent to such mergers. Equally, if innocuous efficiency-enhancing mergers are wrongly prohibited or subject to remedies, this is likely to have a chilling effect on mergers which are economically beneficial. Thus, the effects of both types of error extend far beyond the actual cases involved and are likely to impose significant economic costs. A second issue of interest, therefore, is whether the merger control regime deters anti-competitive mergers. Obviously, this is rather difficult to measure because, if merger controls are effective at deterring anti-competitive mergers, such mergers will not be observed, because firms will not attempt them. UK research indicates that a substantial number of mergers were not pursued because the parties concluded they were likely to be prohibited (Deloitte, 2007).

> *"Actual decisions are only the tip of the iceberg in terms of the impact of merger control, because these decisions along with*

> *guidelines and policy pronouncements influence the type of mergers that firms propose. Given the costs of delay and compliance, firms have a considerable incentive to propose mergers that will be acceptable" (Lyons, 2008, p.50).*

Shapiro, C. (2024) points out that effective enforcement relies heavily on deterrence because competition agencies can only look closely at a small fraction of proposed mergers.

While merger controls should prevent anti-competitive mergers, it is important that they do not impede pro-competitive mergers. In addition to avoiding Type I and II (false positive and negative) errors, effective enforcement requires that the competition agencies' resources are allocated to deterring harmful mergers without imposing unnecessary costs on innocuous mergers (*ibid.*). This requires that such cases should be decided quickly while minimising the cost burden on business. This is a further aspect that needs to be considered in any assessment of the merger control regime.[45]

Ultimately, the test of the effectiveness of a merger control regime depends on whether it has benefitted consumers through lower prices, better quality, greater choice, and more rapid technological progress than would otherwise have been the case (Kwoka, 2015). Such an evaluation is extremely difficult due to lack of data. Competition agencies generally do not collect data on post-merger performance or conduct *ex post* reviews of merger cases (*ibid.*). Kwoka (2003) notes that, since 2003, the US anti-trust agencies have been required to estimate the benefits including savings to consumers from merger actions.

It is important to acknowledge, at the outset, that no agency or regime will get every decision right. Nevertheless, the objective for both policy-makers and competition agencies should be to minimise errors and the resulting welfare losses, to learn from mistakes, and take steps to reduce the potential for repeating errors. Equally any assessment of specific merger cases is subject to the *caveat* that published decisions of competition agencies in merger cases cannot include all the details and explanations that one would like to have (Motta, 2004).

---

45 Trebilcock & Iacobucci (2002) state that ideally a merger review regime should seek to minimise three sets of costs: Type I and Type II error costs, along with (public and private) transaction costs incurred in order to avoid Type I and Type II error costs.

The Structure of this Book

This book is structured as follows:

- **Chapter 2** describes the historical development of Irish merger control legislation, thus setting the context for assessing the current regime;
- **Chapter 3** considers institutional aspects of merger control which Budzinski (2010) argues have an important influence on case outcomes;
- **Chapter 4** provides a broad overview of all CA/CCPC merger cases from 2002-2023, the last year for which data on all cases was available at time of going to press;
- Merger analysis involves comparing the effects of a merger against an alternative scenario of what would happen if the merger did not occur (the counterfactual), which is considered in **Chapter 5**;
- The normal starting point when analysing mergers is to define the relevant market and consider the impact of a proposed merger on market structure – which are considered in **Chapters 6** and **7**, respectively;
- Market structure is not conclusive in determining whether a merger is likely to be anti-competitive. Rather, such an assessment must be based on credible theories of competitive harm. Horizontal mergers are generally considered more likely to raise competition concerns and horizontal theories of harm are analysed in **Chapter 8**, while non-horizontal theories of harm are discussed in **Chapter 9**;
- The need to consider whether a merger might generate cost savings which outweigh any potential anti-competitive effects was originally mooted by Williamson (1968) and the analysis of efficiencies is discussed in **Chapter 10**;
- Where a merger is likely to be anti-competitive, it is standard practice among competition agencies to consider whether the potential anti-competitive effects can be addressed through remedies, rather than prohibiting the merger outright. Thus, **Chapter 11** analyses remedies;
- Finally, **Chapter 12** offers some conclusions and suggests some possible reforms.

2: THE EVOLUTION OF MERGER CONTROL IN IRELAND

Origins

Lyons *et al.* (2012) observe that the historical absence of any effective pro-competition policy lobby in Ireland was reflected in an absence of any effective regulation designed to limit market concentration. They note that, during the 1960s, Government was happy to preside over increased concentration in various economic sectors as the creation of large "domestic" players ("national champions") took priority over competition. The mid-1960s saw the consolidation of 90% of the State's banking sector into two equal-sized groups. Brewing was similarly affected, with Guinness absorbing various rivals, including Smithwick, Cherry and McArdle, while Power, Jameson, Bushmills and Cork Distilleries had Government blessing in forming Irish Distillers. In the construction sector at the end of this period the Irish Cement and Roadstone merger resulted in the establishment of the dominant CRH group.

According to Lyons (2007), legislation to regulate mergers in Ireland was first proposed in the late 1960s. At that time few countries, apart from the US and UK, had merger controls, the latter having introduced merger control legislation in 1965. The then Fine Gael/Labour Coalition Government introduced a bill to regulate mergers in 1974, but it failed to progress beyond a second reading and fell with the dissolution of the Dáil in 1977. Following a change of Government, the *Mergers, Takeovers & Monopolies (Control) Act, 1978* was enacted. During the course of the second stage debate on the 1978

Act in the Dáil, Fine Gael T.D. John Kelly suggested that the 1974 Bill had been held up by opposition from business lobby groups:

> *"At the same time, it would be disingenuous if I did not say that I suspect that the degree of displeasure evinced by Irish industry and business at the main thrust of the Bill played some part – I cannot say how great – in the delay which subsequently overtook the Bill."*[46]

The 1978 Act followed a report by a member of the Restrictive Practices Commission (RPC), which warned:

> *"There remains, however, the need to monitor concentration in a number of sectors where oligopoly, with its attendant risks to competition, is prevalent" (RPC, 1975, p.38).*

The quotation reflected contemporary economic thinking in relation to merger control.

The *Mergers, Takeovers & Monopolies (Control) Act, 1978*

Lyons *et al.* (2012) describe the passage of the 1978 as marking the beginning of an effective and activist competition policy regime. They cite three reasons for this conclusion. First, the legislation created a legal regime that prohibited or permitted a merger on the basis of stated economic criteria that included (but were not confined to) standard *"competition"* concerns. Second, it provided for the undertaking of an objective, third party analysis of transactions where this appeared to be required. Third it defined a set of circumstances in which the provisions of the Act became applicable (in effect, economic importance thresholds).

§3 of the 1978 Act provided that mergers involving enterprises above a certain size had to be notified to the Minister for Industry & Commerce and could not be put into effect until:

a) The Minister had stated in writing that he had decided not to make an Order in relation to the proposal; or

b) The Minister had stated in writing that he had made a conditional Order; or

46 *Dáil Debates*, 305(3), 11.4.1978. Available at https://www.oireachtas.ie/en/debates/debate/dail/1978-04-11/31/. Accessed 15.11.2020.

c) The relevant period had elapsed without the Minister having made an Order, whichever first occurred.[47]

The 1978 Act provided that mergers had to be notified to the Minister if, in the most recent financial year, the value of the gross assets of each of two or more of the enterprises involved was not less than £1.25 million or the turnover of each enterprise was not less than £2.5 million.[48] The Minister could, by Order, vary these thresholds.[49] Following receipt of a notification the Minister was required to either inform the enterprises that he had decided not to make an Order prohibiting the merger, or refer the notification to the Examiner of Restrictive Practices for investigation.[50] The Examiner's report had to state an opinion as to whether or not the proposed merger would operate against the common good in respect of a range of criteria set out in the schedule to the Act:

a) The extent to which the proposed merger would be likely to prevent or restrict competition or to restrain trade or the provision of any service;
b) The extent to which it would be likely to endanger the continuity of supplies or services;
c) The extent to which it would be likely to affect employment and would be compatible with national policy in relation to employment;
d) The extent to which it was in accordance with national policy for regional development;
e) The extent to which it was in harmony with the policy of the Government relating to the rationalisation, in the interests of greater efficiency, of operations in the industry or business concerned;

---

47 The "relevant period" was the period of three months beginning on the date on which the Minister first received a notification of the proposal or, where the Minister requested further information, the date of receipt by him of such information (§6).

48 §2(1)(a).

49 The thresholds were increased to IR£5m and IR£10m respectively in July 1985 (*S.I. No.* 230/1985), and to IR£10m and IR£20m in May 1993 (*S.I. No.* 135/1993). The Minister could also, by Order, declare that the Act applied to certain classes of merger irrespective of the turnover of the enterprises involved. In January 1979 the Minister made an Order requiring any proposed merger, where at least one of the enterprises involved was engaged in the printing and/or publication of one or more newspapers, to be notified (*S.I. No.* 17/1979).

50 §7 Referrals were subsequently transferred to the RPC, which was renamed the Fair Trade Commission (FTC) under the 1987 Act.

f) Any benefits likely to be derived from the proposed take-over in relation to research and development, technical efficiency, increased production, efficient distribution of products and access to markets;
g) The interests of shareholders and partners in the enterprises involved;
h) The interests of employees in the enterprises involved;
i) The interests of the consumer.

The criteria involve a mixture of economic/efficiency factors, e.g. a, b, and f, while others were concerned with social/political considerations.

Having considered the Examiner's report, the Minister could, if he thought that the exigencies of the common good so warranted, after consultation with any other Minister concerned, by Order prohibit a proposed merger either absolutely, or except on specified conditions. An Order had to state the reasons for making the Order, and a conditional Order could have retrospective effect. Every Order had to be laid before the Oireachtas and could be the subject of an annulling resolution within 21 days.[51] An enterprise referred to in an Order could appeal against the making of the Order on a point of law to the High Court within one month of the Order coming into effect. An appeal against a decision of the High Court to the Supreme Court was expressly precluded.[52]

The Minister was required to furnish to the Oireachtas an *Annual Report* stating the number and the nature of investigations into proposed mergers.[53] The Minister could omit from the *Annual Report* any information the publication of which would, in the Minister's opinion, materially injure the legitimate interests of an enterprise, if the information was not essential to the full understanding of the investigation to which it related, but a statement indicating the general character of the information omitted had to be included in the report.[54] Lyons (2007) suggests that it was questionable whether statements were ever included in the Minister's *Annual Reports* regarding the general character of such information. This confidentiality provision was interpreted in a very restrictive manner, so that not even the identity of the enterprises involved in a merger proposal referred for investigation was revealed, though the enterprises had to be named in any Order which was

---

51 §9.
52 §12.
53 §15(1).
54 §15(2).

made, after which their names were included in the *Annual Report* (*ibid.*). There was no obligation to publish a report of the Examiner's investigation of a proposal, and no such report was ever published.

Shortcomings of the 1978 Act

The merger control regime introduced under the 1978 Act had serious shortcomings. Originally it excluded several key economic sectors including banking, electricity, and transport.[55] The *Restrictive Practices (Amendment) Act, 1987,* removed most of these exceptions.[56] The legislation essentially applied a public interest test for deciding whether mergers should be approved. Competition was only one of many potentially conflicting issues that had to be addressed in an investigation of a merger which had been referred by the Minister. Ultimately, however, the Minister's decision was based on *"the exigencies of the common good"*.

A major problem with the 1978 Act was its lack of clarity and transparency (Massey & Daly, 2003; Massey, 2010). Decisions on whether to approve mergers were made by the Minister for Industry & Commerce. The Minister could only prohibit a merger or impose conditions having first referred it to the FTC. Any merger that was not referred was automatically cleared. There was no requirement for the Minister to give reasons for a decision on whether to refer a merger. No reports by the Examiner/FTC on referred mergers were ever published. Prior to the 1990s, the Minister's *Annual Report* on mergers did not even disclose the names of any of the parties involved in notified mergers (Lyons, 2007).

The *Competition Act, 1991*

The *Competition Act, 1991,* abolished the FTC and established the CA whose functions, *inter alia,* included carrying out investigations of mergers referred to it by the Minister. The 1991 Act revised the criteria that were to be considered by the CA when investigating a referred merger. The schedule to the 1978 Act was deleted. Under the 1991 Act, the CA had, firstly,

---

55 Harbour and pilotage authorities, services provided under a contract of employment, and any service provided by a local authority were also excluded.

56 Only banking, employment contracts and services provided by local authorities continued to be excluded (Lyons, 2007).

> *"to state its opinion as to whether or not the proposed merger or take-over concerned would be likely to prevent or restrict competition or restrain trade in any goods or services and would be likely to operate against the common good."*[57]

The 1991 Act thus placed greater emphasis on competition in the assessment of mergers, but the CA was still required to *"give its views on the likely effect of the proposed merger or take-over on the common good"* in respect of a range of other economic, political and social factors.[58]

In *Independent Newspapers/Tribune,*[59] the first merger referral under the 1991 Act, there was a difference of opinion between the CA Members regarding the correct interpretation of the first criterion (Lyons, 2007). The majority took the view that the CA was required to give its opinion on whether the proposal would affect competition and would therefore be likely to operate against the common good.[60] The minority suggested that the CA should give its view about the possible effect on competition and separately state whether the proposal would be likely to operate against the common good, an interpretation which would have required the CA to consider whether competition was in the common good in each individual case.[61]

While the 1991 Act placed an increased emphasis on competition in the assessment of mergers, it still provided that the Minster's decision on whether to prohibit a merger, should be based on *"the exigencies of the common good"* which could include, but was not confined to, the criteria that the CA was required to report on. The 1991 Act introduced a modest increase in transparency by requiring that, if the Minister referred a merger to the CA, the CA's report to the Minister had to be published within two months.[62] However, the number of merger referrals declined sharply after 1991 (see below).

---

57 §17(4)(2)(a).

58 (i) continuity of supplies or services; (ii) level of employment; (iii) regional development; (iv) rationalisation of operations in the interests of greater efficiency; (v) research and development; (vi) increased production; (vii) access to markets; (viii) shareholders and partners: (ix) employees and (x) consumers (§17(4)(2)(b)).

59 CA (1991) – *Independent Newspapers/Tribune.*

60 The author was part of the majority in this case.

61 The target in the case argued that allowing the proposed transaction to proceed was in the common good as it would have resulted in the continued publication of the target's *Sunday Tribune* newspaper (¶5.28).

62 FTC (1990, ¶12.14) had recommended that, in cases where mergers were referred to it by the Minister, the Minister should be obliged to publish its subsequent report.

The Operation of the Merger Regime, 1978-2002

Information on the annual number of merger notifications from 1978 to 2002 is contained in **Table 2.1**. A striking feature of the table is the large number of merger notifications that were deemed to be outside the scope of the Act. Between 1978 and 1991 44% of notified mergers were found to be outside the scope of the legislation. This figure increased to 64% over the period from 1992 to 2002. Excluding transactions that were outside the scope of the legislation, there were 2,066 mergers notified under the *Mergers Acts* between 1978 and 2002.

Forty mergers were referred to the Examiner/FTC over the 1978-2002 period, so that the vast majority of mergers notified were cleared unconditionally. **Table 2.1** also shows that the proportion of mergers referred declined sharply in the 10 years after the introduction of the 1991 Act. Between 1978 and 1991 28 mergers were referred to the Examiner/FTC by the Minister. This represented almost 5% of notified mergers, excluding transactions deemed to be outside the scope of the legislation.[63]

From 1992 to 2002 only 12 notified mergers were referred to the CA, representing just 1.4% of valid merger notifications during this period. Massey (2001) notes that the level of referrals post-1991 was considerably lower than the level of second stage investigations carried out by the EU Commission, the USFTC, and the UKMMC.

Table 2.2 summarises the outcome of the 40 mergers referred over the 1978-2002 period. Half were subsequently cleared unconditionally. Three were cleared with conditions, five were prohibited, while 12 were withdrawn or did not proceed.[64]

---

63 The rate of referrals in Ireland was slightly higher than in the UK up to 1992. Approximately 2-3% of UK mergers were referred to the MMC between 1965 and 1985 (Franks & Harris, 1986). It remained around 3% over the 1984-1990 period (Weir, 1993), rising to 4% between 1990 and 1994 (Howe, 1995).

64 The UKMMC recommended rejection of approximately one-third of mergers referred to it between 1965 and 1985 (Franks & Harris, 1986). The Irish data is not comparable, because no reports of referred mergers were published pre-1992. Information is only available on the number of mergers prohibited by the Minister rather than the number of cases where the FTC may have recommended prohibition.

Table 2.1: Merger Notifications, 1978-2002

	Total Notifications	Outside the scope of the Act	Within the Scope of the Act	Cleared Unconditionally	Referred	Withdrawn/ Did not proceed
1978/79	45	18	27	25	1	0
1980	40	16	24	20	2	0
1981	55	9	46	35	5	2
1982	47	13	34	33	2	1
1983	59	21	38	39	0	0
1984	78	25	53	52	2	0
1985	65	25	40	37	2	1
1986	75	32	43	37	1	0
1987	85	43	42	39	1	0
1988	107	45	62	56	5	1
1989	125	64	61	47	2	1
1990	126	66	60	60	4	3
1991	137	80	57	54	1	1
1992	142	69	73	68	1	0
1993	115	58	57	57	1	2
1994	124	73	51	48	0	0
1995	123	70	53	52	1	0
1996	171	117	54	53	2	0
1997	201	136	65	61	1	3
1998	233	150	83	68	2	0

	Total Notifications	Outside the scope of the Act	Within the Scope of the Act	Cleared Unconditionally	Referred	Withdrawn/ Did not proceed
1999	276	170	106	100	1	0
2000	319	196	123	105	0	0
2001	302	218	84	108	1	0
2002	357	254	103	93	2	0
1978-1991	**1,044**	**455**	**589**	**534**	**28**	**10**
1992-2002	**2,363**	**1,511**	**852**	**813**	**12**	**5**
1978-2002	**3,407**	**1,966**	**1,441**	**1,347**	**40**	**15**

Source: Annual Reports of the Minster for Industry & Commerce in accordance with §15 of the *Mergers, Take-Overs & Monopolies Control Act, 1978* and *Annual Reports* of the FTC and CA.

Table 2.2: Merger Referral Outcomes, 1978-2002

	Total Referrals	Cleared Unconditionally	Cleared with Conditions	Prohibited	Withdrawn/ Did Not Proceed
1978-1991	28	14	1	3	10
1992-2002	12	6	2	2	2
1978-2002	40	20	3	5	12

Source: Annual Reports of the Minster for Industry & Commerce in accordance with §15 of the *Mergers, Take-Overs & Monopolies Control Act, 1978* and *Annual Reports* of the FTC and CA.

Between 1978 and 1987 not a single merger was either prohibited or had conditions attached to its approval (Lyons, 2007). In one 1981 case the Minister issued a prohibition Order but subsequently revoked it and permitted the merger to proceed.[65] In another 1984 case, the Minister authorised a merger subject to conditions, but the Order was subsequently revoked, and the conditions were removed.[66]

Three prohibition Orders were issued between 1988 and 1991. One prohibited an attempted acquisition by GC&C of Irish Distillers.[67] The acquisition of Irish Distillers by Pernod Ricard[68] was subsequently permitted subject to certain conditions. In April 1990, the Minister made an Order prohibiting AIBP from acquiring Master Meats.[69] Effectively the Order constituted a conditional clearance as it ceased to have effect once AIBP had disposed of certain meat plants. It was revoked in 1991 following confirmation that such divestments had taken place. The Minister made an Order in February 1990 prohibiting an acquisition by British Steel of C. Walker & Sons (Holdings) Ltd.[70] The proposed transaction was also notified to the EU Commission under the provisions of the ECSCT as the parties' businesses related to both Treaty (where the EU Commission had exclusive competence) and non-Treaty products. The Commission issued a conditional clearance and, following its decision, the Minister revoked the Order.

The Minister, in a statement dated 8 June 1990, stated that he had decided not to make an Order prohibiting the proposed *Telecom Éireann/Cablelink* merger on the grounds that he had sought and received

---

65 *Proposed Merger or Take-Over Conditional Order, 1981* (*S.I. No.* 331/1981). Smurfit Investments (Ireland) Ltd/Bedstone Ltd (*Smurfit/Bedstone*). The Minister prohibited the proposal except on certain conditions, the most important being that the purchaser divest *Irish Business* magazine. Subsequently, the Minister decided that circumstances had changed sufficiently to allow him to revoke the conditional Order (Lyons, 2007).

66 *Proposed Merger or Take-Over Conditional Order, 1984* (*S.I.* No. 217/1984). Governor & Company of the Bank of Ireland/Irish Civil Service Building Society (*Bank of Ireland/ICS*). The notification involved the acquisition by Bank of Ireland of all the voting shares in ICS. The Minister made an Order making the acquisition conditional on changes to the Society's rules to meet concerns regarding its mutual status. The Order was revoked in 1989, following the commencement of certain provisions of the *Building Societies Act, 1989* (*ibid.*).

67 *Proposed Merger or Take-Over Prohibition Order, 1988 (S.I. No.* 301/1988). *GC&C/Irish Distillers.*

68 *Proposed Merger or Take-Over Conditional Order, 1988 (S.I. No.* 302/1988) *Pernod Ricard/Irish Distillers.*

69 *Proposed Merger or Take-Over Conditional (No. 2) Order, 1990 (S.I. No.* 94/1990). *DJS Meats Ltd/Anglo Irish Beef Processors (Master Meats).*

70 *Proposed Merger or Take-Over Prohibition Order, 1990 (S.I. No.* 42/1990) *British Steel plc/C. Walker & Sons (Holdings) Ltd (Walker Steel).*

undertakings from Telecom Éireann which, in his opinion, provided satisfactory assurances in relation to points identified by the FTC investigation of the transaction, namely that:

i. Cablelink would operate at arms' length from Telecom Éireann;
ii. Telecom Éireann would support whatever optimum level of investment was required to underpin Cablelink's future development; and
iii. Telecom Éireann would support the provision of access to Cablelink on a fair and non-discriminatory basis to third parties for the purposes of providing interactive text services (CA, *Annual Report 1990*. See **Chapter 4**).

The Minister subsequently announced that he had decided not to make an Order in *IAWS/R&H Hall* on foot of undertakings received which provided that IAWS would:

i. Fully respect proposed new competition legislation prohibiting an abuse of dominance;
ii. Ensure that Odlum would not be commercially disadvantaged in any post-merger review of existing commercial arrangements between it and R&H Hall;
iii. Not restrict supplies of animal feed ingredients to commercial compounders;
iv. Ensure that reasonable commercial benefits would accrue to its customers as a result of expected scale economies from the transaction;
v. Maintain existing arrangements with respect to Hall port facilities and if any such facilities were deemed surplus to requirements, permit third parties to use them on commercial terms (CA, *Annual Report 1990*).

Ten of the 28 mergers referred to the Examiner/FTC over the 1978-1991 period were subsequently withdrawn. Lyons (2007) provides some details in relation to some of the withdrawn notifications. One 1981 case involved a proposed acquisition by a UK enterprise, which was engaged *inter alia* in the manufacture of metal cans, of an Irish enterprise engaged in a similar line of activity. The notification was withdrawn following submission of the Examiner's report. It was subsequently re-submitted in 1982, referred again to the Examiner and was once more withdrawn following submission of the Examiner's report. Another merger referred to the Examiner in 1981 involved the proposed acquisition by a UK publicly-quoted company, engaged principally in the engineering sector, of a privately-owned Irish company engaged in similar activities. Following the reference, the notification was withdrawn, and the Examiner did not undertake an investigation. A proposed acquisition by the Irish subsidiary of a UK company involved in the retail grocery trade of an Irish private company also involved in the retail grocery sector was withdrawn following submission of the Examiner's report in 1985.

Overall, only seven prohibition and three conditional clearance Orders were made between 1978 and 2002. Three prohibitions, *Smurfit/Bedstone, Walker Steel* and *Statoil/Conoco I*[71] were subsequently rescinded. *Master Meats* and *Statoil/Conoco II*[72] amounted to conditional clearances subject to divestments, although in the latter case this occurred after the parties had lodged an appeal to the High Court against the original prohibition Order. The limited number of prohibition decisions and conditional clearances tend to indicate a relatively lax approach to merger control during the period before 2002. As against that, several transactions were withdrawn, the majority during the 1978-1991 period, following referral and/or the submission of reports to the Minister by the Examiner/FTC suggesting that some of these withdrawals may have been prompted by the risk of an adverse decision. It must also be recognised that, although there were few prohibitions and conditional clearances, Ireland was ahead of many other countries at the time in having any form of merger control legislation.

Massey & Daly (2003) state that several mergers where a more in-depth investigation appears to have been justified were approved without referral between 1996 and 2002,[73] while *Ladbrokes/Coral*[74] was referred even though the parties had a combined market share of only 20%.

Some mergers were cleared without referral based on informal undertakings offered by the parties, which again serves to highlight a lack of transparency. One example was the 2001 Valentia takeover of eircom,

---

71 *Proposed Merger or Take-Over Prohibition Order, 1996* (S.I. No. 45/1996), *Statoil Ireland Ltd/Conoco Ireland Ltd.* (*Statoil/Conoco I*).

72 *Proposed Merger or Take-Over Prohibition (Amendment) Order, 1996* (S.I. No. 214/1996), *Statoil Ireland Ltd/Conoco Ireland Ltd.* (*Statoil/Conoco II*).

73 These included a merger where the parties accounted for 80% of the liquid milk market in Dublin and a three to two merger of package tour operators (Massey, 2001).

74 CA (1998) – *Ladbrokes/Coral*. Although a member of the CA at the time, the author did not participate in this investigation.

although in this case some information was disclosed in a written Dáil reply by the Tánaiste, which stated that she was *"not empowered to attach terms and conditions to an approval of a merger which is not referred to the Competition Authority. However, following discussions between my Department and the notifying parties in this case, undertakings were voluntarily given by Valentia Telecommunications Limited and Sir Anthony O'Reilly."*[75] The reply went on to state:

> *"Valentia undertook that Sir Anthony O'Reilly would not be given access to information which would reasonably be considered as confidential competitive information and which would confer an unfair competitive advantage on Valentia or Chorus Communications Limited in relation to the current licensed telecommunications operations of Chorus, except for information given to enable Sir Anthony O'Reilly to comply with his statutory and fiduciary duties. Sir Anthony gave a corresponding undertaking to recuse himself from Valentia board discussions relating to Chorus. Sir Anthony O'Reilly also gave an undertaking to recuse himself from any role in Independent News & Media plc relating to Chorus Communications Limited."*

CA Merger Investigations, 1991-2002

The *Competition Act, 1991*, required the Minister to publish the CA's reports in cases where the Minister referred a merger to it. Details of the 13 cases referred to the CA between 1991 and 2002 are outlined in **Table 2.3**.

Five of the cases referred involved horizontal mergers, four had both horizontal and vertical elements, while two were purely vertical mergers. Two merger notifications were withdrawn following referral to the CA and so little information is available in respect of these cases.[76] The referral was withdrawn by the Minister in *GIG/UBH* as it had been made after the statutory deadline for doing so (see below).

The CA recommended that seven of the remaining 10 transactions should be approved, albeit subject to conditions in two cases, while the other three should be prohibited.

---

[75] https://www.oireachtas.ie/en/debates/debate/dail/2001-11-20/53/. Accessed 15.11.2020.

[76] In one of these cases, the parties' identity is unknown.

Table 2.3: Outcome of Mergers Referred to the CA, 1991-2002

Parties	Year	Type of Merger	CA Recommend-ation	Decision
n.a.	1991	n.a.	n.a.	Notification withdrawn
Independent Newspapers/Tribune Group	1992	Horizontal	Prohibit	Prohibited (subsequently appealed)
Ractrayle/Princes Holdings/Suir Nore Relays	1993	n.a.	n.a.	Notification withdrawn
Statoil/Conoco	1996	Horizontal	Prohibit	Prohibited (amended proposal cleared following appeal)
Unilever/Lyons Tea	1996	Horizontal	Approve	Cleared unconditionally
Blockbuster/Xtra-Vision	1997	Vertical	Approve	Cleared unconditionally
GIG/UBH	1997	Horizontal/ Vertical	n.a.	Referral withdrawn due to missed deadline
Coillte/Balcas	1998	Vertical	Prohibit	Prohibited
Ladbrokes/Coral	1998	Horizontal	Approve	Cleared unconditionally
Princes Holdings/Suir Nore Relays/Liberty Media/Aringour	2000	Horizontal	Approve	Cleared unconditionally
GEHE/Unicare	2002	Horizontal/ Vertical	Approve subject to conditions.	Cleared unconditionally
STA Travel/USIT	2002	Horizontal/ Vertical	Approve subject to conditions.	Cleared subject to conditions
Maxol/Busselle	2002	Horizontal/ Vertical	Approve	Cleared unconditionally

Source: CA.

The Minister accepted the CA's recommendations in nine cases,[77] although two of the prohibition decisions were subsequently appealed. The CA's reports provide some insights into the role played by economic analysis in these cases. CA Phase 2 merger investigations under the 1991 Act were subject to much shorter time limits than under the current merger regime. The Minister was required to give the CA a minimum of 30 days to submit its report. The average time afforded to the CA by the Minister to conduct its investigation in the 10 cases where an investigation was carried out was 40 days.[78] Initially, at least, there were limited precedents from other jurisdictions, apart from the US, as the ECMR was only introduced in 1990 while relatively few EU Member States had merger controls at that time.

The majority report in *Independent Newspapers/Tribune Group* expressed concern that the transaction would create or strengthen a dominant position in the market for Irish Sunday newspapers and in the Irish newspaper advertising market stating that *"an increase in market shares from an already high level of concentration is a matter of concern from the viewpoint of competition"* (¶6.8). While acknowledging that there was no competition law prohibition on a firm having a dominant position, the majority report expressed concerns about the potential for predatory or exclusionary conduct which could weaken or eliminate one or more of the remaining competitors in the market, should the merger proceed. The report did not consider a possible increase in newspaper prices post-merger, although it warned that the merger could ultimately lead to increases in newspaper advertising rates if rivals were weakened or eliminated following the merger.[79] The report argued that choice, which was an important feature of a competitive market, was likely to be reduced if multiple newspapers were owned by the same proprietor.

The CA's 1996 report in *Statoil/Conoco* contained several elements of a modern economics-based analysis. At the time there were 13 suppliers of motor fuels in the State, although only six of these had a market share of more than 5% and many of the smaller suppliers only operated in local, mainly,

---

77 The Minister did not accept the CA's recommendation to make an Order in *GEHE* requiring all acquisitions of retail pharmacies to be notified, irrespective of turnover, where the parties' operated pharmacies in close proximity to one another (see below).

78 Three of these investigations encompassed Christmas/New Year. Post-2002 the CA had up to three months to complete a Phase 2 investigation – increased to 90 working days in 2014.

79 The potential for unilateral price increases post-merger was first included in USHMG1992 which were published in April 1992 a few weeks after the CA completed its *Independent/Tribune* investigation.

rural areas. The report argued that the smaller the number of competitors in the market, the greater was the risk of collusion, either tacit or overt.[80] Apart from noting that there were a limited number of competitors in the market, the report did not consider whether the conditions necessary for collusion were satisfied. The report implies, however, that post-merger market shares would be asymmetric which would make collusion more difficult. It suggests that companies monitored each other's retail prices which might help identify cheating but did not analyse whether an effective punishment mechanism for cheating existed. The report did not consider possible unilateral effects, although the transaction would have made the merged entity the largest firm in the market post-merger.[81] Evidence that Conoco was perceived as a low-price operator influenced the CA's conclusions. The CA considered barriers to entry and efficiencies. It stated that it could not accept claims of efficiencies that were not fully substantiated and concluded that even if the claimed efficiencies were fully passed on to consumers, they would have little effect on prices.[82]

In *Ladbrokes/Coral* the CA stated that the *"substantive issue is whether or not the proposed transaction increases the probability of acquiring dominance or otherwise lessens competition in the market"* (¶6.3) rather than collusion. It concluded that the transaction would not affect competition as the market would be relatively unconcentrated post-merger while entry barriers were low. *Blockbuster/Xtra-Vision* was essentially a vertical merger and the CA's analysis focused primarily on the issue of potential foreclosure post-merger.

Princes Holdings/Suir Nore Relays/Liberty Media/Aringour involved a merger of several cable TV providers. The companies were licensed to provide cable TV services by the Office of the Director of Telecommunications Regulation (ODTR). The licences were for a period of 15 years but provided that, after a five-year period of territorial exclusivity, the ODTR could issue licences to other cable operators for the same territory, while cable operators' prices to consumers were regulated by the ODTR. The CA concluded that the

---

80 Explicit collusion aims at putting participants at the joint profit maximising point on the profit frontier. Tacit collusion increases joint profits above the competitive level (defined as the non-cooperative Nash equilibrium) and aims to maximise joint profits. However, maximising joint profits is complicated by the lack of an explicit agreement, usually because such agreements are illegal. Thus, from an economics perspective, explicit and tacit collusion are quantitatively rather than qualitatively different in terms of their implications (Philips, 1995).

81 Economics indicates that unilateral effects are likely in such circumstances (see **Chapter 8**).

82 The Minister made an Order prohibiting the transaction, but this was appealed. The Minister made a subsequent Order permitting the transaction to proceed subject to the parties divesting a number of filling stations (see above).

operators' territorial exclusivity meant that they were not in competition with each other and therefore the transaction would have no effect on competition. The CA decided that entry by rival cable operators was unlikely once the exclusive licence period had expired and did not consider that the parties might constitute potential competitors in the future.[83] The CA did not consider the issue of yardstick competition, whereby the existence of monopoly franchisees in different geographic areas would provide information to the regulator which could be used in regulating prices (Cowan, 1998).[84] The report noted, however, that technological changes meant that cable TV operators would be able to provide telecommunications services over their networks and concluded that the merger would therefore increase competition in such services in the future.

GEHE involved both horizontal and vertical overlaps. The CA concluded that retail pharmacy markets were local in nature and that a national geographic market definition was not relevant for analysing competition at the retail level. The CA also considered the potential for foreclosure due to the vertical aspects of the transaction. It concluded that the transaction did not raise any competition issues but expressed concerns that future acquisitions of individual retail pharmacies, which would not need to be notified to the Minister, could lead to increased concentration in local markets. It therefore recommended that the Minister make an Order that would require notification of any future acquisitions of retail pharmacies where the parties had outlets in close proximity to one another regardless of the merging parties' turnover.[85]

The target in *STA/USIT* was in serious financial difficulties. The CA conducted a close study of the complex vertical relationships involved in the supply and distribution of student tickets and travel products. It recommended that the transaction should be cleared subject to a condition whereby STA was required to supply certain student travel tickets to other

---

83 The period of exclusivity was not due to expire until April 2004, a little over four years after the transaction so that the issue of potential competition was probably too far in the future to be considered.

84 In the UK, for example, the water regulator employed yardstick competition to regulate the prices of monopoly suppliers of water and sewage services. UK legislation required that mergers in the industry had to be referred to the UKMMC which was required to have regard to the principle that the number of water enterprises under independent control should not be reduced so as to prejudice the ability of the regulator to make comparisons between water enterprises. The UKMMC recommended that proposed mergers be prohibited on those grounds in *Severn Trent/South West Water* 1.1.1996 and *Wessex Water/South West Water*.

85 No such Order was made.

Irish retailers of such tickets for a certain period of time on specified terms and the Minister made an Order to that effect.

Maxol/Busselle involved both horizontal and vertical overlaps in relation to motor fuels. The main focus of the CA's report was on competition in local retail motor fuel markets. As in *Statoil/Conoco* the CA focused on the potential for coordinated effects but ultimately concluded that the transaction would not have a negative impact on competition.

Mergers & the *Competition Act*

The CA took the view that the prohibition on anti-competitive agreements in §4 of the *Competition Act, 1991*, which largely mirrored Article 85 of the *Treaty of Rome*,[86] could apply to mergers, based on the CJEU judgement in *Philip Morris* (see **Chapter 1**). In *Cooley/Irish Distillers*, the CA stated that, in its opinion, an agreement between the parties which would have seen Irish Distillers acquire control of Cooley, the only other whiskey distillery in the State at that time, infringed §4(1) and did not satisfy the requirements for an exemption.[87]

In August 1997, the Minister sought to refer the proposed acquisition of United Beverages Holdings (UBH), a drinks wholesaler, by Guinness Ireland Group (GIG) to the CA under the *Mergers Act*. The CA indicated that it could not investigate the proposed transaction as the deadline for the Minister to make a referral had passed. The Minister withdrew the referral, and the parties notified the agreement to the CA under the *Competition Act*. The CA subsequently granted a licence (exemption) to the agreement subject to conditions, which required GIG to reduce its shareholding in C&C, another drinks wholesale distributor, below 10% no later than 15 January 1999, relinquish all rights to representation on the board of C&C, and waive its first option on C&C shares which it did not already own.[88]

In November 1998, the CA sought an injunction to prevent Avonmore Waterford Group (AWG) from acquiring Athboy Co-Op, alleging that the proposed transaction (a) constituted an anti-competitive agreement, contrary to §4(1) of the *Competition Act, 1991*, as amended, and (b) constituted an abuse of a dominant position by AWG, contrary to §5 of the Act. It was agreed by the defendants that there was a fair issue to be tried. The court refused to grant an injunction on the balance of convenience.

---

86 Now Article 101, TFEU.

87 CA Decision No.285 – *Cooley/Irish Distillers*, 25.2.1994.

88 CA Decision No.512 – *Guinness Ireland Group/United Beverages Holdings*, 17.6.1998.

Significantly, the court stated that if the deal were to proceed it could be unscrambled, or an appropriate adjustment made, if it were ultimately held to infringe the *Competition Act* (Mulcahy, 1998).

De-politicising Merger Decisions

The *Competition Act, 2002,* introduced a radical overhaul of Ireland's merger control regime. First, it de-politicised the merger control process by transferring responsibility for merger decisions from the Minister to an independent agency. Second, it established the effect on competition as the sole criteria against which mergers were to be assessed by providing that CA decisions on whether mergers were to be allowed to proceed had to be based on whether they would result in a substantial lessening of competition (SLC). The 2002 Act thus placed economics at the centre of Ireland's merger control regime (Massey, 2002). A member of the CA subsequently warned:

> *"To avoid economic analysis in cases raising competition concerns in the hope that the Authority will elect not to fully analyse the case simply will not work!" (Henneberry, 2004, p.5).*

The CMRG, which had been established to advise on possible legislative reform, had recommended that responsibility for all stages of merger investigations should be transferred to the CA, while the final decision on whether to approve a merger would remain with the Minister (CMRG, 2000).[89] The *Competition Act, 2002,* went considerably further than the CMRG recommendations and completely transferred responsibility for deciding whether or not to approve mergers to the CA, thus completely removing any ministerial involvement in merger cases, other than media mergers. This change was introduced despite opposition from business lobbies and civil servants within the sponsoring Minister's own department to assigning the CA a greater role in merger control.[90] Massey & Daly (2003) cite internal Departmental memos obtained under the *Freedom of Information Act, 2014,* which argued that the existing merger arrangements worked

---

89 In other words, the CMRG recommended that mergers should be notified to, and investigated by, the CA. The CA would then submit a report of its investigation with a recommendation to the Minister, who would be free to accept or reject it. Such a proposal had previously been made in FTC (1990).

90 Opposition T.D. Richard Bruton had called for responsibility for merger decisions to be transferred to the CA during the Dáil debate on the *Competition (Amendment) Bill, 1994. Competition* 3(6), p.163.

well, while another memo stated that *"[m]ost of the pressure to 'give mergers to the Authority' arises from 'empire building' on their behalf when they have yet to fully prove themselves"* (*ibid.*, p.300).

The 2002 Act also provided that decisions on mergers were to be based purely on competition grounds. §20(1)(c) of the Act states the CA must form a view as to whether a merger *"will substantially lessen competition in markets for goods or services in the State"*. §22 provides that, where the CA concludes that a merger will result in an SLC, it may either prohibit the merger, or permit it subject to conditions, where it believes that those conditions would prevent an SLC. The 2002 Act also greatly increased transparency in the merger control process by requiring that the CA (i) publish notice of mergers notified to it within seven days of notification[91] and (ii) publish its merger Determinations giving reasons for its decisions.[92]

The core elements of the regime introduced by the 2002 Act, involving decision-making by an independent body based on whether a proposed merger would result in an SLC, have remained largely unchanged despite subsequent revisions to the legislation. The main exceptions relate to media mergers. Media mergers are subject to a two-tier test, whereby the CCPC is required to consider whether a media merger will result in an SLC. If the CCPC concludes that a media merger will not result in any SLC, the Minister is then required to consider the impact of the merger on media plurality.

The 2002 Act brought all sectors of the economy, including banking, within the scope of the merger regime. The *Credit Institutions (Financial Support) Act, 2008* (CIFSA, 2008) which was introduced in the wake of the financial crash, however, provided that mergers involving credit institutions must be notified to the Minister for Finance instead of the CA on a temporary basis. This facilitated the arrangements put in place by the Government to rescue several banks following the financial crash in 2008. These arrangements were explicitly designed to weaken competition between intermediaries so as to increase their profitability, in order to repair balance sheets (Massey & McDowell, 2021).

---

91 §20(1).

92 §s21(3) and 22(4) provides for publication of Determinations in respect of preliminary and full investigations. §22(7) provides that in the latter case the published Determination must include a report of the full investigation and give reasons for the Determination. Although there is no corresponding obligation in respect of preliminary investigations, the practice, at least until recently, has been to give reasons in such Determinations (see **Chapter 8**).

Conclusions

Ultimately any assessment of Irish merger control prior to 1992 is complicated by the lack of transparency that existed under the then prevailing regime. Very little information was published in respect of merger notifications and decisions. The *Competition Act, 1991*, led to some increase in transparency as it required the publication of CA reports in respect of mergers referred to it by the Minister. However, this was followed by a sharp decline in the number of referrals. Despite its shortcomings, it needs to be borne in mind that the 1978 Act was introduced at a time when few other countries had any form of merger control and was arguably very much a creature of its time.

3: THE INSTITUTIONAL SETTING

Introduction

A key objective of the shift to a more economics approach was to reduce the number of errors in merger cases. Budzinski (2010) argues that this objective had not been achieved because of a failure to take account of lessons from institutional economics resulting in a decline in merger enforcement in the EU and US since the 1980s. Hawk (2020) also observes that there is a tension between developments in economic theory that call for more complex analysis and a desire for simpler legal rules.

Budzinski (2010) argues that the institutional arrangements under which merger control operates have an important impact on case outcomes. For example, should merger control operate on an *ex ante* or an *ex post* basis? An *ex ante* merger control regime generally requires mandatory advance notification of mergers. This in turn, however, raises the question of whether notification should be compulsory for all mergers, or only for those involving firms above a certain size. Further questions arise as to the substantive test that should apply for determining whether a merger should be allowed to proceed and the appropriate level of proof in merger cases. The issue of who are the decision-makers and what level of checks and balances exist is also very important.

Ex Ante versus Ex Post Merger Control

Merger control regimes can be either *ex ante* or *ex post.* An *ex ante* regime requires regulatory approval before the merger can proceed, whereas an *ex post* regime seeks to intervene in the case of anti-competitive mergers after the merger has been initiated. *Ex ante* regimes generally require prior notification of mergers to a regulatory agency. Many countries operate an *ex ante* system of merger control, although there are also examples of *ex post* systems. Motta (2004) argues that *ex ante* merger control is efficient, because it is wasteful to allow mergers to take place and then attempt to unwind them. He also suggests that forced divestments *ex post* would be extremely inefficient.

It may not always be possible to restore the pre-merger situation *ex post*. Beesley (1990) stated that remedies in UK *ex post* merger cases tended to be constrained by the costs of trying to reverse a completed deal. Baer (1997) and Wollmann (2019) both conclude that US merger enforcement was largely ineffective prior to the introduction of compulsory pre-notification. Ottaviani & Wickelgren (2011) find that *ex post* control also has an undesirable chilling effect on *ex ante* incentives to undertake some socially desirable mergers. The risk of false negatives may also be greater in cases that are identified late under an *ex post* regime (Chisholm & Heideman, 2017).[93] Lyons (2008, p.3) states:

> *"Effective merger regulation is the essential ex ante means of filtering merger proposals so that efficient ones are allowed while anti-competitive ones are not."*

Ireland's merger control regime is, primarily, an *ex ante* regime, with a requirement for prior notification to, and approval by, the CCPC before a merger may be put into effect, in cases where the merging parties' turnovers exceed a prescribed threshold. The legislation, however, also provides that parties may voluntarily notify mergers that fall below the thresholds. The CA/CCPC has, on several occasions, carried out an *ex post* review of mergers which fell below the notification thresholds and had not been notified voluntarily before being put into effect. The *Competition (Amendment) Act, 2022*, formally introduced a system of *ex post* review for below the threshold mergers by providing that the CCPC may:

a) Request the parties to notify below the threshold mergers where it believes they could have a negative effect on competition, but the CCPC may review the transaction under the merger rules in any case; and

---

93 The UKCMA must complete its initial investigation of a merger within four months of a merger being concluded or becoming public knowledge, regardless of when it becomes aware of the transaction. After that time, it no longer has jurisdiction in relation to a merger (*ibid.*).

b) Order the unwinding of mergers which had been implemented without having been notified, where the CCPC concluded that the merger would result in an SLC.[94]

The EU operates an *ex ante* merger control system, with prior notification required for mergers that fall within the ECMR thresholds. The US switched from an *ex post* to an *ex ante* merger control regime following the introduction of the *Hart-Scott-Rodino Act* in 1976. The Act was introduced to prevent short-run harm to consumers due to delays in reversing anti-competitive mergers, and because it frequently proved extremely difficult to fully restore competition *ex post* (Baer, 1999). The US anti-trust agencies have, nevertheless, challenged consummated mergers *ex post* (Sher, 2004).[95] An executive order issued by the Biden Administration acknowledged that the law permitted the enforcement agencies *"to challenge prior bad mergers that past Administrations did not previously challenge"* (US White House, 2021).

The UK regime has both *ex ante* and *ex post* elements with a voluntary merger notification system combined with own initiative *ex post* investigations. Parties may proceed to integrate without notifying a transaction, potentially taking steps that cannot be easily reversed if the merger is subsequently deemed to be anti-competitive.[96] Many UK merger investigations involve completed mergers (UKDBIS, 2011). It is acknowledged that the UK system means that some anti-competitive mergers may escape review.[97] Between 2004/05 and 2010/11, 60 of 125 cases referred to the UK Competition Commission (UKCC) for a detailed investigation and 14 of 25 cases deemed to be anti-competitive involved completed mergers (UKDBIS, 2011). Over the 2006/07-2015/16 period there were significantly more own initiative investigations of non-notified than

---

94 The 2022 Act also provides that, where it is not possible to unwind or dissolve a merger or acquisition, the CCPC may require the parties to take such steps as are appropriate to restore the pre-merger situation as far as practicable. Merging parties must therefore weigh up whether to notify a below the threshold merger or risk it being reversed *ex post*.

95 Investigations and challenges to consummated mergers increased after 2001 (Sher, 2004). In December 2020, the USFTC issued proceedings seeking to undo Facebook's acquisitions of Instagram and WhatsApp in 2012 and 2014 respectively, although it had not challenged either transaction at the time.

96 If the UKCMA launches an investigation, it may require the parties to cease taking steps to implement the merger.

97 A report prepared for the UK Office of Fair Trading (UKOFT) concluded that the number of mergers considered unlikely to be cleared unconditionally, of which the authorities were unaware, was approximately equal to the number of investigated mergers deemed anti-competitive (Deloitte, 2007).

notified mergers while own initiative cases accounted for one-third of all cases involving prohibitions or remedies (Chisholm & Heideman, 2017). It is argued that the UK's voluntary notification system reduces the regulatory burden on business and the administrative burden on the competition agency, although, in practice, the UK devotes significant resources to identifying potentially anti-competitive mergers which have not been notified (*ibid.*).

Australia, New Zealand, and Singapore also operate voluntary notification regimes.[98] However, in those countries, the parties bear the risk of completing a merger without making a notification. Giving effect to an anti-competitive merger is prohibited and penalties apply in the case of mergers that have not been notified but are subsequently found to be anti-competitive.

Which Mergers Require Review?

Merger controls are based on the premise that it is more efficient to prevent the acquisition of market power, because it can frequently prove difficult to control the exercise of such power once it has been acquired. Consequently, an efficient merger control regime should:

- Seek to identify and, where appropriate, stop those mergers which would allow a firm or firms to acquire undue market power; and
- Put the minimum difficulties in the way of all other mergers.

Ireland's merger legislation seeks to achieve this balancing act primarily through a mandatory notification scheme for mergers involving firms above a certain size. It thus rests on an implicit assumption that mergers between small undertakings are unlikely to have any significant adverse effect on competition. In a small economy such as Ireland, however, this assumption may be invalid and there may be many markets in which mergers between relatively small undertakings are capable of reducing competition. As noted in **Chapter 2**, the CA in *GEHE* recommended that the Minister should make an Order requiring notification of pharmacy acquisitions if they increased concentration within a 20-kilometre radius.[99]

Merger notification thresholds are imperfect as some anti-competitive mergers will inevitably fall below the thresholds (Shapiro, C., 2024). Achieving

---

98 Ahdar (2020, p.153) describes how the pre-notification requirement for mergers in New Zealand was *"abruptly abolished"* in 1990 and attributes this to *"some effective lobbying by big business"*.

99 The recommendation was not implemented.

the appropriate balance in terms of setting notification thresholds, such that the majority of anti-competitive mergers are notifiable, while innocuous mergers are excluded, has proven difficult.[100] Merger notification thresholds were increased in 2002, substantially reduced in 2014, only to be increased again in 2019. In addition, the legislation provides for voluntary pre-notification of mergers which fall below the notification thresholds and, since September 2023 permits the CCPC to *"call-in"* (request parties to notify) below the threshold mergers and to order the unwinding of below the threshold mergers which have been implemented without its prior approval. The picture is further complicated by the CA/CCPC's approach to voluntary notifications.

The *Competition Act, 2002*, required that all mergers had to be notified to the CA when:

i. Each of two or more of the undertakings involved:
   a) had a world-wide turnover of at least €40 million; and
   b) carried on business in any part of the island of Ireland; and
ii. One or more of the undertakings involved had a turnover in the State of not less than €40 million.[101]

These thresholds represented a significant increase compared with the previous legislation which required mergers to be notified where both parties had a turnover of at least IR£20 million (€25 million).[102]

The 2002 Act contained no definition of *"carries on business"* and the CA originally interpreted this term to include all undertakings making sales into the island of Ireland, even if they did not have a physical presence on the island (CA, 2003, February 18). Gorecki (2011, p.658) observed that *"a few euro internet sales were sufficient"* for a merger to be notifiable. He suggests that the CA originally *"cast the net widely in order to ensure that all mergers that were likely to raise competition concerns were captured"* (*ibid.*, p.659). This led to the notification of many mergers with an insufficient competition nexus to Ireland, raising concerns that the merger notification requirements may have

---

100 It has arguably become even more difficult with the emergence of data-based business models where small companies with low turnover may be extremely valuable due to unique data possession or options. Several countries, including Germany, have introduced an additional threshold based on the transaction value/acquisition price of the merger in an attempt to address this.

101 §18(1)(a).

102 As noted in **Chapter 2**, the previous regime provided that mergers had to be notified if either the parties' gross assets or turnover exceeded a certain threshold. Only a turnover threshold was included in the 2002 Act.

been too broad (Gorecki *et al.*, 2007). In December 2006, the CA announced that it had changed its interpretation of the *"carries on business"* provision in the legislation to the effect that, *"when an undertaking does not have a physical presence on the island, it must make sales of at least €2 million into the island in the most recent financial year to be considered to 'carry on business' on the island"* (CA, *Annual Report 2007*, p.25). This led to a significant decline in total merger notifications and in the proportion of notifications where there was no overlap between the merging parties post-2006.[103]

Another factor contributing to the notification of a large number of mergers with no competition nexus within the State was the requirement to notify any merger involving an undertaking that carried on *"a media business"* in the State regardless of the turnover of the parties concerned.[104] In other words, a merger between an undertaking which carried on a media business in the State and another undertaking operating anywhere in the world had to be notified regardless of whether the other party was engaged in a media business. In 2007 this was amended to provide that all mergers had to be notified irrespective of turnover where an undertaking engaged in a media business in Ireland merged with another undertaking engaged in a media business whether in Ireland or elsewhere.[105] This change also contributed to the reduction in the number of notifications (Gorecki, 2011).[106]

Shortly after the passage of the 2002 Act, the CA called for the merger notification thresholds to be lowered (Henneberry, 2004). The notification thresholds were amended by §55 of the *Competition & Consumer Protection Act, 2014,*[107] which required mergers to be notified, where:

i. The aggregate turnover in the State of the undertakings involved was not less than €50 million, and

ii. The turnover in the State of each of two or more of the undertakings involved was not less than €3 million.

The 2014 Act abolished the worldwide turnover threshold and the *"carries on business on the island of Ireland"* provisions. The €3 million threshold in respect

103 Almost 50% of all merger cases over the 2003-2006 period involved no competition overlap but this declined to just 26% post-2006 (CA/CCPC).

104 *Competition Act, 2002*, §18(5), Order 2002, *S.I. No.* 622/2002.

105 *Competition Act, 2002*, §s18(5) & (6), Order 2007, *S.I. No.* 122/2007.

106 Media mergers accounted for 22% of all merger notifications over the period from 2003 to end 2007 and for 8.6% of notifications over the 2008-2022 period.

107 The 2014 Act also provided for a merger of the CA and the National Consumer Agency to create the CCPC.

of the parties' turnover within the State represented a very significant reduction in the notification thresholds. Many acquisitions of individual hotels and motor dealerships were caught by the new notification thresholds. Documents obtained under the *Freedom of Information Act* show that, within three months of the introduction of the new thresholds, the CCPC's parent Department wrote to it stating that it had received representations suggesting that the new thresholds were too low, had increased the administrative burden on small business, and should be increased. The CCPC subsequently announced that it was *"in the process of reviewing the financial threshold levels and is discussing them with the Department of Jobs, Enterprise & Innovation"* (CCPC, *Annual Report 2015,* p.17). The CCPC recommended to the Department in July 2017 that the thresholds should be increased to *"(i) an individual threshold of €10 million and (ii) €60 million for the aggregate threshold"* (CCPC, *M&A Report 2018,* ¶5.1).

The CCPC concluded, based on a study of mergers notified in 2015 and 2016, that these higher thresholds would reduce merger notifications by 35-40% (*ibid*). Documents obtained under the *Freedom of Information Act* indicate that the CCPC did not consider the possibility that raising notification thresholds may provide an incentive for firms to engage in anti-competitive mergers, which might previously not have been contemplated, because firms would have anticipated they would probably have been prohibited.

An increase in the Hart-Scott-Rodino US merger notification thresholds in 2000 was followed by a significant increase in anti-competitive mergers which fell below the new thresholds (Wollmann, 2019). Of US merger investigations prior to 2000, 32% involved mergers below the higher thresholds. Following the raising of the thresholds, merger notifications fell by 70%. Wollmann (*ibid.*) estimated that 3,240 *"stealth"* mergers, i.e., anti-competitive mergers below the higher thresholds, occurred in the 10 years following the increase in the thresholds. One law firm reportedly advised clients in such cases *"it is prudent to avoid rapid and sudden price increases in the first year after closing, particularly if they are not tied to cost increases"* (Farrington *et al.*, 2015, p.30).[108]

---

108 Wollmann (2023) suggests that firms may strategically not release information about potential anti-competitive stealth mergers, including transaction values, in order to avoid bringing them to the attention of the anti-trust agencies. Based on an analysis of mergers between 1994 and 2011, he finds that mergers where the transaction value was not disclosed were competitively significant and estimates that stealth consolidation may be 40% higher than previously thought.

The Irish notification thresholds were increased from the beginning of 2019. The new thresholds are in line with the CCPC recommendations and require that a merger must be notified to the CCPC if, in the most recent financial year:

i. The aggregate turnover in the State of the undertakings involved is not less than €60 million; and

ii. The turnover in the State of each of two or more of the undertakings involved is not less than €10 million.

Trends in merger notifications to the CA/CCPC by year from 2003 to 2023 are illustrated in **Figure 3.1**.

Figure 3.1: Merger Notifications to the CA/CCPC by Year, 2003-2023

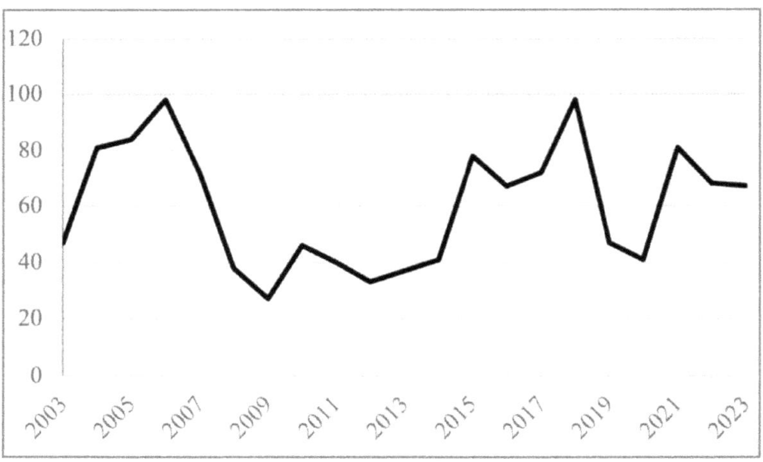

Source: CA/CCPC.

The chart shows a significant drop in merger notifications post-2006 following the CA's decision to amend its interpretation of the *"doing business in Ireland"* provision.[109] The number of notifications increased, significantly, after the notification thresholds were lowered in 2014. Following the subsequent increase in the notification thresholds, merger notifications in 2019 were 52% below the previous year's levels. The CCPC stated that this decline was in line with expectations.

109 It is likely that the financial crash also contributed to the decline in the number of merger notifications as was the case with EU merger notifications (see **Chapter 1**).

> *"The CCPC notes that the change in notification thresholds have had a positive impact by reducing notifications in sectors such as motor fuel – (retail/wholesale) and grocery – (retail/wholesale) which previously involved relatively smaller sized transactions which raised no competition concerns"* (CCPC, M&A Report 2019, ¶1.5).

The statement is puzzling. Motor fuel and grocery retailing are sectors where competition occurs in local markets. Consequently, the acquisition of an individual filling station or grocery outlet could result in a substantial lessening of competition in a relevant local market.[110]

Figure 3.2: Percentage of Notified Mergers Subject to Detailed Investigation by Year, 2003-2023

Source: CA/CCPC.

[110] In *Topaz/Esso*, for example, the CCPC cleared the transaction based *inter alia* on undertakings by the merged entity to dispose of three specific filling stations in order to address concerns that the acquisition of the filling stations concerned would reduce competition in the relevant local markets. Presumably if Topaz had sought to purchase any of these stations individually, the same competition concerns would have arisen. There have been several notifications of filling station acquisitions post-2019, despite the increase in thresholds. Similarly, in *BWG/Londis* the CCPC considered the impact of the acquisition on competition in a number of rural towns based on individual grocery store fascias, although it found in all cases that there would be a sufficient number of competing fascias to prevent any anti-competitive effects (CCPC M/15/009 – *BWG/Londis*,15.6.2015).

Figure 3.2 illustrates the annual percentage of notified mergers that were subject to detailed investigations, suggesting potential competition concerns, over the period from 2003 to 2023.[111]

Apart from a once-off spike in 2012, the proportion of notified mergers identified as posing potential concerns declined from 2004 to 2014. If mergers between small undertakings are generally not anti-competitive, the 2014 reduction in the merger notification thresholds should have resulted in a decline in the proportion of problem cases. The chart shows, however, that the proportion of potential problem cases increased significantly following the lowering of the thresholds in 2014. This trend continued up to 2017, before falling slightly in 2018. This result is inconsistent with the view that mergers between smaller undertakings are unlikely to raise competition concerns. The 2019 increase in the notification thresholds should have increased the proportion of problem cases as it reduced the number of merger notifications between smaller undertakings. The chart shows that the proportion of problem cases increased significantly in 2019 and 2020. While there was a slight decline subsequently, the level of problem cases remains well above the pre 2014 level. This is consistent with a view that the higher thresholds reduced the number of innocuous notifications. The evidence is therefore mixed but the possibility that the 2019 increase in the notification thresholds may have permitted some anti-competitive mergers to go undetected cannot be definitively ruled out.

Voluntary Notifications

The *Competition Act, 2002,* provided that mergers below the compulsory notification thresholds may be voluntarily notified to the CA/CCPC. The Act also provided that §s4 and/or 5 of the Act did not apply to mergers notified and approved by the CA/CCPC.[112] The CA view was that below the threshold mergers could be anti-competitive and this was reflected in its 2002 *Merger Guidelines* (CAMG2002):

111 Defined as cases which were subject to an extended Phase 1 or Phase 2 investigation.

112 §4 prohibits anti-competitive agreements, while §5 prohibits abuse of a dominant position. As noted in **Chapter 2**, the CA had taken the view that mergers could come within the scope of these prohibitions. Making a voluntary notification and obtaining clearance from the CA/CCPC immunises the transaction against a potential legal challenge alleging that it infringes §s4 and/or 5.

> *"The Authority is keen that mergers that clearly raise concerns about competition are notified, while those that clearly do not are not notified" (¶7.3)*

The *Guidelines* suggested a rule of thumb whereby parties should consider notifying below the threshold mergers if post-merger market share was 40% or more, based on any reasonable market definition and should not notify if the post-merger Herfindahl Hirschman Index (HHI) fell within Zone A as defined in CAMG2002.[113]

The CA investigated three below the threshold mergers in 2003 and two in 2004.[114] In September 2003 the CA issued a notice on voluntary notifications:

> *"It is the Authority's policy to seek to prevent implementation of any unnotified merger that would substantially lessen competition in any market in the State. Where such a merger has already been implemented, the Authority may seek to have it reversed." (CA, 2003, September 30).*

The CA reiterated its position subsequently.

> *"In essence, if after a preliminary examination, the Authority considers the transaction may raise competition concerns, it will contact the parties to determine whether they wish to notify voluntarily. If the parties do not voluntarily notify, the transaction will be assessed as to whether it breaches Sections 4 and/or 5" (CA, Annual Report 2003, p.21).*

A CA member expressed disappointment at the lack of voluntary merger notifications, despite the notice. The final sentence below suggests an interesting interpretation of *"voluntary"* notification.

> *"Another disappointing lesson is the question of voluntary notification. So far, only **one** merger has been voluntarily notified. The division's Notice about below threshold mergers last year indicated our policy, and, by and large, we have attempted to hold*

---

113 CAMG2002 defined Zone A as comprising mergers where post-merger concentration as measured by the Herfindahl-Hirschman Index (HHI) was (a) less than 1,000; (b) was between 1,000 and 1,800 and increased by less than 100; and (c) was over 1,800 but increased by less than 50 points. The role of market concentration in merger analysis is considered in **Chapter** 7. Market shares and concentration may not be particularly useful in the case of certain types of below-the-threshold mergers, *e.g.*, digital/data-based businesses, very close competitors in highly heterogeneous markets, dynamic industries, or mergers which eliminate a maverick to restore a non-competitive equilibrium.

114 In one case, the CA issued a decision stating that, in its view, the transaction concerned did not infringe §s4 or 5 of the *Competition Act, 2002*, as amended (CA, *Annual Report 2004*).

> *to that. But, in so doing, we have found that notification of such mergers is not taking place. If we are alerted to a merger, and commence an inquiry because of possible competition issues, parties have been reluctant to notify on the grounds apparently that no they do not feel there will be an adverse effect on competition. This generally results in us having to indicate we will seek an injunction if parties do not agree to hold off closing till our inquiry is completed. The whole process is not what was intended – the Statute seemed to envisage that below-threshold mergers that had competition issues would be notified to give certainty as to their overall effect" (Henneberry, 2004, p.7, emphasis in original).*[115]

In 2012, the CA investigated a proposed merger between the only two wholesale book distributors in the State which fell below the notification thresholds. The parties abandoned the proposed merger when the CA announced that it would bring court proceedings alleging that the proposed transaction involved an agreement which had the object or effect of preventing, restricting or distorting competition contrary to §4 of the *Competition Act, 2002* (CA, *Annual Report 2012*).[116]

CCPCMG2014 contain no references to voluntary notifications apart from stating that the HHI thresholds may be a useful guide for merging parties who are considering a voluntary notification of a below the threshold merger. The CCPC nevertheless continued with its policy of informing merging parties, whenever a below the threshold merger, which it believed might harm competition, came to its attention, that, if they did not *"voluntarily"* notify the transaction, it would launch an investigation into whether the transaction was in breach of §4 and/or 5 of the *Competition Act*. As there is no time limit for such investigations, this left merging parties with little option but to make a *"voluntary"* notification.

---

115 CA/CCPC *Annual Reports* indicate that there were five voluntary merger notifications between 2003 and 2019.

116 The author advised the CA in this case. An internal memo from the CCPC to the Department of Jobs, Enterprise & Innovation dated 30 May 2016 obtained under the *Freedom of Information Act* cited this case when calling for the legislation to be amended to enable the CCPC to require notification of below the threshold mergers where the CCPC had *"prima facie grounds for suspecting that a proposed merger may have the effect of substantially lessening competition in a market for goods or services in the State."* In support of this proposal the memo claimed that *"it would have been very difficult, if not impossible, for the [Competition] Authority to challenge the [Eason/Argosy] transaction had the parties decided to implement it"*.

Kantar Media/Newsaccess[117] provides an example of the CCPC approach:

> *"Following a preliminary assessment of information in its possession, the CCPC was concerned that the proposed merger would result in Kantar Media removing its closest and most substantial competitor from the market. The CCPC therefore **informed the parties that they should make voluntary notification** of the proposed merger (CCPC, M&A Report 2017, ¶3.6, emphasis added)."*

Commenting on the CCPC's subsequent decision to clear the transaction on the basis of remedies, the CCPC Chairperson stated:

> *"It is important for companies and their advisors to take note that even where turnovers fall below the required financial thresholds for mandatory notification, they still have a duty to ensure that any mergers or acquisitions they propose or undertake do not substantially lessen competition in their relevant market. The CCPC will use its powers to ensure that mergers that do not meet the required financial thresholds for mandatory notification, but that are likely to result in a substantial lessening of competition, do not go unchecked" (ibid., ¶3.10).*

The CA/CCPC has cleared several mergers subject to remedies which required the merged entity to notify any future acquisition, even if they fell below the notification thresholds.[118] Such remedies are a further indication that the CA/CCPC considers that below the threshold mergers could result in an SLC.

In *Stena/P&O II*,[119] the CA concluded that the acquisition by Stena of P&O's Fleetwood-Larne business along with two vessels *"would not result in a substantial lessening of competition in any market for ferry freight services in the Central Corridor area of the Irish Sea"* (¶22). It nevertheless made clearance of the transaction conditional on notification of any future merger, even if it fell below the notification thresholds, due to concerns about a possible future acquisition by Stena of P&O's Liverpool-Dublin ferry service.[120] In *CVC/Celtic Rugby*,[121] the transaction was cleared subject to an undertaking

---

117 CCPC M/17/012 – *Kantar Media/Newsaccess*, 11.7.2017.

118 Six cases were cleared subject to such a condition while two more were cleared subject to a combination of behavioural and notification (of future below the threshold mergers) conditions.

119 CA M/04/016 – *Stena/P&O II*, 5.4.2004.

120 The CA indicated that these concerns stemmed from a previous notification which was withdrawn following commencement of a Phase 2 investigation (CA M/03/035 – *Stena/P&O I*, (withdrawn) February 2004).

121 CCPC M/19/034 – *CVC/Celtic Rugby*, 15.1.2020.

to notify any future acquisition by CVC of control over the commercial activities of the Six Nations Rugby Championship.

In *Grafton/Heiton,*[122] the CA concluded that the proposed transaction would not result in any SLC but cleared the transaction on condition that the parties notify future acquisitions of builders' providers businesses that were below the notification thresholds, stating such acquisitions *"could result in an increase in market power in individual markets, as well as a gradual increase in market power nationally"* (¶10.10). In *MJ Gleeson/UBH*[123] and *Eason/Alphyra,*[124] the CA concluded that the proposed transactions would not result in any SLC and did not identify any specific concern in relation to a possible future transaction. In both cases it stated that the notification of future below the threshold mergers by the parties would give it an opportunity to assess whether any increase in market power would result in a detriment to consumers.

> *"The proposed transaction will not substantially lessen competition given the large amount of competitors (both local and national), as well as the relative ease of entry (notwithstanding the importance of "reputational" barriers to entry) into the market for new competitors. The proposal submitted by MJG gives the Authority an opportunity to assess future mergers or acquisitions by MJG to determine whether any increase in market power would result in a detriment to consumers" (*MJ Gleeson/UBH, *¶51).*

> *"While it does not appear that the proposed transaction would substantially lessen competition given the large amount of substitute forms of Etop-ups specifically and top-ups generally, as well as the ability of significant amount of consumers to switch from pre-paid to post-paid accounts, the proposal submitted by Alphyra does give the Authority an opportunity to assess future mergers or acquisitions by Alphyra to determine whether any increase in market power would result in a detriment to consumers" (*Eason/Alphyra, *¶30).*

In *Orpea/First Care*[125] the CCPC again cleared the transaction subject to an obligation to notify future below the threshold mergers.

---

122 CA M/04/051 – *Grafton/Heiton,* 17.2.2005.

123 CA M/05/027 – *MJ Gleeson/UBH,* 23.8.2005.

124 CA M/05/028 – *Eason/Alphyra,* 14.7.2005.

125 CCPC M/21/024 – *Orpea/First Care,* 6.7.2021. Arguably the CCPC's concerns about increased concentration were based on an overly narrow market definition in this case. See **Chapters 6 and 7**.

> *"In light of the above, the Commission has potential concerns regarding Orpea's market share in Co. Kildare post-implementation of the Proposed Transaction and any potential future expansion in this area by Orpea. In particular, should Orpea acquire control over additional residential care and nursing home(s) in County Kildare ...the Commission considers that there is a possibility that such Possible Transaction(s) would not meet the mandatory thresholds for a merger filing to the Commission given the size of the 'Other' competitors in Co. Kildare. In such a scenario, the likely competitive effects of a Possible Transaction on competition in this potential market would not be reviewed by the Commission" (¶31).*

A fundamental question arises regarding the basis for making merger clearance conditional on an obligation to notify a future merger. The CA/CCPC in all six cases acknowledged that the merger that was before it would not result in any SLC.

> *"A sine-qua-non condition for a competition authority to block or condition a transaction is the existence of a strict causal link between the transaction under assessment and the anticipated harm to competition" (OECD, 2009a).*

There is no evidence of such a strict causal link in the CA/CCPC decisions in any of these cases. The concern in each case was that potential future mergers, which might fall below the notification thresholds, might prove anti-competitive. The CA in *Pallas/Crossgar*[126] stated *"it is possible that further consolidation leading to further concentration in the foodservice sector, or categories therein, could give rise to competition concerns should substantial mergers be proposed in the future"* (¶55). The transaction was cleared without any requirement to notify future acquisitions.

The *Competition (Amendment) Act, 2022*, provides that the CCPC may call-in mergers falling below the notification thresholds, if they have not been notified voluntarily, where the transaction *"may, in the opinion of the Commission, have an effect on competition in markets for goods or services in the State"*. This provision explicitly acknowledges that below the threshold mergers may affect competition and introduced a form of *ex post* merger control for such mergers.[127] The 2022 Act also provides that, where a merger has been implemented without CCPC approval, the CCPC may order the

---

126 CA M/12/010 – *Pallas/Crossgar*, 23.8.2012.

127 At the time of writing, it is unclear whether the CCPC will decide that there is no longer any need for remedies requiring future notification of below the threshold mergers given that it can require notification of such transactions under the 2022 Act.

parties to (a) unwind the merger or (b) where unwinding the merger is not possible, require the parties to take steps to restore the situation to that which prevailed pre-merger. The 2022 Act also gives the CCPC the power to impose interim measures in merger cases, effectively requiring the merging parties to refrain from taking any steps to implement the merger pending the outcome of its investigation.[128]

The Substantive Test

The requirement for the CA/CCPC to base merger decisions on pure competition grounds was arguably the most significant change to merger control introduced by the *Competition Act, 2002* (Massey & Daly, 2003). The 1978 Act involved a public interest test, where the Minister was required to decide merger cases based on *"the exigencies of the common good"*. As noted in **Chapter 2**, the *Competition Act, 1991*, retained the *"exigencies of the common good"* as the substantive test to be applied, and specifically provided that the Minister in reaching a decision could take criteria other than those addressed in a report by the CA into account. At the time UK merger control was also based on a public interest test.

Early drafts of the ECMR proposed that the Commission should take account of criteria other than competition when analysing merger cases, but these were ultimately rejected in the final version. Levy *et al.* (2019) state that the Commission has consistently resisted political pressure to take industrial, social or employment considerations into account in its merger appraisals.[129] In 2019, 19 EU Member States called for revisions to the ECMR that would enable industrial policy considerations to be considered (Valero, 2019, January 9). The French and German governments issued a joint Manifesto calling for major changes in the ECMR, following the Commission prohibition of the proposed *Siemens/Alstom* merger (Kotzeva *et al.*, 2019). The primary rationale for that transaction was the alleged need to create a European champion (Massey & McDowell, 2021). The Franco-German Manifesto proposed *inter alia* introducing a degree of political oversight into the merger control process by allowing the Council of Ministers to overturn Commission merger decision. Levy *et al.* (2019, p.30)

---

128 As previously noted, this greatly increases the risks involved in not making a voluntary notification of a below the threshold merger.

129 The Commission's prohibition decision in *Aerospatiale-Alenia/de Havilland* was fiercely opposed by the Industrial Policy Commissioner and several Member States (Levy *et al.*, 2019). (EU Commission Case No. COMP/M.053 – *Aerospatiale-Alenia/de Havilland*, 2.10.1991).

observed that it was difficult to see how introducing political oversight into the merger regime *"would lead to better decision-making or more competitive markets"*.[130]

Most merger control regimes throughout the world apply one of two competition tests:

i. The SLC test, which is contained in Irish legislation; or
ii. The dominance test.

Over the past 25 years many jurisdictions have switched from a dominance to an SLC test.

Modern economic theories have identified two broad categories of competitive harm that may arise from horizontal mergers:

i. Unilateral effects; and
ii. Coordinated effects.

In simple terms, unilateral effects occur where a merger would permit a merging firm to raise prices unilaterally post-merger, while coordinated effects arise where a merger would facilitate collusion (either tacit or explicit).[131]

The US traditionally applied the SLC test.[132] Weitbrecht (2008) states the dominance test was originally included in the ECMR because it was the test contained in German merger control legislation. Lyons (2008) notes that a dominance test could be too harsh on mergers that would create an efficient new enterprise while also allowing anti-competitive mergers which did not satisfy the dominance criterion. Pinkse & Slade (2004) found that the proposed *Bass/Carlsberg-Tetley* UK brewing merger would have resulted in a significant unilateral price increase post-merger, although the parties would not have met the dominance threshold with a combined market share of 40% (Slade, 2004).[133] Massey & Daly (2003) argue that the SLC test is superior to the dominance test for dealing with both unilateral and co-ordinated effects. In particular, they point out that unilateral effects may

---

130 The issue of who should decide on mergers is addressed below.

131 Competitive harm theories are discussed in **Chapters 8** and **9**.

132 §7 of the *Clayton Act* provides that mergers can be prohibited if their effect *"may be substantially to lessen competition, or to tend to create a monopoly"*.

133 The UKMMC had recommended that the merger be allowed to proceed, provided the Acquirer agreed to divest 1,900 tied public houses, although the only economist member of the panel dissented. The Secretary of State rejected the recommendation and prohibited the merger (UKMMC *Bass/Carlsberg-Tetley*, 27.6.1997).

arise in cases where the merging parties would not be considered dominant. EU Competition Commissioner Mario Monti (2002, November 7) argued, however, that the dominance test, if properly interpreted was capable of dealing with all anti-competitive merger effects. It is acknowledged, nonetheless, that the dominance test may lead to both Type I (false positive) and Type II (false negative) errors (Duso *et al.*, 2024).

The EU Commission had sought to overcome the limitations of the dominance test by applying the concept of joint or collective dominance, with mixed success.[134] Unlike Article 102, the ECMR contains no explicit reference to a dominant position enjoyed by two or more undertakings. The CJEU, nevertheless, ruled that the ECMR applied to cases of joint dominance in *Kali und Salz*.[135] Compte *et al.* (2002) claim that the Commission had been seeking to expand the scope of the ECMR and had used *Nestlé/Perrier*[136] as a test case for establishing that it not only prohibited mergers which created or strengthened a dominant position but also prohibited mergers which created or strengthened an *"oligopolistic dominance"*. Venit (1998) notes that the Commission concluded, based on the evolution of prices over the previous five years, that the firms had already recognised the incentive and possibility of raising prices and that the merger would facilitate and reinforce the likelihood of such behaviour. Compte *et al.* (2002) argue that the divestment remedy applied by the Commission actually increased the likelihood of collusion post-merger (see **Chapter 11**). They suggest that the Commission's failure to prohibit the transaction outright may have been prompted by concerns that such a decision might have been overturned on appeal. Motta (2004, p.283) argues that the merger should have been prohibited on the grounds that industry characteristics *"strongly suggest that the firms have been able to tacitly collude over time"*.

In *Airtours* the Commission sought to apply the concept of joint dominance to a four to three merger for the first time, stating that it:

> *"... does not consider that it is necessary to show that the market participants as a result of the proposed merger would behave as if there were a cartel, with a tacit rather than explicit cartel agreement. In particular, it is not necessary to show that there would be a strict punishment mechanism. What matters for collective dominance in the present case is whether the degree of interdependence between*

---

134 Relatively few EU merger decisions involved joint dominance (Davies *et al.*, 2011).

135 *Kali und Salz AG* and *Kali-Chemie AG v. Commission*, Cases 19 and 20/74 of the European Communities, ECLI:EU:C:1975:58.

136 Case No. COMP/M.190 – *Nestlé/Perrier*, 22.7.1992.

> *oligopolists is such that it is rational for the oligopolists to restrict output, and in this sense reduce competition in such a way that a collective dominant position is created."*[137]

The absence of any requirement for a strict punishment mechanism, normally considered essential for tacit collusion, implied a much wider application of joint dominance as a concept (Massey & McDowell, 2010). Jenny (2001) observed that, if the existence of a retaliatory mechanism was not required in order to establish collective dominance, it would mean that situations in which there was no tacit agreement between the parties could be characterised as collective dominance. In effect the decision appeared to broaden the definition of collective dominance to include a non-cooperative oligopolistic equilibrium.[138] The General Court subsequently overturned the decision and set out three necessary conditions for a finding of joint dominance:

i. The market must be sufficiently transparent for each member of the oligopoly to monitor the behaviour of other members;
ii. There must be a clear incentive for individual members of the oligopoly not to cheat by departing from any common policy on the market. Therefore, there should be adequate deterrents to ensure long-term compliance;
iii. It must be established that the reactions of any actual or future competitors, customers or consumers would not be able to jeopardise the results expected from the common policy.

According to Motta (2004), had the Commission decision in *Airtours* been upheld it might have led to the prohibition of other mergers where joint dominance was far from unambiguous. The joint dominance approach failed to fully plug the gap in the EU merger regime. The concept of joint dominance developed by the EU Commission was equivalent to coordinated effects but, single firm dominance under the original ECMR was not equivalent to unilateral effects, leaving a gap in the Commission's ability to police some unilateral effects cases (*ibid.*).

The EU Commission raised the issue of switching from a dominance to an SLC test in a 1998 *Green Paper* (EU Commission, 1998). A majority of

---

137 Case No. COMP/M.1524 – *Airtours/First Choice*, 22.9.1999, ¶150.

138 Firms in oligopolistic markets recognise that their actions are likely to prompt a response by their rivals and will factor such likely responses into their decisions. A non-cooperative oligopolistic equilibrium refers to the outcome that occurs in the absence of collusion, *i.e.*, the parties are competing.

Member States, however, favoured retention of the dominance test to ensure legal certainty (Riesenkampf, 2004). The German competition authority concluded *"there are currently no convincing reasons for changing the prohibition criterion in European or German merger control from the MD [market dominance] test to the SLC test"* (BKA, 2001, p.35). The EU Commission in a December 2001 *Green Paper* sought views on which of the dominance or SLC tests was the more effective (Papaioannou *et al.*, 2002). The Commission then proposed retaining the dominance test but including a definition of dominance that would apply to mergers in a new §2 of the ECMR[139] (EU Commission, 2002). Opponents of switching to an SLC test argued that it would create legal uncertainty (Voelcker, 2004).

The subsequent 2004 revision of the ECMR, however, replaced the dominance test with a new *"significant impediment to effective competition"* (SIEC) test which stated:

> *"A concentration which would significantly impede effective competition, in the common market or in a substantial part of it, in particular as a result of the creation or strengthening of a dominant position, shall be declared incompatible with the common market".*[140]

The SIEC test is generally *"viewed as being nearly identical to the SLC test"* (OECD, 2009a, p.8). Vickers (2006) notes that the change to an SIEC test in the ECMR addressed a problem which arose because dominance had to address different tasks in merger control and the prohibition of abuse. Werden (2008) describes the switch to the SIEC test as a reasonable response to a real problem and suggests that it should lead to appropriate merger prohibitions that would not have been possible under the dominance standard.[141] OECD (2009a) stated that countries which had switched to an SLC test did not report any increase in intervention rates or reductions in legal certainty, although Thomas (2017) argues that the failure to define the meaning of "significant" led to an increasingly discretionary approach in

139 The proposed new §2 stated: *"For the purpose of this Regulation, one or more undertakings shall be deemed to be in a dominant position if, with or without coordinating, they hold the economic power to influence appreciably and sustainably the parameters of competition, in particular, prices, production, quality of output, distribution or innovation, or appreciably to foreclose competition"* (EU Commission, 2002 December 11).

140 *Regulation 139/2004*, Article 2(3). Heimler (2008) and Monti (2003) both argue that the reform was unnecessary and dispute claims that the dominance test resulted in a gap in EU merger enforcement.

141 For a more detailed appraisal, see Levy (2010).

merger decisions. Davies *et al.* (2011) find, however, that the EU Commission was wary of invoking coordinated effects post-2004.[142]

Some commentators argued that harmonisation with the US approach also lay behind the EU's adoption of the SIEC test (see, for example, Riesenkampf, 2004 and Horner, 2006). Prior to the adoption of the SIEC test the EU Commission and US authorities had reached opposing conclusions in *Boeing/McDonnell Douglas*[143] and *GE/Honeywell*.[144]

Akbar (2002) reports that the EU Commission decision to block the *GE/Honeywell* merger, the first time the Commission blocked a merger that had already been cleared by the USDoJ, caused consternation in the US. Motta (2004, p.390) described the Commission arguments in the case as *"novel"* and *"at worst incomplete or incorrect and at best not explained accurately enough"*.[145] Kovacic (2001) claims that both the EU and US believed that the other's decision in *Boeing/McDonnell Douglas* was politically motivated, although he rejects such claims based on an analysis of both decisions.[146] The USFTC decided not to challenge the transaction, but the EU Commission only cleared it subject to restrictions on Boeing's future behaviour in the commercial aircraft sector. Kovacic notes that the USFTC took the rather unusual step of publishing reasons for its decision not to oppose the merger. He also suggests that a proper understanding of EU merger policy *"should have gone a long way to deflect concerns that the EC deviated from orthodox analytical principles and treated the Boeing-MDC merger as an exceptional case"* (*ibid.*, p.847). He argues, however, the EU Commission could have presented its case better and cites claims that, the then Competition Commissioner, Karel van Miert, had made speeches condemning the merger before the Commission's review was complete (ICPAC, 2000). Slade (2004) observed that whether rules of thumb are based on unilateral or coordinated effects can lead to different choices of cases to investigate, and to different conclusion in relation to competitive harm.

Despite the divergences in these high-profile cases, Bergman *et al.* (2005) found that mergers involving at least one US firm were more likely to be

---

142 Aigner *et al.* (2006) argue that, in the aftermath of *Airtours*, the Commission and Courts seemed reluctant to pursue joint dominance theories in merger cases.

143 EU Commission, Case No. COMP/M.877 – *Boeing/McDonnell Douglas*, 30.7.1997.

144 EU Commission, Case No. COMP/M.2220 – *GE/Honeywell*, 3.7.2001.

145 He acknowledges, however, that published decisions cannot include all of the details and explanations that one would like.

146 See also Fox (2003).

cleared by the EU Commission. Duso *et al.* (2013) also found that the EU Commission tended to treat US firms more leniently in merger decisions.

CMRG (2000) recommended that Ireland should adopt a dominance test in line with the ECMR at that time. The CA successfully argued for the adoption of the SLC test, which *"is more suited to addressing both unilateral and co-ordinated effects, and appears, therefore, to be superior to the dominance test"*, in the *Competition Act, 2002* (Massey & Daly, 2003, p.303). The UK *Enterprise Act, 2002*, adopted an SLC test in place of a public interest test. Following the change in the ECMR substantive test, Belgium, France, Spain, and Poland also adopted the SLC test (OECD, 2009a).

Australia initially adopted an SLC test in its 1974 *Trade Practices Act* but switched to a dominance test in 1977. The Australian Government argued that a less restrictive approach to merger control was necessary so that Australian firms could achieve economies of scale and improve their international competitiveness. While this led to increased concentration in several major industries, the dominance test was viewed as having failed to deliver the promised gains in efficiency and international competitiveness. In 1992 Australia reverted back to an SLC test (*ibid.*).

In New Zealand, §27 of the *Commerce Act, 1986*, applied a dominance test. According to Ahdar (2020, p.153):

> *"...the 'dominance' standard proved to be highly permissive. Few mergers were halted and the presence of very large market shares post-merger could still be overcome by an unduly generous view of the likelihood of new entry disciplining the merged firm. An idealized version of potential competition (contestability theory) held sway."*

The dominance test in Australia and New Zealand only applied in cases of single firm dominance. Mergers could not be blocked on the grounds that they would create a strong likelihood of co-ordinated effects which was one of the reasons why the competition agencies in both countries argued in favour of switching to an SLC test (OECD, 2009a). The New Zealand Ministry of Commerce proposed that the dominance test should be replaced by an SLC test, arguing:

> *"...it is likely that the current thresholds for mergers, by ignoring the potential for joint dominance, prevents sufficient scrutiny of mergers that fall short of creating single firm dominance, but may nevertheless result in efficiency losses. In particular, mergers are not scrutinised in terms of whether they facilitate tacit collusion in tight oligopolistic industries". (New Zealand Ministry of Commerce, 1999, p.32).*

A report prepared for the Treasury, however, argued against the adoption of an SLC test because it was unclear whether oligopolistic collusion was (a) a significant problem and (b) could be effectively addressed by merger control (Evans *et al.*, 1999). New Zealand, nevertheless, adopted the SLC test in 2001. Ahdar (2020), states, however, that it is doubtful that this resulted in an increased rate of prohibitions.

A question also arises as to what constitutes a substantial lessening. The CCPC concluded in *PandaGreen/Exomex*[147] that the proposed transaction raised no competition concerns in relation to the supply of domestic waste collection services because:

i. The geographic overlap between the parties in County Louth was limited and according to the purchaser accounted for only [5-10]% of the total number of households in the county.
ii. The target was only active to a limited extent in the supply of domestic waste collection services in the areas where the parties overlapped.[148]

The CCPC took a markedly different approach in *Thornton's/Carducci* where it expressed concerns that the proposed transaction would harm competition in certain overlapping areas within three Dublin local authority areas. According to the Determination, the increment in customer numbers in the overlap area in Fingal County amounted to 92 households (0.1% of all households in the county) within a one square kilometre area.[149] The increment in customer numbers was 1% in Dublin City and 5% in South Dublin County. This begs the question as to whether any competitive harm could be considered substantial given the limited number of customers and very limited geographic areas affected.[150]

---

147 CCPC M/21/016 – *PandaGreen/Exomex*, 30.9.2021.

148 The target indicated that its customers in the overlap areas accounted for [5-10]% of its domestic waste customers in the county (¶87).

149 Table 6 of the Determination lists the number of household customers that were to be divested in each of the three local authority areas. According to the Determination, the parties agreed *"to divest the increment of customers in the area of each postcode which are located within each of the Overlapping Areas"* (¶5.33). FCC has a total land area of 450 square kilometres. (https://consult.fingal.ie/en/system/files/materials/33513/Fingal%20LECP%20Socio-Economic%20Profile_0.pdf). Accessed 15.1.2025.

150 CCPC M/22/067 – *Thornton's Recycling/Carducci*, 13.7.2023. This case also raises questions about market definition, market structure and theories of harm which are discussed in **Chapters 6**, **7** and **8** respectively.

The Consumer *versus* Total Welfare Standard

The necessity to weigh anti-competitive effects against possible efficiency gains when analysing mergers was originally mooted by Williamson (1968). It is now standard practice for competition agencies to consider whether any anti-competitive effects of a proposed merger are likely to be outweighed by merger-related efficiency gains (Massey & Daly, 2003). The treatment of efficiencies constitutes a key test of the welfare standard applied by a competition agency (Lyons, 2002).

Under a consumer welfare standard, the focus is on whether the price-reducing effect of a decline in marginal cost, due to efficiency gains, will at least offset the price increasing effect of reduced rivalry as a result of the merger. A total welfare standard takes account of the impact of a merger on both producers and consumers. If a merger results in higher prices because efficiencies are insufficient to offset the price increasing effect of reduced rivalry, this will increase producer profits. A total welfare standard asks whether the gains to producers from higher profits outweigh the loss to consumers from higher prices.

The consumer welfare standard was formally incorporated in USHMG1997 (Coate & Heimart, 2009).

> *"The Agency considers whether cognizable efficiencies likely would be sufficient to reverse the merger's potential to harm consumers in the relevant market, e.g. by preventing price increases in that market" (USHMG1997, §4).*

A majority of competition agencies across the world apply a consumer welfare standard.[151] Kolasky (2001, p.783) describes the adoption of the consumer welfare standard as *"the single most important advance in anti-trust doctrine over the last quarter-century"*.

Irish legislation does not define what is meant by an SLC. However, CAMG2002 defined an SLC as follows:

> *"The SLC test is interpreted in terms of consumer welfare. Consumer welfare depends on a range of variables including price, output, quality, variety and innovation. In most cases, the effect on consumer welfare is measured by whether the price in the market will rise. The conclusion that an SLC will result from a merger is thus based on whether the price to buyers is expected to rise (or*

[151] Carlton (2007) reported that only Canada and New Zealand applied a total welfare standard.

> *output to fall). Where price is not the appropriate variable, welfare is measured by the changes in the relevant variables" (¶1.3).*

In a December 2010 consultation paper, the CA stated:

> *"Also in addition to a technical description of the SLC test, there should be greater emphasis on its role as a theoretical concept. This would clarify how the SLC test is used by the Competition Authority in forming its opinion on whether or not a proposed transaction will substantially lessen competition" (CA, 2010, December 3, ¶2.9).*

Three years later CA issued a new set of *Merger Guidelines* (CAMG2013), which were subsequently adopted by the CCPC.[152] CCPCMG2014 contained a more detailed description of the SLC test. They define competition as business rivalry, while stating that the object of merger review was not to protect competitors.

> *"Competition in the context of these Guidelines means rivalry between businesses to sell goods and/or services to consumers. Rivalry between businesses, together with the credible prospect of consumers switching from one business to another, provides an incentive for businesses to compete with each other for the benefit of consumers.*
>
> *The strength (or weakness) of the incentive for business rivalry can depend not only on the presence of competitors, and the credible prospect of consumer switching, but also on the anticipated entry of potential competitors (which would further increase the switching options for consumers).*
>
> *It is not the purpose of merger review to protect competitors from the effects of a merger. Rather, it is to ensure that mergers which would result in an SLC are not permitted" (ibid., ¶s1.4-1.6, footnotes omitted).*

In contrast to CAMG2002, CCPCMG2014 contain no specific reference to the consumer welfare standard, although the wording used throughout implies such a standard.

> *"In applying the SLC test the Commission analyses not only the effect on the price of affected products but also other effects that can impact on consumers, such as changes to output (quantity),*

152 CCPCMG2014 contained no revisions to CAMG2013 other than references to the CCPC were substituted for references to the CA (FN2).

quality, consumer choice and innovation (e.g., development of new products or enhancements to existing products)" (¶1.9).

As previously noted, the consumer welfare standard asks whether the price-reducing effect of a decline in marginal cost, due to efficiency gains, will at least offset the price increasing effect of reduced rivalry as a result of the merger (Lyons, 2002). This is the approach followed in CCPCMG2014.

> *"A merger may generate various efficiencies for the merged entity. The Commission's analysis of efficiencies goes beyond the impact of efficiencies on the merged entity and focuses on whether verifiable efficiencies mitigate adverse competitive effects and prevent an SLC.*
>
> *The onus rests on the parties to show that claimed efficiencies are (i) merger-specific, (ii) verifiable and (iii) benefit consumers sufficiently to prevent an SLC" (¶s 8.1 & 8.2).*

The requirement that efficiencies *"benefit consumers sufficiently to prevent an SLC"* clearly indicates a consumer welfare standard.

The Irish Courts have accepted that the object of competition law is to protect consumer welfare. In the only appeal against a merger decision by the CA/CCPC to date, the High Court noted:

> *"In particular, the assessment as to whether a substantial lessening of competition will occur is interpreted in terms of consumer welfare. The effect of the merger on consumer welfare is measured by whether or not the price of the products concerned in the market will rise."*[153]

Similarly, the Supreme Court, albeit in a non-merger case, has stated:

> *"The entire aim and object of competition law is consumer welfare. Competitive markets must serve the consumer. That is their sole purpose."*[154]

CCPCMG2014 provide that the analysis of competitive effects is not limited to the immediate customers of the merged entity.

> *"In applying the SLC test the Authority will examine not only the competitive effects on the immediate customers of the merged entity but also effects on subsequent, intermediate and final customers. For example, retailers or final customers may be*

---

153 *Rye Investments v. Competition Authority* [2009] IEHC 140. This case involved an appeal against the CA's prohibition decision in CA M/08/009 – *Kerry/Breeo*, 28.8.2008.

154 *Competition Authority v. O'Regan & Others* [2007] IESC 22, ¶38.

> *affected by a merger in the supply chain upstream from the retail level" (¶1.10).*

Weitbrecht (2008) argues that the switch to the SIEC test in the ECMR resulted in a move to a consumer welfare standard and away from the German ordoliberal approach without any legislative change and was never subjected to public debate. Then EU Competition Commissioner, José Almunia, in a 2011 speech, described consumer welfare as *"the cornerstone, the guiding principle of EU competition policy"*, a view subsequently endorsed by one of his successors.

> *"Consumer welfare is now well established as the standard the Commission applies when assessing mergers...Our aim is simple: to protect competition in the market as a means of enhancing consumer welfare and ensuring an efficient allocation of resources" (Kroes, 2005, cited in Levy* et al.*, 2019 FN6).*

Many economists, including Williamson (1968), suggest that the total welfare standard is superior to the consumer welfare standard. Farrell & Shapiro (1990) argue that few economists would accept that competition policy should aim to maximise only consumer welfare and that the appropriate objective should be to maximise total welfare. Lyons (2002) also argues that most economists would favour a total welfare standard. Motta (2004) and Carlton (2007) similarly argue that a total welfare standard is preferable.[155]

Lyons (2008) points out, however, that applying a total welfare standard in individual merger cases may not maximise overall welfare, so that a consumer welfare standard may well be superior.[156] Neven & Röller (2005) also observe that, in the absence of regulatory failure, a total welfare standard would be preferable, but suggest that, when institutional and political economy considerations are taken into account, a consumer welfare standard may be superior. Carlton (2007) also states that a short-term consumer welfare standard might lead to better outcomes if courts and/or competition agencies are prone to political influence. Kauper (2008) criticised the consumer welfare standard for placing undue emphasis on oversimplified and unrealistic economic models and too little emphasis on

---

155 Renckens (2007) argues that the concept of an efficiencies defence can only be correctly applied using a total welfare standard.

156 This is because firms may propose any merger they wish, and a competition authority can only adjudicate on mergers proposed by firms. This gives the firms an advantage, and the mergers they propose can block a more desirable market structure that would evolve under a more restrictive consumer welfare standard.

actual market effects. Melamed (2020) rejects criticisms that the consumer welfare standard is flawed, arguing that the focus on price reflects data limitations and difficult problems of proof.

More recently the consumer welfare standard has been criticised on the grounds that it runs the risk of under-deterrence, because it focuses unduly on short-term price effects. It is argued that it fails to sufficiently recognise the implications of imperfect information and the fact that economic agents' decisions may be influenced by strategic and dynamic considerations (Khan, 2017). Lamoreaux (2019) also argues that the preoccupation with consumer welfare ignores wider considerations such as the ability of dominant undertakings to wield undue political influence. Such criticisms reflect a view that the consumer welfare standard has contributed to a narrowing of the scope of US anti-trust law. As Hawk (2020) points out, however, arguments that competition policy should take account of a wider range of issues, including employment, wealth inequality and protection of small business, face the problem that it is difficult to translate such concerns into coherent, administrable, and predictable legal rules.

Lande (2013) advocated an alternative *"consumer choice"* test proposed by Averitt & Lande (2007, p.182) whereby *"[a]n anti-trust violation can…be understood as an activity that unreasonably restricts the totality of price and nonprice choices that would otherwise be available"*. This approach has been dismissed by consumer welfare advocates as inconsistent with economic principles and the preferences consumers express when making trade-offs between price and nonprice values (Wright & Ginsberg, 2013).

The CCPC is following international best practice in applying a consumer welfare standard. Theoretical economic arguments suggest that the total welfare standard is preferable to the consumer welfare standard. Institutional and other factors mean that, while the total welfare standard may be superior in theory, the consumer welfare standard is probably superior in practice.

The Burden of Proof

Proving causation in merger cases *ex ante* is especially complex because it is prospective and multifaceted (Bavasso & Lindsay, 2007).[157] Kolasky (2001) observes that the standard of proof and the allocation of the burden of proof

---

[157] Winston (2021) argues that the main constraint on the effectiveness of anti-trust policy is the inability of competition agencies to predict market outcomes in merger and dominance cases.

both influence the relative frequency of Type I and Type II errors. Kovacic (2001) notes that the EU Commission is subject to a lower burden of proof than the US anti-trust agencies who must go to court if they wish to challenge a merger. He notes that some of the evidence relied upon by the EU Commission in *Boeing-McDonnell Douglas* would have been dismissed by a US Court.[158] Views of customers should be given greater weight than those of competitors as the latter are likely to benefit from price increases due to an anti-competitive merger.[159]

Budzinski (2010) argues that the introduction of sophisticated economic case-by-case analysis in merger cases had raised the standard of proof in EU and US merger cases. He claimed that this had made it virtually impossible for competition agencies on both sides of the Atlantic to challenge mergers based on unilateral effects theories of harm. In *Arch Coal,* the Court held that the USFTC was required to show that anti-competitive coordination was likely based on evidence of past coordination, market structure and dynamics, and the role of fringe players.[160] Gavil (2005, p.594) argued that the *"court has in essence written into the law an economic standard that is unlikely to ever be met"* in *Oracle/PeopleSoft.*[161] Kwoka (2015) states that the implicit commitment in USHMG1992 to identify more explicitly the theory of competitive harm underlying any merger challenge, while meritorious in principle, had made merger challenges more difficult. Shapiro (2019) advocates a re-balancing of the burden of proof in US horizontal merger cases.

Shapiro & Shelanski (2021), while acknowledging that the *Oracle/PeopleSoft* judgement had made it very difficult to win cases based on unilateral effects theories, state that, following changes introduced in USHMG2010 the courts have accepted unilateral effects theories in several key cases, implicitly and, in one case explicitly, rejecting *Oracle/PeopleSoft*. This suggests that the difficulties described by Budzinski (2010) can be overcome, to some extent, by providing greater clarity around the relevant

---

158 He also suggests that a lack of customer opposition to the merger might also have posed problems for the USFTC.

159 Neven & Röller (2002) found that competitors played an important role in favour of anti-competitive transactions during the first 10 years of the ECMR but found surprisingly that they did not play a significant role in opposing competitive mergers. CCPC M/22/062 – *Associated Hardware/National Hardware*, 18.5.2023 cited the fact that the vast majority of the parties' competitors that it had contacted expressed no concerns about the proposed transaction.

160 *FTC v. Arch Coal*, 329 F. Supp. 2d 109 (DDC) 2004 at 138.

161 *United States v. Oracle*, 331 F. Supp. 2d 1098, (N.D. Cal. 2004). See also Parkison Hassid (2007) for a critique of the judgement.

economic concepts, although it may not completely overcome the problem of institutional underenforcement.[162]

The majority in *Coillte/Balcas* expressed the view that the minority had sought to apply a more stringent test than was required by the legislation in arguing that the transaction *"cannot be conclusively presumed to be anti-competitive"* (¶6.25). The *Competition Act, 2002,* as amended, is silent as to the burden of proof that the CCPC is required to meet in order to conclude that a proposed merger would result in an SLC. There is no presumption that a merger will result in an SLC, and it would appear, therefore, that it is for the CCPC to establish that a merger would do so. It would appear that the required burden of proof is on the balance of probabilities, although this is obviously a legal issue.

Surprisingly this issue was not explicitly addressed by the High Court in *Rye Investments*. The Court stated that any material economic conclusions which the CCCPC arrives at must be supported by or consistent with the clear effect of the evidence, information or data upon which it is based.

> *"In other words, where the Authority has, without committing significant error, exercised its specialist expertise in making judgments as to the prospective consequences of the economic and commercial factors which govern or influence competition in the relevant market, this Court should not intervene even if it is demonstrated that an opposite conclusion might plausibly have been reached by placing weight on different aspects of the available evidence or data or by attributing different or greater significance to other pertinent factors in the economic assessment. Nevertheless, the Court will be entitled and obliged to intervene to set aside a material economic conclusion if it is shown to be incorrect because it is unsupported by or inconsistent with the clear effect of the evidence, information or data upon which it is based." (¶5.21).*

The CCPC view is that, in merger cases, *"the relevant standard of proof is the ordinary civil standard, i.e., the balance of probabilities"* (*Bank of Ireland/KBC,* ¶3.8).[163] Such a threshold is in line with EU case law and economic opinion.

The ECMR does not specify the threshold that the EU Commission is required to meet in order to prohibit a merger. Botteman (2006) argued that, despite the General Court's judgements in *Airtours, Schneider Electric/*

---

[162] Shapiro & Shelanski (2021) suggest that one of the reasons why the USDoJ lost in *Oracle* was due to confusion in USHMG1992 with respect to *"targeted buyers"*.

[163] CCPC M/21/021 – *Bank of Ireland/KBC,* 23.5.2022.

Legrand, and *Tetra Laval*, the standard of proof in EU merger cases remained ill-defined but states that the Commission should not be required to prove that a merger will have anti-competitive effects *"beyond reasonable doubt"*. He argues that the Commission is required to get the facts right and describe pre-merger market conditions accurately and ensure that the facts and the conclusions drawn therefrom support the Commission's theory of competitive harm. This would appear to be consistent with the position of the High Court in *Rye Investments*. The CJEU in *Impala*[164] set the balance of probabilities as the standard of proof in EU merger cases.

Lyons (2008) argues that the burden of establishing anti-competitive effects should be higher for non-horizontal than for horizontal mergers, reflecting the fact that economics indicates that vertical mergers are far less likely than horizontal mergers to have a negative impact on competition.[165] He points out that the mechanisms by which anti-competitive effects occur in non-horizontal mergers are more indirect than in the case of horizontal mergers, and may involve several stages, which necessitates establishing that each of these individual steps is likely to occur. The General Court appeared to acknowledge this in *Tetra Laval* stating that, when a merger does not immediately affect the structure of the market, the Commission must be convinced that the merger would *"in all likelihood"* allow the parties to achieve a dominant position in the near future (¶148). The CJEU, however, appeared to apply a lower evidentiary threshold on appeal.

> *"The analysis of a 'conglomerate-type' concentration is a prospective analysis in which, first, the consideration of a lengthy period of time in the future and, secondly, the leveraging necessary to give rise to a significant impediment to effective competition mean that the chains of cause and effect are dimly discernible, uncertain and difficult to establish. That being so, the quality of the evidence produced by the Commission in order to establish that it is necessary to adopt a decision declaring the concentration incompatible with the common market is particularly important, since that evidence must support the Commission's conclusion that, if such a decision were not adopted, the economic development envisaged by it would be plausible."*[166]

---

164 *Bertelsmann AG & Sony Corporation of America v. Independent Music Publishers & Labels Association (Impala)*, Case T-464/04, 2006 II 02289.

165 Stöhr *et al.* (2020), argue, however, that vertical mergers are likely to be harmful in markets where horizontal concentration is high.

166 ¶44.

In *CK Telecoms*, the General Court ruled that the Commission was required to reach a higher *"more likely than not"* burden of proof rather than the balance of probabilities standard in such cases.[167]

> *"In the context of an analysis of a significant impediment to effective competition the existence of which is inferred from a body of evidence and indicia, and which is based on several theories of harm, the Commission is required to produce sufficient evidence to demonstrate with a strong probability the existence of significant impediments following the concentration. Thus, the standard of proof applicable in the present case is therefore stricter than that under which a significant impediment to effective competition is 'more likely than not', on the basis of a 'balance of probabilities', as the Commission maintains. By contrast, it is less strict than a standard of proof based on 'being beyond all reasonable doubt'" (¶118).*

The judgement was subsequently overturned by the CJEU which found that the General Court had erred in law in setting a *"more likely than not"* standard of proof in unilateral effects cases. The CJEU held that the prospective nature of the economic analysis which the Commission was required to carry out under the ECMR precludes a requirement for it to meet a particularly high standard of proof in order to establish that a merger would significantly impede effective competition.[168]

Valetti & Zenger (2019) argue that, while the balance of probabilities threshold is appropriate in the majority of merger cases, it is inappropriate in mergers involving potential competitors and suggest a lower threshold is required to prevent substantial under-enforcement in such cases. They also argue that the likely magnitude of potential harm should influence the required burden of proof.

Bavasso & Lindsay (2007) note that, in order to avail of the failing firm defence in EU merger cases, parties must show that the failing firm's assets would inevitably exit the market in the absence of the merger.[169] They argue that this inevitability standard departs from the general standard of proof under the ECMR. They question whether the standard of proof should vary between cases on the basis of the issues involved. They contrast the EU approach with that in *British Salt*[170] where they found no indication that the UKCC did not apply a balance of probabilities test in a failing firm case.

---

167 *CK Telecoms UK Investments v. Commission*, Case T-399/16, 2020 217.

168 *Commission v. CK Telecoms UK Investments*, Case C-376/20, ECLI:EU:C:2023:561.

169 The CA/CCPC apply a similar test. The issue of failing firms is addressed in **Chapter 5**.

170 UKCC, *British Salt/New Cheshire Salt Works*, Case No. ME/1593/05, 8.11.2005.

Shapiro, C. (2024) states that USHMG2023 clarifies that the anti-trust agencies are only required to show that a merger *may* substantially lessen competition, not that it will do so. He notes that this is already clear from the case law but claims that some US courts had applied too demanding a threshold.

The Phase 2 Threshold

CA/CCPC merger investigations involve a two-stage process similar to that under the ECMR.[171]

There is no statutory requirement for the CCPC to establish that there is a realistic prospect of an SLC before it can embark on a Phase 2 investigation. The CCPC considers that it is not required to have grounds for believing an SLC might occur but merely be unable to conclude that one will not occur.

> *"Where, having considered the information provided and all submissions received, the Commission is unable on the basis of the information before it to form the view that the result of the merger or acquisition will not be to substantially lessen competition in markets for goods or services in the State, the Commission will make a determination to carry out a full investigation, i.e. proceed to Phase Two."*[172]

This contrasts with the position in other jurisdictions.

Article 6(1)(b) of the ECMR provides that the EU Commission must have *"serious doubts"* that a merger would have an adverse effect on competition in order to launch a Phase 2 investigation. The General Court ruled that the standard of proof under the ECMR is the same at both Phase 1 and Phase 2 in *BaByliss*[173] and *easyJet*.[174] Subsequently in *Cisco*[175] it rejected an argument that a decision to clear a merger at Phase 1 should be subject to the *"beyond a reasonable doubt"* standard, re-affirming that the *"balance of probabilities"* was the appropriate standard at both Phase 1 and Phase 2. Kalintiri (2014)

---

171 These are commonly referred to as Phase 1 and Phase 2 investigations. This two-step process is common in many jurisdictions, including the EU, UK and US.

172 CCPC (2021, December), ¶3.1.

173 Case T-114/02 *BaByliss SA v. Commission* [2003] ECR II-1279, ¶169. The Court held that the Commission had failed to meet this test in respect of markets in five Member States and partly annulled the decision.

174 Case T-177/04 *easyJet v. Commission* [2006] ECR II-1931.

175 *Cisco Systems Inc and Messagenet SpA v. Commission*, Case T-79/12 [2013] ECR I-000.

argues that the *Cisco* judgement implies that the correct approach is to institute a Phase 2 investigation if there are serious doubts about the competitive impact of a merger, not least because there is no possibility of correcting a Phase 1 false positive decision.

The UKCMA is required to have a reasonable belief that a merger would result in an SLC in order to initiate a Phase 2 investigation.

> *"At phase 1, the CMA's test for reference (its 'duty to refer') will be met if the CMA has a reasonable belief, objectively justified by relevant facts, that there is a realistic prospect that the merger will lessen competition substantially" (UKCMA, 2021, March 18, ¶3.8).*

Botteman (2006) argues that a decision to initiate a Phase 2 investigation, does not affect the legal position of the merging parties. This argument ignores the fact that a decision to initiate a Phase 2 investigation has significant commercial implications for the merging parties. Mergers are highly time-sensitive and delays arising from a Phase 2 investigation may impose significant costs on the parties. In several merger cases in recent years, it has taken the CCPC more than six months to issue a Determination while a small number of cases have taken a year to be decided. Such lengthy delays obviously create considerable uncertainty. The target business may experience a significant decline during this period as key personnel may choose to leave, staff morale may decline, and customers may also be lost as a result of uncertainty.

Over the 2003-2023 period, the CA/CCPC carried out 45 Phase 2 investigation, excluding withdrawn notifications. In 34 of these cases the Determination stated that the CA/CCPC had decided to conduct a Phase 2 investigation because it was unable to form a view that the proposed transaction would not result in an SLC. Thus in over 75% of these cases, the CA/CCPC had not identified a theory of harm by the end of its Phase 1 investigation.[176] The average time from notification to the adoption of a decision to conduct a Phase 2 investigation was 98 days, which seems to

---

[176] It appears from the Determinations that the CA/CCPC had identified a possible theory of harm in nine of the remaining 10 cases. In seven cases, the Determination indicates that the CA/CCPC had raised specific concerns with the parties (see below). CA M/03/033 – *SRH/FM104*, 23.2.2004 gives no reason for going to Phase 2. In CA M/06/027 – *Tetra Laval/Carlisle*, 11.8.2006, the Determination points out that the notification had indicated that the overlap between the parties was limited to a single product, but the CA's investigations identified a further three horizontal overlaps, while in CA M/10/043 – *Stena/DFDS*, 7.4.2011, the parties ceased operating certain ferry routes post-notification, thus arguably changing the scenario against which the CA had to analyse the proposed transaction.

rule out time constraints as an explanation for the failure to identify a theory of harm at the end of Phase 1.[177]

Table 3.1 provides further details of the time taken to reach a Phase 1 Determination in all Phase 2 cases. Identifying an appropriate theory of harm early on may be helpful in contentious cases for both competition agencies and the merging parties as it can enable both sides to focus on the key issues (Scheffman & Coleman, 2003).

Table 3.1: Duration of Phase 1 Investigation in Phase 2 Cases

Days	Number of Cases	% of Total
<30	9	20.0
31-50	1	2.2
51-75	7	15.6
76-100	6	13.3
101-150	14	31.1
151-200	6	13.3
>200	2	4.4
Total	**45**	**100.0**

Source: CA/CCPC.

The CA/CCPC decided to launch a Phase 2 investigation within 30 days of a transaction being notified in only nine cases (20% of the total) most recently in 2010. In 78% of Phase 2 cases, it took the CA/CCPC more than 50 days to decide to go to Phase 2, while in 49% it took more than 100 days. In two cases the decision to go to Phase 2 was taken more than 200 days after the transaction had been notified. The point is not the length of time taken by the CA/CCPC to reach a decision, not least because this is outside of its control in cases where it has sought information from the parties. However, it would seem reasonable to suggest that the CA/CCPC should be in a position to identify a potential theory of harm in cases where it has had more than 50 days to assess the merger.[178]

177 The legislation provides that the CA/CCPC was required to adopt a Phase 1 Determination within 30 days (prior to 2014) and 30 working days thereafter. If the CA/CCPC issues an RFI, the deadline for taking a decision starts from the date that the parties provide the information requested, rather than the notification date. The decision date is extended by 15 working days (15 days pre-2014) if the parties offer undertakings during Phase 1.

178 The fact that it may be waiting on parties to respond to an RFI does not prevent the CA/CCPC from continuing its analysis of a case.

The absence of any requirement to show that there is a realistic prospect that a merger could result in a SLC prior to launching a Phase 2 investigation, combined with the length of such investigations creates a potential for regulatory hold-up. Parties may offer commitments in order to avoid the lengthy delay and costs associated with a Phase 2 investigation, even in cases where a proposed merger would have no adverse effect on competition (Trebilcock & Iacobucci, 2002). Remedying mergers which are not anti-competitive, in order to avoid a Phase 2 investigation, constitutes a Type I (false positive) error and imposes costs on the parties and society, which are unlikely to be considered by the competition agency.

In addition, if the CCPC proposes to launch a Phase 2 investigation, not on the basis that it has identified a potential threat to competition, but on the grounds that it is not in a position to conclude that there will not be an SLC, it is difficult to see how it could accurately evaluate whether any remedies proposed by the parties would be sufficient to prevent an SLC. The EU General Court in *BaByliss* ruled that, when accepting commitments at Phase 1, the EU Commission has to demonstrate that the commitments were *"sufficient to rule out clearly any serious doubts"* as to whether effective competition would be significantly impeded. The EU Commission Remedy Notice states that for Phase 1 remedies to be acceptable *"the competition problem needs to be so straightforward and the remedies so clear-cut that it is not necessary to enter into an in-depth investigation and that the commitments are sufficient to clearly rule out 'serious doubts' [of competitive harm]"* (EU Commission, 2008, October 22, ¶81).[179]

UKCMA procedures afford the merging parties a significant opportunity to argue against a decision to conduct a Phase 2 investigation. The procedures involve:

i. A *"state of play"* discussion, usually by telephone, where the UKCMA will indicate whether it will hold an issues meeting;

ii. If an issues meeting is held, the UKCMA sends the parties an issues letter outlining the core arguments in favour of a Phase 2 investigation;[180]

---

179 This requirement limits the scope for modifying remedies at Phase 1 (Vande Walle, 2021).

180 The parties are afforded two working days (at least 48 hours, not counting weekends or public holidays) between receipt of the issues letter and the issues meeting.

iii. The merging parties are afforded an opportunity to respond to the issues letter in writing, orally at an issues meeting, or both;[181]

iv. A UKCMA staff member from outside the case team is appointed as a *"devil's advocate"* to comment critically on the case team's recommended outcome (whether or not to go to Phase 2). The *"devil's advocate"* will attend the issues meeting whenever possible;

v. After the issues meeting, the phase 1 decision-maker will meet with case team members and the *"devil's advocate"* to consider whether the Phase 2 reference test is met.

The EU Commission offers parties *"state of play"* meetings at five key points during merger investigations.

The CCPC's procedures do not include similar steps to the EU Commission or UKCMA. It does not, as a general rule, send an issues letter to the parties and afford them either a meeting or time to respond to such a letter. As far as the author is aware, it does not operate a *"devil's advocate"* style procedure at Phase 1. The CCPC (2021, December) procedures contain no provision for *"state of play"* meetings although it has held such meetings with merging parties prior to launching a Phase 2 investigation in several cases.[182] In *Synch* the CCPC held a further state of play meeting with the parties during Phase 2 at which it informed them it still had some concerns and that:

> *"they could agree to extending the date by which the Commission must issue an Assessment should they wish to submit revised proposals to the Commission, and that this would give the*

---

181 The period afforded to the parties to make written submissions typically will be longer than the period of two working days to prepare for the issues meeting.

182 CCPC M/16/040 – *Bon Secours/Barrington's*, 25.12.2016 states that the CCPC met the parties during the course of its Phase 1 investigation to discuss its preliminary views and any potential competition concerns with them (¶14). Similarly, *Kantar/News Access* records that the CCPC met the parties during the course of its Phase 1 investigation to discuss its preliminary views on the competitive effects and concerns with them. The final Determination in eight Phase 2 cases indicates that the CA/CCPC had informed the parties that it had specific competition concerns in relation to the proposed transaction and had received proposals from the parties which sought to address its concerns, prior to its decision to conduct a Phase 2 investigation. In several of these cases, the Determination specifically states that the CA/CCPC had held state of play meetings at which it outlined its concerns to the parties (see, for example, CCPC M/21/071 – *Tesco/Joyce's*, 7.6.2022, ¶1.17) while in others the Determination simply states that the CA/CCPC had informed the parties of its concerns.

> *Commission the opportunity to review the revised proposals in advance of issuing an Assessment"* (ibid., *¶1.63).*[183]

In contrast, the CCPC in *Uniphar/NaviCorp*[184] states that *"...there is no express statutory obligation on the Commission to provide feedback prior to the issue of the Written Assessment"* (¶1.77), arguing that it has wide discretion as to when to inform the parties of the details of its investigation including possible theories of harm. The CCPC procedures provide that it will issue an Assessment within 40 working days of a decision to launch a Phase 2 investigation.

Uniphar/NaviCorp states that the CCPC had provided the parties with an Assessment *"which set out in full the Commission's preliminary competition concerns"* (¶1.77). Gorecki (2023) argues that the reference to *"preliminary concerns"* is inconsistent with the CCPC's *Procedural Guidelines* which state:

> *"The Assessment will* ***set out clearly the Commission's concerns*** *regarding the effect of the proposed merger on competition in the relevant markets." (CCPC, 2021 December, ¶3.8, emphasis added).*

The *Procedural Guidelines* state that parties may propose remedies no later than 15 working days after the CCPC has issued an Assessment, although they provide that the CCPC may accept such proposals after the expiry of this time limit in exceptional circumstances while giving no indication of what might constitute exceptional circumstances (*ibid.*, ¶3.14).[185] This suggests a degree of arbitrariness in the CCPC's procedures with regard to remedy proposals.

Gorecki (2023) is highly critical of the CCPC's procedural approach in *Uniphar/NaviCorp*. The CCPC stated that there was insufficient time to consider a third set of remedy proposals prior to the statutory deadline for a final decision, having rejected two previous sets of proposals as inadequate. It appears that the parties first raised the issue of possible remedies approximately one week before the CCPC issued its Assessment. The Determination argues that the parties could have entered into remedy

---

183 An Assessment outlines the CA/CCPC's views in cases where it considers that a merger will likely result in an SLC. It is issued to the parties before a final decision is taken in the case and they are offered an opportunity to respond in writing and/or at an oral hearing. According to the Determination, the Assessment deadline was extended twice. CCPC M/21/004 – *AIB, BoI, PTSB Synch Payments JV (Synch)*, 16.6.2022 (¶1.6.4).

184 CCPC M/21/079 – *Uniphar/NaviCorp*, 15.12.2022. Note that the review period in this case partially overlapped with that in *Tesco/Joyce's*.

185 In EU merger cases, parties have up to 65 days to submit proposals, although the EU Commission will accept proposals after this deadline provided (a) there is sufficient time for it to assess them and (b) they *"fully and unambiguously resolve the competition concerns identified"* without the need for further market testing (EU Commission, 2008, October 22, ¶94).

discussions much earlier but, as Gorecki (2023, p.6) points out, *"if the parties are unaware of the CCPC's competition concerns until the Assessment, how are they to develop remedy proposals at an earlier stage to mitigate the agency's concerns?"*[186] He argues that the CCPC made it difficult for the parties to develop credible remedies in a timely manner and/or to withdraw the notification and asks whether the CCPC procedures *"bias the outcome"* of the investigation towards prohibition. He concludes that the CCPC's procedures were not in line with international best practice.

Who Are the Decision-makers?

The issue of who makes the decisions in merger cases is also very important (Yarrow, 2002). Decision-makers may be politicians, independent agencies such as the CCPC and EU Commission, or the courts (as in the US).

The *Mergers Act, 1978,* provided that decisions on whether to permit mergers to proceed were made by the Minister prior to 2003. Ireland was not unusual in this regard. In the UK, for example, merger decisions were also made by Government ministers. In Germany, the Minister may overrule merger decisions by the *Bundeskartellamt* (BKA) on public interest grounds, although the evidence does not suggest that this has worked very well.[187] The FTC (1990) noted that politicians may rank other policy objectives above competition when deciding merger cases.

> *"In addition, because a Minister has power to approve a merger or take-over without referral, there is that possibility that issues other than competition will be seen to have a greater significance and a merger which may have an anti-competitive effect may be approved without examination by the Commission" (ibid., ¶12.12)*

In similar vein, Yarrow (1999) argues that having politicians decide merger cases permits decisions based on short-term political considerations rather

---

[186] Gorecki (2009) stated that evidence on countervailing buyer power submitted by the parties in response to the Assessment issued by the CA was provided too late for it to be considered in CA M/08/009 – *Kerry/Breeo*, 28.8.2008. As previously stated, the Assessment outlines the CA/CCPC's competition concerns and affords the parties an opportunity to address them. It is therefore difficult to understand the claim that such evidence was submitted too late.

[187] An analysis of German cases involving Ministerial decisions overruling merger prohibitions found that, with one notable exception, none of the claimed public interest benefits ever materialised post-merger or as a result of the merger. In several cases, the merger adversely affected the claimed public interest goals (Budzinski & Stöhr, 2019 and Stöhr & Budzinski, 2019. For an English summary, see Budzinski & Stöhr, 2021).

than on a more stable set of policy considerations. When decisions are made at a political level, Ministers may succumb to political pressures either to approve potentially anti-competitive mergers, or to refer mergers which do not raise any competition concerns. Massey & Daly (2003) cite a report from the *Financial Times* (1997, May 23) describing a decision by the then UK Secretary of State, to refer the *National Express* merger to the UKMMC against the advice of the UKOFT as a classic case of a political decision where *"symbolism counts more than substance"*. They cite a merger which was referred to the CA for investigation, although the parties had a combined market share of only 20% (see **Chapter 2**). Inappropriate referrals impose unnecessary costs on the merging parties and involve an inefficient use of State resources.

Approving potentially anti-competitive mergers without review is more problematic. A former Minister for Industry & Commerce recounted how, the then Government allowed Telecom Éireann to purchase a controlling interest in Cablelink, its most obvious source of competition at the time.

> *"This decision was made by a government of which I was a member and it is one I argued very strongly against at the time. It was a majority decision" (O'Malley, 1997).*

Massey & Daly (2003) argue that a more in-depth investigation would appear to have been justified in several mergers which were approved without being referred to the CA between 1996 and 2002 (see **Chapter 2**). The lack of any requirement for Ministers to give reasons for their decisions under the 1978 Act compounded the problem.

Scott (2009) reported that some UK Ministers were softer on mergers than others and pointed out that the UKOFT's referral recommendations were rejected 31 times between 1973 and 2001. In 2008 the UK Government amended competition legislation to prevent a Phase 2 investigation of the *Lloyds/HBOS*[188] merger which had been recommended by the OFT. Stephan (2011) states that the case illustrates that merger control based on economic criteria is transparent and preferable to assessments based on public interest criteria, which are unpredictable and open to abuse.[189]

Coate & McChesney (1992, p.406) report that, when faced with the same facts, USFTC lawyers were more likely to claim that a merger raised anti-

188 UKOFT ME.3862/08 – *Lloyds/HBOS*, 24.10. 2008.The Government's decision to allow the merger to proceed was widely criticised. See **Chapter 5**.

189 He suggests that there are other more effective ways of addressing concerns which support arguments for greater political intervention.

trust issues than the agency's economists, a finding *"consistent with the hypothesis that different career incentives induce lawyers to support cases more often than economists."* Garside *et al.* (2013) found that, in monopoly investigations by the UKMMC between 1970 and 2003, the likelihood of a finding of abuse depended on the number of previous investigations that had been chaired by the chairperson of the investigating panel with the likelihood of an adverse finding 30% higher in cases with an experienced chairperson compared to an inexperienced one. An adverse finding was likely in almost every case where the panel chairperson had previously chaired more than 30 investigations.

The CCPC acts as investigator, prosecutor, and decision-maker in merger cases. As in the case of the EU Commission, the same CCPC case team takes a merger case from start to finish, although without the level of checks and balances contained in the EU procedures. As GE CEO Jack Welch remarked following the EU Commission decision to block the proposed *GE/Honeywell* merger: *"It's a tough deal having the prosecutor be the judge"*.[190] Trebilcock & Iacobucci (2002) are also critical of regimes where the same individuals are responsible for both investigations and decisions.

Lyons (2008) notes that, when the same team deals with both Phase 1 and Phase 2 investigations, any preconceptions or prejudices are likely to carry through to Phase 2 and almost invites the investigation team to get locked into a provisional judgement that it had to make during the early weeks of Phase 1. He argues that it is human nature to prefer to prove oneself right rather than wrong, giving rise to a temptation to spend Phase 2 trying to justify the Phase 1 decision to refer.

In contrast, in the UK Phase 1 and Phase 2 decisions are made by a different set of decision-makers.[191] Andrews (2002) argued that the same CCPC personnel should not carry out both the Phase 1 and Phase 2 investigations in a merger case.

---

190 *Financial Times*, 2001, July 12, cited by Akbar (2002).

191 In the UK, decisions at Phase 2 are made by a panel composed of individuals from outside the UKCMA who are not involved at the Phase 1 stage.

Table 3.2: Conditional & Unconditional Clearances at Phase 2 by Year, 2003-2023

Year	Unconditional	Remedy/Prohibition	Total
2003	1	1	2
2004	1	2	3
2005	0	1	1
2006	3	1	4
2007	2	1	3
2008	1	1	2
2009	1	1	2
2010	2	0	2
2012	2	0	2
2013	1	0	1
2014	0	1	1
2015	1	1	2
2016	0	1	1
2017	1	0	1
2018	0	4	4
2020	0	1	1
2021	2	4	6
2022	0	2	2
2023	4	1	5
2003-2012	13	8	21
2013-2022	9	15	24
Total	**22**	**23**	**45**

Note: There were no Phase 2 referrals in 2011 and 2019.

Source: CCPC.

Table 3.2 provides details on the outcome of CA/CCPC Phase 2 investigations. Twenty-two mergers were cleared unconditionally following a Phase 2 investigation over the 2003-2023 period. Thirteen Phase 2 investigations (62%) between 2003 and 2012 resulted in unconditional clearances but only 38% of Phase 2 cases were cleared unconditionally post-2012.[192] The benign interpretation of these results is that the CCPC has become better at identifying genuine problem cases, resulting in fewer innocuous cases going to Phase 2. The alternative interpretation is that it

192 **Table 3.2** does not include cases that were withdrawn during the Phase 2 investigation.

has become far more difficult to persuade the CCPC to change its mind once a Phase 2 investigation has commenced. Recognising this means merging parties may consider it less costly to agree remedies at Phase 1 rather than engage in a long-drawn-out process in which they are unlikely to persuade the CCPC to change its views.

The potential for industry specific regulators to be "captured" by the entities that they are charged with regulating as a result of information asymmetries is widely recognised in the regulatory economics literature (Kahn, 1988). The fact that competition agencies generally deal with a large number of different undertakings is sometimes regarded as making them less prone to capture. However, information asymmetries also arise in merger cases while, in a small economy like Ireland, the CA/CCPC may frequently interact with a relatively small number of large law firms in merger cases. A second aspect of regulatory capture to which the CCPC may be no less immune than industry specific regulators is the temptation to be seen to be *"doing something"* which may give rise to regulatory hold-ups and the application of unnecessary remedies in merger cases.[193]

There is an externality and potential risk involved when mergers are cleared on foot of undertakings and/or commitments by the parties. This arises because the merging parties are anxious to complete the transaction, and their private calculation of costs and benefits will not take account of the effect of such commitments on third parties. Melamed (1995) identified such problems in mergers which were settled by consent decrees in the US. Kolasky (2001) claims that the US anti-trust agencies, in negotiating consent decrees in merger cases where the parties face a strong incentive to avoid further delay, recognise that they have a duty not to demand remedies that they could not obtain if they had to litigate the case. The consent decree process in the US is designed to afford some degree of judicial control in cases where the parties and the anti-trust agencies agree settlements to prevent the agencies engaging in sweetheart deals. In Ireland undertakings or commitments offered in order to address CCPC concerns about possible anti-competitive effects in merger cases are not subject to a judicial oversight equivalent to the US consent decree process. Unlike the EU merger control regime, Irish merger control legislation does not afford third parties a right of appeal in merger cases.

---

193 Fear of losing out in the courts on appeal may equally lead to a preference for remedies over outright prohibitions.

In the US, merger cases are decided by the courts. The role of the competition agencies is to investigate but, if they wish to block a merger, they must challenge it before the courts. In many cases a decision by one of the agencies to litigate is sufficient for the parties to abandon a merger. As pointed out in **Chapter 1**, however, over the past 25 years, the ability of the agencies to win merger cases has declined largely because the courts have adopted a sceptical approach based on outmoded economic theories (Shapiro, 2019). This in turn has affected the agencies' willingness to challenge mergers. The decline in enforcement at Federal level has, to some extent, been offset by increased challenges by States under State anti-trust laws. Hawk (2020) observes, however, that mergers are reviewed, challenged, and often resolved by consent agreement or abandoned with few cases being decided by the Courts. He thus argues that US merger enforcement has become primarily an administrative process which has facilitated the use of economic evidence.

In the US, in certain industries, regulators as well the competition agencies have power to review mergers. The *Telecommunications Act, 1996* removed the Federal Communications Commission's (USFCC) power to exempt telecommunications mergers from review under the anti-trust laws, but it retained the power to conduct its own review of mergers in the sector. Kolasky (2001) described the USFCC's review of mergers as seriously flawed on two counts citing its *Bell/NYNEX* decision.[194] First, he claims that the USFCC required merging parties to demonstrate that a merger would actually enhance competition rather than not substantially reduce it, which is the test under competition law. Second, it failed to apply the consumer welfare standard. He also argued that the USFCC had used merger review to accelerate the opening up of local telephony markets and questioned the legal basis for such actions. Kwoka & White (1999) argue that the Interstate Commerce Commission (USICC) and its successor, the Surface Transportation Board (USSTB), had adopted a relatively lenient approach to railroad mergers. Wilson & Klovers (2021) note that the USDoJ found in *First Union/Core States* that the transaction was likely to involve significant competitive harm and required significant divestments before allowing the merger to proceed although the Federal Reserve which also has jurisdiction in bank mergers had raised no objections to the transaction.

[194] USFCC, *Bell Atlantic/NYNEX*, 12 FCC Rcd 19,985 (August 14,1997).

Checks & Balances

As with any regulatory regime, merger control is vulnerable to regulatory failure. Yarrow (1999) argues that regulators have little incentive to improve their performance. This emphasises the need for appropriate checks and balances in merger cases. Brandenburger & Janssens (2001) argue that unexpected changes in approach by merger regulators need to be considered when setting procedural checks and balances and that parties must have an adequate opportunity to challenge innovative concepts and the factual findings on which they are based, both with respect to theories of harm and market definition.

Following a series of cases in which the General Court overturned a number of its merger decisions, the EU Commission introduced several procedural reforms to address many of the problems identified by Lyons (2008). The UK regime includes a number of similar checks and balances.

The EU Commission has "devil's advocate" panels (known as "a fresh pair of eyes") to provide an internal critique of the arguments provided by case teams in merger cases. In addition, members of the Chief Economist's Team (CET) who are assigned to specific cases have a specific and independent status within case teams, and report directly to the Chief Competition Economist (CCE).[195] The latter can report his opinion directly to the Director-General of DG Competition, as well as to the Competition Commissioner, providing her with an independent opinion with respect to the economic aspects of a case (Kotzeva *et al.*, 2019). The CCE also has the power to offer *"final advice"* to the College of Commissioners immediately prior to a final decision, potentially a very powerful procedure in the event that the CCE disagrees with the case team and relevant senior officials in DG Competition (Lyons, 2008).

Lyons (*ibid.*) argues that the EU checks and balances procedures, while useful, do not eliminate the problem of a single case team taking a merger case from start to finish. As previously pointed out, the UK regime also employs a "devil's advocate" procedure while the final decision following a Phase 2 investigation is made by individuals from outside the UKCMA who were not involved in the Phase 1 investigation.

In the past, critics argued that judicial review of EU Commission decisions was less than fully effective (Bellamy, 2000, p.12). Similarly,

---

195 According to Batzopoulous *et al.* (2021) a CET member is generally embedded in merger review case teams.

Brandenburger & Janssens (2001) argued that judicial control procedure had failed to provide effective protection to merging parties largely because of the length of time taken by proceedings.

CCPC merger investigations are subject to much weaker checks and balances than the EU and UK regimes. The same team is responsible for both Phase 1 and Phase 2 investigations. The CCPC has no formal "devil's advocate"-type procedure. Massey (2010; 2011) urged the CA to incorporate stronger checks and balances into its merger review procedures, in the wake of the High Court's overturning of its *Kerry/Breeo* decision. He suggested that, in contentious cases, external economists should be retained to review the case team's economic analysis.[196] Andrews (2002) called for the appointment of independent hearing officers from outside the CCPC who were competent to adjudicate on both substantive and procedural issues in merger cases. While the final decision rests with the CCPC commissioners, as in the case of the EU, there is no provision for someone outside of the case team, like the CCE, to offer *"final advice"* to them. The CA/CCPC's decisions in cases such as *Kerry/Breeo, PandaGreen/Exomex* and *Uniphar/NaviCorp* raise questions about the need for the CCPC to adopt stronger checks and balances in its merger review procedures.

Cosnita-Langlais & Sørgard (2018) argue that competition agencies are likely to underenforce, *i.e.*, err on the side of making Type II (false negative) rather than Type I (false positive) errors, to avoid the possibility of deterring welfare-improving mergers. Merging parties have a right to appeal against CCPC decisions, but third parties have no right of appeal.[197] This effectively provides a potential check against false positives but there is no corresponding check against false negatives. The lack of any third party right to appeal merger decisions is an obvious weakness in the system and means there is no remedy against possible regulatory capture and false negatives.

The right of merging parties to appeal effectively represents the only significant check in the Irish merger control regime. Ireland's merger legislation requires that the Court should endeavour to decide appeals brought by the merging parties relatively quickly. Only one merger decision has been appealed to the High Court since 2003, so it is difficult to assess whether appeals provide an effective remedy for merging parties.

---

196 CA/CCPC staffing levels may be insufficient to create a CET similar to the EU Commission. External economic peer review could be used to perform a similar role.

197 Both the merging parties and third parties have a right of appeal under the ECMR.

Conclusions

Institutional arrangements can have an important influence on the outcome of merger cases. Differences in the substantive test can affect decisions about which mergers to investigate as well as decisions on cases. Who the decision-makers are, whether politicians, independent agencies or courts, also has an important influence on merger decisions. The decision to transfer responsibility for merger decisions from politicians to an independent agency represented a positive step in Irish merger control. Nevertheless, the current institutional arrangements suffer from a number of shortcomings.

The legislation affords the CCPC considerable leeway in terms of setting its own procedures. As Gorecki (2003) observes, the CCPC view that it is not required to provide any feedback to merging parties in relation to possible competition concerns, prior to issuing an Assessment, may make it difficult for the merging parties to devise effective remedies in a timely manner. This is compounded by the fact that the CA/CCPC has provided feedback at an earlier stage in some cases but not others. To an economist, at least, such procedural inconsistencies appear to raise questions about the fairness of the process. There are potential problems because the same case team is responsible for the conduct of both Phase 1 and Phase 2 investigations, combined with a lack of effective checks and balances to address this. These are all issues which fall within the CCPC's remit to address. A further problem is that the CCPC is not required to have reasonable grounds for believing that an SLC could occur in order to launch a Phase 2 investigation. It also seems anomalous that merging parties have a right of appeal, thus providing a check against false positives, but there is no third party right of appeal in the case of false negatives. Addressing both these issues would require legislative change.

4: MERGER CONTROL POST-2002

Introduction

This chapter provides an initial economic assessment of how well Ireland's merger control regime has performed based on an overview of merger case outcomes between 2003 and 2023. A more detailed analysis of individual merger decisions is provided in later chapters.

As previously noted, two types of errors may arise in merger cases. The merger control agency may wrongly find that a harmless merger was anti-competitive, a false positive, or Type I error, or it might fail to identify a merger that was anti-competitive, a false negative, or Type II error. Imposing remedies that are unnecessary or disproportionate also constitutes a Type I error, while remedies that are not capable of restoring effective competition post-merger constitute another form of Type II error (OECD, 2009a).

Both types of error are harmful. A false positive (Type I error), leads to the prohibition of, or adjustments to, an efficient merger which would have benefitted society. The direct cost of such an error will only be large, however, if the merger would have produced significant cost or demand efficiencies (*ibid.*). In addition, a false positive might discourage future pro-competitive mergers, thus compounding the loss to society. A false negative means an anti-competitive merger is allowed to proceed which will result in direct harm to consumers. The cost of a Type II error will be quite high if it results in a substantial price increase which persists for a lengthy period of time.[198] It is therefore important that the competition agency correctly

---

198 OECD (2009a) suggests that EU law may provide a remedy for such price increases because excessive pricing has been found to constitute an abuse of a dominant position. This,

distinguishes between pro- and anti-competitive mergers. Kwoka (2015) found that Type I errors were rare in US merger cases, but there were far more Type II errors which had considerable adverse effects on competition and consumers. Studies indicate an equal number of Type I and Type II errors in EU merger cases with estimates that one quarter of anti-competitive mergers were cleared without remedy (Lyons, 2008).[199]

An effective merger control regime should not only prevent anti-competitive mergers but should also deter businesses from proposing such mergers in the first place. Deterrence is a key feature of an effective merger control regime. If businesses recognise that anti-competitive mergers are likely to be prohibited, they are unlikely to waste time and resources attempting them. Hence the importance of correctly identifying anti-competitive mergers and providing clear, reasoned decisions which enable businesses and practitioners to identify transactions unlikely to be approved.

In addition to preventing and deterring anti-competitive mergers, it is important that the merger control regime should put the minimum difficulties in the way of innocuous mergers. Such cases should be processed speedily and efficiently, while minimising costs to the merging parties.

Merger Control Post-2002 – An Overview

As pointed out in **Chapter 1** economics indicates that competition problems mainly arise in the case of mergers between direct competitors – horizontal mergers. They arise less frequently in the case of vertical mergers, i.e. mergers between undertakings at different levels in the production/supply chain. Mergers between unrelated businesses, described as conglomerate mergers, are generally less likely to raise competition concerns.

Table 4.1 gives a breakdown of all mergers notified to the CA/CCPC between 2003 and 2023, classifying them as horizontal, horizontal and vertical, vertical and those with no horizontal or vertical overlap. These classifications

---

however, ignores the fact that mergers may result in significant price increases even though the merged entity is not dominant, while excessive pricing cases can be extremely complex.

199 Neven & Röller (2002) found that during the first 10 years of the ECMR there were few Type I errors but a high incidence of Type II errors. They also found that errors were more frequent in cases which were decided at Phase 1 where the probability of waving through an anti-competitive merger (Type II error) was 75% higher, which they describe as a high price to pay. It follows that closer examination at Phase 1 and more frequent Phase 2 reviews may reduce Type II errors considerably. They also identify a possible higher incidence of Type II errors when firms from large Member States were involved. Duso *et al.* (2013) argue that the 2004 reforms of the ECMR have reduced the number of Type I errors and increased the predictability of case outcomes.

are based on information contained in individual CA/CCPC decisions. The CA/CCPC does not publish data breaking down merger notifications in this way in its *Annual Reports* – which is unfortunate because it would be useful to have such information. The table defines cases on the basis of whether the CA/CCPC Determination identifies an overlap between the parties. Cases where the Determination suggests that any overlap was minimal are counted as overlaps. In some cases, it has been necessary to make a judgement call because it is not entirely clear from the Determination how a particular merger should be classified. In a few cases the CA/CCPC concluded there was no overlap, although the decision suggests that the parties may have been potential competitors which constitutes a horizontal merger and they are defined as such in the table.[200] Despite these *caveats*, **Table 4.1** provides a reasonable breakdown of merger notifications over the period 2003-2023.

Table 4.1: Classification of Mergers Notified to the CA/CCPC, 2003-2023

	Mergers Notified	As % of Total Notifications
Horizontal	565	44.7
Horizontal/Vertical	189	15.0
Vertical	100	7.9
No Overlap	392	31.0
Not Classified	18	1.4
Total	**1,264**	**100.0**

Source: CA/CCPC.

Horizontal mergers constituted the largest category of mergers, accounting for 45% of all merger notifications over the entire period. A further 15% of notified mergers involved both horizontal and vertical overlaps. Thus, 60% of all merger notifications were either pure horizontal mergers or a combination of both horizontal and vertical. In other words, the vast majority of notifications fall into a category where competition issues are

200 The CA concluded that there was no overlap between the merging parties in CA M/04/070 – *Rice/Albatross Feeds*, 23.12.2004. The Determination, which runs to just five paragraphs, states that the target was one of only two customers of the purchaser in the State, indicating a vertical relationship between the parties. It was not possible to categorise a small number of cases. Many of these involved withdrawn notifications where there was insufficient information available on the type of merger that was involved, while a small number of Determinations were not available on the CCPC website.

most likely to arise. In contrast only 8% of all notified mergers were purely vertical mergers. Economics indicates that vertical mergers are likely to be efficiency-enhancing but it appears that achieving efficiencies through vertical integration was not a primary motivating factor in most Irish mergers over the 2003-2023 period. There was no overlap between the merging parties in 31% of all merger cases over the period.[201]

Table 4.2 provides a breakdown of merger case outcomes between 2003 and 2023 by type of investigation and outcome. The legislation provides for a two-stage merger review process. Following a preliminary investigation, commonly referred to as a Phase 1 investigation, the CA/CCPC must either permit a merger to proceed or decide to conduct a full Phase 2 investigation. The Phase 1 investigation may, however, be extended (a) if the CA/CCPC issues a formal request for information (RFI) to the parties, in which case the period afforded to the CA/CCPC to reach a Phase 1 decision commences from the time that the parties respond to the RFI in full and/or (b) if the parties offer undertakings designed to address any competition concerns. These cases are defined as extended Phase 1 investigations.[202]

The vast majority of notified mergers, 1,125 (89%), were cleared unconditionally following a preliminary Phase 1 investigation. Another 47 were cleared unconditionally following an extended Phase 1 investigation and 22 were cleared unconditionally following a full Phase 2 investigation. Overall, therefore, 1,194 (94%) of all notified mergers were cleared unconditionally. A total of 46 mergers were cleared subject to remedies, which were designed to address concerns that the merger would have an adverse effect on competition. Over the entire period only five mergers were prohibited outright. In addition, 16 notifications were withdrawn and some of these may have been anti-competitive (*see below*).

Table 4.3 lists the five mergers prohibited between 2003 and 2023.[203] Four of the prohibition decisions involved horizontal mergers, while the fifth involved a merger with both horizontal and vertical overlaps.

---

201 Initially at least, the CA interpreted the requirement to notify a merger where an undertaking *"carries on business in the island of Ireland"* in a very broad fashion (see **Chapter 3**). This led to the notification of a large number of mergers which had no competition nexus with Ireland (Gorecki *et al.*, 2007). The CA changed its interpretation of the requirement in 2006 due to the large number of unnecessary notifications received in the first few years of the new merger control regime. This may account, in part, for the reduction in non-overlapping merger notifications.

202 CCPC, *M&A Report 2023* defines an extended Phase 1 investigation as one in which the CA/CCPC issued an RFI to the parties.

203 The CA's prohibition decision in *Kerry/Breeo* was overturned by the High Court on appeal and it was 14 years before another merger was prohibited. In effect, therefore, only four

Table 4.2: Merger Notification Outcomes, 2003-2023

Year	Total	Cleared Unconditionally			Cleared with Remedies			With-drawn	Prohib-ited
		Phase 1	Ext Phase 1	Phase 2	Phase 1	Ext Phase 1	Phase 2		
2003	47*	43	0	1	0	0	1	1	0
2004	81	77	0	1	1	0	1	0	1
2005	84	76	1	0	2	3	1	1	0
2006	98	90	0	3	1	1	0	2	1
2007	72	65	1	2	0	1	1	2	0
2008	38	36	0	1	0	0	0	0	1
2009	27	25	0	1	0	0	1	0	0
2010	46	42	1	2	0	1	0	0	0
2011	40	38	2	0	0	0	0	0	0
2012	33	27	3	2	0	0	0	1	0
2013	37	34	1	1	0	1	0	0	0
2014	41	40	0	0	0	0	1	0	0
2015	78	73	3	1	0	0	1	0	0
2016	67	63	1	0	0	1	1	1	0
2017	72	61	5	1	0	4	0	1	0
2018	98	87	3	0	0	4	4	0	0
2019	47	42	3	0	0	2	0	0	0
2020	41	31	8	0	0	0	1	1	0
2021	82**	66	7	2	0	2	3	0	1
2022	68	54	4	0	0	2	2	6	0
2023	67***	55	4	4	0	2	0	0	1
Total	**1,264**	**1,125**	**47**	**22**	**4**	**24**	**18**	**16**	**5**

*Includes one notification referred to EU Commission and not included in the table. **Includes one notification referred to EU Commission and not included in the table. ***Includes one notification rejected as invalid by CCPC and not included in the table.

Source: CA/CCPC.

The fact that so few cases have been prohibited outright limits the potential number of false positives. The low prohibition rate raises questions about possible false negatives, i.e., anti-competitive mergers that were not identified by the CA/CCPC. Massey (2010, 2011) and Gorecki (2020) have questioned specific CA/CCPC merger decisions. The potential problem of false negatives is compounded by the absence of any right of appeal in such cases while the merging parties may appeal false positives.

mergers out of 1,264 have been prohibited since January 2003. The Court rejected the CA's findings and concluded that the CA decision constituted a false positive.

Table 4.3: Merger Prohibitions, 2003-2023

Case Number	Case Name	Horizontal/ Vertical	Decision Date
M/04/032	*IBM/Schlumberger*	Horizontal	28.10.2004
M/06/039	*Kingspan/Xtratherm*	Horizontal	25.10.2006
M/08/009	*Kerry/Breeo*[a]	Horizontal	28.08.2008
M/21/079	*Uniphar/NaviCorp*	Horizontal/Vertical	15.12.2022
M/23/011	*daa/Gannon*	Horizontal	21.03.2024

[a] CA decision overturned by High Court on appeal.

Source: CA/CCPC.

Focusing only on prohibitions fails to tell the full story. A further 46 mergers were cleared by the CA/CCPC subject to remedies – 24 following an Extended Phase 1 investigation and 18 at Phase 2.[204] The remedies in two cases related to ancillary restraints,[205] while in six other cases they involved a requirement to notify future mergers, even if they were below the notification thresholds.[206] The actual merger in those eight cases therefore raised no competition concerns and may be excluded when identifying mergers that raised competition concerns. **Table 4.4** lists the remaining 38 remedies cases, of which 23 (61%) were notified over the 2017-2023 period: 82% of these cases involved horizontal mergers, 11% had both horizontal and vertical elements, while 8% were vertical. The preponderance of horizontal mergers that were subject to remedies is consistent with economic theory that horizontal mergers are more likely than non-horizontal mergers to pose competition problems. The application of remedies in these 38 cases indicates that the CA/CCPC considered that these cases were likely to result in an SLC and, presumably, in the absence of remedies, they would have been prohibited.[207] This is subject to the *caveat* that remedies could involve Type 1 errors.

---

204 Four cases were subject to remedies at Phase 1 but there is no indication that they involved an extended Phase 1 investigation. The Extended Phase 1 remedy cases include *Topaz/Statoil* which was cleared when the CA missed the deadline for initiating a Phase 2 investigation. The parties agreed to adhere to remedies that they had offered at Phase 1.

205 CA M/05/009 – *Kingspan/Century Homes,* 13.4.2005; and CC PC M/17/036 – *Sean Loughnane/ Crinkle,* 3.10.2017.

206 See **Chapter 3**.

207 Gorecki (2011, p.656) argues a conditional clearance at Phase 1 suggests that the merger raised *"serious competition issues"*.

Table 4.4: Mergers Subject to Remedies, 2003-2023

Case No.	Case Name	Horizontal/ Vertical	Investigation Stage	Decision Date
M/03/033	*SRH/FM104*	Horizontal	Phase 2	23.2.2004
M/05/024	*UGC/Chorus (NTL)*	Horizontal	Phase 2	4.11.2005
M/05/025	*SRH/Highland Radio*	Horizontal	Ext. Phase 1	12.8.2005
M/05/050	*eircom/Meteor*	Horizontal	Ext. Phase 1	18.11.2005
M/06/044	*Topaz/Statoil**	Horizontal	Ext. Phase 1	9.10.2006
M/06/098	*Premier Foods/RHM*	Horizontal	Phase 1	9.2.2007
M/07/022	*Thomas Crosbie Holdings/South East Broadcasting*	Horizontal	Ext. Phase 1	15.9.2007
M/07/040	*SRH/Communicorp*	Horizontal	Phase 2	7.12.2007
M/09/013	*Metro/Herald AM*	Horizontal	Phase 2	6.11.2009
M/10/026	*ESB/NIE*	Horizontal/Vertical	Ext. Phase 1	29.10.2010
M/13/033	*Sappho/Thomas Crosbie Holdings*	Horizontal	Ext. Phase 1	10.1.2014
M/14/026	*Valeo/Wardell/Robert Roberts*	Horizontal	Phase 2	17.2.2015
M/15/020	*Topaz/Esso*	Horizontal	Phase 2	15.10.2015
M/16/008	*PandaGreen/Greenstar*	Horizontal/Vertical	Phase 2	16.8.2016
M/16/040	*Bon Secours/Barrington's Hospital*	Horizontal	Ext. Phase 1	21.12.2016
M/17/012	*Kantar/Newsaccess*	Horizontal	Ext. Phase 1	11.7.2017
M/17/021	*Applegreen/JFT*	Vertical	Ext. Phase 1	30.6.2017
M/17/027	*Dalata/Clarion/Clayton*	Horizontal	Ext. Phase 1	29.8.2017
M/18/009	*BWG/4 Aces*	Horizontal	Ext. Phase 1	5.5.2018
M/18/016	*Trinity Mirror/Northern & Shell*	Horizontal	Phase 2	12.9.2018
M/18/031	*Uniphar/Sisk Healthcare*	Horizontal	Ext. Phase 1	17.8.2018

Case No.	Case Name	Horizontal/ Vertical	Investigation Stage	Decision Date
M/18/036	*Enva/Rilta*	Horizontal	Phase 2	20.12.2018
M/18/042	*Oaktree/Alannis/Lioncor*	Horizontal	Ext. Phase 1	12.9.2018
M/18/053	*PandaGreen/Knockharley*	Vertical	Ext. Phase 1	6.2.2019
M/18/063	*Berendsen/King's Laundry*	Horizontal	Phase 2	8.7.2019
M/18/067	*LN-Gaiety/MCD Productions*	Horizontal/Vertical	Phase 2	5.7.2019
M/19/010	*Formpress/Midland Tribune*	Vertical	Ext. Phase 1	9.10.2019
M/20/005	*ESB/Coillte*	Horizontal/Vertical	Phase 2	5.2.2021
M/21/004	*Synch*	Horizontal	Phase 2	16.6.2022
M/21/016	*PandaGreen/Exomex*	Horizontal	Ext. Phase 1	30.9.2021
M/21/021	*Bank of Ireland/KBC*	Horizontal	Phase 2	23.5.2022
M/21/071	*Tesco/Joyce's Supermarkets*	Horizontal	Phase 2	7.6.2022
M/22/040	*Q-Park/Tazbell*	Horizontal	Phase 2	15.8.2023
M/22/047	*BWG/McCarrick*	Horizontal	Ext. Phase 1	7.11.2022
M/22/049	*Uniphar/Sam McCauley*	Horizontal	Ext. Phase 1	20.1.2023
M/22/067	*Thornton's Recycling/Carducci*	Horizontal	Phase 2	13.7.2023
M/23/010	*BWG/Tuffy Wholesale*	Horizontal	Ext. Phase 1	3.5.2023
M/23/065	*Phey Topco/Trasmore*	Horizontal	Ext. Phase 1	11.4.2024

* The CA missed the deadline for instigating a Phase 2 investigation in this case. The parties subsequently agreed to honour undertakings they had offered during Phase 1.

CCPC.

Table 4.5: Mergers Cleared Unconditionally Following Extended Phase 1 Investigation, 2003-2023

Case No.	Case Name	Horizontal/Vertical	Decision Date
M/07/064	*Johnston Press/Clonnad*	Horizontal	19.2.2008
M/10/040	*Unilever/Alberto Culver*	Horizontal	23.2.2011
M/11/005	*JD Sports/Champion Sports*	Horizontal	30.3.2011
M/11/022	*Musgrave/Superquinn*	Horizontal/Vertical	28.9.2011
M/12/002	*Millington/Siteserv*	Vertical	21.5.2012
M/12/010	*Pallas/Crossgar*	Horizontal	23.8.2012
M/12/017	*United Care/Pharmexx*	Horizontal	17.11.2012
M/13/001	*Blackrock/CS ETF*	Horizontal	9.5.2013
M/15/039	*Liberty Global/TV3*	Horizontal/Vertical	2.10.2012
M/15/059	*Paddy Power/Betfair*	Horizontal	15.1.2016
M/15/077	*Uniphar/Murrays Medical*	Horizontal/Vertical	23.3.2016
M/16/044	*INM/CMNL*	Horizontal	10.11.2016
M/17/005	*VHI/Swiftcare*	Vertical	10.5.2017
M/17/035	*Dawn Meats/Dunbia*	Horizontal/Vertical	29.9.2017
M/17/040	*INM/Caltray*	Vertical	11.10.2017
M/17/056	*Bay/Radio Nova*	Horizontal	22.1.2018
M/17/064	*Tetrarch/Citywest*	Horizontal/Vertical	30.1.2018
M/18/075	*Irving/Tedcastles*	Horizontal/Vertical	7.1.2019
M/18/082	*Goldreed/Greene Farm*	Horizontal	21.1.2019
M/18/089	*Lakeland/LacPatrick*	Horizontal	5.3.2019
M/19/032	*Boyle Sport/Bruce Betting*	Horizontal	14.2.2020
M/19/042	*Portlon (Parma)/Galway Clinic*	Horizontal	20.4.2020
M/20/001	*Flutter/Stars*	Horizontal/Vertical	20.4.2020
M/20/009	*Portlon (Parma)/Hermitage*	Horizontal	29.7.2020
M/20/010	*Portlon (Parma)/Blackrock*	Horizontal	29.7.2020
M/20/012	*Eason/Dubray*	Horizontal	10.9.2020
M/20/015	*Portlon/Blackrock (Tullycorbett/Xroon)*	Horizontal	29.7.2020
M/20/023	*United Molasses/Premier Molasses & Kruden*	Horizontal/Vertical	25.11.2020
M/20/027	*Uniphar/Hickey's*	Horizontal	19.11.2020
M/20/029	*Brookfield (Greenenergy)/ Amber Oil*	Horizontal/Vertical	26.1.2021
M/21/009	*Citylink/GoBus*	Horizontal	20.8.2021
M/21/011	*Easycash/Bank of Ireland ATMs*	Horizontal	16.8.2021
M/21/012	*AIB/Goodbody*	Horizontal/Vertical	24.6.2021

Case No.	Case Name	Horizontal/Vertical	Decision Date
M/21/031	*Glennon Bros/Balcas*	Horizontal	11.10.2021
M/21/046	*Bank of Ireland/Davy*	Horizontal/Vertical	6.12.2021
M/21/054	*Zeus Packaging/Limerick Packaging*	Horizontal	16.12.2021
M/21/068	*Heineken/Coman's II*	Horizontal/Vertical	16.3.2022
M/22/007	*Assa Abloy/Arran Isle*	Horizontal/Vertical	9.6.2022
M/22/044	*AIB/Ulster Bank (Trackers)*	Horizontal	13.1.2023
M/22/062	*Associated Hardware/ National Hardware*	Horizontal	18.5.2023
M/22/065	*Musgrave/Caulfield*	Horizontal/Vertical	24.3.2023
M/23/004	*John Laing/CCD Group*	Vertical	28.4.2023
M/23/005	*John Laing/Towercomm*	Horizontal/Vertical	31.5.2023
M/23/045	*Proximus Opal/Route Mobile*	Horizontal	27.10.2023
M/23/059	*IFX/Blackhall Facilities Management*	Vertical	21.12.2023

Source: CCPC.

Tables 4.5 and **4.6** provide details of 68 mergers cleared unconditionally following extended Phase 1 or Phase 2 investigations. The fact that these cases were subject to detailed investigations indicates that they raised possible competition concerns. Of these cases, 45 were cleared without remedies following an extended Phase 1 investigation,[208] and 23 following a full Phase 2 investigation.[209] Forty of these cases were notified during the 2017-2023 period. Of the 45 cases cleared without remedies following an extended Phase 1 investigation, 25 were horizontal, 12 had both horizontal and vertical elements, while eight were vertical, meaning 82% had a horizontal element and 18% were vertical. All but one of the cases cleared without remedies at Phase 2 were horizontal.

---

208 This excludes two extended Phase 1 cases involving alleged *"gun-jumping"* rather than any competition concerns (CA M/05/079 – *Radio County Sound/Dooley & Feeney* 1.3.2006 and CCPC M/19/040 – *DMG/JPIMedia*, 20.3.2020). Gun-jumping refers to mergers put into effect prior to being approved by the CA/CCPC. The legislation provides that such mergers are void.

209 This includes *Grafton/Heiton* which was not in the list of remedied cases in **Table 4.4** as it was subject to a future notification remedy. However, it was subject to a Phase 2 investigation due to CA concerns about competitive harm in what it described as the DIY Superstore market. The future notification requirement related to a different market than that for builders' providers.

Table 4.6: Mergers Cleared Unconditionally Following Phase 2 Investigation, 2003-2023

Case No.	Case Name	Horizontal/ Vertical	Decision Date
M/03/029	*Dawn Meats/Galtee Meats*	Horizontal	20.11.2003
M/04/020	*Uniphar/Whelehan*	Horizontal	20.7.2004
M/04/051	*Grafton/Heiton*	Horizontal	6.1.2005.
M/06/027	*Tetra Laval/Carlisle*	Horizontal	10.8.2006
M/06/057	*Coillte/Weyerhaeuser*	Vertical	10.11.2006
M/06/087	*Applied Materials/Brooks Software*	Horizontal	6.2.2007
M/07/030	*Glen Dimplex/Applied Energy*	Horizontal	25.9.2007
M/07/031	*Galco/Sperrin*	Horizontal	2.10.2007
M/08/011	*Heineken/Scottish & Newcastle*	Horizontal	3.10.2008
M/09/024	*Greenstar/Veolia*	Horizontal	11.3.2010
M/10/038	*Barnett/Origin/Hall*	Horizontal	21.1.2011
M/10/043	*Stena/DFDS*	Horizontal	7.4.2011
M/12/027	*Uniphar/CMR*	Horizontal	30.4.2013
M/12/031	*Top Snacks/KP Snacks*	Horizontal	22.4.2013
M/13/036	*Glanbia/Wexford Creamery*	Horizontal	30.4.2014
M/15/026	*Baxter Healthcare/Fannin Compounding*	Horizontal	21.10.2015
M/17/068	*Irish Times/Irish Examiner*	Horizontal	20.4.2018
M/21/040	*AIB/Ulster Bank*	Horizontal	28.4.2022
M/21/076	*PTSB/Ulster Bank*	Horizontal	21.7.2022.
M/23/006	*Dawn Meats/Kildare Chilling*	Horizontal	20.9.2023.
M/23/008	*Aurivo/Arrabawn Co-Op*	Horizontal	15.9.2023.
M/23/060	*Kilsaran/Kilmurray*	Horizontal	26.7.2024.
M/23/068	*McMullan Bros/Naas Fuels*	Horizontal	12.7.2024.

Source: CA/CCPC.

Table 4.7 gives details of the 16 merger notifications that were withdrawn over the 2003-2023 period. Six of the withdrawals occurred in 2022. The CA/CCPC generally provides relatively little information about withdrawn notifications. One possible reason for withdrawing a notification is that the parties, faced with a potential prohibition decision, may have decided to abandon a proposed merger. Of course, the parties equally may have decided not to pursue a transaction for other reasons.[210]

Table 4.7: Withdrawn Merger Notifications, 2003-2023

Case No.	Case Name	Horizontal/ Vertical	Stage at which withdrawn
M/03/035	*Stena/P&O I*	Horizontal	Phase 2
M/05/015	*Tysan/Balcuik*	Horizontal	Phase 1 (Re-notified)
M/06/091	*Barclays/de Smet*	n.a.	Phase 1
M/06/093	*Abbott/KOS*	n.a.	Phase 1
M/07/009	*UTC/SFS*	Horizontal	Phase 1
M/07/059	*Resolution/FriendsProvident*	Horizontal	Phase 1
M/12/018	*Julius Baer/IMWB Merrill Lynch*	Horizontal	Phase 1
M/16/041	*Marino Point/Port of Cork*	n.a.	Phase 1
M/17/055	*Siris Capital/Synchronoss*	Vertical	Phase 1 (Below Threshold)
M/20/003	*Link Group/Pepper*	Horizontal	Phase 2
M/22/015	*East Cork Oil/Misty Lane*	Horizontal	Phase 2
M/22/017	*Linnaeus Veterinary/ Blackhall*	n.a.	Re-notified.
M/22/025	*The Agricultural Trust/ Irish Garden*	n.a.	n.a.
M/22/037	*Thornton's Recycling/ Carducci*	Horizontal	Re-notified
M/22/052	*Linnaeus Veterinary/ Blackhall*	n.a.	n.a.
M/22/063	*Windsor Motors/Green Cars*	Horizontal	Phase 2

Source: CA/CCPC.

At least four withdrawals occurred during the course of a Phase 2 investigation, suggesting that competition concerns were a factor in these cases. *Stena/P&O II*, for example, states that the CA had previously prepared an Assessment in *Stena/P&O I* prior to the withdrawal of the latter notification. According to the Determination, the CA's concerns about a

[210] A few notifications were withdrawn after the CA amended its interpretation of the "carries on business in the island of Ireland" in late 2006 (see **Chapter 3**).

possible future acquisition by Stena of P&O's Dublin-Liverpool ferry service stemmed from its investigation in the earlier case.[211]

In *Link/Pepper*, the CCPC stated:

> *"Our investigation identified potential competition concerns with the proposed transaction and involved extensive engagement with the parties to address the identified potential competition concerns. It was during this process of engagement that the parties announced that they were withdrawing from the proposed transaction" (CCPC, M&A Annual Report 2021, ¶1.8).*

East Cork Oil/Misty Lane was withdrawn following the issuing of an Assessment to the parties by the CCPC which stated that *"the CCPC reached the preliminary conclusion that the proposed acquisition would have likely resulted in a substantial lessening of competition in certain geographic markets"* (CCPC, M&A *Annual Report* 2022, ¶1.8).[212] It seems reasonable, therefore, to identify these three as cases that raised potential competition concerns.[213]

Three notifications were withdrawn and re-submitted, although one of these was withdrawn a second time. The CCPC stated that *Marino Point/Port of Cork "was withdrawn by the parties before a final Determination was issued. Our competitive assessment had been completed on the proposed transaction and therefore the parties forfeited the filing fees"* (CCPC, *Annual Report* 2016, p.18).[214] *Siris Capital/Synchronoss* was withdrawn by the parties on the grounds that it fell below the notification thresholds (CCPC, M&A *Annual Report* 2017). Given the CCPC's practice of informing parties that below the threshold mergers which were not notified would be investigated as potential breaches of §s4 and/or 5 of the *Competition Act*, if they raise competition concerns, the fact that no further action was taken by the CCPC in this case suggests that it did not consider that it raised any competition issues.

Overall, therefore, of the 1,264 merger notifications to the CA/CCPC over the 2003-2023 period, 114 may be said to have raised potential

---

211 *Stena/P&O II* was cleared subject to a requirement that the parties notify any future below the threshold acquisition.

212 No information is available on the fourth case which was withdrawn during Phase 2.

213 As only limited information is available in relation to these cases, it is not possible to consider them in any detail. As previously stated, a small number of notifications were withdrawn after the CA revised its interpretation of "carries on business in the island of Ireland" in late 2006.

214 The wording is somewhat ambiguous. It refers to the CCPC having completed its competitive assessment of the case but there is no suggestion that the CCPC had either issued, or planned to issue, an Assessment to the parties expressing concerns prior to the withdrawal.

competition concerns. This total includes five prohibited mergers and 38 mergers that were subject to remedies.[215] The CA/CCPC may therefore be said to have identified 43 mergers that it considered would result in an SLC, 3.4% of all mergers notified between 2003 and 2023. The low rate of prohibitions/remedies raises the question of potential false negatives. In addition, 45 cases were cleared without remedies following an extended Phase 1 investigation,[216] and 23 were cleared without remedies following a Phase 2 investigation. Although no remedies were applied, the fact that these cases were subject to a detailed investigation suggests that they raised sufficient potential competition concerns to merit close scrutiny. Consequently, they are considered potential problem cases.[217] Three other cases were withdrawn at Phase 2 after the CA expressed competition concerns.

Figure 4.1: Percentage Breakdown of Potential Problem Mergers, 2003-2023

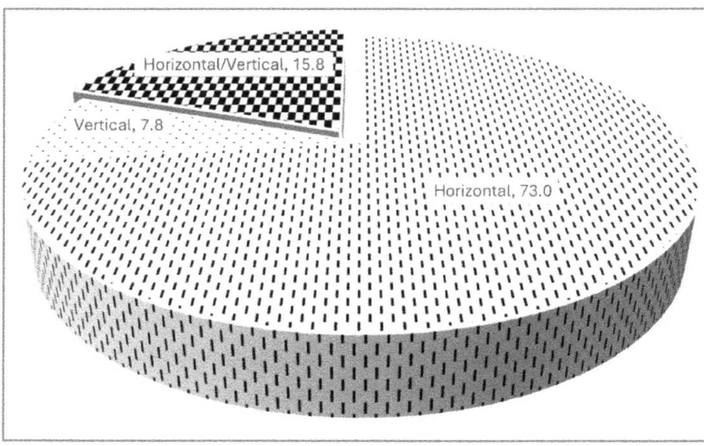

Source: CA/CCPC.

---

215 This figure excludes five of the six cases involving a remedy to notify future below the threshold mergers and two involving remedies that related to ancillary restraints. Although *Grafton/Heiton* was cleared based on a future notification remedy, the fact that the CA's Phase 2 investigation also focused on concerns in relation to DIY superstores, which were not subject to remedy, means that it is included among the problem cases.

216 This excludes two Extended Phase 1 clearance decisions, which involved potential "gun jumping" but did not raise any competition concerns.

217 Gorecki *et al.* (2007) employed a similar approach to identify potential problem cases.

Figure 4.1 gives a breakdown of the 114 potential problem merger notifications by type of merger: 85 (75%) potential problem cases were horizontal mergers, while almost 16% involved both horizontal and vertical overlaps so that 90% of all potential problem cases had a horizontal element. Vertical mergers accounted for just 10% of all potential problem cases.

Deterrence

The fact that only five mergers notified to the CA/CCPC since 2003 were prohibited, while less than 10% were subject to a detailed investigation,[218] raises the possibility of Type II errors (false negatives). An alternative explanation for the low number of cases raising concerns of an SLC is that the system proved highly effective at deterring anti-competitive mergers.

Eckbo (1992) argued that an effective merger policy should create incentives that shape the behaviour of firms. Davies & Majumdar (2002) state that changes in the tenor of merger policy can alter both the number and type of mergers which are actually proposed. Merger decisions do not just affect the undertakings that are the subject of those decisions but may also influence the actions and decisions of others – a deterrent effect (Sørgard, 2009; Salop, 2013). Lyons (2008) argues that effective deterrence requires a clear economics effects approach to merger appraisal and that *"it is necessary to signal this approach in clearly argued decisions as well as in broad messages contained in guidelines and speeches"* (p.4). Firms have a strong incentive to propose mergers that are likely to be approved so that publishing the right argument behind a decision is critical to deterrence.

There is no way of measuring the number of mergers that may have been deterred by the merger control regime because, by definition, such transactions never happened. Lyons (2008) cites a UK study which found that, for every merger blocked by the UK competition agencies, five were abandoned after the parties had received external legal advice. It also found surprisingly that external legal advice was only sought in 25% of all cases where firms abandoned or modified mergers, although the decision not to proceed in some of these cases may have been based on non-competition considerations.

One might reasonably expect *a priori* that the introduction of a more independent and transparent review process under the 2002 Act would have

---

[218] Defined as an extended Phase 1 or Phase 2 investigation.

a greater deterrent effect than the previous regime which lacked transparency. Alternatively, an initial increase in the number of prohibition decisions might be expected in the immediate aftermath of a change in regime, particularly as it involved a change in the substantive criteria against which mergers were assessed. As Budzinski (2010) points out, in such circumstances, the ability of undertakings and legal/economic practitioners to identify the borderline between acceptable and unacceptable mergers should have decreased, resulting in an increase in prohibitions.

Figure 4.2: Percentage of Merger Notifications Involving Detailed Investigation by Year, 2003-2023

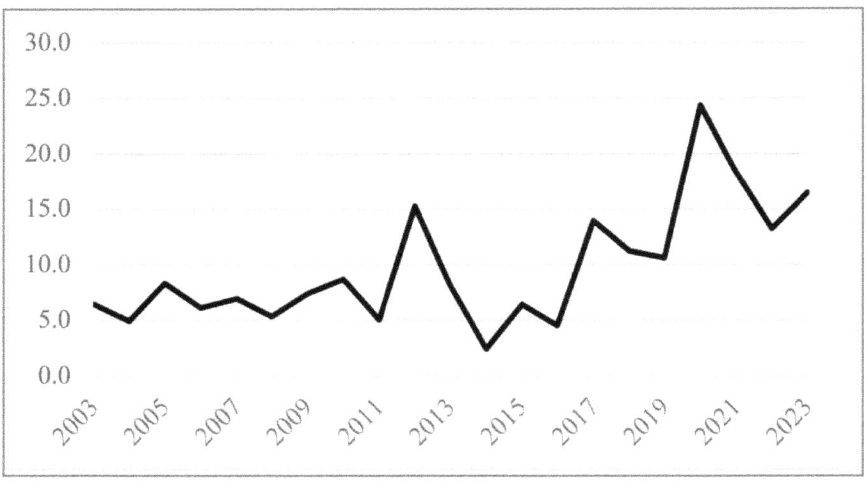

Source: CA/CCPC.

Figure 4.2 shows the number of mergers that were subject to detailed investigation as a percentage of total notifications by year.[219] Up to 2016, the number of potential problem merger cases averaged less than 7% of all notifications. This figure increased to 15% over the 2017-2023 period. In 2020, 24% of all mergers notified raised potential competition concerns. While the proportion of problem cases declined subsequently, it remained well above the levels recorded over the 2003-2016 period. The increase in the number of potential problem cases raises some interesting questions. A regime which is known to be strong on prohibiting anti-competitive measures is likely to have

[219] Defined as all extended Phase 1 and Phase 2 cases, including withdrawals at Phase 2, but excluding seven cases involving remedies relating to ancillary restraints or notification of future below the threshold mergers.

a strong deterrent effect as business undertakings would be unlikely to pursue anti-competitive mergers if they expected they would be prohibited. We might therefore expect that the number of problem cases would decline over time if a merger regime was effective at preventing anti-competitive mergers. Gorecki *et al.* (2007) cited a decline in problem merger cases in the period up to 2006 as evidence that the CA's decisions had deterred anti-competitive mergers. The increase in problem cases post-2016 is inconsistent with the merger regime having a strong deterrent effect. An alternative explanation is that the CCPC may have adopted a stricter approach to reviewing mergers post-2016. This, however, raises the possibility of an overly lenient approach and a higher likelihood of Type II errors in earlier years. Either way, the numbers are problematic.

Many of the CA's early Determinations were rather cursory: 68% of CA merger Determinations during the four years from 2003 to 2006 ran to two pages or less. Such Determinations are unlikely to have provided much guidance to firms or merger advisers in relation to whether mergers were likely to be approved. In fairness, it should be acknowledged that the quality and depth of the analysis in CA/CCPC merger Determinations in the majority of cases has improved over time.

In *Tysan/Balcuik*,[220] an acquisition of a Dublin office development by a consortium of private individuals and companies, for example, the Determination runs to just five paragraphs and simply concludes:

> *"Although some of the owners of Tysan are active in the property market in Dublin, the proposed transaction would not give rise to any significant competitive overlap between the parties' business activities in the State. Therefore, the proposed transaction does not give rise to competition concerns" (¶4).*

The CA explanation for its finding that the printers supplied by the merging parties were not substitutes in *Hewlett Packard/Scitex Vision*[221] is somewhat confusing, if not outright contradictory.

> *"In the Authority's view, from both a demand and supply-side substitutability analysis, it would not appear that the printer products manufactured by HP and Scitex Vision are sufficiently distinct and could not be considered substitutes. Consequently, there would appear to be no overlap in the State between the*

220 CA M/05/018 – *Tysan/Balcuik*, 19.5.2005.

221 CA M/05/054 – *Hewlett Packard/Scitex Vision*, 23.9.2005.

> *operations of the two companies and the proposed transaction does not give rise to competition concerns." (¶13).*

In *Liberty/Princes Holdings*[222] all details of the transaction were redacted.

International Comparisons

Further insights into the effectiveness of Ireland's merger control regime can be obtained by comparing it with merger control regimes in other jurisdictions. **Table 4.8** compares the number of mergers that were (i) subject to Phase 2 investigations; (ii) subject to remedies and (iii) prohibited in Ireland with some other jurisdictions for the period 2003-2023.

Table 4.8: International Comparisons of Merger Case Outcomes, 2003-2023

	Ireland	EU	UK*	US	Denmark	New Zealand
	Case Numbers					
Phase 2 Investigations	48	180	214	1,065	-	-
Remedies	46	351	208	683	16	-
Prohibitions	5	15	23		1	26
	As % of Total Merger Cases					
Phase 2 Investigations	3.8	2.6	11.7	2.9	-	-
Remedies	3.6	5.0	11.4	2.2	12.8	-
Prohibitions	0.4	0.2	1.3		0.8	9.6

*UK data are for fiscal years 2003/04 - 2023/24. New Zealand data for fiscal years 2003/04 - 2022/23. Denmark data is for 2000-2008. US data combines remedies/prohibitions/abandoned cases and relates to 2001 - 2020. For the US Phase 2 is defined as the number of cases involving second stage information requests under the *Hart-Scott-Rodino Act*.

Source: CA/CCPC; EU https://competition-policy.ec.europa.eu/mergers/statistics_en; UK https://assets.publishing.service.gov.uk/media/677e5f37d721a08c0066556e/Merger_outcomes_to_December_24.ods; New Zealand https://comcom.govt.nz/_data/assets/pdf_file/0017/306323/Mergers-determinations-and-enforcement-statistics.pdf; Denmark (Albæk *et al.*, 2010); US *Hart-Scott-Rodino Annual Report*, various years. Available at https://www.ftc.gov/policy/reports/annual-competition-reports. Accessed 10.1.2025.

These results come with a significant health warning as they may not reflect like for like comparisons. Outright prohibition decisions are relatively rare

222 CA M/04/011 – *Liberty/Princes Holdings*, 9.2.2004.

in the various jurisdictions, although New Zealand has a much higher rate than elsewhere, but this may reflect the *ex post* nature of its merger regime. The number of prohibitions in Ireland is low, with just five mergers prohibited, which is just 0.4% of all merger notifications. The Irish rate of prohibitions is higher than the EU Commission but much lower than the UK which had a prohibition rate of 1.3%. The Irish rate is also below that of Denmark and New Zealand. The proportion of Phase 2 investigations was higher in Ireland than in the EU and US but was considerably lower than the UK rate. The UK figures may reflect the fact that it has a largely *ex post* system, and it is perhaps unsurprising therefore that investigations should focus on potential problem cases. The proportion of cases that were cleared subject to remedies was much lower in Ireland than in Denmark, the EU and UK. If prohibitions and remedies combined is taken as a measure of mergers considered to be anti-competitive, this suggests that the CA/CCPC has adopted a more lenient approach to mergers than the EU and UK, although it is higher than the US. This has to be viewed in a context in which, as noted in **Chapter 1**, various authors have suggested that merger control in the US (Kwoka, 2015; Philippon, 2019) and, to a lesser extent, the EU (Duso *et al.*, 2013), has been overly lenient.

Decision Timelines

The speed of decision-making, in particular in the case of mergers considered innocuous, is another measure of the effectiveness of a merger control regime. Irish legislation provides for a two-stage merger review process. As previously noted, under the 2002 Act, the CA had one month to decide whether to conduct a full Phase 2 investigation of the merger, in which case it was required to reach a decision within four months of *"the appropriate date"*.[223] The *Competition & Consumer Protection Act, 2014*, extended these time periods to 30 working days for a Phase 1 investigation and 120 working days from the appropriate date for a full Phase 2 investigation.[224] In the wake of the 2008 financial crash the CA used its discretion to reduce the time allowed

223 *Competition Act, 2002*, §s21(1) and 22(4)(a). The appropriate date is the notification date, or, in cases where the CCPC issues a formal RFI, the date on which it has received a full response to the RFI. In addition, if the parties submitted proposals to address competition concerns during the Phase 1 investigation the deadline for a Phase 1 decision was extended from 30 to 45 days §21(4).

224 §58(c)(i) substituted a limit of 45 working days instead of 45 days for completion of the Phase 1 investigation in cases where the parties submit remedy proposals during Phase 1.

for third party submissions to expedite the assessment process in respect of several mergers involving financially distressed undertakings (CA, *Annual Report 2010*).[225]

The CA/CCPC publishes limited information on the time taken by it to decide on notified mergers. The CCPC's annual *M&A Annual Reports*, for example, state the average time taken for Phase 1 decisions (excluding extended Phase 1 cases), along with the timeline range in such cases. This provides very limited information about the CCPC's overall performance. It excludes cases that were not finished by year end and, more importantly, includes only straightforward cases that raised no competition concerns. It is therefore necessary to analyse the data in more detail in order to obtain a more accurate picture of the efficiency of the merger review process.

Figure 4.3: Average Merger Decision Time (Days) by Year, 2003-2023

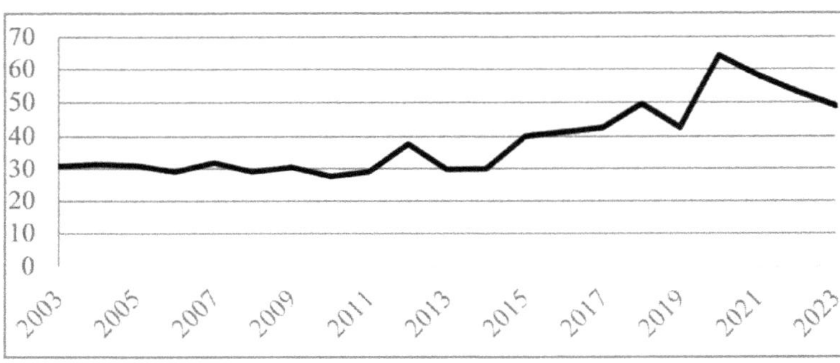

Source: CA/CCPC.

Figure 4.3 gives details on the average duration of CA/CCPC merger investigations defined as the number of days from notification to a final decision.[226] Average case duration remained fairly stable at around 30 days

---

225 See, for example, CA M/09/002 – *HMV Ireland/Zavvi*, 23.1.2009 and CA M/10/041 – *Pilgrim (Oaktree Group)/MHL & MCL*, 3.12.2010. In the former case the CA decision stated that the Provisional Liquidator of Zavvi had agreed to provisionally run the Zavvi stores pending clearance by the CA. *"This was on the expectation that the Authority would expedite the review of the proposed transaction"* (*HMV Ireland/Zavvi*, ¶10). Whether the CA's decision-making schedule should be influenced by third party expectations seems questionable.

226 The 2014 Act sets decision timelines in terms of working days. The CCPC does not publish data on the number of working days taken to reach a decision in all cases. Information on the notification and decision date is posted on the CCPC website for every merger case making it possible to estimate the number of calendar days taken to reach a decision in each case. It would be possible to estimate the number of working days taken to arrive at a decision in

from 2003 to 2013. Following a slight dip in 2014, there was a steady increase in the average duration of merger investigations from 30 days in 2014 to 64 days in 2020. Average case duration declined subsequently but remains higher than in the pre-2020 period. Increases in case duration may partly reflect the fact that the timelines laid down in the legislation were increased in the 2014 Act. It is also, however, due to the fact that the number of quite lengthy investigations has increased significantly in recent years as illustrated by **Figure 4.4**.

Figure 4.4: Percentage of Merger Reviews Exceeding a Given Number of Days by Year, 2003-2023

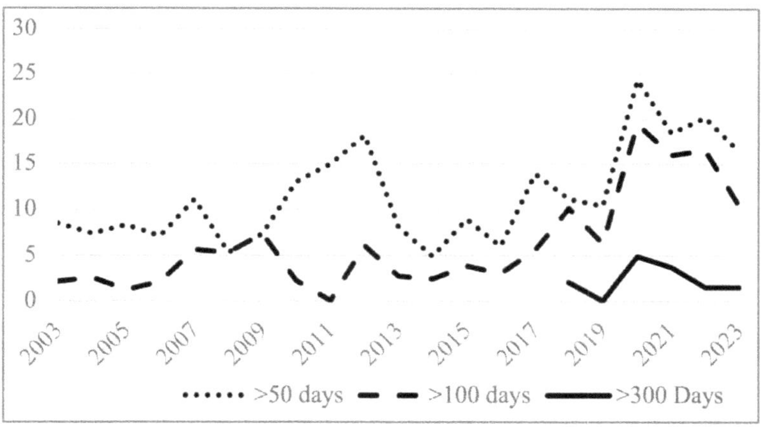

Source: CA/CCPC.

In all but two years up to 2017, less than 10% of merger cases took more than 50 days to be decided. This figure increased from 6% in 2016 to 24% in 2020. Although it declined subsequently, it has remained well above pre-2020 levels. Similarly, in all but two years up to 2017 less than 5% of cases lasted more than 100 days. In 2020, 20% of merger cases ran for more than 100 days, while 16% took more than 100 days in 2021 and 2022. Since 2018, an admittedly small number of cases have taken more than 300 days to be decided. Overall average decision times appear to have increased

every case, but it would obviously be an onerous task. In addition, prior to 2014 the time limits were set in terms of calendar days rather than working days. In the circumstances, the number of calendar days rather than the number of working days taken to arrive at a decision in each case provides a reasonable measure of CA/CCPC performance. The data for 2022 excludes one withdrawn merger notification as it was not possible to ascertain the date of its withdrawal.

significantly, while the proportion of quite lengthy cases has also increased sharply.[227]

The Simplified Merger Notification Procedure

The CCPC introduced a simplified merger notification procedure (SMNP) with effect from 1 July 2020. Mergers which satisfy the SMNP requirements are presumed not to raise any competition concerns. The CCPC indicated that the SMNP would *"have a positive impact on businesses, as review periods for* ***mergers or acquisitions which do not raise significant competition concerns*** *will be shorter and the Irish merger control regime will be less burdensome for notifying parties"* (CCPC, 2020 July, ¶1.2. Emphasis added).[228]

The SMNP applies in cases where:

i. There is no horizontal or vertical overlap between the parties;
ii. Where there is a horizontal overlap, the parties combined market share is less than 15% and where there is a vertical overlap, each of the parties has a market share of less than 25% in each market; or,
iii. An undertaking involved, which already has joint control over a company, is to acquire sole control over that company (¶2.1).[229]

Market definition is clearly critical to the first two conditions (see **Chapter 6**). The presumption that a change from joint to full control is unlikely to raise competition concerns represents a change from the CA approach in *Chevron/Texoil.*[230] Although the proposed transaction in that case involved a change from joint to full control, it was only cleared by the CA following an analysis of its likely competitive effects. In contrast, the CA in *An Post/PostPoint*[231] stated that the transaction would not affect competition *inter alia* because *"An Post already exercises joint control over PostPoint"* (¶9).

---

227 In addition to party response times to RFIs, merger case durations can be affected by numerous factors including (i) the nature of the decision; (ii) size of the transaction; (iii) impact on competition; (iv) complexity; and (v) agency workload (Yang & Pickford, 2016).

228 SMNP notifications are subject to less onerous information requirements.

229 The application of the SMNP in cases involving a move from joint to full control is unlikely where either: *"(a) pre–merger, the controlling shareholders of the joint venture imposed disciplining constraints on one another and consequently on the conduct of the jointly controlled undertaking, which was in, or was soon to be in, competition with the acquiring shareholder; or (b) neither the CCPC nor the European Commission had approved the initial acquisition of joint control of the joint venture by the undertakings involved"* (CCPC, 2020, July, ¶2.12).

230 CA/M/09/008 – *Chevron/Texoil*, 23.4.2009.

231 CA M/10/015 – *An Post/Postpoint*, 31.5.2010.

Figure 4.5 provides details of the proportion of merger notifications that qualified under the SMNP since its introduction on 1 July 2020. The 2020 figure covers only the period from 1 July when the SMNP was introduced. The proportion of merger notifications qualifying for the SMNP increased from 35% in the final six months of 2020 to over 50% in 2022.[232] The SMNP therefore appears to have reduced notification requirements and, presumably costs, in the case of a large proportion of mergers.

Figure 4.5: SMNP Cases as a Percentage of Total Merger Notifications by Year, 2020-2023

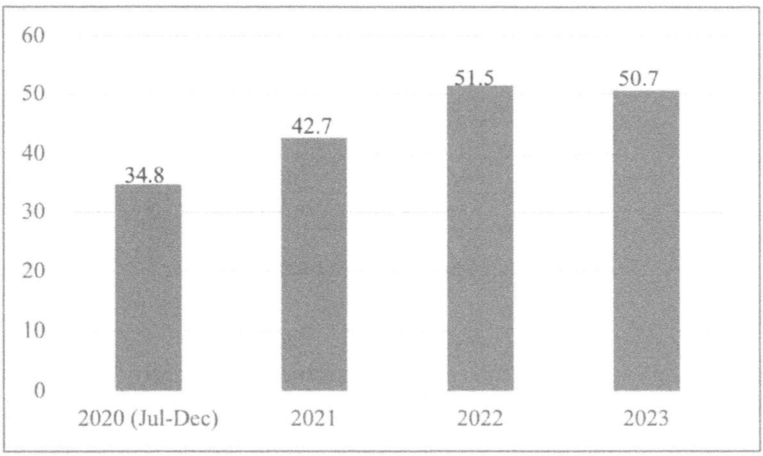

Source: CCPC.

In *Reach/ISL*[233] the CCPC stated that it decided not to apply the SMNP because of competition concerns raised in a third-party submission, although the Determination states that the parties had a combined market share of [15-20]% which is above the SMNP threshold. Other cases were not cleared under SMNP, although they would appear to have satisfied the required criteria based on the published Determinations. In *Caldic/Brand-Nu & B&L,*[234] for example, the CCPC cleared the transaction *inter alia* on the grounds that the parties combined market share was small, although it did not quote a figure. One might expect that the SMNP would apply in cases where market shares

232 The CCPC, *M&A Annual Report 2022* records 37 mergers notified under the SMNP in that year but only 35 Determinations state that the transaction was cleared under SMNP criteria.

233 CCPC M/20/021 – *Reach/ISL,* 28.8.2020.

234 CCPC M/20/031 – *Caldic/Brand-Nu and B&L,* 23.11.2020.

are small.[235] It might be useful in the future for the CCPC to provide some explanation of why the SMNP was not applied in similar cases.

Table 4.9 provides further information on average case duration, distinguishing between SMNP and non-SMNP cases.[236] The table shows that SMNP cases are decided relatively quickly. Average decision time in such cases declined from 19 days in 2020 to 17 days in 2021, although it subsequently increased to 18 days. This is nevertheless impressive, especially when one takes account of the fact that SMNP cases accounted for approximately half of all merger notifications since 2020.

Table 4.9: Average Duration of Merger Cases (SMNP *versus* non-SMNP) by Year, 2020-2023

Year	All Cases	SMNP	Non-SMNP
2020	64.2	18.9	75.2
2021	58.2	17.1	87.9
2022	53.1	17.8	84.6
2023	48.9	17.6	81.1

Source: CCPC.

The other side of the coin illustrated in the table is the lengthy decision times for non-SMNP cases. The average duration of non-SMNP cases increased from 75 days in 2020 to 88 days in 2021, before falling slightly to 85 days in 2022 and 81 days in 2023. It is difficult to draw any definitive conclusions, given that the table covers a period of just three and a half years. One possibility is that, while the SMNP has speeded up the decision process for such mergers, it has enabled the CCPC to devote more time and resources to analysing other mergers. To the extent that the SMNP may enable the CCPC to concentrate on potentially problematic cases, this is a positive outcome. To some extent, therefore, the introduction of the SMNP may represent a win-win by speeding up decisions on innocuous cases, reducing costs to notifying firms in such cases and enabling the CCPC to concentrate its resources on potentially more problematic cases. Some caution is

---

235 See **Chapters 7** and **8.** Other examples where the SMNP was not applied although it appears from the Determination that the criteria were satisfied include CCPC M/20/028 – *Applied Materials/Kokusai Electric*, 9.10.2020; M/21/067 – *Sicon/Sensori*, 7.1.2022; and M/23/027 – *European Bakery Group/Panelto Foods*, 15.8.2023. The CCPC stated in the last case that there was no overlap between the parties.

236 The 2022 numbers exclude one withdrawn merger notification.

required, however, given the limited data available on the operation of the SMNP and the potential risk that incorrect market definitions might allow some potentially problematic mergers to be cleared under SMNP without adequate scrutiny. This is reinforced by the CA/CCPC practice of frequently not defining specific markets in its Determinations (see **Chapter 6**).

Some Preliminary Conclusions

Horizontal mergers accounted for 45% of all merger notifications over the 2003-2023 period. A further 15% of mergers notified involved both horizontal and vertical overlaps. Thus, 60% of all merger notifications were either pure horizontal mergers or a combination of both horizontal and vertical. In contrast only 8% of all notified mergers were purely vertical mergers. Thus, the majority of merger notifications had horizontal elements, and such mergers are considered more likely to raise competition issues.

In the 21-year period following the change in Ireland's merger control regime 1,264 mergers were notified to the CA/CCPC: 89% of mergers notified were cleared unconditionally following a preliminary, Phase 1, investigation, while only five notified mergers have been prohibited and the CA's Determination in one of these cases was overturned by the High Court on appeal. The extremely low proportion of prohibition decisions may be partly explained by the notification in the early years of a large number of mergers which had no competition nexus with Ireland. A further 38 mergers were subject to remedies which indicates that they were originally considered likely to result in an SLC.[237] Overall only 3% of all mergers notified to the CA/CCPC since 2003 were considered by the CA/CCPC as likely to result in a SLC.

It is possible to draw a number of preliminary conclusions based on the analysis in this chapter. The low proportion of prohibition and remedy decisions, by definition, indicates that there have been relatively few false positive (Type I) errors. On the other hand, this raises questions about possible failures to identify anti-competitive mergers, false negative (Type II) errors. Since 2003 Ireland had a lower combined rate of prohibitions and remedies than the EU, UK, Denmark and New Zealand, although it is higher than in the US. This suggests that the CA/CCPC has adopted a more

---

[237] A further six cases were cleared on foot of remedies to notify future mergers, even if they were below the notification thresholds, while two others involved ancillary restraints. Apart from *Grafton/Heiton*, these cases are not included in the number of problem cases as the mergers themselves raised no competition issues.

lenient approach to mergers than competition agencies in these jurisdictions, apart from the US. This has to be viewed in a context in which both the EU and US regimes have been criticised for being overly lenient.

An alternative explanation for the low number of cases raising SLC concerns is that the system proved highly effective in deterring anti-competitive mergers. There is no way of measuring the number of mergers that may have been deterred by the merger control regime. Since 2016, the proportion of problem cases has increased sharply which is inconsistent with the merger regime having a strong deterrent effect. Alternatively, it may be that the increase in the number of problem cases occurred because the CCPC adopted a stricter approach to mergers post-2016. This, however, raises the possibility of an overly lenient approach and a higher likelihood of false negative (Type II) errors in earlier years.

The CA's initial interpretation of the *"doing business in Ireland"* requirement resulted in the notification of a large number of mergers with no competition nexus to the State (Gorecki *et al.*, 2007). This obviously increased the cost burden on the parties involved in such cases. In fairness, the CA altered its approach at the end of 2006, and this was followed by a drop in the proportion of notified mergers which involved no horizontal or vertical overlap from 47% over the 2003-2007 period to 25% post-2007.

Average decision times appear to have increased significantly since 2016, while the proportion of quite lengthy cases has also increased sharply. The introduction of the SMNP in mid-2020 has enabled a large number of cases to be decided relatively quickly, with average decision times in such cases of approximately 18 days. As against this, non-SMNP cases can be quite lengthy. The introduction of the SMNP may nevertheless represent a win-win by speeding up decisions on innocuous cases, reducing costs to notifying firms in such cases, and enabling the CCPC to concentrate its resources on potentially more problematic cases. Some caution is required, however, given that we only have data for three and a half years since the introduction of the SMNP. There is also a potential risk that incorrect market definitions might allow some potentially problematic mergers to be cleared under the SMNP without adequate scrutiny. The fact that more problem cases have been identified following the introduction of the SMNP may also indicate that such cases may previously have gone undetected, i.e. it is consistent with possible false negatives pre-2020.

5: COUNTERFACTUALS IN MERGER ANALYSIS

Introduction

Merger analysis is, by definition, forward-looking. It seeks to identify whether a merger will have anti-competitive effects if it is allowed to proceed. This requires an assessment of what is likely to happen should the merger proceed compared to what would happen in the absence of the proposed merger. The alternative scenario, against which the effects of a merger are assessed, is referred to as the counterfactual.

In most cases the alternative to the merger going ahead would entail the continuation of the existing *status quo*, although this may not always be the case. For example, the pre-merger *status quo* will not be maintained if one of the merging parties constitutes a *"failing firm"* and would go out of business absent the merger. Another scenario in which the pre-merger *status quo* would not be maintained is where it is certain that a merging party would have exited the market even if the merger had never occurred. Such considerations were an important factor in several bank mergers notified to the CCPC in 2021 and 2022, for example.[238] A further scenario in which an alternative counterfactual would arise is where circumstances change during the course of the merger investigation. A distinction needs to be drawn in such cases between a change in circumstances that is a direct result of the merger and one that is not.

Where an alternative counterfactual to the existing *status quo* is appropriate the question arises as to whether an *ex ante* or an *ex post* approach should apply. An *ex ante* approach defines the counterfactual as

---

[238] *Bank of Ireland/KBC; AIB/Ulster Bank; PTSB/Ulster Bank;* and *AIB/Ulster Bank (Trackers).*

the situation that would have prevailed if the merger had never been proposed, whereas an *ex post* approach considers the situation that would arise if the merger were not permitted to proceed (Amelio *et al.*, 2018).

The assessment of the counterfactual is not a matter of considering various possible alternatives. In general, the only scenario against which the merger should be considered is the one that is most likely to occur in the absence of the merger, although multiple alternative scenarios may need to be considered in the case of a failing firm (see below). It is important for merging parties to recognise that, if they wish to argue for an alternative counterfactual, there must be a strong likelihood that such an alternative would occur.

Identifying the Appropriate Counterfactual

In the majority of cases the counterfactual will involve the continuation of the pre-merger *status quo,* although this may not always be the case. CCPCMG2014 refer to a merger involving a failing firm as a specific example where the pre-merger *status quo* would not constitute the appropriate counterfactual.

Establishing the appropriate counterfactual is not a matter of identifying multiple possible alternative scenarios and choosing the one that best supports the case for or against the merger. The only relevant alternative scenario is the one that is most likely to occur. In *Metro/Herald AM,* the merging parties put forward two alternative scenarios, while the CA identified a third possible alternative. It is not clear from the Determination which, if any, of the alternative counterfactuals was chosen as the yardstick against which to assess the competitive effects of the proposed merger.

CAMG2002 made only passing references to the issue of the counterfactual, citing the example of a merger between a new entrant and the *"market leader"* as removing *"a competitive constraint relative to the counterfactual situation of greater rivalry"* (¶4.26(b)).[239] The CA's 2010 consultation on its *Merger Guidelines* defined the counterfactual as the alternative scenario to a merger proceeding:

239 The only other reference to counterfactuals in CAMG2002 states that the SSNIP market definition test is applied using prevailing prices of the merging parties' products and possible substitutes, *"unless such prices are not a relevant counterfactual"* (¶2.6) and so does not relate to the appropriate counterfactual against which a proposed merger should be evaluated.

> *"The 2002 Merger Guidelines should be improved and updated to better describe the concept of the counterfactual (that is, what will or might happen in the absence of the merger going ahead), and its significance for merger review. Given that merger review is necessarily prospective, the counterfactual is an essential element" (CA, 2010, December 3, ¶12.18).*

CCPCMG2014 place a strong onus on merging parties to substantiate any arguments advanced in support of an alternative counterfactual.

> *"In particular, the Commission will expect the merging parties to substantiate any counterfactual they propose with objective evidence supported, where necessary, by independent expert analysis. Such evidence and analysis should obviously be consistent with the parties own internal pre-merger assessments of the likely counterfactual" (¶1.15).*

It is equally incumbent on the CCPC to produce strong evidence in support of any decision involving a non-standard counterfactual. Amelio *et al.* (2018, p.675) point out that *"credible evidence has to be produced if either the [EU] Commission or merging parties propose to deviate from the pre-merger situation as the appropriate counterfactual"*. In rejecting arguments for a non-standard counterfactual in *Tesco/Joyce's*, the CCPC stated *"Tesco appeared to make the argument that the relevant counterfactual is the Proposed Transaction being put into effect"* (¶4.6).[240]

The CCPC in *Q-Park/Tazbell* concluded that, in the absence of the merger, Tazbell would remain in the market and the pre-merger level of competition would be maintained. In its analysis of the competitive effects of the transaction, however, it argued that local authorities were likely to reduce the supply of on-street-car parking in the future and that the level of competition from on-street parking therefore would decline. Thus, the implicit counterfactual applied by the CCPC in analysing competitive effects involved a third party contracting or possibly even exiting the business. In addition, while the CA/CCPC have consistently required that entry must occur within two years in order to offset a potential SLC, it did not apply a time limit for contraction/exit in this case.

---

240 The CCPC concluded that the most plausible counterfactual was that the Target would have continued to operate.

Ex Ante versus *Ex Post* Counterfactuals

A fundamental question arises when one is considering alternative counterfactuals, namely whether the counterfactual should be defined as the situation which would arise if the merger had never been proposed or in the absence of the proposed merger being implemented. The former involves an *ex ante* approach to defining the appropriate counterfactual while the latter involves an *ex post* approach. Economics indicates that the appropriate counterfactual should be determined on an *ex ante* rather than an *ex post* basis (Amelio *et al.*, 2018). In other words, the appropriate counterfactual is what would have happened if the proposed transaction had never occurred.

A potential divergence between the *ex ante* and *ex post* approach towards counterfactuals may give rise to complex trade-offs between deterrence and efficiency considerations. Consider, for example, a situation in which there were other potential purchasers for a target undertaking. This could imply that the appropriate counterfactual to a proposed merger is one in which the target would have been acquired by an alternative purchaser. A question may arise, however, as to whether those unsuccessful bidders would still be interested in acquiring the target firm if a significant period of time had elapsed between their making an offer and the review of the merger. Such offers only constitute evidence of interest at the time they were made. An alternative purchaser may no longer be interested, if the target's commercial situation had declined in the interim. In those circumstances an *ex post* approach may imply that an acquisition should be approved even though it would have a negative effect on competition relative to the situation that would have prevailed if the transaction had not been proposed. Amelio *et al.* (2018) argue that this could lead to a situation where mergers with demonstrably exclusionary intent, whose purpose is to prevent other purchasers from entering the market, would have to be cleared.

Conversely, the *ex ante* approach may require that a proposed merger be blocked even though the applied counterfactual will not in fact materialise. Focusing on what is achievable at the time of the merger decision may allow merging firms to obtain clearance for a merger by presenting authorities with a *fait accompli* because the *ex ante* counterfactual is no longer available as a result of the proposed deal itself. An *ex ante* approach to counterfactuals can deter such hold-up strategies. Amelio *et al.* (2018) caution that an *ex ante* approach may not always lead to the optimal *ex post* outcome. Nevertheless, they conclude that the *ex ante* approach is the correct one.

> *"In our view, the ex ante approach is a more sensible policy approach, since it is directed at preventing anti-competitive outcomes at their root. Arguably, it also comes closest in spirit to the stated aim of comparing 'the competitive conditions that would result from the notified merger with the conditions that would have prevailed without the merger'" (ibid., p.675).*

They cite *Knorr-Bremse/Haldex*[241] as an example illustrating the differences between the *ex ante* and *ex post* approaches. Knorr-Bremse made a last-minute offer for Haldex which outbid a prior takeover offer by ZF Friedrichshafen, which had already secured anti-trust clearance from all of the relevant authorities. ZF had indicated its intention to make significant investments to transform and expand Haldex into a full-service provider that would compete more effectively with the market leaders, Knorr-Bremse and Wabco. This transaction was pre-empted by the higher Knorr-Bremse bid. From an economic perspective, the Commission had to consider whether the Knorr-Bremse proposal had the object or effect of blocking potentially pro-competitive entry by ZF into the brake market. This raised the question of whether the appropriate counterfactual was the pre-merger *status quo* or a counterfactual in which the proposed ZF takeover of Haldex would have gone ahead.

CCPCMG2014 state:

> *"The term 'counterfactual' refers to the state of competition without the merger or acquisition. In other words the 'actual' situation is the merger being put into effect and the 'counterfactual' is the situation in the absence of the merger being put into effect...*
>
> *To establish the relevant counterfactual, it is necessary to:*
>
> *(a) Establish the competitive situation that would prevail but for the merger being put into effect*
>
> *(b) Distinguish between:*
>
> *(i) merger-specific competitive effects, and*
>
> *(ii) non-merger-specific competitive effects, if any, that would occur irrespective of the merger being put into effect" (¶s1.12 & 1.13).*

There are several problems with this definition. First it defines the counterfactual as the state of competition *"without the merger"*. This phrase

241 EU Commission, Case No. COMP/M.8222 – *Knorr-Bremse/Haldex* (notification withdrawn, 4.10.2017).

is somewhat ambiguous in that it is not entirely clear whether it involves an *ex ante* (if the merger never occurred) or an *ex post* (if the merger did not proceed) approach. The *Guidelines*, however, then describe the counterfactual as the situation in the absence of *"the merger being put into effect"*, a phrase that is repeated subsequently. This seems to imply an *ex post* approach which economics indicates is incorrect.

The issue of the appropriate counterfactual arose in *Unilever/Lyons Tea*, which was referred to the CA by the Minister under the 1991 Act. During the course of the Phase 2 investigation, Unilever informed the CA that it had decided to withdraw its *Lipton* brand from the market, although in a submission to the Minister three months earlier it had stated that *Lipton* would remain in the market despite a fall in its market share (*ibid.*, p.72). The CA concluded that the merger, as originally proposed, would be likely to restrict competition in the tea market. The majority of the CA, however, concluded that the withdrawal of the *Lipton* brand meant that it was no longer an actual competitor in the market and that the merger would not therefore have any effect on market concentration or on competition in the market. A minority[242] considered that the merger would be likely to restrict competition in the tea market despite Unilever's decision to withdraw the *Lipton* brand.

Neither the majority nor minority report explicitly discussed the issue of the appropriate counterfactual. The majority accepted that *Lipton* would exit the market regardless of whether or not the merger went ahead and analysed the merger against a scenario in which *Lipton* would not remain in the market. The majority did not consider whether the decision to withdraw may have been causally related to the merger. Under the *ex ante* approach the appropriate question is whether Unilever would have withdrawn from the market if the merger proposal had never occurred. After all, the possibility of the merger being blocked may have influenced the decision to withdraw the *Lipton* brand.[243]

In *Stena/P&O* the CA implicitly accepted that P&O would withdraw its Dublin-Mostyn ferry service irrespective of whether the proposed merger went ahead, although there is no discussion of the appropriate counterfactual in the decision. The parties had previously notified a proposed merger to the CA in November 2003 which was subsequently

242 The minority report was written by the author.

243 The CA also disagreed on the impact of the withdrawal of the *Lipton* brand on potential competition (see below).

withdrawn in February 2004 after the CA had decided to conduct a full Phase 2 investigation. The proposed 2003 transaction was also investigated by the UKOFT (2003) which referred it to the UKCC for a full Phase 2 investigation.[244]

The parties had signed a Memorandum of Understanding on 27 May 2003 setting out the arrangements for the proposed acquisition by Stena of certain assets relating to P&O's ferry operations between Dublin-Liverpool and Larne-Fleetwood. Simultaneously P&O announced the closure of its Dublin-Mostyn route (UKCC, *Stena/P&O*, ¶2). The UKCC concluded that Stena's acquisition of P&O's Dublin-Liverpool service would result in an SLC and should therefore be prohibited.

> *"We therefore concluded that the action that should be taken for the purpose of remedying, mitigating or preventing the substantial lessening of competition was the prohibition of the transfer of the assets used on the Liverpool-Dublin route from P&O to Stena" (ibid., ¶21).*

The transaction which was subsequently notified to the CA in April 2004 involved Stena acquiring all of P&O's assets relating to its ferry business between Larne, in Northern Ireland, and Fleetwood, in Great Britain along with two vessels deployed by P&O on its ferry business between Dublin and Mostyn. The sale of the two P&O vessels deployed on the Dublin-Mostyn route resulted in P&O exiting that route, whilst Stena did not acquire the port infrastructure and facilities necessary to operate on the route. This resulted in the effective closure of the Dublin-Mostyn route as P&O was the only operator on the route. The CA noted *"...P&O's submission that it intends to close its Dublin-Mostyn ferry operation in early course, irrespective of whether its two vessels are acquired by Stena..."* (CA *Stena/P&O*, ¶22).

Implicitly the CA decision accepted that the appropriate counterfactual to the merger was that P&O would have withdrawn the Dublin-Mostyn service. The decision, however, contains no counterfactual analysis. There is no reference to any evidence supporting such a counterfactual and no reasons are given for accepting that P&O would have exited the Dublin-

244 UKOFT ME/1237/03 – *Stena/P&O*, 22.8.2003; UKCC ME/1237/03 – *Stena/P&O*, 5.2.2004. At the time responsibility for merger investigations was shared between the OFT and the CC, the former being responsible for Phase 1 investigations and the latter for Phase 2 investigations. The two agencies were merged to form the UKCMA in April 2014.

Mostyn route irrespective of whether the merger had occurred. The UKOFT decision in relation to the original 2003 transaction noted:

> *"The effect of P&O's decision to withdraw its Mostyn to Dublin service is not a direct effect of this merger – although, potentially, relevant to the counterfactual against which the merger should be assessed" (UKOFT,* Stena/P&O, *p.8).*

The UKCC stated:

> *"Initially we had some reservations about whether or not P&O would close the Mostyn-Dublin route in the absence of the proposed merger. We noted that the intended closure of the route was announced in conjunction with the proposed merger, and that payments in the MoU were expressed as contributions by Stena to the cost of closing Mostyn" (UKCC,* Stena/P&O, *¶5.28).*

Nevertheless, the UKCC ultimately accepted that P&O would have closed the Dublin-Mostyn service had the merger not occurred.[245]

There was no discussion of the appropriate counterfactual in *UTV/FM104*.[246] The proposed transaction related to the acquisition by UTV of a Dublin radio station, FM104, from Communicorp and came about because the CA had raised concerns in relation to the latter's acquisition of three radio stations, including FM104.[247] The acquirer in the latter case agreed to divest FM104 to an upfront purchaser, with UTV ultimately the successful bidder. In considering the impact of the proposed transaction on market structure, the CA compared the post-merger situation in *UTV/FM104* with what it would have been if the *Communicorp/SRH* merger had been implemented without any requirement to divest FM104 to an upfront buyer. That alternative scenario was excluded by the divestment remedy and was therefore not the appropriate counterfactual. Arguably the appropriate counterfactual was one in which Communicorp had not acquired FM104 (see **Chapter 7**).

The CA struggled with the issue of the appropriate counterfactual in *Heineken/Beamish & Crawford*. Beamish & Crawford operated a brewery in Cork City and supplied stouts, ales and lagers to the on- and off-trade throughout the State. It was a subsidiary of Scottish & Newcastle, a UK-based

---

245 The reasons for this are outlined at ¶s5.26-5.32 and in a lengthy Appendix to the report. The fact that Stena reportedly paid part of the costs involved in closing the Mostyn route raises questions.

246 CA M/07/069 – *UTV/FM104*, 17.1.2008.

247 *Communicorp/SRH*.

brewer, which was acquired by Carlsberg and Heineken, who subsequently divided the various Scottish & Newcastle subsidiaries between them with Heineken acquiring Beamish & Crawford. The transaction was notified to the EU Commission under the ECMR, but the Commission agreed to the CA's request to refer the Irish aspect of the transaction (the Heineken acquisition of Beamish & Crawford) to it under Article 9.

The CA Determination states that, in analysing mergers, *"two situations are compared, over a two-year time horizon, to determine if a merger will lead to a substantial lessening of competition"* (¶5.2).[248] It then described these alternatives as the situation where the merger takes place compared with *"the situation that would have been expected to prevail without the merger (sometimes referred to as the counterfactual) is considered"*. This statement appears to suggest an *ex ante* approach to defining the counterfactual.[249]

The transaction arose as a result of the Carlsberg/Heineken acquisition of Scottish & Newcastle. The *ex ante* approach to identifying the counterfactual outlined above indicates that the appropriate counterfactual was the situation that would have applied in the absence of the proposed Carlsberg/Heineken acquisition of Scottish & Newcastle, *i.e.*, the pre-merger *status quo*. Arguably if that transaction went ahead, however, the continuation of the pre-merger *status quo* would not have been possible as Beamish & Crawford's parent would have been acquired by Carlsberg and Heineken and its assets split up between them.

The Determination stated:

> *"...it is possible to consider a variety of scenarios as to what will happen post-merger and what the appropriate counterfactual might be" (¶5.11).*

Beamish & Crawford owned its Beamish stout brand but did not own any of the lager brands that it brewed and distributed.[250] One possibility raised by the CA involved an existing licensor[251] purchasing Beamish & Crawford and using its brewery as a brewing and bottling supply facility to supply its Irish and UK markets. A second possibility was that Beamish & Crawford would

248 The reference to a two-year time horizon is somewhat puzzling.

249 The Determination cites UKCC (2003, ¶1.22) as the source of the quotation. As previously pointed out, CAMG2002 contained no discussion of the counterfactual.

250 Details of the licensing arrangements in relation to the various Beamish & Crawford lager brands are outlined at ¶s5.5-5.10 of the Determination.

251 The owner of a lager brand which had licensed Beamish & Crawford to supply and distribute that brand within the State but see below.

continue but without the Foster's lager brand which was owned by Scottish & Newcastle. The CA, however, chose a third counterfactual.

> *"The Authority has decided, however, to assume that the merged entity will control all of the lager brands currently marketed by B&C post-merger and that, should the merger not proceed, then these brands will continue to be marketed by B&C" (¶5.12).*

The CA advanced the following justification for its approach:

> *"This approach is justified on two grounds. First, the Authority does not know which, if any, of the various alternative outcomes is likely to occur... Second, the approach is likely to be the worst-case scenario from a competition assessment point of view. If it is concluded, on the basis of this approach, that there is no SLC, the merger can proceed. If it is concluded that this approach would produce an SLC, then various possible remedies can be explored" (¶5.13).*

There are several problems with the CA's approach. As previously outlined, the appropriate counterfactual in any merger is the scenario that is most likely to occur without the merger. The CA in this case, by its own admission, stated that it did not know which, if any, of the counterfactuals that it considered was likely to occur. The CA's second argument was that the chosen counterfactual constituted the worst-case scenario from a competition perspective. The most competitive possible alternative scenario to the merger is not the appropriate yardstick against which to evaluate a merger at Phase 2, unless there is strong evidence that such a counterfactual represents the most likely scenario in the absence of the merger (see below). Significantly the CA indicated that, if such an approach had indicated an SLC would occur, then *"various possible remedies can be explored"*. There is no justification for prohibiting or requiring remedies on the grounds that a proposed merger would result in an SLC compared to an alternative scenario unless that scenario is the most likely to occur. The fact that the CA concluded in *Heineken/Beamish & Crawford* that the proposed transaction would not give rise to any SLC when compared to the most competitive counterfactual does not alter the fact that its analysis of the counterfactual was flawed.[252]

Stena/DFDS involved the acquisition by Stena of sole control of vessels, related assets, inventory, employees and contracts related to passenger and

---

252 While not discussed in the Determination, the CA decision assumed that Diageo would proceed with plans to build a new brewery which would expand its capacity. See **Chapter 8**.

freight ferry services operated by DFDS between Belfast-Heysham and Belfast-Liverpool. The merger was announced on 1 December 2010. Stena announced on 2 December 2010 that it was going to close its Larne-Fleetwood route.[253] On 13 January 2011 DFDS announced that it was going to close its Dublin-Heysham and Dublin-Liverpool routes with effect from 31 January 2011. The parties argued that the decisions to close these routes were taken independently of the proposed merger.

Following a Phase 1 investigation, the UKOFT rejected the parties' claims that Stena would have closed the Larne-Fleetwood route irrespective of the merger.

> *"On the basis of the above, the OFT cannot conclude with a sufficient degree of certainty that Stena would have inevitably closed the Fleetwood-Larne route and consequently exit the diagonal corridor market, absent the merger" (¶97).*

It therefore concluded that the appropriate counterfactual was one in which, absent the merger, Stena would have continued to operate its Larne-Fleetwood service. The UKCC subsequently concluded, following a Phase 2 investigation that Stena would have closed the route and not introduced a new service on the same route corridor in the absence of the merger.[254]

The CA concluded that, because the volumes of traffic to and from the State on the target routes and on the Larne-Fleetwood route were minimal, the issue of whether Stena would have closed the Larne-Fleetwood route in the absence of the merger was irrelevant. It acknowledged that the cessation of services on the DFDS Dublin routes had a much greater potential impact on competition within the State because the vast majority of traffic into and out of Dublin was for customers in the State. The CA concluded on the basis of the evidence available that DFDS would have ceased operating the two routes regardless of whether the merger had occurred.[255]

The CA in *Dalata/Moran's Hotel/Bewley's*[256] argued that the portfolio of hotels managed by the purchaser might decline in the future as such management contracts were typically short-term in nature. While there was

---

253 UKOFT ME/4790/10 – *Stena/DFDS*, 8.2.2011, ¶34.

254 UKCC, Case No. ME/4790/10 – *Stena/DFDS*, 29.6.2011. The UK authorities apply different standards for identifying counterfactuals at Phase 1 and Phase 2 (see below).

255 The CA stated that, in reaching this conclusion, it had reviewed internal documents from the parties. The UKOFT did not come to any conclusion on the DFDS Dublin routes at Phase 1, but the UKCC concluded at Phase 2 that DFDS would have closed its two Dublin routes.

256 CCPC M/14/040 – *Dalata/Moran's Hotel/Bewley's*, 29.1.2015.

a possibility of this happening, there was no indication that it was the most likely scenario and should not have been considered as a likely scenario.[257]

Top Snacks/United Biscuits involved the acquisition by Top Snacks of United Biscuits savoury snacks business (KP Snacks), the latter undertaking having decided to exit the market. The parties argued that the most likely alternative to the proposed transaction was that KP would have been acquired by a third party, effectively resulting in a continuation of the pre-merger *status quo* with KP remaining in the market, albeit under different ownership. The CA held that absent the transaction KP would have remained in the market under its existing ownership.

> *"In contrast, were there no acquisition, United Biscuits UK presumably would have continued providing Irish consumers with KP products, [...]. This establishes the relevant counter-factual, i.e., that in the absence of the transaction there would be a continuing United Biscuits UK presence in the State supplying KP-branded savoury snacks products" (¶4.28).*

The question is whether *United Biscuits* had taken an irrevocable decision to exit the market prior to the merger proposal. There may have been a strong likelihood that, in the absence of the merger, the KP business would have been acquired by another party, as the merging parties claimed, although in the absence of supporting evidence such a scenario arguably does not constitute an appropriate counterfactual (see below).

Kepak/Silvercrest[258] involved a rather unusual situation in which the target, which had previously been engaged in the production and supply of frozen beefburgers had lost all of its customer contracts as a result of being caught up in the European equine meat scandal in January 2013 and the target plant had lain idle for several months prior to the transaction. While the Determination contains no specific discussion of the relevant counterfactual, the CA assumed that, following the transaction, the target's contract to supply a fast-food chain in the State would be recommenced and included this in its estimate of the parties' post-merger market share.

The CCPC Determination in *Topaz/Esso* records that Esso had exited from the supply of aviation fuel at Dublin Airport in May 2014, almost a year

---

257 There was no suggestion that whether the purchaser would lose any of its existing management contracts was merger-specific, *i.e.*, arguably it would be equally likely to occur with or without the merger. Thus, if the most likely scenario involved the purchaser losing some of its hotel management contracts, it would have been the appropriate counterfactual.

258 CA M/13/013 – *Kepak/Silvercrest*, 21.05.2013.

before the merger. It had continued to supply aviation fuel to Knock and Waterford until mid-2015 but did not tender when these contracts came up for renewal. Thus, Esso had arguably taken a decision to exit the aviation fuel business prior to the proposed merger. Therefore, in the absence of evidence linking Esso's decision to exit from the aviation fuel market to the proposed transaction, the appropriate counterfactual was one in which Esso was no longer considered a competitor in the aviation fuel market since that was the actual situation at the time of the merger. The CCPC, however, argued that the merger would reduce competition in the aviation fuel market, indicating that it regarded Esso as a competitor in that market. This is inconsistent with the approach taken in the ferry cases described above.

Cedarglade (Musgrave)/Fortunestown Supermarket[259] involved the acquisition of a former supermarket which had not traded during the 20 months prior to the transaction due to fire damage. The CCPC argued that there was a horizontal overlap between the parties because the target business had previously operated, and the acquirer planned to re-open it, as a supermarket. There is no indication in the Determination that the outlet would have re-opened as a supermarket in the absence of the proposed transaction.

In *Eason/Dubray* the merging parties cited evidence of a marked shift away from traditional bookshops to online retailers during the Covid pandemic and argued that the appropriate counterfactual was one in which, post-pandemic, online retailers' market share would be significantly higher than it had been pre-pandemic. The CCPC, however, concluded that the pre-merger (pre-pandemic) market structure represented the most appropriate counterfactual *"as it is uncertain how the market will develop in the future"* (¶40). Arguably this was a case in which there were valid arguments for both scenarios, and it came down to a judgement call.

Whether the counterfactual should be defined on an *ex ante* or an *ex post* basis was critical in a series of bank mergers which were notified to the CCPC during 2021 and 2022.[260] The parties argued that the target undertakings, KBC and Ulster Bank, would have exited the market regardless of the proposed transactions and that the appropriate counterfactual in each case was that they would no longer be present in the relevant market.

In *AIB/Ulster Bank* the CCPC quoted CCPCMG2014 ¶1.12: *"the 'counterfactual' is the situation in the absence of the merger being put into effect"*

---

259 CCPC M/18/054 – *Cedarglade (Musgrave)/Fortunestown Supermarket*, 1.8.2018.

260 *Bank of Ireland/KBC; AIB/Ulster Bank; PTSB/Ulster Bank; AIB/Ulster Bank (Trackers).*

(¶4.2). The following paragraph states, however, that the counterfactual *"involves considering what would have happened if the proposed merger had not taken place"* (¶4.3).[261] There is a fundamental difference between a merger not being put into effect and a merger not having taken place. The former involves an *ex post* approach to identifying the appropriate counterfactual while the latter entails an *ex ante* approach.

Later the Determination states:

> *"To establish the relevant counterfactual, it is necessary to: (a) establish the competitive situation that would prevail in the absence of the merger; and, (b) distinguish between: (i) merger-specific competitive effects; and, (ii) non-merger specific competitive effects, if any, that would occur irrespective of the merger being put into effect" (ibid., ¶4.7).*

This statement combines the *ex ante* and *ex post* standard into a single sentence stating that the relevant counterfactual involves the competitive situation that would prevail in the absence of the merger while defining non-merger specific competitive effects as those that would occur irrespective of whether the merger was *"put into effect"*. The Determination then introduces a third alternative stating that post-notification developments that were unrelated to the proposed transaction were considered, while those that were causally related to the merger were excluded from the counterfactual (¶4.11). The focus should be on events that occurred post the merger proposal rather than post-notification.

The Determination subsequently states that, in analysing the appropriate counterfactual, the CCPC had considered:

> *"...whether the Target Assets would exit the relevant markets identified in Section 3 in the absence of the Proposed Transaction" (¶4.12).*

This statement indicates an *ex ante* rather than an *ex post* approach to defining the counterfactual.

The CCPC subsequently adopted an *ex ante* approach in both *Bank of Ireland/KBC* and *PTSB/Ulster Bank* stating that the assessment of the relevant counterfactual *"involves considering what would have happened if the proposed merger had not taken place"* (*PTSB/Ulster Bank*, ¶4.3; *Bank of Ireland/KBC*, ¶5.3).

The *Bank of Ireland/KBC* decision provides an excellent illustration of the difference between the *ex ante* and *ex post* approach to merger

---

261 ¶4.3.

counterfactuals. The parties advocated an *ex post* approach to defining the appropriate counterfactual, arguing that the CCPC was required to take account of the extent to which KBC's plans and capabilities had changed since the time of entering into an MoU with Bank of Ireland to sell its business, clearly acknowledging in their response to the CCPC Assessment, that the decline in KBC's market share was a result of the merger proposal:

> *"Looking over a longer time horizon and more recent share data, it is clear that the announcement has had a significant effect, with KBCI's market share of new originations having declined substantially to [5-10]% in Q4 2021... In December 2021, KBCI's share of new completions was just [5-10]% and in January 2022 this has fallen again to [5-10]%. In terms of market share of new applications, which is the strongest leading indicator of future originations, KBCI market share of applications has declined to just [5-10]% in December 2021 compared to [15-20]% in December 2020 (i.e. a decline of [✂]%). This share has fallen further still in January 2022 to [0-5]%"* (ibid., ¶5.50.).

The CCPC correctly rejected these arguments pointing out that it was necessary *"to distinguish between competitive conditions and other developments that would have happened irrespective of the proposed transaction (which should be taken into account as part of any counterfactual analysis) and those which are directly related to or the result of the Proposed Transaction (which are irrelevant to the counterfactual analysis)"* (¶5.11). The CCPC advanced three reasons for excluding developments that arose as a result of the proposed merger from the counterfactual analysis:

i. Actions that are directly related to a merger or arise as a consequence of a merger would not have occurred in the merger's absence and are therefore irrelevant to the counterfactual assessment.

ii. Actions taken by the merging parties post-notification should not, in principle, affect the counterfactual or the assessment of an SLC as such actions could affect, or even determine, the outcome of the substantive assessment.

iii. This approach was in line with the EU Commission decision in *General Electric/Alstom*.[262]

The *Bank of Ireland/KBC* decision thus confirms that the relevant counterfactual should be defined on an *ex ante* basis.

---

262 EU Commission Case No. COMP/M.7278 – *General Electric/Alstom*, 8.9.2015.

The CCPC concluded that KBC had not definitively decided to exit the Irish market prior to Bank of Ireland's approach and the signing of the MoU.

> *"The evidence shows that KBC had not decided, until the point of entering the MOU, to cease activities in the State"* (Bank of Ireland/KBC, *¶5.38)*.

Consequently, the appropriate counterfactual in this case was one in which KBC would have remained in the market. Much of the parties' arguments and the reasons for the CCPC's conclusion are redacted in the Determination so that it is not possible to state whether the evidence supported its conclusion. What can be said is that the CCPC correctly adopted an *ex ante* approach in identifying the appropriate counterfactual.

The CCPC concluded in *AIB/Ulster Bank* and *PTSB/Ulster Bank* that Ulster Bank's UK parent, NatWest, had already taken a decision to exit the Irish market prior to the proposed transaction and that the appropriate counterfactual to the merger in both cases was one in which Ulster Bank would not have remained in the market. Again, much of the evidence on which the CCPC relied is redacted in the Determinations, so it is not possible to offer any assessment of the CCPC's conclusions that this constituted the appropriate counterfactual. In *AIB/Ulster Bank (Trackers)* the CCPC concluded that the appropriate counterfactual was one in which Ulster Bank would have exited the market *"with a sale to a potentially less anti-competitive alternative purchaser of their tracker mortgage book"* (¶77). It nevertheless concluded that the sale to AIB would not result in any SLC because *"the acquisition of the assets by a new entrant would provide an acquirer of the Target Assets with limited opportunities to develop new business based on the acquisition"* (¶99).[263]

An *ex ante* approach does not, however, require that developments post-announcement of the transaction should be ignored. Post-announcement developments that are unrelated to the merger should be considered in both the merger scenario and the counterfactual. However, post-announcement developments that are causally related to the transaction can only be attributed to the merger scenario and should be excluded from the counterfactual. In *GE/Alstom* the EU Commission found that a *"recent deterioration of Alstom's financial situation in so far as it would not have occurred in the absence of the proposed merger cannot be taken into account"* (§8.10.3.6). The post-notification decline of the target was causally attributed to the merger.

---

263 According to the Determination this was due to the nature of the Target Assets and would apply regardless of the purchaser (see below).

In *Kerry/Breeo* the CA noted that a retailer had threatened to de-list several of the target's breakfast meat products unless Breeo allowed the retailer improved margins. The Determination acknowledged that the retailer's actions were consistent with the exercise of buyer power as the retailer had threatened to de-list products in order to obtain better financial terms. The CA argued, however, that evidence in relation to market behaviour post the announcement of a merger was *"clearly unreliable"* and could be afforded little weight. This is inconsistent with an *ex ante* approach to counterfactuals which indicates that developments post the announcement of a merger should be considered unless they are causally related to the merger. It is difficult to see how an attempt by a retailer to exercise buyer power could have resulted from the merger announcement.

In *Thornton's/Carducci* the parties argued for an alternative counterfactual to a continuation of the pre-merger *status quo*. The CCPC rejected the parties' arguments and concluded that, in the absence of the transaction, Citybin would have remained in the market thereby maintaining the pre-merger *status quo.* It is not possible to offer an assessment of the CCPC's conclusions in relation to the appropriate counterfactual because the parties' arguments in favour of an alternative counterfactual were redacted in the Determination (¶4.5). In *daa/Gannon* the CCPC defined the appropriate counterfactual as what the owner of the car park would have done had it not sold it to daa.

The Failing Firm Defence

Failing firm cases constitute an exception to the general rule that the pre-merger *status quo* represents the appropriate counterfactual. In failing firm cases there may be several possible counterfactuals against which a proposed merger may need to be assessed including:

i. Exit of the failing firm.
ii. Acquisition of the failing firm by a new entrant.
iii. Acquisition by an alternative incumbent (OECD, 2009b).

A merger or take-over may provide a means of preventing company collapse, and such mergers may be permitted even though they might significantly reduce competition. Scherer & Ross (1990) observe, however, that there are unlikely to be large numbers of such cases, as acquiring firms normally seek healthy acquisition targets. Bouckaert & Kort (2014) find that firms generally prefer exit by failing firms to acquisition, although they note that acquisitions of failing firms may be profitable if they generate scale and/or scope economies.

Economics indicates that consumer welfare will be higher if a failing firm merger is permitted rather than prohibited (Persson, 2005). If the merger were prohibited the output of the failing firm would be lost to the market, assuming there was no alternative buyer, resulting in higher prices and lower consumer welfare. Although a failing firm merger might be anti-competitive and involve some reduction in consumer welfare, provided the assets of the failing firm are retained in the market the reduction in output and consumer welfare is less than would occur as a result of the outright closure of the failing firm. Persson (2005) finds that the failing firm defence generally has a positive impact on consumer welfare.[264] Bouckaert & Kort (2014) conclude that failing firm mergers can be welfare-enhancing when the merging parties' products are sufficiently heterogenous. Kim & Singal (1993) find that the price effects of airline mergers involving distressed airlines differ from those between healthy airlines. Economics, therefore, indicates that, an otherwise anti-competitive merger may be permitted if one of the merging parties constitutes a failing firm, provided certain stringent conditions are satisfied, namely:

i. The failing firm would otherwise exit the market;
ii. The merger would result in the failing firm's assets remaining in the market; and
iii. There is no less anti-competitive alternative to the proposed merger, i.e., there must be no alternative purchaser for the failing firm willing to pay a price higher than the liquidated value of the failing firm's assets.

The counterfactual in a failing firm case is that the failing firm would go out of business and would no longer have any impact on competition in the market (Motta, 2004). Note, however, the inevitability that the failing firm would cease to operate, of itself, is insufficient to justify an otherwise anti-competitive merger. Some or all of the failing firm's assets must be retained in the market so that, post-merger, output would be higher and prices lower than they would be if the failing firm were permitted to close.[265]

---

264 He notes, however, that it may not maximise total welfare.

265 OECD (2009b) notes that some competition agencies consider whether the failure of the firm and the liquidation of its assets could be less anti-competitive than a merger since the

The failing firm defence has been accepted as justifying otherwise anti-competitive mergers under US law since the 1930s.[266] The EU Commission rejected a failing firm argument in *Aerospatiale-Alenia/de Havilland,* concluding that:

i. de Havilland could remain an independent, efficient competitor on the market, and

ii. There could be other potential purchasers of de Havilland which would give rise to fewer, if any, competitive concerns.

The CJEU in *Kali und Salz* agreed with the Commission's finding that the failing firm defence may be invoked under the ECMR, if it could be demonstrated that there was no means of saving a failing undertaking, other than for it to be taken over by a stronger competitor, and there were no less anti-competitive options.[267] The Court rejected an appeal by the French Government which argued that the requirement in the Commission decision that the acquiring firm would absorb all the market share of the failing firm in the absence of the merger was excessively restrictive. The Court held that such a requirement was necessary to ensure that there was no causal link between the deterioration of the market's competitive structure and the merger. The EU Commission applied the *Kali und Salz* criteria in a restrictive manner for a long time and did not accept the failing firm defence again until its 2001 decision in *BASF/Pantochim/Eurodiol*[268] (OECD, 2009b). Significantly in that case, the Commission accepted that the *"absorption of market share"* requirement was overly restrictive and stated that it was sufficient to show that the assets of the failing firm would inevitably exit the market absent the merger and that there was no less anti-competitive alternative to the merger.

OECD (2009b) reports that the requirements for the failing firm defence are similar in most OECD member countries. Ireland, along with the UK and US, however, requires that the anti-competitive effects of the merger must not be more severe than those that would follow from the reorganisation or restructuring of the failing firm *via* the Examinership process.

---

remaining firms in the market might compete for both the failing firm's market share and the assets that otherwise would have been transferred entirely to one purchaser.

266 *International Shoe Co. v. FTC,* 280 US 291 (1930).

267 *France v. Commission.*

268 EU Commission Case No. COMP/M.2314 – *BASF/Pantochim/Eurodiol,* 11.7.2001.

The CA/CCPC's Approach to Failing Firms

The CA draft *Merger Guidelines* published in mid-2002 surprisingly ruled out including a failing firm defence (Compecon, 2002). The CA claimed that the defence would reward failure and that it would open the door to other unspecified defences which it described as inappropriate. The CA also claimed that it *"had not found the defence to be particularly useful or clear in its application"* in previous cases. This statement is somewhat puzzling. Between 1991 and 2002, the CA had only considered 10 mergers referred to it by the Minister under the *Competition Act, 1991,* although failing firm issues arose in two of these: *Independent/Tribune* and *STA Travel/USIT*. The CA accepted in *Independent/Tribune* that there was a risk that the target undertaking could close if the merger did not proceed but the majority concluded that there was a realistic possibility that another buyer might emerge, or that, if the target went into liquidation, the newspaper title might re-emerge under new ownership, and that either outcome would be superior from a competition viewpoint. While acknowledging that the target in *STA Travel/USIT* was in financial difficulties, the CA did not apply a failing firm defence.

CAMG2002, however, included provisions for failing firm mergers.

> *"A merger may not substantially lessen competition in a market if part or all of the merging assets are certain to exit the market in the event of the merger not taking place. The incentives for a firm to exaggerate the extent of its weakness are recognised, and accordingly, in order to consider this 'failing firm' defence, very strict criteria must be clearly demonstrated:*
>
> *(a) The alleged failing firm must be unable to meet its financial obligations in the near future;*
>
> *(b) No possibility exists that the firm will be successfully reorganised under the process of Examinership;*
>
> *(c) The firm has made good-faith and verifiable efforts to elicit reasonable alternative offers of acquisition that would keep its assets, both tangible and intangible, in the relevant market and be less of a threat to competition than the proposed merger. It must be shown that such efforts have resulted in the firms being unable to sell for a price in excess of the liquidation value of its assets; and*
>
> *(d) Without the merger taking place, the assets of the failing firm would definitely exit the relevant market.*

Such conditions may rarely be met in practice" (¶5.17).

The references to firms having an incentive to exaggerate the extent of their weakness and to the necessary conditions being likely to be rarely satisfied suggest a cautious approach by the CA to any failing firm arguments.[269]

The failing firm defence was raised only once in the first 400 mergers notified to the CA (OECD, 2009b). Nevertheless, in a consultation paper issued in November 2010, the CA suggested that its *Merger Guidelines* could be amended to:

i. Clearly indicate what constitutes a "failing firm" for merger analysis purposes;
ii. Identify any issues specific to failing firms that the CA would likely address; and,
iii. Clarify that it is not always necessary to assess whether criteria relevant to failing firms are met because a merger involving a failing firm might not result in an SLC (CA, 2010, December 3, ¶2.14).

Whereas CAMG 2002 devoted only a single paragraph to the failing firm issue, CCPCMG2014 contain a new §9 headed *"Failing Firms and Exiting Assets"*. After briefly outlining the economic rationale for approving mergers involving failing firms, it set out four conditions for satisfying the failing firm test:

i. The firm must be unable to meet its financial obligations in the near future.
ii. There must be no viable prospect of reorganising the business through the process of receivership, examinership or otherwise.
iii. The assets of the failing firm would exit the relevant market in the absence of a merger transaction.
iv. There is no credible less anti-competitive alternative outcome than the merger in question.

The first two conditions are more or less the same as the corresponding conditions in CAMG 2002, while condition (iii) in CCPCMG 2014 is largely the same as condition (iv) in the earlier *Guidelines*. In contrast, condition (iv) in CCPCMG 2014 differs markedly from condition (iii) in the earlier version. There is no requirement in CCPCMG 2014 for the failing firm to

269 Weir (1993) notes that the UKMMC indicated that failing firm arguments would have to be supported by convincing evidence.

have *"made good-faith and verifiable efforts to elicit reasonable alternative offers of acquisition that would keep its assets, ..., in the relevant market and be less of a threat to competition than the proposed merger"*.[270]

The other significant difference compared to CAMG2002 is that CCPCMG2014 do not require the parties to show that a failing firm could not be sold *"for a price in excess of the liquidation value of its assets"*. CCPCMG 2014 says:

> *"Evidence that there is no credible less anti-competitive alternative outcome than the merger in question must show that either (i) the proposed transaction is less anti- competitive compared to other viable transactions with other buyers, or (ii) there are no other viable buyers" (¶9.9).*

This begs the question as to how *"other viable"* transactions and buyers should be defined.

CCPCMG2014 also refer to a *"failing division"* which was not mentioned in CAMG 2002.

> *"The failing division argument (i.e., where the productive assets of part of a firm would exit the market but for a merger) is essentially analogous to the failing firm argument. However, a high level of scrutiny can be anticipated in testing a failing division argument given the potential unavailability [and] ambiguity in division-specific information" (¶9.11).*

Unlike the 2002 version, CCPCMG 2014 contain no reference to a firm having incentives to exaggerate the extent of its weakness. Equally, in contrast to the earlier version, there is no suggestion in CCPCMG2014 that the required conditions for the failing firm defence *"may rarely be met in practice"*.

CA/CCPC Failing Firm Cases

In *Smart Telecom/E-NVI*,[271] the CA did not consider the failing firm issue, although the target undertaking had gone into liquidation prior to the Determination in the case. The CA again did not apply the failing firm

---

[270] OECD (2009b) states that, at that time, Ireland and the US were the only member countries that required evidence that the failing firm had made good faith efforts to elicit alternative, less anti-competitive acquisition offers, while other jurisdictions simply investigated the existence of such alternative transactions. It pointed out that, in practice, evidentiary requirements were likely to be quite similar in various jurisdictions as parties face a very high burden of proof in failing firm cases.

[271] CA M/07/046 – *Smart Telecom/E-NVI*, 17.9.2007.

defence in several mergers notified in 2009 and 2010 following the financial crash, despite evidence that one or more of the parties were in financial difficulty.

HMV Ireland/Zavvi involved the acquisition by HMV Ireland of five of the 11 Zavvi stores operating in the State. Zavvi was an indirect wholly-owned subsidiary of Zavvi Group, a UK-based company, which had been placed into administration on 24 December 2008. As a result, Zavvi Ireland also went into liquidation. On 14 January 2009, HMV Ireland agreed to purchase five of Zavvi's 11 Irish stores, subject to court approval, which was granted on 20 January 2009. The transaction was notified to the CA on 15 January 2009. The CA reduced the time allowed for third party submission from the normal 10 days to five, given the circumstances of the case. The CA concluded that the transaction would not result in an SLC without any consideration of the failing firm issue.

In contrast to the CA's approach, the UKOFT concluded that HMV's acquisition of 15 of Zavvi's former UK stores would not give rise to an SLC on the grounds that Zavvi constituted a failing firm.[272]

> *"As such, the counterfactual against which the merger must be judged in this case is a scenario in which the competitive threat from Zavvi will be lost in any event. Accordingly, the merger itself cannot be regarded as the cause of any lessening of competition" (UKOFT* HMV Ireland/Zavvi, *¶159).*

The CA approach was to first establish whether the proposed merger would result in an SLC and not consider the failing firm issue unless that were found to be the case. The CA concluded that the transaction would not result in an SLC because, there was little if any competitive overlap between the parties, and, in areas where there was a possible overlap, the merged entity would continue to face competition from a large number of competing retailers. The UKOFT decision acknowledges that, in general, the best approach is to first consider whether the proposed transaction would result in a SLC and that an alternative counterfactual to a continuation of the pre-merger *status quo* should be considered *"only where the OFT believes that the merger would in fact otherwise create competition issues"* (¶27). Nevertheless, in *HMV/Zavvi*, the OFT took the view that, because it had sufficient evidence that Zavvi was a failing firm, there was no need to address the possible impact of the transaction on competition, while noting that this was unlikely to apply in all failing firm cases.

---

272 UKOFT ME/4036/09 – *HMV/Zavvi*. 28.4.2009.

> *"In the particular circumstances of this case, the OFT considered that it would be disproportionate to require the parties to carry out an in depth analysis in relation to each of the Overlap Stores given the clarity of evidence indicating the application of the failing firm defence that the OFT was able to attain at an early stage of the investigation. This will clearly not be the case in all failing firm type situations" (¶28).*

A further difference in approach is that the then UK *Merger Guidelines* stated that, in the case of a failing firm, *"it may also be better for competition that the firm fails and the remaining players compete for its share and assets than that the failing firm's share and assets are transferred wholesale to a single purchaser"* (UKMG, 2003, ¶4.37). The CA/CCPC does not apply such a test. The UKOFT concluded that allowing the Zavvi stores involved in the transaction to fail would not have produced a better competition outcome.

The CA made no reference to the failing firm issue in *Tedcastles/Fate Park*,[273] although the Determination noted that the Target business was in examinership and stated that the parties had informed it that the Examiner had concluded that the proposed acquisition *"was the most appropriate proposal to put before the Fate Park creditors and shareholders"* (¶7). The CA cleared the transaction on the grounds that there was minimal horizontal overlap between the parties and a sufficient number of competitors to prevent any possibility of an SLC.

The CA described three mergers notified during 2010 as examples of *"rescue mergers"* but stated that it had not been necessary for it to come to any conclusion in relation to the failing firm argument in those cases.

> *"In these cases, we did not consider it necessary to specifically assess whether there was a failing firm, that is, a firm whose assets would exit the market in the absence of the proposed transaction. Rather, in all three cases, our competition analysis indicated that there were enough grounds to clear the merger irrespective of whether the target undertaking would exit the market" (CA, Annual Report 2010, p.35).*

The target in *Club Travel/Budget Travel*[274] was in liquidation. The parties argued that it constituted a failing firm as it was:

i. Unable to meet its financial obligations in the near future.

---

273 CA M/09/016 – *Tedcastles/Fate Park*, 6.8.2009.

274 CA M/10/003 – *Club Travel/Budget Travel*, 15.2.2010; *An Post/PostPoint*, and *Pilgrim (Oaktree Group)/MHL & MCL*.

ii. No possibility existed of a successful reorganisation *via* an examinership process.

iii. The Liquidator had been unable to sell Budget Travel as a going concern for a price in excess of the liquidation value of its assets.

iv. Absent the proposed transaction, the firm's assets would definitely exit the relevant market (¶s11-13).

The CA concluded that the proposed acquisition would not result in an SLC as post-acquisition the parties would have a combined market share of less than 15% in any potential relevant market and would face competition from a number of other suppliers. It was, therefore, unnecessary, in the CA's opinion, to consider whether Budget Travel constituted a failing firm.

Although the CA's 2010 *Annual Report* states that a failing firm argument was advanced in *An Post/PostPoint*, there is no reference to this in the Determination which stated that the transaction was unlikely to raise competition concerns as An Post already exercised joint control over PostPoint and the transaction would not affect the competitive structure of any of the markets in which the parties were involved.[275] Again, in *Kepak/McCarren*,[276] the CA did not consider a failing firm argument, although the parties had submitted that McCarren was insolvent and reliant on temporary financing from its bank.

All of the cases described above involved a possible failing firm. It is clear from the CA decisions in all these cases that a relatively brief analysis was sufficient to confirm that there was little prospect that the transactions would pose any competition concerns. Consequently, there was no need to specifically address the failing firm issue and the decision not to do so in these cases ought not be interpreted as indicating a reluctance by the CA to accept a failing firm defence, despite the scepticism displayed in CAMG 2002.

The first case in which a failing firm defence was accepted was *AIB/EBS*,[277] a case which was decided by the Minister for Finance, under the CIFSA (2008), rather than by the CA. CIFSA (2008), which was introduced in the wake of the financial crash, *inter alia* temporarily transferred responsibility for deciding on mergers of financial institutions from the CA

---

275 The CA's *Annual Report 2010* also stated that a failing firm argument had been advanced in *Pilgrim (Oaktree Group)/MHL & MCL*. In that case the targets, were in examinership. Again, there is no reference to a failing firm argument in the CA's Determination which noted that there was no horizontal or vertical overlap between the merging parties.

276 CA M/13/026 – *Kepak/McCarren*, 26.10.2013.

277 CIFS Act 11/001 – *AIB/EBS*, 27.6.2011.

to the Minister for Finance. On 9 June 2011, the Minister for Finance requested the views of the CA under §7(7) of the CIFSA on the proposed transaction whereby Allied Irish Banks plc would acquire sole control of EBS Building Society. The proposal was part of a government plan to restructure the Irish banking system through the creation of two pillar banks alongside a smaller third bank (Noonan, 2011, March 31). The Minister requested the CA to submit its views by 15 June, but this deadline was subsequently extended by two days until 17 June 2011.

The CA stated that its views were based primarily on the information provided by the merging parties in their joint notification to the Minister of 8 June 2011, along with information provided to it by the Department of Finance on 23 May 2011, particularly in relation to the relevant counterfactual *i.e.*, what would have happened in the absence of the merger. It pointed out:

> *"Due to the urgency attached to the provision of these views, we were not in a position to conduct our own market enquiries into the proposed transaction" (CA, Annual Report 2011, p.36).*

The CA went on to say that, based on the information provided by the Department of Finance, and, in the absence of information to the contrary

> *"The Authority is not in a position to conclude whether there would be, or would not be, competition concerns as a result of the proposed transaction in relation to the residential mortgages market segment.*
>
> *The Authority considered whether the failing firm argument is applicable to EBS for the purposes of reviewing proposed acquisition of EBS Building Society by Allied Irish Banks plc and concluded that there is strong evidence in support of EBS being a failing firm" (*ibid.*).*

The Minister for Finance approved the transaction on 27 June 2011 on the basis that the acquisition would not substantially lessen competition in the Irish banking market because *"there is no realistic alternative which would ensure that competition from EBS would be preserved"* (*ibid.*).

Based on the limited information available, it is difficult to conclude whether EBS satisfied the failing firm defence as set out in CAMG 2002. Gorecki (2012) observes that the two-page published assessment in the case *"raised more questions than it answered"* while any analysis of the decision is hampered by the fact that significant information was redacted on the grounds of commercial confidentiality.

Massey & McDowell (2021) suggest that policy measures implemented by the authorities in the wake of the financial crash acquiesced in the potential for reduced competition between financial intermediaries to help finance recapitalization costs. The EU Commission, in approving state aid for the merged *AIB/EBS*, explicitly acknowledged that its restoration to profitability was contingent on charging higher mortgage interest rates to new and existing customers.

> *"With regard to the return to profitability, the plan sets out an appropriate mix of planned actions. New lending will be granted at higher interest rates. In addition, the pricing of (back-book) loans and deposits will be improved where possible. These measures, together with the discontinuation of the ELG scheme guarantee fees, will enable the Bank to progressively drive the recovery of its NIM" (EU Commission, 2014, May 7).*

Nevin (2018) reports that Irish banks' profitability recovered sharply after the crisis and that they recorded a more rapid return to a higher rate of return on assets (and profits) than comparator euro zone banks (see also Reynolds *et al.*, 2011).

The EU Commission decision in *AIB/EBS* was by no means unique. Lyons & Zhu (2009) cite the Commission state aid decision in *Fortis Bank*[278] as imposing conditions that restricted competition while they argue that the Commission failed to address anti-competitive aspects in the UK *Lloyds/HBOS*[279] merger when approving state aid for the merged entity after HBOS' assets proved to be more toxic than previously realised.[280]

> *"... it may not be too strong to say that the Commission colluded with the UK government to facilitate an anti-competitive merger with an incomplete remedy. At the very least, it should have required a competitively effective divestiture" (Lyons & Zhu, 2013, p.63).*

The UKOFT, in recommending a Phase 2 investigation in *Lloyds/HBOS*, rejected failing firm arguments advanced by the parties on the grounds that, absent the merger, the UK Government would not have allowed HBOS to fail:

---

278 EU Commission, SA NN 42/2008; NN 46/2008 and NN 53/A/2008 – *Fortis Bank*, 3.12.2008.

279 The transaction was also notified to the CA which cleared it on the grounds that there was only a limited overlap between the parties in the supply of invoice discounting services within the State (CA M/08/036 – *Lloyds TSB/HBOS*, 17.12.2008).

280 EU Commission Case No. SA N 428/2009 – *Restructuring of Lloyds Banking Group*, C (2009) 9087 final, 18.11.2009.

> *"...the OFT considers that the application of the failing firm defence in this case is not appropriate given that it is not realistic to consider that HBOS would have been allowed to fail or that its assets would have been allowed to exit the market" (UKOFT, Lloyds/HBOS, ¶159).*

The UK government amended competition legislation to prevent the recommended Phase 2 investigation.

Lyons & Zhu (2013) observe that the *Lloyds/HBOS* merger would almost certainly not have been allowed at any other time. Vickers (2008, December 15) argued that the Government's decision to permit the merger was unnecessary and an economic mistake, risking an irreversible loss of competition in banking services because Government provision of systemic support for the UK banking system had removed the risk that HBOS would collapse. Reynolds *et al.* (2011) express a similar view, noting that the decision to allow the merger to proceed was widely criticised.

The first case in which the CA considered a failing firm defence was *Musgrave/Superquinn.* At the time, *Musgrave,* a grocery wholesaler/franchisor had franchise agreements with approximately 870 independently-owned retail grocery outlets which operated under the Musgrave-owned *Supervalu, Centra, Day Today* and *Daybreak* fascias (brands). Musgrave also supplied grocery goods to other independent retail stores. Superquinn was a vertically-integrated grocery retailer with 18 supermarkets and six convenience stores, along with a distribution depot which supplied only Superquinn outlets. Prior to the notification of the transaction, joint receivers had been appointed to Superquinn and its parent company. The CA Determination acknowledged that an important issue in the case was *"whether or not Superquinn constitutes a failing firm"* (¶48) as the parties claimed.

The CA Determination re-iterated that all four criteria for a failing firm set out in CAMG2002 had to be satisfied in order for an undertaking to be considered to constitute a failing firm. The CA accepted that Superquinn satisfied the first two criteria, *i.e.*:

i. it would be unable to meet its financial obligations in the near future; and
ii. there was no possibility of it being successfully reorganised via an Examinership process.

The CA acknowledged that a process had been entered into to identify potential purchasers other than Musgrave but noted that there was a strategy to sell Superquinn on an *"all or nothing"* basis, rather than to sell assets separately. There was, according to the CA, evidence that alternative purchasers would have been interested in buying some, but not necessarily all of Superquinn's assets. The CA concluded:

> *"This does not suggest that the third criterion has necessarily been met" (¶58).*

The parties stated that there was no buyer willing to pay a higher price for the Superquinn assets than that offered by Musgrave but acknowledged that another serious bidder had submitted what the parties described as an inferior offer. The CA pointed out, however, that:

> *"The parties did not show that Superquinn could not be sold for a price in excess of the liquidation value of the business and assets to be acquired" (¶53).*

The parties acknowledged that it was not possible *"to say with certainty that all Superquinn assets would exit the market in the absence of the proposed transaction"* (¶54). The CA concluded:

> *"It is clear that the final criterion is not met in this instance. That is, it is not necessarily the case that output attributable to Superquinn and/or Superquinn assets prior to the proposed transaction would no longer be available in the absence of the merger. Rather, notwithstanding the preference of the creditor banks and the Joint Receivers, a viable alternative counterfactual would involve the sale of at least some assets to competitors and/or new entrants" (¶59).*

The CA went on to state that the fact that Superquinn was in receivership did not of itself mean that it was a failing firm because receivership did not imply that Superquinn assets would necessarily no longer be productive in the retail grocery market.

> *"Furthermore...it is clear that the assets would not have left the market, as this would not have been in the interests of the creditor banks that had appointed the Joint Receivers" (¶61).*

Several other CA/CCPC Determinations where the Target undertakings were in receivership made no reference to the failing firm defence.[281] The

---

[281] See, for example, CCPC M/14/035 – *Dalata/White's Hotel*, 9.1.2015; CCPC M/14/036 – *Dalata/Clayton Hotel (Galway)*, 12.1.2015; CCPC M/14/037 – *Dalata/Pillo Hotel (Galway)* 13.1.2015; CCPC M/15/002 – *Atlantic Troy/Charleville Park Hotel*, 20.2.2015; CCPC M/15/028 – *Atlantic Troy/Killeshin Hotel*, 3.7.2015; CCPC M/15/035 – *Tetrarch/Dawson Hotel*, 21.8.2015;

parties in *House of Fraser (Dundrum)/Sports Direct*[282] had argued that *"there was a very real prospect that the survival of House of Fraser would not have been secured"* in the absence of the proposed transaction (¶14) but the CCPC did not consider a failing firm argument.

The only case to date in which the CA/CCPC accepted a failing firm defence was *Baxter Healthcare/Fannin Compounding*. The CCPC concluded, following a full Phase 2 investigation, that the proposed transaction would result in an SLC but stated:

> *"In this instance, a question arises as to whether, as argued by the parties, Fannin Compounding is a failing division within Fannin and whether the assets of Fannin Compounding will exit the relevant market in the near future" (¶150).*

Fannin was a wholly-owned subsidiary of DCC. In considering whether Fannin would be unable to meet its financial obligations in the near future, the CCPC stated:

> *"A strict interpretation of this element of the failing division test would focus solely on whether DCC has the ability to continue supporting Fannin Compounding without jeopardising its financial survival. The Commission considers, however, that a more sensible approach, in the context of the relevant counterfactual, is to assess whether DCC has both the ability and incentive to meet Fannin Compounding's financial obligations in the near future" (¶152).*[283]

The CCPC concluded that DCC had the ability to continue supporting Fannin but lacked any incentive to do so because Fannin had been loss-making since 2013 and the CCPC accepted that there was no possibility of it returning to profitability in the near future. The CCPC concluded, based on a report by accountants retained by it, that there was no prospect of a successful restructuring of Fannin. It also found that the assets of Fannin would exit the market, absent the transaction, based on internal DCC documents which showed that it had been considering exiting the relevant market since August 2014. Finally, the CCPC also concluded that there was no alternative less anti-competitive purchaser of Fannin.

CCPC M/15/045 – *Pat the Baker/Irish Pride*, 18.11.2015; and CCPC M/16/005 – *Dalata/Clarion Sligo*, 19.2.2016.

282 CCPC M/18/071 – *House of Fraser (Dundrum)/Sports Direct*, 2.10.2018.

283 The CCPC stated that this was consistent with the EU Commission approach in Case No. COMP/M.6360 – *Nynas/Shell/Harburg Refinery*, 2.9.2013.

In *Irish Post/Irish TV*,[284] the High Court had ordered that the vendor be wound up prior to the notification of the transaction. The vendor had no business apart from the target. However, the Determination contains no reference to the possibility that the target might have been a failing firm. Similarly, there was no reference to the Target possibly being a failing firm in *Formpress/River Media*.[285] The parties had submitted that the Target business had been loss-making for several years and could no longer be sustained by its existing owners who were looking to dispose of the business, which would be closed immediately if no buyer was found.

The UKCMA indicated in *Lakeland/LacPatrick*[286] that the merging parties had advanced an alternative counterfactual, although the specific details were redacted. The decision states that there was no need to consider the alternative counterfactual because the transaction did not raise any competition issues.[287]

The CA/CCPC has accepted a failing firm defence in only one case since 2002. In fairness it should be acknowledged that the EU Commission only accepted a failing firm argument in four merger cases over the 1990-2010 period, while the UKOFT accepted failing firm arguments in only five merger cases between 2002 and 2010 (Reynolds *et al.*, 2011). Motta (2004) states that the failing firm defence has been rarely used in either the US or the EU.

Alternative Mergers

The CA argued in *Heineken/Beamish & Crawford* that, in reviewing a proposed merger, it could not consider alternative, potentially less anti-competitive, transactions.

> *"The Authority has to examine the merger as notified. Frequently in mergers the Authority is aware that there are credible but unsuccessful firms that also bid for the target. However, it is not the remit of the Authority to consider these alternative merger possibilities, even if they were less restrictive of competition" (FN50).*

Contrary to the view expressed by the CA, a competition agency is not precluded from considering alternative less anti-competitive mergers. In certain circumstances an alternative merger may be regarded as the

---

284 CCPC M/17/009 – *Irish Post/Irish TV*, 8.3.2017.

285 CCPC M/18/092 – *Formpress/River Media*, 28.12.2018.

286 UKCMA, Case No. ME/6779/18 – *Lakeland/LacPatrick*, 5.3.2019.

287 The CCPC Determination in this case makes no mention of an alternative counterfactual.

appropriate counterfactual against which a proposed merger should be analysed. Amelio *et al.* (2018) state that a competition agency cannot assess a proposed merger against arbitrary alternative combinations involving one of the parties which leads to a potentially more competitive outcome. In circumstances where there is reliable evidence that a specific alternative transaction is the most plausible alternative to a proposed merger, however, *"it would make little sense to evaluate the proposed merger against a* status quo ante *that may no longer be relevant for the future or against other counterfactuals that ignore the existence of the alternative transaction"* (p.675). In other words, a competition agency cannot simply argue that some unspecified alternative purchaser would emerge or choose a scenario involving an alternative purchaser that would have a less adverse effect on competition as the appropriate counterfactual in the absence of any evidence that such a transaction would likely occur absent the merger. It may, however, consider a counterfactual involving an alternative purchaser where there is reliable evidence that such a transaction is the most likely alternative to the proposed merger.

As noted previously, the EU Commission rejected a failing firm argument in *Aerospatiale-Alenia/de Havilland inter alia* on the basis that there could be an alternative purchaser for the Target. In *Lufthansa/Austrian Airlines*, the EU Commission found that, in the absence of the proposed transaction, Austrian was likely to have been acquired by Air France-KLM and that this constituted the appropriate counterfactual. In *Lufthansa/Certain Air Berlin Assets*[288] there was a horizontal overlap between the merging parties on 130 routes, of which around 70 would become monopoly or near-monopoly routes if the transaction went ahead. In addition, it would have led to increased airport dominance at Düsseldorf airport. Lufthansa argued that the proposed acquisition would not reduce competition because there were no viable alternative bidders for Air Berlin's assets. The EU Commission rejected the claim that the assets would not have been commercially viable absent a sale to Lufthansa. Several other carriers had made offers for the target's Austrian subsidiary, NIKI, but those bids had been discarded by the insolvency administrator in favour of initiating exclusive negotiations with Lufthansa.[289] The question then becomes whether an alternative takeover of the target company was a more

---

[288] Case No. M.8633 – *Lufthansa/Certain Air Berlin Assets*, 21.12.2017.

[289] Commission press release of 17.12.2017. Available at: http://europa.eu/rapid/press-release_IP-17-5402_en.htm.

appropriate counterfactual against which the proposed transaction should be assessed. As Amelio *et al.* (2018, p.674) observe *"it would* prima facie *not appear implausible that a strong incumbent airline might have an incentive to block entry of a competitor by acquiring a struggling rival instead of allowing that competitor to acquire the struggling firm".*

In *ArcelorMittal/Ilva*[290] the EU Commission had to assess whether there would have been a viable alternative purchaser for the target, Ilva, in the absence of the proposed acquisition by ArcelorMittal. A parallel state aid investigation had identified viable alternatives.[291] Amelio *et al.* (2018) point out that the case involved thorny questions on the degree to which these alternatives would have materialized and would have been comparable, since they involved different business models and planned approaches toward a necessary restructuring.

In contrast to the approach taken by the CA in *Heineken/Beamish & Crawford,* the CCPC considered less anti-competitive alternatives in the various bank mergers cited earlier.

> *"In general terms, when considering if there were alternative less anti-competitive purchasers, the Commission seeks to identify who the alternative purchaser(s) might have been and takes this into account when determining the counterfactual. The Commission does not restrict its analysis to alternative purchasers who were willing to pay the same or similar price that was agreed in the merger, but rather if there was an alternative purchaser willing to acquire the firm at any price above liquidation value" (AIB/Ulster Bank, ¶4.56).*[292]

The CCPC statement that its consideration of alternative less anti-competitive purchasers includes any alternative purchaser willing to pay a price above liquidation value is problematic. In the case of a failing firm any price above the liquidation value may be regarded as a reasonable return, compared with the next best option, for the owners. *AIB/Ulster Bank* did not involve a failing firm. It is not obvious that *"any price above liquidation value"* is appropriate in a non-failing firm case. The CCPC failed to advance any rationale for such a requirement. The CCPC could argue that an excessively high purchase price was an indication that an acquisition was anti-

290 Case no. M.8444 – *ArcelorMittal/Ilva,* 7.5.2018.

291 EU Commission press release of 21.12.2017. Available at: http://europa.eu/rapid/press-release_IP-17-5401_en.htm.

292 This argument was repeated in *Bank of Ireland/KBC* (¶5.62).

competitive but there would appear to be no sound economic rationale for the argument that an alternative purchaser willing to pay *"any price above liquidation value"* should be regarded as a credible alternative purchaser. Arguably such a requirement would constitute a barrier to exit.

The CCPC concluded that the appropriate counterfactual was one in which there was likely to be an alternative less anti-competitive purchaser for at least some of the Target's assets on the basis that, in the absence of the proposed transaction, NatWest/Ulster Bank would have had an incentive to sell the assets to another party.

> *"The Commission considers that, in the absence of the Proposed Transaction, there are credible potential purchasers of Ulster Bank's GPLs for CRE, and that NatWest and Ulster Bank would have had an incentive to sell these loans to an alternative purchaser. The Commission is, therefore, of the view that the counterfactual for GPLs for CRE is the sale to an alternative less anti-competitive purchaser, for example, [...]" (¶4.73).*

In *Bank of Ireland/KBC*, the CCPC noted that, given its conclusion that the appropriate counterfactual was that KBC would have remained active in the mortgage market in the State, it was not necessary for it to consider whether KBC's assets in the State could have been sold to a potentially less anti-competitive alternative purchaser. It nevertheless decided to consider such an alternative.

The CCPC concluded in PTSB/Ulster Bank that there were *"alternative (and potentially less anti-competitive) purchasers in respect of Ulster Bank's performing mortgage book and book of lending to microenterprises"* (¶4.72). The Determination states that a party had *"informed the Commission that it would be interested in acquiring some or all of Ulster Bank's microenterprise lending assets"* (¶4.63). The decision also stated that one or more parties had expressed an interest in acquiring part of the Ulster Bank mortgage book, but no party had expressed an interest in acquiring the entire mortgage book (¶4.68). The CCPC concluded:

> *"Therefore, the Commission has reached the view that the appropriate counterfactual is that, absent the Proposed Transaction, Ulster Bank would have exited the State and that it would have proceeded with: (i) a sale to a potentially less anti-competitive alternative purchaser of its whole book of lending to microenterprises; and (ii) a sale to a potentially less anti-competitive alternative purchaser of a proportion of the Mortgage Book" (¶s4.72 & 4.73).*

As previously stated, a competition agency cannot assume that some unspecified alternative purchaser would emerge or choose a scenario involving an alternative purchaser that would have a less adverse effect on competition as the appropriate counterfactual, in the absence of evidence that such a transaction would likely occur absent the merger. It should only consider a counterfactual involving an alternative purchaser where there is reliable evidence that such a transaction is the most likely alternative to the proposed merger. As in *AIB/Ulster Bank* and *Bank of Ireland/KBC* any analysis of the CCPC Determination in this case is subject to the *caveat* that much of the reasoning for the CCPC's conclusions is redacted.

There was evidence in *PTSB/Ulster Bank* of other parties expressing an interest in acquiring some of the target assets. The CCPC stated *"that potential alternative purchasers of some of the Target [mortgage] Assets could be identified"* (¶4.67). The Determination suggests that there was more than one party interested in acquiring part of the Ulster Bank mortgage book. There is no explanation for the CCPC choosing as the counterfactual a scenario in which only one purchaser acquired part of the mortgage book, as opposed to one in which several parties each acquired parts of it. The question is whether the latter outcome would have been less likely to occur than the counterfactual adopted by the CCPC. If one accepts that Ulster Bank would have exited the market absent the merger then this would necessarily entail it disposing of its entire mortgage book. §5 of the Determination, which considers potential unilateral effects theories of harm, provides further detail in relation to the chosen counterfactual.

> *"The Commission has considered the impact of the Proposed Transaction compared to a counterfactual of the acquisition of a portfolio of €1 billion of mortgages, a proportion of the Mortgage Book, by a new entrant" (¶5.22).*

No explanation is offered as to how the figure of €1 billion was arrived at. Similarly, no explanation is offered for why the portfolio of mortgages is assumed to be acquired by a new entrant as opposed to one of the smaller existing players in the market.

The Determination then states there was little difference between the proposed merger and the chosen counterfactual in terms of impact on market concentration in relation to either the flow or stock of mortgages, finding in both cases that the HHI would increase by less than 150 points. It appears somewhat contradictory for the CA to suggest that the chosen counterfactual was considered less anti-competitive than the proposed transaction and its conclusion that there was only a minimal difference between the effects of both transactions on market concentration.

The approach to the counterfactual in *PTSB/Ulster Bank* appears particularly unsatisfactory. No explanation is offered:

i. For adopting a counterfactual involving one rather than multiple purchasers of a portion of the *Ulster Bank* mortgage book;

ii. For the size of the portfolio that would be acquired; and

iii. For assuming this portfolio would be acquired by a new entrant rather than one of the smaller incumbents.

This is compounded by the fact that the counterfactual chosen was subsequently found to be virtually no less anti-competitive than the notified merger.

The CCPC in *ESB/Coillte (JV)* considered whether, in the absence of the proposed transaction, Coillte might have entered into an alternative joint venture arrangement with one or more other parties but stated that it had not been provided with evidence that Coillte had given detailed consideration to such an alternative. It thus concluded that the appropriate counterfactual was the continuation of the pre-merger *status quo,* i.e. absent the proposed joint venture, Coillte would have continued to engage in the development and construction of on-shore wind farms itself. It would not appear from the Determination that an alternative joint venture was the most likely alternative scenario to the proposed transaction.

A non-standard counterfactual may be justified where there are parallel mergers in the same market because the competition agency, in considering each of the individual mergers, has to predict how the market would evolve in the absence of that merger, i.e. it must take account of the impact on the market of the second merger (Bavasso & Lindsay, 2007). In *Sanitec/Sphinx,*[293] for example, the EU Commission noted that, if another announced merger proceeded, the merging parties involved would have a substantial market share. In *Verizon/MCI*[294] the EU Commission assumed that a second announced merger would proceed but found that no competition concerns would arise even if it did.

---

[293] EU Commission Case No. COMP/M.1578 – *Sanitec/Sphinx*, 1.12.1999.

[294] EU Commission Case No. COMP/M.3752 – *Verizon/MCI*, 7.10.2005.

Phase 1 & Phase 2 Counterfactuals

As noted in **Chapter 3**, the UKCMA is required to establish that there is a realistic prospect of an SLC in order to conduct a Phase 2 investigation. Consequently, at Phase 1 the UKCMA is required to *"assess whether the merger creates the realistic prospect of an SLC"* (UKCMA, 2021, March 18, ¶3.12). This has implications for the appropriate counterfactual.

> *"In Phase 1 investigations, if the CMA must consider multiple potential counterfactual scenarios where each of those scenarios is a realistic prospect, it will choose the one where the merger firms exert the strongest competitive constraint on each other, and where third parties exert the weakest competitive constraints on the merger firms" (¶3.12).*

In other words, at Phase 1 the UKCMA considers the effect of the merger compared with the most competitive counterfactual, provided that there is a realistic prospect of such a counterfactual occurring. A different approach applies at Phase 2 since the UKCMA at that stage has to reach a conclusion as to whether the merger is likely to result in an SLC. At Phase 2 the UKCMA may consider several possible counterfactual scenarios, but *"will select the most likely conditions of competition as its counterfactual against which to assess the merger"* (¶3.13).

The difference in the approach to counterfactuals at Phases 1 and 2 was illustrated in *Linergy/UFBP II*[295] which involved a proposed merger between two Northern Ireland-based animal rendering businesses. The UKOFT had referred a previous merger proposal by the parties to the UKCC for a Phase 2 investigation.[296] UFBP's parent, Glenfarm Holdings Limited, decided not to pursue the transaction because it did not believe that UFBP would be able to stay in business for the time required to conduct a Phase 2 investigation (UKCMA, *Linergy/UFBP II*, Phase 2 ¶3.7). Linergy subsequently signed a memorandum of understanding with SAPI, an Italian undertaking, expressing the parties' intention to merge Linergy and UFBP, in the event that the latter was acquired by SAPI (UKCMA *Linergy/UFBP II*, Phase I, ¶26). In June 2012, SAPI acquired UFBP from Glenfarm. On 8 June 2015, Linergy purchased the whole of the issued share capital of Ulster Farm from SAPI. The UKCMA subsequently launched an investigation into the transaction.

---

295 UKCMA, Case No. ME/6514/15, *Linergy/Ulster Farm By-Products (UFBP) II*, Phase 1, 17.7.2015, Phase 2, 6.1.2016.

296 UKOFT, ME/5294/11, *Linergy/UFBP I*, 15.3.2012.

The UKCMA's Phase I investigation noted that, prior to signing the MOU, both parties operated Category 1 rendering plants. UFBP also operated a Category 3 rendering plant. Linergy did not have a Category 3 plant, but its Board had approved plans to construct one and it had also secured the necessary licensing and planning approvals for its construction. The UKOFT Phase 1 decision, in relation to the previous 2012 proposal, found that *"absent the merger, there was a realistic prospect that Linergy would have built its own Category 3 plant which would have competed with that of Ulster Farm"* (UKOFT, *Linergy/UFBP I*, ¶19).

In October 2012, UFBP closed its Category 1 plant, and, in December 2012, Linergy's Board resolved not to build a Category 3 plant. Thus, the parties submitted that, contrary to the position at the time of the UKOFT's March 2012 decision, they were operating in separate product markets and there was no horizontal overlap between them (*Linergy/UFBP II*, Phase I, ¶30). They argued that Linergy's decision not to construct a Category 3 plant,[297] and UFBP's decision to close its Category 1 plant, were based on commercial considerations and were taken independently of each other and the MOU (¶42). The UKCMA in its Phase 1 decision argued, however, that the parties' actions post-31 May 2012 had been influenced by the MOU and that the appropriate counterfactual was the situation which prevailed immediately before it was signed. It further concluded that, in the absence of the MOU, Linergy would have built a Category 3 plant while UFBP would not have closed its Category 1 plant.

> *"Therefore, for the purposes of its competitive assessment, the CMA has used as its counterfactual the situation in which each of Linergy and UFBP operate both a Category 1 and a Category 3 plant" (ibid., ¶56).*

The Phase 2 decision noted that the UFBP Category 1 plant had been in poor condition and had closed following a fire at the plant in October 2012. The UKCMA accepted SAPI's arguments that there was no commercial case to keep the plant open, even if the October 2012 fire had not occurred. It also accepted that Linergy's decision not to proceed with a Category 3 plant was a result of changed circumstances which meant that the commercial case underlying the Linergy Board's earlier decision to build a Category 3 plant no longer applied. The Phase 2 investigation concluded that:

---

[297] Animal health regulations mean that Category 1 and Category 3 plant outputs are not substitutes and therefore constitute separate markets.

i. SAPI would have acquired UFBP irrespective of the MOU;
ii. SAPI would have closed UFBP's Category 1 plant irrespective of the MOU; and
iii. Linergy would not have built its own Category 3 plant (*Linergy/UFBP II*, Phase II, ¶6.79).

The UKCMA applied a different counterfactual at Phase 2 to that adopted at Phase 1. This difference can be understood, however, when it is recognised that a different standard is applied when choosing a counterfactual at Phase 1 and Phase 2. The Phase 1 standard is whether there is *"a realistic prospect"* that an alternative, more competitive counterfactual could occur. At Phase 2, the appropriate counterfactual is the alternative scenario that is most likely to occur.

The CCPC is under no requirement to establish that there is a realistic prospect of an SLC before launching a Phase 2 investigation but may decide to do so on the grounds that it is unable to conclude that an SLC would not occur (see **Chapter 3**). On that basis, it could be argued that a different standard in relation to the counterfactual could be applied at Phase 1 and Phase 2 and that various alternative counterfactuals should be considered at Phase 1 provided there was a realistic prospect of their occurring. Such an approach may be problematic for several reasons.

Applying the *"realistic possibility"* rather than the *"most likely to occur"* standard when identifying the appropriate counterfactual at Phase 1, raises the possibility of a false positive, i.e., an initial finding that a merger is likely to result in an SLC on the basis of a counterfactual, which a more detailed analysis would show is unlikely to occur. The UKCMA's procedures, which were described in **Chapter 4**, provide the merging parties with significant opportunities to argue against launching a Phase 2 investigation. The CCPC's procedures contain no such provisions (CCPC, 2021). Merging parties may, therefore, be faced with having to choose between offering undertakings or facing a potentially lengthy Phase 2 investigation, at relatively short notice, without any opportunity to put forward a detailed case against the holding of a Phase 2 investigation. Applying remedies to a merger which will not result in an SLC constitutes a Type I error, i.e., a false positive. Such an error imposes costs on the parties and ultimately on consumers as they attach conditions to the merger which are unnecessary because the transaction would not result in any SLC. In the absence of sufficient checks in the CCPC's procedures to prevent false positives at

Phase 1, the same standard should apply for identifying the counterfactual at both Phases 1 and Phase 2, namely, the *"most likely to occur"* standard.

Potential Competitors

A merger between a market incumbent and a potential market entrant could reduce competition in two ways:

i. Competition could be reduced in a market if the potential entrant would have entered the market thereby increasing competition in the absence of the merger.

ii. Competition could also be reduced if the threat of entry by the potential entrant exercised a competitive constraint on market incumbents preventing them from raising prices.

The first of these scenarios is known as the *"actual potential entrant"* theory and the second is referred to as the *"perceived potential entrant"* theory (Brenner, 1999). The two theories have quite different implications for the appropriate counterfactual.

Under the actual potential entrant scenario, the appropriate counterfactual is that, in the absence of a merger, the potential entrant would have entered the market. In order to apply the actual potential entrant scenario, it is necessary to show that the most likely alternative in the absence of the merger is that such entry would have occurred. In contrast, the appropriate counterfactual under the perceived potential entrant theory is the pre-merger *status quo.* In other words, under this scenario, absent the merger, the threat of entry by the potential entrant would have continued to exercise a competitive constraint on the parties.

The issue of potential competition was considered in *Unilever/Lyons Tea.* The CA disagreed as to whether Unilever's *Lipton* tea brand would exercise a competitive constraint as a potential competitor if it exited the market absent the merger. Both the majority and minority applied a perceived potential entrant theory. The majority of the CA concluded that, if the *Lipton* brand were withdrawn and the merger did not proceed, the market incumbents would not be constrained by the threat of possible re-entry of the *Lipton* brand (¶7.2). The minority report expressed a contrary view.

> *"The possibility of future entry by Unilever might be expected to act, to some extent, as a constraint on the ability of incumbent firms to raise prices since they must take account of the possibility of such re-entry...Nevertheless if the merger proceeds Unilever will clearly*

cease to be a potential competitor in the market and any disciplining effect which may have existed by virtue of the possibility that it might re-enter would be eliminated" (p.73).

Conclusion

Merger analysis by definition is forward-looking and involves assessing the impact of a proposed merger on competition relative to an alternative scenario in which the merger had not occurred. Identifying the appropriate alternative scenario, the counterfactual, is thus a key element in the assessment of any merger. In the majority of cases the alternative to the merger involves the continuation of the pre-merger *status quo*, although this will not be true for all mergers.

An *ex ante* rather than an *ex post* approach should be adopted when identifying alternative counterfactuals to the pre-merger *status quo*, i.e. the appropriate counterfactual is the situation that would have prevailed if the proposed merger had never occurred, rather than if it had not been implemented. The appropriate test, in cases involving exit by non-failing firms, is whether the firm would have exited in the absence of the merger as otherwise the possibility would arise for an undertaking to effectively buy off a competitor. The CCPC in *Bank of Ireland/KBC* correctly concluded that the *ex ante* approach should be employed when defining the appropriate counterfactual, although CCPCMG2014 are somewhat confused on this point.

The CA in *Heineken/Beamish & Crawford* claimed, arguably incorrectly, that it was precluded from considering possible alternative mergers of which it was aware, but the CCPC subsequently adopted a different approach in relation to various bank mergers. The appropriate counterfactual in any merger case is the one that is most likely to occur. This is particularly relevant in the case of alternative mergers. A competition agency cannot assume that some unspecified alternative purchaser would emerge or choose a scenario involving an alternative purchaser that would have a less adverse effect on competition as the appropriate counterfactual, unless there is strong evidence that such a transaction would likely occur absent the merger. It should only consider a counterfactual involving an alternative purchaser where there is strong reliable evidence that such a transaction is the most likely alternative to the proposed merger.

6: MARKET DEFINITION

Introduction

Market definition was the traditional starting point in merger analysis (Massey, 2000). Defining the market involves identifying both the range of products – the relevant product market – and the geographic area – the relevant geographic market – within which competition is likely to be affected by a merger.[298] At the outset, it should be acknowledged that market definition is a means to an end rather than an end in itself and it is not always necessary to define the relevant market in merger cases.

Market definition has often proved controversial in merger cases. The more narrowly a market is defined, the more likely firms will be found to have market power. Not surprisingly, merging firms generally tend to advocate broad market definitions (Shapiro, 2024). The merging parties in *FTC v. Coca-Cola*[299] proposed a market definition comprising a wide range of beverages including milk, tea, and beer in what was dubbed the "Lake Erie defence" (Kaserman & Zeisel, 1996).[300] Competition agencies, at times, have been accused of arbitrarily defining markets in order to support claims

298 There may also be a temporal element to market definition. The CCPC acknowledged the existence of temporal markets in *ESB/Coillte (JV)*. The EU Commission identified temporal markets in generation and wholesale supply of electricity in EU Commission Case No. COMP/M.5467 – *RWE/Essent*, 23.6.2009. It identified seasonal markets in air transport in EU Commission Case No. COMP/M.8869 - *Ryanair/Laudamotion*, 12.7.2018. Temporal markets may also exist for hotel rooms and airport car parking.

299 *FTC v. Coca-Cola*, 641 F. Supp. 1128, 1133 (1986). For a more detailed description, see White (1989).

300 Armentano (1986) criticised the USFTC for challenging the merger based on this wide market definition.

of competitive harm (Morris & Mosteller, 1991). Incorrect market definitions may result in both false positives and negatives.

Many of the market definitions applied in 1960s US Supreme Court merger judgements have been widely criticised (Werden, 1981). The Court's failure to clarify the degree of substitutability necessary for products to be in the same market provided enormous leeway for *"rigging"* market definitions with *"the appearance of* ad hoc *gerrymandering to reach a predetermined outcome"* (Simons & Williams, 1993, p.799). Kauper (1996) states that, while the EU Commission has been accused of tailoring market definitions to reach particular outcomes in some dominance cases, this was not true in merger cases. The Commission, however, was criticised for its geographic market definitions in *Volvo/Scania*[301] and *SEB/FSB*[302] (Brandenburger & Janssens, 2001). The CA/CCPC approach to market definition frequently has been unsatisfactory.

The Role of Market Definition in Merger Cases

Market definition plays an important role in merger analysis, in:

i. Providing a logical way to organise information;
ii. Helping to screen out implausible theories;
iii. Focusing the scope of competitive effects analysis;
iv. Imposing analytic discipline on investigators (Glasner & Sullivan, 2020).

The last point bears emphasising.

> *"The discipline of forcing decision-makers to have a reasonable market definition in mind... is likely to be valuable in constraining agencies... from making decisions based on arbitrary criteria" (Turner, 1980, p.1150)*

Market definition identifies the line of business and geographic area in which competition concerns may arise which enables the identification of market participants and measurement of market shares which can be informative of likely competitive effects (Shapiro, 2010). Market concentration can help identify mergers that are unlikely to raise competition concerns but it *"is critically dependent on a correct market*

301 EU Commission Case No. COMP/M.1672 – *Volvo/Scania*, 15.3.2000.

302 EU Commission Case No. COMP/M.2380 – *Skandinaviska Enskilda Banken/ FoeningsSparbanken*, withdrawn 19.9.2001.

definition" (Hovenkamp, 2024, p.74). Glasner & Sullivan (2020), while acknowledging that market definition is not always necessary in every case, state that it is important to understand the correct approach to defining and interpreting markets.

Defining relevant markets provides useful guidance to merging parties and practitioners. The EU Commission stated that one of the reasons for publishing its 1997 *Market Definition Notice* (1997MDN) was to increase transparency in relation to its competition decisions (¶5), a theme repeated in the 2024MDN.

> *"By publishing the methodology that it follows and by indicating the main criteria and evidence on which it relies when defining relevant markets, the Commission aims to increase the transparency of its policy- and decision-making when applying Union competition law. The Commission also aims to reduce the burden on the resources of its own services and those of external stakeholders, making competition assessments more efficient.*
>
> *Increasing the transparency and consequently the predictability of the Commission's assessments under Union competition law will also increase legal certainty for undertakings and their advisers. They will be able to better assess the scope of the relevant markets and the likelihood that the Commission may identify competition concerns in a particular case. They will be able to take these factors into account in their internal decision-making when contemplating, for instance, acquiring other undertakings, creating joint ventures, concluding certain agreements, or engaging in certain behaviour unilaterally. The guidance provided in this Notice will also assist undertakings in anticipating the type of information the Commission considers relevant for the purposes of market definition" (¶s 4&5).*

In contrast, CCPCMG2014 states:

> *"Decisions relating to market definition in previous merger investigations by the Commission may provide only limited guidance" (¶2.6).*

The objective of merger control is to identify and prevent mergers that would increase market power. However, the more widely the market is defined, the less concentrated it will be and the less likely the merging parties will be found to have market power potentially resulting in false negatives.[303] Equally defining markets too narrowly will result in the exclusion of close substitutes capable of exercising an effective competitive constraint on the merging parties leading to potential false positives.

The economics literature emphasises that markets in merger cases should be defined to include those products and geographic areas which are close substitutes for the merging parties. Distant substitutes should be excluded from the market because they will not exercise a sufficient competitive constraint to prevent a post-merger price increase. The existence of some competition or substitutability between products or areas is an insufficient basis for concluding that they are in the same market (Werden, 1992). The question is whether the degree of substitutability between products is sufficient to restrain market power (Neven *et al.*, 1993). The relevant market should include *reasonable* substitutes for the merging firms' products, not all substitutes in order to avoid *"false negatives"* due to markets being incorrectly defined too widely (Shapiro & Shelanski, 2021).

This is recognised in the 2024MDN (EU Commission, 2024):

> *"Only products that exert effective and immediate competitive constraints within the relevant timeframe form part of the same relevant market as those of the undertaking(s) involved, while other less effective, or merely potential, constraints are considered as part of the competitive assessment (¶6).*[304]

The CCPC in *LN-Gaiety/MCD Productions* stated:

> *"Some degree of substitutability or competition is not sufficient in itself to regard the outdoor and indoor venues as forming part of the same relevant market" (¶3.82).*

Several CA/CCPC decisions, nevertheless, have cited weak substitutes as potentially exercising a significant constraint on the merging parties. *MJ Gleeson/UBH* argued that, although non-alcoholic beverage wholesaling and distribution was not a substitute for combined alcoholic and non-alcoholic beverage wholesaling, *"they would be likely to have a discernible level of influence"* on the parties' behaviour post-merger. No evidence was advanced to support

303 This is known as the *"cellophane fallacy"* or *"cellophane trap"* referring to the US Supreme Court judgement which found that, although du Pont produced 85% of all cellophane wrapping, the relevant product market was wider because, in the Court's view, other packaging materials were substitutes for cellophane at prevailing market prices (*United States v. E.I. du Pont de Nemours & Co.*, 353 US 586 (1957)).

304 The 1997MDN stated that the rationale for defining markets in merger cases was to identify the competitive constraints facing the merging parties (¶2).

this claim. It is difficult to see how non-alcoholic wholesalers and distributors would constrain the merging parties from raising the wholesale price of alcoholic beverages post-merger unless they constitute supply-side substitutes (see below). *CapVest/Origin Foods/Maiden*[305] observed that consumers might *"consider buying readymade cakes or breads as an alternative to baking with readymade baking mixes"* (¶30). It is unclear what significance, if any, the CA attached to this statement. While there may be some substitutability between baking mixes and readymade cakes, they are unlikely to be sufficiently close substitutes to exercise an effective competitive constraint on each other because quite a large increase in the price of readymade baking mixes would likely be required before consumers would switch to buying readymade cakes and bread. Similarly, in several hotel mergers the CA/CCPC argued that B&Bs, hostels, other non-hotel accommodation providers and Airbnb could exercise some competitive constraint on three/four-star hotels, without offering any supporting evidence for such a claim.[306] In the absence of strong supporting evidence, claims that such alternatives would exercise a significant competitive constraint on three/four-star hotels seem questionable to say the least.[307]

The Economic Approach to Market Definition

Until the 1980s economists paid scant attention to market definition in merger cases (Horowitz, 1981). Stigler (1982, p.9) described market definition as *"an undeveloped area of economic research at either the theoretical or empirical level"*. Neo-classical economists such as Cournot (1838) and Marshall (1890) defined markets as comprising the range of products and geographic areas for which arbitrage kept price linked. Such a definition does not establish whether a firm or firms have market power, i.e., the ability to increase prices (Werden, 1981).

Areeda & Turner (1978, p.347) proposed the following market definition for competition analysis:

---

305 CA M/10/031 – *CapVest/Origin Foods/Maiden*, 18.11.2010.

306 *Dalata/White's Hotel; Dalata/Clayton Hotel (Galway); Dalata/Pillo Hotel (Galway); Dalata/Moran's Hotel/Bewley's*; CCPC M/16/047 – *Dalata/DoubleTree Hilton*, 2.11.2016.

307 Empirical studies indicate that the impact of Airbnb on hotels has been limited and is largely confined to those at the lower end of the market (*Yang et al.* 2022) or to times of peak demand when hotels are capacity constrained (Farronato & Fradkin, 2022).

"In economic terms a 'market' embraces one firm or any group of firms which, if unified by agreement or merger, would have market power in dealing with any group of buyers."

Werden (1981, p.721) offers a similar definition:

"A market for ***anti-trust purposes*** *is any product or group of products and any geographic area in which collective action by all firms (as through collusion or merger) would result in a profit maximizing price that significantly exceeded the competitive price" (emphasis in original).*

Economists traditionally defined markets based on the cross-price elasticity of demand which measures the responsiveness of the change in demand for a product, to changes in the price of another product.[308] Cross-price elasticities are inadequate for market definition purposes because:

i. It is unclear how high the cross-price elasticities need to be for goods to be considered to be in the same market;
ii. A small increase in the price of product A may cause sufficient consumers to switch to product, B, to render a unilateral price increase for A unprofitable but the reverse need not be true. Both sets of cross-elasticities must be high to support a conclusion that products are in the same market (Werden, 1998);
iii. Cross-price elasticities only measure whether one product is a substitute for another rather than the collective competitive significance of all substitutes. Werden (1998), citing the case of breakfast cereals, points out that, if there are many brands in a market, the cross elasticities between any two brands may be quite small. A small increase in the price of an individual brand may induce substitution to several other brands, with each gaining only a small fraction of switching customers.

Shrieves (1978) and Horowitz (1981) advocated using price correlations to define markets on the basis that prices of substitutes cannot move too much out of line with one another.[309] The prices of products will be perfectly

---

308 The cross-price elasticity is estimated using the following formula:

$$(\delta q_i / \delta p_j) / (q_i / p_j) \quad [6.1],$$

where q_i and p_j denote the quantity and price of products i and j respectively. Cross-price elasticities were first accepted by the US Supreme Court for defining markets in *Times-Picayune Publishing Co. v. United States,* 345 US 594 (1952).

309 CCPCMG2014 (¶2.14(d)) includes price correlations among the types of evidence that may be considered when evaluating demand-side substitution.

correlated if a specified percentage change in the price of one results in a consistent percentage change in the price of the other, whether one price increases by 100% and the other by .01% or whether they both increase by 10% at a time. Avoiding inaccurate results due to spurious correlations generally requires specifying a formal model, although it was claimed that price correlations did not require complex models (Stigler & Sherwin, 1985). A high price correlation is a necessary but not sufficient condition for establishing that two products are in the same market. If prices are uncorrelated then products are not close substitutes and are in different markets (Areeda & Turner, 1978).

Figure 6.1: On- and Off-Trade Packaged Lager Prices (2002 = 100)

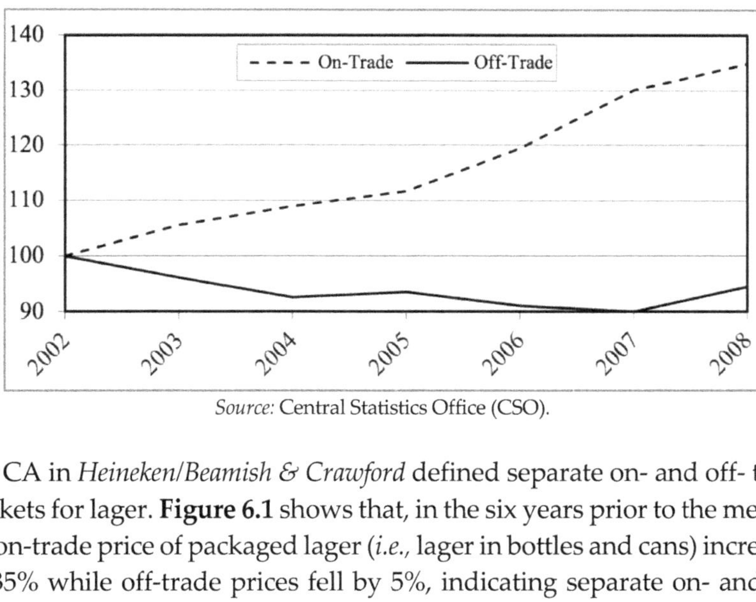

Source: Central Statistics Office (CSO).

The CA in *Heineken/Beamish & Crawford* defined separate on- and off- trade markets for lager. **Figure 6.1** shows that, in the six years prior to the merger, the on-trade price of packaged lager (*i.e.*, lager in bottles and cans) increased by 35% while off-trade prices fell by 5%, indicating separate on- and off-trade markets. The CA did not cite price correlations in this case but stated that Granger[310] causality tests indicated separate product markets for stout,

310 Slade (1986) proposed using such tests to define markets. According to the causality literature a variable Y is "caused" by another variable X if one obtains significantly better predictions of Y when X is included as an explanatory variable along with all other explanatory variables than when X is excluded (see Granger, 1969; Sims, 1972; and Wu, 1983). Causality tests are highly sensitive to the model specification and will yield biased results if important variables are excluded which is likely due to data limitations (Kaserman & Zeisel, 1996). Kimmel (1987) and Coe & Krause (2008) also criticised such tests.

ale, and lager.[311] On-trade draught and bottled lager prices also diverged prior to the merger, albeit to a lesser extent. Between 2005 and 2008 the price of bottled lager in pubs increased by 21% *versus* 11% for draught lager (see **Figure 6.2**). The CA concluded that there was a single on-trade lager market for draught and bottled lager, although it cited no analysis supporting this conclusion. The price divergence suggests possible price discrimination indicating separate markets.

Figure 6.2: National Average On-Trade Lager Prices (2002 = 100)

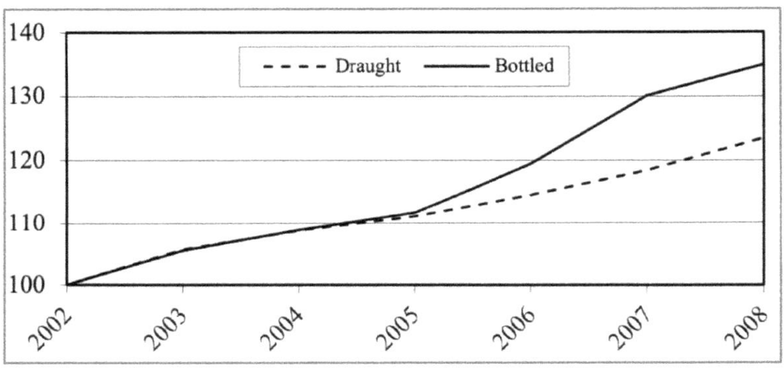

Source: CSO.

The merging parties in *Britvic/C&C*[312] cited price correlations in support of a broad market definition *"for all soft drinks that includes water, carbonated soft drinks, fruit juices and squashes"* (¶11). The CA rejected this pointing out that:

i. A high degree of correlation was unsurprising as two of the price series were subsets of a third price series;

ii. Correlation analysis is only valid if price series are stationary (stable);[313] and

---

311 The CA again concluded that stout, ale, lager, and cider constituted separate markets in CA M/09/018 – *C&C/Tennents*, 17.9.2009. Somewhat confusingly, however, the CA referred to the *"beer market"* in CA M/12/030 – *C&C/Gleeson*, 27.2.2013 with no explanation for applying a different definition. The CCPC in M/16/017 – *Molson Coors/Miller*, 13.5.2016 analysed the impact of the transaction in six different potential markets: separate on- and off-trade and combined on- and off-trade markets for all beer and for lager.

312 CA M/07/027 – *Britvic/C&C*, 13.8.2007.

313 The CA's own price correlation tests found that the price series were (a) non-stationary, rendering the results unreliable; and (b) were not co-integrated, indicating a narrower market than that claimed by the parties.

iii. The analysis did not control for external factors which could affect the price series.

In *Galco/Sperrin* the parties cited high price correlations as evidence that steel corrosion protection systems and various alternative building materials were in the same market. The merging parties also argued that price correlations supported a broad market definition in *Top Snacks/KP Snacks* but the CA stated, correctly, that while this evidence supported a wide market definition it was not conclusive.

Elzinga & Hogarty (1973 & 1978) proposed defining markets based on product flows, arguing that, in most cases, such analysis only required data on product shipments. The Elzinga-Hogarty test measures the percentage of a product consumed in an area that is produced there and the percentage of a product produced in an area that is consumed there. They state that, if both values are high, the area in question should be regarded as a distinct geographic market and proposed critical values for the test.[314]

The presence or absence of trade flows between areas is neither a necessary nor a sufficient condition for establishing that they constitute a single market (Stigler & Sherwin, 1985). Despite trade flows between two geographic areas, differences in demand elasticities between them creates the potential for price discrimination, indicating separate markets (Baker, 2007). The Elzinga-Hogarty test treats different locations as separate geographic markets if there are no shipments between them, even though cross elasticities of demand between the locations may be quite high.[315]

In *Pabst*[316] the market was defined as that for beer in the State of Wisconsin because Wisconsin had the highest *per capita* beer consumption in the US and imports of beer into the State were low, ignoring the fact that 75% of the beer brewed in Wisconsin was shipped out of the State (Schrank & Roy, 1991).[317] The EU Commission in *Italian Flat Glass*[318] argued that market definition should be based on actual product shipments, not those that were *"theoretically possible"*. It concluded that there was *"no doubt"* that the geographic market was Italy because Italian producers supplied 80% of

---

312 Kaserman & Zeisel (1996) state that there was no theoretical or practical justification for these critical values.

315 Elzinga (1981) acknowledges that the absence of substantial shipments in or out of a particular area does not establish that it constitutes a distinct geographic market and argued that the test only estimated minimum market size.

316 *United States v. Pabst Brewing Co.*, 384 US 546 (1966).

317 Admittedly ignoring such "exports" is not consistent with the Elzinga-Hogarty test.

318 Case 89/93 – *Italian Flat Glass*, 7.12.1988.

Italian flat glass. The absence of trade flows provides no information as to how consumers and non-Italian suppliers would have responded to a price increase by Italian producers. The threat of potential imports may have exercised a sufficient constraint on Italian prices to render actual shipments unnecessary. Documentary evidence indicated that Italian producers took account of competition from non-Italian producers suggesting that the market was wider than Italy (Kauper, 1996).

The CCPC in *Bon Secours/Barrington's Hospital* concluded that the Mid-West region was an appropriate regional geographic market based on the percentage of Barrington's Hospital patients living in that region. However, a significant proportion of Mid-West residents may have attended private hospitals in other regions.[319] The CCPC in *Xtratherm/Ballytherm* concluded that, although imports of PIR insulation materials were minimal, they were capable of exercising a competitive constraint on the parties post-merger.[320]

Natural experiments which involve relatively large price changes or changes in the number of competitors over time or between areas may also provide useful information for defining markets (Coleman *et al.*, 2003).[321]

The Characteristics, Price & Intended Use Test

The EU Commission has repeatedly stated that a relevant product market comprises all products that consumers regard as interchangeable based on their characteristics, price and intended use. This was first stated in the Commission's *Notice on Agreements of Minor Importance* (EU Commission, 1986, September 3, ¶11) and was subsequently included in the 1997 and 2024MDNs (¶12). CCPCMG2014 state that the characteristics and functions of products may indicate demand-side substitution but acknowledge that they are insufficient to reach a definitive conclusion as to the relevant

---

319 CCPC M/20/036 – *UPMC/Aut Even* noted that a significant cohort of patients in the South-East Region obtained hospital treatment outside of that region.

320 CCPC M/21/033 – *Xtratherm/Ballytherm*, 13.8.2021.

321 The CCPC noted in *LN-Gaiety/MCD Productions* that none of Ticketmaster's largest customers switched to self-supply of ticketing services following an October 2016 increase in Ticketmaster's charges, citing this as *"an actual example of a demand-side response to an increase in the price… where Ticketmaster was able to increase its prices without losing customers"* (¶3.118). *Q-Park/Tazbell* cites another natural experiment where off-street car parking charges increased following a 2022 reduction in public transport fares indicating that public transport and off-street parking are not substitutes.

product market while relative price levels may also be used to evaluate demand side substitution.[322]

A major problem with the *"characteristics, price and intended use"* formula is that it is necessarily subjective. Neven *et al.* (1993) state that the test has serious shortcomings because differences in characteristics provide no information on the degree of substitutability between products. Motta (2004) states that a relevant market should not consist of a set of products that resemble one another on the basis of certain characteristics but should comprise the set of products (and geographical areas) that exercise a competitive constraint on each other. In *Timac/Grassland Fertilizer* the CA stated that a reasonable case could be made that fertilizer products distributed by the parties were *"sufficiently different in terms of both use and sales channels that they may not be considered direct competitors"* (¶12).[323]

Evidence on price levels is also unsuitable for defining markets. Motta (2004) states that defining markets based on price differentials is *"unsound"* because they provide no information on the extent to which products exert a competitive constraint on each other. Similarly, Baker (2007) notes that price differentials ignore possible substitution between high price/high quality and low price/low quality products. Although the price of one product, A, may be twice that of another product, B, even a small increase in the price of A may cause enough consumers to switch to B as to render a price increase unprofitable. This may apply particularly when there are quality differences between products. A difference in price tells us that some consumers are prepared to pay more for A than B because they believe the difference in quality justifies a higher price. However, even a relatively small additional increase in price may cause enough consumers of A to conclude that it is not worth the additional extra cost to render the price increase unprofitable. UKCMA (2017, April 10) notes that price differentials between on-line and bricks and mortar retailers do not preclude competitive interaction between them.

---

322 The CCPC has not always adhered to this approach (see below). CAMG2002 listed product characteristics as a factor that could be used to determine substitutability.

323 CA M/12/032 – *Timac/Grassland Fertilizer*, 17.1.2013. The CA did not reach a conclusion because the acquirer accounted for less than 1% of a market for all fertilizers. Previously in M/04/064 – *Timac/Albatross*, 1.12.2004, the parties argued that the specialised nature of the acquirer's fertilizers meant that the parties' products were in separate markets, but the CA did not define the market. In CCPC M/19/044 – *Timac/Grassland Fertilizer*, 27.5.2020, the CCPC concluded that there was no horizontal overlap between the parties because they operated at different levels in the supply chain.

In *eircom/Meteor* the CA concluded that fixed and mobile phone calls constituted separate product markets based on price differentials and product characteristics. In *Permira/Griggs*[324] the CA argued that the merging parties' products *"are not close substitutes as their price ranges generally target different customer types"* (¶18). However, the CCPC in *Aurivo/Arrabawn* concluded that branded and own label milk were in the same product market despite a significant price difference (¶3.35).

The SSNIP Test

USHMG1982 introduced a new approach to market definition with the *"SSNIP"* test which seeks to identify the smallest market within which a hypothetical monopolist could impose a *"small but significant non-transitory increase in price"*.[325] It asks whether the hypothetical monopolist could sustain a price increase of 5% for at least one year. To be sustainable, profits after the price increase must be higher than they were before it. Because a price increase will result in some decline in sales, the question is whether the profits foregone on those lost sales will exceed the additional profits due to the higher price on the remaining sales (Morris & Mosteller, 1991). If enough consumers would switch to alternative products to render the price increase unprofitable, then the monopolist lacks the power to raise price. The market must therefore be expanded by adding the next closest substitute. The process is repeated until the point is reached where a 5% price increase would be profitable.[326] The range of products and the geographic area so defined constitutes the relevant market. The SSNIP test provides a logical approach for distinguishing between substitute products that are in the market and more distant substitutes that are not, by defining the market to include all those products that would be necessary to sustain

---

324 CA M/13/031 – *Permira/Griggs*, 29.11.2013.

325 The basic idea behind the SSNIP test was first outlined by Adelman (1959) (Werden, 2003b).

326 The SSNIP test involves repeated iterations whereby the market is gradually expanded by adding the closest substitute until the point is reached where a 5% price increase would be profitable. Cross-price elasticities can be used to rank substitutes in order of closeness (Werden, 1998; Motta, 2004). Coate & Fischer (2008) provide a detailed analysis of the application of the SSNIP test in 116 USFTC cases. The SSNIP threshold represents a benchmark for assessing buyer substitution and does not constitute a tolerance level for anti-competitive post-merger price increases (Baker, 2007).

a SSNIP and excluding those that would not prevent such a price increase (Simons & Williams, 1993).[327]

Applying the SSNIP test at prevailing market prices may lead to errors in defining markets in dominance cases. A profit-maximising monopolist will generally raise price to the point where other products become close substitutes. Measuring the degree of product substitution at prevailing prices involves considering the position after the dominant firm has already raised prices above the competitive level.[328] In merger cases, the crucial issue is not whether one of the merging parties already has a degree of market power, but whether the merger will increase market power. Thus, in merger cases the SSNIP test is based on prevailing market prices (*ibid.*).

The SSNIP test can be applied by estimating the critical elasticity of demand (ε) defined as:

$$\varepsilon = 1/(m+t) \qquad [6.2]$$

where m is the pre-merger price cost margin (defined as the gap between price and marginal cost) and t is the minimum price increase considered significant, usually 5%.[329] Thus, estimating the critical elasticity of demand requires information on firms' price-cost margins. If the pre-merger elasticity of demand exceeds the critical elasticity, the sales decline due to the price increase will be large enough to render the price increase unprofitable and the products concerned do not constitute a relevant market. Goods characterised by high fixed costs or sharply upward-sloping cost curves will have lower critical demand elasticities than those with low fixed costs or relatively flat cost curves.

Harris & Simons (1989) proposed estimating the critical loss to apply the SSNIP test when demand elasticities cannot be estimated. The critical loss is defined as the maximum sales loss resulting from a price increase such that profits would remain unchanged. If the actual loss of sales is less than

---

327 USHMG1992 clarified that the SSNIP test assumes that *"the terms of sale of all other products are held constant"*. Consequently, the SSNIP test should be based on the own elasticity of demand rather than the residual elasticity of demand. The residual demand curve is the demand curve faced by an individual firm which is the total market demand curve less the supply of all other firms in the market. It recognises that a price change by one firm may result in changes in the prices of competing products and takes account of such changes. Following publication of USHMG1982 several studies applied the SSNIP test using residual demand elasticities (Baker & Bresnahan, 1988; Kamerschen & Kohler, 1993; Amel & Hannan, 2000).

328 This is an example of the "cellophane trap" (see above).

329 This formula applies in the case of linear demand. Where demand is non-linear, the critical elasticity is defined as [log(m+t) - log(m)]/Log (1+t). Werden (1998) provides a detailed description on calculating critical elasticities of demand.

the critical loss, then a 5% price increase would be profitable, and the market would be defined. The critical loss (y) may be expressed as:

$$y = t/(m+t) \qquad [6.3]$$

where t and m again refer to the level of price increase and the pre-merger price-cost margin.[330] Morris & Mosteller (1991) defined geographic markets for supermarkets using critical loss. Strand (2006) proposed a relatively simple critical loss test for defining geographic markets. Critical loss analysis is more complicated in the case of differentiated products and is best suited to homogenous products (Coate, 2006).[331]

Table 6.1 illustrates critical elasticity of demand and critical loss values for a 5% price increase for various price-cost margins. The table illustrates that the critical elasticity of demand and critical loss both decline as the price-cost margin increases. For example, a decline in sales of more than 16.7% would be required to render a 5% price increase unprofitable for a price-cost margin of 25%. For a 50% price-cost margin, however, a sales decline greater than 9.1% would render a 5% price increase unprofitable. The table also shows that, in many cases, a large sales decline is not required to render a 5% price increase unprofitable. A majority of customers do not need to switch in order to render a 5% price increase unprofitable. What matters is the number and response of marginal rather than average customers.[332] **Table 6.1** also indicates that a low critical loss implies relatively high price-cost margins, indicating that demand is relatively price insensitive (Katz & Shapiro, 2003).[333] Merging parties need to be careful

---

330 Harris & Simons (1989) suggest using average variable cost as a proxy for marginal cost so that the only information required is data on average variable cost and price.

331 EU Commission 2024MDN describes critical loss analysis as a way of applying the SSNIP test (¶59). For a detailed description of how to conduct critical loss analysis in the case of differentiated products, see Meyer & Wang (2012).

332 The UKOFT concluded that, while individual live music festivals were not particularly close demand substitutes, and therefore placed only a weak constraint on each other, there was likely to be at least a proportion of marginal customers who would switch between certain festivals. The issue is whether this marginal group is sufficiently large to defeat a SSNIP (UKOFT ME/1680/05 – *Mean Fiddler/Clear Channel*, 17.6.2005).

333 Davis & Garcés (2010) observe that high price-cost margins imply that the actual loss in response to a price increase is likely to be low. Claims that markets should be defined widely, because critical loss is small while expected losses are likely to be high, are therefore inconsistent (EU Commission, 2021). High rates of cost pass-through also indicate that demand is relatively inelastic (Scheffman & Spiller, 1987), a sufficient (but not necessary) condition for defining a relevant market (Kaserman & Zeisel, 1996). For market definition

therefore when arguing that actual loss is likely to exceed the critical loss, because the latter is very low and such claims should be viewed sceptically.

Table 6.1: Critical Elasticity of Demand & Critical Loss for a 5% Price Increase

% Price-marginal cost margin	Critical Elasticity of Demand	Critical Loss
10	6.67	33.3
15	5.00	25.0
20	4.00	20.0
25	3.33	16.7
30	2.86	14.3
35	2.50	12.5
40	2.22	11.1
45	2.00	10.0
50	1.82	9.1

Rather than asking whether the likely loss in the event of a price increase exceeds the critical loss, USHMG2010 posited that, under certain specific assumptions, the SSNIP test is satisfied if the aggregate diversion ratio exceeds the critical loss. Simons & Coate (2014) argue that this rests on assumptions that may only apply in a small minority of cases and claim that this change reduced the burden of proof and was likely to result in many more mergers being fully investigated and possibly condemned.[334] They claim that this test may have been accepted in *H&R Block Inc.*[335] because the Court did not understand the controversy surrounding it or its significance.[336] Shapiro & Shelanski (2021, p.62) argue that the changes *"corrected an erroneous method of critical loss analysis that had been used with some success by defense economists"* and made it more difficult for merging parties to argue that products are in the relevant market just because there is *some* substitution between them.

---

purposes, it does not matter whether a price increase is due to the exercise of market power, or a cost increase unique to the product concerned.

334 Ezrielev & Simons (2011) also argue that the approach to critical loss in USHMG2010 rests on assumptions that are unlikely to be met in many cases.

335 *United States v. H&R Block, Inc.*, 833 F. Supp. 2d 36 (D.D.C.2011).

336 They state that it appears from the judgement that the defendant's economic expert did not raise these issues.

The EU Commission 1997 and 2024 MDNs both refer to the SSNIP test.[337] In *Nestlé/Perrier*, the EU Commission concluded that *"an appreciable non-transitory increase in the price of source waters"* (¶13) would not cause a significant shift to soft drinks.

The CCPC application of the SSNIP test in *Topaz/Esso* was somewhat novel and has potentially far-reaching implications. In defining the relevant geographic market for a Dublin oil import terminal, the CCPC argued that the SSNIP test should be based on, what it described as, the price of *"terminalling services"* rather than the price of purchasing fuel from the terminal. There is no suggestion in the Determination that customers purchased fuel from overseas refineries, arranged for its importation and then paid terminal owners to unload and store it pending collection.[338] Consequently, there was no actual price for *"terminalling services"*. The CCPC estimated this price as the difference between the price at which terminal operators bought and sold fuel products, i.e., the terminal operator's margin. If this approach were applied in a grocery merger it would imply that the SSNIP test should be based on retailers' margins rather than the retail price of groceries. The parties in *Applegreen/Joint Fuel Terminals* stated the terminal *"does not have any actual turnover, as all products are sold by Topaz and Valero, rather than the JFT itself"* (¶22).[339]

The CCPC stated that the SSNIP test was just one of the tools used to define markets in *Tesco/Joyce's* and went on to say:

> *"A substantial emphasis should also be placed on product characteristics, price and intended use as well as observed substitution patterns between various products that can potentially be included in the same product market" (¶3.10).*

The CCPC repeated this in *Thornton's/Carducci* while stating that the SSNIP test's *"applicability varies depending on pricing practices in the sector"* (¶3.7). Such statements appear inconsistent with CCPCMG2014 (see above). Hovenkamp (2024) argues that the best approach is to apply the SSNIP test whenever adequate data is available and only use other approaches when it is not.

---

337 CAMG (2002) also referred to the SSNIP test.

338 In the US, for example, gas shippers pay the operators of long-distance pipelines to transport natural gas from its source to various cities so there is a price and a market for gas transmission services.

339 This transaction involved the subsequent divestment of the fuel import terminal in Dublin Port involved in *Topaz/Esso*. Notably it refers to the terminal owners selling fuel products from the terminal rather than providing terminalling services. **Appendix 6.1** provides further details on the application of the SSNIP test in *Topaz/Esso*.

USHMG2023 introduced a modified version of the SSNIP test, described as the SSNIPT test, which also sought to include purchasers' responses to non-price variables. Hovenkamp (2024) notes that the only practical way to factor in non-price variables is to assign them a monetary value as they would otherwise greatly complicate merger analysis.

Narrow Market Definitions

As a general rule, if a merger will not result in an SLC in a narrowly-defined market, then it is unlikely to do so in a more widely-defined market. This is because the likelihood of a firm or firms being found to have market power is greater, the more narrowly the market is defined. Consequently, where no competitive harm is found if a merger is evaluated with respect to a narrowly-defined market, in many cases this will be sufficient to establish that a transaction will not give rise to an SLC. Analysing the effects of a merger based on the narrowest possible market definition thus provides a useful means of identifying mergers that will not result in an SLC, eliminating the need to define the market. This approach is subject to two important *caveats*:

i. If the narrowest possible market definition places the merging parties in separate markets, such a definition may result in a false negative;

ii. The narrowest possible market may exclude competing products that would exercise an effective competitive constraint on the merging parties, resulting in a false positive.

In both of these situations, it is necessary to define the market correctly in order to establish whether the merger will/will not result in an SLC.

CCPCMG2014 acknowledge the potential for a false negative but fail to recognise the potential for a false positive if the market is incorrectly defined too narrowly.

> *"Where no competitive harm is found if a merger is evaluated with respect to a narrowly defined market, the Commission may also find that no competitive harm may be found in a broader market in which the merging parties' market shares are further diluted. In other circumstances, expanding the market may lead to a finding of competitive harm in the wider market. (¶2.4).*

In *DSM/Martek*[340] the CA noted that a narrow market definition would have placed the parties in separate markets but noted that there was a minimal overlap between them in a wider market. The CA acknowledged the potential for a false positive in *Glen Dimplex/Applied Energy* where the merging parties had a combined market share of 55-60% in the narrowest possible market but had a much lower market share in a wider market.

> *"Thus, defining the precise product and geographic market in which the parties compete is essential to enable the Authority to examine the competitive effects of the proposed acquisition." (¶1.19)*

Dunnes/Whelan's Tipperary[341] noted that a narrow market definition would have placed the merging parties in different product markets (FN12) and analysed the transaction based on a wider market definition, acknowledging the potential for a false negative. In *PRL/Custodian,*[342] the CCPC, having found no overlap between the parties based on a narrow market definition, analysed the effect of the transaction in a wider market. In *Arrow/Commtech*[343] and *Accenture/Rothco*[344] the CCPC applied wide product market definitions. In the former case it stated that it had not uncovered any information that the parties would have market power in any narrower market post-merger. The latter Determination stated that *"the parties' activities are not substitutable when assessed on a narrow basis"* (¶20).[345] In *Dawn Meats/Dunbia,* the CCPC considered an all-island geographic market for the procurement of lamb as the target's processing plant was located in Northern Ireland.[346]

In several other cases where narrow market definitions place the parties in separate markets, the CA/CCPC failed to consider the possibility of a false negative. In *Barnett/Origin/Hall* the CA analysed the transaction on the basis of the narrowest possible market definition which placed grain and non-grain feed ingredients (NGFI) in separate products markets.

340 CA M/11/003 – *DSM/Martek*, 11.2.2011.

341 CCPC M/16/002 – *Dunnes/Whelan's Tipperary*, 26.2.2016.

342 CCPC M/17/028 – *PRL/Custodian,* 29.6.2017.

343 CCPC M/17/063 – *Arrow/Commtech*, 19.12.2017.

344 CCPC M/17/069 – *Accenture/Rothco*, 25.1.2018.

345 The target's customers indicated that they did not view the acquirer as an alternative supplier (¶22), implying that they were in separate markets. Nevertheless, applying a wider market definition provided a check against a possible false negative.

346 A geographic market limited to the State would have placed the parties in separate geographic markets.

Novasep/Pharmachem[347] contained no discussion of market definition, but the CA concluded that the parties' products were not substitutes placing them in separate product markets. In *eircom/Meteor* the CA concluded that there was no overlap between the parties because fixed and mobile telecommunications constituted separate markets.[348] As Meteor had a small share of mobile telecommunications services at the time it is unlikely that the case outcome would have been different if fixed and mobile telephony services had been defined as a single market. However, whether there was one or two markets could have been critical to avoiding a false negative in a merger between eircom and a larger mobile operator. In *Kingspan/CRH Insulation*[349] the CA decided that there was no competitive overlap between the parties citing its *Kingspan/Xtratherm* conclusion that PIR and EPS insulation materials constituted separate product markets.

An extreme example of narrow markets incorrectly placing the merging parties in separate markets occurred in 14 motor dealership cases in which the CCPC concluded that individual car marques (brands) constituted the narrowest possible market although, in every case, the merging parties operated several dealerships selling multiple new car marques.[350] These cases are summarised in **Table 6.2**.

The CCPC concluded that there was a minor overlap between the parties in the market for new Volkswagen cars, although the acquirer had dealerships for nine other car marques in *JDM Automotive/Commons Road Cars* and *JDM Automotive/Karmann Auto*. In *Frank Keane/Doran Motors* the CCPC identified no competition concerns because there was no overlap between the parties in respect of individual car marques, although they operated dealerships for seven different car marques between them.

---

347 CA M/07/054 – *Novasep/Pharmachem*, 9.10.2007.

348 The CA focused on a fixed-line telecommunications market in CA M/09/15 – *Vodafone Ireland/BT Ireland*, 21.8.2009, while the CCPC referred to *"the potential market for the provision of retail mobile telecommunications services"* in CCPC M/17/037 – *Tesco Ireland/Tesco Mobile*, 26.7.2017 (¶12). Neither Determination discussed whether fixed and mobile might constitute a single market. CCPC M/17/045 – *IIF/GMC*, 12.9.2017 assessed the effects of the proposed transaction *"in the potential market for the provision of telecommunications services"* (¶20) but provided no explanation of what this market definition included.

349 CA M/10/039 – *Kingspan/CRH Insulation*, 2.12.2010. UKOFT, ME/4807/10, *Kingspan/CRH Insulation*, 13.4.2011 reached a similar conclusion.

350 In most cases the parties sold new cars and light commercial vehicles (LCVs).

Table 6.2: CCPC Motor Dealership Merger Cases

Case	Date	Overlap Markets Defined by CCPC	Other New Car Marques Sold by Merging Parties
CCPC M/14/041 – *JDM Automotive/Commons Road Cars*	22.1.2015	New Volkswagen	Audi, BMW, Ford, Land Rover, Mazda, Mini, Porsche, Seat, Volvo
CCPC M/15/071 – *JDM Automotive/Karmann Auto*	22.1.2016	New Volkswagen	Audi, BMW, Ford, Land Rover, Mazda, Mini, Porsche, Seat, Volvo
CCPC M/16/014 – *Frank Keane/MSL*	25.4.2016	New Volkswagen	BMW, Mini, Mitsubishi.
CCPC M/18/019 – *JDM Automotive/Motorpark*	22.3.2018	New Ford & Volvo	Audi, BMW, Kia, Jaguar, Land Rover, Mazda, Porsche, Volkswagen
CCPC M/18/020 – *Armalou Spirit Ford – Lillis O'Donnell*	22.3.2018	New Ford	Jaguar, Land Rover, Skoda, Volvo
CCPC M/18/073 – *Alavina/J. Donohoe Motors*	12.10.2018	New BMW and Mini	Citröen, Hyundai, Opel, Skoda
CCPC M/18/074 – *Quarry Park Motors/Linden Copse*	12.10.2018	New Skoda	Mazda, Peugeot, Volkswagen, Volvo
CCPC M/18/086 – *Brightstone/Fitzpatrick Motors*	7.12.2018	New Ford	Citröen, Seat, Suzuki
CCPC M/19/031 – *Windsor Motors/Holcroft*	21.11.2019	New Peugeot	Dacia, Mazda, Nissan, Opel, Renault
CCPC M/21/057 – *JDM Automotive/CAB Motor Company*	19.11.2021	New Ford	Audi, BMW, Mini, Motorrad, Jaguar, Kia, Land Rover, Mazda, Porsche, Volkswagen, Volvo
CCPC M/22/016 – *Keary Motors/Renault Retail Group*	13.5.2022	New Renault & Dacia	BMW, Hyundai, Mini, Nissan
CCPC M/22/048 – *Frank Keane/Doran Motors*	20.10.2022	None	BMW, Hyundai, MG, Mini, Skoda, Suzuki, Volkswagen
CCPC M/23/017 – *MMM/John Morrison Motors*	2.6.2023	New BMW and Mini	Citröen, Hyundai, Opel
CCPC M/23/035 – *Bright Motor City/Gowan Group*	30.8.2023	New Citröen	Cupra, Ford, Hyundai, Suzuki, Seat

Source: CA/CCPC.

In *MMM/John Morrison Motors*, the parties both sold new BMW and Mini cars and three other new car marques, but the Determination analysed the effect of the transaction in separate markets for new BMWs and Minis, although, unlike many of the other cases, it acknowledged that sellers of other car marques would exert a competitive constraint on the merged entity. The Determination cites two UK cases in support of such narrow market definitions. One of these cases stated that the UK competition agencies *"did not consider it appropriate to segment the supply of new or used cars by type… or marque… on the basis of the considerable overlap in types of vehicle and the evidence of competition between marques"*.[351]

The CCPC analysed markets for individual car marques and all new cars in three other motor dealership cases.[352] It defined a single market for all car marques in mergers of wholesale distributors of new cars[353] and concluded that there was a single market comprising all car marques for pre-owned cars.[354] There is no economic basis for concluding that different car marques constitute separate product markets, i.e. that new Ford cars are in a separate market to other new cars. Competition law permits selective distribution agreements for new cars because, although they reduce intra-brand competition, they increase inter-brand competition, i.e., competition between different car marques, indicating a single market for all new cars.[355]

Analysing transactions based on an implausible narrow market definition does not constitute best practice, risks creating dubious precedents and may result in false negatives. The possibility that a merger between retailers of multiple car marques could result in an SLC in a local geographic market at least should have been considered.[356] The fact that this

---

351 UKCMA, Case No. ME/6685/17 – *Steven Eagell/Lancaster Motor Company*, 24.7.2017, ¶21. The Determination noted that evidence in the case supported this approach.

352 CCPC M/17/015 – *Avanacar/Citröen*, 5.5.2017; CCPC M/19/018 – *Connolly Motor/Hyundai Galway*, 8.8.2019; and CCPC M/19/037 – *Connolly Motors/Volkswagen Letterkenny*, 18.12.2019. In CCPC M/18/080 – *JDM Automotive/TKF Autos*, 9.11.2018 the CCPC only considered a wider market for all new passenger cars, although the transaction did not involve the acquisition of a motor dealership but related to the premises from which the vendor had previously operated such a business.

353 CCPC M/19/021 – *Gowan Group/Opel*, 20.8.2019 citing EU Commission Case No. Comp/M.9070 – *Europcar/Vicentini*,10.9.2018 which found a horizontal overlap between wholesale distributors of all new car marques. The CCPC adopted a similar approach in M/23/041 – *Nissan Ireland/Renault Ireland*, 28.9.2023.

354 In the majority of the cases in **Table 6.2**, the parties also sold pre-owned cars.

355 Such arrangements are permitted under both Irish and EU competition law.

356 The marques involved in *JDM Automotive/Commons Road Cars* accounted for 37% of new car sales nationally (SIMI: https://www.simi.ie/en/motorstats. Accessed 4.12.2024). In some of

approach was repeated so frequently raises questions about internal quality control procedures.

The CA concluded that replica football kits for individual teams each constituted a separate product market in *Nike/Umbro*.[357] The UKOFT[358] noted that consumers purchased replica football kits to show their support for a particular team and would not purchase another team's kit if the price of their favourite club's kit increased. A 5% increase in the price of Arsenal shirts is unlikely to cause Arsenal supporters to switch their allegiance to Tottenham Hotspur, justifying such a narrow market definition. Thus, in contrast to the car cases, the evidence in this case suggests that shirts/replica kits for individual teams are likely to constitute separate product markets.

In a limited number of cases, the CA/CCPC concluded that an SLC would not arise in a particular market based on market share data for a different market. Thus, in *ILHAWK/Ark Life* the CCPC analysed the impact of the transaction *"in respect of the narrowest relevant product market (i.e. the provision of Closed Book life insurance products), with reference to the broader relevant product market for the provision of all life insurance products"* (¶22).[359] In *AIG/Laya Healthcare* the CCPC stated that the parties overlapped in *"the provision of travel insurance and the provision of medical case management services"* (¶14) but concluded that the transaction would not result in any SLC partly because the parties accounted for a small share of what appears to be a different market, *"the combined travel/personal accident (PA) insurance sector"* (¶19).[360] The merging parties in *Premier Group/Imprint* were engaged in the provision of permanent and temporary recruitment services in the State. The CA concluded that the transaction would not result in an SLC based, in part, on the parties' estimates that their combined market share was less than 10% in the accountancy and finance recruitment *"segment"*.

---

these cases the merging parties were arguably in separate local geographic markets, but the CCPC did not advance that argument.

357 CA M/07/068 – *Nike/Umbro*, 23.1.2008.

358 UKOFT, CA98/06/2003, *Price-fixing of Replica Football Kit*, 1.8.2003.

359 CCPC M/21/045 – *ILHAWK/Ark Life*, 24.9.2021. The Determination justified this approach on the grounds that *"industry reports do not provide any market share data on Closed Books, and as a result there is very little information available regarding the size and value of Closed Books in the State"* (¶23).

360 CCPC M/15/005 – *AIG/Laya Healthcare*, 13.3.2015. It adopted a similar approach in CCPC M/23/049 – *AXA/Laya Healthcare*, 3.10.2024, citing EU Commission Case No. COMP/M.9056 – *Generali CEE/AS*, 10.12.2018, which stated that the characteristics and purpose of travel insurance were distinct from other types of insurance while different types of insurance were not demand-side substitutes.

According to the parties this was the only part of the market for which market share data was available.[361]

In *PandaGreen/Exomex*, the CCPC stated that it was not necessary to define precise geographic markets but nevertheless expressed concerns about possible anti-competitive effects in certain towns and townlands *"in Co. Louth where the Parties overlap in the supply of individual C&I waste collection services…"* (¶68). In *Thornton's/Carducci*, the CCPC expressed concerns that the transaction would reduce the number of competitors in domestic waste collection services from three to two in what were described as *"overlapping areas"* in three Dublin local authority areas. Contrary to the CCPC's assertions that geographic market definition did not affect the outcomes, the competition concerns raised by the CCPC in both cases rested on a questionable implicit assumption that the overlapping areas constituted relevant geographic markets, raising the possibility of false positives in both cases. The CCPC acknowledged in *Thornton's/Carducci* that *"in terms of supply side substitution, the geographic market may be* ***slightly wider*** *than the Overlapping Areas"* but stated that it was not necessary to consider that possibility because it had *"analysed the* ***narrowest potential geographic market****"* (FN52).[362] There is no indication in either Determination that conditions of competition in the *"overlap"* areas were sufficiently different to those in surrounding areas. The small size of some of the overlapping areas, particularly in *Thornton's/Carducci*, raises doubts that they constituted separate markets but were in fact part of a wider market comprising the entirety of the relevant local authority area.[363] The CCPC cited no direct evidence of market power and failed to advance any theory of competitive harm in either case. The CCPC failed to consider the possibility of a false positive due to an implicit overly narrow market definition in both cases.

The CCPC approach in both these cases introduces a degree of arbitrariness into the market definition process.[364] It is inconsistent with its

---

361 CA M/08/016 – *Premier Group/Imprint*, 19.5.2008. This ignores the possibility that they may have had much higher combined shares in the overall market. It is akin to saying that the merging parties compete in a state-wide market but arguing that the merger will not result in an SLC because they have a small share in Kerry which is the only part of the State that market share data is available for.

362 As pointed out applying an overly narrow market definition may result in a false positive. Confusingly the CCPC suggested that the market could be defined even more narrowly *"by reference to very limited local geographic markets"* (¶3.34).

363 Many of the overlap areas were quite small and involved very few customers (see **Chapter 11**).

364 The possibility that a plausible theory of harm could apply based on a wider market definition in *Thornton's/Carducci* is considered in **Chapter 8**.

own *Guidelines* and the High Court *Rye Investments* judgement which stated that market definition was crucial to a finding that a proposed merger would affect competition.

> *"It must be recalled that the definition of the product market is crucial to the reliability of the assessment of any change in competition resulting from the proposed merger. The primary source of possible constraint upon the ability of the merged entity to raise prices lies in the possibility that consumers of the product will react by switching to acceptable alternative products already on offer to them" (¶7.21).*

CCPCMG2014 (¶2.5) states:

> *"However, where there is significant horizontal and/or vertical overlap between the merging parties and competition concerns are likely to arise post-merger, the Commission **will normally identify one or more relevant markets** in which the merger may result in an SLC" (emphasis added).*

Market Segmentation

CCPCMG2014 states:

> *"Market definition is not an exercise in drawing a definitive line and then ignoring market realities on either side of that line. Market definition should not restrict the range of competitive effects to be assessed by the Commission in its merger review. The Commission may consider segmentation within the relevant product or geographic market or factors outside the relevant market which impose competitive constraints on firms in the relevant market" (¶2.1).*

The opening sentence seems inconsistent with the economic literature which stresses the need to distinguish between close and distant substitutes. It also appears to be at odds with the EU Commission MDNs. The suggestion that a relevant market may be further sub-divided into segments echoes a 1960s US Supreme Court judgement which concluded that aluminium and copper were in the same market but this did not preclude their division *"into separate submarkets"*.[365] The judgement was widely criticised for its apparent inconsistency in finding that aluminium and copper constituted a single market but could also be divided into separate sub-markets (Simons & Williams, 1993). Kauper (1996, p.2400)

---

[365] *United States v. Aluminium Company of America*, 377 US 271 (1964).

described it as the *"best example of gerrymandering of 'sub-markets' to find a merger unlawful"*. Baker (2007) states that sub-markets may play a useful role in some cases, but cautions that the term must be applied carefully and does not provide a justification for discarding standard demand-side market definition criteria. Hovenkamp (2024, p.42) describes sub-markets as *"a Supreme Court fabrication out of practically nothing"* which resulted in lower courts concluding that it was unnecessary to apply established criteria for market definition to a smaller grouping of sales if they were characterised as a sub-market.

The High Court, in *Rye Investments*, rejected the CA's division of the processed cheese market into sub-segments when overturning its prohibition decision in *Kerry/Breeo*.

> *"It is immediately apparent therefore, that there is in the conclusion expressed at para. 8.115 an ambiguity and a lack of coherence as to the manner in which the Authority is drawing its conclusion from its analysis of the relevant market as it has been defined, as opposed to the significance it appears to attach to the fact that the Kerry and Breeo brands are one another's closest competitors in the 40% of that market represented by the slices segment. Thus it is not clear, at least from para. 8.115 itself, what significance the Authority attaches to the sub-division of the relevant market into the three segments. The section clearly contains no finding, as such, that the slices segment constitutes a distinct product market. Nor does the paragraph appear to indicate that the fact that the Kerry and Breeo brands are one another's closest competitors within the slices segment necessarily result in their also being closest competitors to one another in the product market as a whole when the remaining 60% of that market is taken into account" (Rye Investments, ¶7.7).*

The Court went on:

> *"Accordingly, it is difficult to avoid the impression that while the Authority does not make any finding to the effect that the standard/ sliced cheese segment or the sliced cheese segment is a distinct product market in itself, it nevertheless appears to base its conclusion as to the closeness of competition between the Kerry and Breeo brands upon the competitive effect in that segment alone as if it was the relevant product market" (ibid., ¶7.11).*

The CA defined the market as the procurement of cattle for slaughter in *Dawn Meats/Galtee Meats* but stated this did not *"preclude analysis of market segments for different types and ages of cattle, and possibly for each grade therein"* (¶2.9). The CA did not define a relevant product market in *Bunzl/DGD* but confusingly described catering supplies as *"the segment in which the most significant overlap occurs…primarily through activities in the contract catering supplies sub-segment"*[366] (¶7).

These three cases pre-dated the *Rye Investments* judgement. Nevertheless, the CA/CCPC continued to divide markets into segments and sub-segments subsequently. In *Kepak/John Kelly Meats,*[367] the CCPC stated that there were no reasons to depart from its approach in *Dawn Meats/Galtee Meats. Dawn Meats/Dunbia* made no reference to possible market segments and defined the relevant product market as that for the purchase of all cattle types for slaughter.

The *Top Snacks/KP Snacks* Determination refers at various junctures to a *"sharing crisps segment"* (¶1.39); a *"private label segment"* (¶4.20); a *"crisps-only segment"* (¶4.49); *"a snacks-only segment"* (¶4.49); *"a combined hypothetical crisps and snacks segment within the State for each of the impulse, multipack and sharing* segments" (¶4.51). To paraphrase *Rye Investments,* it is not clear what significance the CCPC attached to the sub-division of the relevant market into these various segments. In *Permira/Griggs,* the CA speculated:

> "It may be possible to segment the market for the retail sale of footwear, clothing or accessories further by providing sub-segments in each constituent group or based on whether the products are luxury or non-luxury" *(¶17).*

The Determination, however, cited market share data *"in the overall market for the retail sales of footwear, clothing and accessories within the State"* (¶20).

In *Elvery's/Mahers,*[368] the CCPC stated that, because there was an overlap between the parties in the retail sale of branded leisurewear, footwear, sports goods and sports equipment, it had considered the competitive effects of the transaction *"on this **possible** product market **segment**"* (¶11, emphasis added). Conclusions should relate to the correct relevant market not to a *"possible"* market segment.

In *Heineken/Coman's I,*[369] having stated that it would analyse the impact of the proposed transaction in the wholesale supply of packaged alcoholic and non-alcoholic beverages, the CCPC, cited a third party that claimed that

---

366 CA M/07/055 – *Bunzl/DGD,* 17.10.2007.

367 CCPC M/16/060 – *Kepak/John Kelly Meats,* 21.12.2016.

368 CCPC M/15/062 – *Elvery's/Mahers,* 1.12.2015.

369 CCPC M/16/011 – *Heineken/Coman's I,* 5.4.2016.

it was the largest wholesaler of such products in the State *"with an estimated* ***segment share*** *of approximately 30-35%"* and states that, post-merger, the parties would have a *"**segment share**"* of 25-30% (¶29). The Determination subsequently refers to an *"off-trade beer segment"* (¶35); *"a beer segment"* (¶36); a *"lager segment (off-trade and on-trade)"* (¶37); and an *"off-trade lager segment"* (¶37) with no indication as to the relevance of these various segments.[370] It concluded that Heineken would have insufficient market power in *"the lager segment"* to foreclose rival wholesalers.

CapVest/Origin Foods/Maiden provides a particularly confusing and troubling example of the CA/CCPC use of segments and sub-segments. The CA speculated that consumers might not switch from baking mixes to individual baking ingredients in response to a 5-10% increase in the price of the former but advanced no evidence on this point and reached no conclusion.[371] The Determination stated that the CA would analyse the effects of the proposed transaction in the readymade baking mixes *"segment"* because this was where the parties' activities overlapped while arguing that *"the competitive effects…will be unaffected whether the relevant product market is narrow – readymade baking mixes – or broad, encompassing all home baking products"* (¶31). The Determination subsequently stated that only the supply of *"sweet readymade baking mixes"* would be affected and the remaining *"[55-65]% of the readymade baking mixes segment"* (¶56) would be unaffected by the transaction. If only sweet readymade baking mixes would be affected, then those products constitute a separate market.

Supply-side Substitution

When defining a relevant market, it is also necessary to consider the potential for supply-side substitution because firms that do not currently produce products that are close substitutes for those of the merging parties could switch to producing such products in the event of a post-merger price increase.[372] Kauper (1996) notes that the CJEU stressed the importance of supply-side substitution in *Continental Can* but attached less significance to it in subsequent cases. Neven *et al.* (1993) criticised the EU Commission for

---

370 An empirical study by Gürkaynak & Kalkan (2017) of the Turkish beer market rejected the hypothesis that the premium beer segment constituted a separate product market and supported the Turkish Competition Authority's finding that there was a single market for beer.

371 The Determination stated that one retailer regarded readymade baking mixes as a distinct product market.

372 The CA/CCPC treat supply-side substitution as a constraint which is external to the market.

its inconsistent approach to supply-side substitution and claim that its failure to take it into account resulted in excessively narrow market definitions in several cases. The EU Commission accepted a wide market definition in *Tommas/Sarrio*[373] based on supply-side substitution on the grounds that it was relatively easy for paper manufacturers to switch between producing different quality papers (Motta, 2004). It rejected supply substitution arguments in *Nestlé/Perrier* because soft drinks manufacturers would have had to incur huge advertising costs to compete with producers of mineral spring waters.

CCPCMG2014 state:

> *"The boundaries of the relevant product market are generally determined by reference to demand-substitution alone. The reaction of suppliers to price changes is generally considered in the analysis of the competitive effects of the merger, either under rivalry or potential new entry, rather than as part of market definition. However, there may be circumstances where the Commission will consider the responses of suppliers to changes in price" (¶2.15).*[374]

Evidence considered in evaluating supply-side substitution includes, but is not limited to:

i. Evidence that substitution by potential suppliers is technically possible;
ii. Costs and time for switching production and distribution between products;
iii. Evidence that suppliers had previously switched production capacity in response to price changes. (Evidence that suppliers had considered switching may be considered but is given less weight.);
iv. Evidence potential suppliers have spare capacity (¶2.18).

---

373 EU Commission COMP/M.166 – *Tommas/Sarrio*, 24.2.1992.

374 Theoretically supply-side substitution should be considered in the context of defining the market, although the CCPC practice is in line with the approach adopted by many competition agencies. Baker (2007, p.134) argues that the agencies' approach is correct because *"it can be both difficult and confusing to ask one analytical step, market definition, to account for two economic forces, demand and supply substitution"*. However, he also states the US anti-trust agencies will assign market shares to supply-side substitutes which reflects the capacity that they would switch in response to a post-merger price increase, to avoid overstating the merging parties' market shares.

The CA ruled out possible supply-side substitution in *Tetra Laval/Carlisle*,[375] stating that it appeared unlikely that manufacturers of other types of limited purpose equipment could easily begin producing cheddaring machines in a timely fashion. It also stated that manufacturers of other limited purpose equipment might be deterred by the level of intellectual property rights involved in such equipment. In *Uniphar/Whelehan* the CA concluded that the relevant product market was the market for services provided by full-line pharmacy wholesalers. Short-line wholesalers were not considered to be in the same market as full-line wholesalers because the former provided a more limited service to pharmacies. The Determination did not consider the possibility that a price increase by full-line wholesalers might induce short-line wholesalers to provide a full-line service, i.e., it did not address the issue of supply-side substitution.[376] The CA in *Sarcon/Barlo*[377] concluded that neither of the parties could easily switch to producing products that were substitutes for those of the other in finding that there was no overlap between them. In *GDG/AEPL* the CA accepted that secondary space heating products might be part of the relevant market based on supply-side substitution.

In *Greenstar/Veolia*[378] the CA indicated that the provision of waste collection services to large and small (C&I) customers and to construction and demolition (C&D) customers were substitutes from both the demand and the supply-side. However, it analysed the transaction in the market for the provision of waste management services to large and small C&I

---

375 The UKOFT also concluded that manufacturers of other types of cheese processing equipment would not be easily able to move into the manufacture of cheddaring machines and block formers although it found that producers supplying the American market could easily adapt their equipment to meet the requirements of UK customers (UKOFT ME/2415/06 – *Tetra Laval/Carlisle*, 20.7.2006).

376 The CCPC took a similar approach in *Uniphar/CMR*. In *Uniphar/Murrays Medical*, however, the CCPC stated that it had assessed the impact on competition *"by reference to the narrowest possible relevant product market, namely the wholesale supply of ostomy and urinary medical products to community pharmacies"* without indicating whether this market included only full-line wholesalers or all wholesalers. The Determination cites market share data for both market definitions.

377 CA M/04/019 – *Sarcon/Barlo*, 22.4.2004.

378 The Determination concluded that the geographic market for large C&I customers with multiple sites was much wider than for individual C&I customers implying separate markets for large and small C&I customers. In *PandaGreen/Greenstar* the CCPC explicitly stated that there were separate markets for the provision of waste services to large C&I customers at multiple locations and individual C&I customers.

customers rather than a combined market for C&I and C&D customers, on the basis that the former constituted the narrowest possible market.

In a 2005 decision in relation to an alleged abuse of dominance, the CA concluded that domestic and C&I waste services were not interchangeable from either a demand or a supply-side perspective.[379] The CCPC subsequently defined separate markets for domestic and individual C&I waste collection services in *PandaGreen/Greenstar, Thornton's/A Plus*[380] and *PandaGreen/Exomex*. The EU Commission[381] and the High Court in *Panda Waste* also found that domestic waste collection services constitute a distinct product market.

> *"There is no dispute in this case as to the relevant product/service market; that is the provision of household waste collection services, excluding apartment complexes."*[382]

A CCPC report on household waste collection services stated, however, that in smaller towns, domestic and C&I waste collection services were usually combined.

> *"Side-by-side competition in waste collection...can provide waste operators with the opportunity to* ***combine the collection of household and commercial waste*** *which can increase efficiencies and lead to synergies.* ***In smaller towns, commercial collection is usually combined with household collection****...competition in the household waste collection market increases competition in the commercial collection market, as certain areas would not be viable as commercial collection only" (CCPC, 2018, September 30, ¶12.22, emphasis added).*

The fact that the two services can be combined implies that they are supply-side substitutes because it indicates that it is relatively easy for a supplier of one service to supply the other.[383]

---

379 CA Enforcement Decision E/05/002, 30.8.2005.

380 CCPC M/18/005, *Thornton's/A Plus,* 2.3.2018.

381 EU Commission Case No. COMP/M.4576 – *AVR/Van Gansewinkel*, 3.4.2007.

382 *Nurendale Limited t/a Panda Waste Services v. Dublin City Council, Dun Laoghaire/Rathdown County Council, Fingal County Council & South Dublin County Council*, [32009] IEHC 488, *(Panda Waste)*, ¶73.

383 In several mergers in the waste management sector the CA/CCPC also identified markets for waste processing; the sale of (non-glass) recyclables; management of local authority recycling facilities; and disposal of residual waste, *i.e.,* waste that cannot be recycled or composted (CA M/07/012 – *Bord na Móna/AES*, 2.5.2007; *PandaGreen/Greenstar*; and *PandaGreen/Exomex*). It has stated that the market for residual waste disposal includes

The CA concluded in *Kerry/Breeo* that natural and processed cheese were not supply-side substitutes based on the responses of two natural cheese suppliers to *"a detailed questionnaire"*. It also concluded that poultry (PCM) and non-poultry cooked meats (NPCM) were not supply-side substitutes, citing an unnamed respondent who suggested that the two products were produced in separate plants for health reasons.[384] In *Esso/Topaz* the CCPC stated that *"both demand and supply side substitution need to be considered"* in defining the market for terminalling services (¶68).

The CA/CCPC have defined motor fuels as a single product market in several cases, although petrol and diesel are not substitutes from a demand-side perspective.

> *"While recognising that motor fuels may not constitute a single unified market, the Authority nevertheless believes that...they share a number of common characteristics and the impact of the proposal on each of the segments is likely to be broadly similar" (Statoil/Conoco, ¶4.2).*

The CA subsequently concluded that there was a single retail market for motor fuels in *Maxol/Busselle, Statoil/Topaz, Topaz/Esso* and in several filling station cases. The EU Commission[385] and UK competition agencies[386] have also defined motor fuels as a single product market. In *Statoil Hydro/Conoco Phillips* the EU Commission acknowledged that petrol and diesel were not demand-side substitutes but were supply-side substitutes.

> *"There is no demand-side substitutability between these products because motorists must use the type of fuel appropriate to their vehicle. From a supply-side perspective, however, at least petrol and diesel are always distributed in the same retail outlets,*

---

landfill, incineration, and cement kilns. *"Incineration is therefore considered a substitute for landfill disposal"* (*PandaGreen/Knockharley*, ¶37).

384 The CA asked competitors of the merging parties whether plants could easily switch between producing PCM and NPCM but gave no indication of the number of parties who were asked, the number who responded, or the questions asked. There is no indication if other respondents shared this view. The CCPC concluded that all cooked meats constituted the narrowest possible market definition when analysing the subsequent sale of the *Kerry Foods* business (CCPC M/21/041 – *Pilgrim's Pride/Kerry Foods*, 10.9.2021).

385 EU Commission Case Nos. COMP/M.1383 – *Exxon/Mobil*, 29.9.1999; COMP/M.3291 – *Preem/Skandinaviska Raffinaderi*, 1.12.2003; COMP/M.3516 – *Repsol YPF/Shell Portugal*, 13.9.2004; COMP/M.4348 – *PKN/Mazeikiu*, 7.11.2006; COMP/M.4532 – *Lukoil/Conoco Phillips*, 21.2.2007; and COMP/M.4919 – *Statoil Hydro/Conoco Phillips*, 21.10.2008.

386 See, for example, UKOFT, ME/5139/11 – *Rontec/Total UK*, (¶s17-21), and UKCMA, Case No. ME/6471/14, *Motor Fuel/Murco.*

because service stations seek to serve the maximum number of automotive customers" (¶23).

Supply-side substitution describes a situation where, in response to a price increase for a particular product, producers of products which are not demand side substitutes switch to supplying the product which has increased in price. The suggestion by the CA in *Statoil/Conoco* that, although petrol and diesel constitute separate product markets from the demand side, competitive conditions are the same in both is arguably a more accurate description than the suggestion that they are supply-side substitutes.

The CCPC noted that there was some supply-side substitution between live music events and music festivals but, nevertheless, concluded they were in separate markets in *LN-Gaiety/MCD Productions*. In *Fane Valley/Smyths*[387] the CCPC stated that there was *"strong supply side substitutability between categories of animal feed producers as illustrated by the large number of animal feed producers supplying a variety of animal feed types"* (¶19).

Cluster Markets

The term cluster markets has sometimes been applied in cases where parties sell a range of non-competing products. Areeda & Hovenkamp (2021) list three conditions for a market to be regarded as a cluster market:

i. "Many customers" need or "prefer" the convenience of purchasing the combined range of products rather than any single product;
ii. economies of scope make it cheaper to supply the cluster rather than each good separately; and
iii. entering into competition with the cluster is difficult.

Although the CA/CCPC has not used the term, a number of its decisions involving wholesale and retail grocery, wholesale supply of alcoholic and non-alcoholic beverages, DIY stores and pharmacies (see above) could arguably be described as cluster markets. It has also suggested in several Determinations that the supply of food and drink to food service outlets may constitute a single product market, even in cases where the parties supplied only a sub-set of food and drink products,[388] which would tend to rule out the existence of a possible cluster market comprising the full range

---

387 CCPC M/19/020 – *Fane Valley/Smyths*, 14.8.2019.

388 See, for example, CCPC M/23/036 – *Musgrave/Doyle's Veg Prep*, 12.9.2023 in which the target supplied *"over 400 products, with a focus on the supply of fresh fruit, vegetables, exotics, salads, juices, cheese, and dairy products"* (¶6).

of such products. Baker (2007) cautions that cluster markets may prove misleading if competition from sellers of a partial range of products constrains the prices of sellers of the full range of cluster products.

Shapiro & Shelanski (2021) describe *Staples/Office Depot*[389] as a good example of a cluster market. The USFTC defined the relevant market as the sale and distribution of consumable office supplies to large business customers. The Court rejected the parties' arguments against such a market definition.

> *"Although a pen is not a functional substitute for a paperclip, it is possible to cluster consumable office supplies into one market for analytical convenience. Defining the market as a cluster market is justified in this case because 'market shares and competitive conditions are likely to be similar for the distribution of pens to large customers and the distribution of binder clips to large customers.'" (¶117).*

Banking services have also been viewed as cluster markets in several cases. The US Supreme Court in *Philadelphia National Bank* held that the relevant product market was *"the cluster of products (various kinds of credit) and services (such as checking accounts and trust administration) denoted by the term 'commercial banking.'"*[390] The Court applied the same market definition in six further bank merger cases over the following 12 years (Wilson & Klovers, 2021). The USDoJ rejected the cluster market approach and defined separate product markets for individual banking services in *First Union/Core States*.[391]

The Australian Trade Practices Commission (ATPC) adopted a cluster market definition in *Westpac/Challenge*[392] but its successor, the Australian Competition & Consumer Commission (ACCC), rejected this approach in *Westpac/Bank of Melbourne*,[393] defining a series of separate product markets, although it identified a cluster market for SME banking services. OECD (2000) observed that it was costly for SMEs to unbundle loans from other banking services because providers of current account services to SMEs enjoy an information advantage enabling them to better assess credit risk.

---

389 *Federal Trade Commission v. Staples, Inc.*, 970 F. Suppl. 1066 (DDC) 1997.

390 *United States v. Philadelphia National Bank*, 374 U.S. 321 (1963) at 356.

391 The parties were required to divest 32 branches and $1.1 billion in assets. The Federal Reserve, which also has a role in approving bank mergers, has continued to define cluster markets resulting in some inter-agency conflict (McCarthy, 1997). Technological changes including the development of online banking may have made it far easier for customers to obtain individual banking services from different suppliers.

392 ATPC, *Westpac/Challenge*, 1995.

393 ACCC, *Westpac/Bank of Melbourne*, 25.7.1997.

Cruickshank (2005) found that the provision of overdrafts and term loans to SMEs was effectively tied to the provision of current account services in the UK. The EU Commission has considered whether individual retail banking products represent separate relevant product markets or whether several retail banking products may form part of a cluster market, without reaching a definitive conclusion.[394]

The CCPC in *Bank of Ireland/KBC* concluded that *"the relevant product market is that for the provision of mortgages to all types of customer… and that there is no reason to find a wider product market, nor to further segment the market"* (¶4.46). It took a similar view in *PTSB/Ulster Bank* (¶3.49). The CCPC noted that there were horizontal overlaps between the parties in relation to other banking services but concluded that there was no need to define product markets for such services as the overlap was minimal. The conclusion that the provision of mortgages constituted a separate product market to other banking services seems justified. If the market were defined as comprising a cluster of banking services competition from specialist mortgage providers would be excluded (OECD, 2000). In financial services, different products within a particular cluster could have very different geographic markets which is inconsistent with their being part of a single product market (Rozanski & Rubinfeld, 1997). In *AIB/Ulster Bank* and *PTSB/Ulster Bank* the CCPC, in addition to a mortgage market, also defined a relevant product market for lending to microenterprises, i.e., enterprises with an annual turnover of less than €2m, which constituted a different market to lending to larger SMEs.

Digital markets have also been viewed as examples of cluster markets (Hovenkamp, 2022). In this context the EU Commission (2021, p.7) defines cluster markets in the following terms:

> *"A cluster market exists when transactional complementarities are such that consumers do not consider unbundling as a suitable alternative to purchasing the bundled products."*

Market definition may be extremely complicated in such markets (*ibid.*), although Hovenkamp (2022) suggests that in such cases it may be best to avoid market definition altogether, noting that digital markets are

---

394 See, for example, Case No. COMP/M.3894 – *Unicredito/HVB*, 18.10.2005 and Case No. COMP/M.4844 – *Fortis/ABN Amro*, 3.10.2007.

particularly susceptible to direct measures of market power that do not require market definition.[395]

Two-sided Markets

Media mergers accounted for almost 13% of all mergers notified to the CA/CCPC between 2003 and 2023. Many of these involved newspapers and/or local radio stations, with some involving television broadcasters. Newspapers and commercial broadcasting (both radio and television) are classic examples of what economists refer to as two-sided markets.[396] A two-sided market is one in which:

i. Two sets of agents interact through an intermediary or platform; and
ii. Decisions of each set of agents affects outcomes for the other set of agents, typically through an externality (Rysman, 2009).

The CA/CCPC has repeatedly acknowledged that newspapers and radio stations cater for two different customer types: readers/listeners and advertisers.[397] The higher their readership/listenership, the more attractive they are to advertisers.

Market definition is more complicated in two-sided markets than in traditional markets. In two-sided markets the profitability of a price increase on one side of the market will also depend on the reactions of users on the other side of the market and induced feedback effects due to indirect network effects. Where a SSNIP test is possible, it is unclear whether only the price on one side of the market should be increased and, if so, which one, or whether both should be increased simultaneously (Caccinelli & Toledano, 2018).[398]

While the CA/CCPC has recognised the two-sided nature of media markets, it has frequently analysed them as separate markets.[399] *Irish Times/Sappho*, for example, refers to *"separate markets for readers and advertisers given the two-sided nature of the newspaper industry"* (¶3.3). Two-sided markets involve two inter-connected markets rather than two

---

395 In many cases, digital platforms offer services to consumers for free which makes market definition difficult.

396 On-line platforms are another example of two-sided markets (Hesse, 2007).

397 See, for example, *SRH/FM104*; CA M/05/065 – *Johnston Press/Leinster*, 2.12.2005; and *Metro/Herald AM*.

398 There is no universally accepted or valid criterion for defining markets in the case of two- or multisided platforms (EU Commission, 2021).

399 See, for example, *INM/CMNL*.

separate markets. Filistrucchi *et al.* (2012; 2014) point out that many competition agencies have struggled with the two-sided nature of newspaper markets, failing to fully consider the presence, sign and the extent of indirect network effects in such markets and have sometimes considered only one side of the market or considered each side separately.[400] Both the EU Commission and UKCC recognised that the type of reader differentiates newspapers from advertisers' point of view but failed to acknowledge that the quantity of advertising may affect reader demand.[401] CA/CCPC Determinations involving mergers of television broadcasters have also analysed the market for viewers and television advertising as two separate markets.[402]

The CA in *Independent Newspapers/Tribune* and in its 1995 *Interim Report on the Newspaper Industry* (CA, 1995, March 30) defined separate markets for national newspapers, local newspapers, and freesheets; for daily and Sunday newspapers; and for Irish and UK titles. The latter report also defined separate markets for quality and tabloid newspapers. The CA adopted a similar approach in two subsequent *"enforcement decisions"*.[403] In *Irish Times/Sappho* the CCPC implicitly concluded that quality and tabloid titles were part of a single market comprising all daily national newspapers but advanced no explanation for this conclusion. Although the CCPC stated in *Reach/ISL* that, in light of a third-party submission, it would consider whether there were separate markets for quality and tabloid newspapers, the Determination contained no new analysis and simply stated that there was no need to depart from its views on market definition in *Trinity Mirror/Northern & Shell.*

---

400 Examples of the former include UKCC ME/1618/04 – *Archant/Independent News & Media*, 22.9.2004. UKOFT ME/1586/05 – *Future/Highbury House*, 14.4.2005, is an example of the latter.

401 EU Commission Case Nos. COMP/M.423 – *Newspaper Publishing*, 14.3.1994; COMP/M.1455 – *Gruner+Jahr/Financial Times/JV*, 20.4.1999; and COMP/M.3420 – *GIMD/Socpresse*, 16.6.2004. The CA recognised this in *Johnston Press/Leinster Leader*.

402 See, for example, CA M/08/021 – *TV3/Kish Media*, 18.8.2008; CCPC M/15/069 – *ITV/UTV*, 12.1.2016. CCPC M/16/038 – *Liberty Global/UTV Ireland*, 7.9.2016 suggests that broadcasting platforms also constitute two-sided markets as the number of channels on a platform is important for attracting subscribers. *Liberty Global/TV3* (¶69) also cited the interaction between a platform's channel numbers and its ability to attract viewers.

403 CA E/03/003 – *Agreements between Independent Newspapers (Ireland) Limited and newspaper retailers allegedly fixing the retail price of Independent newspaper titles*, 10.11.2003; and CA E/03/004 – *Agreements between The Irish Times Limited and newspaper retailers allegedly fixing the retail price of The Irish Times newspaper*, 24.7.2003.

In *Johnston Press/Leinster Leader* the CA implied that regional newspapers constituted a distinct product market stating that the proposed transaction's *"impact on the structure of regional newspaper publishing in the State, post-merger is minimal"* (¶37). The CA stated in *Independent/Champion*[404] that it considered national and regional/local newspapers to be different product markets (¶12).

The CA in *Metro/Herald AM* stated that *"the relevant market for readership encompasses all daily (morning and evening) paid-for and free newspapers"* (¶3.7). The CA had previously concluded that the merging titles were not in the same market as national daily newspapers, pointing out that *Metro* was targeted at ABC1 readers in the GDA, *"half of whom would not have read a morning newspaper"*, whereas *The Irish Times* was targeted at a national readership. It further stated that there were significant differences in content between *Metro* and *The Irish Times*.[405] The *Metro/Herald AM* Determination states:

> *"Contrary to some initial expectations of the parties, neither of the free daily newspapers developed a readership unique to themselves" (¶3.9).*

The statement is a further indication that the merging parties' freesheet newspapers were not substitutes for daily national titles and were, therefore, not part of the same market.[406] The CCPC in *INM/CMNL* stated that in previous Determinations it *"has consistently held"* that local/regional newspapers constituted a distinct market from national daily/evening newspapers (¶21) a claim repeated in *Formpress/River Media*.[407]

The CA/CCPC has frequently concluded that different media channels constituted separate advertising markets, although it has not always been consistent.[408] The CA stated in *SRH/Capital Radio* that radio advertising:

---

404 CA M/08/003 – *Independent/Champion*, 10.3.2008.

405 CA M/05/071 – *Associated Newspapers/Irish Times/Metro/Fortunegreen* (*Fortunegreen JV*), 1.12.2005.

406 The SSNIP test cannot be used to define markets for freesheets since it depends on the impact on sales of a 5% price increase.

407 US evidence suggests some substitutability between national and local newspapers, although not necessarily sufficient for them to be regarded as constituting a single market. Increased availability of the *New York Times* in more than 100 US cities in the late 1990s resulted in a decline in local newspaper circulation among better educated consumers and an increase among those with lower education levels while local newspapers reduced their national and foreign news coverage and increased local news coverage (George & Waldfogel, 2006).

408 The CCPC's competition analysis distinguished online from offline advertising in *INM/Caltray* (*op .cit.*); *Trinity Mirror/Northern & Shell*; CCPC M/21/052 – *DMG/Nalac*, 18.6.2023; and CCPC M/23/038 – *Mediahuis/Euractiv*, 19.9.2023. The EU Commission

i. Had distinguishing features from other forms of advertising;
ii. Involved substantially less production and placement costs;
iii. Less production time; and
iv. Could be placed at short notice.[409]

The CA found no overlap between the merging parties in *Emap/SRH*[410] on the grounds that radio and magazine advertising and local newspaper and magazine advertising constituted separate product markets (¶s19 & 22). US studies have reached different conclusions. Dertouzos & Trautman (1990) found little evidence that broadcasting, and newspaper advertising were in the same market, while Frank (2008) found that different media channels were highly substitutable for alcoholic drinks advertisers.

In *Trader Publishing/Webzone*,[411] a merger of two providers of online motor vehicle advertising services, the CA implied that different forms of media advertising were substitutes, stating that the proposed transaction raised no competition concerns because *"dealers and private parties will continue to be able to choose from a wide variety of print and broadcasting media and/or in an increasing number of online motor vehicle advertising websites in which to advertise"* (¶24).[412] In *Irish Times/MyHome* the CA adopted a narrow market definition limited to online property advertising.[413]

The CA/CCPC has been inconsistent in relation to whether advertising in national and regional/local newspapers constitutes one or two markets. In *Johnston Press/Leinster Leader* the CA argued that national newspapers were alternatives to the merging parties' titles for advertisers wishing to advertise in the limited number of local areas in which there was an overlap

---

concluded that online advertising was in a separate market to offline or print advertising in EU Commission Case No. COMP/M.4731 – *Google/DoubleClick*, 11.3.2008.

409 The CA concluded that radio advertising was a separate market from other forms of advertising in CA M/04/003 – *Radio 2000/News 106*, 5.3.2004; *SRH/Highland Radio*; CA M/06/067 – *Connacht Tribune/Galway Bay FM*, 24.10.2006; *Thomas Crosbie Holdings/WKW FM*; and CCPC M/16/033 – *NewsCorp/Wireless Communications*, 2.8.2016. The CA noted that the EU Commission had adopted a similar approach in EU Commission Case No. COMP/M.779 - *Bertelsmann/CLT*, 7.10.1996.

410 CA M/05/036 – *Emap/SRH*, 28.7.2005.

411 CA M/05/061 – *Trader Publishing/Webzone*, 3.11.2005.

412 Ratliff & Rubinfeld (2010) note that, while online advertising may exert a competitive constraint on other advertising channels, it is less certain that offline advertising constrains the price of online advertising.

413 CA M/06/059 – *Irish Times/My Home*, 25.9.2006 states: *"To the extent that print property advertising is a substitute for online property advertising and there are competition concerns, such advertising will be viewed as a possible competitive constraint"* (¶11). This issue was not subsequently addressed in the Determination.

between the parties' newspaper titles.[414] In *Irish Times/Gazette*[415] the CA concluded that there was limited or no overlap between the parties because the *Gazette* titles' advertising was specific to the Dublin suburbs in which they were distributed. Similarly, in *Irish Times/Relevance*[416] the CA stated:

> *"The difference in the target demographic audiences of the ITL as a national daily newspaper and the six Gazette titles as local weekly newspapers indicates that these publications would not be considered substitutes by advertisers" (¶12).*

In *Johnston Press/Clonnad* and *Independent/Champion* the CA argued that local/regional and national newspaper advertising constituted separate markets.

In *Metro/Herald AM,* however, the CA *"concluded that daily paid-for and free newspapers are part of the same advertising market"* (¶3.27). This is inconsistent with the earlier *Fortunegreen JV* decision which noted that *Metro* was targeted at readers within the GDA:

> *"Due to the geographic coverage and demographics of Metro's target audience, advertising on* Metro *is **complementary rather than substitutable** for the joint venture partners' [national] newspaper advertising.*
>
> *The Authority concludes that the introduction of* Metro *expands the target advertising audience to include customers who would not have bought or read a morning newspaper" (¶s 19-20, emphasis added).*

The CA in *Metro/Herald FM* asked advertising agencies *"to indicate which newspapers **would also be included** in the advertising mix when they advise their clients to advertise in* Metro *or* Herald AM*"* (¶3.23, emphasis added). The question suggests that the merging titles were complements rather than substitutes for advertising in national newspaper. The correct question is whether advertisers would switch advertising in national titles to the merging parties' freesheets or *vice versa* in response to a 5% increase in their respective advertising rates. Evidence of advertiser switching following the launch of the merging titles was inconclusive.[417]

---

414 The decision also stated that 60-70% of advertising in the parties' newspaper titles was local in nature.

415 CA M/07/010 – *Irish Times/Gazette,* 22.03.2007.

416 CA M/08/007 – *Irish Times/Relevance,* 25.3.2008.

417 According to the Determination, two-thirds of advertising agencies who responded indicated that there had been some reallocation of advertising spend away from other

In *CMNL/North Dublin Publications,* the CCPC stated that it had followed the approach in *Metro/Herald AM* in analysing the impact of the transaction on competition in the market for *"the sale of newspaper (both free and paid-for)* advertising" (¶16).[418] The CCPC stated in *INM/CMNL* that it *"has consistently held"* that *"the supply of advertising space in local/regional newspapers can be treated as a distinct market from the supply of advertising space in national daily/evening newspapers"* (¶21).[419]

Irish Times/Sappho cited *Metro/Herald AM* in support of a conclusion that advertising in quality and tabloid national newspapers constituted a single market (¶3.4).[420] This is inconsistent with *INM/CMNL* which stated that advertisers' demand for newspaper advertising depended on the demographic characteristics of a newspaper's readership (¶43). Several EU Commission decisions also concluded that the type of readers differentiates newspapers from advertisers' point of view, implying separate advertising markets for quality and tabloid newspapers (Filistrucchi *et al.*, 2012).

The CA in *SKY/VMtv*[421] distinguished between advertising on premium content and non-premium content TV channels and found that there was a horizontal overlap between the parties in respect of the latter. However, it concluded that the transaction would not result in an SLC because the transaction resulted *"in a minimal increase in Sky's share of total [television] advertising revenue in the State"* (¶20).

Measuring Market Power Directly

Market definition may not be necessary, particularly in unilateral effects cases, if market power can be measured directly (Baker & Shapiro, 2008;

---

newspapers following the launch of the merging parties' freesheet titles, while a similar proportion of direct advertisers and more than 50% of indirect advertisers reported no reallocation of advertising spend following their launch. The Determination states that three internal documents of the parties indicated that they viewed freesheets as competing with paid-for newspapers, while another document from one of them suggested that it considered freesheets were in a separate advertising market.

418 CCPC M/18/001 – *CMNL/North Dublin Publications*, 8.2.2018. The purchaser published several regional newspaper titles while the target published three weekly freesheets.

419 It subsequently treated advertising in national and local/regional newspapers as separate markets in *Formpress/River Media; Formpress/Midland Tribune; Trinity Mirror/Northern & Shell* and *Reach/ISL*.

420 The latter Determination stated that daily paid for and free newspapers constituted a single advertising market but included no analysis of whether there was a single newspaper advertising market comprising quality and tabloid newspapers.

421 CA M/10/020 – *Sky/VMtv*, 29.6.2010.

Werden, 2009) a point acknowledged in both CAMG2002 and CCPCMG2014. Glasner & Sullivan (2020) observed that it is doubtful that such measures could replace market definition in all cases. Frequently measuring market power directly is not possible due to data deficiencies and few, if any, CA/CCPC Determinations have relied on direct measures of market power.

Economists have proposed various methods for measuring market power directly. The Lerner Index, for example, uses the difference between price and marginal cost to measure of the degree of firms' market power (Lerner, 1934).[422] Kamerschen & Kohler (1993) state that a firm's market power can be measured by its residual elasticity of demand. The steeper (more inelastic), a firm's residual demand curve, the greater its market power. Werden (1998) states that it has become common for US courts to accept economic evidence on residual demand elasticities. The US Supreme Court cited Areeda & Kaplow (1988) in *Eastman Kodak*, stating *"[w]hat constrains [a] defendant's ability to raise prices... is 'the elasticity of demand faced by the defendant – the degree to which its sales fall... as its price rises.'"*[423] In several cases US courts have stated that market share was just a mechanism for estimating market power and the court should use better measures of market power when available.[424]

Motta (2004) cautions that, even where market power can be measured directly, it may be a good idea to complement such analysis with a more traditional approach based on an analysis of the market in which merging parties operate. Although USHMG2010 placed less emphasis on market definition in favour of a greater focus on direct evidence of competitive effects, §4 states that, in any enforcement action, the agencies would normally identify relevant markets in which the merger may substantially lessen competition. Shapiro & Shelanski (2021, p.60) note that *"the [antitrust] agencies have continued, without exception, to define relevant markets and measure market concentration when they challenge mergers in court."*

---

422 The Lerner Index is expressed as:

$$(p-c)/p \quad [6.4],$$

where p equals price and c is marginal cost. The index is the left-hand side of the profit maximisation condition for a monopolist which is equal to the inverse of the elasticity of the monopolist's demand curve, i.e.:

$$(p-c)/p = 1/e \quad [6.5].$$

423 *Eastman Kodak Co. v. Image Technical Services Inc.*, 540 US 451 (1992).

424 See, for example, *Allen-Myland, Inc. v. IBM Corporation*, 33 F.3d 194, 209 (3rd Cir. 1994); *United States v. Baker Hughes, Inc.*, 908 F 2d 981, 992 (DC Cir. 1990) and *Ball Memorial Hospital Inc. v. Mutual Hospital Ins.*, 784 F.2d 1325, 1336 (7th Cir., 1986).

The CA/CCPC's Approach to Market Definition

While it is not always necessary to define the relevant market in merger cases, this should not be interpreted as a *carte blanche* to ignore market definition. The CA/CCPC has frequently asserted that it was not necessary to reach a definitive conclusion on market definition because the outcome would be the same irrespective of whether the market was defined narrowly or broadly. There are several problems with this approach.

A broad market definition may suggest that an SLC will not occur because it includes products or geographic areas which are not close substitutes and are unlikely to exercise a significant competitive constraint on the merging parties, i.e. it may result in a false negative. Hovenkamp (2024) notes that casual market definitions which ignore the link between market definition and market power can result in overly broad market definitions as in the *Cellophane* case.[425]

The CA in *European Refreshments/Fresh Trading* advanced an Irish version of the "Lake Erie defence" (see above) stating that possible product market definitions ranged from a narrow market definition limited to smoothies to a wide definition comprising all non-alcoholic beverages (NABs), including carbonated soft drinks, packaged water, non-carbonated drinks, iced teas, fruit juices, waters, sports and energy drinks, dairy and hot tea and coffee (¶21).[426] There appears to be no evidence for such a wide market definition which is inconsistent with previous CA/CCPC cases and international precedents.[427] Although the CA did not reach a conclusion on market definition, the suggestion that the market could include all NABs affords a degree of validity to such a market definition which is unwarranted and creates a somewhat dubious precedent.

---

425 It can also sometimes result in errors in the opposite direction.

426 CA M/13/009 – *European Refreshments/Fresh Trading*, 17.4.2013. The parties combined market share ranged from [5-10]% to [30-40]% depending on market definition.

427 The CA previously rejected such a wide market definition in *Britvic/C&C*, based on a quantitative analysis, while in an earlier Determination involving the acquisition of a minority shareholding by the Purchaser in the Target, the CA indicated that the widest possible market was that for all juices (CA M/09/009 – *European Refreshments/Fresh Trading*, 7.5.2009). Subsequently, CCPC M/18/018 – *SHS/3V*, 15.3.2018 followed *Britvic/C&C* and analysed competitive effects in the squashes market. See also EU Commission Case Nos. COMP/M.833 – *Coca-Cola/Carlsberg*, 11.9.1997; COMP/M.2276 – *Coca-Cola/Nestlé/JV*, 27.9.2001; COMP/M.2504 – *Cadbury Schweppes/Pernod Ricard*, 29.10.2001; COMP/M.6924 – *Refresco/Pride Foods*, 4.10.2013; UKOFT, ME/1955/05 – *Cott Beverages/ Macaw*, 12.12.2005; ME/4091/09 – *Coca-Cola/Fresh Trading*, 11.6.2009; UKCC, Case No. ME/5801/12 – *A.G. Barr/Britvic*, 9.7.2013; UKCMA, Case No. ME/6705/17 – *Refresco/Cott*, 3.1.2018; and *FTC v. Coca-Cola*.

In *Citylink/GoBus* the CCPC argued that the outcome would be the same whether the market was defined narrowly as express coach services on the Galway-Dublin/Dublin Airport route or all interurban public transport services including bus and rail. For passengers wishing to travel from Dublin to Belfast, an express coach service from Galway to Dublin is clearly not a substitute. Thus, the wider market definition proposed by the CCPC includes products which are not close substitutes for those of the merging parties resulting in a potential false negative.

The notifying parties in *Chadwicks/Haylen*[428] argued that the market could be defined broadly as the distribution of all types of building materials. The target supplied a limited range of specialised products which were not substitutes for other building materials such as concrete blocks, timber, plasterboard and so on. Although the CCPC analysed the transaction based on the narrower market definition, it stated that the outcome would have been the same had the market been defined to include all building materials, although this would have included a wide range of products which were clearly not substitutes for those supplied by the target.

In many cases, while stating that the outcome would be the same if the market was defined narrowly or broadly, the CA/CCPC has applied a narrow market definition. As applying a narrow market definition will frequently suffice to establish that an SLC will not occur, there is no obvious reason for stating that the outcome would be the same whether the market was defined narrowly or broadly when the latter definition may constitute a false negative. Referring to potential wider markets may afford them a degree of plausibility which is not justified by the evidence.[429] The

428 CCPC M/20/040 – *Chadwicks/Haylen*, 4.2.2021. The target supplied specialist architectural hardware products including ironmongery products used in the functioning of doors such as locks, hinges and door handles, as well as non-door-related products. Other building supply products are clearly not substitutes for such products. The CCPC applied a broad product market for all building supplies as well as narrower product markets in CCPC M/21/080 – *Grafton (Chadwicks)/Sitetech*, 2.2.2022, although again the Target only supplied a limited range of products which were not substitutes for all building materials. The Determination acknowledged that the parties were not close competitors. It adopted a similar approach in CCPC M/22/022 – *Wolseley Group/Cooperstorm*, 27.5.2022, where the parties supplied plumbing and heating products. In contrast a broad market definition was appropriate in *Associated Hardware/National Hardware* as the parties distributed a broad range of building materials.

429 As previously stated, if a narrow market indicates that an SLC is unlikely, then it is generally safe to conclude that an SLC is unlikely in a broader market, unless the narrow market definition puts the parties in separate markets. If a narrow market suggests a possible SLC, however, the correct market must be defined in order to avoid a false negative.

CA/CCPC approach also arguably establishes a worrying precedent that *"market definition does not matter"*.[430]

The CA/CCPC has also argued on occasion that the outcome would be the same if the market was defined narrowly or broadly despite evidence ruling out a broader market definition. The CCPC in *Baxter/Fannin Compounding* stated that its conclusions would be the same whether the market was defined narrowly as compounded chemotherapy medicines or broadly comprising all types of compounded medicines. The Determination acknowledged that cancer patients could not switch from compounded chemotherapy medicines to other compounded medicines in response to a 5-10% price increase for the former. It also acknowledged that producers of other compounded medicines had no interest in supplying compounded chemotherapy medicines largely because of high costs and onerous regulatory requirements which provided that the latter products had to be compounded in separate facilities to other compounded medicines, ruling out supply-side substitution. The CCPC argued that the outcome would be the same whether the market was defined as the State or wider, although the Determination stated that importing compounded chemotherapy medicines from outside the State was not a viable option for customers, ruling out a possible geographic market wider than the State.

In *Elvery's/Mahers*, which involved the acquisition of a sport goods store in Cork City, the CCPC stated that the outcome would be the same whether it adopted a national market, or a narrow market limited to Cork City.[431] It seems highly unlikely that an individual outlet in Cork City would exercise a significant competitive constraint on sports retail outlets throughout the State or *vice versa*. The CCPC stated that the acquirer's nearest store, which was 60 kilometres from the Target store, was unlikely to be a close competitor, ruling out a possible national market. In *Heineken/Coman's I* the CCPC stated that the parties *"operate, to a large extent, in different parts of the*

[430] It is perhaps significant that notifying parties regularly submit that it is not necessary to define the relevant market because the impact on competition will be the same whether the market is defined narrowly or broadly.

[431] Previously the CA had stated that *"it is unreasonable to maintain, from a demand-side perspective, that the relevant geographic market is as wide as the State"* and only considered local geographic markets in *JD Sports/Champion Sports*, although the merging parties operated multiple sports retail outlets throughout the State. The Determination noted that the UKOFT and UKCC had defined local geographic markets in UKOFT ME/3986/08 – *Sports Direct/JJB*, 1.5.2009 and UKCC, Case No. ME/3986/08 – *Sports Direct/JJB*, 16.3.2010.

State" (¶28) but nevertheless considered both a national market and local markets in each of four counties.

DCU/St. Patrick's College Drumcondra et al.[432] described *"the narrowest possible relevant product markets"* as *"undergraduate and postgraduate programmes in teacher education"* (¶23) but went on to state that some of the parties' teacher education programmes were *"not substitutable with each other"* (¶25).[433] This indicates the existence of separate markets and is inconsistent with the narrowest possible market including all of the various programmes.

DekaBank/Whitewater[434] involved the acquisition of a shopping centre in Newbridge, County Kildare by the owner of another shopping centre 210 kilometres away in Cork City. The CCPC, while stating that it had not come to a definitive conclusion, analysed the transaction based on the narrowest possible market definition which placed the centres in separate markets. The prospectus for the Mahon Shopping Centre stated that 62% of shoppers visiting the centre lived within its core catchment of Cork City and suburbs, a further 28% came from other parts of County Cork and the remaining 10% from the wider Munster area (¶18). There appears to be no obvious reason for not coming to a definitive conclusion and leaving open the possibility of a wider geographic market given clear evidence that the two centres were in different geographic markets. *Enva/Rilta* described the State as the narrowest possible geographic market, while stating that it was not necessary to reach a conclusion on the relevant geographic market for hazardous waste products.[435]

In some cases, the outcome clearly depended on market definition, despite CA/CCPC claims to the contrary. *Glanbia/Wexford Creamery* cited econometric evidence indicating that the target was a significant competitor of the purchaser within a County Wexford market but not in a wider national or regional market comprising the province of Leinster excluding Dublin, suggesting that any conclusions in relation to competitive effects

---

432 CCPC M/16/032 – *DCU/St. Patrick's College Drumcondra et al.*, 9.8.2016.

433 The CCPC found that the primary teacher education programmes of two institutions were not substitutable because they were for teachers in Catholic and non-Catholic schools respectively. The other merging parties' post-primary teacher training programmes were not substitutes because they *"cover different subjects"* (¶25).

434 CCPC M/16/004 – *DekaBank/Whitewater*, 3.3.2016.

435 According to the Determination, Northern Ireland-based operators provided little, if any, competition in hazardous waste collection due to the costs and difficulties involved in transporting such material across the border, ruling out a geographic market wider than the State.

depended on geographic market definition. The CA concluded that the transaction would not result in an SLC in the wider regional market having stated that it would consider the impact of the transaction in a market limited to County Wexford (¶3.26).

In *Orpea/First Care* the CCPC expressed *"potential concerns regarding Orpea's **market share** in Co. Kildare"* (¶31, emphasis added), implicitly acknowledging that no concerns arose in respect of three alternative broader market definitions which were also considered. No evidence was advanced that Kildare constituted a distinct market or that nursing home operators in Kildare were not subject to an effective competitive constraint from competitors outside the county. **Table 6.3** shows that concentration levels in more widely-defined markets were not problematic confirming that the CCPC's concerns depended on a specific, narrow market definition.[436]

Table 6.3: Market Concentration in Nursing Home Beds

Geographic Market	Parties Combined Market Share	Post-Merger HHI	HHI Change
State	6.1	544.6	15.2
GDA	13.0	493.0	76.2
County Dublin	10.9	959.7	39.2
County Kildare	25.7	1,069.2	193.0

Source: Orpea/First Care.

In *CVC/Celtic Rugby*, the CCPC raised concerns in a potential narrow market for the sale of broadcast rights for Rugby Union events, while stating that no issues arose in relation to a wider market for the broadcast rights for all major sports events.[437] It is incorrect to claim that the outcome of these cases

436 CAMG2002 and CCPCMG2014 both state that competition concerns are unlikely in markets where post-merger concentration as measured by the HHI is less than 1,000 (see **Chapter 7**), which was the case for all of the other possible market definitions in *Orpea/First Care*. This case and the two waste cases described previously illustrate the potential for *"regulatory hold-up"* due to the lack of procedures affording parties an opportunity to argue against a Phase 2 referral (see **Chapter 4**). The US anti-trust agencies do not apply the narrowest possible market definition when challenging mergers due to concerns that courts may look sceptically on markets that appear to have been defined too narrowly (Nocke & Whinston, 2022).

437 The two tournaments were in separate temporal markets (see below). Subsequently, in *CVC/Six Nations Rugby*, the CCPC decided that it was not necessary to consider the potential

would have been the same whether the market was defined narrowly or broadly. When a narrow market definition indicates potential concerns, it is necessary to define the correct market in order to avoid a false positive. In both these cases the failure to define the market correctly arguably resulted in false positives, resulting in the unnecessary application of remedies.

In *Grafton/Heiton* the CA defined the market narrowly as DIY superstores rather than all DIY outlets but argued that its competitive analysis *"would not be affected by a broader market definition"* (¶3.14). It is highly unlikely, however, that the case would have gone to a Phase 2 investigation if a wider market definition had applied as the parties had a combined market share of 25% in the wider market but 70% in the narrower market (Massey, 2010).[438]

The CCPC in *Pat the Baker/Irish Pride* stated that it did not consider that the relevant product market was necessarily that for all packaged bread as claimed by the parties. Market enquiries, a consumer survey and a review of the parties' econometric analysis of scanner data, *"indicate a number of possible narrower markets"* (¶24). The CCPC considered separate markets *"for packaged white bread and packaged brown bread and for buns, baps and rolls"* (¶25).

In numerous cases where the CA/CCPC stated that it did not need to reach *"a definitive conclusion"* on the relevant market it, nevertheless, based its conclusions on an analysis of a specific market. The CA implicitly concluded that whisky constituted a distinct product market in *Möet Hennessy/Glenmorangie.*[439] Subsequently in *Diageo/Bushmills*[440] it concluded that an SLC would not arise *inter alia* because Pernod Ricard was the market leader in the state *"in relation to the Irish whiskey market"* (¶19).

---

narrow market for Rugby Union broadcast rights and concluded that the transaction would not result in an SLC in the wider broadcast market for all sports events.

438 The CA cleared the proposed transaction on the basis that entry barriers were low. CCPC M/23/051 – *Chadwicks/Rooney's*, 23.10.2023 stated that the CCPC saw *"no need to endorse"* the *Grafton/Heiton* market definition and it analysed a market comprising all DIY stores because (i) although the target was not a DIY superstore, it was a large DIY store and (ii) offered a product range comparable to that offered by DIY superstores.

439 CA M/04/065 – *Möet Hennessy/Glenmorangie*, 29.11.2004. The CA found no overlap between the parties as Glenmorangie only produced and supplied scotch whisky which was not produced or supplied by Möet Hennessy.

440 CA M/05/039 – *Diageo/Bushmills*, 4.8.2005. Diageo argued for a narrow market defined on the basis of origin, while Bushmills argued for a broad market comprising all whiskies. The CA cited EU Commission decisions in Case Nos. COMP/M.938 – *Guinness/Grand Metropolitan*, 15.10.1997 and COMP/M.2268 – *Pernod Ricard/Diageo/Seagram*, 9.5.2001, which identified separate whisk(e)y markets based on origin.

In *Hachette/Time Warner* the CA noted that the parties would have a combined share of [10-20%] of total book sales. It concluded that the transaction raised no competition concerns because (i) it resulted in only a small increase in market concentration and (ii) post-merger there would be a sufficient number of large competitors. Both findings rest on an implicit, albeit unstated, assumption that there is a single market for books. The Determination, however, went on to say that *"because the proposed acquisition would not substantially lessen competition in the State, it is not considered necessary to define the relevant market, or markets"* (¶7).[441] In *DCC/Kent* the CCPC stated that it did not need to come to a definitive view on the relevant product market but cleared the transaction based on the parties' low market shares.[442]

The CA claimed in *LL/TPDL/FIL/Freshmills/Drummonds*[443] that its conclusions would be the same if the market was defined narrowly or broadly, although the evidence for a broad product market was rather weak.

> *"However, given the complementary nature of agricultural inputs from the perspective of the end customer (i.e., the farmer), the Authority considers that the supply of agricultural inputs by agri-merchants to farmers* ***could*** *represent a single relevant product market" (¶25, emphasis added).*

The CA did not define a geographic market but indicated that it was likely to be regional:

> *"...if a farmer decides to source supplies of agricultural inputs from an agri-merchant located outside the farmer's locality, he will face additional transport costs...Thus, it is likely that agri-merchants compete in regional geographic markets for the retail supply of agricultural inputs to farmers" (¶29).*

Subsequently, the CCPC stated that a regional geographic market for agricultural inputs would be consistent with this case and stated that stores

---

441 CA M/06/009 – *Hachette/Time Warner Book Group*, 4.3.2006. In an earlier decision, the CA implicitly acknowledged the possible existence of several different book markets, citing market share data for various book genres. It concluded that it was not necessary to define the market because the proposed transaction would not result in a significant increase in concentration in any potential market. CA M/04/048 – *Hachette/Hodder Headline*, 13.9.2004. The UKOFT took a similar view, although it indicated that *"third parties broadly support the parties' view that there is substitutability across genres: the available evidence suggests that most publishers are active across the range of general literature genres and customer purchasing patterns tend to be similarly varied* (UKOFT, ME/1219/04 - *Hachette/Hodder Headline*, 15.9.2004).

442 CA M/12/033 – *DCC/Kent*, 27.2.2024.

443 CA M/09/010 – *LL/TPDL/FIL/Freshmills/Drummonds*, 18.6.2009.

located more than 100 kilometres apart did not compete with one another in *Fane Valley/Lakeland Dairies*.[444]

In *Valeo/Wardell/Robert Roberts* the CCPC identified an overlap between the merging parties in relation to 20 *"product categories"*. It concluded that no competitive issues would arise in 16 of these categories because the increment in [market] share would be small, implying that each category constituted a relevant market. The CCPC concluded that there would be sufficient competitors to prevent a post-merger price increase in three other product categories, which again implies that these categories constituted relevant product markets.[445]

The CA in *First Choice/Sunshine Cruises*[446] cleared the transaction largely on the basis that the merging parties had a combined market share of less than 30% *"of ocean cruise holidays to passengers in the State"* (¶14). Although the Determination contains no discussion on market definition, the conclusion rests on the implicit assumption that there was a single market for ocean cruise holidays. It ignored the possibility that cruises to different destinations might not be close substitutes and might therefore constitute separate markets, i.e., an Alaskan cruise might be in a different market to a Mediterranean cruise. The parties' may have had a higher combined share in a more narrowly defined market.[447] The EU Commission found that package holidays to short- and long-haul destinations constituted separate product markets.[448] Cruise holidays also involve short- or long-haul flights to/from cruise departure locations.

In *Largo Foods/Tayto*[449] the CA cited estimated market shares in savoury snacks, trends in the merging parties' market shares over time and described a third party as having entered and gained a significant share of this market. The Determination concluded that the transaction would not result in an SLC *"[d]espite the appearance of a high market share post-merger…"*

---

444 CCPC M/15/058 – *Fane Valley/Lakeland Dairies*, 27.11.2015. It applied a similar approach in CCPC M/18/012 – *North Cork/Feales Bridge & Hedleys Bridge*, 16.3.2018.

445 The CCPC specifically defined a market for one product category, brown sauce.

446 CA M/08/032 – *First Choice/Sunshine Cruises*, 24.10.2008.

447 If both parties offered cruises to the same destinations, this would place them in the same market, but the Determination provided no information on this point. The USFTC concluded that there was a single market for ocean cruises that was distinct from a wider holiday market (Coleman *et al.*, 2003).

448 See, for example, *Airtours/First Choice* and EU Commission Case No. COMP/M.4600 – *Tui/First Choice*, 4.6.2007. This distinction was upheld by the General Court in *Airtours v. Commission*.

449 CA M/06/051 – *Largo Foods/Tayto*, 4.9.2006.

(¶26). In *Blackstone/Tangerine*[450] the CA stated that it did not need to reach a conclusion on the relevant market but concluded that the transaction raised no competition concerns as the parties had small market shares and there were several other suppliers in the *"bagged snacks"* market.[451] *Intersnack/Largo Foods*[452] included no discussion of the relevant market although the CA cleared the transaction on the basis that (a) the increment in market share was minimal and (b) there were alternative suppliers of both branded and private label snack foods.

Subsequently in *Top Snacks/KP Snacks*, however, the CA claimed that it had not defined a savoury snacks market in *Largo Foods/Tayto* despite citing market shares and evidence of market entry in support of its conclusion that the transaction would not result in an SLC. The analysis of market definition in *Top Snacks/KP Snacks* is particularly confusing. The CA argued that there were differences in the characteristics of savoury snacks but stated that it was unclear if such differences *"necessarily imply distinctly separate product markets"*. It claimed that there were *"substantial arguments for defining a relevant market smaller than all savoury snacks"* but failed to articulate those arguments (¶3.22).[453] The Determination states *inter alia* that transporting crisps and snacks *"involve the opportunity costs of not transporting products with a greater density (e.g. canned goods, liquids, dried goods etc.)"* (¶3.21) with no explanation of how this was relevant to geographic market definition.

In *Lisavaird/JDS*[454] the CCPC stated that it was not necessary to define the relevant product market before concluding that *"the Proposed Transaction raises no competition concerns in the State with respect to **the manufacture and sale of dairy spreads**"* (¶13).

The CCPC in *Musgrave/La Rousse*[455] claimed that the outcome would be the same whether it adopted a narrow or a broad product market definition

450 CA M/11/018 – *Blackstone/Tangerine*, 24.6.2011.

451 The Determination stated the merging parties' *"bagged snacks"* products included crisps, nuts, other snacks, popcorn and chocolate-covered nuts and fruits.

452 CA M/11/021 – *Intersnack/Largo Foods*, 3.8.2011.

453 The Determination includes reference to market enquiries and internal documents of the parties suggesting that crisps and snacks constitute a separate market to popcorn and nuts but provides no details. It states that several third parties involved in the sector told it that consumers do not view popcorn or nuts as substitutes for crisps/snacks. No information was provided as to the number of parties asked, the questions asked, the number of responses received, or whether any respondents expressed contrary views.

454 CCPC M/17/038 – *Lisavaird/JDS*, 1.8.2017.

455 CCPC M/17/067 – *Musgrave/La Rousse*, 19.1.2018.

but analysed the transaction based on a broad market definition comprising the supply of food and drink products to all food service outlets. The evidence pointed toward a narrower market. The Target was described as *"a premium food business specialising in the supply of fine foods to premium foodservice operators"* which *"concentrates on customers who have a 'premium' offering such as 4-5 star hotels and full service restaurants, as well as some catering operations"* (¶7). The Determination also stated that *"Musgrave and La Rousse operate at different levels within the foodservice sector"* and that there was only a *"minor overlap"* between them (¶s28&29).

In *Amber/Grove Farm*[456] the CCPC argued that the outcome would be the same whether the market was defined narrowly as *"the supply of frozen breaded chicken products"* or broadly *"to encompass processed chicken products in general"* before stating that the wider processed chicken food products market constituted *"the narrowest possible relevant product markets"* (¶16).[457] The CCPC stated that it did not need to come to a definitive view as to whether advertising in newspapers and magazines constituted separate product markets in *Irish Post/Irish TV*, despite having done so in previous cases.[458]

The CCPC stated in *DekaBank/DoubleTree Hilton Dublin*[459] that its conclusion would be the same irrespective of whether the market was defined broadly or narrowly but went on to state:

> *"Therefore,* ***if*** *the relevant product market were to be defined as the supply of rentable commercial property for use as hotel accommodation, there would be no overlap between the activities of the parties in the State" (¶15, emphasis added).*

The Determination also states:

> *"Therefore,* ***if*** *the relevant geographic market were to be defined as regional, there would be no overlap between the parties' activities in the State" (¶16, emphasis added).*

---

456 CCPC M/16/018 – *Amber/Grove Farm*, 23.5.2016.

457 The CA previously decided that the supply of primary chicken products and processed chicken food products constituted separate product markets. (CA M/10/018 – *Moy Park/O'Kane*, 23.6.2010).

458 See, for example, *Johnston Press/Clonnad*; and *Trinity Mirror/Northern & Shell* and CCPC M/21/008 – *DMG/New Scientist*, 12.4.2021. CA M/06/061 – *Irish Times/Gloss*, 22.9.2006, while not reaching any conclusion, includes a brief discussion of differences between advertising in newspapers and what is described as *"a female magazine"* implying different product markets.

459 CCPC M/16/046 – *DekaBank/DoubleTree Hilton Dublin*, 2.11.2016.

It is inherently contradictory to argue, on the one hand, that the impact on competition would be the same regardless of market definition and then to conclude that there would be no impact on competition provided the market were defined in a particular way.[460] This amounts to saying that a merger *"will/will not result in an SLC in the market for x, but we are not definitely saying that x is the relevant market"*. If x is not the relevant market, then what is the basis for concluding that the merger will/will not result in an SLC?

The CCPC in *Carechoice/TMNH Holdings*[461] again argued that product market definition would not alter its competitive assessment of the transaction but stated that it had analysed its impact by reference to *"the potential product market of the provision of residential care and nursing home services"*. It is not immediately obvious that there are any close substitutes for residential care and nursing home services. A conclusion that a proposed transaction will/will not result in an SLC in a potential market only applies if that potential market is the correct market. The CCPC subsequently suggested in *Arthopoda (Orpea)/Brindley Healthcare* that home care provision was an alternative to residential care without indicating if they were in the same market.[462] It seems unlikely that home care is a close substitute for residential care.

In *Aviva/Friends First* the CCPC considered separate life insurance markets for (i) pure protection products; (ii) savings and investment products; and (iii) pension products and described these as *"the narrowest potential relevant product markets"* (¶26).[463] Subsequently, in *AXA/Laya Healthcare* it analysed the transaction based on a wider market definition comprising all life insurance products.[464]

---

460 Geographic markets for hotels appear to be local, which would indicate that the parties in this case were in separate geographic markets (see below).

461 CCPC M/18/083 – *Carechoice/TMNH Holdings*, 27.11.2018.

462 CCPC M/20/020 – *Arthopoda (Orpea)/Brindley Healthcare*, 6.8.2020.

463 CCPC M/18/002 – *Aviva/Friends First*, 20.2.2018. In the case of protection and pension products, however, the Determination quotes separate market share data for individual and group customers and for single and regular premium savings and investment products. The Determination notes that the EU Commission had considered dividing the three product markets into individual and group segments in Case Nos. COMP/M.4701 – *Generali/PPF Insurance Business*, 3.12.2007 and COMP/M.5075 – *Vienna Insurance Group/EBV*, 17.6.2008.

464 The Determination contains no reference to *Aviva/Friends First* but notes that the EU Commission, having considered the possible existence of separate life insurance markets by product type in previous cases, analysed the impact on competition in a broader life insurance market in EU Commission Case No. COMP/M.6883 – *Canada Life/Irish Life*, 31.5.2013, a decision which predates *Aviva/Friends First*.

The EU Commission 2024MDN states that the Commission is not bound to apply market definitions from previous cases.[465] It, nevertheless, states that the Commission may start its analysis based on market definitions applied in previous cases *"and verify whether the definition of the relevant market used in those past decisions may be applied to the case at hand"* (¶14). The CCPC is free to adopt a different market definition from that applied in a previous case where the *"facts, circumstances, and evidence"* are different. Changes in consumer tastes and technology can justify changes in market definition over time (Motta, 2004). Nevertheless, in order to provide greater clarity and certainty, definitions from previous cases appear to represent a useful starting point and where the CCPC concludes that they are not applicable it should provide a clear explanation setting out why, in its opinion, a different market definition is justified.[466] It is equally incumbent on merging parties to consider whether changes in market circumstances may mean that market definitions from previous cases may not apply to a subsequent transaction.

Determinations which state that it is not necessary to come to a definitive conclusion on market definition provide limited guidance to merging parties and practitioners. Merging parties and practitioners should be able to place some reliance on previous CA/CCPC Determinations, including their findings with respect to market definition, when contemplating a merger. What appears to be a policy of not defining markets in merger cases reduces transparency; makes it difficult for firms and practitioners to accurately predict whether a proposed merger is likely to raise competition concerns; and creates the potential for arbitrary market definitions. This has a wider negative effect as effective guidance affects deterrence.

In some cases, it may be obvious that a merger will not raise any competition concerns based on any plausible market definition. For example, the parties may have relatively small shares and/or face a large number of competitors irrespective of how the market is defined. This may represent a sensible and pragmatic approach on occasions, although **Chapter 7** suggests that caution is required. In several cases the CA/CCPC has analysed several potential markets before concluding that an SLC

---

465 Affeldt *et al.* (2019) report that the EU Commission left the geographic market open in 12% of cases between 1990 and 2014.

466 *Heineken/Coman's II*, for example, cited changed circumstances in the wholesale distribution of packaged beverages as grounds for applying only a national market definition whereas *Heineken/Coman's I* and CCPC M/16/062 – *Counterpoint/East Coast/Knockton*, 31.1.2017 both analysed national and local geographic markets.

would not arise.[467] This begs the question as to whether it would be easier to define the correct market and analyse the impact of the transaction in that market rather than considering multiple markets. Compiling market share data for multiple markets may place an onerous burden on merging parties.

CCPCMG2014 argues that it is not necessary to define the market if there is evidence that a merger will result in an SLC based on a number of possible market definitions.

> *"However, if an SLC can be shown when a merger is evaluated with respect to a number of alternative markets, there is no need to choose between them; it will be sufficient to show that the merger will result in an SLC regardless of the choice of market definition" (¶2.4).*

An SLC finding that is not based on the correct market definition may constitute a false positive. This applies if several alternative market definitions are considered but none of them is the correct market.[468] How many alternative market definitions need to be considered? If different market definitions produce inconsistent results, it will be necessary to identify the correct market. It is unclear that analysing whether a merger would result in an SLC in several different potential markets is less onerous than identifying and analysing competitive effects in the correct market.

Quantitative Analysis

Neven *et al.* (1993) argue that quantitative evidence is important in cases where market definition matters. In *FTC v. Staples* the USFTC successfully argued that the relevant market was limited to office equipment superstores and not all office equipment outlets, as the merging parties had argued. The USFTC success in this case surprised many anti-trust practitioners because there were many office supply retailers, and the parties accounted for only a small share of total sales. Econometric evidence demonstrated that, where the parties competed directly with one another, their prices were lower than in locations where they did not, while the presence of smaller suppliers in a given geographic location did not

---

467 For example, *Portlon (Parma)/Blackrock* and *Portlon/Blackrock (Tullycorbett/Xroon)* each analysed market shares in 24 different potential markets. Ten or more markets were considered in *Brookfield (Greenenergy)/Amber Oil, UPMC/Aut Even*, CCPC M/20/038 – *DCC/Campus Oil*, 2.2.2021; and CCPC M/21/034 – *Arachas/Hooper Dolan*, 23.8.2021. Several other Determinations referenced six or more markets.

468 For example, because the various market definitions are all too narrow and exclude some products that are close substitutes for the merging parties' products.

constrain the pricing behaviour of the merging parties.[469] Evidence that office supply superstores constituted a distinct product market proved critical in establishing that the merger would be anti-competitive (Dalkir & Warren-Boulton, 1999). Documentary evidence also supported a narrow market definition, although Baker (1999) states that it was unlikely that the merger would have been challenged without empirical evidence supporting the documentary evidence.

In *Grafton/Heiton* the CA commissioned econometric analysis *"similar to that conducted in FTC v. Staples"* (¶5.4).[470] The results indicated that prices in *Woodies* stores were not affected by either the number of DIY superstores or the number of independent stores in a particular area and therefore did not support a conclusion that DIY superstores constituted a distinct product market. Nevertheless, the CA concluded that *"superstore characteristics, consumer surveys, competitors' views and the parties' internal documents... indicate that a DIY superstore market provides a useful point from which to analyse the proposed acquisition"* (¶3.5). As previously noted, defining markets based on their *"characteristics"* is unsatisfactory.

In *Heinz/HP Foods*[471] the CA cited econometric evidence that barbeque and Worcester sauces were part of a wider product market, although it defined ketchup as a distinct product market, citing EU Commission decisions.[472] The CA rejected the merging parties' claims of a broad market definition in *Britvic/C&C* citing econometric evidence. The CA commissioned econometric analyses in *Unilever/Alberto Culver* and *Top Snacks/KP Snacks* but described the results as inconclusive in the latter case. In *Valeo/Wardell/Robert Roberts* the CCPC's econometric analysis supported a conclusion that brown sauce was in a separate product market to other cold sauces contrary to econometric evidence submitted by the parties.

---

469 For a more detailed account of the econometric evidence in this case, see Baker (1999). Manuszak & Moul (2008) report that the USFTC relied on similar evidence in opposing a 2005 merger, *Blockbuster Video/Hollywood Video*, which was abandoned as a result.

470 The parties had submitted econometric evidence showing that they set prices nationally. Gorecki *et al.* (2007) report that the CA conducted a similar exercise to define the geographic market in *Uniphar/Whelehan*.

471 CA M/05/033 – *Heinz/HP Foods*, 11.8.2005.

472 The CA cited EU Commission decisions in Case Nos. COMP/M.1802 – *Unilever/Amora-Maille*, 8.3.2000 and COMP/M.1990 – *Unilever/Bestfoods*, 28.9.2000.

Surveys

Kaserman & Zeisel (1996) describe how the USFTC used consumer survey results to estimate price elasticities in soft drinks mergers, noting that a well-designed survey can provide a reliable measure of demand-side product and/or geographic substitutability. Half of UKCC merger decisions between 2004 and 2008 relied on survey data (Hurley, 2011). Reynolds & Walters (2008) state that, provided they are carefully conducted, customer surveys can provide useful insights, but, due to the complications involved, the UKCC always considered them along with other evidence.

A robust survey requires a number of distinct steps which may not be possible within the merger review timetable. Hurley (2011) points out that time constraints may result in a competition agency commissioning a survey before it fully understands the questions it wants answered.[473] Merging parties should be afforded an opportunity to comment on a survey in advance and it is important that they fully engage in the process because the wording, ordering and content of questions can have a dramatic effect on responses.[474] Surveys can be unreliable at best and, at worst, result in incorrect conclusions if not carefully conducted (*ibid.*). A low response rate may be more damaging than a small sample because non-responses are not random. It is impossible to infer the characteristics of non-respondents. There is a risk of bias, reinforced by the fact that those who have strong views one way or another are more likely to respond. Relying on a biased survey may be more damaging than not doing a survey at all. Hurley (2011) argues that competition agencies should publish data on survey response rates, error margins and confidence levels, criticising the UKCC for generally failing to do so. A sufficiently large sample is required to ensure that survey results are robust and statistically meaningful (EU Commission, 2021).[475]

Neven *et al.* (1993) state that it was not surprising that an EU Commission survey of major customers and suppliers in *Solvay-Laporte/Interox*[476] proved inconclusive given that it only sought information

473 Reynolds & Walters (2008) express similar views.

474 The UK competition agencies generally provide the merging parties with an opportunity to comment on survey questions in advance (Hurley, 2011), as does the EU Commission which suggests that, if parties intend to conduct a consumer survey, they *"might want to involve the Commission in the questionnaire development and design"* (DG Competition, 2011 November 17, ¶48).

475 *Grafton/Heiton* and *Q-Park/Tazbell*, for example, involved limited numbers of consumers (see below).

476 EU Commission Case No. COMP/M.197 – *Solvay-Laporte/Interox*, 30.4.1992.

in relation to secondary variables such as import and market shares and prices in different countries. They suggest that it might have been simpler to ask whether customers would have switched purchases in response to a 5% price increase directly. They argue such an approach might also have been useful in the *Pay-TV*[477] case.

Hurley (2011) criticised aspects of the EU Commission passenger survey in *Ryanair/Aer Lingus I* which sought to test Ryanair's claim that passengers did not regard the two airlines as close substitutes. He argues that a question asking passengers if they would have flown with another airline if the price had been 10% lower than they had paid for their ticket could be regarded as leading, giving rise to potential bias.[478] Another question asked respondents to state the reason for their trip and offered them 10 options but the Commission failed to indicate whether the ranking of these options varied in order to neutralise the effect of question order. The General Court rejected Ryanair's criticisms of the survey, noting the tight time limits within which the Commission must decide on merger cases.[479]

In *Grafton/Heiton* the CA commissioned a survey which interviewed 423 shoppers as they exited five of the merging parties' large DIY outlets. Shoppers were asked where they would go if they could not find an item that they had been looking for in the outlet that they had just visited. The Determination states that *"crucially"* a high proportion indicated that they would go to another large DIY outlet with only a small proportion stating that they would go to a smaller outlet (¶3.11). The survey was flawed in two respects. First, it asked the wrong question. In order to establish whether large DIY stores constituted a separate market, shoppers should have been asked how they would respond if all DIY superstores raised their prices by 5-10% while prices in smaller outlets remained unchanged. The survey thus failed to address whether smaller outlets exercised a competitive constraint on larger stores. Gorecki (2014) argues that it is unclear how the hypothetical monopolist question should be framed given the large volume of products typically carried by DIY superstores, while claiming that the purpose of the survey was *"to gain an understanding of DIY superstore customers"*. Second, the survey was limited to five (out of 35 of the parties' outlets) which were selected on the basis that the merging parties had stores that *"were located nearby one another"* (¶1.12), giving rise to sample

---

477 EU Commission Case No. COMP/M.110 – *ABC/Generale Des Eaux/Canal+/W.H. Smith TV*, 10.9.1991.

478 It appears that Ryanair did not object to the question.

479 Case T-342/07, *Ryanair v. Commission*, 6.7.2010, 2010 II-03457.

bias and increasing the likelihood that respondents would indicate that they would go to another DIY superstore.[480] The Determination states that the survey *"was not intended to represent the entire DIY market of the State"* (¶3.9). Given these flaws the survey could not be relied upon to support the CA's conclusion that customers regarded DIY superstores as the closest substitutes for each other.[481]

In *Glen Dimplex/Applied Energy* the parties commissioned a survey of property developers asking if they would consider switching to other heating sources in response to a 5-10% permanent increase in the relative price of electric radiators (¶3.4). Twenty said they would definitely consider switching, while 17 said they might consider switching. The question posed by the SSNIP test is whether customers would switch in response to a 5-10% price increase not whether they might or would consider doing so. The CA conducted a Phase 2 investigation because it *"was unable to form a view as to the precise product and geographic market in which the parties compete"* (¶1.21) primarily due to a low response rate to questionnaires that it had issued to customers.[482] The CA ultimately concluded that the relevant market included gas and oil-fired heating systems as well as electric radiators in which the parties had a combined share of 6%. It is highly unlikely that the CA would have launched a Phase 2 investigation had it been clear that the parties had such a small market share. The parties might have avoided a Phase 2 investigation if their survey had asked the right questions.

The CA commissioned a consumer survey in *Top Snacks/KP Snacks*.[483] There is no indication that the merging parties were consulted about the questions in advance. The first question posed was whether respondents considered crisps and peanuts *"to be close substitutes for one another?"* It

---

480 DG Competition (2011, November 17) states that individuals included in a survey must accurately represent the survey population. Similarly, Gorecki *et al.* (2007) cite the need to ensure that opinion evidence is based on a representative sample of customers or competitors.

481 The author requested a copy of the actual survey and results under the *Freedom of Information Act* but was informed that the relevant records could not be found.

482 The CA ultimately received 11 responses, five of which indicated that they would switch to other heating products following a 5-10% increase in the price of electric radiators, while three stated that they would not. Two others indicated that they did not purchase electric space heating systems for their housing projects and were excluded (the CA appears not to have asked them if they would switch to electric radiators in response to a 5-10% increase in the price of other heating systems), while a third stated energy efficiency was the deciding factor and price was irrelevant.

483 The author obtained copies of the survey questionnaire and results under the *Freedom of Information Act*.

would have been far better to ask respondents if they would have switched from crips to peanuts or *vice versa* in response to a specific price increase. The term *"close substitutes"* has a precise technical meaning in the context of market definition, and it is unlikely that respondents would have interpreted it in this way. Limiting the choice to crisps and nuts also pre-empted the outcome to some extent because it implicitly assumes that other snacks such as popcorn are not part of the relevant market. Respondents were then asked if they purchased either of the merging parties' crisp brands and, if so, how they would respond to a price increase for that brand. They were then asked to indicate which alternatives from a list of brands they would consider switching to.[484] The Determination states that the survey results were *"supportive of nuts as a possible alternative product to crisps"* (¶4.72).

In *Valeo/Wardell/Robert Roberts*,[485] the CCPC survey asked consumers whether they considered other products to be *"close substitutes"* for brown sauce and, if they purchased brown sauce, which alternative brands would they consider switching to in the event of a 10% price increase for a particular brown sauce brand.

In *Pat the Baker/Irish Pride*[486] the CCPC survey asked consumers whether they regarded sliced white and brown bread as close or distant substitutes based on whether they *"regularly/freely"* switched between the two but also asked how respondents would react if either of the parties increased the price of their branded breads by 5-10%. In *Q-Park/Tazbell* a survey commissioned by the CCPC asked car park customers how they would respond (a) in the event that a particular car park was closed for up to six months and (b) to a 30c per hour increase in the price of off-street car parking. Only the latter question is helpful from the point of view of market definition.[487]

---

484 Respondents could choose multiple alternative brands. Had they been asked to nominate the brand that they were most likely to switch to, it would have been possible to measure the likely degree of switching between brands, information that would have been useful for analysing the likelihood of an SLC (see **Chapter 8**).

485 The author obtained copies of the survey questionnaire and results under the *Freedom of Information Act*.

486 The author obtained copies of the survey questionnaire and results under the *Freedom of Information Act*.

487 The closure of a car park is equivalent to an infinite increase in price and thus will not assist in identifying close substitutes for the car park in question. Although the survey was conducted over several days in March 2023, only 102 customers of the Target's Galway car park responded to this question. The CCPC acknowledged that this constituted a small sample.

The CA in *Premier Foods/RHM* cited grocery retailers' replies to questionnaires as the basis for concluding that there were separate markets for sauces, soups and gravies. The Determination does not state what questions were asked, what the response rate was, nor the basis for concluding that a hypothetical monopolist could profitably raise prices for each of the three product groupings.[488]

In *Metro/Herald AM* and some local radio cases the Authority asked advertising agencies how they would respond to a hypothetical price increase. A significant number of respondents stated that the response would depend on their customers, indicating that the latter group were the appropriate people to ask. In *Communicorp/SRH*[489] the merging parties commissioned a survey to identify the market, but the results were inconclusive, mainly because it asked the wrong questions.

In a number of cases the CA/CCPC attempted to conduct a SSNIP test by asking customers whether, in the event of a hypothetical 5% price increase, they would:

i. Maintain their level of spending and buy less;
ii. Buy the same amount and spend more; or
iii. Switch to some other product.

In order to apply the SSNIP test one needs quantitative data on the likely decline in sales volumes in response to a price increase but in many cases the CA did not ask respondents to quantify the extent to which they would reduce purchases. Information on the number of customers who chose each option is insufficient for a proper application of the SSNIP test.

In *Kerry/Breeo* the CA sent a questionnaire to the merging parties' main customers – the major grocery multiples. The CA acknowledged that the questionnaire responses were inconclusive for market definition purposes in the case of cooked meats (¶6.17). The High Court in *Rye Investments* held that, the question of whether PCM and non-PCM constituted one or two

---

488 In *Heineken/Beamish & Crawford* the CA surveyed publicans asking for their views on how consumers would respond to price changes for different beer types when a consumer survey would arguably have been better but more costly (see **Chapter 8**).

489 In CCPC M/07/021 – *Thomas Crosbie Holdings/WKW FM*, 17.8.2007, advertisers who responded to a CA survey stated that they would not switch to other media if the price of radio advertising increased by 5-10%.

markets was really a judgement call, observing that *"it may well be possible to make plausible judgments as to the existence of one or two product markets"*.[490]

In relation to cheese, of the nine parties surveyed, two failed to respond, two provided what the CA described as *"unclear responses"*, one retailer indicated that it did not know how it would respond to a price increase for processed cheese, while the remaining four indicated they would either spend the same amount in monetary terms and purchase a smaller volume or purchase the same volume at a higher price. The CA argued:

> *"Thus, the survey results, although not conclusive, lean towards supporting a view that processed cheese occupies a distinct product market from natural cheese" (¶8.19).*

It is not possible to infer from the reported responses whether a SSNIP for processed cheese would have been profitable, a necessary condition for defining a separate market.

Opinion evidence suffers from a number of serious weaknesses. Gorecki *et al.* (2007) describe it as the least reliable type of evidence. The CA accepted retailers' claims that private label brands were not close substitutes for the merging brands despite evidence that the retailers had been substituting private label brands for those of the merging parties on their shelves over a number of years. Customer responses need to be assessed in light of evidence regarding their actual behaviour.

Product Market Definition in Individual Cases

Grocery Retailing

In retail grocery mergers the CA/CCPC has repeatedly considered all types of grocery retail outlets including large multiple supermarkets, franchise stores, independents, convenience outlets and filling station forecourt stores to be part of a single product market. This is in contrast to *Grafton/Heiton* where the CA decided that DIY superstores were in a separate product market to smaller DIY/hardware stores.

The CA concluded in *Musgrave/Superquinn* that *"the relevant product market is the retail sale of grocery goods"* (¶84). The Determination lists several factors which *"might suggest some merit in a product definition or set of definitions based on shopping services or business models"* (¶78):

---

490 *Rye Investments* (¶8.12). In CCPC M/17/002 – *Silvereed/Tombolo*, 16.2.2017 the CCPC analysed the proposed transaction in both the market for *"cooked bulk beef and pre-packed beef products"*, which it described as *"the narrowest potential relevant market"*, and in the wider non-PCM market.

i. Different shopping behaviours (e.g., *"one-stop"*, *"convenience"* or *"top-up"* shopping) and different retailer business models.
ii. Parties' documents *"disaggregate the grocery goods sector into various sub-segments such as 'multiples', 'symbols', 'discounters' and 'convenience' sectors"* (¶76).
iii. Asymmetric constraints i.e., *"larger retailers place a stronger competitive constraint on smaller retailers than* vice versa*"* (¶77).

In support of a single market including all grocery retailers regardless of size the CA cited:

i. Reports on switching indicated that Supervalu, a franchisee retailer was a competitor of multiples such as Dunnes Stores, Tesco and Superquinn (¶80).
ii. Reports prepared for Musgrave aggregate market shares of Supervalu and the typically smaller Centra but also report their market shares separately (¶81).
iii. The fact that *"fascias offer a range of shopping services. For example, Superquinn Select and Tesco Express are examples of vertically-integrated stores targeting **smaller shopping baskets**, whereas some franchisee stores such as Eurospar and larger Londis stores target **larger shopping baskets**"* (¶82, emphasis added).

According to CA (2008, ¶4.44 & ¶4.84) SuperValu supermarkets were similar in size and in many other respects to those of the large multiple supermarket groups, indicating that they were in the same market as large multiple supermarkets. It does not follow that smaller symbol franchise stores are also part of this market. The fact that some internal reports combined market shares for SuperValu and Centra while others did not is hardly conclusive. Evidence that vertically-integrated and franchise stores target different shopper types with different brands/fascias arguably indicates separate markets rather than a single market including all retail outlets.[491] The CA/CCPC, nevertheless, followed this approach in many subsequent cases.[492]

491 The reference to smaller and larger shopping baskets may be indicative here.

492 In *BWG/Londis*, the CCPC stated that it would not *"seek to distinguish between so–called multiples, discounters or convenience stores"* (¶44). The CCPC treated all grocery outlets as a single market in CCPC M/17/050 – *Joyce's/Nestor's*, 5.10.2017; CCPC M/17/058 – *Musgrave/Whelan Centra*, 7.12.2017. In *BWG/4 Aces* the CCPC stated that the parties overlapped in the retail sale of grocery goods.

The CA/CCPC defined forecourt convenience shops as being in the same market as multiple supermarkets in several cases.

> *"The sector encompasses (i) a wide spectrum of large supermarkets known as 'multiples'...(ii) medium-sized shops which are usually part of a 'symbol' group... and (iii) smaller stores...categorised as 'convenience' stores. Forecourt convenience stores fall within the latter category..." (Topaz/Esso, ¶60).*

> *"Forecourt convenience stores also compete with other retail grocery outlets, such as Centra, Spar, Londis and Costcutter, as well as larger multiples, such as Tesco, Dunnes and SuperValu".*[493]

The majority of filling station convenience shops are much smaller and carry a far more limited range of grocery products than a large supermarket. It seems highly unlikely that many consumers would go to a filling station convenience shop to do a weekly shop. The suggestion that there is a single grocery retail market which includes forecourt convenience shops seems questionable. Supermarkets may exert a competitive constraint on forecourt shops, but the opposite is unlikely to be the case. Evidence of asymmetric competitive constraints indicates separate markets for different shop types. Hosken *et al.* (2002) suggest that convenience store shoppers are likely to be less price sensitive than supermarket shoppers.

The CCPC in *Dunnes Stores/JC Savage*[494] stated that it did not consider it *"necessary to include in its local market analysis the numerous smaller retailers of grocery goods present in the JCSS Catchment Area"* (¶20), implying separate markets for large and small grocery stores. In *Tesco/Joyce's* the CCPC acknowledged that convenience shops, kiosks and service station forecourt shops were unlikely to pose an appreciable competitive constraint on large and small supermarkets and defined the relevant product market as:

> *"The retail sale of grocery goods and general merchandise in Large and Small supermarkets" (¶3.31).*[495]

---

493 CCPC M/15/024 – *Petrogas/Knockmitten Petroleum*, 30.6.2015, FN7. CCPC M/17/052 – *Cedarglade (Musgrave)/Ballybrit Service Station*, 11.10.2017 referred to *"the potential relevant market for the sale of grocery goods"* (¶17).

494 CCPC M/19/022 – *Dunnes Stores/JC Savage*, 30.7.2019.

495 Large supermarkets were defined as stores of 1,000-2,500m^2 while small supermarkets were defined as stores of 400-1,000m^2. The Determination also defined stores larger than 2,500m^2 as hypermarkets but failed to indicate whether such outlets were in the same market as large and small supermarkets or constituted a separate market.

Subsequently, in *Maxol/Kinsella's Fuel Services,*[496] the CCPC analysed a distinct market *"for the operation of forecourt convenience stores"* (¶13).

Competition agencies in other jurisdictions have concluded that grocery retailing includes a number of separate product markets which can be distinguished by type of outlet e.g., hypermarket, supermarket etc., floor area and shopping type. In *Kesko/Tuko*[497] the EU Commission defined the market as that for *"a basket of daily consumer goods sold in a supermarket environment"*. In *Tesco/ABF,*[498] which involved the acquisition by Tesco of an Irish-owned multiple supermarket group, the EU Commission, without reaching a definitive conclusion, stated *"the most appropriate definition…would cover the multiples and perhaps some of the larger symbol stores, but not smaller stores or more specialist retail outlets"* (¶9).

UKCC (2000, ¶2.53) concluded that the relevant market was that for one stop shopping in stores of 1,400m² or more. *Safeway/Asda*[499] defined the relevant product market as that for one stop grocery shopping in stores of 1,400m² or more.[500] *Somerfield/Morrison*[501] concluded that larger grocery stores exercised a greater competitive constraint on smaller stores than smaller stores exercised on larger ones but defined the relevant market as the market for secondary as opposed to one-stop shopping because, in contrast to *Safeway*, most of the stores involved in the proposed transaction were mid-range stores, i.e., between 280m² and 1,400m². UKCMA (2008) concluded that competitive constraints in grocery retailing were asymmetric and defined three product markets for the supply of groceries:

i. Large grocery stores i.e., 1,000-2,000m²;
ii. Mid-sized stores including all stores larger than 280m²; and
iii. Convenience stores including convenience, mid-sized and large stores.

The UKCMA defined a separate product market for stores of over 1,400 m² in *Asda/Co-Op.*[502] In *Sainsbury's/Asda,* while stating that competitive

[496] CCPC M/23/018 – *Maxol/Kinsella's Fuel Services,* 8.6.2023.
[497] EU Commission Case No. COMP/M.784 – *Kesko/Tuko,* 19.2.1987.
[498] EU Commission Case No. COMP/M.914 – *Tesco/ABF,* 5.5.1997.
[499] UKCC (2003), *Safeway,* 26.9.2003.
[500] The UKCC acknowledged that, in particularly remote areas or areas where the population was insufficient to support stores of 1,400m², stores just below this threshold might operate and compete as one-stop shops but this did not alter its conclusions in respect of the relevant product market.
[501] UKCC Case No. ME/1456/04, *Somerfield/Morrison,* 23.3.2005.
[502] UKCMA, ME/6466/14 – *Asda/Co-Op,* 22.12.2014.

constraints were asymmetric, the UKCMA acknowledged that mid-sized stores exercised some competitive constraint on larger stores (¶7.38) and defined the relevant product market as including large and medium-sized stores (¶7.40).[503]

The French competition authority also concluded that competitive constraints in grocery retailing were asymmetric and that hypermarkets constituted a separate product market to other retail grocery outlets[504] (Allain *et al.*, 2017). In *Von's Grocery* in the early 1960s the US Supreme Court defined the market as the market for *"retail grocery sales"*. In the 1990 *California v. American Stores Co.* case,[505] the Supreme Court implicitly accepted a narrower market for *"supermarkets"*, defined as grocery stores of at least 10,000 square feet. In the 2008 *Whole Foods* case, the D.C. Circuit accepted an even narrower market definition advanced by the USFTC as the marker for the *"operation of premium natural and organic supermarkets"*.[506]

Motor Fuel Retailing

In *Maxol/Tom Chawke*[507] the CCPC stated that the target comprised two businesses – motor fuel retailing and a convenience store – implying two separate product markets. *Topaz/Esso* stated that, while convenience stores located on filling station forecourts formed part of the relevant filling station, they *"were not considered to be part of the same product market"* (¶60). In *Petrogas/Knockmitten Petroleum,* the CCPC somewhat confusingly described the narrowest product market affected as *"the retail sale of motor fuels (petrol and diesel) with associated forecourt convenience stores"* (¶20), a phrase repeated in many subsequent cases.[508] Filling stations with and without forecourt convenience stores compete for the sale of motor fuels while forecourt convenience stores compete with non-forecourt

---

503 UKCMA, ME/6752/18 – *Sainsbury's/Asda*, 25.4.2019. In contrast to a number of earlier decisions the product market definition included Iceland, along with discounters such as Aldi and Lidl.

504 Hypermarkets are defined as grocery stores with sales space of 2,500m² or more (*ibid.*)

505 *California v. American Stores Co.*, 495 U.S. 271 (1990).

506 *FTC v. Whole Foods Market, Inc.*, 548 F.3d 1028 (D.C. Cir. 2008), ¶s1037-1041.

507 CCPC, M/14/038 – *Maxol/Tom Chawke*, 22.1.2015.

508 See, for example, CCPC M/16/009 – *Tedcastles/Sirio*, 23.3.2016; CCPC M/16/043 – *Petrogas/MKMH*, 4.10.2016; CCPC M/17/006 – *Topaz/Casey's of Bantry*, 1.3.2017; CCPC M/17/011- *Maxol/Melia's Harold's Cross*, 27.3.2017; CCPC M/17/016 – *Petrogas/Westmeath Motors*, 28.4.2017; CCPC M/17/019 – *Petrogas/PR Reilly*, 9.5.2017; CCPC M/17/020 – *Maxol/Great Gas*, 10.5.2017; CCPC M/17/039 – *TOP/KEC*, 24.7.2017; CCPC M/18/004 – *Maxol/Brennan's*, 9.2.2018; CCPC M/18/006 – *Valero/Riverside Service Station*, 14.2.2018; CCPC M/18/023 – *Petrogas/Carranstown*, 29.3.2018 and CCPC M/18/050 – *BWG/Keating's Londis*, 11.7.2018.

convenience stores in respect of grocery goods. Most of these Determinations analysed the transactions on the basis that the filling station and convenience store businesses were in separate markets.[509]

Other Retail

In *Champion Sports/JD Sports,* the CA defined the narrowest possible markets as the retail sale of:

i. Branded sports clothing; and,

ii. Branded sports footwear (¶25).

In *Eason/Dubray* the CCPC concluded that the market for the retail sale of books included both traditional bricks and mortar stores and on-line retailers in line with the EU Commission and the UKCC in *Egmont/Bonnier (Books)*[510] and *HMV/Ottaker's*[511] respectively. In the latter case the UKCC noted that the parties had increased discounts in response to increased discounting by other retailers, including on-line retailers. Empirical evidence for the US indicates that traditional bookshops' book prices were similar to those of online retailers (Clay *et al.,* 2002). Goldmanis *et al.* (2010) found a higher rate of bookshop closures, particularly of smaller bookshops, in areas with the fastest growth rates in internet usage. Both findings indicate that traditional and on-line book retailers are in the same market.[512]

Hotels

Although in most instances it has not reached a definitive conclusion, the CA/CCPC approach to market definition in hotel merger cases has arguably been inconsistent. In several cases the CA/CCPC applied a wide market definition comprising all hotels.[513] Applying a wide market definition,

---

509 In *Cedarglade/Ballybrit Service Station* the CCPC stated that there was no overlap between the parties in respect of motor fuel and focused only on grocery goods. CCPC M/16/027 – *Maxol/Topaz Ballindine,* 8.7.2016 and CCPC M/17/053 – *TOP/H2 Blakes,* 28.9.2017 do not refer to the existence of two separate markets.

510 EU Commission Case No. COMP/M.4611 – *Egmont/Bonnier (Books),* 15.10.2007

511 UKCC, Case No. ME/1974/05 – *HMV/Ottakar's,* 12.5.2006.

512 CCPC M/15/054 – *Sports Direct/Heatons,* 13.11.2015 implied that traditional "bricks and mortar" and on-line sports goods retailers constituted a single market. The Determination stated that, although *Sports Direct* had no outlets within the State, Irish consumers could order from its UK-based online operation. This does not establish that the two are close substitutes.

513 CA M/04/071 – *Kantaka/RBS,* 21.12.2004; CA M/07/007 – *Bernard McNamara/Conrad International/ECHPL,* 21.2.2007; *Tetrarch/Dawson Hotel* (although the Determination in this case noted the parties were not particularly close competitors); CCPC M/15/044 – *Thornmont/Hilton Kilmainham,* 17.9.2015; and CCPC M/16/010 – *Halstonville/Diminuto,* 30.3.2016.

without establishing that such a definition is correct, is likely to understate the parties' market share and the degree of market concentration, while overstating the level of competition in the market by including more distant substitutes, giving rise to a potential false negative.[514]

In *Bernard McNamara/Conrad International/ECHPL* the CA stated that *"it is possible to consider defining the relevant product market according to price and/or comfort level based on the grading or stars awarded to the particular hotel"* (¶9). In *Dalata/White's Hotel,* the CCPC argued that it was unclear whether *"these differences necessarily imply distinctly separate markets"* (¶14). In other cases, the CA/CCPC has asserted that, despite quality differences, different hotel categories are a competitive constraint on each other without citing any evidence for such claims.

> *"Although 3 and 4 star hotels can be distinguished in terms of the services offered, the Commission's market enquiries suggest that* ***in certain circumstances*** *4 star hotels* ***may*** *compete with 3 star hotels" (Dalata/Moran's Hotel/Bewley's, ¶25, emphasis added).*[515]

Irish Property/Ballsbridge Holdco[516] described the market for five-star hotels as the narrowest possible market but added that *"top end 4 star hotels* ***may*** *also act as a competitive constraint on the merged entity"* (¶18, emphasis added).

The CA/CCPC analysed narrow markets (based on hotels' star ratings) in several cases. As previously noted, a narrow market definition is sufficient to establish an SLC will not arise provided it does not place the parties in separate markets, in which case the possibility of a false negative may arise.[517] In other cases, the CA/CCPC considered the impact of the transaction in several possible markets. In *Atlantic Troy/Athlone Springs* the CCPC analysed the transaction in markets for four-star hotels and all hotel types.[518] In *Dalata/Moran's Hotel* the CCPC considered separate three- and

---

514 This is a possible example of the "cellophane trap".

515 The CCPC repeated such claims in *Atlantic Troy/Charleville Park Hotel; Atlantic Troy/Killeshin Hotel* and *Dalata/Clarion Sligo.*

516 CCPC M/15/014 – *Irish Property/Ballsbridge Holdco,* 22.4.2015.

517 Examples include *Dalata/DoubleTree Hilton Dublin* where the only overlap related to four-star hotels and CCPC M/17/072 – *Irish Holdings/Galway Leisure Investments,* 2.2.2018, where there was no geographic overlap between the parties. In CCPC M/19/006 – *Wicklow Hotel Partnership/Powerscourt Hotel Resort & Spa,* 3.5.2019, the CCPC only considered a five-star hotel market although the acquirer operated both four- and five-star hotels – nonetheless, given the number of hotels involved, a false negative seems highly unlikely.

518 CCPC M/18/048 – *Atlantic Troy/Athlone Springs,* 10.7.2018. The parties only operated four-star hotels and as the narrower market definition indicated that an SLC would not arise, there is no obvious reason for considering a wider market for all hotels. The CCPC adopted

four-star hotel markets and a combined three/four-star market. As the parties did not overlap in the first two markets, analysing a combined market eliminated the potential for a false negative.[519]

Hospitals

The CCPC in *Bon Secours/Barrington's Hospital* stated that it made no difference whether the product market was defined narrowly as private hospital services or widely as encompassing private healthcare services in general, without actually defining the latter term. The Determination stated that it had analysed the market on the basis of the narrower market definition (private hospital services) but subsequently stated that the merging parties each provided different private healthcare services.

Subsequently, in *Portlon (Parma)/Hermitage,* the CCPC claimed that it made no difference whether the market was defined narrowly on the basis of individual procedures or widely as the market for all private healthcare services. The Determination cites evidence indicating that all hospitals were not close substitutes:

i. Not all hospitals offer complex procedures. The more complex the procedure the further a patient may have to travel and the wider the geographic market (¶34). Different geographic markets indicate different product markets.

ii. Private health insurers differentiate between different private hospital categories depending on the complexity of services offered (¶49).

---

a similar approach in CCPC M/18/010 – *SCIF/McWilliam Park Hotel,* 7.3.2018 and CCPC M/18/037 – *SCIF/Connemara Coast Hotel,* 12.6.2018. In CA M/13/011 – *OIF/Mount Kellett/UBIL/Jury's Inn,* 7.5.2013, the CA considered markets for three-star hotels and all hotels. In CCPC M/17/044 – *Kennedy Wilson Holdings/Kennedy Wilson Real Estate Europe,* 8.9.2017, the CCPC analysed the transaction in a combined market for four- and five-star hotels, although the Determination suggests the parties only operated five-star hotels.

519 It followed this approach in *Dalata/White's Hotel*; *Dalata/Clayton Hotel*; and *Dalata/Pillo Hotel.* In the latter two cases, the parties both operated four-star hotels but did not overlap in the case of three-star hotels. Thus, there was arguably no need to apply a wider market definition. In CCPC M/16/006 – *Dalata/Cavenford/Vizmol,* 8.3.2016, having stated that the narrowest relevant market was that for four-star hotel accommodation, the CCPC also analysed the transaction in a combined three- and four- star market. While the target operated four-star hotels, it is unclear whether the Purchaser operated both three- and four-star hotels and if a wider market definition was necessary to avoid the risk of a false negative. In CCPC M/18/078 – *Tetrarch/Seed Portfolio Hotels,* 22.10.2018, the CCPC considered markets for (i) four-star; (ii) five-star and (iii) four- and five-star hotels which, given that the parties had hotels in different categories, eliminated the risk of a false negative.

iii. Certain hospitals provide high-intensity complex procedures while others do not. The former group commanded higher re-imbursement rates from insurers (¶50).

The Determination argued that it was not necessary to decide if the market included private healthcare services in public hospitals because regardless of whether such services were included *"the Merging Clinics' combined estimated market share would not significantly exceed the market share of their nearest competitor"* (¶38), a claim repeated in *Portlon (Parma)/Blackrock* (¶39). There is no economic basis for linking market definition to differences in market shares.[520] In the case of cardiothoracic procedures, however, the Determination stated that few private hospitals offered such services and the CCPC considered *"the inclusion of private provision in public hospitals in the estimated combined market share of the Merging Clinics most relevant in respect of private cardiothoracic procedures/cardiac procedures"* (¶69).

Bookmakers

In *Ladbrokes/Coral* the CA simply stated that the relevant market was that for off-course betting, implying that licensed betting offices (LBOs) and telephone betting ("telebetting") constituted a single market without any discussion.[521] *William Hill/Stanley Racing*[522] stated that the parties only overlapped in respect of telephone/on-line betting, implying that LBOs and tele/online betting constituted separate markets. In *Ladbrokes/Chronicle*[523] the CA analysed the impact of the transaction in a telebetting and a combined online and telebetting market but did not consider whether LBOs were part of this market. While not coming to a definitive conclusion, the CCPC in *Ladbrokes/Gala Coral*[524] treated online and telebetting as separate markets. In *Paddy Power/Hacketts*, the CCPC again offered no view as to whether LBOs

---

520 Including private healthcare services provided by public hospitals had a very significant impact on market concentration in this case which is inconsistent with the CCPC assertion that it made no difference to the outcome (see **Chapter 7**).

521 The CA report stated that the parties claimed telebetting was still underdeveloped in the State (¶5.3).

522 CA M/05/021 – *William Hill/Stanley Racing*, 2.6.2005. The transaction involved the acquisition by *William Hill* of 52 *Stanley Racing* LBOs but did not include *Stanley Racing's* telebetting and online bookmaking business in the State. Prior to the transaction William Hill had no LBOs in the State.

523 CA M/13/018 – *Ladbrokes/Chronicle*, 24.6.2013. The CCPC expressed no view on whether LBOs, telebetting and online betting were in the same or separate markets in CCPC M/15/013 – *Paddy Power/Track*, 31.3.2015.

524 CCPC M/16/007 – *Ladbrokes/Gala Coral*, 10.3.2016.

and online betting constituted one or two markets. *Boyle Sports/Bambury I*[525] acknowledged the possibility that LBOs and online betting might be part of the same market, but analysed the transaction based on the narrowest potential market definition, *i.e.*, LBOs. In *Star Group/Sky Betting*[526] the CCPC analysed an online betting market, excluding telebetting.

Sports Broadcast Rights

In *BT/ESPN Global*[527] the CA analysed the impact of the transaction in the upstream market for the purchase of all sports broadcast rights. The CCPC in *CVC/Celtic Rugby* analysed the likely competitive effects in markets for (i) TV rights for all sports and (ii) TV rights for rugby. Subsequently in *CVC/Six Nations*[528] it only considered a market for TV rights for all sports. The weight of evidence indicates that different sports are not close substitutes and even different rugby tournaments are not close substitutes for each other. Football (soccer) is far and away the most popular sport in most European countries, with other sports a distant second (see, for example Cave & Crandall, 2001; Robertson, 2002; Hoehn & Lancefield, 2003).[529]

The EU Commission in *UEFA Champions League*[530] rejected claims that there was a single market for sports broadcast rights and concluded that *"there is a separate market for the acquisition of TV broadcasting rights to football which is played regularly throughout every year"* (¶79). The EU Commission noted in *FAPL*[531] and *UEFA Champions League* that those competitions were particularly attractive to broadcasters as stand-alone drivers of paying subscribers, a point acknowledged by the CCPC in *CVC/Six Nations*.

Differences in scheduling mean that different rugby competitions are unlikely to be close substitutes for viewers and broadcasters, a point made

---

525 CCPC M/17/003 – *Boyle Sports/Bambury I*, 10.2.2017. The Vendor's telebetting service was not part of the transaction. In CCPC M/17/061 – *Boyle Sports/Bambury II*, 13.12.2017 and CCPC M/18/007 – *Boyle Sports/JP Bookmakers*, 19.2.2018, the CCPC analysed the transactions in a narrow LBO product market as the Targets were not engaged in online or telebetting. Despite the common name, *Bambury I* and *II* involved different vendors.

526 CCPC M/18/038 – *Star Group/Sky Betting*, 18.6.2018.

527 CA M/13/003 – *BT/ESPN*, 25.4.2013. The CA previously applied a market for the acquisition of Irish sports broadcasting rights in CA M/06/089 – *Doughty Hansen/Setanta*, 5.1.2007.

528 CCPC M/21/026 – *CVC/Six Nations*, 24.6.2021.

529 UK subscribers cited access to live Football Association Premier League (FAPL) football matches as a major reason for subscribing to *Sky Sports* (Ofcom, 2005; 2007; 2015).

530 EU Commission, Case C.2-37.398 – *Joint selling of the commercial rights of the UEFA Champions League*, 23.7.2003, 2003 OJ L271/25, 8.11.2003.

531 EU Commission, Case C.2-38.173 – *Joint selling of the media rights to the FA Premier League*, 22.3.2006, 2004 OJ C115/02, 30.4.2004.

by the parties in *CVC/Six Nations*. The Six Nations runs over five weekends in February/March while the autumn rugby internationals take place over three or four weekends every November. The United Rugby Championship (URC), which was the subject of the *CVC/Celtic Rugby* Determination, runs from September to late May every year and matches typically do not coincide with international match broadcasts. Two free-to-air broadcasters informed the CCPC that other rugby tournaments were not close substitutes for the Six Nations due to *"differences in scheduling, viewership levels, and demographics of viewers"* (¶49).[532] According to the Determination home country events attract viewers, indicating that Irish audiences are unlikely to regard the English Rugby Premiership as a close substitute for the URC which involves Irish teams.

Other Product Markets

In *IBM/Schlumberger*, one of only five mergers prohibited by the CA/CCPC, the CA defined the relevant market as the market for business recovery hotsite services. The CA stated that a significant number of customers that it had contacted indicated that, in the event of a 5-10% price rise, they would still choose to purchase business recovery hotsite services. As the Determination contains no precise information on the number of customers who would and would not switch, it is impossible to evaluate whether the likely loss as a result of a hypothetical 5-10% price increase would be less than the critical loss.

The Determination noted that the demand for such services varied considerably between customer types. Significantly the Determination stated that the proposed transaction would have enabled the merged entity to price discriminate. Customer heterogeneity and differences in their willingness to pay point to the existence of separate markets. This is further supported by the suggestion in the Determination that non-merging firms may have exercised an effective competitive constraint on the merging parties in respect of smaller customers, but not larger ones, combined with indications that the majority of high-end users would not switch providers or accept lower levels of service in return for a lower price, following a 5% price increase (¶3.26). It is unlikely, however, that a finding that there were two separate markets

---

532 This is an example of a temporal market. A Six Nations match on a Saturday afternoon in February is not a substitute for a Pro-14 match on a Friday night in October or April from either a viewer or a broadcaster perspective. The CCPC in *LN-Gaiety/MCD Productions* concluded that live music events and music festivals were not substitutes for one another, partly because they occurred at different times of the year.

would have affected the outcome of the case. While the merging parties might have faced an effective competitive constraint in a market for smaller customers, they were the only suppliers to high-end users. It is likely, therefore, that the transaction would have resulted in an SLC in the market for high-end users had it been defined as a separate market.

Kingspan/Xtratherm, another prohibition case, contains an extensive analysis of market definition running to 13 pages out of a total of 45 (excluding annexes). The parties manufactured and supplied PU/PIR insulation products. They argued that the relevant market included various other types of insulation materials in addition to PU/PIR. The CA concluded, however, that PU/PIR insulation products constituted a distinct product market. The CA cited evidence provided by architects and other users that, although PU/PIR was more expensive, other insulation materials would have required much thicker amounts of insulation. As a result, buildings would either have to occupy a larger land area which had significant cost implications or have a smaller amount of internal space. Subsequently in *Xtratherm/Ballytherm* the CCPC stated that the transaction would not raise any competition concerns regardless of whether the market was defined narrowly as PU/PIR or broadly to include all insulation materials but that it saw no reason to depart from the market definition in *Kingspan/Xtratherm.*[533]

Tetra Laval/Carlisle highlights the importance for merging parties to define markets correctly. According to the Determination, the notifying parties had indicated that they only overlapped in respect of the supply and sale of heat exchangers based on actual sales to customers within the State. However, the CA found that the parties had competed with one another in several tenders for the supply of other types of *"limited purpose equipment"*.[534] The CA concluded that, although the parties had never actually sold such equipment to customers in the State, there was a competitive overlap between them because they regularly tendered for contracts to supply it.[535]

533 The parties argued that market circumstances had changed since the CA's 2006 decision. As previously noted, if a narrow market definition indicates that a merger will not raise any competition concerns, then it is unlikely that it would do so if the market were defined more widely.

534 Limited purpose equipment was described as equipment which had specific limited uses, in contrast to general purpose equipment which had a variety of different uses.

535 In *Q-Park/Tazbell* the parties identified a market for the provision of car parking services in the original notification but did not mention the upstream market for the provision of car park management services where they also overlapped.

In *Applied Materials/Brooks Software* the CA simply stated that there was an overlap between the parties in the supply of manufacturing execution software (MES) and that this constituted the relevant market without any discussion or analysis.[536] In *Coillte/Weyerhaeuser* the CA concluded that there was no horizontal overlap between the parties although Weyerhaeuser produced medium-density fibreboard (MDF) and a Coillte subsidiary produced oriented strand board (OSB). Both products could be manufactured from pulpwood suggesting a potential horizontal overlap on the buying side.

Gorecki (2020) states that there was general agreement between the parties, customers, competitors and the CCPC in *Berendsen/King's Laundry* that the healthcare and hospitality sectors constituted separate product markets, citing demand-side differences between customers in terms of the type of linen items and hygiene standard specification. The parties argued, that both markets should have included customer self-supply, *inter alia,* because:

i. Some hospitals and hotels operated on-premises laundries (OPLs);
ii. There was a ready market for the supply of laundry equipment; and
iii. The costs of setting up an OPL were relatively low.

The CCPC rejected these claims as larger customers *"unanimously considered that setting up OPLs would not be a viable option in response to a 5% to 10% price increase"* (¶3.9).

In *Green Reit/Central Park*[537] the CCPC analysed the competitive effects of the transaction in a potential market for the supply of rentable commercial office property. Less than a month later in *Starwood/Elm Park* it considered a market for the supply of rentable commercial property (i.e., office and retail).[538] In *Hammerson/Teba,*[539] which involved a shopping centre, the CCPC analysed the transaction in the *"potential"* market for the supply of rentable retail space. The UKCMA in *Hammerson/Grand Central*

---

536 The Determination states *"MES software is deployed in an assortment of complex manufacturing environments such as semiconductor fabrication plants ('fabs'), flat panel display plants, automotive plants and life sciences manufacturing plants, among others"* (¶2.6). In fairness, the CA may have concluded that it was self-evident that there were no substitutes for MES software.

537 CCPC M/15/065 – *Green Reit/Central Park,* 23.12.2015.

538 CCPC M/15/070 – *Starwood/Elm Park,* 18.1.2016. It is not obvious why the CCPC applied two different market definitions as there was a minor overlap between the merging parties in retail property in the former case. The CCPC subsequently reverted to a market for rentable commercial office property in CCPC M/16/028 – *Standard Life/Block B Elm Park,* 14.7.2016.

539 CCPC M/17/046 – *Hammerson/Teba,* 14.9.2017.

Shopping Centre[540] considered a market for retail space in shopping centres and on-street, whereas the EU Commission in *Hammerson/Irish Life/ILAC Shopping Centre*[541] based its competitive analysis on a market limited to retail space in shopping centres.

In *ESB/NIE* the CA analysed the impact of the transaction *inter alia* in the market for electricity generation and wholesale supply. The CA/CCPC stated that it had followed a similar approach in *SSE/Endessa*[542] and *EP UK Investments/Tynagh Energy*.[543] The problem is that there is arguably no single market for electricity generation but multiple individual temporal markets because electricity is still largely non-storable. Market shares based on generation capacity are a poor indicator of market power in electricity generation where market power stems from the ability of generators to set the market price at peak demand periods (Borenstein *et al.*, 1999). Failing to recognise this may have resulted in a false negative.

Geographic Market Definition in Individual Cases

Geographic markets may be local, regional, national or in some cases may be even wider than the State. Low transport costs would usually, but not always, imply a wide geographic market (Motta, 2004). Benson (1980) observes that to establish whether two firms are in the same geographic market it is necessary to examine the reactions of one firm to price changes by the other. Affeldt *et al.* (2021) note that the EU Commission has been criticised in the past for defining geographic markets too narrowly when in many sectors competition is arguably global. They found that, in over 5,000 EU merger cases over the 1990-2014 period, markets were defined as national in 64% of cases; EU-wide in 25% of cases; and worldwide in the remaining 11% of cases. There was some evidence of a shift toward wider geographic markets over time, excluding the final year of the sample.

In *Coffee (General Foods Corp.)*,[544] the majority of the USFTC adopted a wide geographic market definition on the grounds that transport costs were

---

540 UKCMA ME/6597/16 – *Hammerson/Grand Central Shopping Centre*, 28.7.2016.

541 EU Commission Case No. COMP/M.8229 – *Hammerson/Irish Life/ILAC Shopping Centre*, 14.12.2016.

542 CA M/12/008 – *SSE/Endessa*, 17.7.2012.

543 CCPC M/19/025 – *EP UK Investments/Tynagh Energy*, 30.9.2019. The CCPC stated, somewhat confusingly, in this case that it had *"assessed the likely competitive impact of the Proposed Transaction on the potential product market for the supply of electricity generation capacity"* (¶23). If it was applying the same market definition as in the two earlier cases it would have been helpful to have used the same wording.

544 *General Foods Corp.*, 3 Trade Reg. Rep. (CCH), 142 (April 6, 1984).

low although price data and company planning documents indicated a narrower geographic market definition (Hilke & Nelson, 1989). Werden (2000), in an expert witness report in *Interstate Bakeries*,[545] noted that bread was commonly shipped over long distances and transportation costs were low, suggesting a wide geographic market. Most of the evidence pointed toward highly localised retail markets for white sliced bread. This apparent contradiction was explained by evidence that price discrimination was possible between different areas, indicating that geographic markets were local. Stigler & Sherwin (1985) point out that large price differences may persist between different geographic areas even with large trade flows if price discrimination is possible. Defining markets around targeted customers also referred to as *"price discrimination markets"* was originally included in USHMG1992 but was given much greater prominence in USHMG2010 (Shapiro & Shelanski, 2021). The CA in *United Care/Pharmexx* cited the lack of price discrimination between customers in different parts of the country as evidence of a State-wide market.

CCPCMG (2014) state:

> *"The relevant geographic market consists of all supply locations that would have to be included for the hypothetical monopolist to find it profitable to impose a small but significant non-transitory increase in price" (¶2.21).*[546]

EU2024MDN defines the relevant geographic markets as follows:

> *"The relevant geographic market comprises the geographic area in which the undertakings involved supply or demand relevant products, in which the conditions of competition are sufficiently homogeneous for the effects of the conduct or concentration under investigation to be able to be assessed, and which can be distinguished from other geographic areas, in particular because conditions of competition are appreciably different in those areas" (¶12(b)).*[547]

Retail Geographic Markets

Competition agencies frequently analyse the impact of retail mergers on competition in both national and local markets. Whether a market is national or local will depend firstly, on whether the parties operate nationally or only

545 *United States v. Interstate Bakeries Corp. and Continental Baking Co.*, (ND Ill., 1995).

546 Although the wording differs from CAMG2002, there is little difference in practice.

547 The definition is similar, but not identical, to that in ¶8 of the EU1997MDN.

within particular areas. The fact that the parties operate nationally does not necessarily mean that they operate a national competitive strategy. In both grocery and motor fuel retailing, a small number of undertakings which operate multiple retail outlets throughout the State account for a large share of the respective markets. Supermarket multiples generally charge uniform national prices whereas motor fuel prices diverge considerably between different areas (CCPC, 2022, November).

The degree of competition faced by multiple retailers may vary at local level, providing scope to charge different prices in different areas. Operating a national pricing policy and failing to exploit market power at local level may be costly in terms of profits foregone. Nevertheless, a national pricing policy may be beneficial due to (i) the benefits of having a uniform retailer image and (ii) economies of scale in price setting, price labelling and advertising.

National pricing policies may also allow scope for local variations. Although the parties in *Somerfield/Morrison* had national pricing policies, Somerfield operated tiered pricing which resulted in local price variations. The UKOFT found that some retailers had centrally set strategies which provided for local actions and responses such as targeted discounts, margin support, or order of store refurbishments. Thus, centrally set strategies may allow for important variations depending on local market competition. Where retailers apply uniform national pricing policies, other key elements of their retail offer may reflect competition at local level.[548]

Where a merger reduces competition in local areas the parties may increase prices and/or reduce service quality thereby lowering a store's costs and increasing its profit margins. The CCPC acknowledged in *Tesco/Joyce's* that while multiple supermarket chains pursued national pricing strategies, *"local flexing"* meant that non-price elements of competition could vary depending on the degree of local market competition. If a merger increases the number of local areas where a retailer has market power post-merger, this may alter the costs and benefits of adhering to a national pricing policy. In *Grafton/Heiton* the CA considered why the parties would not switch to a local pricing strategy post-merger.

---

548 Such elements include promotions, vouchers, offers; local advertising; quality of management and staff training; staffing levels and number of checkouts; product range, availability and quality; levels of pre- and after-sales service; store aspect: layout, size, maintenance, facilities and opening hours.

Entry analysis, which measures the impact of new store openings, can assist in defining local geographic markets. The UKCC in *HMV/Ottakar's*[549] cited econometric evidence showing that new store openings had a significant impact on existing outlets within a one-mile radius but had less impact on those located further away. An *ex post* analysis of this case confirmed the existence of local competition but found no evidence of any negative impact on price, service quality or product variety post-merger (Aguzzoni *et al.*, 2016). The UKOFT has cited parties' internal documents on the effect of store openings in several cases.

The UK authorities have frequently defined catchment areas as the area accounting for 80% of a retail outlet's sales.[550] The extent of catchment areas has varied depending on the type, size and location of retail outlets involved. Evidence used to identify the origin of sales includes loyalty card data, home delivery records, customer contact details, customer surveys and company documents (UKCC/OFT, 2011 March and UKCMA, 2017, April 10).

In *Safeway* the UKCC concluded that catchment areas for large supermarkets with a floor area of 1,400m^2 or more were limited to a 10-minute drive-time in urban areas and a 15-minute drive-time in rural areas. Smaller shops were found to have a catchment area of a five-minute drive-time in urban areas and a 10-minute drive-time in rural areas. The French competition authority defined catchment areas based on a 30-minute drive time for hypermarkets and 10-15 minutes for supermarkets (Allain *et al.*, 2017). The UKOFT concluded that catchment areas for large out-of-town carpet stores were wider than for smaller independent outlets.[551] The UKMMC considered that there were separate geographic markets for town centre and out-of-town electrical goods retailers.[552]

---

549 In *Thomas Crosbie Holdings/South East Broadcasting* the CA cited internal party documents indicating that the entry of Beat FM had impacted on the incumbent WLF FM's advertising sales.

550 UKCMA (2017, April 10). This threshold, which was first applied by the UKCC in *Safeway/Asda*, is designed to exclude statistical outliers. The UKCMA centres catchment areas around the stores of both merging parties (2017, April 10, ¶2.3). The CA/CCPC have generally only considered catchment areas in respect of target outlets, although it followed the UK approach in *Maxol/Busselle* and *McMullen Bros/Naas Fuels*. The EU Commission in *Veolia/Suez* identified catchment areas around each of the merging parties' waste treatment sites and estimated market shares based on the total volume treated by each site included in the relevant catchment area (EU Commission Case No. COMP/M.9699 – *Veolia/Suez*, 14.12.2021).

551 UKOFT ME/4570/10 – *Carpetright/Allied Carpets*, 13.9.2010.

552 UKMMC – *Kingfisher/Dixons*, 1990. Consumers typically shop around before purchasing large electrical items, indicating a single market for town centre and out of town electrical retail outlets

Grocery retail markets are regarded as localised because consumers tend not to travel long distances to do their grocery shopping. Empirical research shows that travel costs, rather than price or variety, is the main factor in consumers' choice of grocery stores (Marshall & Pires, 2018). The CA/CCPC have generally analysed the impact of grocery mergers at both national and local level, in line with the approach adopted by competition agencies in other jurisdictions. In the first merger notified under the 2002 Act,[553] the CA concluded that there was no horizontal overlap between the parties because the acquirer only operated grocery stores in Galway and South Dublin while the vendor operated stores in Counties Kildare and Meath. In *Musgrave/Superquinn* the CA identified both a national and a regional grocery market comprising Dublin City and County but also noted *"it is possible for the competitive environment at a local level to differ from that at a national or regional level"* (¶113).

In retail grocery mergers, the CA/CCPC has generally applied wider catchment areas in rural compared to urban areas but its approach has not always been uniform. In *BWG/Mangan's*[554] the CA accepted catchment areas of *"at least 15-20 minutes, particularly in rural areas"* (¶16). Although not explicitly stated, the CA appeared to accept catchment areas of a 10-minute drive-time/10-kilometre radius of the target outlets in *Musgrave/Superquinn*. *BWG/Londis* applied *"an approximate 20-minute drive-time catchment area"* (¶80). The CCPC applied a 10-minute drive-time/10-kilometre area in *Joyce's/Nestor's*,[555] *Cedarglade (Musgrave)/Fortunestown Supermarket*[556] and *TOP/Garrycastle (Spar) Athlone*.[557] *Musgrave/Whelan Centra* cited an analysis of competing outlets within five miles/eight kilometres of the target's retail outlets, without distinguishing between urban and rural locations, although two of the six stores involved were described as being in rural locations (¶21).

---

while the fact that the main national retailers of electrical goods employed national advertising and pricing policies was very important for market definition (London Economics, 1997).

553 CA M/03/001 – *Musgrave/Express Check-out*, 13.3.2003.

554 CA M/08/014 – *BWG/Mangan's*, 2.5.2008.

555 The Determination noted that only one of the Acquirer's five supermarkets was located within 10 kilometres of any of the Target's shops.

556 The CCPC oddly stated that it did not need to come to a definitive view as to whether the relevant geographic market was local, regional, or national even though the proposed transaction involved an individual supermarket and was thus extremely unlikely to have had a national or regional impact.

557 CCPC M/18/056 – *TOP/Garrycastle (Spar) Athlone*, 20.8.2018. The CCPC did not state whether the target was located in an urban or a rural area.

In *Dunnes/Whelan's Tipperary*[558] the parties had suggested a 10-kilometre/10-minute drive-time but the CCPC stated that a wider area might be appropriate for two of the Target outlets which were located in rural areas. The CCPC applied a 10-minute drive-time (without referring to distance) in *Musgrave/Donnybrook Fair*.[559] *BWG/4 Aces* stated that an analysis provided by the parties indicated that there would be a number of stores competing with the target's franchise outlets post-merger, without identifying the relevant catchment areas. *Maxol/Tom Chawke* cited (i) the number of forecourt convenience stores within 15 kilometres; and (ii) the number of non-forecourt convenience stores within eight kilometres of the target's forecourt convenience store (¶20ii).[560] *Cedarglade (Musgrave)/ Ballybrit Service Station* stated that the transaction was unlikely to raise any competition concerns because (a) there would be no change in the number of grocery fascias and sufficient competitors *"in the Greater Galway City Area"* while (b) there were five competing store fascias within a three-kilometre radius of the target shop (¶17).[561]

The CCPC in *Dunnes Stores/JC Savage* stated that it would analyse the transaction based on the *"narrowest potential geographic market, the JCSS Catchment Area"* (¶14) without stating whether this was narrower than catchment areas applied in previous grocery mergers.[562] *Tesco/Joyce's* noted that drive-times from the target's Oranmore supermarket to the nearest Dunnes Stores outlet varied depending on traffic conditions and while the average was seven to 12 minutes, it could be as high as 28 at peak times.[563]

Although the UK authorities have historically analysed the effects of retail grocery mergers at national and local level, Haydock & Smith (2019) note that *Sainsbury's/Asda* placed an increasing focus on the national market. UKCMA (2017, April 10) stated that the incentive for the parties to reduce competition

---

558 In this case the target did not operate grocery shops but operated four butcher's shops.

559 CCPC M/18/079 – *Musgrave/Donnybrook Fair*, 1.11.2018.

560 It is unclear why the Determination (a) only referred to the number of convenience stores given the CA/CCPC view that such stores are part of a wider grocery market and (b) defined different catchment areas for forecourt and non-forecourt convenience stores.

561 It is unclear, therefore, whether the relevant catchment area comprised the *"Greater Galway City Area"*, which was not defined in the Determination, or was limited to a three-kilometre radius around the target shop.

562 The furthest competing store included in the catchment area was 7.5 kilometres from the target outlet.

563 This raises the question of whether it may be necessary to specify a time of day when using drive-times to define local markets. UKCMA (2017, April 10, ¶2.16) states that assumptions about driving speeds must be clearly stated in any submissions in respect of catchment areas. The CCPC concluded that the store was within the relevant local market but suggested that it exercised a materially weaker competitive constraint on the merging parties' Oranmore stores.

at national level reflects the aggregate loss of competitive pressure at local level, i.e., there is no additional unilateral incentive over and above that resulting from any loss of competition at local level.

The CA in *Debenham's/Roches Stores*[564] appeared to adopt a contradictory approach to local geographic markets. It stated that Dublin City centre was the *"only area where the parties' retail outlets are located in close proximity to each other"* (¶15). It argued, however, that in addition to multicategory retailers and specialist retailers in the City Centre, the parties also faced competition from multi-category retailers and specialist stores in out-of-town shopping centres with transport links to the city centre. The target also had three stores in out-of-town shopping centres although the Determination did not consider this overlap.[565] Subsequently, in *Fitzwilliam/Wittington Canada/ Arnotts* the CA analysed the competitive impact of the transaction in a County Dublin geographic market, although the Target's two stores were located in the City Centre.[566]

The CA in *JD Sports/Champion Sports* concluded that the relevant catchment areas for the merging parties' sports goods stores *"may exceed 15km"* (¶32) citing *inter alia* information on customers' addresses obtained from a 2010 JD Sports customer survey before concluding that a 20-minute drive time constituted *"the narrowest possible geographic markets where the proposed transaction is likely to raise competitive concerns"* (¶38).[567]

In *Eason/Dubray,* a merger of two book retailers, the CCPC, while adopting a three-kilometre threshold for catchment areas in respect of the parties' stores in Dublin city centre, Galway city centre and Dún Laoghaire, accepted that a wider catchment area was appropriate for the parties' stores in the Liffey Valley shopping centre in West Dublin based on loyalty card data which indicated that many of the customers that had made purchases at Eason's Liffey Valley store lived more than three kilometres away.

---

564 CA M/06/052 – *Debenham's/Roches Stores*, 6.9.2006.

565 The Target's out-of-town stores were located in Blackrock, Blanchardstown and Tallaght, all of which had transport links to the city centre.

566 Confusingly it referred to a GDA market but described this as limited to County Dublin. It subsequently followed this approach in CCPC M/15/036 – *Fitzwilliam/Wittington Canada/ Arnotts II*, 21.8.2015) and *House of Fraser/Sports Direct*. The CCPC in *Arthopoda (Orpea)/Brindley Healthcare* stated *"The GDA is generally considered to include Dublin City, Fingal, South Dublin, Dún Laoghaire-Rathdown, Meath, Kildare and Wicklow…"*, noting that this definition was also used by the CSO and the National Transport Authority (FN6). The CA/CCPC also applied this definition of the GDA in *Greenstar/Veolia* and *Wicklow Hotel Partnership/Powerscourt Hotel.*

567 In contrast, the UKCC in *Sports Direct/JJB* concluded that local markets for sports retail outlets were limited to a two- to five-mile radius around a store.

In *GEHE* the CA stated that retail pharmacy markets were local rather than national and applied a one-mile radius when considering local markets in two Dublin suburbs, although it stated *"that in rural areas the catchment area of a pharmacy could be considerably more than this"* (¶4.16).[568] In *Lloydspharmacy/Walsh's & Friary Allcare*[569] the CCPC cited the distances between the target's outlets and the purchaser's closest outlets without indicating whether it considered them to be in the same or in separate geographic markets.[570] *Lloydspharmacy/Dargle Pharmacies*[571] noted that the closest Lloyds outlet was located 3.3 kilometres from the Target's Shankill pharmacy (¶13) without indicating whether it was in the same geographic market as the vendor's Bray outlets. In *Uniphar/Lindchem,*[572] the CCPC identified a horizontal overlap between the parties in two local markets in Dublin 6 and Ballyvolane, a suburb of Cork City, noting in the latter case that the closest *Uniphar* outlet was three kilometres away (¶19).[573] In *Uniphar/Riverchem*[574] analysed six local areas, although the distances between the merging parties' pharmacies ranged from 400 metres (in Limerick City) to 35 kilometres (in County Kildare). In *Carlyle/Fermoy Medical Hall*, the CCPC concluded that there was no horizontal overlap between the parties because the purchaser's closest outlet was 27 kilometres from the target (¶17).[575]

In *Lloyds Pharmacy/McSweeney,*[576] the CCPC considered both national and local markets, although the transaction involved only four pharmacies. The CCPC found no horizontal overlap between the parties in respect of three of the target outlets because the purchaser's closest pharmacies were between 68 and 79 kilometres away (¶s19-21) but identified a horizontal overlap in Limerick City *"comprising a catchment area of within a radius of 2km from Charlotte Quay Pharmacy"* (¶22).[577]

---

568 UKCMA Case No.ME/6558/15 – *Celesio/Sainsbury's (Pharmacy Business)*, 29.7.2016 found that pharmacies varied aspects of their retail offer based on the level of local market competition.

569 CCPC M/15/021 – *Lloydspharmacy Ireland Ltd./Walsh's & Friary Allcare*, 21.5.2015.

570 The distances varied from 2.2 up to 43 kilometres (¶s 13-16).

571 CCPC M/15/025 – *Lloydspharmacy Ireland Ltd/Dargle Pharmacies*, 30.6.2015.

572 CCPC M/15/076 – *Uniphar/Lindchem*, 29.1.2016.

573 It referred to other pharmacies being closer, indicating a unilateral effects approach which implies the parties' outlets were considered to be in the same market.

574 CCPC M/16/015 – *Uniphar/Riverchem*, 26.4.2016.

575 CCPC M/18/022 – *Carlyle/Fermoy Medical Hall*, 27.3.2018.

576 CCPC M/18/024 – *Lloyds Pharmacy Ireland Ltd/McSweeney Group*, 28.3.2018.

577 The CCPC subsequently followed a similar approach in CCPC M/18/052 – *Sam McAuley (Carlyle)/Nolan's*, 14.8.2018; CCPC M/18/097 – *Uniphar/Inischem*, 1.2.2019 and CCPC M/19/019 – *Lloyds Pharmacy/Median BOFH*, 13.8.2019.

In *Uniphar/Bradley's Pharmacy Group,* having applied a two-kilometre catchment area, the CCPC concluded that the proposed transaction would not result in an SLC in Ardee, partly because there were two other pharmacies within two kilometres of the merging parties' outlets but went on to state that pharmacies in Drogheda and Dundalk:

> *"...will exert a competitive constraint on Uniphar, following implementation of the Proposed Transaction. Therefore, the Commission considers that the Proposed Transaction will not substantially lessen competition in the supply of prescription and non-prescription medicines in retail pharmacies in the potential local market comprising the local area around Bradley's Pharmacy in Ardee, Co. Louth" (¶44).*[578]

The conclusion is totally inconsistent with previous pharmacy cases. It seems highly unlikely that pharmacies in Drogheda and Dundalk, which were 20-25 minutes' drive-time away, would exert a competitive constraint on those in Ardee. No evidence was advanced in support of this conclusion nor is there any suggestion in the Determination that there were particular circumstances justifying a much wider market definition in this case. The CCPC subsequently applied a two-kilometre radius when analysing the impact on competition in local pharmacy markets in *Uniphar/Hickey's.*

In *Uniphar/LXV Remedies (Sam McAuley)* the CCPC applied a six-kilometre radius around the target outlet which was located in the Mahon Shopping Centre in Cork City because it was the largest shopping centre in the county and drew customers from a wider area than two-kilometres. Similar arguments would arguably apply to pharmacies in large shopping centres in any of the State's major cities.[579] Two of the target's other pharmacies in this case were located 3.4 kilometres apart in the town of Navan in County Meath. The CCPC identified two different local markets based on a two-kilometre catchment area. Both pharmacies faced competition from the same seven pharmacies, all of which were within two-kilometres of both. An eighth pharmacy was within two kilometres of one of the target outlets but was 3.6 kilometres away from the other. Arguably

---

578 CCPC M/18/085 – *Uniphar/Bradley's Pharmacy Group*, 16.11.2018. Drogheda is at the southern end of the county and Dundalk at its northern end, while Ardee is on its western edge, 21km from Dundalk and 24km from Drogheda (*Google Maps* Accessed 30.3.2023). Thus, this would imply a local geographic market encompassing virtually all of County Louth.

579 The UKCMA concluded that pharmacies located in supermarkets had wider catchment areas than stand-alone pharmacies (*Celesio/Sainsbury's (Pharmacy business)*).

conditions were sufficiently similar to support a single geographic market comprising all of Navan town.

The CA in *Statoil/Conoco* noted that competition *"particularly at the retail level for motor fuels, may be rather localised by virtue of the fact that any savings from lower purchase prices are quickly dissipated if one has to travel any distance to obtain supplies at a lower price"* (¶4.5). The report, nevertheless, focused exclusively on competition at national level with no analysis of competition at local level.[580] Subsequently, in *Maxol/Busselle* the CA considered competitive effects at national level and in several local geographic markets, based on a five mile catchment area.[581] The CA identified local markets in *Statoil/Topaz* based on a two-mile radius in urban areas and a five-mile radius in rural areas (CA, *Annual Report 2006*).[582] The CA applied a five-mile/eight-kilometre catchment area in *Chevron/Texoil* stating it was only within that radius *"that the locations of the parties' service stations could raise competition concerns"* (¶23). The CA/CCPC subsequently applied catchment areas of 3.2 and eight kilometres in urban and rural areas, respectively, in various filling station mergers.[583]

---

580 The parties claimed that there were only 12 cases where they had filling stations in close proximity of each other, although there is no indication of how close proximity was defined.

581 The local markets all comprised rural areas.

582 There was no Determination in this case because the CA missed the deadline for deciding to conduct a Phase 2 investigation.

583 See, for example, *Tedcastles/Fate Park*; *Topaz/Esso*; CCPC M/16/021 – *Maxol/Topaz Bull*, 19.5.2016; *Maxol/Topaz Ballindine*; *Petrogas/MKMH*; *Topaz/Casey's of Bantry*; *Maxol/Melia's Harolds Cross;* CCPC M/17/007 – *Petrogas/Excol*, 16.3.2017; *Petrogas/Westmeath Motors*; *Maxol/Great Gas*; *TOP/KEC*; *TOP/H2 Blakes*; *Maxol/Brennan's*; *Valero/Riverside Service Station*; *Petrogas/Carranstown*; CCPC M/18/072 – *Petrogas/Glenview Motors*, 2.10.2018 (for some reason, the CCPC considered a national as well as a local market, although the transaction involved an individual filling station); and *Maxol/Kinsella's Fuel Services*. Despite the large number of cases, the CA/CCPC has never advanced any economic justification for catchment areas of 3.2/8 kilometres and has never advanced evidence suggesting that such areas account for 80% of a filling station's customers or sales: in *Tedcastles/Sirio* the CCPC applied an eight-kilometre catchment area, although two of the four stations appear to have been located in urban areas; in *BWG/Keating's Londis*, it applied an eight-kilometre radius for motor fuels and a three-kilometre radius for convenience stores; and in *Petrogas/PR Reilly*, it considered filling stations both within a 3.2-kilometre radius and within 3.2 kilometres along a straight road from the target outlet. In the majority of these cases, the CA/CCPC did not define what constituted an urban or a rural area. Two filling stations in Sligo town were deemed to be in a rural area in *Petrogas/Excol*. The CCPC adopted the CSO definitions of urban and rural areas in *McMullan Bros/Naas Fuels*. Houde (2012) suggested that geographic markets for filling stations should be defined based on consumers' commuting paths that depend on the structure of the road network and the direction of traffic flows rather than

In *Maxol/Tom Chawke* the CCPC concluded that the transaction would not result in an SLC because there were 48 competitors within 15 kilometres of the target filling station but offered no explanation for applying a wider radius than in other filling station cases. In *TOP/Ashbourne Oil*[584] the CCPC stated that there were eight filling stations which sold road diesel within a [redacted] radius of the Target's premises.[585] In *East Cork Oil/Tara Oil*[586] the CCPC listed 12 competing service stations, along with estimated market shares for each, but redacted details of the relevant catchment area within which these stations were located (¶29). It is difficult to understand why the extent of the relevant catchment areas was redacted. In *Petrogas/Knockmitten* the CCPC did not identify specific catchment areas, although the Purchaser's closest filling stations were between 19 and 53 kilometres away.

It is perhaps surprising that the CA/CCPC has not sought to define local geographic markets more accurately in the case of grocery shops, filling stations and pharmacies, rather than relying on rules of thumb, given the number of cases involved. Equally, while catchment areas may well differ depending on the nature of the products concerned, it has offered no explanation for why catchment areas for grocery shops are three times those for filling stations in urban areas or 2.5 times as large in rural areas.

The CA/CCPC has tended to only define catchment areas centred around the target undertaking's outlets in retail mergers. This is out of line with international best practice and is likely to underestimate the extent of catchment areas and to exclude outlets which would exercise a competitive constraint on the merging parties, giving rise to potential false positives. Consider, for example, a situation in which the purchaser and the target have filling stations in an urban area 3.2 kilometres apart. Now suppose that there are three competing stations within one kilometre of the purchaser station in the opposite direction to the target. A catchment area centred around the target filling station will exclude these three competitors although they are all likely to be closer competitors of the purchaser's station than the target station is.

The CA/CCPC has also been inconsistent in its approach to different retail categories. For example, in the case of grocery retailing it has frequently defined catchment areas based on drive-times and distance whereas in other cases, notably motor fuel retailing, it has only considered

---

isochrones. UKCMA (2017, April 10, ¶2.15) provides that isochrones should follow local road networks.

584 CCPC M/15/019 – *TOP/Ashbourne Oil*, 15.5.2015.

585 Catchment areas for kerosene and marked gas oil were also redacted in the Determination.

586 CCPC M/15/061 – *East Cork Oil/Tara Oil*, 14.12.2015.

distances. Drive-times rather than distance-based measures should be used to define catchment areas as the former take account of geographical barriers to travel such as topography and the relevant road infrastructure (EU Commission, 2021).

In *Grafton/Heiton*, the CA stated that *"the catchment area of a typical DIY superstore is 4-5 miles for a large urban area, and 10-15 miles elsewhere"* (¶3.16) while the catchment area for a builders' merchants was about five to 10 miles in Dublin and Cork cities and 20-25 miles elsewhere (¶7.7).[587] The CA in *Wolseley/Brooks Group* stated that market enquiries indicated catchment areas for wood flooring retail outlets of three to five miles in Dublin and up to 30 miles in the rest of the country but stated that *"this does not constitute a determination as to the relevant geographic market"* (¶8).[588] In *Chadwicks/Haylen* the CCPC considered a State-wide market, and a market limited to a five-mile radius of the Target's premises. The purchaser in this case operated a nationwide chain of outlets while the Target distributed its products throughout the island of Ireland from its premises in Inchicore in Dublin. It is unclear why the CCPC felt it necessary to consider a possible local market. There is no indication that conditions of competition within the local market differed from those in the rest of the State.[589]

In several motor vehicle dealership mergers the CCPC defined catchment areas as encompassing a radius of 90 kilometres/one-hour drive-time.[590] In *Connolly Motor/Hyundai Galway*, however, the CCPC stated that it was not

---

587 The CCPC applied similar catchment areas in CCPC M/16/012 – *HPC/St. Gobain*, 11.4.2016. The Determination, however, stated that ancillary restrictions included in the agreement were excessive because they were *"broader than the markets affected by the proposed transaction, which are regional/local in scope"* (¶27).

588 CA M/04/042 – *Wolseley/Brooks Group*, 26.8.2004. The parties operated wood-flooring retail outlets in Dublin, Cork, Galway, Limerick, Sligo, Tralee and Waterford. The parties also had outlets in Sligo which supplied heating and plumbing equipment to the building trade.

589 The CCPC adopted a similar approach in *Grafton (Chadwicks)/Sitetech*, while applying a 10-mile radius for local markets. Again, the target distributed its products nationwide while the CCPC concluded that parties outside the relevant local markets who also distributed their products nationwide would exercise a constraint on the merging parties, making it unlikely that conditions of competition differed between local geographic markets. The CCPC stated in *Associated Hardware/National Hardware* that there was no reason to depart from the approach taken in both *Chadwicks/Haylen* and *Grafton (Chadwicks)/Sitetech* where it had conducted a competitive analysis of building materials on a national basis while failing to mention that it had also considered local markets in both those cases (see below).

590 *JDM Automotive/Commons Road Cars*; *JDM Automotive/Karmann Auto*; and *Frank Keane/MSL*. In *MMM/John Morrison Motors* the CCPC noted that a large proportion of the merging parties' new car sales were to customers located outside such a catchment area, indicating that this definition may be too narrow.

necessary to come to a conclusion as to whether the geographic market was limited to County Galway, where the target business was located, or the entire State and analysed the impact on both possible definitions.[591]

Ladbrokes/Coral acknowledged that LBO markets were localised but included no analysis of specific local markets. In *Ladbrokes/Chronicle* the CA implicitly accepted that individual racecourses constituted separate markets for on-course betting. The CCPC has considered both local and national geographic markets for LBOs. The UKCMA in *Ladbrokes/Coral*[592] found evidence of local market flexing, although bookmakers did not consider local market competition when competing to offer the best odds for specific events in national newspapers. The parties argued in *Boyle Sports/Tully Bookmakers*[593] that large bookmaking chains set prices (odds) nationally but acknowledged that non-price competition was important at local level.

The CCPC in *Paddy Power/Track* concluded that there was no horizontal overlap between the parties as the nearest Paddy Power LBO was 6.8 kilometres from the target LBO. In *Paddy Power/Hacketts*[594] the CCPC concluded that the transaction raised no competition issues based on the number of LBOs within two kilometres of the target LBOs. In *Paddy Power/Mulholland*[595] the CCPC considered the number of competing LBOs within a one-kilometre radius of five of the target's LBOs but adopted a five to 10-kilometre radius in respect of a sixth. In *Boyle Sports/Bambury I*, the CCPC cited the UKCMA in *Ladbrokes/Coral* that *"a catchment area of 400m was appropriate for the assessment of the competitive effects of the transaction"* (¶6.106).[596] The CCPC analysed the proposed transaction based on (a) a 400-metre and (b) a three-kilometre radius around the Target LBOs.[597]

---

591 The suggestion that the market may have been State-wide seems inconsistent with the view that catchment areas of motor dealerships are limited to a 90-kilometre radius. The Purchaser's Mayo and Sligo dealerships were more than 90 kilometres from the target's dealership (*Google Maps*. Accessed 25.9.2024). In *JDM Automotive/Motorpark*, the CCPC ruled out any overlap between the parties as they were located 110 kilometres from each other.

592 UKCMA ME/6556/15 – *Ladbrokes/Coral*, 11.1.2016, ¶6.106.

593 CCPC M/21/066 – *BoyleSports/Tully Bookmakers*, 22.12.2021.

594 CCPC M/15/022 – *Paddy Power/Hacketts*, 4.6.2015.

595 CCPC M/15/033 – *Paddy Power/Mulholland*, 6.8.2015.

596 In *Grand Metropolitan/William Hill*, the UKMMC recommended that the parties be required to divest LBOs that were within a quarter-mile of each other if there were no other LBOs within a quarter-mile of the parties' outlets.

597 Given that no overlaps arose within a 400-metre radius, also applying a wider market definition avoided a false negative. There was an overlap between the parties in three of the nine wider catchment areas. The CCPC applied a similar approach in *Boyle Sports/Bambury*

Hotels

There are frequent reports of substantial increases in hotel prices in a particular city or town coinciding with large concerts or sporting events. Such episodes provide a useful natural experiment. Such price spikes are largely confined to the city or town in question indicating that hotel markets are local in nature.[598] Hotels frequently apply dynamic (or surge) pricing where prices vary in response to demand again indicating that geographic markets are local (Crowe, 2023, December). A 5% increase by a hypothetical hotel monopoly in Galway city might result in sufficient customers switching to other hotels within a reasonably short drive-time to render such a price increase unprofitable. However, it is unlikely to cause consumers to switch to hotels in Cork, Donegal or Waterford. The CA/CCPC has generally applied local geographic markets in hotel mergers, although it has not always defined such markets consistently.

In *Kantaka/RBS* the CA implicitly concluded that Dublin constituted the relevant geographic market. In other cases, involving Dublin hotels, the CA/CCPC referred to a Dublin city market,[599] a county Dublin market[600] and a GDA wide market.[601] *Bernard McNamara/Conrad International/ECHPL* referred to *"the local hotel accommodation market"* (¶9) without defining it. In *Atlantic Troy/Killeshin Hotel* the CCPC stated that it had based its analysis

---

II; Boyle Sports/JP Bookmakers; and *Boyle Sports/Tully Bookmakers* while also considering a national market.

598 Oasis: Dublin hotel rates rising – but still too early to count cost of reunion concerts, *Irish Times* (2024, August 27).

599 *Tetrarch/Dawson Hotel* identified various Dublin city centre hotels as providing sufficient competition to the parties post-merger, implying a Dublin City geographic market. *Thornmont/Hilton Kilmainham* stated the parties were not particularly close competitors, based on distances and travel times, without indicating whether it considered them to be in the same geographic market.

600 *Irish Property/Ballsbridge Holdco* stated that Dublin was the narrowest relevant geographic market for five-star hotels. The CCPC applied a County Dublin geographic market in *Dalata/Caverford/Vizmol; Dalata/DoubleTree Hilton;* CCPC M/17/062 – *DekaBank/Gibson,* 15.12.2017; *Tetrarch/Citywest.* In the last case the merging hotels were arguably in separate geographic markets as they were located 16.5 kilometres (34 minutes' drive-time) from one another. Applying a wider market definition provided a check against a possible false negative. The Determination states the hotels were unlikely to be each other's closest competitors, given their locations.

601 *Wicklow Hotel Partnership/Powerscourt Hotel* analysed the impact in both County Dublin and the GDA which it defined as counties Dublin, Wicklow, Meath and Kildare because the target hotel was located *"in County Wicklow on the Dublin/Wicklow border"* (¶22). The Determination stated that limiting the market to County Wicklow would not alter the conclusions.

on *"the narrowest geographic market possible"* (¶20) without identifying it.[602] In several cases involving individual hotels the CCPC, having found no overlap between the parties in local markets, based on a 20-minute drive-time, also analysed the impact of the transactions in a national market.[603] A national geographic market definition appears inappropriate when the acquisition involves an individual hotel.

In *Dalata/White's Hotel* the CCPC analysed the transaction based on a 20-minute drive-time from the target hotel in Wexford Town.[604] In *Dalata/Moran's Hotel/Bewley's* the CCPC, again without coming to a definitive conclusion analysed the transaction based on markets comprising (i) Cork City and surrounding areas; and (ii) County Dublin but indicated that relevant geographic markets could be narrower (FN23).

Hospitals/Nursing Homes

In several private hospital mergers, the CCPC considered both regional and national geographic markets.[605] In *Bon Secours/Barrington's Hospital* the CCPC noted that, while both hospitals were located in the HSE West Region, they were in different sub-regions so that while they overlapped at regional level *"such overlap is likely to be limited"*. It advanced a similar argument in *UPMC/Bon Secours/Druid Stone.* Such areas constitute administrative public hospital regions *"for the HSE's purposes"* and provide little or no information about the degree of competitive overlap between private hospitals. In *Bon Secours/Barrington's Hospital* the CCPC identified the *"Mid-West Region"* (comprising counties Clare, Limerick and North Tipperary) as *"an appropriate regional geographic market"* (¶22). Three years later in *Portlon (Parma)/Galway Clinic* the CCPC identified a regional market for private healthcare services comprising Counties Clare, Donegal, Galway, Leitrim, Mayo, Roscommon, Sligo, and North Tipperary, which it described as the West Region.[606]

---

602 The target hotel was located between 120 and 155 kilometres from the purchaser's three hotels.

603 *SCIF/McWilliam Park Hotel; SCIF/Connemara Coast Hotel; Atlantic Troy/Athlone Springs Hotel;* and *Irish Holdings/Galway Leisure Investments.*

604 It followed a similar approach in *Dalata/Clayton Hotel (Galway).*

605 CCPC M/16/055 – *UPMC & Bon Secours/Druid Stone JV*, 9.12.2016; *Portlon (Parma)/Galway Clinic; Portlon (Parma)/Hermitage*; and *Portlon (Parma)/Blackrock.* While the relevant geographic market for an individual hospital is likely to be regional, a national market appears appropriate where the merging parties operate hospitals throughout the State.

606 The Determination found no horizontal overlap between the parties and reached a similar conclusion in *Portlon (Parma)/Hermitage* and *Portlon (Parma)/Blackrock.* The Determination contains no reference to *Bon Secours/Barrington's* and offers no explanation for moving Clare

Care Choice/TMNH Holdings analysed competition in a national market, a Dublin market and a local market, although the Target only operated one nursing home in South Dublin. Subsequently, in *Arthopoda (Orpea)/Brindley Healthcare* the CCPC did not define a geographic market but analysed the impact of the transaction in (i) Kildare, the only county where the parties overlapped; (ii) the GDA; and (iii) the State. Geographic markets for individual nursing homes appear to be local.[607]

Airlines

In airline mergers individual routes are generally considered to constitute separate markets. A question arises as to whether routes should be defined in terms of flights between two specific airports ("airport pairs") or between specific cities ("city pairs"). In *Ryanair/Aer Lingus I*, the EU Commission defined routes as city pairs based on:

i. Whether both airports were within 100km/one-hour driving time of a city;
ii. Views of airport operators;
iii. Views of other airlines;
iv. Passengers' views as indicated in survey responses;
v. Internal documents of the merging parties;
vi. Price correlations.[608]

The Commission stated that *Ryanair's* marketing and advertising indicated that it viewed certain routes from Dublin to secondary European airports as competing with *Aer Lingus* services to primary airports in the same city. For example, *Ryanair* marketed its Dublin-Beauvais service as being to Paris (Beauvais), indicating that it viewed it as competing with *Aer Lingus'* Dublin-Paris service. *Ryanair's* website included tourist information on the relevant city, indicating that the service was aimed at passengers wishing to visit that city.

---

and North Tipperary from a Mid-west to a West regional market. The CCPC reverted to a Mid-West regional geographic market comprising counties Clare, Limerick and North Tipperary in CCPC M/21/037 – *Bon Secours/Alliance Medical/Barrington's JV*, 26.8.2021.

607 Gaynor *et al.* (2013) report that *ad hoc* methods of market definition resulted in geographic markets being significantly overestimated in many US hospital merger cases.

608 *Ryanair/Aer Lingus I*. Price correlation tests were not run for all routes.

Waste Collection

The CA/CCPC has stated that domestic waste collection markets were local on the basis that waste service operators provided services within a certain radius of transfer stations. Over time it has applied increasingly narrow definitions to local domestic waste collection markets. The CA in *Greenstar/Veolia* identified three regional geographic markets for C&I waste:

i. The GDA;[609]
ii. Cork City and County; and
iii. The South-East Waste Region.

The Determination cited *"compelling reasons"* in the latter case for defining the relevant market as comprising the entire South-East Region rather than Waterford City and County, including the fact that the parties operated in adjoining counties, while waste collected in Waterford City was shipped to transfer stations located outside the city (¶s3.28-3.31). Such arguments appear equally applicable to domestic waste collection services.

The CCPC decided in *PandaGreen/Greenstar* that the four individual Dublin local authority areas each constituted separate geographic markets despite a previous High Court judgement which had defined the relevant geographic market for domestic waste collection services as the GDA. Referring to EU case law, the Court stated:

> *"The question in this case therefore is, within what area are the terms of competition sufficiently homogeneous with regards to the provision of household waste collection services? This question is in fact easily answered. The WMP applies to the areas of all four respondents. The conditions of competition in these areas are therefore homogenous, or at least sufficiently homogenous within the above test. The Variation too applies to what one could call the greater Dublin area. This is therefore the geographic market for the purposes of applying ss. 4 and 5 CA 2002 and/or Articles 81 and 82 of the EC Treaty" (¶77).*

In an interesting interpretation of the judgement, the CCPC claimed:

> *"initially the judgment appears to start from the viewpoint that the geographic market is the GDA... later in the judgment when discussing dominance and collective dominance the High Court*

---

609 Comprising the four Dublin local authority areas and the adjoining counties of Kildare, Meath and Wicklow.

> *finds that each individual local authority is dominant within its local authority area" (¶3.21).*

A subsequent CCPC report on domestic waste collection suggested that geographic markets could be narrower than individual local authority areas:

> *"Within local authority areas, therefore, smaller, local geographic markets exist for household waste collection, which are serviced by an even smaller number of operators than the local authority area level" (CCPC, 2018, September 28, ¶2.30iv).*

In *Thornton's/Carducci* the CCPC stated that *"the relevant geographic market for the supply of domestic waste collection services may be geographically smaller than each of the local authority areas in the GDA taken separately"* (¶3.34).

Media Mergers

The CA/CCPC has frequently concluded that geographic markets for local/regional newspapers are quite narrow, often after a relatively perfunctory analysis. The CA Determination in *Celtic News/Westmeath Examiner*[610] simply states:

> *"The competitive overlap between the parties' newspapers is minimal, since the newspapers concerned are targeted at different regions and only overlap in the border areas of the geographic areas where they are circulated" (¶5).*

Where there was some circulation overlap, the CA/CCPC has generally concluded that it was insufficient to give rise to any competition concerns, without any detailed analysis. Dertouzos & Trautman (1990) found evidence of vigorous competition between newspapers located in different US cities in cases where there was an overlap in circulation.

In *Alpha Publications/Midmedia*, the CA concluded that the proposed transaction raised no competition concerns although both parties had newspaper titles which circulated in County Roscommon.[611] In *River Newspapers/Olok*[612] the CA concluded there was no geographic overlap in respect of newspaper advertising because the Target's advertising was local to the Inishowen peninsula area of County Donegal. In *Irish Times/Gazette*

---

610 CA M/04/030 – *Celtic News/Westmeath Examiner*, 30.6.2004.

611 CA M/05/022 – *Alpha Publications/Midmedia*, 30.5.2005. The Determination, which runs to just over a page, notes that the target's *Athlone Voice* newspaper circulated in South Roscommon, while the acquirer's titles, including the *Roscommon Champion*, were focused *inter alia* on County Roscommon, with no analysis of this apparent overlap.

612 CA M/07/005 – *River Newspapers/Olok*, 9.2.2007.

the CA concluded that *"the geographic scope of the relevant advertising market co-exists with that of the underlying readership market served"* by each of the target's local titles (¶11).

The CA/CCPC applied narrow geographic markets to local radio and local radio advertising. In *SRH/Capital Radio,* a merger involving a national radio station and a local Dublin station, *FM104,* the CA concluded that the relevant geographic market for advertising was national, on the grounds that approximately 65% of the target's advertising was national. In *SRH/Highland Radio* the CA concluded there was no overlap between the parties because most of the target's advertising was local, while the acquirer's was national. In *Radio 2000/News 106* the CA concluded that the relevant geographic market was Dublin local radio advertising, as this was where all three stations involved broadcast. In *UTV/Coderidge* the CA stated that there was no overlap between the parties in respect of national advertising because there was no geographic overlap between the local radio stations involved.[613] In *Thomas Crosbie Holdings/South East Broadcasting,* the CCPC identified a geographic overlap between the parties in Waterford City and County.[614]

Other Sectors

Dawn Meats/Galtee Meats stated that local markets for export-approved meat processing plants could exceed 60 miles (100 kilometres), although such plants obtained at least 90% of their cattle supply from within a 60-mile radius; and approximately 60% from within a 30-mile radius. It noted that cattle prices showed little geographic variation suggesting a possible national market due to a *"chain of supply"* effect (¶2.13). The CA analysed the impact of the transaction in a national and a local market comprising a 100-kilometre radius of the target plant in *Kepak/John Kelly Meats.*[615] The EU

---

613 CA M/04/078 – *UTV/Coderidge,* 21.1.2005. Advertisers conducting a national radio advertising campaign can choose between a national station or a combination of local stations in order to achieve nationwide coverage.

614 In *UTV/Coderidge* and CA M/13/006 – *Clare FM/Tipp FM,* 10.4.2013, the CA acknowledged that, while local radio stations were restricted to broadcasting in particular areas, there could be signal overspill between stations in contiguous areas. In the former case the CA argued that switching would result in the advertiser largely reaching listeners outside of its target area, while in the latter, it concluded that the level of competition was minimal. There was no reference to signal overlap in CCPC M/19/002 – *Kerry FM/Clare Radio,* 5.3.2019.

615 There was no overlap between the parties in this local market. The CCPC also considered a national and a local market limited to a 100-kilometre radius in *Dawn Meats/Dunbia.*

Commission in *ABP/Fane Valley/Slaney Foods*[616] considered both national and local markets for the purchase of cattle for slaughter, defining the latter as comprising a 100-kilometre radius around a meat plant. The CCPC in *ABP/Good Herdsmen* did not consider a local market for the purchase of cattle for slaughter because the target did not own slaughtering facilities.[617]

In *Stena/P&O* the CA identified three geographic markets for ferry services between the island of Ireland and Britain:

i. A northern corridor comprising routes between South-West Scotland/North-West England and Northern Ireland;
ii. A central corridor comprising routes between North Wales/North-West England and Dublin Bay;
iii. A southern corridor with routes between South Wales and the South of the State.[618]

In *Stena/DFDS* the parties claimed that there were four geographic markets arguing that routes between Northern Ireland and South-West Scotland and between Northern Ireland and North-West England constituted separate markets. The CA focused its analysis on the Central Corridor and on routes between Northern Ireland and North-West England, which it described as a *"diagonal corridor"*. The CA stated that this Diagonal Corridor was *"the narrowest relevant geographic market"* but indicated that the choice of geographic market would not materially alter the competitive impact of the transaction. The UKOFT adopted a similar approach to this case[619] but in Phase 2 the UKCC defined a single market for freight ferry services across the Irish Sea, while acknowledging that routes within the same corridor were likely to be closer substitutes for one another than those on different corridors.

UGC (Chorus)/NTL involved a merger of two cable TV operators who operated in different geographic areas of the State. The CA argued that premerger prices were independently set by the parties at a regional level and *"the effect of the proposed acquisition on each region should be taken into account"* (¶66). The Determination noted that the UKCC had concluded that

---

616 EU Commission Case No. COMP/M.7930 – *ABP/Fane Valley/Slaney Foods*, 7.10.2016.

617 CCPC M/17/051 – *ABP/Good Herdsmen*, 13.10. 2017.The target competed with the buyer for the purchase of cattle which it sent to one of the buyer's plants for slaughter. The purchaser operated a slaughtering plant in Cahir, County Tipperary, where the target was based, suggesting that a local market analysis may have been appropriate.

618 The UKOFT and UKCC also concluded that the three main corridors between Ireland and Britain constituted separate geographic markets.in this case.

619 UKOFT, *Stena/DFDS*.

the Pay-TV market was national even though suppliers had different local franchise territories.[620] The test posed by the EUMDNs is whether conditions of competition are sufficiently homogeneous or appreciably different between areas. The parties in *UGC (Chorus)/NTL* competed with BSkyB, which offered Pay-TV services throughout the State and applied a national pricing policy. Although the merging parties did not compete directly with each other *"their pricing decisions reflect the BSkyB retail and wholesale prices"* (¶88).

The CA concluded in *Eirgrid/SONI*,[621] a merger of the electricity transmission system operators (TSOs) in the State and Northern Ireland, that there was no geographic overlap because the parties were legally confined to operating within their own separate jurisdictions. It subsequently concluded that there were separate geographic markets for the electricity transmission systems in both parts of Ireland for similar reasons in *ESB/NIE*.[622] The CA acknowledged that parties wishing to build power stations on the island of Ireland could choose to locate them in either jurisdiction. Therefore, theoretically, the transmission networks were competitors, but the CA concluded that there was no competitive overlap between the parties as the State and Northern Ireland constituted separate markets for electricity transmission.

The CA in *One51/Hegarty/A1/Galway Metal*[623] acknowledged that the transaction *"will result in three metal merchants in the State coming under common control"* (¶10) but was silent on whether there was a horizontal overlap between the target undertakings. The Determination notes that metal merchants *"may obtain supplies of scrap metal from anywhere on the island of Ireland"* (¶16). It cited market share figures which seem to suggest a market that was at least state-wide and concluded that the transaction raised no competition concerns *inter alia* because of the large number of competitors in the State. Thus, it appears that the CA considered that the relevant geographic market was state- or island-wide, although this was not explicitly stated.

The CA in *Topaz/Statoil* argued that markets for fuel terminalling services were regional and identified *"Leinster and Connacht with fuel terminals located*

---

620 UKCC, *NTL/Cable & Wireless*, 22.3.2000.

621 CA M/08/028 – *Eirgrid/SONI*, 25.9.2008.

622 This case involved the acquisition by ESB, which owned the electricity transmission and distribution systems within the State, of the electricity transmission and distribution systems in Northern Ireland.

623 CA M/07/043 – *One51/Hegarty/A1/Galway Metal*, 6.9.2007. There was no horizontal overlap between the purchaser and the three target undertakings.

in Dublin and Galway, respectively" as separate regional markets (*Topaz/Esso*, ¶95). In *Topaz/Esso* the CCPC argued that *"inter-port competition in terminalling services is unlikely within a radius of 100 kilometres and perhaps less"* (¶96). In *Irving/Tedcastles* the CCPC stated that the Enwest terminal in Galway Port exercised a competitive constraint on the Whitegate refinery in Cork, which is arguably inconsistent with *Topaz/Esso*.[624]

In *Green Reit/Central Park, Starwood/Elm Park* and *Standard Life/Block B Elm Park* the CCPC based its analysis on a geographic market comprising Dublin City and the surrounding areas. It is unclear whether this geographic market includes all of county Dublin or extended into adjoining counties, although presumably if it had intended to define the market as County Dublin or the GDA it would have said so. The EU Commission in *Hammerson/Irish Life/ILAC Shopping Centre* analysed the effects of the transaction within the GDA, as it was *"the only plausible definition that would give rise to affected markets"* (¶25). In *Hammerson/Teba,* which involved a shopping centre in North County Dublin, the CCPC, while not coming to a definitive conclusion, applied a geographic market comprising a 50-kilometre radius around Dublin which it said *"substantially encompasses"* the entire GDA.[625] The CCPC in *Colas/SIAC*[626] concluded that the parties were in separate geographic market because asphalt plants only supplied within a 40-kilometre radius and the parties' plants were more than 40 kilometres apart.

Price Discrimination Markets

The possibility of price discrimination means that shipments data and low transport costs are insufficient to establish a geographic market wider than the State. Overseas suppliers should, nevertheless, be included if the geographic market is defined as the State.[627] CCPCMG2014 ¶2.7 acknowledges that price discrimination implies the existence of separate markets.[628] However, the CCPC has rarely addressed this when defining geographic markets as being wider than the State. The EU Commission has

624 The Enwest terminal is 242 kilometres from Whitegate. While the Dublin terminal is slightly further away, drive-times are similar in both cases. (*Google Maps*. Accessed 26.8.2024).

625 Most of counties Kildare, Meath and Wicklow lie within 50 kilometres of Dublin city centre. (*Google Maps*. Accessed 26.8.2024).

626 CCPC M/21/043 – *Colas/SIAC*, 9.9.2021.

627 *"When the geographic market is defined based on customer locations, sales made to those customers are counted, regardless of the location of the supplier making those sales"* (USHMG2010, §4.2.2).

628 CAMG2002 made no reference to price discrimination markets.

identified national geographic markets in cases where suppliers had the ability to discriminate between Member States.[629] In *Celsa/BRC/McMahon* the CA concluded that the market may have been EEA-wide purely on the grounds that all of the relevant product was imported.[630] In *Givauden/Naturex*[631] the CCPC analysed the impact of the transaction within the EEA but gave no reasons for this market definition.

Merging parties' claims that markets are EEA-wide or global require careful scrutiny.

> *"...undertakings may say that they are active in a global market where they consider that they compete globally for revenues against undertakings from all continents. However, that does not mean that the products of all globally active undertakings are substitutable for customers in the EEA, or that customers face sufficiently homogeneous conditions of competition globally, which are the relevant criteria for the Commission's market definition under Union competition law..." (EU Commission, 2024MDN, ¶19).*

The CA in *Kingspan/Xtratherm* concluded that the relevant geographic market was limited to the island of Ireland, rejecting the parties' claims for a wider Ireland/UK market, because prices were higher in the UK and transport costs were also relatively high.[632] In *Amazon/Book Depository*,[633] the CA, while noting that it was not necessary to come to a definitive conclusion, stated that it *"considers that the relevant geographic market is likely to be as wide as the State and the United Kingdom"* (¶22). In *Eason/Dubray* the CCPC stated that *Amazon/Book Depository* had analysed the impact of the transaction on *"the sale of books to consumers in the State"* (¶22).[634] In *Top Snacks/KP Snacks* the CA rejected arguments that the relevant geographic

---

629 EU Commission Case No. COMP/M.4257 – *Smithfield/Oaktree/Sara Lee Foods Europe*, 28.7.2006.

630 CA M/08/030 – *Celsa/BRC/McMahon*, 23.10.2008. EU Commission (2021) states that a large share of imports does not automatically indicate a broader geographic market and notes that most national competition agencies do not regard evidence of trade flows by itself as decisive for defining geographic markets.

631 CCPC M/18/029 – *Givauden/Naturex*, 24.5.2018. The Determination states that the parties cited two (unnamed) EU Commission decisions, which supported an EU-wide market without coming to any conclusion.

632 The Determination included charts showing that Irish and UK PU/PIR prices had not tracked each other closely over time. Price differences do not establish that markets are separate but evidence that prices do not track closely over time (are uncorrelated) demonstrates the existence of separate markets.

633 CA M/11/019 – *Amazon/Book Depository*, 26.7.2011.

634 EU Commission (2021) states that there is no evidence that on-line retailing has resulted in broader geographic markets.

market comprised Ireland and the UK but acknowledged *"the importance of UK-based constraints"* (¶4.53).

Market Definition in SMNP Cases

The SMNP applies where:

i. The parties are not in the same markets, or in any market(s) upstream or downstream of one another; or
ii. Where they are in the same market(s), they have a combined share of less than 15% or, where they are in market(s) which are upstream/downstream of each other, their share of such market(s) is less than 25% (CCPC, 2020, May, ¶2.1).

Clearly market definition is determinative for establishing whether the merging parties are in separate markets or satisfy the relevant market thresholds.[635] The SMNP *Guidelines* provide that, for the purpose of estimating market shares under condition (b) the parties are required *"to identify all potential product and geographic markets which are likely to be impacted by the merger or acquisition"* (¶2.5). Arguably it is equally necessary to identify all potential markets in order to establish if condition (a) is satisfied, although the SMNP *Guidelines* are silent on this point. The CCPC is unlikely to apply the SMNP under condition (b) if *"it is difficult to determine the market shares of the undertakings involved"* (¶2.13).

The CCPC stated in *Kavanagh Retailing/Clarke's Barna*[636] that the parties satisfied the SMNP requirements because, although they were in the same product and geographic market, their combined market share was less than 15% (¶4). As both parties operated supermarkets, previous CA/CCPC Determinations would suggest that the retail grocery market was the relevant product market, although *Dunnes Stores/JC Savage* would indicate a narrower market limited to supermarkets. The target operated a single supermarket, indicating a local geographic market.[637] The CCPC again found that the parties combined market share was below 15% in *Dunnes Stores/BV Trading*. As the acquirer accounted for 20% of the national grocery market at the time of the transaction, this again implies a local geographic

---

635 The SMNP also applies to a change from joint to sole control, but market definition is irrelevant in such cases.

636 CCPC M/22/054 – *Kavanagh Retailing/Clarke's Barna*, 18.10.2022.

637 The target supermarket was 11.4 kilometres (14 minutes' drive-time) from one operated by the acquirer (*Google Maps*. Accessed 14.9.2023).

market definition.[638] It would have been helpful if both Determinations had identified the relevant market and stated the basis for concluding that the parties' combined market shares were below 15%, as independent market share data is generally unavailable for local markets.[639] *Garvey Group/Blarney Filling Station* was cleared under the SMNP on the basis that the parties were not active in the same product or geographic markets. As both operated filling stations, they were obviously considered to be in separate geographic markets.[640] A number of subsequent SMNP cases have identified relevant markets. This should be done in all SMNP cases.

Some Conclusions

Market definition in merger analysis is a means to an end. Nevertheless, it is extremely important as it provides a context and framework for analysing the likely competitive effects of a merger. It enables identification of market shares and concentration, which provides a useful mechanism for identifying harmless mergers (see **Chapter 7**). Defining markets also provides important guidance for businesses and may improve deterrence.

Adopting the narrowest possible market definition may be sufficient to conclude that an SLC will not arise in many cases, making a precise market definition unnecessary. This approach cannot be relied upon, however, if (a) it places the parties in separate markets or (b) it indicates a possible SLC. In both these scenarios it is necessary to define the market correctly. Several CA/CCPC Determinations have defined markets too narrowly, implicitly or explicitly, giving rise to both potential false positives and negatives.

The CA/CCPC regularly states that its conclusions would be unaffected whether the market was defined narrowly or widely. A broad market definition may yield a false negative by including products/areas which are not close substitutes and will not therefore exercise an effective constraint on the merging parties post-merger. It may also afford overly wide market definitions an unwarranted validity. It would be better to either define the

---

638 CCPC M/24/019 – *Dunnes Stores/BV Trading*, 12.5.2024. Dunnes' Naas and Maynooth stores were 8.5 and 14.1 kilometres respectively from the target (*Google Maps.* Accessed 5.6.2024).

639 The CCPC concluded in CCPC M/23/016 – *Belbyford/Imperial Hotel (Cork)*, 30.5.2023 that the parties were in separate geographic markets. The purchaser operated hotels in Dublin, Galway and Kildare while the target hotel was in Cork City. The CCPC also identified the market in CCPC M/23/022 – *VPO/Lumcloon*, 9.6.2023.

640 The nearest filling station operated by the purchaser was 74 kilometres from the target, well outside the range applied by the CA/CCPC for defining local markets in motor fuels (*Google Maps*. Accessed 18.12.2024).

market correctly or apply the narrowest possible market definition. The CA/CCPC has also argued, on occasion, that it had not come to any conclusion on market definition and that this would not affect the case outcome while basing its conclusions on market shares and competitor numbers in a specific market. It has repeated claims that whether the market was defined narrowly or broadly would not affect case outcomes when the evidence clearly ruled out a wider market definition. In other cases, it has referred to potential markets, implying that its conclusions are dependent on the potential market definition being the correct one.

Local market definitions are frequently based on a rule of thumb approach rather than any detailed analysis. Given the number of cases involved in sectors such as grocery, motor fuel and pharmacy retailing, the CA/CCPC needs to undertake some analytical research to establish a more reliable approach to defining catchment areas in such cases. In retail mergers it is necessary to consider catchment areas for both purchaser and target outlets in order to correctly identify all competitors capable of exercising an effective competitive constraint on the merging parties post-merger and avoid a potential false positive.

Market definition is unnecessary when market power can be measured directly, although data deficiencies preclude this in many cases. Even where it is possible, it is arguably best practice to also define the relevant market.

In all cases involving a potential SLC, it is important to define the market correctly to avoid a possible false positive. The CA/CCPC have failed to recognise this in some cases. Failing to define markets creates a worrying potential for arbitrary market definitions and decisions.

Appendix 6.1: The SSNIP Test in *Topaz/Esso*

The SSNIP test asks whether customers would switch in the event of a hypothetical 5% price increase. In the case of the fuel terminals in Dublin Port the question is whether a 5% price increase would exceed the cost to customers of obtaining fuel from other terminals on the island of Ireland. The CCPC Determination included data on fuel transport costs which is reproduced in **Table A.6.1**.

The cost difference between transporting petrol and diesel 150 kilometres *versus* 50 kilometres was 0.69 and 0.78 cent per litre (cpl) respectively. CCPC (2022, November) provided a breakdown of the retail price of motor fuel which indicated that the retail margin accounted for

10.5% of the final retail price. Assuming no change in margins since the *Topaz/Esso* Determination would indicate a wholesale ex-terminal price of 62.6cpl at the time of the merger. This would yield a 5% (SSNIP) increase of 3.1cpl, well above the additional cost of transporting fuel 150 *versus* 50 kilometres, indicating a catchment area of up to 150 kilometres. While retail margins may have increased in the intervening period it is extremely unlikely that they would have increased to such an extent as to significantly affect these results.

Table A.6.1: Fuel Transport Costs in *Topaz/Esso*

	Petrol (cent/litre)	**Gasoil (cent/litre)**
50km	0.62	0.69
150km	1.31	1.47
250km	2.01	2.25
Add Cost 150 *v* 50km	0.69	0.78
Add Cost 250 *v* 50km	1.39	1.56

Source: Topaz/Esso.

The CCPC estimated that the *"price of terminalling services"* as 0.24cpl, i.e. less than one fifth of a cent, which implied that a 5% price increase would amount to 0.012cpl, well below the additional transport cost for 150 kilometres, although the Determination does not indicate how this figure was arrived at.

The Determination cited a report by this author which stated that the additional transport cost was less than 1% of the ex-tax retail price of motor fuel at the time but pointed out that this was not the correct price for applying the SSNIP test. Working backwards, however, the additional transport cost would have been less than 5% of the ex-terminal price provided the ex-terminal price was more than 20% of the ex-tax retail price.

7: MARKET STRUCTURE

Introduction

During the 1960s conclusions in relation to competitive effects in US merger cases were largely based on market shares (Shapiro, 2019). Even quite small market shares were sufficient for mergers to be blocked[641] (Kovacic & Shapiro, 2000). USHMG1968 encapsulated a highly structural approach to merger analysis stating that, in markets with a CR4 of 75% or more, the anti-trust agencies would challenge mergers where each of the merging parties had market shares of 4% or more. Such thresholds were considered conclusive except in exceptional cases (Kwoka, 2015). This approach reflected the then prevailing structure-conduct-performance paradigm, which posited a one-way causal chain whereby structure (the level of concentration) determined market conduct which in turn determined industry performance (Sutton, 1991).

USHMG1982 introduced a more sophisticated approach but still reflected a view that anti-competitive conduct was a function of increased market concentration (Farrell & Shapiro, 1990). Willig (1991) developed a simple model of a homogenous goods market which supported the reliance on market concentration in USHMG1982. Weiss (1989) claimed that there was overwhelming evidence of a correlation between increases in market concentration and prices. Morris & Mosteller (1991) stated that mergers resulting in an individual firm controlling an undue percentage of the relevant market and in a significant increase in market concentration were

[641] In *Brown Shoe* the Supreme Court blocked a merger where the parties had a combined market share of 5%.

inherently likely to reduce competition in the absence of strong evidence to the contrary.

It is now recognised in the economics literature and by competition agencies that high market concentration does not necessarily mean that a merger will harm competition (Shapiro, 2019).[642] Nevertheless, market structure continues to play an important role in merger analysis.

> *"A central element in assessing the competitive impact of a merger is identifying its effect on market structure" (CCPCMG2014, ¶3.1).*[643]

Shapiro & Shelanski (2021) state that, since the US Supreme Court *Philadelphia National Bank* judgement in the early 1960s, mergers which significantly increase market concentration are presumed anti-competitive and successful merger challenges by the anti-trust agencies are generally based on establishing that a merger will significantly increase market concentration.[644] While some commentators argued that the downgrading of market definition in USHMG2010 would make it easier for merging parties to rebut this structural presumption, *"in almost every case where the government establishes the structural presumption, the government wins"* (Shapiro & Shelanski, 2021, p.60).

The main determinants of EU merger cases and of the likelihood of Phase 2 investigations during the first 15 years of the ECMR were market shares, increases in market shares, entry barriers and the EU Commission's views on the ease of collusion post-merger (Bergman *et al.*, 2005). The importance of market shares and concentration in EU merger decisions has declined over time, while the importance of barriers to entry has increased (Affeldt *et al.*, 2019).

Market Concentration & Competition

As pointed out in **Chapter 1**, there is strong evidence that increased concentration in many US markets has coincided with increased prices, higher profit margins and a decline in investment and innovation over the past 20-30 years (Philippon, 2019). Increased market concentration in

---

642 Lancieri & Valetti (2024), however, proposed much stricter rebuttable structural presumptions.

643 It is obviously necessary to define the relevant market in order to assess the impact on market structure.

644 Hovenkamp & Shapiro (2019) state that this presumption was critical to effective merger enforcement.

various UK retail sectors over the 1984-1991 period coincided with an increase in retailers' gross margins (Dobson & Waterson (1996).[645] Similar results have been observed for US grocery retailing (Lande, 2001). Highly concentrated markets, nevertheless, may be characterised by vigorous competition (Sutton, 1991).

The economics literature indicates that most horizontal theories of competitive harm, which are discussed in **Chapter 8**, require concentrated markets. Coate (2006) states that unilateral effects work best when there are a limited number of significant competitors in a market. EUHMG state:

> *"The larger the market share, the more likely a firm is to possess market power. And the larger the addition of market share, the more likely it is that a merger will lead to a significant increase in market power. The larger the increase in the sales base on which to enjoy higher margins after a price increase, the more likely it is that the merging firms will find such a price increase profitable despite the accompanying reduction in output. Although market shares and additions of market shares only provide first indications of market power and increases in market power, they are normally important factors in the assessment" (¶27).*

The EU Commission rejected claims by the merging parties in *Danfoss/Eaton Hydraulics* that high market shares were not informative of competitive conditions in differentiated product markets. The Commission noted that virtually all standard economic models predict that increased concentration will lead to increased prices absent significant efficiencies and product differentiation did not justify dismissing evidence of high market shares in a properly defined market[646] (Batzopoulous *et al.*, 2021).

Similarly, collusion, whether explicit or tacit, is more likely in more concentrated markets (Salinger, 2024).[647] This is because:

i. Cheating is easier to detect;

---

645 They point out that this may have been due to achieving scale economies, improved productivity and integrating into wholesaling, but may also reflect an increased ability to exercise market power.

646 EU Commission Case No. COMP/M.9820 – *Danfoss/Eaton Hydraulics*, 18.3.2021. The target in this case was an Irish-based undertaking. Entry, countervailing buyer power and product repositioning may also prevent price increases following increases in market concentration.

647 Standard Cournot oligopoly models, which assume that firms compete on output, posit a direct link between the number of firms and the degree of competition. Thus, the more concentrated are such markets, the greater the degree of market power (Lancieri & Valetti, 2024).

ii. Being part of a competitive fringe, i.e. opting out of any cartel, becomes more attractive the larger the number of firms in a cartel;

iii. If there are too many cartel members it may not be possible for them to reach an agreement that induces truthful revelation of necessary information (Philips, 1995).

Measuring Market Concentration

One way of measuring market concentration is to combine the market shares of the largest firms in the market. The CR4, which measures the combined market share of the four largest firms in a market, was frequently used historically in US cases and was cited in USHMG1968. The CR4, however, constitutes an arbitrary measure as there is no obvious justification for focusing on the aggregate market shares of the four largest firms rather than the three or five largest.[648] It also provides relatively limited information about market structure. For example, when the four largest firms each have a 22.5% market share, the CR4 will be the same as when one firm has 60% and the next three have 10% each, although clearly the actual market structure differs considerably between these two cases.[649]

The HHI is generally considered a superior measure to simple concentration measures, and it replaced the CR4 in USHMG1982 (Coate & McChesney, 1992). Werden (1991) argued that the level of, and change in, HHI were reasonably good predictors of the effects of mergers on prices. The HHI is calculated as the sum of the squares of the market shares of all the firms in the relevant market. In contrast to the CR4, the HHI reflects both the number of firms in a market and differences in their relative size. The HHI declines as the number of firms in a market increases. The greater the degree of inequality in firm size, the higher is the HHI. The HHI has a maximum value of 10,000 which occurs in the case of a monopoly. The inverse of the HHI indicates the number of theoretically equal-sized firms that corresponds to that HHI value.[650] Hovenkamp (2024) states that the

---

648 The New Zealand Commerce Commission (NZCC) used the CR3 to define safe harbour thresholds in its 2002 *Merger Guidelines* (CCNZ, 2002).

649 The CR4, nevertheless, may provide some information about market structure. A CR4 of 50 means that the fourth largest firm would have a market share of at least 12.5% and implies that there are a minimum of eight firms in the relevant market.

650 For example, if the HHI equals 2,000, then dividing 10,000 by 2,000 indicates that this is equivalent to a market with 5 theoretically equal-sized undertakings. This represents a useful way of interpreting the meaning of any particular HHI value.

SSNIP test provides the theoretically correct market definition for applying the HHI, while some alternative approaches to market definition are inadequate for identifying competition concerns.

Strictly speaking market share data for every firm in the market are required to calculate the HHI correctly. However, firms with small market shares will not greatly affect the overall HHI. Consequently, it is possible to make a reasonably accurate estimate of the HHI if market share data for all of the larger firms in a market are available, provided the aggregate share of the remaining firms is relatively small.[651]

Shapiro (2010) states USHMG1992 emphasised a link between market shares and unilateral price effects which rested on a strong assumption that market shares were good proxies for diversion ratios which is frequently not justified. He points out that the merging parties' market shares and the change in the HHI are more informative than the level of the HHI in unilateral effects cases.

The CA/CCPC's HHI Thresholds

The CA cited both the CR4 and HHI in *Statoil/Conoco* and the three-firm concentration ratio (CR3) and HHI in *Ladbrokes/Coral*, although there is no obvious reason for applying different CR measures in different cases. The CA adopted the HHI as its preferred measure of market concentration in CAMG2002, in line with international best practice.[652] High levels of market concentration constitute a necessary, but not sufficient, condition for establishing that a merger will result in an SLC. It follows that a merger is unlikely to raise any competition concerns where post-merger concentration levels are relatively low. Many competition agencies, including the CA/CCPC, therefore use market concentration as a screening device to identify those mergers that are unlikely to have potential anti-competitive effects.

> *"A merger is unlikely to create or enhance market power or to facilitate its exercise unless it significantly increases concentration*

---

651 Market shares and HHIs were significantly overstated in *Fitzwilliam/Wittington Canada/Arnotts* because the data excluded two significant market participants (¶47). The market share data was therefore not very useful.

652 CAMG2002 (¶3.2) stated that, in rare cases, usually if the HHI was unavailable, the CR4, firm's individual market shares or the number of firms might be used to measure concentration. CCPCMG2014 (FN7) contains no reference to using the CR4 but notes that it does not take account of differences in firm size.

and results in a concentrated market, properly defined and measured. Mergers that either do not significantly increase concentration or do not result in a concentrated market ordinarily require no further analysis" (USHMG1992, p.3).

The CA/CCPC applies a combination of the post-merger level of the HHI and the change in the HHI due to a merger to identify mergers that are unlikely to raise competition concerns. The CA originally defined HHI thresholds below which it considered mergers were unlikely to infringe §s4 and 5 of the *Competition Act, 1991*[653] (CA, *Annual Report 1997*). These thresholds were subsequently adopted unchanged in CAMG2002. The thresholds were revised in CCPCMG2014. The HHI thresholds applied by the CA/CCPC are set out in **Table 7.1**.

Table 7.1: CA/CCPC HHI Merger Thresholds

	CAMG2002		CCPCMG2014		Competition Risk
Zone	**HHI**	**Change**	**HHI**	**Change**	
Unconcentrated (A)	<1,000	Any	<1,000	Any	Low
	1,000-1,800	<100	1,000-2,000	<250	
	>1800	<50	>2,000	<150	
Concentrated (B)	1,000-1,800	>100	1,000-2,000	>250	Moderate
	>1,800	50-100			
Highly Concentrated (C)	>1,800	>100	>2,000	>150	High

Source: CAMG2002 & CCPCMG2014.

CAMG2002 distinguished between unconcentrated, concentrated and highly concentrated markets which it defined as Zones A, B and C and provided that:

i. Zone A mergers were considered less likely to have adverse competitive effects;

653 As pointed out in **Chapter 3**, the CA had taken the view that mergers could infringe §s4 and 5 of the *Competition Act, 1991*. Under the 1991 Act, the CA could issue a certificate stating that, in its opinion, an agreement was not in breach of §4. Such certificates were the domestic equivalent of EU negative clearances. The CA issued a Category Certificate outlining the circumstances in which, in the CA's opinion, a merger would not be considered anti-competitive. The thresholds were based on USHMG1992.

ii. Zone B mergers could raise competition concerns;

iii. Zone C mergers were regarded as occurring in already highly concentrated markets and thus were more likely to raise competition concerns.

CAMG2002 specifically stated that *"the zones do not constitute a 'safe harbour'"* (¶3.11). This was repeated in various decisions, *e.g.*, *Heineken/Beamish & Crawford*. The CA's 2010 consultation on the *Guidelines* confusingly, however, refers to *"'safe harbour' thresholds"* (CA, 2010, December 3, ¶2.7). The Consultation offered no view on whether the 2002 thresholds should be changed beyond stating that they were based on those applied by the US competition agencies at the time, which had subsequently been changed.

The subsequent 2013 Consultation proposed revising the thresholds but advanced no reasons for the proposed changes (CA, 2013, September 13). CCPCMG2014 simplified the HHI thresholds. The reference to zones was dropped. The threshold for defining a market as highly concentrated was increased from 1,800 to 2,000.[654] The thresholds for changes in the HHI required to trigger concerns were also increased considerably. In the case of concentrated markets, the threshold more than doubled from 100 to 250, while in highly concentrated markets it increased by 50% from 100 to 150.[655]

The right-hand column in **Table 7.1** defines mergers as representing a low, moderate, or high risk to competition. These correspond with Zones A, B and C in CAMG2002. CCPCG2014 classifies mergers as either low or high risk with no moderate risk category. Thus, CCPCMG2014 defines low risk mergers as those (a) with a post-merger HHI below 1,000; (b) a post-merger HHI of between 1,000 and 2,000 and an increase of less than 250; and (c) a post-merger HHI of more than 2,000 with an increase of less than 150. CCPCMG2014 defines mergers with a post-merger HHI of 1,000-2,000 and an increase of more than 250 and a post-merger HHI above 2,000 with an increase of more than 150 as highly likely to raise competition concerns. **Table 7.1**, however, defines the former as posing a moderate competition risk and the latter as high risk.

---

654 The increase in the upper threshold equated to a reduction in the number of theoretically equal sized firms in a market from 5.6 to 5.

655 In a 2022 report on competition in motor fuel retailing, however, the CCPC applied different HHI thresholds, defining concentrated markets as those with a HHI above 1,500 and highly concentrated markets as those with a HHI greater than 2,500. No explanation was advanced for these thresholds (CCPC, 2022, November).

The focus on the impact of mergers on market structure mainly arises with respect to horizontal mergers. In general, vertical mergers are considered unlikely to raise competition concerns unless one or more of the parties involved have market power. High market shares, of themselves, are insufficient to establish that a firm has market power. However, a firm with a relatively low market share is unlikely to have market power. Thus, although it has not been addressed in CA/CCPC *Merger Guidelines*, vertical mergers are unlikely to raise competition concerns if the parties have limited market shares in any relevant market.[656]

Mergers between potential entrants and market incumbents will not affect concentration as they do not affect the number of competitors in the market, but such mergers may, nevertheless, have anti-competitive effects because they may remove a constraint on firms in the market raising their prices.[657]

Market Concentration & Merger Case Outcomes

An analysis of USFTC merger cases in the decade following the introduction of USHMG1982 found that a high proportion of cases that exceeded the HHI limits were not challenged. Rather market concentration was used to identify which cases should be investigated rather than to establish that a merger was anti-competitive, consistent with economic theory (Coate & McChesney, 1992). Kwoka (2015) similarly found that many mergers that exceeded the HHI thresholds between 1999 and 2003 went unchallenged, prompting some commentators to conclude that merger policy was more lenient than indicated by the *Guidelines* (Baker & Shapiro, 2008).

Affeldt *et al.* (2021) conducted a detailed review of market concentration in all EU merger cases between 1990 and 2014 based on data from 2,000 EU Commission merger decisions involving over 20,000 markets. They found that mergers where the post-merger HHI was greater than 2,000 and increased by more than 150 points were more likely to be remedied or

656 EUNHMG2008 state that competition concerns are unlikely to arise in non-horizontal mergers if both parties' markets shares are below 30% and the post-merger HHI is less than 2,000 (see **Chapter 9**).

657 The CA/CCPC has considered but generally rejected the possibility that the parties might constitute potential competitors in a limited number of cases. CA M/12/007 – *Nestlé/Pfizer Nutrition*, 15.6.2012; CA M/12/021 – *Henry Schein/C&M Vetlink*, 29.11.2012: CA M/13/002 – *Capita/Northgate*, 6.3.2013 (see **Chapter 8**). In several other cases, it could be argued that there were grounds for regarding the parties as potential competitors, but this was not addressed in the CA/CCPC Determinations.

blocked. They also reported an average HHI of 3,000 in cases where geographic markets were defined as national, with little increase over time.

Table 7.2: HHIs in CA Phase 2 Horizontal Merger Investigations, 1992-2002

Case	Relevant Market	Pre-Merger HHI	Post-Merger HHI	Change
Independent/Tribune	Irish Sunday Newspapers	4,363.7	5,717.4	+1.353.7
	Irish & UK Sunday Newspapers	2,278.2	2,906.5	+628.3
Statoil/Conoco	Motor Fuels	1,502.0	1,883.0	+381.0
Ladbrokes/Coral	Off-course Betting	966.8	1,150.3	+183.5
STA Travel/USIT	ISIC Cards; Youth Cards; USIT Travel Stamp; and Interail Tickets	10,000	10,000	0.0
	SATA Tickets J1 Visas	n.a.	10,000	n.a.
Maxol/Busselle	Motor Fuel – State	1,504	1,542	+38.0
	Retail Motor Fuel – State	1,646	1,721	+75.0

Notes: The CA defined the relevant market as that for Irish Sunday Newspapers in *Independent/Tribune,* but HHI estimates based on an alternative market definition of all Sunday (Irish and UK) newspapers were also included. The estimated HHIs in *Ladbrokes/Coral* differ slightly from those cited by the CA. This is due to different assumptions in relation to the market shares of smaller competitors. The CA estimated market shares assuming that "others'" market share of 46.6% was split between (a) 100 equally-sized shops with 0.466% each or (b) 20 equally-sized shops with 2.33% each. The estimates in this table account for the fact that there were two other Irish undertakings with multiple LBOs at the time and it is assumed that each of them had a 5% market share with the remaining 36.6% split equally between 500 independents as the report indicates that others had a combined total of 566 LBOs.

Source: CA various merger reports.

Information on the role of market concentration in Irish mergers pre-2002 is limited to the nine published reports on horizontal mergers referred to the CA between 1991 and 2002. **Table 7.2** provides details of HHIs for these cases where the relevant data is available.[658] *Independent/Tribune* and

658 The CA did not estimate HHIs in *Princes Holdings/Suir Nore Relays Liberty Media/Aringour,* arguing that it involved the consolidation of a number of smaller monopolies into a larger

Statoil/Conoco would be defined as high risk under CAMG2002, while *Ladbrokes/Coral* and *Maxol/Busselle* would have been classed as moderate risk. The CA recommended that *Independent/Tribune* and *Statoil/Conoco* should be prohibited while *Ladbrokes/Coral* and *Maxol/Busselle* should be permitted. The CA did not cite HHI data in *STA Travel/USIT*.[659]

The CA/CCPC has only published HHI data or actual market share data in a relatively small number of Determinations. It was possible, however, to estimate approximate HHIs in many other cases based on market share ranges included in the Determinations in line with an approach adopted by Affeldt *et al.* (2021). It was possible to estimate HHIs for 382 (51%) of the 754 mergers with a horizontal element notified over the 2023-2023 period. These 382 cases, which involved 835 different market definitions, were then defined as low-, moderate- and high-competition risk based on CAMG2002 and CCPCMG2014 HHI thresholds as outlined in **Table 7.1**. The results are presented in **Table 7.3**.[660]

Over the entire 2003-2023 period, 64% of horizontal mergers which could be defined came within the low risk category, with 31% in the high risk category. The table also shows a significant increase in the proportion of low risk cases, from 56% to 69%, and a corresponding decline in high risk cases from 37% to 27% following the change in HHI thresholds in CCPCMG2014. This begs the obvious question whether this was due to changes in the HHI thresholds. In order to test this proposition, post-2013 horizontal mergers were re-classified using the CAMG2002 HHI thresholds. It was possible to classify 178 post-2013 cases using the

---

one, or in *GEHE* where it said HHI estimates would not be meaningful in the absence of an exact [local] geographic market.

659 USIT had a monopoly in four markets (ISIC cards, Youth cards, the USIT Travel Stamp and Interail Tickets) giving an unchanged HHI of 10,000 post-merger. The transaction resulted in a merger to monopoly in the markets for SATA air tickets and J1 visas. The CA recommend it be cleared subject to remedies.

660 **Table 4.1** defined 565 merger notifications as purely horizontal, with a further 189 that had both horizontal and vertical elements. A detailed description of the methodology used is included in **Appendix 7.1**. The number of markets is far higher than the number of cases because many transactions involved multi-product firms operating in several different markets while, in many other instances, the CA/CCPC, rather than define a specific market, analysed the impact of the transaction in a number of potential markets. Even though the data includes 50% of all horizontal mergers, there may be a potential sample bias problem. It may be that cases for which no market share data was included were mainly low risk cases so that the proportion of high risk cases could be overstated.

CAMG2002 thresholds and **Table 7.4** compares the results for these cases with the actual outcomes under the CCPCMG2014 HHI thresholds.[661]

Table 7.3: Percentage Distribution of Horizontal Mergers by Competition Risk Category, 2003-2023

Competition Risk	Merger Cases			Markets		
	2003-2013	2014-2023	2003-2023	2003-2013	2014-2023	2003-2023
Low	56.0	69.0	63.9	56.0	72.7	67.3
Moderate	6.7	4.3	5.2	8.6	3.9	5.4
High	37.3	26.7	30.9	35.4	23.5	27.3

Source: CA/CCPC Determinations.

Table 7.4: Percentage Distribution of Horizontal Merger Cases by Competition Risk, 2014-2023

Competition Risk	2002 Thresholds	2014 Thresholds
Low	52.8	63.5
Moderate	14.0	4.5
High	33.1	32.0
Total	**100.0**	**100.0**

Source: CA/CCPC Determinations.

Under the 2014 thresholds, 64% of the cases where comparisons were possible were defined as low-competition risk but only 53% would have been defined as such if the 2002 thresholds had been applied. Only 5% of cases were classed as moderate risk using the 2014 thresholds but 14% would have fallen into this category using the 2002 thresholds, while 32% of cases were defined as high risk using the 2014 HHI thresholds compared with 33% if the 2002 thresholds had applied. This suggests that the change in thresholds had virtually no impact on the proportion of high risk cases post-2013. Rather the main impact of the change was that a significant proportion of cases that would previously have been classed as moderate risk, were classed as low risk under the 2014 HHI thresholds.

661 It was possible to define 232 cases using the CCPCMG2014 thresholds but only 178 of these could be categorised using CAMG2002 and the comparison is limited to those 178 cases, which represent 39% of all horizontal mergers notified post-2013 (see **Appendix 7.1**).

Between 2003 and 2023 118 horizontal mergers notified were defined as high risk based on estimated HHIs. **Table 7.5** provides details of investigation outcomes in these cases. It bears repeating that there is no presumption that high levels of concentration mean that a merger is likely to harm competition. High post-merger concentration levels simply indicate that a closer examination is required. In **Chapter 3** it was suggested that the introduction of the SMNP in 2020 may have freed up CCPC resources to focus on potentially harmful mergers. Consequently, **Table 7.5** includes data for the periods before and after 2020.

Table 7.5: Outcomes in High Risk Cases (%)

	2003-2013	2014-2019	2020-2023	2003-2023
Phase 1 Clearance	51.8	41.4	27.3	42.4
Ext. Phase 1	19.6	34.5	48.5	31.4
Phase 2	28.6	24.1	24.2	26.3
Total Ext. Phase 1/ Phase 2	48.2	58.6	72.7	57.7
Remedied/Prohibited	23.2	34.5	24.2	26.3

Source: CA/CCPC Determinations.

Pre-2014 more than half (52%) of high risk cases were cleared following a preliminary Phase 1 investigation, while 48% were subject to a detailed investigation, i.e. an extended Phase 1 or Phase 2 investigation, of which 29% were subject to a Phase 2 investigation. During the 2014-2019 period 41% of high risk cases were cleared following a preliminary Phase 1 investigation, with 59% subject to a more detailed investigation. The percentage of high risk cases subject to Phase 2 investigation declined slightly but this was more than offset by an increase in the proportion of cases involving an extended Phase 1 investigation to 35%. During the 2020-2023 period the proportion of high risk cases subject to a detailed investigation increased to 73% of which 24% involved a Phase 2 investigation. The proportion of high risk cases cleared based on a preliminary Phase 1 investigation fell dramatically to 27%. Over the 2020-2023 period 24% of high risk mergers were remedied/prohibited compared to 23% pre-2013 and 35% over the 2014-2019 period.

The data indicates that pre-2020 a significant number of cases involving high post-merger concentration levels were not subject to a detailed investigation, even though the CA/CCPC *Guidelines* would indicate that one was required.[662] Thus, in practice, merger policy pre-2020 appears to have been far more lenient than indicated by the *Merger Guidelines*, adding to questions raised earlier about possible false negatives during this period. Although there was some improvement during the 2014-19 period, 41% of high risk cases were still cleared based on a preliminary Phase 1 investigation. The dramatic increase in the proportion of high risk cases that were subject to more detailed scrutiny from 2020 onwards is welcome, as it reduces the risk of false negatives. The tighter approach coincides with the introduction of SMNP freeing up CCPC resources to focus on high risk cases.

Chapter 4 defined all extended Phase 1 and Phase 2 cases, of which there were 114, as potential problem cases; 102 of these cases involved horizontal or horizontal/vertical overlaps. **Table 7.6** classifies these cases by risk category.[663]

Table 7.6: Risk Classification of Extended Phase 1 & Phase 2 Cases by Case Outcome

	Low	Moderate	High	n.a.
Prohibited	0.0	0.0	100.0	0.0
Remedied	20.0	0.0	57.1	22.9
Ext. Phase 1 Cleared	17.5	0.0	60.0	22.5
Phase 2 Cleared	22.5	4.7	72.7	0.0
Total	18.6	1.0	63.7	16.7

Source: CA/CCPC Determinations.

As might be expected the majority of cases (64%) which were subject to more detailed investigations by the CA/CCPC came within the high risk category based on our HHI estimates. However, 19% of detailed investigations and 20% of remedied cases came within the low risk category based on our estimates; and 17% involved cases that could not be classified, i.e. the Determinations contained insufficient data to estimate HHIs.[664] All

662 The CCPC stated in *Q-Park/Tazbell*, for example, *"in line with the Merger Guidelines, the high level of concentration indicates that the Commission should intensify its analysis of the competitive effects of the Proposed Transaction"* (¶5.44).

663 Some of these cases are included in the 118 high risk cases in **Table 7.5**.

664 Many of these cases involved retailing, whether grocery, pharmacy or motor fuel. Market share data is frequently not available for local markets, although the CA/CCPC has attempted to estimate market shares in some cases. In effect, close scrutiny in these cases is not prompted by evidence of high market concentration, but rather to establish whether local markets might be highly concentrated.

five prohibition cases came within the high risk category. It is notable, however, that a significant proportion of cases subject to detailed investigation would be defined as low risk based on market concentration levels. Several cases that were subject to close scrutiny involved the potential for information exchange leading to coordination due to cross-shareholdings or other ongoing links between the parties. The concern in *eircom/Meteor* involved vertical aspects of the transaction. The issue in two other cases, *Stena/DFDS* and *PTSB/Ulster Bank,* appears to have involved the appropriate counterfactual and in particular whether decisions by the vendor to exit the market were merger-related (see **Chapter 5**).

Table 7.7 provides data on market concentration for these cases, broken down into different time periods. Interestingly, the table indicates that the percentage of low risk cases subject to detailed review increased over time, while the proportion of high risk cases declined. It is unclear why some low risk cases were subject to a detailed investigation.

Table 7.7: Risk Classification of Extended Phase 1 & Phase 2 Cases by Time Period

	Low	Moderate	High	n.a.
2003-2013	14.3	2.9	71.4	11.4
2014-2019	14.8	0.0	63.0	22.2
2020-2023	25.0	0.0	57.5	17.5
2003-2023	18.6	1.0	63.7	16.7

Source: CA/CCPC Determinations.

Individual Cases

Greenstar/Veolia was subject to a Phase 2 investigation, even though, as **Table 7.8** illustrates, the HHI in all the relevant markets was well below 1,000 classifying them as low-competition risk. There is no obvious explanation in the Determination for the decision to conduct a Phase 2 investigation in that case.[665]

Relatively few horizontal merger Determinations cite HHI data. Arguably this is inconsistent with the *Merger Guidelines*. It is also puzzling, because HHI

665 77 days after the transaction had been notified, the CA concluded that it *"was unable to form the view at the conclusion of the Phase 1 investigation that the result of the proposed acquisition would not be to substantially lessen competition in any markets for goods or services in the State"* (¶1.14).

data provide a relatively straightforward mechanism for identifying cases that are unlikely to raise competition concerns. In many cases, it may only be necessary to estimate the change in the HHI, which is twice the product of the market shares of the merging parties, in order to identify a merger as low-competition risk. Simply put, CCPCMG2014 provides that, in a horizontal merger, a HHI increase of less than 150 points involves a sufficiently small increase in market share as to rule out the possibility of an SLC. Thus, citing evidence that the HHI would increase by less than 150 points would be sufficient to discount the need for a more detailed investigation in many cases.[666] Providing information on market share ranges and estimated HHIs would provide greater clarity and increase transparency, provide a far more accurate picture of the likely effect on competition and would be consistent with the CCPC's own *Guidelines*.[667]

Table 7.8: C&I Waste Collection Market HHIs in *Greenstar/Veolia*

Market	Pre-merger	Post-merger	Change	Zone
GDA	475	571	+96	A
Cork City & County	680	890	+210	A
South-East Region	426	726	+300	A

Source: Greenstar/Veolia, Tables 1-3.

Instead of citing the HHI, the CA/CCPC has concluded in many horizontal merger cases that no SLC would arise because the parties combined market share and/or increase in market share was *"small"* and/or because there would be a sufficient number of competitors in the market post-merger.

666 It would not have been possible to identify low risk cases as easily under CAMG2002, which provided that only cases where the HHI increased by less than 50 points could be considered low risk without estimating post-merger HHI levels.

667 For example, the HHI in all of the markets analysed in *Zeus Packaging/Limerick Packaging* appear to have increased by less than 150, based on information in the Determination. The case took 76 days to decide, although there is no reference to any RFI having been issued to the parties. Following the *Guidelines* and applying the HHI thresholds might have resulted in a speedier outcome. The CCPC adopted the approach advocated here, at least partially, in CCPC M/23/052 – *NPP Packaging/Wraptite,* 15.11.2023. The case involved at least 10 different markets. The Determination includes data showing that the change in HHI was less than 150 in seven markets. Information on market shares suggest the change in HHI in two other markets was also below 150 but the Determination instead advanced an argument based on the increase in market share and the number of competitors. Data for the remaining market suggests it was in the high risk category.

Such measures are vague and subjective and beg questions as to how small is small and how many competitors is sufficient? In *BWG/Heaney Meats*,[668] for example, the CCPC stated that the merging parties would have market shares of between [0-10]% and [10-20]% for different meat products, which it described as *"a relatively small market share"* (¶25). A market share below 10% might reasonably be described as relatively small but it is not clear that a 10-20% market share would be universally regarded as such.[669]

The assumption that small increases in market shares will not have an adverse effect on competition is incorrect. Considering only changes in market shares and failing to estimate HHIs meant that many cases, which merited a detailed investigation according to CA/CCPC *Guidelines*, were cleared based on a preliminary investigation. Even small increases in concentration can result in higher prices post-merger (Baker, 1997). The failure by the US authorities to subject mergers with small increases in market shares to closer scrutiny resulted in significantly more false negatives, i.e. anti-competitive mergers being cleared (Kwoka, 2015). Stöhr (2024) also reports evidence for EU cases that post-merger price increases were higher the greater were the differences in the parties' turnover pre-merger, which she suggests may be due to an overly lenient approach in cases involving the acquisition of small firms by larger ones.[670] Nocke & Whinston (2022) state that it is the change in the HHI that matters in merger cases, not its level, and point out that even mergers which result in relatively small increases in the HHI may be anti-competitive.[671] The CCPC

---

668 CCPC M/19/039 – *BWG/Heaney Meats*, 10.1.2020.

669 HHI estimates would, however, place this transaction in the low risk category as defined in CCPCMG2014.

670 Such arguments were advanced in *Unilever/Alberto Culver*; *CapVest/Origin Foods/Maiden*; and CCPC M/22/027 – *Ferrero International/Fulfil*, 9.6.2022. In *Goldreed/Greene Farm*, the CCPC did not even refer to the number of competitors but concluded there would be no effect on competition, purely on the grounds that it involved a minimal [0-10]% increase to the acquirer's existing [50-60]% market share. HHI estimates indicate that all of these cases would be classified as posing a high-competition risk under both CAMG2002 and CCPCMG2014.

671 They also suggest that the thresholds in USHMG2010 were too lax and cite various studies which found evidence of post-merger price increases in support of this conclusion. They caution that this may apply particularly to mergers which fall into the low risk category based on post-merger HHI levels and are waved through without further investigation. USHMG2024 reverted to the pre-2010 HHI thresholds. In contrast, Simpson & Hosken (1998) report no anti-competitive effects in supermarket mergers with post- merger HHIs below 2,000 but significant evidence of anti-competitive effects for post-merger HHIs of approximately 2,500. It should be noted, however, that their study included only four mergers and is therefore hardly conclusive.

acknowledged in *Dawn Meats/Kildare Chilling* that small market shares did not rule out the possibility of adverse effects on competition.

> *"Conversely, mergers between suppliers with relatively low combined market shares may raise competition concerns if the suppliers are close competitors and exert strong competitive constraints on one another (¶5.26).*[672]

To be defined as posing a high-competition risk under CCPCMG2014, the post-merger HHI must exceed 2,000 (1,800 under CAMG2002) and increase by more than 150 points (50 under CAMG2002). If the larger firm has a market share of 40% or more then the post-merger HHI will almost certainly exceed 2,000.[673] As the change in HHI is double the product of the merging firms' market shares, it is relatively easy to calculate, for a given market share for the larger firm, the maximum market share for the smaller firm necessary to ensure that the HHI will increase by less than 150 (50) points. The results are shown in **Table 7.9**.

Table 7.9: Maximum Market Share of Smaller Firm Required to Stay Below HHI High Risk Threshold

Market share (%) of larger firm	**Maximum market share (%) of smaller firm for merger to avoid high risk**	
	150 points (CCPCMG2014)	**50 points (CAMG2002)**
40	1.90	0.63
50	1.50	0.50
60	1.25	0.42
70	1.07	0.36
80	0.94	0.31

Even when the larger firm has only a 40% market share, the smaller firm would require a market share below 2% for the merger to fall below the high risk HHI threshold in CCPCMG2014.[674] The *Guidelines* set a threshold

672 It repeated this in *Q-Park/Tazbell* (¶6.92).

673 A market share of 44.7% means that a firm's individual market share will contribute 2,000 to the HHI. A 40% market share means that it would contribute 1,600 points and with 60% split between the remaining firms the HHI will almost certainly exceed 2,000 except in highly unusual circumstances.

674 In all cases the smaller undertaking would need to have a market share of less than 1% to produce a HHI increase of less than 50.

for the increase in the HHI which implicitly defines the maximum increase in market share necessary to rule out the possibility of competitive harm. Ignoring the *Guidelines* and concluding that a merger poses no competition risk on the basis that the increase in market share is *"small"* or *"minimal"* creates the potential for Type II errors (false negatives).

The CA/CCPC has cleared several mergers in which the merged entities had very high market shares, ranging from 50-90%, on the grounds that the increase in market share was small/minimal. Examples of these cases are provided in **Table 7.10**.

Table 7.10: Examples of Mergers Involving High Market Shares Cleared by the CA/CCPC without Remedy

Case	Relevant Products	Level of Investigation
Unilever/Alberto Culver	Hairstyling Products >90% Deodorants >70%	Extended Phase 1
CapVest/Origin Foods/Maiden	Tinned Tomatoes >70% Readymade Baking Mixes >60%	Preliminary Phase 1
Ferrero International/Fulfil	Energy Snack Bars >80%	Preliminary Phase 1
Goldreed/Greene Farm	Bulk and Pre-pack Cooked Beef Products [50-70]% PCM [50-70]%	Extended Phase 1
Easycash/Bank of Ireland	Supply of ATMs to Site Owners in the State [50-60]%	Extended Phase 1
Uniphar/Sisk Healthcare	Supply of Orthopaedic Products [45-60]% Diagnostic Imaging Products [40-50%]	Extended Phase 1
Apcoa Parking/NCPS	Car Parking Management Services *via* PAC Contracts [40-50]%	Preliminary Phase 1

Source: CA/CCPC.

Unilever accounted for [80-90%] of hair styling products and [60-70%] of deodorants in *Unilever/Alberto Culver* which would place both product markets in Zone C as defined in CAMG2002. For some reason, the CA cited CR3 rather than HHI data for both products. The transaction was cleared without remedies following an extended Phase 1 investigation because (a) the increase in market share was *"minimal"* and (b) there were a number of competitors, although by definition these would have been quite small. *CapVest/Origin Foods/Maiden*, *Boyle Sports/Tully*, and *Ferrero International/Fulfil* were all cleared following a preliminary Phase 1 review, although the HHIs would place all three cases in the high-competition risk category. These cases illustrate how focusing exclusively on increases in market shares without considering the HHI may result in high-competition risk cases avoiding proper scrutiny.[675] It cannot be assumed that even a relatively small increase in market share will have no impact on competition.

The CCPC in *CapVest/M&M Walshe* described the merging parties as having *"a moderate share"* in the markets for the supply of own label rashers to retailers(¶31).[676] The parties had a combined market share of [30-40]% and the merged entity was the largest undertaking in the market by some distance. Subsequently in *CapVest/CCIF Core* the CCPC described the parties as having *"a moderate share of [20-30]% of the potential market"* for sliced cooked ham (¶35).[677] Both transactions would appear likely to have come within the high-competition risk category based on HHI estimates. In *MM/ESNT/Essentra*,[678] the CCPC stated that, although the transaction would result in a substantial increase in the acquirer's market share, *"it is unlikely to significantly alter the existing structure of competition in this sector"* (¶26). In several other cases the CA/CCPC have described the overlaps between the merging parties as minimal without providing any details of the basis for this conclusion.[679]

---

675 Based on HHI thresholds in CAMG2002 in the first and CCPCMG2014 in the latter two cases.

676 CCPC M/20/017 – *CapVest/M&M Walshe*, 19.6.2020.

677 CCPC M/20/041 – *CapVest/CCIF Core*, 5.2.2021.

678 CCPC M/22/033 – *MM/ESNT/Essentra*, 5.9.2022. Based on data in the Determination the HHI probably increased by more than 150 points in both markets but the post-merger HHI could not be estimated.

679 CA M/04/004 – *DaimlerChrysler/Mitsubishi*, 6.2.2004, states there was a minimal competitive overlap, but the parties' market shares were redacted. The parties' market shares were also redacted in CA M/04/028 – *Abbott/Aventis*, 19.5.2004, where the acquirer was described as having a *de-minimis* market share. The parties' market shares of sales of fresh beef and lamb were redacted in *Dawn Meats/Dunbia* although the transaction was cleared *inter alia* on the grounds that they had small market shares. The CCPC cleared CCPC M/17/049 – *Vermillion/SEPIL*, 21.9.2017 on the basis of market shares and the number of competitors in the market for the supply of natural gas but market share data for all suppliers was redacted and there is no indication of whether the market was regarded as concentrated. There appears to be no good reason for not publishing market share ranges in Determinations. CA M/04/073 – *Nestlé/Wagner*, 10.1.2005 stated that there was minimal overlap between the parties. According to the Determination Nestlé sold chilled pizzas while Wagner sold frozen pizzas. It is not clear whether the parties were considered to be in the same market.

In contrast *Orpea/First Care* resulted in a HHI increase of 193, from 887 to 1,080 (see Table 6.3). The CCPC nevertheless expressed concerns about future increases in concentration resulting from future acquisitions, while offering no reasons for not adhering to its own *Guidelines*.[680] The transaction was cleared subject to a remedy requiring the notification of future below the threshold mergers. Imposing remedies where no SLC arises constitutes a false positive.

The CCPC in *Portlon (Parma)/Hermitage* argued that that it did not need to decide whether private healthcare services provided by public hospitals were part of the relevant market. HHI data reproduced in **Table 7.11**, however, indicate that the transaction would be defined as low-competition risk if public hospitals were included in the market but as high-competition risk if they were excluded.[681]

Table 7.11: Market Concentration in Private Hospital Services

	Including public hospitals	Excluding public hospitals
Pre-merger HHI	711	1,299
Post-merger HHI	883	1,726
HHI Change	+172	+427
Competition Concerns	Low risk	High risk

Source: CA *Portlon (Parma)/Hermitage,* Table 3.

The CA analysed the impact of *UTV/FM104* on market structure compared with the situation that would have arisen if the earlier proposed *Communicorp/SRH* merger had been allowed to proceed without the requirement to divest FM104. It was argued in **Chapter 5** that the appropriate counterfactual in this case involved comparing the situation post the *UTV/FM104* transaction with that which would have prevailed assuming the proposed *Communicorp/SRH* merger did not include the acquisition of FM104, because the CA's clearance of the latter transaction

680 The Determination cited the fact that the Kildare market was concentrated but curiously failed to mention that the increase in HHI was significantly below the 250 threshold which, according to CCPCMG2014, indicates that it was *"unlikely to cause concern"* in a market with a post-merger HHI of 1,000-2,000. As noted in **Chapter 6**, although the CCPC claimed that the outcome would be the same regardless of market definition and thus would not affect its conclusions, Kildare was the only one of four potential geographic markets where the post-merger HHI exceeded 1,000.

681 A similar situation arose in *Portlon (Parma)/Blackrock (Tullycorbett/Xroon)*.

was subject to an up-front divestment of that station. **Table 7.12** illustrates that the impact on market structure differs significantly depending on the counterfactual.

The CA argued that the transaction was low risk as defined by CAMG2002 because it resulted in an actual decline in the HHI. The alternative counterfactual would have placed the transaction in the high risk category.[682] If *UTV/FM104* had been a standalone transaction unrelated to a divestment, it arguably would have been subject to a more detailed investigation than was the case.[683]

Table 7.12: *UTV/FM104* – Comparison of HHI Estimates Under Alternative Counterfactuals (Dublin Listenership)

	CA Counterfactual	Alternative Counterfactual
Pre-Merger	6,176	3,297
Post-Merger	4,298	4,298
Change	-1,878	+1,001

Source: Communicorp/SRH, Table 5 and *UTV/FM104,* Table 1.

In *Vodafone Ireland/BT Ireland* the CA stated that its conclusions would not be affected *"whether the product markets are defined in terms of the platform type or customer type"* (¶51). It went on to state, however, that market share data was only available for all customer types and concluded that the transaction would not result in an SLC, in part, because of the parties' low combined market share in fixed line broadband services for all customer types.

Three to Two Mergers

Mergers involving a reduction in the number of competitors in a market from three to two are generally considered likely to harm competition. In such mergers, both the post-merger HHI and the increase in HHI are likely to be relatively high and fall within the high competition risk category. The CA/CCPC have been inconsistent in their approach to three to two mergers.

---

682 The CA did not cite HHI data for the Dublin radio advertising market, although the HHI under the alternative counterfactual would have increased by 1,039 from 3,357 to 4,396, also placing it within the high risk category.

683 The transaction was cleared unconditionally at Phase 1, 27 days after notification, a period which included the Christmas/New Year holidays.

Smurfit/Lithographic Universal[684] involved a merger between the two largest of the three providers of heat offset web printing services located in the State. The CA cleared the transaction following a preliminary Phase 1 investigation, arguing, not entirely convincingly, that the *"moderate competitive constraint"* of the third domestic competitor and of UK-based suppliers in respect of time-sensitive print jobs over 20,000 copies combined with the threat of entry would be sufficient to prevent any SLC.

In a brief, three-page Determination, the CA in *ExxonMobil/BP*[685] stated:

> *"The share estimates indicate that, although the proposed transaction would result in the removal of a large competitor, BP, from the European IPA industry, a sufficient number of alternative IPA suppliers would remain to ensure effective competition" (¶14).*

Table 7.13 illustrates that there were only three other suppliers in the market, one of which had a market share of less than 10%, while imports from outside the EU also accounted for less than 10% of the market.[686]

Table 7.13: The European Isopropanol Market

Company	% Market Share
Shell-Chemical	40-50
Sasol	25-35
BP	10-20
ExxonMobil Chemical	0-10
Dow Chemical	0-10
Other Imports	0-10

Source: ExxonMobil/BP.

Communicorp/SRH involved a proposed merger between the two largest local radio broadcasters in Dublin, which between them accounted for more than 75% of both local radio listenership and advertising. A third broadcaster had a market share of approximately 15%. It was not a strict three to two merger as there were two smaller stations, each with quite limited market shares. The CA required the merging parties to divest one of their three Dublin local radio stations and sought an up-front buyer in this case.

684 CA M/03/012 – *Smurfit/Lithographic Universal*, 17.7.2003.

685 CA M/04/015 – *ExxonMobil/BP*, 6.4.2004.

686 The Determination also pointed out that the acquirer ExxonMobil *"has no presence in the Irish IPA industry"* although it did not define the relevant geographic market as being limited to Ireland.

Heineken/Beamish & Crawford involved a merger of two of the three major brewers in the State, which between them accounted for 90% of on-trade and 70% of off-trade lager sales.[687] The Determination noted that HHI data for the on- and off-trade lager markets, placed the transaction in Zone C as defined by CAMG2002. The transaction was, however, cleared without remedies following a Phase 2 investigation (see **Chapter 8**).

Uniphar/CMR, a three to two merger of full-line pharmacy wholesale distributors, was cleared without remedies following a Phase 2 investigation. The CA acknowledged that HHI data placed the transaction in Zone C as defined by CAMG2002. In this case the merging parties were the second and third largest in a market where the largest supplier had a market share of [50-55]% which had increased in the years prior to the merger. The Determination pointed out that the customers who were community pharmacies *"typically use two full-line wholesalers: a primary full-line wholesaler that supplies most of the pharmacy's needs and a secondary full-line wholesaler that is used if there are supply problems with the primary wholesaler"* (¶2.8). The market share of the largest firm in the market tends to suggest that it was the primary full-line wholesaler for a majority of pharmacies, with the merging parties competing for the role of secondary wholesaler to those customers. The merger therefore eliminated competition between the parties for the position of secondary wholesaler.

Similar issues arose in *Uniphar/Murrays Medical* which involved a three to two merger of full-line wholesale suppliers of ostomy and urinary medical products. Again, the merging parties were the second and third largest in the market while the largest supplier had a market share of [60-70]%. Consequently, the transaction may have eliminated competition between the merging parties for the role of secondary wholesaler to a large number of pharmacies. The transaction was cleared following an extended Phase 1 investigation.[688]

There appear to be similarities between both these cases and the US *Heinz/Beech Nut*[689] case which involved a merger of two US baby food manufacturers. Gerber, the largest firm in the market had a market share of

---

687 Most off-trade sales involved packaged lager, *i.e.*, bottles and cans, and some wholesale distributors imported and sold packaged lager to the off-trade.

688 In response to a survey conducted on behalf of the CCPC, however, only 12% of pharmacists expressed the view that the transaction would result in a price increase by their secondary wholesaler.

689 *FTC v. H.J. Heinz Co.*, 246 F.3d 708 (D.C. Cir. 2001). For an economic analysis of this case, see Baker (2004).

65%. The merging parties had market shares of 17% and 15%, respectively. The majority of retail grocery outlets stocked Gerber's products and one of the two merging brands' baby food products. The USFTC successfully challenged the proposed merger on the grounds that the merging parties competed with each other to be the second brand in the majority of grocery outlets and the proposed merger would therefore eliminate competition between them.

There is no indication that the CA/CCPC considered this possibility in either *Uniphar/CMR* or *Uniphar/Murrays Medical*. This omission is quite striking as CAMG2002 acknowledged that where customers require a primary and a secondary supplier *"if the market only had two suppliers, there would be no choice of secondary supplier"* (¶4.14(d)). CCPCMG2014 states:

> *"The number of suppliers may be particularly relevant to the intensity of competition if customers seek to have more than one supplier, e.g., a primary supplier and a secondary supplier, as might be the case if continuity of supply is important" (¶4.40).*

In *Topaz/Esso,* Topaz owned one of the three terminals in Dublin Port, while the target Esso was the joint owner of one of the other terminals and was also responsible for its operation. The proposed transaction, therefore, involved a reduction in the number of owners of oil import terminals in Dublin Port from four to three. The CCPC argued, quite reasonably, that, if the geographic market was regional rather than national, the transaction really amounted to a three to two merger given that Topaz would exercise operational control over two of the three terminals if the merger was to proceed.[690] The CCPC also argued that the transaction would involve a three to two merger in several local retail markets for motor fuels.[691]

In *Boyle Sports/Bambury I,* the CCPC stated that there would be three LBOs operated by competitors within three kilometres of the target undertaking post-merger which would act as a competitive constraint on the merging parties and the transaction was cleared unconditionally

---

690 The transaction was cleared subject to the divestment of the Esso interest in the terminal. As outlined in **Chapter 6**, the relevant geographic market was arguably wider than Dublin.

691 The Determination acknowledged that this ignored potential intra-brand competition from dealer-owned/dealer-operated (Do/Do) filling stations operated under one of the merging parties' fascias, a point which is considered further in **Chapter 8.** *"The use of fascia rather than the number of individual motor fuel filling stations assumes that branded sites are controlled by the supplier. However, while that is the case for CoCos, it is not the case for DoDos. Hence this approach ignores possible [intra]-brand competition"* (¶163). The CCPC also required the parties to divest some filling stations.

following a preliminary Phase 1 investigation.[692] One of the three LBOs involved was owned by the acquirer, while the other two were both operated by the same third party. Thus, in this local market, contrary to the CCPC's claims, the proposed transaction reduced the number of competitors from three to two.

The CCPC highlighted the reduction in competitor numbers from three to two in *Berendsen/King's Laundry* which was subject to remedies:

> *"Thus, the Proposed Transaction will result in the removal of an important and significant competitor to both Berendsen and Celtic Linen and reduce the number of important and significant competitors in the healthcare market from 3 to 2" (¶4.302).*

The CCPC identified two local LBO markets in *Boyle Sports/Bruce Betting* within which the transaction would reduce the number of competitors from three to two. The transaction was cleared unconditionally after a preliminary Phase 1 investigation on the grounds that the CCPC:

> *"... found very specific market conditions in the local areas including that: all towns will have at least one competitor who is geographically close to the LBOs of the parties; pricing and discounts are done on a national basis; there is good competition on the national market; brand loyalty is low and entry barriers are low in the local areas." (¶35).*

As the Determination acknowledged, the transaction would leave only one competitor to the merging parties post-merger. The reference to there being *"at least one competitor"* to the merging parties in the relevant local markets is therefore puzzling. The Determination implies that a reduction in the number of competitors from three to two would have no effect on competition. The fact that pricing is determined nationally and that there was effective competition at national level was not unique to the relevant local markets.[693] Similarly, it seems extremely unlikely that low brand loyalty and the lack of entry barriers were unique to the two local markets in question rather than common features of local LBO markets generally.

---

692 The situation is further confused by the fact that the Determination refers not to the Target's Lucan LBO but, in an apparent typographical error, to one in Swords, which was discussed elsewhere in the Determination.

693 National pricing could indicate that the LBO market is national rather than local. However, there may be scope for local flexing with respect to non-price competition, *e.g.*, in-store facilities, staffing levels, frequency of store upgrades.

Citylink/GoBus concerned a merger between two of the three undertakings operating inter-city bus services between Dublin and Galway. It was cleared unconditionally by the CCPC following an extended Phase 1 investigation.[694] Following the announcement of the merger, the third operator, Bus Éireann, indicated its intention to withdraw from the route. However, a new entrant was granted a licence to operate on the route. The CCPC indicated that the transaction would have constituted a merger to monopoly in the absence of the new entrant. The Determination states that the CCPC conducted a survey of interurban bus services which found that there was a mean number of two operators per route but provides no further details or even any indication of the number of routes surveyed. It would have been useful for the CCPC to have sought information on fares in its route survey in order to establish whether fares were lower with three operators than with two.[695] The parties had stated that the proposed transaction would *"permit certain efficiencies"* (¶47) in timetabling as there was *"a degree of duplication around the most popular departure times."* The CCPC argued that *"Citylink will not have the incentive to* ***substantially reduce*** *its offerings of departure slots"* (¶48, emphasis added). A reduction in service frequency constitutes a reduction in output which would negatively impact consumer welfare.

In *Bank of Ireland/KBC*, a four to three merger, the CCPC stated:

> *"Therefore, the more concentrated a market is and the fewer effective competitors that remain to constrain one another, the more likely it is that a proposed transaction will enable the merged entity to raise prices" (¶6.21).*

In *Tesco/Joyce's* the CCPC identified three local markets in which the parties' supermarkets overlapped based on a 10-minute drive-time. **Table 7.14** provides details of competing outlets in each case.

The CCPC concluded that there would *"remain a sufficient number of* ***competitors****"* (¶5.18, emphasis added) post-merger in respect of the Ballybane and Father Griffin Road stores but stated that it had competitive concerns in relation to Oranmore. As **Table 7.14** illustrates, post-merger there

694 Unusually for a detailed investigation, the Determination runs to just 13 pages.

695 Barrett (2004) reports that fares on interurban bus routes were lower where there was competition on the route compared with a monopoly. He also reported that fares per mile on the Galway-Dublin route with three operators were 6% and 22% lower for single and return tickets respectively than on the Waterford-Dublin route which had two operators. This is another example of a natural experiment. The fact that the level of competition may be lower in other markets does not justify finding that a merger will not result in an SLC. The new entrant subsequently withdrew from the market (see **Chapter 8**).

would be eight grocery outlets competing with the merged entity in Ballybane and 10 at Father Griffin Road compared to four in Oranmore. However, the crucial issue from a competition perspective is the number of competitors rather than the number of stores. Several of the competing stores at both Ballybane and Father Griffin Road were part of the same multiple chain. Thus, post-merger the merging parties faced three competitors in both Oranmore and Ballybane and four at Father Griffin Road.[696]

Table 7.14: *Tesco/Joyce's* Effective Competitors within a 10-minute Drive-time of Target Supermarkets

	Oranmore	**Ballybane**	**Fr. Griffin Road**
Tesco	1	1	1
Dunnes Stores	1	3	4
Aldi	1	2	3
Lidl	2	3	2
Supervalu	0	0	0
Marks & Spencer	0	0	1
Joyce's	0	3	1
Total Outlets	**5**	**12**	**12**
Total Competing Outlets Post-Merger	**4**	**8**	**10**
Total Competing Fascias Post-Merger	**3**	**3**	**4**

Source: Tesco/Joyce's, Table 7.2.

During the course of its Phase 1 investigation in *PandaGreen/Exomex*, the CCPC expressed concerns with respect to individual C&I waste collection services in certain townlands in County Louth where the Parties overlapped. The Determination did not outline any theory of harm but merely stated that the supply of individual C&I waste collection services in the overlapping towns was highly concentrated and that the proposed transaction would likely remove an important competitive force and reduce the number of competitors from three to two. There is no indication in the Determination whether there were other suppliers of C&I waste collection active in the county or adjacent counties that customers could have

696 While the number of competitors was the same in both Ballybane and Oranmore, the CCPC also raised a closeness of competition issue in the latter case (see **Chapter 8**). The transaction was cleared subject to the divestment of the target Oranmore outlet.

switched to in the event of any post-merger price increase.[697] Equally there is no indication that prices in the overlap areas were lower than in other areas where the parties did not overlap. The transaction was cleared subject to a remedy involving a divestment of customers.

In *Thornton's/Carducci,* the CCPC stated that the transaction raised concerns in relation to domestic waste collection services because it resulted in a reduction in the number of competitors from three to two within the *"overlap areas"*:

> *"The acquisition of Carducci by Thornton's Recycling could weaken competition in the Overlapping Areas. The Proposed Transaction would lead to a reduction in the number of domestic waste collection service providers in each of these areas from three to two. This reduced competition could lead to increased prices and/or lower levels of service" (¶5.27).*

The transaction was cleared subject to a remedy involving a divestment of customers. The Determination stated that, in light of the remedy, it was not necessary for the CCPC to conclude in relation to the competitive effects of the original transaction (¶5.35). As in *PandaGreen/Exomex, Thornton's/Carducci* cites no evidence apart from references to increased market concentration in support of an SLC.[698]

The CCPC in *Phey Topco/Trasmore* expressed concern that a reduction in the number of competitors from five to four could lead to reduced customer choice, increased prices and/or otherwise harm competition in two different markets. It did not consider any specific theory of harm but cited high post-merger market concentration and a significant increase in the HHI in both

---

697 The Determination noted that the purchaser provided individual C&I waste collection services in County Louth, operating from its depot in County Meath where the waste was subsequently processed, so clearly it was possible for suppliers in adjoining counties to provide individual C&I waste collection services in the overlapping areas. The CA in *PandaGreen/Greenstar* had indicated that switching costs were low for individual C&I waste customers and accepted in that case and in *Greenstar/Veolia* that geographic markets for individual C&I waste collection services were regional. In contrast to domestic waste, the CA/CCPC has not advanced a case for a narrower C&I waste geographic market as far as the author is aware.

698 Again, it would have been useful to identify whether prices were lower in the overlap areas than elsewhere. *Thornton's/Carducci* would have constituted a four to three merger if the market had been defined as the relevant local authority area as in previous domestic waste merger cases. The possibility of competitive harm in such a wider market cannot be ruled out without considering possible theories of competitive harm (see **Chapter 8**).

markets.[699] The transaction was cleared subject to a divestment remedy which addressed *"the preliminary competition concerns identified by the Commission because they restore to five the number of suppliers active in the market"* (¶49). The Determination identified no specific theory of harm.[700]

The Determination in *Uniphar/LXV Remedies* (*Sam McAuley*) records that the CCPC had identified preliminary competition concerns during its Phase 1 investigation in relation to two local markets: Athy, County Kildare and Navan, County Meath. The Determination provides no explanation of the nature of these concerns. It then states that, as the parties had proposed remedies which addressed the concerns in both cases, *"it is not necessary for the Commission to conclude on the competitive effects of the Proposed Transaction in the absence of the Proposals"* (¶s66 & 70). The CCPC's concerns in both instances are difficult to understand given the number of competitors remaining post-merger, combined with the fact that the remedies did not appear to affect that number. In Athy the transaction involved a five to four merger, with three other pharmacies in the town. The Determination states that the remedies meant that there would be three pharmacies within the catchment area which would have been the case anyway. In the case of Navan, the Determination involved a seven to six and eight to seven merger, leaving six competitor pharmacies within two kilometres of one of the target outlets and seven within two kilometres of the other, which would also have been the case without any divestment.[701] The divestments appear to have reduced the merged entities' pharmacy numbers but it is unclear from the wording of the Determination whether they had an effect

---

699 The parties had combined market shares of [45-55]% in both markets which is certainly sufficient to raise potential competition concerns, although, as noted above, the CA/CCPC has approved several mergers involving much higher market shares and concentration levels so, in the absence of any theory of harm, it is not clear why it adopted a different approach in this case.

700 In *McMullan Bros/Naas Fuels* the CCPC expressed the view that a reduction in the number of competitors from five to four did not raise competition concerns. Valetti & Zenger (2019) state that the increase in profit margins observed in many countries over recent decades exacerbates the change in market power due to horizontal mergers and argue that, as a result, the effect of a five to four merger may be comparable to that of a four to three merger previously. Salinger (2024) argued that five to four was not an appropriate upper limit for challenging mergers.

701 In contrast, *Petrogas/Excol* stated: *"A reduction of the number of brands of service stations and associated forecourt convenience stores from eight to seven is unlikely to give rise to a concern of a substantial lessening of competition because there will remain six competing brands within a 5mile/8km radius of the two retail motor fuel service stations and associated forecourt convenience stores to be acquired by Applegreen"* (¶23).

on the number of competing outlets.[702] Data on pharmacy numbers indicates entry is relatively easy (see **Table 7.15**). The number of pharmacies in counties Kildare and Meath in 2020 was two and a half times the 2009 total. In the absence of any clear explanation this looks like a false positive, particularly, in the case of Navan.[703]

Table 7.15: Registered Pharmacies in Kildare & Meath

	Kildare	Meath	State
2009	32	25	935
2020	79	62	1960
% Change 2009-2020	+146.9	+148.0	+109.6

Source: https://www.thepsi.ie/gns/Registration/public-registers/Statistics.aspx. Accessed 3.9.2020.

Taken together *PandaGreen/Exomex*, *Thornton's/Carducci*, *Phey/Topco* and *Uniphar/LXV Remedies (Sam McAuley)* raise some troubling questions. In these cases, the CCPC expressed concerns about a potential harm to competition, solely on the basis that the transaction would increase concentration, arguably based on overly narrow market definitions in the two waste cases (see **Chapter 6**) without outlining any theory of harm. Economics and CCPCMG2014 state that increased concentration is a necessary but not sufficient condition for establishing that a merger is likely to have an adverse effect on competition. In other words, if the post-merger level and increase in HHI exceed the HHI safe harbour thresholds, this constitutes valid grounds for conducting a more detailed investigation but, of itself, is not a sufficient basis for expressing competition concerns. Expressing concerns, which may ultimately prove unfounded, arguably places pressure on parties to offer remedies, in order to avoid the delay involved in a Phase 2 investigation, which may be unnecessary if the merger has no effect on competition. This constitutes a potential false positive (Type I) error. It is extremely unsatisfactory for the CCPC to apply remedies without offering any clear explanation as to the nature of the alleged competition concern.[704]

---

702 The Determination clearly indicates that the number of competitors post-merger in Athy would be the same with, and without, the remedy.

703 The approach in this case is in sharp contrast to *Uniphar/Bradley's*, a four to three pharmacy merger where the CCPC argued that pharmacies in towns up to 25 minutes' drive-time away would exercise a competitive constraint on the merging parties (see **Chapter 6**).

704 The subsequent Determinations failed to identify any theory of harm, stating in some cases that it was not necessary to do so in light of the remedy (see **Chapter 8**).

Bidding Markets

There are many markets in which sales are based on tenders or auctions whereby State agencies and large private sector buyers issue tenders and invite suppliers to bid for the right to supply the required products. In addition to such formal tender processes, many business-to-business transactions may involve a more informal bidding process.

It has been suggested that bidding (auction) markets by their nature are unlikely to give rise to competition problems and that the presence of just two bidders in an auction may suffice to secure a competitive outcome (OECD, 2006). Consequently, it is claimed that there are no grounds for concern about market concentration and power and that mergers involving bidding markets require little competition scrutiny.[705] Such claims have frequently been made to the UK competition authorities with the result that *"they seem also to have seeped into some anti-trust agency thinking"* (Klemperer, 2007, p.2).

Klemperer is extremely critical of such claims, arguing that it is simply incorrect to assume that competition problems cannot arise in bidding markets. He acknowledges that this may be true in a *"perfect"* bidding market which satisfies the following conditions:

i. Competition is 'winner take all', so each supplier either wins all or none of the order and there is no smooth trade-off between the price offered and the quantity sold;

ii. Competition is 'lumpy' – each contest is large relative to a supplier's total sales in a period (the value of each individual contract is typically significant for competitors);

iii. Competition begins afresh for each contract, and for each customer. There is no 'lock-in' by which the outcome of one contest significantly determines another.

He also states that bidding markets sometimes display two further characteristics.

iv. Entry is easy;

v. A 'bidding system' or 'bidding process' is involved (*ibid.*).

---

705 Klemperer (2007) claims that this was argued in at least five cases reviewed by the UKCC over the previous 12 months. The UKCC accepted that a reduction in the number of providers of helicopter services in the UK Northern Zone of the North Sea would not have an adverse effect on competition in *CHC/HSG* (UKCC, 2000).

Competition concerns are unlikely to arise if conditions (i)-(iii) are met because these conditions satisfy the requirements for a competitive market. If condition (iv) is also satisfied, then the market is perfectly contestable. In other words, if it is assumed that all of the conditions for effective competition are satisfied, this leads to the conclusion that there is no competition problem. Klemperer (2007) points out, however, that many markets described as bidding markets violate at least one of conditions (i)-(iii), while (iv) is often not satisfied and, in particular, rarely applies if (i) and (ii) are satisfied. He further notes that once any of these extreme assumptions is not satisfied the question of dominance and unilateral and coordinated effects arises. In simple terms the argument that bidding markets do not give rise to competition problems is flawed because many so-called bidding markets fail to satisfy the necessary conditions for such conclusions to hold. Klemperer (2007) therefore concludes that bidding markets require a stricter, rather than a more lenient, application of competition law. The EU Commission rejected claims by the parties that the relevant markets constituted perfect bidding markets in *Danfoss/Eaton Hydraulics*, pointing out that tenders could not be regarded as *"winner-takes-all"*.

Economic analysis indicates that the greater the number of participants in a tender, the more aggressively each of them will bid and thus the more competitive the tender will be and the lower will be the price to the purchaser (see, for example, Philips, 1995; Scheffman & Coleman, 2003; Marshall & Marx, 2012). Baker & Shapiro (2008) state that mergers in bidding markets typically cause prices to increase. In preparing tenders, suppliers will take account of their costs, their beliefs about their rivals' costs and capabilities as well as their view of the potential number of rival bidders in order to determine their best offer.

There was little mention of bidding markets in CAMG2002, although it stated that *"the presence of three or more firms may increase the intensity of bidding"* (¶4.14(d)) but went on to suggest that market concentration may not be a concern in bidding markets ((¶4.16).

The CA stated somewhat confusingly in *Tetra Laval/Carlisle*:

> *"Customer evidence shows the importance of several bidders in the market for the supply of their limited purpose equipment requirements, with several customers noting that it is sufficient to have two bidders in order to provide leverage against price increases" (¶2.44)*

It subsequently repeated the latter point:

> *"Several customers have noted that two bidders are sufficient and the presence of three bidders is not essential" (¶3.8)*

Surprisingly, in light of the reference in CAMG2002 to three or more bidders increasing the intensity of competition, the Determination failed to analyse customer claims that two bidders may suffice and makes no reference to the economics literature on bidding markets.[706]

The UKOFT, in contrast, rejected Tetra Laval's claims that the market was a perfect bidding market and that two bidders was sufficient to ensure a competitive outcome because:

i. The products were not homogenous;
ii. Bidders were not homogenous;
iii. While demand was lumpy, competition was not for the market as (a) there were a considerable number of low value contracts and a more limited number of high value contracts and (b) only a small proportion of the manufacturing capacity of suppliers was devoted to the relevant products; therefore winning or losing a contract did not appear to significantly affect capacity utilisation or profitability which affected bidders' incentives to bid aggressively;
iv. There was no evidence (e.g., relative prices and/or profit margins) indicating that the presence of two (or more) bidders was sufficient to ensure a competitive outcome.

The CA Determination indicates that at least two of Klemperer's conditions for perfect bidding markets were not met.[707] In those circumstances, a reduction in the number of bidders would be expected to have a negative effect on competition.

---

[706] Although Klemperer (2007) post-dates the CA's Determination in this case, his paper was originally published as a discussion paper by the UKCC in June 2005.

[707] Evidence that *"many customers do not want to change from their incumbent supplier"* violates the requirement that the outcome of a tender should not be significantly affected by the result of a previous one, while the ease of entry condition was not satisfied as the CA accepted that entry was unlikely in the case of block formers. Having concluded on the basis of a *"preliminary analysis"* that the transaction would not affect competition, the CA did not address the issue of entry in the other two markets.

Some months later in *Applied Materials/Brooks Software,*[708] the CA stated:

> *"Where a genuine bidding market exists, the outcome of competition in the market is that the existence of two firms is enough to imply perfect competition, or in extreme circumstances that one firm is enough. However the existence of a genuine bidding market is quite rare and requires a number of criteria to be perfectly satisfied" (¶2.21).*

It concluded that the relevant market constituted a perfect bidding market in which the existence of two or possibly just one participant would produce a competitive outcome.[709]

The CA's 2010 consultation on its *Merger Guidelines* contain no references to bidding markets. USHMG2010 introduced auction and bidding models into unilateral effects analysis (Shapiro, 2019). The only reference to bidding markets in CCPCMG2014 acknowledges that the larger the number of bidders in a tender, the more intense competition is likely to be:

> *"For example, in tendering processes the greater the number of firms able to tender for the supply of products or services, the more likely it is that there will be intense competition" (¶4.39).*[710]

The CCPC in *Apcoa Parking/NCPS*[711] found that the market for parking management services was not an idealised bidding market as the vast majority of contracts were awarded informally. Subsequently in *Q-Park/Tazbell* the CCPC stated that, where either a formal or informal bidding process has taken place, the procurement of car park management services had the characteristics of a bidding market.[712]

Bulow & Shapiro (2004) state that, in mergers involving bidding markets, it is important to consider whether the merging parties' have the

---

708 The Determination cites Klemperer's UKCC Discussion Paper (see above).

709 The Determination identified an incumbency effect, to the extent that customers would be unlikely to use anyone other than their existing suppliers when developing new plants using the same technology, but that competition begins afresh when a new technology is introduced. Whether all conditions for a perfect bidding market existed thus depended on the interpretation of what constituted a new tender. The CA also stated that it was difficult to identify any harm to consumers in the State, as purchasing decisions were made outside the State and Irish-based customers exported virtually all of their output.

710 Similar wording was included in the *Draft 2013 Guidelines* (CA, 2013, September 13, ¶4.30).

711 CCPC M/19/012 – *Apcoa Parking/NCPS*, 27.6.2019.

712 It did not express a view as to whether the market satisfied the conditions for a perfect bidding market.

key assets necessary to be effective bidders as well as their shares in winning or submitting bids. They argue that the merging parties in *BP Amoco/Arco*[713] had advantages over other potential bidders because information was critical in oil lease auctions and bidders with better information will win most of the bids.

Market Concentration in SMNP Cases

Since mid-2020 horizontal mergers where the parties have a combined market share of less than 15% are analysed under the SMNP. A combined market share of 15% implies a maximum possible HHI increase of 112.5. The implicit HHI threshold under SMNP is thus consistent with the HHI thresholds in CCPCMG2014. If a combined market share of less than 15% is considered to pose a low risk to competition, combined market shares in excess of the 15% SMNP threshold should not be regarded as small. The CCPC concluded that no SLC would arise in *Egis Ingenerie/JB Barry & BeMRA Engineering* because the parties market share was *"minimal"* and because of competitive constraints from competitors. The case did not meet the SMNP criteria and the Determination indicated that the parties had market shares of [10-15]% and [5-10]% with a combined market share of [15-20]%.[714] It cannot be assumed in cases above the SMNP thresholds that even small increases in market shares do not raise possible competition concerns and it is therefore not a valid basis, in itself, for clearing a transaction.

Conclusions

Pre-1980s US merger control focused almost exclusively on the impact of mergers on market structure. It is now generally recognised that high market shares and market concentration are a necessary but insufficient condition for a merger to be anti-competitive. Market concentration can be useful for distinguishing between mergers which are unlikely to be anti-

---

713 The transaction was cleared subject to a consent decree requiring divestments: https://www.ftc.gov/news-events/news/press-releases/2000/04/ftc-clears-merger-bp-amoco-atlantic-richfield-company.

714 CCPC M/23/012 – *Egis Ingenerie/JB Barry & BeMRA Engineering*, 3.5.2023. In fairness to the CCPC, the parties were unable to provide market shares for other firms in the market which meant that it was not possible to estimate the HHI, although, as pointed out, the change in HHI can be estimated based on the parties' market shares and it may have been possible to establish whether the increase was below 150 points which would place it in the low risk category.

competitive and those that require closer scrutiny and may permit large numbers of harmless mergers to be approved quickly at a low cost (Schmalensee, 1987). The US anti-trust agencies have used the HHI to identify cases that require further investigation. CA/CCPC *Guidelines* define HHI thresholds as a means of differentiating between innocuous mergers and competitively harmful ones. The CA/CCPC has frequently failed to estimate HHIs and apply these thresholds in practice.

An analysis of horizontal mergers notified to the CA/CCPC over the 2003-2023 period indicates that merger policy over much of this period may have been overly lenient, raising the possibility of false negative (Type II) errors in cases which were not subject to detailed investigation when arguably CAMG2002 and CCPCMG2014 would indicate they should have been.

In several individual cases the CA/CCPC concluded that the transaction was unlikely to raise concerns because it would only result in a small increase in market share, without considering the impact on market concentration. Economics indicates that even small increases in market shares may harm competition. The CA/CCPC also on occasion has simply argued that there were a sufficient number of competitors in the market to exercise an effective competitive constraint on the merged entity, even in cases where the merging parties had very high market shares (up to 90% in at least one case). Such cases also raise the possibility of false negatives.

CCPCMG2014 provides that an increase in the HHI of less than 150 points is unlikely to raise competition concerns irrespective of the post-merger HHI level. As only the parties' market shares are required to estimate the increase in the HHI due to a merger, this offers a relatively simple means for identifying many harmless mergers. Stating in merger Determinations that a transaction would not result in any SLC because it would result in a HHI increase of less than 150 points would be consistent with CCPCMG2014 and would provide greater clarity than references to small or minimal increases which are vague and arguably somewhat subjective and likely to lead to Type II errors.

There are examples of potential false positives (Type I) errors where the CA/CCPC has raised competition concerns solely on the basis of market concentration, based in some cases on overly narrow market definitions. This is inconsistent both with economics and the CCPC's own *Guidelines* which indicate that high market concentration is a necessary but not sufficient condition for a merger to result in competitive harm.

The CA/CCPC has been inconsistent in its approach to three to two mergers which might usually be expected to raise potential competition concerns. It has cleared several such cases without remedies, sometimes based on a preliminary investigation but has prohibited or required remedies in others, although the reasons for the difference in outcomes are not always clear. In one 2023 case the CCPC raised concerns in a five-to-four merger which was cleared subject to a divestment remedy which maintained five market competitors, while another was cleared subject to divestment remedies involving two local markets where the transaction reduced the number of competitors from eight to seven and seven to six. It is too early to judge whether these decisions are a harbinger of a tougher approach to merger control.

Appendix 7.1: Categorising Horizontal Merger Notifications According to the Degree of Competition Risk

This Appendix describes the methodology used to classify horizontal mergers as low-, medium-, and high-competition risk cases. HHIs were estimated for all horizontal mergers where the Determination contained sufficient data to permit such estimates. It was possible to estimate HHIs in respect of 382 (51%) of horizontal merger notifications encompassing 835 different market definitions. Based on the HHI results these markets were then defined as representing a low, moderate, or high risk to competition as defined in **Table 7.1**.

A small number of CA/CCPC Determinations contain actual HHI data or market shares from which it is possible to calculate the actual HHI. In many other cases it was possible to estimate the HHI from market share data included in the Determination, while in others it was possible to arrive at an approximate estimate of the HHI.[715] In yet other cases it was only possible to identify the change in the HHI based on information on the parties' market shares included in the Determination. As in Affeldt *et al.* (2021), where CA/CCPC Determinations quote a range for undertakings' market shares, the mid-point of the range was used to estimate HHIs. In some cases, the CA/CCPC used a range of 10% while in others it has used a range of 5%,

---

[715] For example, in a market in which there are only three firms the minimum possible value of the HHI is approximately 3,300, which arises when all three firms are the same size. If one firm is larger than the others, the HHI will be greater than 3,300.

sometimes in the same Determination. Obviously HHI estimates will be more accurate where they are based on narrower market share ranges.

In many instances the mid points of the market share ranges sum to over 100%. In those cases, the market share estimates were adjusted downward on a *pro rata* basis to ensure that they summed to 100%. Determinations frequently do not include market share data for all market participants, including an aggregate for "others". In such cases it is assumed that other parties' market shares are no higher than that of the undertaking with the smallest reported market share. This market share is then divided into the total market share of others to arrive at an estimate of the minimum number of undertakings within this category in order to estimate the HHI. In other words, if the smallest undertaking for which market share information is provided had a market share of 5%, it is assumed that none of the parties included in the "others" category had a market share greater than 5%. If others had a combined market share of 25%, it is assumed that the others category includes at least five undertakings. The contribution of these undertakings to the total HHI, therefore is estimated as 5×5^2, i.e. each firm is assumed to have a market share of 5%, which is squared, and the result is then multiplied by five because there are assumed to be five such undertakings. If the others category has a significant aggregate market share, using their aggregate share in the HHI calculations would lead to a substantial upwards bias in the result. If others have a small aggregate market share, say less than 10%, any upward bias will be relatively limited. For example, if their aggregate 10% share was used in the calculations this would equal 100 but if there were five undertakings with 2% each, their correct input to the HHI would be 20, i.e. 5×2^2 Thus, if the aggregate share of others is 10% or lower, their aggregate share can be used when estimating the HHI as the resulting overstatement would be less than 100 points.

8: HORIZONTAL THEORIES OF COMPETITIVE HARM

Introduction

Horizontal mergers, by definition, involve a reduction in the number of competitors in a market. Nevertheless, they are unlikely to raise competition concerns unless there are relatively few competitors, and the market would be highly concentrated post-merger. As noted in **Chapter 7**, high levels of concentration are not sufficient to establish that a merger will harm competition. It is also necessary to identify a credible theory of competitive harm.

> *"Any Commission finding in relation to the presence or absence of an SLC will be based on all available information considered in the light of all credible theories of consumer harm arising from possible adverse competitive effects" (CCPCMG2014, ¶1.7).*

Competitive harm may occur if the merger:

i. Enables the merged entity to raise prices (or lower quality) unilaterally – unilateral effects; or

ii. Enables the firms remaining in the market post-merger to collectively raise prices (or lower quality) – coordinated effects.

iii. Reduces innovation or harms competition in some other way.

Historically coordinated effects were the main concern in merger cases and were the exclusive focus of USHMG1968. As noted in **Chapter 2**, the 1978 *Mergers Act* followed an RPC report warning of the threat posed by oligopoly in many business sectors. USHMG1982 continued to focus exclusively on coordinated effects. Unilateral effects theories were first included in USHMG1992. Innovation theories of harm were added in USHMG2010 (Shapiro, 2019). USHMG2023 identify additional ways in which a merger may result in an SLC (Shapiro, 2024).

Identifying an Appropriate Theory of Harm

Scheffman & Coleman (2003) state that an analysis of the pre-merger state of competition in a market is required in order to identify the appropriate theory of competitive harm. This is not just a matter of choosing between unilateral or coordinated effects theories but identifying which theory from within each category is most appropriate in a particular case. As pointed out in **Chapter 3**, in many cases the CA/CCPC failed to put forward a theory of harm in reaching a Phase 1 decision.

Unilateral and coordinated effects can both arise in any given case and the distinction between them may be blurred on occasion (USHMG, 2010). Lyons (2008), for example, observes that a merger creating the second or third largest firm in a market may result in both unilateral and coordinated effects.[716] Unilateral effects are more likely in the case of differentiated products, while coordinated effects are more likely with homogenous products (Werden & Froeb, 1998).

> *"Reaching terms of coordination is easier in the case of homogenous products than in a differentiated product market"* (Irish Times/Sappho, *¶4.50).*

Consumer goods markets are more likely to be differentiated, while business customers are less likely to view products as differentiated on the basis of brand names. Unilateral effects theories of harm may therefore be more appropriate in mergers involving consumer goods, while coordinated effects may be more appropriate in business-to-business markets. Shapiro (1996) observes, however, that virtually all markets involve some element of product differentiation. Products are differentiated because consumers

---

716 The CCPC concluded in M/17/024 – *UPS/Eirpost*, 14.6.2017, that, *"the fact that the merged entity will become the second largest player in the potential market does not of itself, in the particular circumstances of this case, give rise to competition concerns"* (¶21). It stated that the merged entity would be subject to competitive constraints from An Post and DHL and several others with market shares of at least 5%.

believe that they are and shop accordingly (Carlton & Perloff, 2000).[717] Product differentiation is almost always multi-dimensional in nature (Caplin & Nalebuff, 1986).[718] The nature of the products and markets involved thus provide some insights into the kind of competitive harm theory that may be relevant in a particular case. If evidence indicates that the number of competitors matters, as is often the case for bidding markets, then a merger which results in the removal of a significant competitor is likely to prove harmful (Scheffman & Coleman, 2003).[719]

Following their introduction in USHMG1992, unilateral effects theories of harm were initially largely endorsed by the US courts.[720] The Court in *Staples/Office Depot* employed the logic of unilateral effects theory without referring to it by name (Baker, 1997). Although unilateral effects theories were rejected in *Oracle/PeopleSoft* they have been accepted in several key cases subsequently (Shapiro & Shelanski, 2021). Since 1992 USDoJ horizontal merger investigations generally have focussed on unilateral effects unless there were structural factors facilitating collusion post-merger or a history of collusion in the market (Shapiro, 1996). Shapiro (2010) described the shift by the US anti-trust agencies to unilateral effects as their most frequently applied theory of competitive effects as the biggest change in US merger enforcement between 1992 and 2010. Post the 2004 reform of the ECMR, unilateral effects theories have featured far more frequently in EU Commission decisions which have developed further, particularly in their assessment of closeness of competition (Duso *et al.*, 2025). Slade (2004) points out that market shares and entry barriers play a key role in unilateral effects analysis, while coordinated effects involve consideration of a range of additional factors.

---

717 For example, the CA reported that own brand milk accounted for 14% of supermarket milk sales although it was 41% cheaper than branded milk in October 2003, indicating that many consumers are prepared to pay a higher price because they regard a branded product as superior to the own brand product (CA M/05/006 – *Glanbia/Dairygold*, 9.3.2005).

718 They point out that cars, for example, vary in size, comfort, fuel economy, reliability, and various other dimensions.

719 Shy (2001) points out that, in mobile telephony, prices drop with each new entrant.

720 In *State of New York v. Kraft General Foods, Inc., Nabisco Cereals Inc. et. al.*, 862, F. Supp. 1030, (S.D.N.Y., 1993), for example, the Court accepted *"that the Merger Guidelines' concern for this effect is valid"*.

Table 8.1 provides some data on the number of CA/CCPC horizontal merger cases where it was possible to identify a theory of harm.[721] Specific competitive harm theories were identified in 117 (16%) of the 754 CA/CCPC merger cases with a horizontal element over the 2003-2023 period. At first sight, this figure looks relatively low. Recall, however, that **Table 7.3** indicated that two-thirds of horizontal mergers where it was possible to calculate HHIs were defined as low risk, while many horizontal mergers defined as high risk were not subject to detailed investigation.[722]

Table 8.1: CA/CCPC Cases by Theory of Harm Applied

Theory of Harm	Number of cases				%			
	2003-2013	2014-2019	2019-2023	2003-2023	2003-2013	2014-2019	2020-2023	2003-2023
Unilateral	20	32	28	80	46.5	82.1	80.0	68.4
Coordinated	2	2	1	5	4.7	5.1	2.9	4.3
Both	21	5	6	32	48.8	12.8	17.1	27.4
Total	**43**	**39**	**35**	**117**	**100.0**	**100.0**	**100.0**	**100.0**

Source: CA/CCPC Determinations.

Over the entire 2003-2023 period, 68% of horizontal mergers where specific harm theories were cited involved unilateral effects, with a further 27% involving both unilateral and coordinated effects. Coordinated theories on their own were cited in only 4% of cases. The results indicate a shift post-2014 with over 80% of cases involving only unilateral effects compared to 47% pre-2014, while the proportion of cases where both unilateral and coordinated effects were considered declined from 49% pre-2014 to 17% from 2020. The focus on unilateral effects is consistent with practice in other jurisdictions.[723] Several cases involved unilateral effects based on closeness

721 Cases were identified based on whether the Determination mentioned unilateral or coordinated effects or some other indication of a competitive harm theory, *e.g.*, such as closeness of competition between the merging parties.

722 The proportion of cases where competitive harm theories were identified increased from 14% pre-2020 to 20% from 2020 onwards. It is significantly lower than the percentage of horizontal mergers which met the HHI threshold for more detailed investigation according to **Table 7.3**. In several cases the CA/CCPC stated that it had not identified a credible coordinated effects theory of harm, and such cases are not counted as involving this theory.

723 Gorecki *et al.* (2007) report that the CA analysed theories of harm in 18 horizontal mergers over the 2003-2006 period. Eleven of these involved unilateral effects, six considered both unilateral and coordinated effects, while only one involved coordinated effects only.

of competition even though they related to homogenous products.[724] In other cases involving consumer goods markets with differentiated products the CA/CCPC did not consider a unilateral effects theory of harm.[725]

Unilateral Effects Theories

Coate (2006) identifies three types of unilateral effects theories of harm applied by the USFTC in single product merger cases between 1993 and 2003:

i. Monopoly;
ii. Spatial;
iii. Nash-Bertrand.

Monopoly (Dominance) Theory

A monopoly-creating merger is likely to result in price increases since the merged entity will face no competitive constraints from rivals (Motta, 2004). A dominant firm is one which, although not a monopoly, has sufficient market power to enable it to significantly raise prices above the competitive level or act in some other way independently of its rivals. Consequently, a merger that creates or strengthens a dominant position is likely to give rise to unilateral effects. McAfee & Williams (1992) state that mergers which result in a new largest firm, and which increase the size of the largest firm, always reduce welfare.

> *"One scenario is where the merger results in monopoly, near-monopoly or single firm dominance by the merged firm. The larger the market share of the merged firm relative to its competitors, the more likely it is that market power of the kind described as monopoly would be created by such a merger" (CAMG2002, ¶4.13).*

CCPCMG2014 state that competitive constraints on merging parties will be weak where *"there is an absence of substantial competition from other firms in the market or firms likely to enter in a timely manner"* (¶4.11).

The EU Commission analysis in *Ryanair/Aer Lingus I* involved a monopoly theory of harm.[726] All previous EU airline merger cases involved airlines which had their main centres of operations at different airports,

---

724 See, for example, *Kingspan/Xtratherm* and *Barnett/Origin/Hall.*

725 See, for example, *Glanbia/Dairygold.*

726 While the proposed merger had potentially far-reaching implications for Irish consumers, as noted in **Chapter 1**, the EU Commission concluded that it fell within the scope of the ECMR.

often in different countries and raised concerns on a relatively limited number of overlapping routes. *Ryanair/Aer Lingus I* concerned *"the two main airlines in Ireland with a significant base at the same airport, namely Dublin Airport"* (¶335). The parties were, respectively, the first and third largest airlines in Europe in terms of weekly sales of *"no-frills"* seats during summer 2006.[727] They overlapped on 32 routes out of Dublin Airport, accounting for approximately 70% of all passengers on intra-European routes, including eight of the 10 most important routes to/from Dublin.

Each of the parties accounted for [30-40]% of all passengers ex-Dublin in 2005 and for [40-50]% and [30-40]%, respectively of intra-European traffic. The combined entity would also have been the largest short-haul carrier at Cork and Shannon airports.[728] Including the latter two airports, the two airlines overlapped on 35 routes in total. Details of their market shares and their main competitors on these routes are provided in **Table 8.2**. The merger would have created a monopoly on 22 routes where the parties were the only operators, while they had a combined market share in excess of 60% on the remaining 13 routes.

Both airlines monitored each other's fares and reacted regularly to the other's fare changes. Both used specific software to adjust capacities and prices on a daily basis in response to competitive actions of the other. The Commission found that the advertising strategies pursued by the two airlines indicated that each considered the other to be its closest competitor noting that they both routinely published advertisements in which they compared fares and services with those of the other.[729] Both monitored and sought to react to the other's promotional fares.

> *"The proposed merger would eliminate this actual competition between the Merging Parties, giving the merged entity significantly increased market power with the likely consequence of increased fares and/or a reduction of the number flights for passengers wishing to travel to or from Ireland. Indeed, post-merger, as predicted by standard 'non-coordinated effects' analysis...both carriers would internalise the effects of setting higher fares on each other. In particular, the merged entity would*

---

727 Citing the Association of European Airlines.

728 The two airlines together operated to around 20 destination airports from both airports.

729 The Commission subsequently noted in *Danfoss/Eaton Hydraulics* that it was very unlikely that two undertakings in a highly concentrated oligopolistic market would not be close competitors.

> *have the incentive to set higher fares for Aer Lingus since most of the customers lost would be captured by Ryanair" (¶491).*

The Commission found that the proposed merger was likely to lead to higher prices, lower quality services and less consumer choice. It also found that it would reduce potential competition with less pressure on the merged entity to establish new routes.[730]

Rejecting Ryanair's appeal against the Commission decision, the EU General Court stated:

> *"If Aer Lingus did not exist, the temptation would be great for Ryanair to maximise its profits to take account of the lack of competitive pressure resulting from the acquisition of its main actual or potential competitor on the relevant markets. Ryanair's intentions in relation to the use of Aer Lingus or its former pricing practices do not affect the credibility of that structural risk, which is apparent from the analysis of the anti-competitive effects connected with the elimination of competition between the parties to the concentration" (Ryanair v Commission, ¶1251).*

Two of the five mergers prohibited by the CA/CCPC, *IBM/Schlumberger* and *daa/Gannon,* involved a merger to monopoly. *IBM/Schlumberger* involved the two largest suppliers of business recovery hotsite services with an estimated 70-95% of the relevant market. Neither of the two non-merging firms identified by the CA in this case provided recovery services for mainframe computers. The Determination states that both were capable of meeting the requirements of some low-end customers but not high-end customers. The CA stated that the merging parties were each other's closest competitors, citing views of customers and internal documents of the parties. *daa/Gannon* involved an attempt by daa, which owns and operates Dublin Airport, to acquire a former car park located close to the Airport which would have given it control of approximately 90% of car parking capacity at the airport.

---

730 The Commission stated that Ryanair had established several new routes out of Dublin in response to expansion by Aer Lingus, increasing the number of routes on which both airlines competed from six in 2001 to 35.

Table 8.2: Ryanair/Aer Lingus Overlap Routes

Route	Ryanair	Aer Lingus	Combined	Existing Competitors	
Dublin to	% Share			Airline	% Share
Alicante	[50-60%]	[40-50%]	100% [95-100%]	Charter	[0-5%]
Barcelona	[40-50%]	[30-40%]	[70-80%] [65-70%]	Iberia Clickair Charter	[20-30%] [0-5%]
Berlin	[50-60%]	[40-59%]	100%	None	0
Bilbao-Vitoria	[50-60%]	[40-59%]	100%	None	0
Birmingham	[60-70%]	[30-40%]	100%	None	0
Bologna	[50-60%]	[40-59%]	100%	None	0
Brussels	[50-60%]	[40-59%]	100%	None	0
Edinburgh	[70-80%]	[20-30%]	100%	None	0
Faro	[50-60%]	[40-59%]	100% [95-100%]	Charter	[0-5%]
Frankfurt	[40-50%]	[40-50%]	[80-90%]	Lufthansa	[20-30%]
Glasgow	[50-60%]	[30-40%]	[90-100%]	Loganair	[0-10%]
Hamburg-Lubeck	[60-70%]	[30-40%]	100%	None	0
Krakow	[30-40%]	[40-50%]	[70-80%]	Sky Europe	[20-30%]
London	[40-50%]	[30-40%]	[70-80%]	BMI British Airways Cityjet	[10=20%] [0-10%] [0-10%]
Lyon	[30-40%]	[60-70%]	100% [95-100%]	Charter	[0-5%]
Madrid	[20-30%]	[30-40%]	[70-70%]	Iberia	[30-40%]
Malaga	[30-40%]	[60-70%]	[95-100%] [85-95%]	Spanair Charter	[0-10%] [0-5%]
Manchester	[70-80%]	[20-30%]	[90- 100%]	Luxair	[0-10%]
Marseille	[50-60%]	[40-50%]	100%	None	0

Route	Ryanair	Aer Lingus	Combined	Existing Competitors	
Dublin to	% Share			Airline	% Share
Milan	[30-40%]	[60-70%]	100% [95-100%]	Charter	[0-5%]
Newcastle	[70-80%]	[20-30%]	100%	None	0
Paris	[40-50%]	[30-40%]	[80-90%]	AF Cityjet	[10-20%]
Poznan	[60-70%]	[30-40%]	100%	None	0
Riga	[40-50%]	[20-30%]	[70-80%]	Air Baltic	[20-30%]
Rome	[40-50%]	[50-60%]	100%	None	0
Salzburg	[50-60%]	[40-50%]	100% [95-100%]	Charter	[0-5%]
Seville	[50-60%]	[40-50%]	100%	None	0
Tenerife	[50-60%]	[40-50%]	100% [95-100%]	Charter	[0-5%]
Toulouse-Carcassonne	[60-70%]	[30-40%]	100%	None	0
Venice	[40-50%]	[50-60%]	100%	None	0
Vienna-Bratislava	[20-30%]	[50-60%]	[70-80%]	Sky Europe Austrian Airlines	[20-30%] [0-10%]
Warsaw	[30-40%]	[30-40%]	[60-70%]	LOT Shuttle	[10-20%] [10-20%]
Cork to					
London	[50-60%]	[40-50%]	100%		
Manchester	[40-50%]	[10-20%]	[60-70%]	BMI Baby Aer Arann	[30-40%] [0-10%]
Shannon to					
London	[50-60%]	[40-50%]	100%		

Source: Ryanair/Aer Lingus I, Table 2.

The CA/CCPC cleared several cases involving monopoly unilateral effects subject to remedies. The merging parties in *Premier Foods/RHM* had a market share of [70-85]% in respect of gravies. The CA concluded that they would have the ability and incentive to raise prices unilaterally post-merger and the transaction was cleared subject to a divestment remedy. In *Thomas Crosbie Holdings/South East Broadcasting* the CA referred to the *"limited competition"* that existed between the merging parties who were the only two competitors in the sale of local radio advertising in Waterford City and County pre-merger (¶41). The merging parties in *PandaGreen/Greenstar* would have had a post-merger market share in excess of 95% of domestic waste collection services in both Dún Laoghaire/Rathdown and Fingal counties. The CCPC concluded that the transaction would result in an SLC in both markets, but the transaction was cleared subject to a divestment of customers. *Kantar/News Access* involved a merger of the only two suppliers of the relevant products.

Enva/Rilta, a merger between two waste service operators, was a particularly complicated case involving 12 different product markets, all of which were national in scope. The CCPC concluded that the transaction was likely to result in an SLC in the markets for hazardous oily tank and interceptor waste treatment services and hazardous waste lubricant oil treatment services where the parties were the only competitors.[731] The CCPC concluded that the proposed transaction was also likely to result in an SLC in two further markets where the merging parties had a [90-95]% market share – the markets for hazardous waste lubricant oil collection services and the market for hazardous contaminated soil collection services. The CCPC accepted remedies designed to address the competition concerns in respect of these markets. The parties had a combined market share of [75-85]% in hazardous oily tank and interceptor waste collection services but the CCPC concluded that competition from six small suppliers would prevent an SLC. The suggestion that a competitive fringe would be capable of constraining the merging parties seems highly questionable, particularly in light of inconsistencies in the Determination in relation to market shares.[732] The

731 The CCPC also concluded that the transaction would result in vertical foreclosure in the markets for collection services of both waste streams (see **Chapter 9**).

732 **Table 3** states that the parties respective market shares were [40-45]% and [30-35]% in 2013 and [45-50]% and [30-35]% in 2017 but then states that their combined market share had fallen from [80-85]% to [75-80]% over the period which seems inconsistent (¶4.87). To add to the confusion the Determination states: *"There is a long tail of smaller competitors, with market shares that never exceed [0-5]% in either 2013 or 2017"* (*ibid.*) but also said: *"As illustrated in Table*

transaction effectively reduced the number of competitors from four to three in the market for hazardous waste management/brokerage services. The merged entity became the second largest in the market with a market share of [25-30]%, while the three largest firms accounted for [70-95]% of the market. The CCPC concluded that competition from the two other large providers and some smaller operators would prevent any SLC. The transaction also effectively reduced the number of competitors from three to two in the market for non-hazardous aqueous waste treatment services. According to the Determination, Irish Water was the main supplier of such services in the State, while there were a number of very small providers but no information on market shares was provided. The CCPC concluded that Irish Water and the smaller operators would exercise a sufficient competitive constraint on the parties to prevent any SLC.

The Determination identified no competition concerns in five other markets. In the market for the supply of hazardous lead acid battery collection services, the parties had a combined market share of 21% and faced nine competing suppliers which would tend to exclude unilateral effects theory of harm. The parties were the only two suppliers of re-processed fuel oil but the CCPC stated that customers had indicated that they would switch to other fuels in the event of a post-merger price increase, implying a wider fuel market.[733] The CCPC concluded that brokers and smaller suppliers would exercise a sufficient competitive constraint on the parties post-merger in the market for the supply of non-hazardous contaminated soil collection services in which the merging parties had a combined market share of [30-35]%. In the market for the supply of hazardous contaminated packaging collection services the CCPC concluded that the transaction *"raises no competition concerns since Enva and the Rilta Group subcontract the collection of the vast majority of hazardous contaminated packaging in the State to third party hauliers"* (¶4.47). No explanation is offered for the conclusion that the subcontracting of services eliminated any competition concerns. According to the Determination the

---

3 above, there were six competitors… with market shares in excess of [0-5]% in the State in 2017. These six competitors increased their combined market share from [10-15]% in 2013 to [15-20]% in 2017. Some of these collectors have grown considerably over the period from 2013 to 2017… increased its market share from [0-5]% to [0-5]% between 2013 and 2017… increased its market share from [0-5]% to [0-5]% over the same period (¶s4.91&4.92). These figures appear not to add up.

733 This illustrates how incorrectly applying an overly narrow market definition could have resulted in a false positive.

overlap between the parties in the market for the supply of hazardous contaminated packaging treatment services was minimal.

As noted in **Chapter** 7 the CA/CCPC has cleared several mergers where the merged entities had very high market shares, ranging from 50-90%, following a preliminary Phase 1 investigation. The CCPC acknowledged in *Baxter/Fannin* that the merged entity would be able to raise prices unilaterally as it would be the only supplier of compounded chemotherapy medicines to hospitals but accepted that the target was a failing firm. *Johnston Press/Clonnad* involved two local newspapers with a combined market share of [90-100%] of the newspaper advertising market in South Tipperary.[734] The transaction was cleared following an Extended Phase 1 investigation on the basis that entry barriers were relatively low (see below).

Chapter 7 highlighted several cases where the CA/CCPC argued that the transaction would not result in an SLC because the increase in market share was small and there would be sufficient competitors in the market post-merger to exercise a competitive constraint on the merged entity despite the merging parties having high combined market shares.[735] As was pointed out, such claims are insufficient to rule out a monopoly/dominance theory of harm.

The analysis in *Wavin/Hepworth Building Products* amounted to a single paragraph, although the parties may have had a share of almost 50% in one market.[736] The Determination argues that the remaining competitors would be capable of exercising a competitive constraint on the merged entity, while imports would exercise *"some competitive constraint"*. The information in the Determination is too vague to draw any definitive conclusions, although the limited data on the parties' market shares suggest that it was probably in the high risk category. A single paragraph seems insufficient by way of analysis and explanation for the decision.

---

734 The Determination stated the HHI in the case of newspaper advertising post-merger would be 9,140. A HHI of 10,000 corresponds to a monopoly. While no market share figures were quoted for newspaper circulation, the Determination stated that the HHI in this market was also in Zone C as defined in CAMG2002. Thompson (1984) reported that local newspaper advertising rates in Ireland were higher in more concentrated markets.

735 These include *Unilever/Alberto Culver* and *CapVest/Origin Foods/Maiden.*

736 CA/05/007 – *Wavin/Hepworth Building Products,* 22.3.2005. The Determination states that the parties had market shares of less than 40% and 10% respectively in *"below ground drainage"*. Presumably, it would not have stated that one of the parties had less than 40% unless their share exceeded 30%. The CA did not define a relevant market or indicate whether there were substitutes for below ground drainage products. Based on the limited information in relation to the parties' market shares it is likely that the transaction would have come within Zone C as defined in CAMG2002 implying a high risk of competitive harm.

Ferrero International/Fulfil considered several possible markets including one for the supply of energy snack bars in the State in which the Target had a [70-80]% market share, while the acquirer had a [0-10]% share. The CCPC, nevertheless, concluded that the addition of the Acquirer's share to that of the Target *"represents a relatively small increment"*. It claimed unconvincingly that *"the combined entity will continue to face* ***some*** *competitive pressure from other significant competitors"* (¶30, emphasis added).

The parties in *Easycash/Bank of Ireland* had a combined market share of [50-60]%. The Determination, however, contains a fairly extensive unilateral effects analysis. It considered the number of competitors remaining post-merger, citing customer views indicating that the parties did not compete more closely with each other than they did with other competitors in the market. They had not competed in the same tenders to supply ATMs to customers.[737] It also found that barriers to customers switching supplier and to entry and expansion were relatively low. The evidence appears to rule out a monopoly/dominance unilateral effects theory in this case.

In 2012 the CA threatened to issue proceedings alleging a below the threshold merger involving the only two book wholesalers in the State was in breach of §4 of the *Competition Act, 2002,* as amended. The parties subsequently abandoned the proposal. The CA indicated that it believed that *"the proposed transaction would result in increased prices and a reduction in the range of new books to consumers"* (CA *Annual Report, 2012,* p.30). Based on the limited information available, the CA's case would appear to have rested on a monopoly unilateral effects theory (see also **Chapter 9**).

Spatial

Economics has demonstrated that a merged entity could unilaterally raise prices post-merger in circumstances where it would not satisfy traditional definitions of dominance. This can occur if competitive interactions between the merging firms are particularly important (Coleman *et al.*, 2003). In those circumstances, the elimination of the direct competition between the merging parties as a result of the merger will lead to higher prices even if all the remaining non-merging firms in the market continue to compete independently (Shapiro, 1996).

Prior to the merger, the merging parties are constrained from raising prices unilaterally because the resulting loss in sales would render a price increase unprofitable. Post-merger some of the sales lost by one of the

737 See discussion on bidding markets below.

parties as a result of a price increase will accrue to the other merging party. The extent to which sales lost by one of the merging parties is captured by the other will depend on the extent to which consumers consider the merging parties' products to be close substitutes for one another. If a significant proportion of sales lost by one of the merging parties accrues to the other merging party, then a price increase, which was not profitable pre-merger, would become profitable post-merger, giving the merged entity the ability and the incentive to increase price post-merger. Spatial unilateral effects theories of harm focus on the relative closeness of the merging firms' products because the risk of unilateral effects is greater, the closer are the merging brands in the eyes of consumers and thus the higher the proportion of sales lost by one that will accrue to the other. However, the parties do not need to be the closest substitutes for one another for a post-merger price increase (Shapiro, 2010; Hovenkamp, 2024).

The CA/CCPC's analysis of spatial unilateral effects has been inconsistent, focusing incorrectly on whether the merging brands are each other's closest competitors in some cases, while in others recognising correctly that this is not a necessary requirement for unilateral effects. In *Johnston Press/Clonnad*, for example, the CA stated:

> *"In other words, if the two products are each other's* ***closest substitute****, a pre-merger price increase of Product A would result in customers switching their purchases to Product B (and other rivals). Post-merger, the merged entity would internalise consumer substitution away from Product A, thereby avoiding at least some of the penalty otherwise associated with raising price" (¶45, emphasis added).*

The parties in *Galco/Sperrin* had a combined share of [40-70]% in an island-wide market, depending on the source and methodology used. The CA concluded that:

> *"... although Galco has a strong presence in Leinster and Munster, as Sperrin has a minimal presence in these regions, the parties do not compete closely with each other there...*
>
> *in the regions where Galco and Sperrin compete with each other, i.e. various non-merging undertakings are therefore present who could constrain the merged entity's ability to raise price" (¶s6.25 & 6.26).*

Such conclusions are open to serious question. Sperrin had a 4% market share in Leinster and Munster while Galco had market shares of 75% and 47%

respectively. Thus, the fact that Sperrin had a small market share did not necessarily rule out a potential post-merger price increase (see **Chapter 7**). In Connacht, the parties had a market share of 49% while none of their five competitors had a market share greater than 15% and two had 4% and 2%, which again would not automatically preclude a post-merger price increase.[738]

In *Heineken/Beamish & Crawford*, the CA stated that a pre-condition for the merged entity to have an incentive to unilaterally raise prices post-merger was that their lager brands *"should be the closest substitutes"* for one another" (¶5.169). The CA concluded that an SLC would not occur in *Fitzwilliam/Wittington Canada/Arnott*,[739] because the parties were not each other's closest competitors.

The CCPC in *Valeo/Wardell/Robert Roberts* stated (correctly) that unilateral effects required that the parties should be close competitors rather than each other's closest competitors.

> *"Valeo will only have the incentive to exercise market power and increase price if it would be profitable to do so. In order for this to occur, the Chef and YR brown sauce brands should be* ***close competitors*** *to each other in the supply of brown sauce to the retail sector in the State such that a price rise in one product (e.g., YR) will result in a sufficient diversion of sales revenue to the other (e.g., Chef) and* vice versa *(¶106, emphasis added).*

The CCPC concluded that the parties were *"**sufficiently close competitors** in the brown sauce market such that post-transaction the merged entity will find it profitable to raise prices"* (¶107, emphasis added).

Irish Times/Sappho stated that the CCPC had *"found there is no evidence to suggest that the newspapers are each other's* ***closest*** *competitors"* (¶4.16, emphasis added). In *Petrogas/PR Reilly* the CCPC concluded that further analysis was necessary *"in order to identify the* ***closest*** *competitors of the Applegreen retail motor fuel service station and the Target Assets on Howth Road"* (¶21, emphasis added).

---

[738] In Ulster, the parties combined market share was [37-42]% with four rivals, the largest of which had a 31% market share while two others had 14% each suggesting unilateral effects were less likely.

[739] The parties were both engaged in *"multi-category retailing"*, *i.e.*, both operated department stores, in Dublin. As previously noted, the transaction was referred to the CA by the EU Commission under Article 4(4), ECMR. The EU Commission had previously cleared the acquisition of Arnotts by Anglo Irish Bank and Royal Bank of Scotland (Case No. COMP/M.5826 – *Anglo Irish Bank/RBS/Arnotts*, 9.8.2010).

Pat the Baker/Irish Pride acknowledged that unilateral effects did not require the parties to be each other's closest competitors:

> *"Consequently, depending on the circumstances, it is possible for competition concerns to arise even when merging parties are not closest competitors" (FN28).*[740]

Similarly, *Bank of Ireland/KBC* stated:

> *"In considering closeness of competition between BOI and KBC, the Commission is not required to demonstrate that KBC is a particularly close competitor of BOI and in particular, that it constrained BOI from otherwise raising prices or lowering quality profitably. Rather, in determining whether the Proposed Transaction will lead to unilateral effects, the correct question is whether the merged entity will be able, as a result of the merger, to exercise market power" (¶6.140).*

Paddy Power/Betfair stated that a spatial unilateral effects theory required the parties to be close competitors rather than closest. The CCPC reverted to a *"closest competitors"* test in *Joyce's/Nestor's.*

The CA considered a spatial unilateral effects theory of harm in *SRH/FM104* due to the possibility that the merging parties' radio stations may have been close competitors in the radio advertising market but ultimately concluded that empirical evidence did not support such a theory of harm. In *Bay/Radio Nova,* which involved a merger of local radio stations in Dublin, the CCPC concluded that the parties were not close competitors based on audience demographics. The CCPC somewhat cryptically argued in *Bauer Media/Siteridge*[741] that the acquirer's two national radio stations did not compete for listeners (or advertisers) with the Target, a local radio station in Cork *"in the same way as other radio stations with a BAI franchise area of Cork City and County"* (¶21).[742]

---

740 An econometric analysis commissioned by the CCPC showed that a 10% increase by one of the parties would result in only a 1% increase in the market share of the other. Consumer survey results also indicated that the parties were not close competitors.

741 CCPC M/22/059 – *Bauer Media/Siteridge (Red FM)*, 22.12.2022.

742 As noted in **Chapter 6**, while the CA/CCPC recognised the two-sided nature of local radio markets, it has tended to analyse the effect of mergers on the two sides of the market separately or to focus on only one side, usually the advertising market. An analysis of the effect of the 1996-2006 US local radio merger wave, prompted by changes in ownership rules in the *Telecommunications Act, 1996,* found that local radio mergers increased consumer surplus mainly due to increased product variety, but reduced advertisers' surplus due to changes in product variety and a reduction in advertising quantity (Jeziorski, 2014).

The purchaser in *Glanbia/Dairygold* was the largest supplier, by some distance, of liquid milk in the State, while the target was the joint third largest supplier.[743] The CA argued that competition from retailers' own label milk, along with increased imports from Northern Ireland, would prevent a post-merger price increase. Bonanno & Lopez (2005), however, found that increases in the market share of own label milk in the US resulted in price increases for branded milk, an increase in price differentials between branded and own label and increased own label prices once they had become dominant in the market.[744]

The CA prohibition decision in *Kerry/Breeo*[745] concluded that the transaction would result in unilateral effects in the markets for rashers, NPCM and processed cheese because the merging parties' brands were each other's closest competitors.[746] The CA concluded that private label was not a close competitor of the merging brands in rashers and NPCM, even though it had a 45-50% share in both markets which was approximately equal to the merging parties' combined market share. The CA argued that consumers would not switch to private label brands in the event of a 3% increase in the price of the merging parties' brands of rashers and NPCM.[747] Two years after this Determination, the CA conceded:

---

743 The Determination indicated that the purchaser had a market share of [40-50]% while the target was one of three firms with a [5-10]% market share, and only one other undertaking had a larger market share of [10-20]%.

744 The study was based on price data for 2,759 supermarkets in 10 US cities. It suggests that own label may facilitate price discrimination as it enables supermarkets to define consumers based on their willingness to pay as an explanation for the increase in branded prices, while own label prices tend to increase to a lesser extent. Bontemps *et al.* (2005) find that prices of many branded grocery products increased with the development of own label. The CA's claim in *Glanbia/Dairygold* that milk imports from Northern Ireland would also constrain the merged entity's ability to raise prices is also questionable. Subsequently, in *Glanbia/Wexford Creamery*, the CA stated that the market for liquid milk may be limited to the State, citing *inter alia* the introduction of a quality control mark by the National Dairy Council that only applied to milk produced and processed in the State. In *Aurivo/Arrabawn* the CCPC noted that several retail grocery operators stated that they only purchased liquid milk originating within the State.

745 As previously stated, the CA decision was overturned by the High Court on appeal (*Rye Investments v. Competition Authority).*

746 The Determination found that the merger would not have any anti-competitive effects in several other markets.

747 CAMG (2002) provided that closeness of competition within a market should be assessed on the basis of consumer responses to a 3% price increase rather than the 5% SSNIP threshold: *"This test for substitutability within the market involves a lower threshold than the test for substitutability at the market definition level, with a 3% price increase being typically used"* (¶4.6).

> *"This approach is not consistent with current best international practice which does not specify the magnitude of a price increase as a measure of substitutability" (CA, 2010, December 3, ¶2.16).*

The CA argued that, because private label was largely sold at a significant discount to branded products, the two were not close substitutes.[748] As noted in **Chapter 6**, price differences do not mean that different products do not exercise a competitive constraint on one another. The CA in *Kerry/Breeo* relied heavily on the evidence of retailers that the merging parties' brands were "must have" and private label was not a close substitute for the merging brands although the main retailer groups had significantly increased shelf space allocated to their own label rashers and NPCM at the expense of branded products. The CA quoted from the parties' internal documents, although these also contained suggestions that Kerry viewed private label as the main threat to its brands.[749] Both the CA and the parties produced a considerable amount of econometric evidence based on retail scanner data, although data on private label was limited.

In *Heineken/Beamish & Crawford* the CA cited a survey of pub owners which indicated that Diageo's lager brands were regarded as the closest substitutes to those of Heineken while Heineken's brands were considered the closest substitutes to those of Beamish & Crawford. The CA acknowledged that this would indicate that a post-merger price increase of the target's *Miller* lager would be partially internalised by the merged entity but argued that this needed to be qualified because the evidence on closeness of substitution was based on expert opinions rather than actual evidence of switching behaviour in response to price changes. This *caveat* applied equally to publicans' views that Diageo's lager brands were the closest substitutes to Heineken's. The CA nevertheless conceded:

> *"Thus the evidence suggests that post-merger the merged entity will have a weak incentive to raise the price of MGD" (¶5.175).*[750]

The CA cited no independent source to justify this threshold. Gorecki (2009) referred to the CAMG2002 threshold as supporting the CA decision without citing any supporting source.

748 The main retail groups all differentiated their private label offerings in terms of price and quality and some of the higher quality private label brands were actually more expensive than the merging brands.

749 The quotation was redacted in the CA's Determination but was read into the record of the appeal hearing.

750 The CA also argued that any such incentive would be further weakened by Heineken's requirement to market itself as a brewer for other brands, *i.e.*, to secure licence agreements to brew and supply other lager brands. This argument is unconvincing.

It went on to state:

> *"In a differentiated market such as lager there might be expected to be both a price rise-but by less than the merged entity-and some output expansion. However, the discussion in this paragraph suggests that Diageo will lean more to the output expansion than price rise" (¶5.177).*

The statement appears to implicitly accept that the transaction would result in a unilateral price increase because Diageo would increase its lager prices to some extent in response to a post-merger price increase by Heineken which suggests a potential false negative.[751] The CA argued that Diageo would lean more toward output expansion than raising price because:

i. Its market share had been declining; and
ii. it had announced plans to expand capacity.

According to the Determination, Diageo had regularly increased its prices between 2002 and 2007 despite its market share falling from 56% to 41% over that period and it is difficult to see any reason for it to change its behaviour post-merger. Diageo's proposed new brewery was not scheduled to come on stream until 2013, five years after the merger and well outside CA/CCPC's standard two-year time-frame for entry (see below).[752]

The CCPC in *Valeo/Wardell/Robert Roberts* cited econometric evidence, results of a consumer survey, and internal documents of the parties, as evidence that the parties were close competitors and concluded that the proposed transaction would result in an SLC.

The CCPC opposed *Topaz/Esso inter alia* because it involved a three to two merger in respect of fuel import terminalling services based on a geographic market definition that was limited to Dublin/Leinster. Arguably the CCPC could have advanced an alternative harm theory. There were two other fuel import terminals in the State at Galway and Foynes. According to the Determination, the Galway terminal was operated by Topaz, which

---

751 Unilateral effects theories indicate that the optimal response of non-merging firms to a post-merger unilateral price increase may be to raise their own prices, albeit to a lesser extent (see below). Miller *et al.* (2021) developed a model for the US brewing industry which shows that price leadership resulted in profits above the competitive level largely due to industry consolidation.

752 Diageo subsequently announced in January 2009 that it was postponing its planned expansion. It informed staff in January 2010 that the investment programme *"remains on hold and will be revisited when the economic context is more certain"* (*Irish Times*, 30 January 2010). More recently it has commenced work on a new brewery, but this is yet to be completed at the time of writing, some 16 years after the Heineken/Beamish & Crawford merger.

also had a throughput agreement to import fuel through Foynes. Thus, post-merger Topaz would have controlled and/or imported fuels through four of the five terminals in the State. The Determination notes that a small amount of fuel was imported from a terminal in Derry in Northern Ireland. Wholesale fuel customers could also purchase fuels from the Whitegate refinery in Cork. Even then Topaz would arguably control a sufficient share of total supply to pose competition problems, although such arguments would have been weaker if the geographic market was defined as the island of Ireland.[753] The CCPC also could have advanced a spatial theory that the three Dublin terminals were much closer substitutes for each other than were any of the other terminals on the island or the Whitegate refinery.

In *Petrogas/PR Reilly* the CCPC considered the number of filling stations within a 3.2-kilometre radius of the target and within a 3.2-kilometre *"straight road distance"* on either side of the target filling station in order to identify close competitors of the target. It concluded that there were sufficient competitors to exercise an effective competitive constraint on the merging parties. In *BWG/Londis* the CA concluded that the parties were not close competitors in the wholesale grocery market based on data on franchisee switching between wholesaler/franchisors.

The CCPC in *Dawn Meats/Dunbia*[754] concluded that the parties were not close competitors in the market for the purchase of live cattle for slaughter. All beef processors purchased all types of cattle and neither of the merging parties specialised in the purchase of particular cattle types or breeds. The target plants were located a considerable distance from any of the purchaser's plants with other plants closer to the purchaser's plants, supporting a conclusion that, from the viewpoint of sellers, the parties were not particularly close competitors.

Irish Times/Sappho cited the fact that the majority of sales of *The Irish Times* were in Leinster while the majority of sales of the *Irish Examiner* were in Munster as evidence that the parties were not each other's closest competitors. Such evidence is consistent with the CCPC's conclusions but not conclusive. Sales in Munster may account for a small proportion of total *Irish Times* circulation but *The Irish Times* could still be the closest competitor to the *Irish Examiner* in Munster. In *Fitzwilliam/Wittington Canada/Arnotts* a

---

753 The Determination only referred to the Derry terminal supplying fuel to customers in the State. CCPC (2022, November) referred to four import terminals in Northern Ireland that supplied motor fuels to service stations in the State.

754 It came to a similar conclusion in *Dawn Meats/Kildare Chilling*.

survey of the target undertaking's customers commissioned by the CCPC indicated that 44% expressed concerns that the transaction would prove anti-competitive and lead to higher prices, but the CA dismissed such concerns as lacking *"credibility"* (¶79).[755]

Paddy Power/Betfair refers to *"numerous"* internal documents of both parties which indicated that they *"perceive themselves to be competing not only with each other but also with a number of other large online betting service providers"* (¶49). A customer survey conducted on the CA's behalf found that 64% of Paddy Power customers who said they would switch in response to a price increase said they would switch some or all of their betting spend to Betfair, while 65% of Betfair customers indicated they would switch to Paddy Power, indicating that the parties were relatively close competitors.[756] The Determination described the parties' brands as distinct and aimed at somewhat different market segments but this amounts to little more than acknowledging that their products were differentiated and is inconsistent with the consumer survey switching results. The CCPC concluded that the parties would not be able to raise prices post-merger because customers would switch to other competitors.[757]

The CCPC in *Joyce's/Nestor's* found that only two of the target's four supermarkets were within 10 kilometres of one of the purchaser's five stores. The Determination states that there were several competing grocery stores that were significantly closer to the target stores than the purchaser's closest store, indicating that the parties were not close competitors.

The CCPC treated *Reach/ISL* as resulting in a decline in market concentration in the markets for daily newspapers and advertising in daily newspapers because it involved the sale by INM (the largest newspaper

---

755 The survey indicated that 70% of the customers who expressed such concerns indicated that they would switch to another store in the event that the target raised its prices post-merger, but the CA argued that, because most of them indicated they would switch to stores other than those of the purchaser, this ruled out a possible unilateral price increase. As customers were asked about their views regarding the merger, this may have influenced the responses, *i.e.*, customers who believed the merger would harm competition may have felt that it would make little sense to switch to the other merging party post-merger.

756 Betfair was the third most popular choice for Paddy Power customers behind Boyle Sports (71%) and Ladbrokes (65%). Paddy Power was the fourth most popular choice for Betfair switchers behind Boyle Sports (75%) and Ladbrokes and Bet365 (both 70%). The survey asked customers to list all of the alternatives that they would switch to rather than the one they would be most likely to switch to.

757 Several of the alternatives listed by the CCPC were cited as likely switching options by less than 50% of the survey respondents, indicating that they were far more distant competitors of the merging parties than the merging parties were for each other.

group) in the State of its 50% shareholding in the *Irish Daily Star* to the other 50% shareholder. Consequently, it fell within the CCPCMG2014 safe harbour thresholds. The CCPC nevertheless considered a unilateral effects theory of harm but concluded that the *Irish Daily Star* was not a close competitor of the purchaser's newspaper titles including the *Irish Daily Mirror*. As both titles were tabloid newspapers it might have been worth considering evidence on both papers' readership demographic.[758]

The CCPC in *Xtratherm/Ballytherm* cited the CA's conclusions in *Kingspan/Xtratherm*[759] that Xtratherm and Ballytherm were not each other's closest competitors because Ballytherm produced a more limited product range while an economic submission on behalf of the parties indicated that Xtratherm had lost business or been forced to reduce its prices in response to competition from rivals other than Ballytherm.

Tesco/Joyce's involved a five to four supermarket merger in two local geographic markets in Galway City. According to the Determination the parties were the fourth and fifth largest grocery retailers in the city (¶2.14).[760] The CCPC argued that the three non-merging supermarkets were not particularly close competitors of the merging parties' Oranmore stores. It noted that, while there was a Dunnes Stores outlet within a 10-minute drive-time of the target, during peak hours the journey between the two outlets could take up to 28 minutes (see **Chapter 6**). On that basis the Tesco (purchaser) store would appear to be a closer competitor of the target. The CCPC argued that the two other competing stores, Aldi and Lidl, *"could be differentiated because of their 'low-cost' operating model"* (¶2.11). It cited CA (2008) in support of this claim. It is doubtful whether much reliance can be placed on a 13-year-old report, given that Aldi and Lidl had both significantly increased their market shares and store numbers in the intervening period.

The CCPC considered a spatial unilateral effects theory in the markets for pharmacy buying group services and common management and branding (CMB) services in *Uniphar/NaviCorp*. The CCPC found that the parties were close competitors in both markets which were characterised by

---

758 The Determination also noted that the purchaser's market shares would increase by [5-10]% from [10-15]% to [15-20]% and that it would continue to face competition from three larger newspaper groups.

759 It could be argued that the products were homogenous, in which case Ballytherm's small market share would indicate that other market participants were closer competitors of Xtratherm (see below).

760 Internal documents provided to the CCPC by the purchaser included an e-mail describing the target as "the market leader" in Galway (¶1.13).

significant barriers to entry. It prohibited the proposed transaction on the grounds that the merged entity would have the ability and the incentive to unilaterally raise prices and/or degrade service quality.

In *Arthopoda (Orpea)/Brindley Healthcare*, the CCPC concluded that the transaction would not result in any SLC in County Kildare, given the parties combined 21% market share and the fact that they would face competition from three other named nursing homes. It would appear that the merging parties' nursing homes near the town of Maynooth were located close to each other, suggesting that some consideration of a spatial theory of harm may have been appropriate.[761]

The CCPC in *Portlon (Parma)/Hermitage* and *Portlon (Parma)/Blackrock* argued that there would be sufficient competitors capable of exercising a competitive constraint on the merging parties post-merger, describing *"Bon Secours (Glasnevin), Mater Private Group, St. Vincent's Private Hospital and the Beacon Hospital"* as offering a similar range of procedures to the Hermitage and Blackrock clinics.[762] The Determination, however, stated that hospitals differed in the type and quality of services provided:

> *"... the Blackrock Clinic, Mater Private Dublin and the Beacon Hospital are considered as high tech private hospitals which have the ability to provide a range of high-intensity, complex procedures which other private hospitals do not provide... Hermitage Clinic and the Galway Clinic are categorised alongside the Mater Private Cork and Bon Secours hospitals and these hospitals generally command a lower reimbursement rate" (¶50).*

This suggests that the Hermitage and Blackrock were not close competitors, at least in the wider market for private healthcare services. Rather the Beacon and Mater Private Dublin were the closest competitors to Blackrock while Bon Secours was closest to the Hermitage. The Hermitage and Galway may have provided similar levels of services, but several other private hospitals were geographically closer to the Hermitage than Galway

761 The Determination cites market share ranges but includes figures for bed numbers for all market players, making it possible to estimate precise market shares. It seems highly unlikely that the three competing nursing homes mentioned by the CCPC would have accounted for the remaining 79% (more than 1,300) nursing home beds in the county, suggesting that there would have been sufficient competitors to rule out the possibility that other suppliers would have acquiesced to a post-merger price increase by raising their prices, but it would have been helpful if the Determination had made this clear. Consideration of a spatial theory of harm could have clarified whether there were other nursing homes closer to the parties' Maynooth facilities, rather than simply citing market share and referring to three rivals.

762 *Portlon (Parma)/Galway* (¶59) and *Portlon (Parma)/Blackrock* (¶60).

was.[763] In other words, there would appear to have been reasonable grounds for concluding that the merging parties were not sufficiently close competitors for either merger to have resulted in unilateral effects rather than simply relying on arguments about the number of competitors.

In *Chadwicks/Rooney's* the CCPC argued that the target did not meet the strict definition of a DIY superstore in *Grafton/Heiton* due to its size but stated that it was a large DIY store and offered a product range comparable to that offered by DIY superstores (¶27). The Determination considered the geographical closeness of competitors in the local market around the target store and found that there were several DIY superstores which were geographically closer to the purchaser's Navan store than was the target's store in Kells (¶53).[764] As previously noted, in *Associated Hardware/National Hardware* the CCPC only considered a national market and did not analyse local geographic markets although the transaction involved two co-operative groups, both of which were described as having members located throughout the State. The Determination gives no reason for not considering local geographic markets.[765]

The CCPC in *Q-Park/Tazbell* analysed competition in eight local markets for the provision of off-street-car parking services, five in Dublin City, along with Dún Laoghaire, Galway and Limerick. **Table 8.3** summarises the key elements in this case.

The CCPC concluded that the proposed transaction would not result in an SLC in five markets: ILAC Centre, Irish Life Centre, and Smithfield in Dublin, along with Dun Laoghaire and Limerick. It concluded an SLC was likely in the case of the target's Drury Street and Fleet Street car parks in Dublin and in Galway city.[766] The CCPC considered a spatial theory of

---

763 The CCPC argued that the Galway Clinic was not a close competitor of the Blackrock Clinic, based on its small market share in the provision of neuro-spinal services.

764 In the case of the market for building materials, the Determination simply referred to the large number of competitors in the relevant catchment area, although it appears from a map in the Determination that many of these were located nearer to the purchaser's Navan outlet than the target store was.

765 In fact, the Determination provides no information with respect to the number of outlets affiliated to each group or any indication as to their locations within the State, so it is not possible to establish if there was an overlap between the groups' members in any local market.

766 The CCPC rejected arguments by the parties that they did not control parking charges of the car parks which they managed as the car park owners had the ultimate say over whether to accept price changes proposed by management companies. It argued that the interests of owners and management companies were aligned and that car park management service providers strongly influenced parking charges and noted that, when recommending price

harm based on closeness of competition, although arguably a monopoly theory of harm might also have been considered in the case of the five Dublin car parks given the parties' combined market shares and the fact that post-merger they would be by far the largest operator in each market and much larger than their largest competitor. In five cases the CCPC ruled out an SLC based on the number of competitors and the fact that several were geographically closer to the target than any car park operated by the purchaser, although arguably in the three Dublin cases at least, it is not clear that such constraints would be sufficient given the parties' combined market share and the gap between them and their largest competitor.

Table 8.3: *Q-Park/Tazbell* – Summary of Key Elements in Local Markets for Off-street Car Parking Services

	Dublin City					Dún Laoghaire	Galway City	Limerick City
	ILAC Centre	Irish Life Centre	Smith-field	Drury Street	Fleet Street			
Combined Market Share	[55-65]%	[50-60]%	[50-60]%	[65-75]%	[55-65]%	[30-35]%	[20-30]%	[25-30]%
Parties' Rank Post-Merger	1	1	1	1	1	1	1	1
400m Overlap	No	No	No	Yes	No	No	Yes	No
Competitor Nos.	5	4	3	5	10	8	3	6
Closer Competitors	5	0	0	1	10	5	1	4
Post-Merger HHI	4,055	3,687	4,257	5,419	3,728	2,300	1,727	1,697
HHI Change	+1,370	+1,295	+1,680	2,236	1,624	+493	+394	+351
CCPC SLC Finding	No	No	No	Yes	Yes	No	Yes	No

Source: Q-Park/Tazbell.

The CCPC defined the local market for off-street car parking services as an area of 800 metres around each of the target's car parks. However, it also defined a narrower area of 400 metres around the target's car parks but

increases to owners, they would inform them of proposed price changes at other car parks operated by them.

claimed that it was not suggesting that there was a geographic market limited to a 400-metre walking distance radius.[767]

> *"Rather, the Commission uses the 400-metre radius to as [sic] a heuristic to illustrate competition between Tazbell's car parks in the Off-Street Car Parking Relevant Markets and their (geographically) closest set of competitors. This is an analysis of the closeness of competition, rather than an alternative geographic market" (¶6.105).*

The Determination, nevertheless, includes market share and market concentration data for the 400-metre catchment areas and includes these among a list of factors indicating an SLC was likely.[768] Significantly, the Determination states:

> *"It is not correct to say that the Commission's preliminary conclusion in the Assessment was based* ***solely*** *on the market structure of a 400-metre catchment" (¶6.175, emphasis added).*

The CCPC also argued that differences in the prices charged by car parks was an indicator of closeness of competition without citing a supporting source for this claim (¶6.182).[769] The Determination cited internal Tazbell documents indicating that Q-Park exerted a strong competitive constraint over it in Galway but concluded that the transaction would remove a strong competitive constraint on Q-Park (¶6.198).[770] The CCPC also considered a wider 1.2-kilometre geographic area in all eight markets but found that this made little difference to market shares, concentration and competitor numbers.[771]

In contrast to many previous cases involving filling stations which simply considered the number of competitors within the relevant local catchment area, the CCPC in *McMullen Bros/Naas Fuels* considered whether

---

767 Tazbell, in its response to the CCPC Assessment, observed "[i]*t is notable that the Assessment uses the 400m radius when the 800m radius does not produce a problem*" (¶6.103).

768 The Determination states that, in Galway, the merged entity would be the largest within the 400m catchment area with a market share of [50-60]% while the next largest operator would have [15-20]%. It expresses similar views in relation to Drury Street in Dublin.

769 As pointed out in **Chapter 6**, differences in price do not determine whether products exert a competitive constraint on each other. The suggestion that a narrower area and/or price differences should be used to identify closer competitors has echoes of the 3% threshold that the CA applied in *Kerry/Breeo* for defining close competitors, a threshold which it subsequently acknowledged was not in line with international best practice.

770 This implicitly assumes that competitive constraints were symmetric, as the Tazbell documents provide no indication of the extent to which it exerted a competitive constraint on Q-Park.

771 This arguably provides a check against false positives arising from overly narrow market definitions as discussed in **Chapter** 6.

the parties were close competitors in the three local geographic markets where they overlapped, although its approach was somewhat inconsistent. Following the transaction the merged entity was the second largest in the Maganey catchment area with a [20-25]% market share. The CCPC argued that the merging parties would face a sufficient competitive constraint from the remaining competitors and that two of the largest suppliers in the area (Circle K and Inver) *"will exert a strong competitive constraint"* post-merger. The Circle K stations which had a [40-45]% market share were the two furthest away from the target filling station at 8.3 and 9.1 kilometres respectively, while the Inver station and one of the purchaser's Maxol stations were closer at 6.43 and 6.46 kilometres respectively. In Wicklow town, the target was the largest in the market and the parties had a combined market share of [50-55]%. The CCPC nevertheless argued that the parties were not each other's closest competitors as the two remaining non-merging filling stations were located in between the parties' stations, although all four appear to have been on the same road from Wicklow town to the M11 motorway.[772] The CCPC cited the fact that the non-merging stations had the capacity to increase sales but did not address whether they would have an incentive to acquiesce to any unilateral post-merger price increase. The Determination also referred to competitive constraints outside of the catchment area, identifying two additional filling stations in Ashford within 3.2 kilometres of the purchaser's Maxol station. Ashford is located on the other side of the M11 motorway to the four stations within the target's catchment area so that motorists leaving Wicklow town and accessing the M11 would not pass those stations, although the Determination notes that the target monitored prices in one of the Ashford stations. In the case of Gorey, only one of the four competing stations was located closer to the target than the purchaser's station (0.49 *versus* 0.66 kilometres).

Nash-Bertrand[773]

A merger may lead to unilateral effects because it alters the non-cooperative market equilibrium (CAMG, 2002, ¶4.4). In an oligopolistic market with few competitors each of them recognises that its actions will prompt a response

[772] As Houde (2012) points out shopping (price comparison) costs are the same for all filling stations on consumers' commuting routes. The non-merging stations were 0.6 and 2.57 kilometres from the target's filling station while the purchaser's was 2.99 kilometres away.

[773] In contrast to Cournot oligopoly models which assume firms compete in terms of output, Bertrand oligopoly models assume firms supply differentiated products and compete on price.

by its rivals. Consequently, when deciding on a particular course of action, firms take account of their rivals' likely responses. The Nash equilibrium is defined as the set of actions, such that, for each of the market participants, each action is the best response to the actions of all other market participants. Alternatively, a set of actions constitutes a Nash equilibrium if none of the market participants has an incentive to deviate from its actions given the actions of all other market participants (Philips, 1995 and Motta, 2004). A reduction in the number of competitors may alter the non-cooperative Nash equilibrium resulting in higher prices. Froeb *et al.* (2005) observe that, because the merged firm will internalise demand interactions between its jointly owned products, a horizontal merger will change the non-cooperative market equilibrium and describe this as the unilateral effect of the merger.

In differentiated product markets, rivals of the merging parties may have an incentive to raise their prices, in response to a unilateral price increase by the merged firm, albeit to a lesser extent (see, for example, Salant *et al.*, 1983; Deneckere & Davidson, 1985; Werden & Froeb, 1998; Shapiro, 1996). Motta (2004) points out that the gains from a merger accruing to non-merging firms may exceed those of the merging parties. Weinberg (2008) states that several US merger studies reported post-merger price increases by both the merging parties and their rivals. Allain *et al.* (2017) also found that non-merging supermarket groups increased their prices and market shares, with higher price increases in more concentrated local markets, following a merger between the second and fifth largest supermarket undertakings in France. The potential for non-merging parties to acquiesce to any post-merger unilateral price increase by raising their own prices is acknowledged in both EU and CA/CCPC *Guidelines*.

> *"A merger may significantly impede effective competition in a market by removing important competitive constraints on one or more sellers, who consequently have increased market power. The most direct effect of the merger will be the loss of competition between the merging firms. For example, if prior to the merger one of the merging firms had raised its price, it would have lost some sales to the other merging firm. The merger removes this particular constraint. Non-merging firms in the same market can also benefit from the reduction of competitive pressure that results from the merger, since the merging firms' price increase may switch some demand to the rival firms, which, in turn, may find it profitable to increase their prices. The reduction in these competitive*

> *constraints could lead to significant price increases in the relevant market" (EUHMG, 2004, ¶24).*[774]

CAMG2002 stated:

> *"The analysis of the reaction of other firms may also... include a change in the non-cooperative equilibrium that formerly operated in the market. If the merger creates a change in circumstances such that some or all firms may have the power to unilaterally raise price, this will be considered in the analysis" (¶4.8).*

CCPCMG2014 acknowledge that a merged entity may raise prices unilaterally if *"competitors do not have a strong incentive to compete (for example, if they might also benefit from increased prices), also referred to as price accommodation"* (¶4.11).

The larger the number of competitors remaining post-merger, the lower the likelihood of a merger having a negative effect on consumer welfare, other things being equal. This provides the rationale for using concentration measures such as the HHI as an initial screening device for unilateral effects (Motta, 2004). When the HHI exceeds the safe harbour thresholds, the possibility of a post-merger price increase cannot be ruled out solely on the basis of the number of competitors remaining post-merger. It is important in such circumstances to consider whether the remaining competitors might have an incentive to accommodate a unilateral price increase post-merger.

Carlyle/Sam McAuley stated that the increase in the parties' market share would be very small and that there were several competitors who would exercise a post-merger competitive constraint.[775] *United Care/Pharmexx* expressed the view that the two remaining competitors would be sufficient to prevent a post-merger price increase. In *Counterpoint/East Coast/Knockton* the three largest suppliers post-merger had a combined market share of [55-70]% with the merged entity apparently the largest with [25-30]%. In *CapVest/CCIF Core,* three parties accounted for approximately 90%+ of the market for the supply of branded sliced cooked ham to the retail sector post-

---

774 FN28 to the quotation adds: *"Such expected reactions by competitors may be a relevant factor influencing the merged entity's incentives to increase prices".*

775 CCPC M/17/030 – *Carlyle/Sam McAuley Chemists,* 3.7.2017. The merging parties had market shares of [25-30]% and [0-5]% respectively. It was not possible to establish whether the transaction fell within the HHI safe harbour thresholds based on information contained in the Determination.

merger.[776] In *John Laing/Towercomm* the parties were the second and fourth largest in the market with a combined market share of [25-35]% while the two largest firms would account for [55-75]% of the market post-merger. The merging parties in *KTC Edibles/Trilby Trading* had a combined market share of [35-45]%.[777] None of these Determinations considered whether it might have been in non-merging parties' interests to go along with any unilateral price increase post-merger.

The CCPC acknowledged that the more concentrated the market and the fewer competitors remaining post-merger, the greater the likelihood of a unilateral price increase in *Bank of Ireland/KBC*.

> *"Where a proposed transaction materially changes the market structure and eliminates an important competitive force from the market, it will reduce the competitive pressure faced by both the merged/post-transaction entity and other competing suppliers. Competing suppliers may respond to a price rise by the merged/post-transaction firm by raising their own prices. Therefore, the more concentrated a market is and the fewer effective competitors that remain to constrain one another, the more likely it is that a proposed transaction will enable the merged entity to raise prices" (¶6.21).*

Homogenous Products

In order to unilaterally increase price post-merger in a homogenous products market, the merged entity would have to reduce output. A price increase could not be sustained, however, if other non-merging firms expanded their output to offset the reduction by the merged firm. Thus, unilateral effects in homogenous product markets require that the merging parties must have a high market share and that the remaining firms must be capacity constrained.

The CA prohibition Determination in *Kingspan/Xtratherm* stated that the merging parties were each other's closest competitors although it described the products as homogenous.[778] The Determination noted that Kingspan had previously attempted to raise prices but had been unable to do so,

---

776 The merged entity was not the largest operator in the market post-merger. According to the Determination it and another party would each have market shares of [20-30]% while the largest supplier had a market share of [40-50]%.

777 CCPC M/23/037 – *KTC Edibles/Trilby Trading*, 13.9.2023. The parties claimed that the market was highly fragmented, although this is inconsistent with market share data and claims that they faced several large competitors.

778 The literature also indicates that business customers are less likely to regard products as differentiated.

which is not surprising if products are homogenous. The CA argued that it would be in the remaining firms' interests to accept a higher price in response to any unilateral price increase by the merging parties.

> *"It should be noted, however, that it would not be in the interest of the market participants to compete vigorously on price where there are only two major suppliers, the product is homogenous and there is limited potential growth in the market. Price competition could trigger a price war to the detriment of all market participants" (¶6.10)*

The merging parties had a combined market share of [70-90]%. The two other firms in the market, Quinn Therm and Ballytherm, had market shares of [10-20%] and [0-10%] respectively. The CA acknowledged that Quinn Therm had spare capacity, stating that it could increase the number of shifts at its plant.[779] The CA argued that, in considering whether increased capacity utilisation by Quinn Therm would prevent a post-merger price increase, it would have to satisfy the test for entry, i.e. an increase in capacity utilisation would have to be (i) timely; (ii) likely; and (iii) sufficient. The CA accepted that some or all of Quinn Therm's spare capacity could be brought on stream within two years and would be sufficient to restore prices to their pre-merger levels.[780] The CA concluded, however, that it was unlikely that Quinn Therm would bring spare capacity on stream arguing that *"substantial extra demand would be needed in order to justify an additional shift given the non-marginal addition to capacity of such a shift"* (¶5.24), having stated that a substantial increase in demand was likely (¶5.23). Arguably some additional capacity could have been brought on stream relatively quickly through overtime working on existing shifts, an option not

---

[779] According to the Determination, Kingspan operated three shifts, Xtratherm and Quinn Therm two, while Ballytherm operated a single shift. The Determination stated that market investigations indicated that Quinn Therm was the only credible alternative to the merged firm and limited its analysis of increased capacity utilisation to Quinn Therm. Apart from a reference to market investigations, no reason is given for excluding Ballytherm.

[780] The Determination stated that sufficient amounted to *"40-50% of the current output of the merging parties sold in Ireland"* (¶5.25). The merging firms accounted for 75-85% of the market. This implies that buyers would have had to offer Quinn Therm 30-42.5% of the market in order to encourage it to bring spare capacity into production, even though its existing market share was 10-20%. It is difficult to make any sense of such estimates. If the overtime option had been considered, the required increase in sales necessary to justify bringing additional capacity on stream would have been relatively small.

considered by the CA, which would have been easy to reverse if increased capacity utilisation proved unprofitable.[781]

The CA acknowledged that Quinn Therm could respond to any post-merger price increase by raising output but argued that *"a more profitable strategy for Quinn Therm is to partially match the price increase and increase market share/output"* (¶6.17). No quantitative evidence was adduced to support this contention which seems doubtful given Quinn Therm's market share of less than 20%. In those circumstances it would appear far more profitable for it to increase output and market share in response to any attempted price rise by the merged firm. A similar argument applies to Ballytherm which had a market share of less than 10%. The CA also argued that it would be in Quinn Therm's interest to raise prices because the market was declining. A declining market means lower future sales and hence the gain from deviating from any price increase in the short-run is likely to exceed the cost in terms of future profits forgone.

The Determination stated that Quinn Therm had indicated that its business model was to increase output in response to demand, as opposed to fixing a given level of capacity, and supplying that amount thereby allowing the market to determine the price (¶5.24). More significantly the Determination stated:

> *"However Quinn is capable and willing to offset any supply contraction by the merged entity" (¶5.43).*

It is difficult to reconcile such views with the CA's conclusion that Quinn Therm was unlikely to increase output in response to a reduction in output by the merged firm and that customers would therefore be unable to exercise countervailing buyer power (because they would not have an alternative source of supply unless Quinn Therm increased output). Evidence on prices included in the Annex to the Determination indicated that Quinn Therm entered the market even though prices had fallen over the previous two years, following Xtratherm's entry in August 2002. Quinn Therm subsequently increased its market share even though prices continued to fall up to the time of the notification in 2006. This tends to support the view that it would be more profitable for Quinn Therm to increase output and market share in the event

---

781 The merging parties appear not to have advanced this argument. In *Ballytherm/Xtratherm* the CCPC accepted that, if the merged entity reduced its output in order to raise prices, other suppliers had the capacity to increase output in response. It is also inconsistent with *Galco/Sperrin* where the CA concluded that the parties could expand shifts almost immediately with overtime payments being the only additional cost involved.

that the merged entity sought to raise prices. The Determination stated that several customers indicated that they expected that the proposed merger would result in higher prices. Such evidence is obviously important, but it does not identify any clear theory of competitive harm.

In *Barnett/Origin/Hall*, which also involved homogenous products, the CA *"examined two possible theories of harm... (a) unilateral effects and (b) coordinated effects"* (¶3.6). The most relevant unilateral effects theory would involve the merged firm reducing output in order to raise prices, which requires that the remaining non-merging firms must be capacity constrained.[782] The CA argued that customers could easily switch to other suppliers of both grain and NGFI in response to an attempted post-merger price increase by the merged entity implying that non-merging parties were not capacity constrained.[783] In *Dawn Meats/Dunbia* the CCPC noted that the existence of spare capacity in beef processing meant that the parties could not reduce the price paid for cattle by reducing purchases (output) as other processors would increase their purchases.[784]

The Diversion Ratio

The diversion ratio is a mechanism which can be used for measuring the closeness of the merging parties' products in spatial unilateral effects cases (Shapiro, 1996). It measures the proportion of the sales lost by one merging brand, in the event of an increase in the price of that brand, that accrues to the other merging brand, assuming the price of all other brands remains unchanged. The closer the degree of substitution between the merging products, the higher will be the diversion ratio and consequently the higher

---

782 The Determination did not refer to a specific unilateral effects theory. The parties' combined market share tends to rule out a dominance theory, while homogenous products would tend to rule out a spatial theory based on closeness of competition.

783 The CA also stated that customers indicated that they did not believe prices would increase post-merger.

784 The CCPC similarly argued in *Lakeland/LacPatrick* that, if the merged entity reduced the price it paid to farmers for raw milk, they would switch to other milk processors. The CCPC did not state whether other processors had spare capacity, although the UKCMA stated that there was *"significant spare capacity"* (¶115). The CCPC failed to mention in either case that reducing purchase prices would require the merged entity to reduce the quantity purchased, resulting in a loss of market share (and revenue) in downstream export markets where they did not have power to raise prices, although this was mentioned by the UKCMA (¶108). The UKCMA decision also contains a more detailed analysis of closeness of competition between the parties in the market for the procurement of raw milk from farmers than the CCPC Determination in the case.

will be the likely post-merger price increase. If pre-merger price cost margins are known, the diversion ratio can be used to estimate the potential magnitude of a post-merger price increase using the formula:

$$M.D/(1-M-D) \quad [8.1]$$

where D is the diversion ratio and M is the price-marginal cost margin (*ibid.*).[785] Diversion ratios are frequently employed in UK and US merger cases. The CA estimated diversion ratios in *SRH/Capital Radio*. Consumer surveys may enable diversion ratios to be estimated. In some cases where the CA/CCPC has commissioned consumer surveys the questions posed did not permit such estimates.[786] Shapiro (1996) suggested diversion ratios could be estimated based on market shares when information necessary to estimate them was unavailable.[787] Diversion ratios involve a static analysis and will generally indicate that a merger is likely to result in a post-merger price increase even in highly fragmented markets. Consequently, it is essential that the dynamic responses of competitors, potential entrants, and customers, to a post-merger price rise are also considered in order to establish whether a merger will result in a price increase.

Upward Pricing Pressure

USHMG2010 introduced the concept of upward pricing pressure (UPP), based on Farrell & Shapiro (2010a), to measure the likely impact of a merger on price.[788] Their model asks whether, in the event of fall in the price of one of the merging products, product A, the profits lost on those sales of product B that switch to product A, exceed any cost savings on product A due to efficiencies. The UPP is given by the formula:

---

785 Assume that the gross margin is 30%. Suppose that, if the price of brand A increases, 25% of the sales lost would go to its closest competitor, brand B, while 10% would go to its furthest competitor, Brand X. Based on the formula, a merger between A and B would imply a likely price increase of 16.7% but a merger of A and X would imply a likely price increase of 5%.

786 In *Top Snacks/KP Snacks* consumers were asked to indicate all of the crisp brands that they would consider switching to in response to a 10% increase in each of the merging parties' crisp brands from a list. If consumers had been asked which particular brand they would be most likely to switch to in response to such a price increase it would have been possible to estimate diversion ratios for each of the alternative brands. A similar situation arose in relation to brown sauce in *Valeo/Wardell/Robert Roberts*.

787 This assumes that all brands are equally close substitutes so that sales lost by the firm raising its prices accrue to the remaining brands in proportion to their overall market shares.

788 The authors posted an earlier version online in 2008. They acknowledged that the test may yield false negatives.

$$UPP_a = D_{ab}(P_b - C_b) - E_aC_a \quad [8.2]$$

where P_a P_b and C_a C_b are the prices and marginal costs of the merging parties' respective products, D_{ab} is the diversion ratio, i.e. the proportion of sales gained by product A, as a result of a decline in its price, that are achieved at the expense of product B and E_aC_a is the reduction in the marginal cost of product A due to efficiencies.

The then Chief Economist of DG Competition expressed serious reservations about UPP (Neven, 2010, September 29). Carlton (2010) was also highly critical of the proposal to replace market definition/concentration with UPP as the starting point in merger analysis. Schmalensee (2009) argued that UPP should be used carefully along with other relevant evidence and proposed an alternative measure, UPP*, which unlike UPP, recognises that efficiencies on Product B will increase its margin and thus increase upward pricing pressure for Product A. Farrell & Shapiro (2010b), while acknowledging the validity of this point, expressed reservations about its application, because (i) it echoes a discredited approach that merger efficiencies are detrimental and (ii) it is more complicated and less intuitive than UPP. Simons & Coate (2010) argue that UPP may not generate reliable predictions of likely merger effects and, in the absence of efficiencies, is likely to predict that all horizontal mergers will result in price increases. Coate (2011) cautioned against using a UPP index as a screening device in merger cases. Mathiesen *et al.* (2012) warned that the UPP may yield false positives as well as false negatives. The Gross Upward Price Pressure Index (GUPPI) is the UPP excluding any efficiency gains (Coate, 2011). Haydock & Smith (2019) point out that it is better to rely on wider evidence than the GUPPI alone, no matter how carefully it has been calculated. UPP in its various guises may be a useful tool but needs to be used carefully. UKCMA (2017, April 10) states that diversion ratios and price pressure indices are unlikely to determine case outcomes on their own.

Merger Simulations

Merger simulations are another mechanism for estimating the likely impact of differentiated product mergers. Their reliability depends on the reliability of the data and assumptions used.[789] Simulation models only consider static

---

789 For a description of merger simulation models, see Epstein & Rubinfeld (2002, 2004). Hausman & Leonard (2005) describe methods employed to test simulation results in the EU

short run effects and fail to take account of the extent to which entry, repositioning by other suppliers, and buyer responses may constrain the merged firm's ability to raise prices (Botteman, 2006). Lyons (2008, p.25) describes full-blown merger simulations as *"a dangerous black box"*. Merger simulations have proved unsatisfactory for several reasons:

i. Basic simulation models always predict that a merger is likely to raise prices;
ii. The magnitude of the predicted price increase depends crucially on assumptions about the demand system and the shape of the demand curve which requires judgements and assumptions introducing some ambiguity in the results;
iii. By design, simulations only capture price competition (Kwoka, 2015).

Tenn *et al.* (2010) find that simulation models which only focus on price are likely to yield biased results if firms compete in other ways, *e.g.*, promotional activity, although they suggest that multi-dimensional competition can easily be incorporated into simulation models. Budzinski & Ruhmer (2010) state that merger simulation is not a magic bullet and must be used in conjunction with more traditional analytical instruments. UPP models offer better qualitative predictions but less accurate quantitative estimates than merger simulations (*ibid.*). Merger simulations have rarely been employed by the EU Commission (Duso *et al.*, 2024). To date, the CA/CCPC has not employed simulation models. Gorecki *et al.* (2007) suggested that, given their limitations, investing resources in simulation models might add little value for a small agency which had dealt with relatively few harmful mergers.

Competitor Repositioning

Following a differentiated products merger, competitors of the merged entity may try to reposition their products so as to make them closer substitutes for the merging brands.[790] It may well pay for a non-merging rival to reposition its

---

Volvo/Scania case. They were acting for the merging parties and the EU Commission provided them with details of the simulation during the course of its investigation.

[790] Suppose there were four brands: one aimed at the top end of the market, one at the bottom, and the other two mid-market. If the latter two merged, the issue is whether either the top or bottom market brand would seek to reposition themselves towards the mid-market. Product repositioning increases the diversion ratio between the repositioned brand and the merging brands.

brand, or to introduce a new brand, located closer to the merging brands (Shapiro, 1996). The threat of repositioning may, of itself, be sufficient to prevent a post-merger price increase. Gorecki *et al.* (2007) speculate that, in fast-moving consumer goods markets, a non-merging firm could reposition its product to increase its diversion ratio with the merging parties and that large buyers such as supermarkets would redistribute shelf space or promote a rival seeking to reposition itself. The likelihood of post-merger brand repositioning by non-merging rivals depends on the likely costs of doing so. The further a brand needs to be *"moved"* in order to position it close to the merging brands, the more costly product repositioning is likely to be and thus the lower the likelihood of it occurring.[791] An alternative scenario posited by Gandhi *et al.* (2008) is that merging firms may reposition their products, by distancing them from each other, in order to avoid cannibalisation post-merger, citing mergers of radio stations, newspapers and cruise lines as examples. Such repositioning by the merging parties may facilitate repositioning by non-merging firms. They suggest that product repositioning by the merging parties may be more important than repositioning by non-merging firms in terms of mitigating the anti-competitive effects of a merger. They caution, however, that product repositioning may frequently be quite expensive and time-consuming, reducing the likelihood of it occurring in the short-term.

The CA/CCPC has rarely considered the potential for repositioning by non-merging brands in unilateral effects cases, although Shapiro (2010) noted that it had rarely featured in US cases either. Rather the CCPC has tended to focus on the existing closeness of competition between the merging brands. It may be important, therefore, for merging parties to provide evidence of the potential for non-merging brands to reposition their products post-merger.

Coordinated Effects

Coordinated effects arise where a merger increases the risk of collusion either tacit or explicit. Coate (2006) distinguishes between structuralist and regime shift coordinated effects theories. The former relates to a situation where the market is already behaving in a less than competitive manner in

---

791 Ashenfelter *et al.* (2013) report that rivals may have changed their product offerings following the US *Maytag/Whirlpool* merger. Over the past decade Dunnes Stores has arguably repositioned itself toward the quality end of the Irish retail grocery market. This may well have been a response to entry by discounters such as Aldi and Lidl, although the *Musgrave/Superquinn* merger may also have provided a repositioning opportunity.

which case the issue is whether the merger will make collusion more sustainable going forward. The regime shift approach applies if the merger may lead to coordinated behaviour where it had not previously occurred. Assessing the likelihood of coordinated effects post-merger involves analysing why a merger:

i. Would make coordination more effective if it was occurring already; or

ii. Might cause it to occur if it had not occurred previously (Scheffman & Coleman, 2003).

The CA in *Barnett/Origin/Hall* cited instability in market shares for NGFI ruling out the possibility of coordinated behaviour pre-merger.[792] In the grain market, however, the transaction left the two largest firms with similar post-merger market shares, but the presence of several smaller firms reduced the likelihood of coordination.

It is generally acknowledged that coordinated effects are more likely to arise with homogenous rather than differentiated products. While product differentiation reduces the likelihood of collusion, it may, nevertheless, still be possible (OECD, 1999).[793]

The analysis of coordinated effects is far more complicated than unilateral effects and economists have not developed a method of quantifying the increased likelihood of collusion post-merger (Shapiro, 1996). Economics has identified various factors which may give rise to coordinated effects, but it is generally not possible to predict with any degree of certainty whether coordinated behaviour will actually occur (Scheffman & Coleman, 2003). Lyons (2008), nevertheless, identified the emergence of a consensus on coordinated effects based on a repeated game model of the sustainability of collusion.[794]

Analysing the potential for coordinated effects post-merger involves a check-list approach based on various factors identified as facilitating coordinated behaviour including:

- A small number of firms in the market;
- Firms are symmetric;

---

[792] The Determination stated that no customer contacted by the CA expressed concerns about coordinated effects post-merger.

[793] Levy & Reitzes (1992), for example, dispute the view that homogeneity is a key factor in collusion.

[794] He notes that the General Court in *Airtours v. Commission* implicitly adopted the model's basic tenets.

- A high level of transparency particularly as regards prices;
- An ability to punish firms that deviate from the potential collusive outcome; and
- Repeated interaction between firms in various markets.

Davies *et al.* (2011) observe, however, that the empirical economics literature provide few insights on some basic questions, specifically how few is few and how symmetric is symmetric. A reduction in the number of competitors as a result of a merger may make cheating easier to detect and police or make behaviour more predictable and transparent or make firms more likely to realise that they can gain by competing less vigorously (Philips, 1995). Where firms' market shares are sufficiently asymmetric, it is likely to be more profitable for those with smaller market shares to try and increase their market share by competing rather than colluding. Thus, a merger may increase the likelihood of collusion if it increases market symmetry. A merger may also eliminate a firm which had previously pursued an independent low-pricing strategy thereby removing an obstacle to coordination.[795]

The CA concluded in *Chevron/Texoil* that the presence of three rival fascias would be sufficient to prevent any post-merger price increase in local motor fuel markets without considering a specific theory of harm. Four firms are few enough for coordinated effects, while retail motor fuel prices are highly transparent due to legal requirements requiring filling stations to display their prices. Arguably the possibility of coordinated effects merited further discussion.

Evidence of significant price variation in a market suggests coordination is likely to be difficult, although it is not conclusive. A lack of price variation does not constitute evidence that coordination is occurring but suggests it may be more feasible. The USFTC concluded in its cruise ships merger investigation that a price consensus would have been difficult to achieve due to the complexity of the market and would also have required price discrimination while variability in demand and in the number of passengers booking early would have made it difficult to detect cheating (Coleman *et al.*, 2003). The UKCC in *Safeway* did not consider that the vast range of products sold by supermarkets necessarily precluded a sufficient

---

795 Such firms are referred to in the economic literature as "mavericks" (see below). A merger which does not involve a maverick may also increase the likelihood of coordination by altering the incentives for a non-merging maverick firm (see below).

degree of price transparency for coordinated effects post-merger.[796] In *Sainsbury's/Asda*[797] the UKCMA found that coordinated effects could arise in respect of delivery charges for online grocery sales in local markets, particularly those not served by Ocado, an online-only competitor.

Lyons (2008) notes how the EU Commission in the early years of the ECMR tended to look favourably on mergers that would create a strong rival to an existing large market player, overlooking the increased risk of coordinated effects. Pilsbury (2007) criticised the General Court finding that coordinated effects were likely in *Impala* because transparency could be inferred if there was evidence that prices were closely aligned, exceeded the competitive level and if there was no other reasonable explanation for such outcomes. Davies *et al.* (2011) find that findings of tacit collusion have been rare in EU cases and have been largely confined to markets with just two more or less equal-sized undertakings.

Capacity constraints also play a key role in the analysis of tacit collusion. Asymmetric market shares make collusion difficult when aggregate capacity is limited but may facilitate collusion when aggregate capacity is much larger than the market (Compte *et al.*, 2002). Capacity constraints reduce the incentive for parties to deviate and increase the severity of price wars. They could also lead firms to view competition as mutually destructive and thus futile. Lyons (2008) emphasises the need to consider the individual circumstances of a merger, particularly in the presence of capacity constraints, and states that the importance of capacity distribution was not recognised at the remedies stage in *Nestlé/Perrier* (see **Chapter 11).** Kühn & Van Reenen (2009) criticised the EU Commission for advancing fairly implausible concerns in relation to coordination of capacity expansion in *UPM-Kymmene/Haindl*[798] but acknowledged that it eventually accepted that the merger would not enhance coordination.

The CA summarily dismissed the possibility of coordinated effects in *Kingspan/Xtratherm*:

---

[796] Albæk *et al.* (2010) criticise the Danish competition authority's finding that a merger of two wholesalers of plumbing supplies would yield to coordinated effects, arguing that the vast range of individual products involved, combined with the widespread practice of individual discounts, meant that there was insufficient transparency for coordination to occur. The transaction would have resulted in a four to three merger in relation to two broad product categories and a three to two merger in respect of another product category.

[797] This was the first time that online sales were considered in a UK grocery merger.

[798] Case No. COMP/M.2498 – *UPM-Kymmene/Haindl*, 21.11.2001.

> *"Since there were no concerns with respect to co-ordinated effects the discussion is confined to unilateral effects" (¶16.1).*[799]

The CCPC Determination in *Dawn Meats/Dunbia*[800] contains a detailed discussion of the likelihood of coordinated effects post-merger. It notes that there was no evidence of pre-merger coordination indicating that a finding of coordinated effects required a regime shift theory of harm. Although the transaction increased symmetry between the two largest beef processors and prices were transparent, the CCPC noted that coordination would be difficult with nine competitors in a market subject to demand fluctuations. It concluded that coordinated effects were unlikely in *Lakeland/LacPatrick* for broadly similar reasons.[801]

The merging parties in *Irish Times/Sappho* had combined market shares of 23%, making them the second largest in the national daily newspaper market post-merger, while the market leader, Independent News & Media, had a 30% market share. The CCPC concluded that post-merger market shares would be sufficiently asymmetric to eliminate the risk of co-ordination.

The CA/CCPC ruled out the possibility of price coordination in *Uniphar/CMR* and *Uniphar/Murrays Medical* noting that, although in both cases there would be only two competitors in the market post-merger, pricing was sufficiently opaque. In both cases, it concluded that the incentives for the parties to compete to retain their primary customers was sufficient to rule out possible coordination in respect of delivery services. In *Xtratherm/Ballytherm* the CCPC concluded that, although the transaction would result in some increase in symmetry, market shares would remain sufficiently asymmetric, while prices were sufficiently opaque due to discounts off list prices, to rule out possible coordinated effects.

A coordinated effects theory was one of four competitive harm theories considered by the CCPC in *Synch (JV)* which involved the main banks in the State establishing a joint venture to develop and operate a mobile payments system. The CCPC concluded that conditions conducive to coordinated behaviour were likely to exist in the market for the provision of banking products and services, including current account services. There were a

---

799 Arguably market shares post-merger would have been sufficiently asymmetric to rule out coordination, but this was not stated.

800 The Determination noted that the EU Commission had previously concluded that coordinated effects were unlikely in *ABP/Fane Valley/Slaney Foods*. The CCPC subsequently ruled out possible coordinated effects for similar reasons in *Dawn Meats/Kildare Chilling*.

801 The UKCMA reached a similar conclusion in that case.

limited number of competitors, with the four JV Parents having a combined market share of 81-83% in current account services which was expected to increase as two other banks were in the process of exiting the market. The JV parents were close competitors while the CCPC considered that their products were largely homogenous. The CCPC further argued that the proposed transaction would make it easier to agree transparent focal points for coordinated behaviour, *e.g.*, fees for peer- to-peer (P2P)[802] Mobile Instant Payments Services (MIPS) or person-to-business (P2B) mobile payments services or the introduction of new payment products or services. It also believed that the proposed transaction could facilitate the potential exchange of information with the JV parents of:

i. Requests for access to the Synch Mobile Payments Service;
ii. Information about the value, volume, and type of payments made by participants in the Synch Mobile Payments Service;
iii. Information about payments to merchant participants *via* Synch;
iv. Potential exchange in relation to fees charged by the JV Parents to merchants or their respective customers for making a payment *via* Synch.

The CCPC stated that the exchange of information could harm competition in:

i. The provision of P2P Mobile Instant Payments Services; and
ii. The market for P2B mobile payments services in the State.

It expressed a particular concern that the potential exchange of information between Synch and the JV Parents could result in less vigorous competition, resulting in higher prices than in a normally functioning competitive market. The CCPC also expressed concern that the exchange of information between the JV Parents *via* Synch could adversely affect competition for banking products and services (including current account services).

Maverick Firms

Certain firms may pursue more aggressive pricing strategies than other market participants. Such undertakings are described as *"mavericks"*. The removal of a maverick firm would support a regime shift coordinated effects theory. The concept has rarely featured in EU Commission merger

802 Effectively payments between individuals.

decisions and mainly in potential unilateral effects cases since the 2004 reform of the ECMR (Bromfield & Olczak, 2018).

The CA in *Statoil/Conoco* noted that the target had a reputation as a low-price retailer of motor fuels and observed that post-merger *"the strong price competition which in the past was offered by Conoco would simply disappear, lessening the competitive pressure on the remaining suppliers"* (p.50).

A maverick undertaking may have an effect on competition that is disproportionate to its size. CAMG2002 noted that the removal of a maverick could (i) alter the non-cooperative equilibrium (¶4.8); (ii) result in unilateral market power even if the maverick had a low market share (¶4.14(e)); and (iii) make collusion easier (¶4.24).

The CA concluded in *Heineken/Beamish & Crawford* that Beamish & Crawford was not a maverick firm. Beamish & Crawford had regularly failed to increase the price of its draught lager brands when the other two brewers raised theirs with the result that its Foster's lager was significantly cheaper than other lager brands.[803] According to the Determination, in the five years prior to the merger, Diageo led in announcing increases in the wholesale price of draught lager to the on-trade and Heineken always applied identical price increases to its draught lager brands a few weeks after the Diageo announcement. Beamish & Crawford did not follow such price increases between 2003 and 2005 but followed them before and after this period, although in 2007 it did not raise the price of its Foster's brand but applied a higher rate of increase to its *Miller* brand.[804] Beamish & Crawford arguably satisfied the EUHMG definition of a maverick as a firm with *"a history of preventing or disrupting coordination"*. CAMG2002 contained a narrower definition of a maverick.

> *"A maverick is a firm that has a history of cutting price or otherwise deviating from conventional market behaviour in a pro-competitive manner" (¶4.14(e)).*

CCPCMG2014 includes no definition of a maverick firm but describes maverick behaviour as *"competing more vigorously (e.g., in terms of price, quality, innovation etc.) relative to other firms"* (¶4.22). They state that a merger

---

803 The Determination indicated that Foster's lager was approximately 90c per pint cheaper than other lagers which was approximately 20% lower than the average national price of a pint of lager at the time as recorded by the CSO.

804 Presumably, this means that the wholesale price increase for Miller's was greater than the increase applied by the other two brewers on their lager brands. The CA also quoted internal Beamish & Crawford documents which stated: *"Maintain price parity on MGD Draught with competitor set in the on-trade."* (¶5.156).

involving a maverick firm could have a disproportionate effect on competition (*ibid.*) while also noting that a maverick undertaking makes coordination difficult (¶4.33(c)). Baker (2002) argues that a maverick firm is one that constrains coordination from becoming more likely or effective without necessarily starting price wars or otherwise appearing observably disruptive, which may be more consistent with the EUHMG definition. Viewed in this light, a maverick firm may not actually prevent a price increase but may constrain other undertakings from increasing price to the extent that they would like.[805] Thus the fact that Beamish & Crawford did not always deviate from, or prevent price increases, by the other two brewers was not sufficient to support a conclusion that it was not a maverick.

The CA/CCPC consideration of maverick firms has also been limited to mergers which eliminated a maverick firm from the market. A merger that does not involve a maverick firm may, nevertheless, make coordination more effective and result in price increases, if it alters the maverick firm's incentives (*ibid.*).[806] Baker & Shapiro (2008) state that a merger which eliminates a maverick should be presumed to harm competition. They also point out a merger involving a non-maverick firm may make coordination more likely or effective if it (a) alters the maverick's incentives or (b) results in the maverick preferring a higher coordinated price post-merger.

Innovation Theories of Harm

Firms may compete in terms of innovation (developing better products) because it may enable them to capture customers from rivals. USHMG1992 were widely criticised for paying little attention to innovation (Shapiro, 2010). Markets which are characterised by dynamic competition and rapid innovation may be less likely to suffer reduced competition than those

805 Baker (2002) cites the behaviour of Northwest Airlines in the US as an example of such maverick activity. He also suggests that a maverick may not be easily identifiable to outside observers.

806 The CA/CCPC view provides no explanation for maverick behaviour but simply defines a maverick as a firm that behaves in a particular way and fails to recognise that changes in circumstances, including those resulting from a merger of rival undertakings, may change the incentive for maverick behaviour. According to Baker (2002), USHMG1992 implied that maverick firms were a special case and were regarded as an afterthought in merger analysis. He argues, however, that mavericks may be central to the analysis of coordinated effects. CAMG2002 were influenced by USHMG1992, which is unsurprising as the EU Commission did not publish its horizontal merger guidelines until 2004.

characterised by stable and widely-used technology. Sidak & Singer (2008), however, rejected calls for a more lenient approach to merger control in cases involving nascent, high-technology sectors characterised by dynamic demand. Valetti & Zenger (2019) dismiss claims that potential competition concerns are unwarranted in technology markets and point out that safeguarding potential competition against dominant incumbents has become far more important than previously.

Shapiro (2012) reports considerable empirical evidence that competition spurs innovation. In contrast a merger between rivals reduces the incentive to innovate as there is no benefit to the merging parties in taking sales from each other.[807]

USHMG2010 introduced a new section on *"Innovation and Product Variety"* which provided for a two-stage analysis of innovation. The first considers the short-term impact of a merger on the introduction of new products by focusing on whether new products being developed by one of the merging parties are likely to cannibalise a significant proportion of the profits arising from products sold by the other merging party in which case the parties may have an incentive to discontinue the development of such products post-merger. The second step considers the longer-term impact of the merger, looking beyond the parties' current products and possibly those being developed and focusing on the parties' R&D plans and capabilities (*ibid.*). Buehler *et al.* (2017) state that the EU Commission has pursued innovation theories of harm in several mergers since 2014.[808] Valetti & Zenger (2021) state that the EU Commission applied innovation theories of harm, which were influenced by USMG2010, in several cases while Duso *et al.* (2025) also refer to the Commission's application of more novel theories of harm in relation to innovation and digital markets since the 2010s.

Related to the issue of whether a merger would result in the cancellation or delay of new products is whether it might lead to the withdrawal of existing products resulting in a reduction in product variety. This involves a very similar analysis to the treatment of short-term innovation effects and focuses on diversion and cannibalization of profits. Shapiro (2010) points

---

807 This is analogous to unilateral price effects (see above), where some of the sales lost in the event of a price increase by one of the merging parties are captured by the other merging party (Lancieri & Valetti, 2024).

808 Reference to innovation theories of harm first appeared in EU Commission Case No. COMP/M.7932 – *Dow/Dupont*, 27.3.2017 (Duso *et al.*, 2024). They have subsequently featured in several other cases including Case Nos. COMP/M.9294 – *BMS/Celgene*, 29.7.2019; and COMP/M.8084 – *Bayer/Monsanto*, 29.5.2018.

out that anti-competitive reductions in product variety are likely to be accompanied by a price increase on the remaining product.

> *"An anti-competitive incentive to eliminate a product as a result of the merger is greater and more likely, the larger is the share of profits from that product coming at the expense of profits from products sold by the merger partner" (USHMG2010, §6.4).*

As noted in **Chapter 1**, concerns have emerged in recent years regarding the ability of large firms, particularly in the IT and pharmaceutical industries, both of which have a strong presence in Ireland, to acquire entrants in order to eliminate potential competition, known as "killer acquisitions". Essentially acquisitions by incumbents of new entrants, which could grow and pose a significant competitive threat, may avoid scrutiny if the entrant is below the merger notification thresholds. Incumbents may be better placed to identify potential competitive threats long before regulatory agencies become aware of them (Rose & Shapiro, 2020). It may also be difficult for competition agencies to prove that nascent or potential rivals constitute a competitive threat because they may lack any track record showing what they can do. A potential rival that has been acquired for a high price would have little incentive to support a case against the merger (Baker, 2021).

A study of over 1,000 pharmaceutical mergers estimated that 5-7% constituted killer acquisitions (Cunningham *et al.*, 2021). A disproportionate number of such acquisitions fell just below thresholds for anti-trust review. Bon *et al.* (2021) point out that mergers which eliminate potential entrants may harm dynamic competition even though entry may have been unsuccessful.[809] Jean *et al.* (2019) report that *"the GAFAMs"*[810] between them made a total of 634 acquisitions at a total cost of €142 billion between 1991 and 2018.[811] The high prices paid in several instances raise concerns that the transactions may have been anti-competitive. Furman (2019) identified almost 250 acquisitions by these five companies over the previous five years, none of which was subjected

---

809 They cite an example where an incumbent acquires a potential entrant which was trying to develop an alternative method for administering a drug supplied by the incumbent, *i.e.*, tablet rather than injection. The incumbent has little incentive to continue developing the alternative product post-merger as it would mainly take sales from the incumbent's existing product. Even if the likelihood of the entrant successfully developing the new product was less than 50%, the merger would reduce dynamic competition.

810 GAFAMs is a collective reference to Google, Amazon, Facebook, Apple and Microsoft, although some of these firms have since rebranded under new names.

811 For further details on acquisitions by these undertakings see Parker *et al.* (2021).

to a merger review. As Valetti & Zenger (2019, p.6) observe, while the majority of these were likely to be pro-competitive *"it would hardly be a surprise if at least some of them might raise significant potential competition concerns"*. Ederer & Pellegrino (2023) report that the GAFAMs were disproportionately active in acquiring start-ups and that this coincided with them becoming increasingly insulated from product market competition. The USFTC quoted a 2008 e-mail by Meta (formerly Facebook) Chief Executive, Mark Zuckerberg, in which he allegedly stated, *"it is better to buy than compete"*.[812]

Sabre/Farelogix, which was prohibited by the UKCMA two days after a US Court refused an injunction application by the USDoJ to block the transaction, involved a merger of two undertakings providing technology applications used by airlines to sell flights. The UKCMA advanced two theories of harm. First, it concluded that the transaction would cause the purchaser to cease developing rival products for those of the target (dubbed a reverse killer acquisition), thereby limiting the number of competitors in the relevant market to two rather than three.[813] Second, it would have eliminated the growing threat which the target posed in the supply of distribution applications for airlines (Bon *et al.*, 2021). Shapiro (2019) advocates lower evidentiary thresholds for acquisitions of potential competitors in order to reduce the ability of powerful firms to acquire potential rivals before they mature into actual rivals, a view echoed by Gilbert & Melamed (2024). The EU Commission had urged national competition authorities to refer mergers in pharmaceutical and digital markets that fell below their national notification thresholds to it under Article 22 ECMR as a means of policing killer acquisitions (Karlinger *et al.*, 2020).[814] The CJEU held that the EU Commission did not have jurisdiction to review mergers if national authorities had no jurisdiction to review mergers below their national notification thresholds.[815] However, where national law permits a national authority to review mergers below the national notification thresholds the agency may refer the transaction under Article 22.[816] The effectiveness of such

812 *The Irish Times*, 2025, April 15.

813 Giving evidence during the USFTC challenge to Meta's acquisition of Instagram and What's App, Meta Chief Executive Mark Zuckerberg was reported as stating that Meta had been in the process of building a camera app but purchased Meta because he believed it had a better camera app (*ibid.*). This is a good example of a possible reverse killer acquisition.

814 In 2021 the CCPC referred one case, *Facebook/Kustomer*, to the EU Commission under Article 22.

815 The General Court had previously rejected the merging parties' appeal (Case T-227/21, *Illumina & Grail v Commission*, ECLI:EU:T:2022:447).

816 The *Competition (Amendment) Act, 2022* allows the CCPC to review below the threshold mergers (see **Chapter 3**). Several other national authorities have similar powers and other

arrangements depends on national authorities identifying such acquisitions.[817]

USHMG2024 place greater emphasis on dynamic competition and innovation than previous versions. They seek to address the issue of killer acquisitions by providing that mergers which eliminate a potential entrant in a concentrated market are considered anti-competitive. They apply a reasonable probability of entry test to define potential entrants. Shapiro, C. (2024) describes this approach as sound because a requirement that a potential entrant had made specific plans to enter in the near future would undermine effective enforcement, as firms would be unlikely to create written records of such plans if they were contemplating a merger.

Network effects in online platforms frequently result in the emergence of a dominant or monopoly platform operator. Baker (2021) notes that such outcomes are not inevitable in all cases, pointing out that multiple platforms may successfully co-exist where user preferences for platform features vary. Where a platform is dominant, Baker (2021) suggests that potential entrants and fringe competitors may represent the main source of competition. The loss of any rival, even a very small one, therefore may prevent the emergence of competition. Berry *et al.* (2019) state that acquisitions of potential competitors may have important competition implications when competition is for the market as is frequently the case with on-line platforms. Cases involving multi-sided platforms are complicated because traditional merger analytical tools may result in biases (Evans & Noel, 2008).

Duso *et al.* (2024) state that theories of harm advanced by the EU Commission in digital markets cases were similar, in some respects, to those applied in conglomerate mergers. The EU Commission developed an ecosystem theory of harm in *Booking/Etraveli*,[818] the first prohibition of a merger between digital platforms.

The CCPC stated in *Synch (JV)* that the arrangements could stifle innovation in the provision of MIPS in the State. It posited that this could lead to coordination with innovative features being developed collectively *via* Synch and made available to all participants simultaneously, at the expense of the JV Parents independently developing and improving their own proprietary mobile payments services in order to increase the

---

Member States are reportedly considering amending their legislation to include similar provisions.

817 Gilbert & Melamed (2024) observe that mergers involving potential entrants may harm competition in markets that do not yet exist.

818 EU Commission Case No. COMP/M.10615 – *Booking/Etraveli*, 25.9.2023.

attractiveness of their payments and current account services. The CCPC expressed concerns that because the parent undertakings held a substantial combined market share in current account services, the Proposed Transaction would reduce the prospects for potential competition to emerge in MIPS and related markets for banking products and services (including current accounts).

A further concern raised by the CCPC related to the possibility that network effects would discourage the JV Parents and other Synch participants from further developing their own individual mobile payments services. It claimed that the Proposed Transaction could reduce the incentive for innovation in respect of new and/or improved individual mobile payments services.[819] The CCPC also argued that the JV Parents might seek to limit innovation within Synch which was not aligned with their own commercial interests through their ability to influence Synch Board decisions. It noted that some of the JV Parents had been slow to innovate in the introduction of SEPA Instant payments which had slowed the development of Synch.

Other Theories of Harm

In addition to considering a unilateral effects theory of harm, the CA in *Glanbia/Wexford Creamery* also considered what it described as a possible blocking of an alternative acquirer theory.[820] The CA in *Musgrave/Superquinn* also considered whether the transaction would enable the merged entry to strategically block entry but ruled it out on the grounds that the bulk of any resulting increase in profits would accrue to the parties' rivals.

The CA also considered a *"waterbed"* theory of harm in *Musgrave/Superquinn*.[821]A waterbed effect occurs where powerful buyers are able to extract better price or other supply terms from suppliers while less-powerful buyers experience a decline in their terms of supply resulting in them raising prices to consumers (CCPCMG2014 ¶7.5). The CA concluded that the post-merger market structure would not support a waterbed effect theory because Musgrave's buyer power would not increase significantly.

---

819 Gastelum (2024), argues that a lack of competition has disincentivised Ticketmaster from making improvements to its products, resulting in systemic failures in relation to ticket sales for highly popular live events.

820 The UKCC raised similar concerns in relation to Ryanair's minority shareholding in Aer Lingus (see below).

821 For a more detailed description of waterbed effects, see Dobson & Inderst (2008).

The CCPC in *Tesco/Joyce's* quoted from an internal purchaser e-mail in relation to the target's Oranmore store which stated:

> *"...Would we consider leasing part to a competitor, so instead of restricting the full 14k sq ft, limit it to 7,000 sq ft or below. That way they can still attract a convenience operator but it limits the potential impact on our own store ..." (¶5.51).*[822]

Tesco argued that the comments had been made in *"the heat of negotiations"* (¶5.53) and that it intended to operate the store as a full range supermarket (¶5.54).

Several rivals of the merging parties in *Fitzwilliam/Wittington Canada/ Arnotts* expressed concerns that the merged entity could use its increased buyer power to raise rivals' costs and/or harm suppliers. The Determination states that the parties' internal documents raised no concerns in this regard but offered no further detail. The CA issued a survey to 35 of the merging parties' suppliers. Four expressed concerns about the merged entities increased buyer power but *"the vast majority of suppliers who provided a written response to the questionnaire expressed no concerns about the impact of the proposed transaction"* (¶88). It would have been helpful to include details of the number of suppliers who had responded in the Determination.

In *Synch* the CCPC identified a possible liquidity risk theory of harm because payments to customers *via* Synch would be instantaneous but interbank payments would not be cleared and settled instantaneously. The CCPC argued that this might deter entry or expansion into P2P MIPS, P2B mobile payments services and the related market for banking services including current account services. Liquidity risk was more likely to affect smaller competitors and new entrants as they were likely to have a greater proportion of interbank payments which would not be cleared and settled instantaneously. Larger operators were likely to be better placed to absorb the impact of any time lag between settlement and clearance of interbank transactions.

The CA stated in *UGC Chorus/NTL* that an internal document included a proposal to increase the price of NTL's cable analogue TV services to the level offered by Chorus which it stated would impact approximately 250,000 NTL subscribers. The Determination stated:

822 The statement that a convenience store would have limited impact on the purchaser's supermarket indicates that they are not close competitors and is inconsistent with the CA/CCPC view that there is a single retail grocery market.

> *"This is attributable to the management strategy...to migrate subscribers from analogue to digital services, and is not a result of a substantial lessening of competition" (¶113).*

The issue is whether a merger would enable the merged entity to raise prices, not why it would raise prices. The Determination also stated that NTL or any other purchaser of NTL could pursue a similar strategy. This implies that NTL already had the power to raise prices, which begs the question why it had not done so. According to the Determination, NTL had been more successful in negotiating wholesale content terms and conditions from BSkyB, which had allowed it to price its retail product more keenly, but the CA failed to consider whether the benefit to consumers of such behaviour might be lost as a result of the transaction. The CA stated that it had also been more creative than Chorus when differentiating its product *vis-à-vis* BSkyB's satellite offering and in retaining its Pay-TV customers.

Fuelplus/Valero[823] involved the acquisition of the vendor's high volume fuel card business in the state by a party that was engaged in the fuel card business as an issuer of own brand fuel cards and as a reseller of other fuel cards. The Determination advanced no theory of competitive harm but argued that, provided other parties exercised a constraint on the merged entity, no competition concerns would arise.

> *"Consequently, to the extent that cards supplied by resellers provide a competitive constraint on own brand cards issued directly, the activities of other resellers within the State can be expected to continue to provide a competitive constraint on Radius subsequent to the implementation of the proposed transaction" (¶130).*

The purpose of merger review is to establish whether the parties will be subject to sufficient competitive constraints post-merger. The Determination further stated:

> *"Consequently, to the extent that fuel sales in Northern Ireland provide a competitive constraint within the State, Valero's activities in Northern Ireland can be expected to act as a competitive constraint on Radius subsequent to the implementation of the proposed transaction" (¶132).*

---

[823] CCPC M/15/007 – *Fuelplus/Valero*, 26.3.2015.

It is unlikely that cross-border competitive constraints would be significant, except in border areas, particularly for fuel card customers.[824]

CVC/Celtic Rugby involved the acquisition of control over the approval of broadcasting and sponsorship arrangements for the Pro14 (now URC) rugby tournament. The CCPC stated that post-merger the *"Rugby Six Nations and the Autumn Internationals would continue to provide a competitive constraint in the market for the sale of broadcasting rights for rugby union sporting events in the State"* (¶62) but went on to say that it *"may have concerns regarding the likely competitive impact of the Proposed Transaction in the absence of the Six Nations as a continuing competitive constraint post transaction"* (¶64). Such concerns rested on an assumption that the Six Nations and Autumn Internationals exercised a competitive constraint on the Pro-14 for the sale of broadcast rights. As noted in Chapter 6, the tournaments were in separate temporal markets. Nevertheless, the transaction was subject to a remedy requiring the parties to notify any future acquisition of an interest in the Six Nations should such a transaction fall below the notification thresholds.[825] When the latter transaction was subsequently notified, the CCPC made no reference to the tournaments exercising a competitive constraint on each other.[826]

In *Glennon Bros/Balcas* the CCPC cleared the transaction following an extended Phase 1 investigation on the grounds that there were sufficient competitors to exercise an effective competitive constraint on the merging parties. Based on data on market share ranges in the Determination, it appears that the HHI was within the CCPCMG2014 safe harbour thresholds in three of the four markets where the parties overlapped. In a fourth market for the supply of pallets and packaging timber products in the State, it seems quite likely that the transaction exceeded the safe harbour thresholds, and a more detailed consideration of possible competitive harm theories would arguably have been appropriate.[827]

---

824 There is some historical evidence that quite large price differentials may affect cross-border fuel sales.

825 As noted, applying remedies where an SLC is unlikely to arise constitutes a false positive.

826 *CVC/Six Nations.* The CCPC decided that there was no need to consider a possible market for rugby broadcast rights, in contrast to *CVC/Celtic Rugby.* UKCMA ME/6930/21 – *CVC/Six Nations Rugby,* 14.7.2021, concluded that the parties were not close competitors for the sale of broadcast rights.

827 The Determination states that the merging parties had market shares of [20-30]% and [5-10]% respectively. Given information on other parties' market shares the post-merger HHI would have exceeded 1,000 and individual market shares of 22% and 6% would have put the increase in HHI above the 250 safe harbour threshold. The transaction was also notified to the UKCMA which concluded that it would not result in any SLC because the merging

In *DFDS/McBurney Transport* the merging parties each accounted for [0-5]% of the markets for inland [freight] transportation services and for warehousing services in the State. Both markets were highly fragmented. According to a report on freight transport services cited in the Determination *"the industry is dominated by microbusinesses that consist of a single owner-driver or have only one or two employees"* (¶19). The CCPC, *"out of an abundance of caution"* also considered a *"market"* comprising the merging parties and their principal competitors and concluded that the transaction raised no competition issues as the parties' would have a market share of less than [20-25]% in that case, while noting that this excluded several significant competitors. As both unilateral and coordinated effects work best when the number of competitors is limited, the highly fragmented nature of both markets and the merging parties' small market shares was arguably sufficient to rule out any possibility of an SLC in the absence of evidence supporting a narrower market definition.[828]

The CCPC expressed concerns in *PandaGreen/Exomex*[829] in relation to the market for individual C&I waste collection services without advancing any theory of harm. The customers were businesses and prices were thus likely based on individual negotiations which would tend to rule out coordinated effects.[830] The CCPC claimed that the proposed transaction would mean that there would be only two providers in the overlapping towns and townlands post-merger. The Determination failed to consider whether customers could have switched to other waste operators in adjoining areas, although it acknowledged that switching costs were low. According to the Determination the parties argued that the geographic market for individual C&I waste collection services was regional in line with previous CA/CCPC decisions in *PandaGreen/Greenstar* and *Greenstar/Veolia.* The target and a third operator both had processing facilities in Dundalk in County Louth

---

parties would have a market share of less than 20% in any UK potential market (UKCMA ME/6939/21 – *Glennon Bros/Balcas*, 9.9.2021).

828 CCPC M/23/001 – *DFDS/McBurney Transport,* 27.2.2023. The transaction appears to have come within the CCPCMG2014 safe harbour thresholds. See also CCPC M/15/016 – *PRL/Moran Freight Services*, 11.5.2015 and M/17/004 – *Primeline/Johnson Bros*, 16.2.2017.

829 As pointed out in **Chapter 3**, the CCPC concluded that no issue arose in respect of domestic waste collection services because the geographic overlap between the parties was limited, and the target was only active to a limited extent in the overlap areas. The target indicated that its customers in the overlap areas accounted for [5-10]% of its domestic waste customers in the county (¶87).

830 The Determination provided no market share data, so it is not known whether market shares were symmetric.

which were significantly closer to most of the overlapping areas than the purchaser's facility in County Meath.[831] The Determination also stated that the target mainly operated in the Northern part of County Louth while the purchaser provided individual C&I waste collection services throughout the county.

In *Thornton's/Carducci* the CCPC expressed concerns in relation to domestic waste collection services in certain overlapping areas within three of the four Dublin local authority areas. The number of customers and the areas within which the CCPC alleged competition was harmed were arguably insufficient to substantially lessen competition (see **Chapter 3**). **Chapter 6** suggested that the CCPC's concerns implicitly assumed market definitions which were overly narrow, while **Chapter 7** pointed out that they were based purely on market structure and concentration within those limited areas. Together, these factors suggest a potential false positive. In contrast to *PandaGreen/Greenstar,* the Determination did not consider whether the transaction could have had adverse competitive effects beyond the overlap areas. An analysis of pricing data across each of the local authority areas could have provided useful insights in this regard. Market shares for the three local authority areas are outlined in **Table 8.4**.

Table 8.4: Domestic Waste Collection Services Market Shares in Dublin Local Authority Areas

	DCC	FCC	SDCC
Thornton's	[5-10]%	[10-15]%	[30-35]%
Citybin (Carducci)	[30-35]%	[10-15]%	[5-10]%
PandaGreen	-	[35-40]%	-
Greyhound	[60-65]%	[35-40]%	[55-60]%
Advanced	[0-5]%	[0-5]%	[0-5]%
Total	**100.0**	**100.0**	**100.0**
Customer Increment	1.0%	5.0%	0.1%

Source: Thornton's/Carducci, Tables 3-5 and CSO *Census of Population* Profile 2 – Housing in Ireland F2063 – Private Dwellings in Permanent Housing Units. Accessed 5.12.2023.

The transaction involved a four to three merger in two local authority areas and a five to four merger in FCC. Market symmetry increased in all three

[831] The purchaser's waste processing facility was 53 kilometres from Dundalk which the Determination listed as one of the overlapping areas (Google Maps, visited 9.1.2025).

cases. In FCC, the transaction would have left three operators with quite similar market shares and a combined market share of [90-95]%. It would have increased symmetry between the two largest operators with a combined market share of [90-95]% in Dublin City and SDCC. Prices for domestic waste collection services are likely to be reasonably transparent. In Dublin City and Fingal, the merging parties were the second and third largest operators with [35-45]% of the market between them. Arguably both unilateral and coordinated effects were possible in all three local authority areas and should at least have been considered.[832] In other words, by focusing on very narrow areas, the CCPC may have failed to recognise the potential for competitive harm in a wider geographic market. This highlights the importance of considering appropriate theories of harm rather than basing competition concerns solely on market concentration levels. This has implications for the effectiveness of the remedies applied a point which is considered in **Chapter 11**.

The CCPC in *Landmark/BenchWarmers*[833] advanced a rather unusual argument that, even if the parties were competing in the same market, the transaction would not give rise to any competition concerns because the target *"is likely to generate minimal turnover in the State from the sale of online advertising space"* (¶17).[834] This begs the question of why someone would acquire a firm that had a minimal turnover.

Potential Competition

As pointed out in **Chapter 4,** a merger between an incumbent and a potential entrant may harm competition:

i. If the potential entrant would have entered the market in the absence of the merger thereby increasing competition in the market (the *"actual potential entrant"* theory);

ii. If the threat of entry by the potential entrant exercised a competitive constraint on market incumbents preventing them from raising prices (the *"perceived potential entrant"* theory) (Brenner, 1999).

---

832 Arguably waste collection services are homogenous. There is some evidence of attempts at product differentiation in domestic waste collection services. Some operators provide a free bin washing service, while others include bin liner bags (for compost waste bins) as part of their service. This might complicate attempts at coordination.

833 CCPC M/17/017 – *Landmark/BenchWarmers*, 2.5.2017.

834 This statement is repeated at ¶19. According to the decision, all of BenchWarmers' revenue was generated from the sale of online advertising within the State (¶12).

Gilbert & Melamed (2024), however, argue that there is little economic support for distinguishing between actual and perceived potential entrants, which they describe as largely a product of historic US court decisions. They further suggest that US courts have over-estimated benefits of perceived potential entry by underestimating effect of actual potential entry.

The threat of entry by Southwest Airlines on US internal air routes resulted in price cutting by incumbents (*ibid.*). Kwoka & Shumilkina (2010) reported fare increases of 9% on routes where the parties were competitors and 5% on routes where the merging parties were potential competitors following the *US Air/Piedmont* merger.

A merger between an actual potential competitor and an incumbent has no effect on the number of competitors in the market. Hovenkamp (2024) notes that there is some doubt whether US legislation applies to actual potential entry because §7 of the *Clayton Act* prohibits mergers which *"may substantially lessen competition"* not mergers which fail to increase competition. He suggests that such a merger may only be unlawful to the extent that it prevents the increased competition that would have occurred had the firm entered *de novo* rather than *via* a merger, although this view is rejected by Gilbert & Melamed (2024). If there are a large number of potential entrants, then a merger involving one of them will have relatively little impact on competition. Thus, an actual potential entrant theory of harm is only likely to apply if there are very few potential entrants (Hovenkamp, 2024). The US Supreme Court recognised this in *Procter & Gamble* noting that *"the number of potential entrants was not so large that the elimination of one would be insignificant"*.[835] The US anti-trust agencies are required to show that, absent the merger, the potential entrant would have entered the market rapidly and been viable, and that there were few other likely potential entrants.[836]

Gilbert & Melamed (2024) note that mergers between market incumbents and potential or nascent competitors can be harmful even if there is a relatively low probability of entry occurring absent the merger. They suggest that, rather than focusing on the probability of harm due to the elimination of potential competition, the analysis should adopt a sliding scale taking account of the magnitude of the benefits that would accrue to consumers or suppliers from successful entry.

---

835 *FTC v. Procter & Gamble Co.*, 386 US 568, 581 (1967).

836 *FTC v. Steris Corp.*, 133 F. Supp. 3d 962 (N.D. Ohio, 2015). Shapiro (2019) called for a lowering of this evidentiary threshold in order to prevent killer acquisitions (see above).

USHMG2023 devotes considerable attention to potential competition, the first time in 50 years that this issue has been addressed in the *Guidelines* (Gilbert & Melamed, 2024). §2.4.A states that the anti-trust agencies will examine whether:

i. One or both of the merging firms had a reasonable probability of entering the relevant market other than through an anti-competitive merger' and
ii. Such entry offered *"a substantial likelihood of ultimately producing deconcentration of the market or other significant procompetitive effects"*.

The EU Commission has applied actual potential competitor theories in several merger cases.[837] It applied a perceived potential entrant theory in *Deutsche Börse/NYSE Euronext*.[838]

The CA/CCPC has rarely raised potential competition concerns. In *STA Travel/USIT* the CA acknowledged that the purchaser was a potential entrant in several markets in which USIT held a monopoly but argued that it was no more likely to enter than two other potential entrants without advancing any supporting evidence. Gilbert & Melamed (2024) state that whether other firms are equally likely to enter is irrelevant. The issue is whether the merger reduces the likelihood of disruptive entry in the future.

In a Determination that runs to just six paragraphs, the CA in *Ryanair/Buzz*[839] stated that Buzz was unlikely to be a substantial potential competitor on point-to-point services without any explanation for its conclusion. The CA concluded that the parties were not potential competitors in *Millington/Siteserv* as there was no evidence of the acquirer having considered entering the market prior to the merger implying an actual potential entrant theory. In *Abbott/Natural Supplements Association*[840]

---

837 EU Commission Case Nos. COMP/M.1630 – *Air Liquide/BOC*, 18.1.2000; COMP/M.1853 – *EDF/EnBW*, 14.9.2006; *General Electric/Alstom*; *Dow/Dupont* and *Bayer/Monsanto*. The latter two cases involved agricultural pesticides which require a series of regulatory approvals before they can be put on the market. As in the case of pharmaceuticals, when such products have secured the necessary approvals, the probability of entry is high as the product development costs are sunk (Gilbert & Melamed, 2024).

838 EU Commission Case Nos. COMP/M.6166 – *Deutsche Börse/NYSE Euronext*, 1.2.2012.

839 CA M/03/005 – *Ryanair/Buzz*, 4.3.2003. *Buzz* did not operate any routes to/from Ireland. Bachis & Piga (2006) report that, in EU markets where the parties overlapped, post-merger Ryanair reduced fares booked in advance on routes previously operated by Buzz, but sharply increased fares on bookings close to departure dates. Whether the merger had a harmful effect on consumer welfare thus depends on the numbers of early and late bookers.

840 CA M/04/058 – *Abbott/Natural Supplements Association*, 1.11.2004.

the CA concluded that, although both parties supplied nutritional products in the State, there was no competitive overlap between them as one supplied products designed for individuals with specific medical conditions, while the other supplied products aimed at fitness enthusiasts and athletes. According to the Determination in *Pfizer/CLS Animal Health* both parties were engaged *inter alia* in the manufacture and supply of animal health products. However, the CA found there was no overlap between them because they did not supply substitute products within the State.[841] The possibility that the parties may have been potential competitors was not raised in either case. The CA in *Uniphar/Whelehan* concluded that short-line wholesalers were not substitutes for full-line wholesalers but did not consider the possibility that they might constitute potential competitors, i.e. that a short-line wholesaler might enter the full-line wholesale market in response to a price increase or that the threat of such entry might exercise a competitive constraint.[842]

In *Southbank/Travel Channel*[843] the CA concluded that *"but for this transaction, it would only have been a matter of time before Scripps brought its highly successful Travel Channel to Europe, including to the State"* (¶13), although the Determination acknowledged that the CA had no *"concrete evidence of such a plan"* (*ibid.*). The CA, nevertheless, concluded that the transaction would not result in an SLC.

The CA considered the possibility that the parties were potential competitors in *Nestlé/Pfizer*. Both parties produced and supplied infant milk formula. Nestlé had previously supplied such products in the State but had withdrawn its brands due to their low sales levels. The CA concluded that Nestlé could not be considered an actual potential competitor despite its global leadership in infant nutrition as there was no evidence that it had considered re-entering the Irish market, apart from through the proposed acquisition. The CA also rejected a potential entrant theory in *Henry*

---

841 CA M/04/009 – *Pfizer/CSL Animal Health*, 4.3.2004. The Determination cites the fact that Pfizer's manufacturing plants in the State only produced human pharmaceutical products. The issue is whether Pfizer could have entered the market by importing products that were substitutes for those of CSL in response to a price increase (actual potential entrant) or whether the threat of such entry was sufficient to prevent any such price increase (perceived potential entrant).

842 **Chapter 6** suggested that short-line wholesalers might have constituted supply-side substitutes to full-line wholesalers. Supply-side substitution and potential entry are normally distinguished on the basis of the length of time required for entry to occur.

843 CA M/12/004 – *Southbank/Travel Channel*, 20.4.2012.

Schein/C&M Vetlink on the grounds that there was no evidence that the acquirer had previously considered entering the market.

The CA concluded that there were both horizontal and vertical overlaps between the parties in *Future/Wrapports/Aggrego*[844] based on the fact that, while Aggrego was not operating in the State at the time, there was evidence that it had considered entering. The CA concluded that there would be a reduction in potential competition in *Irish Wind/SMS*[845] but that it was insufficient to raise any competition concerns. The CA acknowledged that the purchaser in *Oasis Dental/Smiles*[846] might be a potential competitor but stated that the transaction raised no competition concerns, without giving specific reasons for this conclusion.

mytaxi/Hailo[847] involved a merger of two taxi dispatch services providers. The transaction was cleared unconditionally on the grounds that the purchaser was not active in the State and there was therefore no horizontal overlap between the parties without any consideration of potential competition. Similarly, potential competition was not considered in *Big Bus Tours/Irish City Tours*,[848] which involved the acquisition of an undertaking that provided hop-on/hop-off bus tours of Dublin city by an undertaking that provided similar services in 19 other European cities.

In *March UK/GUS Ireland*[849] the target undertaking carried on a home shopping catalogue business in the State, while the acquirer, through its Littlewoods business, operated a similar business in the UK, including Northern Ireland. The CA considered both an actual and a perceived potential competitor theory.

> *"As Littlewoods had no entry plans, and as a potential entrant it was not found to currently constrain the behaviour of existing competitors within the State, the Authority found that the acquisition would not result in the removal of a significant competitive constraint from the market" (¶7).*

The CA decided in *Abbott/TheraSense*[850] that, although the merging parties both produced glucose monitoring systems for diabetes patients, there was no competitive overlap in the State because the Target did not sell product

---

844 CA M/14/003 – *Future/Wrapports/Aggrego*, 24.2.2014.
845 CA M/14/010 – *Irish Wind/SWS*, 17.4.2014.
846 CA M/14/011 – *Oasis Dental/Smiles*, 2.5.2014.
847 CCPC M/16/037 – *mytaxi/Hailo*, 2.9.2016.
848 CCPC M/18/034 – *Big Bus Tours/Irish City Tours*, 7.6.2018.
849 CA M/03/016 – *March UK/GUS Ireland*, 15.7.2003.
850 CA M/04/006 – *Abbott/TheraSense*, 26.2.2004.

in the State. The Determination did not consider potential competition even though TheraSense sold its products in Northern Ireland.[851]

Downstream Competition

The CA/CCPC has argued in several mergers between grocery wholesalers that the parties overlapped in both the retail and wholesale grocery markets because of franchise agreements with retailers who traded under a brand name (fascia) that was owned by the wholesaler.[852] In arguing that grocery wholesaler/franchisors are active in the retail grocery market by virtue of their agreements with retail franchisees, the CA/CCPC is implicitly treating the franchisors and franchisees as if they were fully vertically-integrated. In other words, it assumes that franchise stores are no different to wholesaler-owned and -operated stores. If a wholesaler/franchisor owns and operates a retail outlet it can set the retail price, but the CA acknowledged in *BWG/Mangan's* that the wholesalers did not control the selling prices of their affiliated retailers (¶19). The CA also stated that it was relatively easy for franchisees to switch between franchisors. Wholesaler-owned stores can only switch if the wholesaler decides to sell the store.

The parties in *BWG/Londis* argued that the proposed transaction could not give rise to unilateral effects in any local market because franchisees cannot internalise the diversion in sales from a unilateral price increase post-merger.

> *"It may well be the case that if a Spar store raises its prices, some of the lost sales will be captured by a Londis store in the same local market. However, the Spar store's profits would be reduced and it would not benefit from the fact that some of its lost sales would accrue to the Londis store. There is no reason why the Spar owner would want to increase the profits of a rival. The stores will still be*

---

851 The Determination states that TheraSense had a small share of the market in the UK, including Northern Ireland. It is not clear whether TheraSense was a new entrant in the UK. The Determination refers to Abbott acquiring all the issued shares in TheraSense which it did not already own but provides no information as to Abbott's level of shareholding in TheraSense prior to the transaction. CA M/04/043 – *ABF/Littlewoods/St. James*, 25.7.2004, and CA M/06/084 – *BT/PlusNet*, 18.12.2006, both involved cases where the Target operated in Northern Ireland but included no reference to potential competition. Similarly, there was no reference to potential competition in CA M/07/002 – *Eason/Menzies*, 1.2.2007 a joint venture between two newspaper wholesale distributors. Menzies operated mainly in Northern Ireland although it distributed newspapers in County Donegal.

852 See, for example, *BWG/Mangans* (¶11) and *BWG/Londis* (¶33).

separately owned and so the merger will not lead to any internalisation of profits arising from a diversion of sales from one to the other."[853]

The CCPC did not address this point but acknowledged that franchisees *"have some discretion in the setting of prices"*. It argued that competition between franchise stores with different fascias (inter-brand) was stronger than that between franchise stores with the same fascia (intra-brand) (¶79).

The merging parties in *Topaz/Esso* pointed out that dealer-owned and dealer-operated (Do/Do) filling stations would have no incentive to raise their prices post-merger *"because they have no means of benefiting from demand driven to other sites served by the merged entity"* while the agreements for the supply of fuel to Do/Do filling stations limited the supplier's ability to increase the wholesale price. The CCPC acknowledged that fuel wholesalers did not control prices in Do/Do filling stations and that this claim had some merit but argued that it was overstated. It claimed that, if the merged entity raised prices at some or all of its Co/Co stations post-merger, it would capture some of the returns from retail sales lost to Do/Do stations *via* wholesale sales. Whether this would render a retail price increase at Co/Co stations profitable would depend on whether a sufficient proportion of sales lost would be captured by the Do/Do stations, but the CCPC advanced no evidence on this point. It also argued that the Do/Do stations might accommodate a price increase by raising their own prices due to possible tacit understandings between the merged entity and its Do/Do stations. It speculated that the parties could share the increased Do/Do profits through a slightly higher wholesale price or a lump sum payment, which would seem to require more than a tacit understanding between the parties (¶173-175).[854]

Musgrave/Caulfield involved the acquisition by a grocery wholesaler of three supermarkets operated by a franchisee under the wholesaler's fascia. The CCPC only considered whether there were overlaps between the target stores and stores that were owned and operated by the wholesaler franchisor and excluded other franchise-operated outlets trading under the same store fascia. Having acknowledged in *BWG/Londis* that grocery franchisees had some discretion in setting retail prices the CCPC argued

---

853 Compecon Economic Report *Economic Analysis of Proposed Acquisition by BWG Foods Limited of ADM Londis Limited,* February 2015, submitted with Notification documents, p.23, quoted at ¶75.

854 CCPC (2022, November) acknowledged that a fuel supplier *"has no control over the retail price set by Do/Do stations in its wider network"* FNxxi.

that the franchise arrangements meant that the target was not a close competitor of a supermarket owned by the purchaser trading under the same fascia so that the competitive landscape would not change as a result of the merger.[855]

Barriers to Entry

Firms cannot exercise market power if a market is characterised by relatively free entry and exit. In the absence of entry barriers, any attempt to raise prices will simply cause new firms to enter the market, forcing prices down again. Lamoreaux (2019) observes that few of the giant firms that emerged from the US Great Merger Movement around the beginning of the 20th century maintained their dominant positions for long, as most of them were unable to create entry barriers. Consequently, even where mergers result in markets being highly concentrated, they are unlikely to adversely affect competition provided entry barriers are relatively low. Conversely, market power may prove durable in markets where barriers to entry exist.[856]

Contestability theory argues that, in the absence of entry barriers, markets will operate competitively as the threat of entry will exercise a sufficient constraint on incumbents even in highly concentrated markets (Baumol *et al.*, 1986). According to this theory entry costs only constitute a barrier to entry if they cannot be recouped if the entrant is subsequently forced to exit the market. Costs that cannot be recouped on exit are said to be *"sunk"*. Schwartz (1986) states that the theory has limited applications, while Schmalensee (1987) stated that contestable markets were extremely rare. Armstrong *et al.* (1994) observe that one of its key assumptions, that firms can enter a market faster than incumbents can respond by cutting prices, is unrealistic. Even minor relaxations in the conditions required for perfect contestability generate very different outcomes to those predicted by the theory. It is now recognised that few, if any, industries satisfy the requirements for contestable markets (Gilbert & Melamed, 2024).

The US anti-trust agencies adopted a relatively lenient approach to airline mergers in the 1980s based on a mistaken view that airline markets were contestable. Bailey & Baumol (1984) suggest, however, that airlines' behaviour resembles that suggested by standard oligopoly models rather

855 CCPC M/22/065 – *Musgrave/Caulfield*, 24.3.2023, ¶49.

856 Collard-Wexler (2014) reported that, in cases of merger to monopoly in the US ready-mixed concrete industry, the merged entity's monopoly position persisted for up to a decade.

than that of competitors in a contestable market. Schmalensee (1987) also rejected the view that airline markets were contestable. Airline hub and spoke route networks (Shy, 2001) and difficulties in acquiring take-off and landing slots at airports constitute entry barriers. The EU Commission concluded in *British Midland v. Aer Lingus*[857] that airlines wishing to enter the Dublin-London Heathrow route would require scarce take-off and landing slots at Heathrow which could be used for other routes. UK competition agencies arguably adopted an overly lenient approach to consolidation in newly-liberalised local bus markets based on a mistaken view that such markets were contestable (Beesley, 1990).

The CA in *Coillte/Balcas* stated that the sawmilling industry in Ireland was characterised *"by low entry barriers and high exit barriers"* (¶4.28). As Carlton & Perloff (2000) observe, sunk costs make exit costly and therefore prevent entry, i.e. exit costs constitute a barrier to entry. McAfee *et al.* (2004) point out that because an incumbent has already incurred "sunk costs" it will be reluctant to exit the market. In homogenous goods markets even low levels of sunk costs may act as an entry barrier (Shy, 1995).

There has been considerable debate in the economics literature on the question of what constitutes a barrier to entry and the assessment of entry in merger cases (Coate, 2008). The lack of quantitative analysis of entry in merger cases has been criticised (Cabral, 2003; Schmalensee, 2004). USHMG1992 provided for a more detailed and sophisticated analysis of entry (Shapiro, 2010) and introduced the concept of minimum viable scale (MVS), developed in Salop (1991), for assessing whether successful entry was possible.[858] A high MVS makes entry unlikely for three reasons:

i. Successful entry is less likely to be achieved;
ii. Incumbents are more likely to fight by cutting prices;
iii. The greater are sunk costs, the greater the entrant's exposure.

McAfee *et al.* (2004) observe that the failure by economists to reach a consensus on the definition of entry barriers had probably hindered the development of efficient anti-trust policy. Carlton (2004) claims that application of the concept of entry barriers in competition cases had misled courts and regulatory agencies.

---

857 Case 92/213 – *British Midland v. Aer Lingus*, 26.2.1992, OJ 1993 L96/34, 10.4.1992.

858 *"The concept of minimum viable scale (MVS) differs from the concept of minimum efficient scale (MES). While MES is the smallest scale at which average costs are minimized, MVS is the smallest scale at which average costs equal the premerger price."* (USHMG1992, §3.3).

One view of entry barriers focuses on factors that enable firms to enjoy supernormal profits in the long-run without attracting new entrants - long-run barriers to entry. This view defines entry barriers as a cost which must be borne by firms seeking to enter an industry but is not/was not borne by incumbents (Stigler, 1968). It is now widely recognised that incumbents can act strategically to discourage entry. Consequently, a distinction is drawn between exogenous entry barriers, which are determined independently of the firms in a market, and endogenous, or artificial, entry barriers, which are the result of strategic behaviour by incumbents that is designed to impede entry by exploiting some asymmetry between the incumbent and the new entrant, increasing the latter's costs. Such barriers may enable firms to maintain prices above their competitive level for a time, i.e. they may constitute barriers to entry in the short-run but not in the long-run.

Geroski (1994) states that any durable features of a market which inhibit the ability of outsiders to enter and compete with incumbents constitute a barrier to entry. Barriers to entry thus exist if entrants are attracted to a market due to high incumbent profits but cannot successfully enter because their expected post-entry profits are negative or lower than could be earned from other activities. McAfee *et al.* (2004) suggested that, from a competition perspective, a barrier to entry should be defined as a cost that delays entry and thereby reduces social welfare relative to immediate but equally costly entry. Coate (2008) suggests defining entry barriers as structural conditions or strategic behaviour that prevent market forces from quickly deterring or countervailing anti-competitive effects. Salop (1991) argues that the issue in the case of unilateral effects theories is whether the threat of entry would deter anti-competitive mergers rather than deter unilateral price increases post-merger whereas with coordinated effects the issue is whether the threat of entry would prevent co-ordinated price increases. Werden & Froeb (1998) suggest that, in the absence of strong evidence that an otherwise anti-competitive merger would generate significant efficiency gains, there are strong grounds for presuming entry barriers would prevent entry post-merger.

Entry is unlikely if entrants have plenty of time to respond before the entrant becomes established. The threat of entry is therefore unlikely to prevent price increases if there are entry lags (Salop, 1991). Entry barriers may be entrant-specific (Geroski, 1994). Brand loyalty and customer switching costs may make entry more difficult.[859] Advertising costs cannot be recouped in the event of exit and therefore constitute a sunk cost and may constitute an important entry barrier (Martin, 2002), as was recognised by the UKMMC in *Kingfisher/Dixons*.[860] In *Unilever/Lyons Tea* the CA cited evidence of high advertising expenditure by the two main tea brands, which between them accounted for over 90% of the market. The CA acknowledged that distribution and marketing costs could constitute a barrier to entry in *Top Snacks/KP Snacks*. Carlton & Perloff (2000) describe patents as a good example of a long-run entry barrier. Patents may confer an absolute cost advantage on incumbents because they restrict entrants' access to up-to-date, state-of-the-art technology, although this will also depend on how difficult it may be to imitate or invent around an incumbent's patent (Geroski, 1994).

Evidence of entry is not conclusive proof of the absence of entry barriers. Carlton & Perloff (2000) reported that half of all new entrants fail. Morris (2002) points out that many markets experience low survival and high exit rates. Thus, entry must be sustainable (Baker & Shapiro, 2008) and even then, may have little competitive impact if entrants are confined to market niches. The CA noted in *Top Snacks/KP Snacks* that, while some entry had occurred, *"establishing a significant market presence is challenging"* (¶4.58.) Nevertheless, it concluded that there was a significant argument that entry would constrain anti-competitive conduct post-merger. The merging parties in *Enva/Rilta* cited an example of a recent entrant in the market for the supply of hazardous waste lubricant oil collection services but the CCPC noted that the entrant had subsequently exited and suggested that its entry was due to particularly high international oil prices at the time suggesting that entry was unlikely under more normal conditions. The CCPC cited entry in *Citylink/GoBus* as evidence that entry barriers were low, although the entrant subsequently exited the market three years later (NTA, 2024, April 12).[861] The absence of past entry does not prove that there are significant barriers to entry but may

---

859 Brand loyalty may reflect perceptions that the entrant's product is of lower quality (Salop, 1991). The CCPC stated that brand loyalty was strong in the brown sauce market in *Valeo/Wardell/Robert Roberts*.

860 Based on an analysis of 129 frequently purchased consumer goods, Urban *et al.* (1984) found that the second entrant in a market would have to spend three and half times as much on advertising to match the first mover's market share.

861 Of course, the CCPC does not have the benefit of hindsight when making its decisions. The fact that entry proved unsuccessful in this case does not mean that the CCPC got it wrong. Rather it illustrates the difficulty in identifying whether entry will be successful.

be because market prices are at competitive levels or the fact that the market is declining (Baumol *et al.*, 1986).

The EU Commission rejected claims that entry would prevent competitive harm in Ireland and the UK in *Kimberly/Clark/Scott* due to:

i. High post-merger concentration;[862]
ii. Strong brand loyalty;
iii. Saturated and mature nature of market;
iv. Heavy advertising and promotional costs of entry;
v. Limited retail shelf space and retailers' practice of devoting major share of space to the two leading brands;
vi. Major investment required to build a new production plant (Levy, 1996).

In *Courtaulds/SNIA*,[863] the EU Commission concluded that any attempts by the merging parties to raise prices post-merger would attract imports from the US and Far East. Neven *et al.* (1993) criticised the EU Commission's analysis of entry barriers in *Alcatel/AEG Kabel*.[864] They also suggest that a more careful analysis of previous entry attempts in *Nestlé/Perrier* could have yielded interesting insights. The EU Commission concluded in *Ryanair/Aer Lingus I* that new entry or expansion by existing operators was unlikely. It stated that *"the strength of both airlines at the same airports combined with their low frills/low cost business model would increase the already high barriers to entry or expansion for actual and potential competitors"* (¶338). It pointed to numerous unsuccessful attempts at entry on routes, and airlines pulling out of routes, in and out of Ireland. The Commission highlighted the fact that there was no example of entry by a third carrier on a Dublin route where Ryanair already operated.

> *"In contrast to other competitors, Aer Lingus has 'survived' on a number of routes against Ryanair" (¶512).*

The EU Commission rejected claims by the parties and concluded that entry was unlikely in *Siemens/Alstom* (Kotzeva *et al.*, 2019).

CAMG2002 and CCPCMG2014 state that entry must be:

---

862 Affeldt *et al.* (2021) found that barriers to entry unambiguously increase market concentration and that such effects were greatest in national markets where the average HHI was 1,400 higher than in markets without barriers to entry.

863 Case No. COMP/M.113 – *Courtaulds/SNIA*, 19.12.1991.

864 Case No. COMP/M.165 – *Alcatel/AEGKabel*, 18.12.1991.

i. Timely;
ii. Likely; and
iii. Sufficient.

In effect these requirements combine the divergent economics theories on entry barriers. The likelihood requirement reflects concerns with long-run barriers to entry while the timeliness condition addresses the issue of strategic behaviour designed to impede or delay entry, i.e. short-run barriers (Coate, 2008). CCPCMG2014 states that entry within a two-year time-frame is generally considered timely (¶6.5).[865]

When considering the likelihood of entry, the question is whether entry would be profitable at pre-merger price levels since entry needs to offset any post-merger price increase. If production is characterised by economies of scale, an entrant may fear being unable to win enough sales to justify entry.[866] This will depend on factors such as the MVS and the volume of sales required for entry to be profitable. McAfee *et al.* (2004) suggest that scale economies constitute an ancillary barrier that reinforces the primary barrier of brand loyalty.[867] Coate (2008) states that the starting point in analysing entry is to consider what is required in order to duplicate one of the merging parties in the market. He cautions that entry analysis is complex and that simply running down an entry checklist may lead to analytical oversights.[868]

---

865 CAMG2002 applied a similar two-year threshold. The possibility that entry in five to 10 years' time might restore competition does not address competition concerns because consumers would suffer in the meantime, while such entry might never happen (Kolasky & Greenfield, 2001, July 30).

866 Where scale economies exist, entrants that attempt to enter at the efficient scale may end up depressing the market price. Alternatively, if they enter on a smaller scale, their production costs will be higher than the incumbent's. Both alternatives result in lower margins for the entrant. If scale economies are large enough, and incumbents respond to entry aggressively, while the market does not expand significantly, prices may fall below the entrant's expected post entry costs of production, blocking entry (Geroski, 1994). Coate (2008) argues that the fact that scale economies may push price below the competitive level does not constitute an entry barrier.

867 They distinguish between primary and ancillary entry barriers, defining the former as a cost that constitutes a barrier to entry on its own, while the latter do not constitute a barrier to entry by themselves but reinforce the effects of other barriers.

868 A number of different approaches to entry is possible in differentiated product markets, each of which may require a unique analysis, as they are likely to involve different combinations of sunk, fixed, and variable costs. He also notes that the sufficiency test requires a critical loss analysis.

The CA claimed that barriers to entry in the Irish video rental market were relatively low in *Blockbuster/Xtra-Vision* without citing any supporting evidence (¶4.16). The parties had claimed in written submissions to the Minister, prior to the referral of the transaction to the CA, that barriers to entry and exit were low (¶5.8). The purchaser subsequently indicated during a meeting with the CA that it would take up to four years to set up an operation similar in size to the target from scratch, *"given the problems in acquiring suitable locations, etc."* (¶5.38).

The CA concluded in *Johnston Press/Clonnad* that, despite the parties having a near monopoly market share post-merger, entry would be timely, likely, and sufficient to prevent a post-merger SLC based on it being relatively easy for freesheet papers to enter the market. The question is whether such entry was sustainable.[869]

The CA concluded that entry was likely to be timely, likely, and sufficient to prevent any SLC in *Galco/Sperrin* following a detailed analysis based on information that entry was likely within a two-year time-frame, while the market was expanding.[870]

Regulation may constitute an entry barrier in many markets. The CA stated that licensing requirements meant that *"regulatory restrictions on entry amount to high barriers to entry into the market"* for local radio in *SRH/FM104* (¶12).

The CA concluded in *Kingspan/Xtratherm* that entry was unlikely, although there had been three new entrants during the previous few years. It argued that this had led to significant excess capacity in the market which represented a barrier to further entry.[871] The CA found that entry was likely to offset any SLC in *Smurfit/Universal Lithographic* but the Determination contains no analysis of the sufficiency and timeliness of entry. In *United Care/Pharmexx* the CA concluded that entry would prevent any SLC, although the basis for this conclusion is unclear as the merging parties failed to provide sufficient supporting evidence.

---

869 The rationale for the subsequent *Metro/Herald AM* merger was that the market was not capable of supporting both titles.

870 Entry is likely to be easier in an expanding market, other things equal (Geroski, 1994).

871 Previous investment decisions by incumbents could influence a potential entrant's view of how the incumbent would respond to entry which the incumbent may try to exploit to its advantage (Dixit, 1980). Similarly, threats of aggressive post-entry behaviour by incumbents are more credible if they have already incurred significant sunk costs, which discourages entry (McAfee *et al.*, 2004).

> *"On balance, although the parties have not provided sufficiently detailed information to establish that entry in response to a modest price increase would be timely, likely and sufficient to prevent any harm to competition, the Authority considers that there is a* ***realistic prospect*** *that entry* ***could occur at some point in the future*** *should prices* ***rise sufficiently****." (¶104,* emphasis added*).*

It is not entirely clear that *"a realistic prospect that entry could occur at some point in the future should prices rise sufficiently"* satisfies the timely, likely and sufficiency conditions for entry in CAMG2002 and CCPCMG2024.

In *Kerry/Breeo* the CA identified several likely entrants but concluded that individual entry by each of them would be insufficient to prevent an SLC. Coate (2008) points out that if multiple forms of entry are possible, considering whether each of them individually would be sufficient could lead to an incorrect conclusion that entry would be insufficient to prevent an SLC. The correct approach is to assess whether their combined entry would be sufficient.

The merging parties in *Sean Loughnane/Crinkle* accounted for [70-80]% of the wholesale supply of own label breakfast puddings. The CCPC noted that contracts for supply of own-label were generally of relatively short duration and concluded that suppliers of branded breakfast puddings could easily bid for contracts to supply own label in the event of any post-merger price increase. The CCPC also concluded that it would be relatively easy for producers of sausages to produce breakfast puddings.[872] In *Kantar/News Access* the CCPC identified long-term customer contracts as potential entry barriers but approved the transaction based on remedies that it deemed adequate to facilitate entry (see **Chapter 11**).[873] The CCPC stated in *Direct Fuels/DCI*[874] that there were *"no insurmountable barriers to entry in the provision of fuel cards"* (¶21) with no discussion of whether entry would be timely, likely or sufficient.

In *Enva/Rilta* the CCPC rejected the parties claims that *de novo* entry or entry by existing EPA waste licence holders would prevent an SLC in the market for hazardous oily tank and interceptor waste treatment services. The CCPC stated that the time span and costs for *de novo* entry were likely to be substantial. Customers contacted by the CCPC did not view other existing EPA licence holders as credible alternatives to the merging parties,

---

872 Arguably both could be viewed as examples of supply-side substitution rather than entry. As previously noted, the distinction between the two depends on the time taken to switch/enter.

873 Aghion & Bolton (1987) and Ziss (1996) analyse how contracts may impede entry.

874 CCPC M/17/042 – *Direct Card/DCI*, 29.8.2017.

while several EPA licence holders informed the CCPC that they had no intention of entering the market.

Barriers to Expansion

Smaller firms already operating in the same market as the merging parties might be able to expand their activities to offset any post-merger reduction in competition. It is therefore necessary to consider whether there are any barriers that would prevent expansion by smaller firms already in the relevant market(s). In differentiated product markets where reputation matters, it may be difficult for small undertakings to expand sales (Schmalensee, 1987).

The CA in *Grafton/Heiton* concluded that no SLC would arise as entry barriers were low (¶5.18). The decision pointed to evidence of successful entry prior to the transaction but also cited plans by existing rivals to significantly expand their store numbers within two years, particularly in local geographic markets where the merging parties overlapped.[875] In *BWG/Mangan's* the CCPC concluded that expansion by existing competitors would be timely, likely and sufficient, citing evidence of recent expansion and planned announcements of further expansion by various grocery symbol groups (¶19). In *Galco/Sperrin* the CA concluded that barriers to expansion were not a constraint. It noted that non-merging firms had plenty of spare capacity and could easily increase output through overtime working or adding additional shifts,[876] in response to any attempt by the merging parties to raise price by reducing output post-merger.

Countervailing Buyer Power

Large buyers may have sufficient bargaining strength to be able to resist any pressure for higher prices post-merger. Buyer power depends on customers' ability to obtain supplies elsewhere. Dobson & Waterson (1996, p.33) point out that multiple grocery retailers have significant buyer power because the range of grocery products has increased much faster than retail

875 B&Q had stated that it planned to expand its Irish operations to 10 stores. At the time of writing, it had eight. The Determination recorded that Homebase also planned to significantly expand its operations. Homebase had four outlets in 2004. When it went into liquidation in November 2024 it had eight (https://www.rte.ie/news/business/ 2024/1113/1480802-uk-retailer-homebase-falls-into-administration/. Accessed 13.1.2025.)

876 The merging parties were reported to be operating close to full capacity.

capacity enabling them to *"credibly threaten to replace an individual supplier with minimal disruption"*. Countervailing buyer power arises where buyers, either because of their size or commercial significance to their suppliers, have the ability to prevent suppliers raising their prices. The key issue is not the relative size of the buyers and the merged entity but whether such buyers could effectively refuse to buy or defer purchases in the event of an attempted price increase. It is not necessary for a buyer to be able to permanently replace a supplier in order to exercise countervailing buyer power. It may be sufficient that the buyer can impose costs on the supplier by delaying purchases or temporarily replacing it with another supplier. Buyer power depends on the buyer's:

i. Ability to find alternative suppliers in the case of a price rise;
ii. Ease of switching supplier;
iii. Ability to threaten to establish their own supply arrangements;
iv. Ability to impose costs on suppliers, *e.g.*, by delaying purchases.

The EU Commission in *Enso/Stora*[877] found that, even though the merged entity would account for 60% of the market in liquid packaging board, the presence of two competitors with a market share of 10-20% each, would ensure that customers would have sufficient countervailing buyer power to resist any post-merger price increase. Fixed costs were high in the production of liquid packaging board which meant that customers switching even a relatively small proportion would have a drastic impact on Enso/Stora's profitability. In addition, the largest customer, Tetrapak, accounted for 60-80% of sales and was therefore in a position to encourage entry by committing to purchase a large-fixed quantity from an entrant, which would reduce the risk associated with entry.

CAMG2002 stated:

> *"Effective buyer power requires that buyers have alternative sources of supply, or are capable of credibly threatening to set up alternative supply arrangements." (¶4.10).*

The CA's approach to the issue of countervailing buyer power in *Kerry/Breeo* and *Heineken/Beamish & Crawford* was inconsistent, although both cases were decided at around the same time. It concluded in the former case that the major supermarket multiples would not be able to exercise countervailing buyer power post-merger. In the latter case it argued that individual pubs

877 Case No. COMP/M.1225 – *Enso/Stora*, 25.11.1998.

would be able to exercise countervailing buyer power post-merger *vis-à-vis* Heineken and Diageo, the only remaining brewers, despite evidence that they had been unable to do so previously when there were three brewers (Massey, 2011). In *Kerry/Breeo* the CA argued that, to exercise countervailing buyer power, the retail multiples would need alternative sources of supply to replace the merging brands but failed to consider in the latter case what beers pubs might replace Heineken and Diageo brands with.

As pointed out in **Chapter 3**, the CA dismissed evidence of the exercise of buyer power by one of the supermarket multiples in *Kerry/Breeo* claiming that it was *"clearly unreliable"* and could be afforded little weight (¶2.63) because it post-dated the merger announcement. The High Court found that the CA's rejection of this evidence was *"unwarranted"* and went on say *"there would not appear to be any basis for supposing"* that the threat of de-listing *"was in any way influenced"* by the merger (*Rye Investments*, ¶9.57). Gorecki (2009) argued that the CA had insufficient time to investigate whether the threat may have been merger-related. A sceptical view is appropriate in the case of merging party documents prepared in contemplation of a merger, but it cannot be assumed that customer's post-merger actions are merger-related and should, therefore, be discounted, because a customer has no obvious incentive to portray an anti-competitive merger as innocuous.[878]

The CA accepted that the larger retail and wholesale groups would be able to exercise countervailing buyer power in *Top Snacks/KP Snacks* but did not consider the position of smaller customers. The CCPC argued in *Valeo/Wardell/Robert Roberts* that retailers might acquiesce to a price increase for brown sauce because it was not an important item for them.

In contrast to CAMG2002 which contained only a brief discussion of countervailing buyer power (CA, 2010, December 3), CCPCMG2014 devote a full section to the topic and defines countervailing buyer power as the *"ability of a customer or customers, because of their position in the market successfully to resist supplier price increases"* (¶7.1). A merger may reduce customer buyer power and merging parties must therefore demonstrate that buyer power would remain effective post-merger. It may also be the case that only some (usually larger) customers will be able to exercise countervailing buyer power, while smaller customers will not be able to

---

878 The CA/CCPC in *Irish Times/Sappho* and *Fitzwilliam/Wittington Canada/Arnotts* cited merging party internal documents in support of a conclusion that they were not each other's closest competitors. In the former case the comments were contained in an indicative offer letter from the purchaser to the target, while in the latter the document referred to discussions about *"risks associated with the proposed transaction"*.

resist a post-merger price increase. If pricing is transparent and price discrimination is not possible then the exercise of buyer power by large customers may benefit all buyers. Where sales are based on individual negotiations customers with buyer power will not protect those with less bargaining power. In *Glanbia/Cold Chain*[879] the CCPC stated that *"the bargaining power of at least some food service operators indicate that the proposed transaction will not lead to a substantial lessening of competition in the supply of dairy products in the food service sector"* (¶19). This ignores the position of those customers without buyer power in a market likely characterised by individual negotiations.

The CCPC in *CapVest/CCIF* reported that the merging parties had claimed that the customers included large retail chains and supermarkets who could easily and quickly switch between suppliers. The Determination contains no analysis of such claims. The CCPC concluded in *CapVest/M&M Walshe* that the merged entity would not be capable of unilaterally raising prices post-merger because it would face competition *"from a significant number"* of other suppliers[880] (¶32) along with countervailing buyer power. The CCPC would appear to be correct in suggesting that large retailers and wholesalers would be able to exercise countervailing buyer power post-merger as there was evidence of spare capacity, although the Determination is silent with regard to smaller retailers.

Retailers' ability to switch suppliers may be limited if consumers display a high degree of brand loyalty to the merging parties' brands, limiting the degree of countervailing buyer power. The CA argued in *Kerry/Breeo* that several of the parties' brands were *"must have"* and the supermarket multiples therefore would be unable to exercise countervailing buyer power. The question is whether consumers would purchase another brand or go elsewhere if a *"must-have"* brand was unavailable in a particular store. Few shoppers are likely to switch supermarkets if they are unable to find an individual item in a shop but obviously customer switching will increase as the number of unavailable brands increases. A large supermarket may be

---

879 M/15/023 – *Glanbia/Cold Chain*, 11.6.2015.

880 The Determination identified four rivals to the merging parties but failed to consider whether it might be in their interest to go along with a post-merger price increase. The Determination did not refer to a specific unilateral effects theory, although from the retailers' point of view, own label gammon steaks and rashers are likely to be homogenous. The Determination's discussion of capacity and the lack of any discussion of whether the parties were close competitors is consistent with a homogenous theory of harm.

able to de-list several products without losing a significant number of customers.[881]

Retailers may have mixed incentives where they sell their own label brands which compete with the merging parties' branded products. As customers they might be expected to resist price increases by suppliers but, as competitors, they may be happy to acquiesce to price increases as it would enable them to raise the price of their private label brands.[882]

The CCPC advanced a somewhat confusing argument about the competitive constraint exercised by private label in *Pat the Baker/Irish Pride.*

> *"The merged entity's revenue from the sale of private label packaged bread, and the proportion relative to total revenue, would not, however, create an incentive for the merged entity to compete less vigorously in the supply of branded products, for example by reducing the price of its private label products relative to its branded products. At the retail level while some consumers might switch to the merged entity's private label product others might switch to competitor branded products. The presence of competing branded products and the switching by consumers to competitor products would reduce the overall revenues earned by the merged entity" (¶149).*

The supplier sets the wholesale price not the retail price so any reduction in the supplier's price for own label bread may or may not be passed on. Assuming that it was passed on, however, then, while some consumers might switch to the own label bread supplied by the merged entity, there is no reason for them to switch to other branded brands since the price of branded breads is unchanged in the example given.[883]

---

881 Massey (2010) points out that in order to exercise countervailing buyer power multiple retailers did not need to permanently replace the merging parties' products.

882 The EU Commission in *Kimberly/Clark/Scott* concluded that retailers had little incentive to resist a price increase for branded tissue products because such an increase would enable them to raise the price of their own label tissue products (see also the example of own label milk described above).

883 Not only would consumers of the merged entities' branded bread switch to its own label but consumers of other bread brands would also switch to its own label in such circumstances. This may simply be the result of an unintended drafting error. If instead of reducing the price of its own label, the merged entity increased the price of its branded bread, then it is correct to say that, while its own label might capture some of the sales lost by its branded bread, some sales would be lost to other brands.

Minority Shareholding

A minority interest in a rival firm that stops short of conferring control over the rival firm may soften competition and thus lead to higher prices and lower output to the detriment of consumers. A firm holding shares in a rival is likely to compete less aggressively with that rival because it will benefit from the rivals' success. Alternatively, if a firm competes aggressively with a rival in which it has a shareholding, any resulting financial losses suffered by the rival will have an adverse effect on the value of the shareholding firm's investment, reducing its incentive to compete (OECD, 2008). Even though the potential investment losses are likely to be smaller than the gains from winning business from a rival, having a minority shareholding reduces the incentive to compete compared to the situation in which a firm has no financial interest in its rival. The minority shareholding by linking the profits of the two undertakings increases the incentive for each of them to unilaterally adopt behaviour conducive to joint profit maximization (DotEcon, 2010).[884]

Before launching its ultimately unsuccessful public bid for Aer Lingus (see above), Ryanair had acquired a 19.1% shareholding in its rival following the latter's privatisation.[885] Although it blocked the merger, the EU Commission subsequently decided that it did not have the power under the ECMR to order Ryanair to divest its shareholding as the planned takeover had not been implemented and Ryanair only held a minority shareholding which did not enable it to exercise control over Aer Lingus. The EU General Court rejected an appeal by Aer Lingus against the Commission decision.[886] The Court held that Ryanair could not exercise decisive control over Aer Lingus. It concluded that there was no concentration as defined by the ECMR because the Commission had

---

884 The report also noted that a minority shareholding may give the shareholding firm access to information about the other firm that would not normally be available to it, which could also have implications for competition. The issue of access to information has featured in several CA/CCPC Determinations (see below). The competition implications of minority shareholdings in competitors were included in USHMG2010.

885 Ryanair subsequently increased its stake to 29%.

886 The Commission had ruled that the acquisition of shares by Ryanair before and during the public bid constituted a *"single concentration"*. It seems strange that, if the acquisition of shares was part of a concentration, the shareholding could be retained after that concentration had been prohibited.

prohibited the merger, and the Commission did not therefore have the power to order Ryanair to dispose of its shareholding.[887]

The Court also rejected a claim by Aer Lingus that a minority shareholding in a competitor in a duopolistic market inherently distorts competition because it reduces the incentive for the shareholding company to compete with a company in whose profitability it is interested. The Court said that this claim was disproved by the fact that, after acquiring its shareholding in Aer Lingus, Ryanair entered four routes previously served only by Aer Lingus and increased its frequencies on six other routes where it competed with Aer Lingus. Ryanair might have competed more aggressively if it did not have a shareholding in Aer Lingus.

Arguably the three-part *Airtours* test for joint dominance was satisfied in this case. The Commission's decision stated that both airlines monitored each other's fares and reacted regularly to changes in fares and employed specific software to adjust their capacities and prices on a daily basis in response to competitive actions by the other. Thus, the market would seem to have displayed the required degree of transparency. Ryanair's minority shareholding would arguably have reduced its incentive to deviate while, as the Commission had noted, Aer Lingus was the only airline to have successfully competed with it so that the reactions of any actual or future competitors, customers or consumers would not jeopardise the results expected from a common policy.

The General Court stated that its judgment *"was without prejudice to the Member States' powers to apply, if necessary, their national legislation on competition to Ryanair's acquisition of a minority shareholding in Aer Lingus"* (¶19). The UKOFT subsequently took up the cudgels, launched an investigation and referred Ryanair's minority shareholding in Aer Lingus to the UKCC for a Phase 2 investigation.[888] The UKCC found that the acquisition of the minority shareholding constituted a merger situation, under UK law and that it gave rise to an SLC.[889]

---

[887] *Aer Lingus v. Commission*, Case T-411/07, ECLI:EU:T:2010:281, 2010 II-03691. The EU Commission subsequently objected to parties holding minority shareholdings in competitors in a number of merger cases (Moavero Milanesi & Winterstein, 2002). Examples include Case Nos. COMP/M.1080 – *Thyssen/Krupp*, 2.6.1998; COMP/M.1082 – *Allianze/AGF*, 8.5.1998; COMP/M.1712 – *Generali/INA*, 12.1.2000; COMP/M.1980 – *Volvo/Renault*, 1.9.2000; and COMP/M.2567 – *Nordbanker/Postgirot*, 8.11.2001.

[888] UKOFT, ME/4694/10 – *Ryanair/Aer Lingus*, 15.6.2012.

[889] UKCC, ME/4694/10 – *Ryanair/Aer Lingus*, 28.8.2013.

> *"The CC found that Ryanair would have the incentive to use its influence to weaken Aer Lingus's effectiveness as a competitor, which would not exist for a shareholder that was not in competition with Aer Lingus, and that it would expect Ryanair to act on this incentive. The CC assessed the various ways in which Ryanair's minority shareholding could serve to weaken Aer Lingus as a competitor by influencing its commercial policy and strategy relative to the counterfactual and concluded that Ryanair's shareholding in Aer Lingus had led or may be expected to lead to a substantial lessening of competition (SLC) in the markets for air passenger services between Great Britain and Ireland. (¶2).*

The UKCC concluded that the potential for Ryanair's minority shareholding to impede or prevent Aer Lingus from being acquired by, or entering into a joint venture with another airline, including its ability to deter another airline from combining with Aer Lingus was particularly significant (¶21). It ordered Ryanair to reduce its shareholding in Aer Lingus to 5%, not to have representation on the Aer Lingus board and not to acquire further shares in Aer Lingus without having obtained approval for an acquisition under the ECMR.

Ryanair appealed unsuccessfully to the Competition Appeals Tribunal (UKCAT)[890] and to the UK Court of Appeal.[891] Following the latter judgment International Consolidated Airlines Group S.A. (IAG) launched a formal bid for Aer Lingus. Ryanair sought a full re-examination of the UKCC's Determination and remedies on the basis that there had been a material change in circumstances since the decision.[892] It argued that the IAG bid clearly demonstrated that the finding that its minority shareholding would prevent another airline from acquiring Aer Lingus was incorrect. The UKCMA rejected Ryanair's claims and upheld the UKCC remedies, noting that IAG announced its bid after the UKCC ordered Ryanair to reduce its shareholding in Aer Lingus and had made its offer conditional on Ryanair agreeing to sell its shares to IAG.[893]

Interestingly Ryanair was ultimately forced to divest its shareholding in Aer Lingus by the UK competition agencies, rather than the CA/CCPC. Irish

---

890 UKCAT, Case No. 1239/4/12/15, *Ryanair v. Competition & Markets Authority and Aer Lingus* [2015] CAT 14, 15.7.2015.

891 Case No: C3/2014/1376 *Ryanair v. Competition & Markets Authority and Aer Lingus* [2015] EWCA Civ 83, 12.2.2015.

892 The UKCMA was established on 1 April 2014 replacing both the UKOFT and UKCC.

893 UKCMA Case No. ME/4694/10 – *Ryanair/Aer Lingus* (Possible Material Change of Circumstances), 11.6.2015.

consumers were more severely affected by any anti-competitive effects as the airlines overlapped on routes from Ireland to many European destinations while the harm to UK consumers was limited to routes between Britain and Ireland.

In *SRH/Capital Radio*[894] the CA raised concerns about potential coordinated effects on the grounds that the merged entities' minority shareholding in another radio broadcaster could facilitate exchange of confidential information but did not allude to a minority shareholding in a competitor lessening the incentive for the parties to compete. The CA in *UGC (Chorus)/NTL* stated that cross shareholding would reduce the incentive for the merged entity to compete with BSkyB as a firm that owns a financial interest in a rival would recognise when setting its prices, that a portion of sales lost due to increasing its prices, would accrue to its rival and, as a shareholder, it would share in the rival's resulting profits on such sales. It stated that the cross ownership/management issue would heighten the incentives for co-ordination in the retail Pay-TV market where there would be only two competitors post-merger and many of the conditions necessary for coordination were present.[895] The CA also argued that common board membership between the two undertakings could act as an information conduit between them so that any difficulties the firms might have previously had in coordinating tacitly could be bypassed by direct communication between the boards. The CA cleared the transaction subject to remedies designed to overcome the problems caused by the cross-shareholding.

The possibility that the acquisition of a minority shareholding in a competitor may be anti-competitive is not mentioned in CCPCMG2014. The only mention of minority shareholdings involves a vague statement that the CCPC may *"consider competitive effects that may arise where any one or more of the merging parties have non-controlling minority shareholdings in relevant third parties prior to the merger"* (¶1.11).

The issue of information exchange facilitating coordination arose in several acquisitions by BWG, a grocery wholesaler, of several smaller wholesalers that were shareholder members and had representation on the board of two wholesaler buyer groups. The transactions were cleared

---

[894] The CA rejected a standard coordinated effects theory of harm due to a lack of price transparency.

[895] The Determination noted that retail prices were transparent; products were relatively homogeneous; one party (BSkyB) controlled the supply and pricing of key inputs to the other; and the potential for margin squeeze provided an effective punishment mechanism.

subject to remedies involving the disposal of the target's shareholding and relinquishing their representation on the board of the groups concerned.[896]

The CCPC dismissed the risk of information exchange in *Kepcar/Greene Farm Foods*[897] on the grounds that (i) the purchasing JV partners submitted that they would not use the target to exchange information; (ii) the purchasing JV partners operated at different levels in the supply chain; and (iii) one of the purchasing JV partners had only a small market share in the relevant markets (¶41). The CCPC raised concerns in *ESB/Coillte (JV)* about the potential for exchanges of confidential information between the JV and ESB in relation to auction bids for renewable energy.[898]

Bidding Markets

When considering mergers in bidding markets, competition agencies frequently analyse the historical bidding behaviour of the parties. For example, they will assess the extent to which the parties have historically participated in the same tender. Win/Loss and other bidding data is frequently used to analyse how often one of the merging parties has been the runner-up in tenders where the other submitted the winning bid.[899]

> *"Unilateral effects will be most likely where the parties ranked first and second in tenders merge...the merger is most likely to be harmful in situations where the merger parties were the two most competitive bidders for a customer as this constraint is then removed."*[900]

In *GE/Instrumentarium* a regression analysis produced by Philips, a rival of the merging parties showed that it offered higher discounts when both of the merging parties were present compared with when only one was present, indicating that the merger would reduce the competitive constraint on Philips. The parties produced their own analysis which yielded contrary results, but the EU Commission rejected this on methodological grounds and because data on discounts offered by the target in all bids in which it had participated were based on the company manager's recollections rather

---

896 See, for example, *BWG/4Aces; BWG/McCarrick; BWG/Tuffy Wholesale.*

897 M/16/066 – *Kepcar JV (Kepak & Oliver Carty)/Green Farm Foods*, 2.2.2017.

898 The CCPC also raised concerns in relation to possible vertical theories of harm, see **Chapters 9** and **11**.

899 Shapiro (2010) describes this as the bidding analogue of the diversion ratio. Botteman (2006) describes the EU Commission's application of Win/Loss analysis in Case No. COMP/M.3083 – *GE/Instrumentarium*, 2.9.2003.

900 UKCC Case No. ME/6132/13 – *Tradebe Environmental Services/Sitka*, 28.3.2014, ¶6.52.

than documentary records (Botteman, 2006). Kotzeva *et al.* (2019) describe the detailed analysis of bidding data undertaken by the EU Commission in *Siemens/Alstom*. The EU Commission concluded that the merging parties were particularly close competitors in *Veolia/Suez* based on evidence of how often the parties bid against and lost out to each other in tenders (Buettner *et al.*, 2022).

The parties in *Jacob/Babtie*,[901] which involved two undertakings that supplied engineering consultancy services on public sector projects, provided data on the results of tenders to the CA. The Determination contains no analysis of the tender results but concluded that the parties' market shares were minimal and there were a large number of competitors in the market.

In *Tetra Laval/Carlisle* the CA concluded that the proposed would not result in an SLC. This conclusion was based on a preliminary analysis in the case of two of three relevant markets.

> *"On the basis of the Competition Authority's **preliminary analysis** in this respect, the Competition Authority concluded to narrow the focus of its investigation and analysis to those concerns identified above in relation to block formers" (¶3.21, emphasis added).*

The merger reduced the number of potential bidders from three to two as only one firm apart from the merging parties, APV, submitted bids in response to tenders by Irish customers for block formers. While Tetra Laval and CPS both produced block formers, cheddaring machines and cheese vats, APV only produced the latter two pieces of equipment although it had supplied CPS block formers to Irish customers. Based on an analysis of bids from 1995, the CA concluded that Tetra Laval was the market leader in cheese vats and block formers, but not cheddaring machines, where APV was the market leader.

The CA concluded that CPS was not a direct competitor of Tetra Laval[902] because, although it regularly submitted tenders to supply equipment to Irish customers, it had failed to win a tender since 1995. It therefore

---

901 CA M/04/040 – *Jacob/Babtie*, 9.8.2024.

902 It is difficult to reconcile this conclusion with the CA's finding that there was a competitive overlap between the parties by virtue of the fact that CPS had bid for tenders even though it had not been successful (see **Chapter 6**). According to the OFT there had been 15-25 orders for the products in the UK over a six-year period from 2000 to 2005. Only two of those orders had been for all three items, while there had been only one order for a cheddaring machine over this period. As the Irish market was considerably smaller, it seems likely that there would have been very few tenders for such equipment from Irish customers over the period since 1995.

concluded that the transaction would have no effect on the number of competitors in the market. In contrast, the UKOFT[903] considered that APV was a credible bidder, despite having won no contracts in the UK over the 2000-2005 period. There are costs involved in bidding for contracts so presumably CPS would not have bid unless it was seriously interested in trying to win the business.[904]

The CA also failed to consider whether the presence of CPS as a bidder, may have influenced Tetra Laval's bidding behaviour. The CA noted that *"many customers do not want to change from their incumbent supplier and that bids submitted by other suppliers may be used to reduce the price of the bid made by the incumbent supplier"* (¶3.10). Thus, CPS may have exercised a competitive constraint despite its failure to win a contract. It would have been worth exploring whether there were specific instances of customers using bids from CPS to obtain better terms from other suppliers, most notably Tetra Laval. The CA stated that Tetra Laval documents indicated that it did not regard CPS as a competitor. According to the UKOFT, the merging firms were the first and second largest world-wide suppliers of the relevant products and switching data indicated that they were each other's closest competitors in the UK. The fact that CPS regularly bid for such business suggests that it ought to have at least been regarded as a potential competitor, but the CA did not consider this.

The CA also noted that some customers had raised concerns in respect of block formers because the only alternative supplier to the merged entity, APV, did not manufacture such equipment and would therefore be heavily reliant on the merged entity to supply it, without which it would not be able to supply a full range of limited use equipment to customers. APV submitted that post-merger it would be dependent on its closest rival for such equipment. The CA rejected these arguments on the grounds that APV had purchased block formers from other sources in the past and because of

---

903 UKOFT, *Tetra Laval/Carlisle*.

904 In *Siemens/Alstom* the EU Commission concluded that, given the significant costs involved in preparing tenders, firms only submitted bids if they believed they had a significant chance of winning. It, therefore, regarded participation in tenders to be indicative of each player's commitment/strength in the market (Kotzeva *et al*., 2019). Buettner *et al*. (2022) state that, on the one hand, an undertaking that frequently tenders but is never successful would not be considered a credible competitor. However, they state that win/loss analysis may yield fewer observations and where sample sizes based on win/loss analysis are too small, the EU Commission places greater weight on the number of tenders submitted by the parties. The CA did not provide any information on sample size for win/loss data in *Tetra Laval/Carlisle*.

evidence that firms which supplied equipment to cheese processors had purchased block formers produced by other manufacturers. The UKOFT pointed out that APV faced capacity constraints in respect of the production of cheddaring machines, raising further questions about its ability to exercise a competitive constraint on the merged entity in respect of such equipment in the Irish market. The UKOFT concluded that the transaction was likely to result in an SLC in respect of all three products. It found that neither APV nor other suppliers not already active in the UK would be capable of exercising a sufficient competitive constraint on the merging firms to prevent a post-merger price increase.[905] It cleared the transaction subject to the merged entity divesting CPS's *Wincanton* brand.[906]

The CA claimed that the difference in the conclusions reached by the two agencies could be explained by differences in market conditions between the two jurisdictions:

i. CPS competed directly with Tetra Laval in the UK because it both bid for *and supplied* cheddar cheese processors whereas although it bid for contracts in Ireland it had not won a tender since 1995;

ii. Although demand for limited purpose equipment in both countries was "lumpy", the Irish market was much smaller, with less than 10 customers;

iii. Both undertakings had manufacturing plants and/or operations located in the UK, but did not have any in the State.

The claim that CPS was not a competitor in the Irish market because it had failed to win a bid for a number of years is questionable and inconsistent with the approach of the UKOFT in the case and that of the EU Commission in *Siemens/Alstom*. It is difficult to see any logic in the claim that the smaller number of customers in Ireland would support a different conclusion in respect of the transaction's impact on competition. The argument that the parties did not have any manufacturing operations in the State was irrelevant.

In *Nike/Umbro* the CA noted that suppliers of replica sports kits bid for the right to supply kits to top-tier sports teams. The CA did not conduct a bidding market analysis to analyse the extent to which the merging parties bid against each other for the same contracts and whether they were particularly close

905 The UKOFT's conclusion that potential entry by Stoelting, a US producer, would not exercise a sufficient competitive constraint was in direct contrast to the CA's findings.

906 All of CPS's sales of the relevant products in the UK during the previous six years had been under the *Wincanton* brand.

competitors. The Determination concluded that there were sufficient firms in the market to prevent unilateral or coordinated effects.

The CCPC Determination in *Kantar/News Access* implied that between them the merging parties had won most of the tenders they bid for between 2012-2017, although the actual percentage won was redacted (¶44). As noted in **Chapter 7**, the CCPC concluded that the market for car parking management services was not a perfect bidding market in *Apcoa Parking/NCPS*. Subsequently in *Q-Park/Tazbell* the CCPC concluded that the parties were not close competitors based on an analysis of tenders for the provision of car park management services and concluded that the transaction would not result in an SLC in that market, although information on the percentages of contracts won by the parties was totally redacted. The inclusion of data giving a percentage range for contracts won would have been useful given the CCPC conclusion that an SLC would not occur because there were several other undertakings which competed closely with the merging parties in respect of such tenders. In *Cathexis/Jones Engineering* the CCPC noted that, prior to the merger, the purchaser had rarely tendered in respect of process engineering and mechanical engineering projects that the target had tendered for and concluded that the parties were therefore not close competitors.[907]

The CCPC rejected the parties' claim that the relevant markets constituted perfect bidding markets in *Berendsen/King's Laundry*. Gorecki (2020, p.13) states that the analysis of tendering and diversion ratios was *"probably more thorough and extensive"* than in any previous merger Determination and describes the CCPC's finding that the merger would have resulted in an SLC in the healthcare market as *"persuasive"* but was critical of the redaction of information in relation to tenders (see **Chapter 12**).

Conclusions

In order to establish if a merger is likely to result in an SLC, it is necessary to define a mechanism by which it will harm competition. Traditionally the primary concern was on coordinated effects: the risk that a merger would facilitate collusion whether tacit or overt. Since the early 1990s the focus has been mainly on unilateral effects: the possibility that a merger will enable the merged entity to unilaterally raise price post-merger. More recently,

---

[907] CCPC M/22/032 – *Cathexis/Jones Engineering*, 30.8.2022.

increasing attention has focused on the risk that mergers will harm innovation and product development: innovation theories of harm.

Where the evidence suggests that a merger may be anti-competitive it is also necessary to consider whether new entry, expansion by existing rivals, countervailing buyer power, and, in the case of unilateral effects, product repositioning by rivals may prevent any competitive harm.

As indicated in **Chapter 7**, a large proportion of horizontal mergers fell below the level of concentration where competition harms are considered likely to arise and thus did not require a detailed analysis. However, many cases which were above these thresholds were cleared without any detailed analysis resulting in potential false negatives. In most cases which were subject to detailed review, it appears from the published Determinations that the CA/CCPC's analysis of theories of harm was sound. In several cases, however, there are strong grounds suggesting possible Type I (false positive) or Type II (false negative) errors. In a small number of Determinations, the redaction of information makes it impossible to come to any conclusion. The CCPC has analysed potential theories of harm in a relatively limited number of cases.

9: COMPETITIVE EFFECTS: NON-HORIZONTAL MERGERS

Introduction

Mergers between firms that are not direct competitors are referred to as non-horizontal mergers. Unlike horizontal mergers, non-horizontal mergers do not entail a direct loss of competition between the merging parties. Consequently, non-horizontal mergers are considered less likely to raise competition concerns (see, for example, CAMG2002, ¶6.1; CCPCMG2014, ¶5.5; EUNHMG2008, ¶11). Non-horizontal mergers are generally considered to be efficiency-enhancing rather than harmful. Lyons (2008) argues that guidelines for non-horizontal mergers cannot therefore be as precise as those for horizontal mergers. Nevertheless, non-horizontal mergers may raise competition concerns if the parties have significant market power in one or more markets. The EU Commission has increased its focus on non-horizontal mergers since the 2010s (Duso *et al.* 2024).

Non-horizontal mergers frequently involve complementary activities or products.[908] Complements have positively correlated demand, so that a higher price for one reduces the demand for both. Combining complementary activities or products within a single undertaking may yield significant efficiency gains because:

[908] Products are complementary if they are more valuable to buyers when consumed together.

i. Efforts to increase the sales of one product will benefit sales of the other, and more effort will be exerted to increase sales if both products are sold by the same entity;
ii. Integration increases the incentives to cut price, as a price reduction for one product generates higher demand for both, and the benefits of the increased demand for the complementary product accrue to the integrated firm;
iii. Complements are frequently purchased together by consumers and integration may facilitate one-stop shopping (CAMG2002, ¶6.3).

In addition, on the supply side, combining different product lines under common control may result in (or be motivated by) economies of scope.

There are two broad types of non-horizontal mergers:

i. Vertical mergers involve companies operating at different levels of the supply chain, *e.g.*, a merger between a manufacturer of a product and a distributor of the product;
ii. Conglomerate mergers involve firms which have neither a horizontal (as competitors in the same relevant market) or vertical relationship (as suppliers or customers).

Vertical mergers may raise competition concerns if they block rivals' access to essential raw materials or to distribution outlets. Conglomerate mergers are generally considered unlikely to pose a threat to competition, although in a small number of cases they may do so.

Vertical Mergers

The traditional structure-conduct-performance paradigm viewed vertical integration suspiciously. Modern economics theories indicate that firms vertically integrate in order to achieve efficiencies. Transaction costs economics, for example, identified new efficiency rationales for vertical mergers. Vertical mergers also allow for the internalisation of double mark-ups.[909] Salinger (2024) criticises USHMG2023 for providing that the

[909] Double mark-ups or double marginalisation arises where both the supplier and the retailer of a product enjoy some degree of market power. Each will add a margin when they sell the product. CCPCMG2014 ¶5.5 acknowledges that vertical integration will eliminate the double mark-up so that prices will be lower and output higher than when the supplier and retailer are not integrated. Based on an analysis of ticket price data for 393 cinemas in 26 US cities, Gil (2015) found that vertical integration resulted in lower prices and a lower rate of increase in

elimination of double marginalisation would be analysed as part of an efficiencies defence rather than as a primary economic effect of a vertical merger, stating that this suggests a fundamental misunderstanding of the economics of vertical mergers.

Where neither of the merging parties has significant market power, vertical mergers are considered likely to be efficiency-enhancing. However, if either of the parties in a vertical merger has significant market power, the merger may have anti-competitive effects, in certain circumstances, and may lead to price increases and/or market foreclosure (Scheffman & Higgins, 2003). Firms with market power may have strategic goals for vertical integration that are poorly aligned with consumer welfare. Theories of strategic vertical integration using game theory have identified circumstances in which vertical integration alters industry conduct to the detriment of competition and consumers (Riordan, 2008).

A firm is unlikely to have significant market power unless it has a large market share, although market shares by themselves are insufficient to establish that a firm has significant market power, The EU Commission uses market share thresholds as a preliminary screening device in non-horizontal merger cases. EUNHMG2008 state that competition concerns are unlikely to arise in non-horizontal mergers *"where the market share post-merger of the new entity in each of the markets concerned is below 30% and the post-merger HHI is below 2,000"* (¶25).[910] The CA/CCPC has not used market shares as a screening device although, in many individual vertical and horizontal/vertical mergers, it has ruled out potential foreclosure on the basis that the parties had low market shares.[911] This begs the question as to whether there would be some merit in adopting a formal safe harbour threshold in vertical cases. Since July 2020 vertical mergers where neither party has a market share in excess of 25% are subject to SMNP. Whether it makes sense to have separate thresholds of 25% under SMNP and a second

---

prices over time. Luco & Marshall (2020) found that, in the case of multi-product firms, vertical integration reduced prices where double marginalisation was eliminated but resulted in price increases for other products, based on a study of the US carbonated soft drinks industry where Coca-Cola and Pepsi vertically-integrated with bottlers in some areas but not in others. As some bottlers also distributed other carbonated drinks brands, the mergers did not eliminate double marginalisation for those brands. The double marginalisation argument for vertical integration breaks down if price discrimination is possible (Riordan, 2008).

910 CAMG2002 and CCPCMG2014 do not include any "safe harbour" thresholds for non-horizontal mergers.

911 See, for example, *Musgrave/Caulfield* (¶s57-66); *Dawn Meats/Dunbia* (¶s7.4-7.10); and *McMullan Bros./Naas Fuels* (¶7.2).

30% threshold for non-horizontal mergers which exceed the SMNP threshold is open to question.[912]

As in the case of horizontal mergers, vertical theories of competitive harm distinguish between:

i. Unilateral effects,[913] whereby the merged entity can raise prices unilaterally as a result of market foreclosure; and
ii. Coordinated effects where the merger makes collusion easier.

Unilateral Effects – Foreclosure

CAMG2002 focused on whether vertical integration could necessitate simultaneous entry in both upstream and downstream markets leading to market foreclosure. which could occur if:

i. Integration covered such a high share of the market that an entrant to one market must simultaneously enter the second (*i.e.*, the entrant is not able to buy the second product on the open market because integration had eliminated most or all of this market);
ii. Simultaneous entry to both markets was far more difficult than entering just one market or entering them sequentially, e.*g*., if the minimum efficient scale differed between the two markets;
iii. Raising the barrier to entry in the first market had a negative effect on competition, *e.g*., if rivalry was already weak in that market (¶6.5).

Foreclosure is now viewed in a wider context as vertical integration has become the primary focus of the economics literature on raising rivals' costs. Vertical integration may create an incentive to increase price or foreclose the supply of inputs to rivals, increasing the firm's market power by raising rivals' costs (Granitz & Klein, 1996). Strategies that raise rivals' costs represent a more attractive and less costly option than predation for a dominant firm wishing to deter entry, especially if such strategies do not significantly raise the firm's own costs (see, for example, Salop & Scheffman, 1983 & 1987; Krattenmaker & Salop, 1986; Gilbert & Katz, 2001; Scheffman & Higgins, 2003). However, a dominant firm can gain from cost-raising strategies even when they increase the dominant firm's own costs to

---

912 Of 76 merger notifications involving a vertical link between July 2002 and end December 2023, approximately one-third satisfied the SMNP criteria.

913 The CA/CCPC refer to unilateral whereas the EU Commission uses the term non-coordinated.

the same extent as those of its rivals.[914] Thus, vertical integration by a firm with market power in one market can, in certain circumstances, lead to anti-competitive price increases and/or market foreclosure in another market (Scheffman & Higgins, 2004; Normann, 2011). Merger analysis recognises the risk of foreclosure through a denial of access to inputs (input foreclosure) or to customers/markets (customer foreclosure). Thus, EUNHMG2008 state:

> *"A merger is said to result in foreclosure where actual or potential rivals' access to supplies or markets is hampered or eliminated as a result of the merger, thereby reducing these companies' ability and/or incentive to compete. Such foreclosure may discourage entry or expansion of rivals or encourage their exit. Foreclosure thus can be found even if the foreclosed rivals are not forced to exit the market: it is sufficient that the rivals are disadvantaged and consequently led to compete less aggressively. Such foreclosure is regarded as anti-competitive where the merging companies - and, possibly, some of its competitors as well - are as a result able to profitably increase the price charged to consumers" (¶29).*

Note that it is not necessary to establish that the merger would force rivals to exit the market or prevent entry in order to establish a threat of foreclosure. It is sufficient that rivals are disadvantaged and that their ability to compete is reduced.

Input foreclosure arises where the merger is likely to raise the costs of downstream rivals by restricting or denying them access to an important input or raising their costs by making it harder for them to obtain supplies of the input under similar prices and conditions as they would if the merger had not occurred.[915] The concern is that such behaviour will foreclose rivals

---

914 The demand curve facing the dominant firm is the residual demand curve, *i.e.*, the total market demand curve less the supply curve for the competitive fringe firms. Raising costs will reduce the competitive fringe supply, effectively shifting the residual demand curve facing the dominant firm outwards resulting in higher prices. Provided price increases by more than marginal costs, such a strategy will be profitable.

915 Martin (2002) notes that a dominant firm may purchase all of the best sources of raw material even though this exceeds its requirements, in order to force rivals to use lower quality inputs. Riordan (2008) points out that a vertically-integrated firm may raise the price of inputs by artificially increasing its own demand, while self-supply insulates it from such a price increase. Carlton & Perloff (2000) suggest that an incumbent would be willing to bid more than a rival for access to a scarce resource that would allow entry. Heavner (2004) notes that, in some circumstances, downstream firms may be reluctant to purchase inputs from the upstream arm of a vertically-integrated competitor due to expected quality reductions. They cite this as a reason why Burger King and Wendy's restaurants in the US sold Coca-Cola rather than Pepsi,

in the downstream market by denying them proper access to essential inputs, with the intent of extending monopoly power from the upstream market to the downstream market. This is likely to harm consumers if it enables the merged entity to raise the price of the final product in the downstream market. Suzuki (2009) reports that the US *Time-Warner/Turner* merger resulted in the foreclosure of rival TV channels which were not vertically-integrated with cable distributors, led to a reduction in the quality of channel bundles provided to consumers, while efficiency gains were not passed on to consumers.[916]

Salop (2000) states that a two-step analysis is required to establish if input foreclosure will harm consumers. First, it is necessary to establish whether rivals' input costs will be raised or their efficiency otherwise degraded. If so, then one needs to establish if prices to consumers in the downstream market will be raised above the competitive level. Merger efficiencies may cause the merged entity to reduce its prices, in which case the overall effect of foreclosure on consumers may be neutral or even positive. Karlinger *et al.* (2020) note that it may also be necessary to take account of the price-reducing effects of eliminating double marginalisation.[917]

Therefore, whether a vertical merger is likely to harm competition through input foreclosure depends on whether, post-merger:

i. The merged entity would have the ability to substantially foreclose access to inputs;

ii. It would have the incentive to do so; and

iii. The foreclosure strategy would have a significant detrimental effect on competition downstream.

---

as the latter owned a number of competing restaurant chains. Similarly, they state that rivals of American Airlines were reluctant to use reservation systems produced by Sabre which was owned by American's parent company (AMR). Heavner (2004) claims that Pepsi sold its restaurant businesses and AMR sold Sable because rivals' reluctance to purchase from them rendered vertical integration unprofitable.

916 The USFTC permitted the merger to proceed subject to behavioural remedies (*In the matter of Time-Warner/Turner,* File Number 9610004). For a detailed analysis of the case, see Besen *et al.* (1999). Chipty (2001) finds that US vertically-integrated cable TV companies exclude rival content distributors but that consumers are not harmed and may benefit due to efficiency gains from vertical integration.

917 Raising the costs of inputs to downstream rivals benefits the integrated firm's downstream arm while eliminating double marginalisation benefits the upstream arm so that it is not a matter of simply balancing one against the other (*ibid.*).

This is the approach followed in CCPCMG2014. The ability to foreclose is greater if the input accounts for a significant proportion of the downstream competitor's production costs and there are no close substitutes (¶5.11). Input foreclosure may be (i) total, whereby the merged entity refuses to supply an essential input to a downstream competitor or (ii) partial, whereby the merged entity raises prices or offers less attractive terms to a competitor. Input foreclosure may not be possible if customers can obtain supplies elsewhere. However, the existence of alternative suppliers may not be sufficient to prevent foreclosure if (i) those suppliers are capacity-constrained; (ii) have higher production costs; or (iii) their products are of inferior quality to those of the merging parties (Salop, 2000). The incentive to foreclose downstream competitors will depend on whether increased profits due to higher prices and sales in the downstream market exceed profits lost on upstream sales to a downstream rival (CCPCMG2014, ¶5.12).[918]

> *"The Commission's principal concern when conducting such analysis is not with harm to a merged entity's downstream competitors. Rather the Commission's analysis focuses on the impact on consumers and, particularly in the context of input foreclosure, the effect on prices to consumers in the downstream market" (¶5.13).*

The USFTC challenge to the proposed *Barnes & Noble/Ingram* merger was based on an input foreclosure theory that the merger would have foreclosed competition in the upstream wholesale distribution market for books. Barnes & Noble which had its own distribution network had announced that it was considering providing wholesale services to other book retailers which would have brought it into direct competition with *Ingram*, the largest book wholesaler in the US, which responded by offering better services and lower prices in order to retain its customers. The USFTC concluded that the proposed merger threatened to raise rivals' costs by foreclosing rival book retailers from an important upstream supplier. Absolute foreclosure was not required in order to establish competitive harm. The fact that rival retailers would be required to use more costly or less efficient suppliers was sufficient to give rise to competition problems (Anthony, 2000). The merger was abandoned following the USFTC challenge. As noted in **Chapter 8**, a

918 Motta (2004) points out that, in the presence of less efficient upstream suppliers of the input, the vertically-integrated firm would prefer to supply downstream rivals itself rather than allow others to do so. It will raise the price of such inputs but by less than it would in the absence of other upstream suppliers. Matsushima (2009) developed a model showing that vertical integration may enhance downstream product differentiation and does not always harm downstream rivals.

proposed merger between the only two book wholesalers in Ireland was abandoned after the CA threatened to challenge the proposed transaction.[919] The proposed transaction had both horizontal and vertical elements as the purchaser, Eason was active at both the wholesale and the retail level. The CA's brief description of the case refers only to a horizontal unilateral effects theory of harm, although had the case proceeded, arguably the CA could also have alleged a vertical foreclosure theory of harm as in *Barnes & Noble/Ingram.*

Duso *et al.* (2025) report that non-horizontal conglomerate and vertical theories of harm focusing on foreclosure have become much more common in EU merger cases. The EU Commission was criticised, however, for finding input foreclosure in the Dutch market for raw milk in *Friesland Foods/Campina.*[920] Kamphorst & Pruzhansky (2012) state that the Commission's theory of harm was unlikely to be supported by economic theory or the facts in the case. The CA/CCPC ruled out possible input foreclosure in relation to raw milk in *Kerry/Newmarket*[921] on the grounds that rivals had their own supplies of raw milk, and *North Cork Co-op/Feales Bridge & Hedleys Bridge* because the volumes involved were too small. In *Lakeland/LacPatrick*[922] the CCPC did not consider possible foreclosure in liquid milk although it considered and rejected possible input foreclosure in respect of bulk supplies of buttermilk and yoghurt. The UKCMA concluded in *Lakeland/LacPatrick* that the merged entity would not have the ability to engage in input foreclosure in respect of raw milk.

Customer foreclosure may occur when an upstream firm integrates with an important downstream customer. The merger may foreclose rivals' access to a sufficient customer base thereby reducing their ability or incentive to compete. This could reduce competitors' sales below the MVS forcing them to exit the market. Even if rivals are not forced to exit, customer foreclosure may increase their marginal costs, limiting their ability to compete effectively (Salop, 2000). In turn, this may raise downstream rivals' costs by making it harder for them to obtain supplies of

---

919 *Eason/Argosy.*

920 EU Commission Case No. COMP/M.5046 – *Friesland Foods/Campina*, 17.12.2008. The Commission sought additional remedies to divestments offered by the merging parties to address horizontal concerns.

921 CA M/10/029 – *Kerry/Newmarket*, 5.10.2010.

922 The CA/CCPC did not consider the issue of input foreclosure in several other cases involving milk processors (see, for example, CA M/03/021 – *Pritchitts/Lakeland*, 17.7.2003, where foreclosure was unlikely given the parties market shares; *Glanbia/Dairygold*; CA M/11/004 – *Glanbia/Dawn Dairies & Golden Vale*, 1.4.2011; and *Glanbia/Wexford Creamery*).

the input under similar prices and conditions as absent the merger. This may then allow the merged entity to profitably raise prices on the downstream market (EUNHMG2008, ¶58).

Customer foreclosure is more likely if the merger involves a significant customer and hence is a significant source of sales revenue for upstream rivals. The incentive to foreclose upstream competitors depends on whether increased production costs as a result of not purchasing inputs from upstream competitors are outweighed by increased profits in both upstream and downstream markets (CCPCMG2014, ¶5.16). The *Guidelines* indicate that the full effects of customer foreclosure may take time to occur as some time may elapse before upstream competitors exit the market as a result of lost sales revenues. Such exit could then result in the merged entity further increasing its market power in the upstream market and further increasing rivals' input costs in the downstream market potentially leading to further price increases for downstream consumers (*ibid.*, ¶5.17). Although there are certain similarities between input and customer foreclosure, the competitive effects of the latter are generally more protracted and uncertain (Duso *et al.*, 2024). This begs the question of how far into the future one needs to look when considering the likelihood of customer foreclosure.

As in the case of input foreclosure, customer foreclosure can be total, where the merged entity refuses to purchase from a rival in the upstream market, or partial, where the merged entity reduces the price it is willing to pay or otherwise imposes less attractive terms on an upstream competitor. *TOP/KEC* involved the acquisition of two filling stations in County Cork. The CCPC concluded that the purchaser would not have the ability to engage in customer foreclosure within an eight-kilometre radius of the two filling stations. The eight-kilometre radius defines the potential retail market, not the wholesale market, and it is difficult to see how two rural filling stations could possibly constitute significant customers from a wholesaler perspective, so it is not clear why the CCPC felt it necessary to discuss possible customer foreclosure in this case.

The CCPC concluded that the merging parties would not have the ability to engage in either input or customer foreclosure in *Uniphar/Allcare*.[923] The purchaser was one of only two full-line pharmaceutical wholesalers in the State accounting for [40-45]% of the market. The CCPC concluded that the parties could not engage in customer foreclosure

[923] CCPC M/15/027 – *Uniphar/Allcare*, 10.7.2015.

requiring the target's customers to obtain their pharmaceutical supplies from the purchaser as the target had no market power in the provision of professional management services to pharmacies. Similarly, they could not foreclose the market for the provision of professional management services by requiring customers of the purchaser to purchase such services from the target as its pharmacy customers would switch to the other full-line pharmacy wholesaler.

Coordinated Effects

A vertical merger may facilitate coordination between the merged entity and some or all of its competitors in either the upstream or downstream market.[924] For example, the efforts of upstream firms to collude might be undermined by competition at the downstream level and vertical integration into the downstream market by upstream firms might represent a means of overcoming this. A vertical merger may also encourage other suppliers of the input to raise their prices, *i.e.*, it may facilitate tacit or explicit collusion in the upstream market. Salop (2000) argues that this last point is sometimes overlooked in analysing vertical effects which creates significant potential for error.

A vertical merger may increase the likelihood of coordinated behaviour in various ways:

i. By reducing the number of effective competitors through foreclosure;
ii. By increasing market symmetry through increased prevalence of vertical integration;
iii. By raising entry barriers, e.g., requiring simultaneous entry in both markets;
iv. Increasing transparency by making market information available to firms participating in coordinated behaviour, possibly including information on non-participating firms;
v. The merger increases the effectiveness and enforcement of coordination;
vi. By eliminating or reducing the incentives for maverick behaviour (*e.g.*, through vertical integration with the maverick firm).

CAMG2002 noted that vertical integration could facilitate collusion among upstream firms either by making entry more difficult or making it easier to

---

[924] Nocke & White (2007) show how vertical mergers facilitate upstream collusion.

coordinate behaviour by controlling downstream prices (¶6.6). However, vertical integration may also reduce the incentive for the parties to participate in coordinated behaviour either in upstream or downstream markets.

Other Vertical Harm Theories

Salinger (1991) develops a model showing that a vertical merger involving a multiproduct downstream firm merging with the supplier of the inputs for one of the downstream products could raise prices. Stefanadis (1997) argues that vertical mergers can result in downstream customer foreclosure in markets where R&D in the upstream market is important. Acquiring a downstream customer may enable a firm to engage in customer foreclosure. Reducing potential future sales of upstream rivals may make it more difficult for them to recoup the costs of R&D, thereby reducing their incentive to innovate.[925]

Higgins (1997) defines diagonal mergers where an upstream input supplier merges with a downstream rival of users of the input which does not itself use that input. He argues that diagonal mergers are almost as anti-competitive as comparable horizontal mergers but may be overlooked by competition agencies as they are neither horizontal nor vertical. Karlinger *et al.* (2020) cite *Deutsche Börse/London Stock Exchange Group* as an example. The transaction involved the proposed acquisition by Deutsche Börse, which was already vertically-integrated into clearing services, of a clearing house that was an essential input for competing stock exchanges.[926] Innes (2006) developed a model showing that vertical (and conglomerate) mergers could deter entry.

CA/CCPC Vertical Merger Cases

Table 2.3 indicated that only two of the of the 13 mergers referred to the CA by the Minister under the *Competition Act, 1991,* were purely vertical mergers: *Blockbuster/Xtra-Vision* and *Coillte/Balcas.* The CA recommended that the Minister approve the *Blockbuster/Xtra-Vision* merger without conditions on the grounds that it was unlikely to prevent or restrict competition. It considered and rejected the possibility that the transaction

---

925 This is more likely in industries where R&D costs are high or where there are large economies of scale.

926 EU Commission, Case No. COMP/M.7995 – *Deutsche Börse/London Stock Exchange Group,* 29.3.2017. The parties agreed to divest the clearing house, but the transaction was prohibited on other grounds.

would result in either foreclosure or coordinated effects. *Coillte/Balcas* involved the proposed acquisition by the State-owned forestry company Coillte of a sawmilling firm based in Northern Ireland. At the time Coillte was dominant in the upstream market for the supply of roundwood in the State with a market share of 97%. Unlike sawmills within the State, Balcas was not subject to regulations which prevented timber imports. Thus, it could purchase inputs from suppliers other than Coillte. The CA concluded that this provided some constraint on Coillte's ability to raise prices which would be eliminated if the merger were to proceed and recommended that the Minister prohibit the merger.[927]

The overwhelming majority of vertical mergers notified between 2003 and 2023 were cleared unconditionally following a preliminary Phase 1 investigation. **Chapter 4** indicated that only one purely vertical merger was subject to a Phase 2 investigation, while just seven were subject to an extended Phase 1 investigation. These cases represented 8% of all vertical mergers notified. Only three vertical mergers were subject to remedies. These numbers suggest a relatively relaxed approach by the CA/CCPC to vertical mergers. **Table 9.1** provides a summary of these eight cases.

Coillte/Weyerhaeuser involved the acquisition by the State-owned forestry company of a producer of MDF which is manufactured from pulpwood and wood chippings. Coillte already had a wholly-owned subsidiary which produced OSB, which can also be manufactured from pulpwood. Coillte was the major producer of timber in the State, and the acquisition gave it control of the only two board plants in the State.[928] Forests must be thinned regularly after about 12-15 years to maximize output of the final crop. Thinnings are sold as pulpwood to board plants and the revenue from such sales offsets the costs incurred in growing and maintaining the crop until harvesting. Coillte's main customers for its mature timber (roundwood) were domestic sawmills.[929]

---

927 The Minister subsequently made an Order prohibiting the merger.

928 At the time of the transaction, Coillte accounted for approximately 76% of roundwood supplies in the State, with 11% percent coming from Northern Ireland and 6% from private growers. Imports were effectively prohibited on plant health grounds, with the exception of a limited area in Scotland, which accounted for the remaining 7% of supplies. While private forestry planting in Ireland had increased since the mid-1990s, Coillte was expected to remain dominant in the production of timber for approximately 15-20 years after the proposed transaction due to the time required for forests to mature under Irish growing conditions.

929 A proportion of the final roundwood ends up as wood chippings and residues, which the sawmills sold to board plants.

Table 9.1: Extended Phase 1/Phase 2 Vertical Mergers, 2003-2023

Case No.	Case Name	Decision Date	Investigation Stage	Outcome
M/06/057	*Coillte/ Weyerhaeuser*	10.11.2006	Phase 2	Cleared without conditions
M/12/002	*Millington/ Siteserv*	21.5.2012	Extended Phase 1	Cleared without conditions
M/17/005	*VHI/ Swiftcare*	10.5.2017	Extended Phase 1	Cleared without conditions
M/17/021	*Applegreen/ JFT*	30.6.2017	Extended Phase 1	Cleared with remedies
M/17/040	*INM/ Caltray*	11.10.2017	Extended Phase 1	Cleared without conditions
M/18/053	*PandaGreen/ Knockharley*	26.9.2019	Extended Phase 1	Cleared with remedies
M/23/004	*John Laing/ CCD Group*	28.4.2023	Extended Phase 1	Cleared without conditions
M/23/059	*IFX/Blackhall Facilities Management*	21.12.2003	Extended Phase 1	Cleared without conditions

Source: CA/CCPC.

The CA identified three main competition concerns.

i. **Tying:** As private growers were dependent on Coillte's board plants to sell thinnings, Coillte could require growers wishing to sell thinnings to the board plants to commit to sell their final crop through the Coillte auction system, thus effectively allowing Coillte to retain control of all timber sales as private forests matured;

ii. **Raising rivals' costs:** Private growers would recognize that Coillte would have the power to reduce the price for thinnings, effectively raising their costs and thus discouraging entry in the forestry market;

iii. **Margin-squeezing:** Coillte could increase the price of timber to sawmills, while simultaneously reducing the price its board mills paid for sawmill residues.

Although the CA accepted that Coillte would have the ability and incentive to engage in such strategies in order to maintain its dominant position in the roundwood market post-merger, it concluded that it was unlikely to do so and/or such actions would not result in an SLC.

The CA rejected possible tying on the basis that it would not be in growers' interests to allow Coillte to sell their final crop through its auction system, although this would arguably result in higher (monopoly) timber prices for private growers.[930] It also argued that, given the relative prices of thinnings and sawlog, growers would have no incentive to agree to a tie and would, if necessary, forgo the small income arising from the sale of thinnings. This again overlooks the fact that growers would benefit from a higher monopoly price by allowing Coillte to sell their roundwood. The CA further argued that any attempt by Coillte to induce farmers to enter into long-term contracts committing their pulpwood and sawlog to Coillte would likely result in intense efforts by farmers' organisations to have the government subsidise the development of alternative markets for pulpwood which would discourage growers from entering into long-term supply contracts with Coillte (¶6.20). To speculate that any adverse competitive effects were likely to be offset because customers would be able to lobby the government to protect them is an extremely unsatisfactory reason for concluding that a transaction will not substantially lessen competition.[931] The CA also argued that, to the extent that Coillte would have the power to raise rivals' costs by depressing the price of thinnings, this would not discourage entry because the forestry business was already subject to considerable uncertainties, and the merger would only result in a marginal increase in the level of uncertainty facing potential entrants. Marginal changes matter, particularly for SMEs, and even a marginal increase in risk would increase the return required to justify investment. The CA also claimed that any sharp unexpected decline in forest planting *"might bring about a change in the subsidy regime"* (¶6.40). To repeat, speculation that any competition harm would be offset by State intervention represents an unsatisfactory basis for a decision.

VHI/Swiftcare involved the acquisition by VHI, the largest private health insurer in the State of the 50% shareholding in a business operating three

930 Gorecki (2014) argues that it is unclear why the merged entity would share the monopoly rents with private growers but acknowledges that private growers would have an incentive to sell roundwood *via* Coillte's auction system and share rents with the merged entity if this yielded higher returns than selling independently.

931 Gorecki (2014) states that this was only one of three arguments advanced by the CA.

primary care clinics that it did not already own. VHI indicated that the clinics which had previously been open to all-comers in future would only provide services to VHI members. The CCPC concluded that the transaction would not enable VHI to foreclose rival private health insurers from accessing primary care services in the State because:

i. There were a large number of alternative primary care providers within the catchment areas of the three Swiftcare clinics;
ii. The number of patients who attended the clinics was a small proportion of potential customers indicating that the clinics were not significant providers of the relevant services;
iii. The majority of private health insurance policy holders were not covered for attending the clinics;
iv. There were no significant barriers to entry which would prevent rival health insurers establishing their own primary care clinics.

The CCPC also ruled out possible customer foreclosure because VHI would have neither the ability nor the incentive to prevent its members using other providers of primary care services.

PandaGreen/Knockharley involved the acquisition by an undertaking engaged in the provision of waste collection and processing services of a landfill site used for the disposal of residual waste material.[932] The CCPC ruled out possible customer foreclosure for several reasons:

i. Significant capacity shortages in upstream markets for the recovery and disposal of waste reduced PandaGreen's importance as a customer for those services;
ii. PandaGreen would continue to deliver waste, for both disposal and recovery, to Knockharley's competitors' post-transaction because additional available capacity at Knockharley was insufficient to meet PandaGreen's waste disposal/recovery needs;
iii. Diverting waste from competing sites to Knockharley would have increased PandaGreen's transport costs as the proximity of waste processing facilities to disposal/recovery outlets is an important cost factor.

The CCPC, however, concluded that the merged entity could have market power in the market for the recovery of waste at landfill sites because

---

932 Residual waste is waste that cannot be recycled or disposed of other than *via* landfill.

Knockharley accounted for 53% of total waste recovered at landfills within the GDA with the balance split between the only two other landfills within the GDA. Rival operators expressed concern that PandaGreen might deny them access to the Knockharley landfill post-merger and they would have difficulty finding alternatives. The CCPC also pointed to the fact that the ability to foreclose downstream competitors was increased if capacity was constrained upstream which it said was the case in this instance. The transaction was approved subject to remedies which addressed the CCPC's foreclosure concerns (see **Chapter 11**).

In *Millington/Siteserv* the CCPC noted that the vertical overlap between the parties was minimal and concluded that the transaction raised no vertical competition concerns because *"there are viable alternative suppliers and customers available"* (¶28).[933] Similarly, in *INM/Caltray* the CCPC ruled out possible foreclosure as the parties could not require advertisers and advertising agencies to only use the JV Company and IN&M's online platform in the market for the production, sale/licensing and distribution/disclosure of digital video content for branded advertising in the State. There was a relatively minor potential vertical overlap between the parties in *John Laing/CCD Group* as the purchaser's parent KKR indirectly owned and controlled Q-Park, an undertaking which provided car parking management services in Dublin City. The target owned a car park, the operation of which it had licensed to another car parking management services provider. The CCPC concluded that there was no likelihood of input or customer foreclosure. In *IFX/Blackhall Facilities Management* the purchaser supplied animal nutritional products to the target for resale but as the parties had market shares of less than 5% at both the wholesale and retail level, the CCPC concluded that there was no risk of foreclosure.

Horizontal/Vertical Cases

Table 4.1 (see **Chapter 4**) indicated that 15% of mergers notified over the 2003-2023 period had both horizontal and vertical elements. Of these 189 cases, 22 were subject to an extended Phase 1/Phase 2 investigation and details of these cases are outlined in **Table 9.2**. In the majority of these cases

[933] As noted in **Chapter 8** the Determination also considered whether the parties might be potential horizontal competitors but dismissed this possibility.

the focus of the investigation was on horizontal aspects of the transaction (see **Chapter 8**). Fourteen of the 22 cases were cleared unconditionally.

The CA considered the possibility of foreclosure in *Barnett/Origin/Hall* because rival firms had in the past sometimes used storage facilities belonging to R&H Hall in Dublin Port. The CA noted that other firms had storage facilities in various locations and that there was no shortage of alternative storage facilities located close to the R&H Hall facility. It noted that some of the Hall facilities were underutilised and that it would have no incentive to refuse access given the cost of maintaining such facilities. In addition, the CA argued that, because Barnett had no storage facilities in the State, the foreclosure threat did not arise as a result of the merger but was already present, *i.e.*, the merger did not alter the incentives for Hall to grant or refuse access to its storage facilities. If the transaction had led to the creation of a dominant position in the market, which it did not, then it could have increased the incentive for the merged firm to deny access to such facilities in order to foreclose the market.[934]

The CCPC considered an essential facilities argument in *PandaGreen/Greenstar*. Both merging parties were vertically-integrated, operating in both waste collection and in waste processing.[935] The CCPC therefore analysed whether, post-merger, the parties would have the ability and the incentive to foreclose operators providing waste collection services in Dublin City and County by denying waste collection operators, that did not have their own waste processing facilities, access to such facilities.[936] It noted that foreclosure could be total or partial.

---

934 Under the pre-2002 legislation the Minister had approved the *IAWS/R&H Hall* merger, based on informal undertakings by the parties to *inter alia* maintain existing arrangements with respect to Hall port facilities and to permit third parties to continue using them on commercial terms if they were deemed surplus to the merging parties' requirements (see **Chapter 2**).

935 The CA had not raised this issue in *Greenstar/Veolia* where it only considered the horizontal overlap between the parties in C&I waste collection services.

936 At the time of the transaction, all of the firms providing waste collection services in Dublin City and County, with the exception of Citybin, had their own waste processing facilities. The issue of possible foreclosure would also have arisen in respect of a new entrant wishing to enter the waste collection business.

Table 9.2: Horizontal/Vertical Mergers Subject to Extended Phase 1/Phase 2 Investigation, 2003-2023

Case No.	Case Name	Decision Date	Case Outcome
M/10/026	*ESB/NIE*	29.10.2010	Extended Phase 1 Non-vertical Remedy
M/10/038	*Barnett/Origin/Hall*	21.1.2011	Phase 2 Cleared Unconditionally
M/11/022	*Musgrave/Superquinn*	28.9.2011	Extended Phase 1 Cleared Unconditionally
M/15/039	*Liberty Global/TV3*	2.10.2015	Extended Phase 1 Cleared Unconditionally
M/15/077	*Uniphar/Murrays Medical*	23.3.2016	Extended Phase 1 Cleared Unconditionally
M/16/008	*PandaGreen/Greenstar*	6.3.2018	Phase 2 Non-vertical Remedy
M/17/035	*Dawn Meats/Dunbia*	28.9.2017	Extended Phase 1 Cleared Unconditionally
M/17/064	*Tetrarch/Citywest*	30.1.2018	Extended Phase 1 Cleared Unconditionally
M/18/036	*Enva/Rilta*	20.12.2018	Phase 2 Horizontal & Non-Horizontal Remedies
M/18/067	*LN-Gaiety/MCD Productions*	5.7.2019	Phase 2 Vertical Remedy
M/18/075	*Irving/Tedcastles*	7.1.2019	Extended Phase 1 Cleared Unconditionally
M/19/010	*Formpress/Midland Tribune*	9.10.2019	Extended Phase 1 Vertical Remedy
M/20/001	*Flutter/Stars*	12.5.2020	Extended Phase 1 Cleared Unconditionally
M/20/005	*ESB/Coillte*	5.2.2021	Phase 2 Non-vertical Remedy
M/20/023	*United Molasses/Premier Molasses & Kruden*	25.11.2020	Extended Phase 1 Cleared Unconditionally
M/20/029	*Brookfield (Greenenergy)/Amber Oil*	26.1.2021	Extended Phase 1 Cleared Unconditionally
M/21/068	*Heineken/Coman's II*	16.3.2022	Extended Phase 1 Cleared Unconditionally
M/21/079	*Uniphar/NaviCorp*	15.12.2022	Phase 2 Prohibition (Horizontal)
M/22/007	*Assa Abloy/Arran Isle*	9.6.2022	Extended Phase 1 Cleared Unconditionally
M/22/049	*Uniphar/LXV Remedies (Sam McAuley)*	20.1.2023	Extended Phase 1 Non-vertical Remedy
M/22/065	*Musgrave/Caulfield*	24.3.2023	Extended Phase 1 Cleared Unconditionally
M/23/005	*John Laing/Towercomm*	31.5.2023	Extended Phase 1 Cleared Unconditionally

Source: CA/CCPC.

The CCPC concluded, however, that there was no risk of foreclosure because:

i. There were several other providers of waste processing services to whom waste collection firms could turn if the merging parties were to refuse or restrict access to their facilities;

ii. The expected opening of the Poolbeg incinerator would significantly increase waste processing capacity within the GDA;

iii. The purchaser had a contractual commitment to supply a specified volume of material to the Poolbeg incinerator, providing it with an incentive to increase, rather than decrease, the volumes of waste it accepted from competing waste collectors (¶s4.40-4.44).

The transaction was cleared subject to remedies in relation to horizontal competitive issues.[937]

Liberty Global/TV3 involved a merger between a television channel provider and the operator of a broadcasting platform. The CCPC focused primarily on vertical competitive effects and the impact of advertising revenues on the merged entity's incentives. It stated that, while TV3 had a significant share of the television viewing market, this would be insufficient for it to have the ability or incentive to engage in input foreclosure. It also ruled out possible customer foreclosure partly on the basis of the merged entity's share of broadcast platform services but also because it would not be in the parties' interests to disadvantage rival broadcasters by placing their channels in less advantageous positions on its platform as this would induce customers to switch to other platforms. It also noted that there was a regulatory requirement for platforms to prioritise the positioning of certain FTA channels, while there was also an obligation on TV3 to make its channels available to any network on fair, reasonable and non-discriminatory (FRAND) terms. The transaction was cleared unconditionally following an extended Phase 1 investigation.[938]

---

937 Remedies in *Uniphar/LXV Remedies (Sam McAuley)* and the prohibition decision in *Uniphar/NaviCorp* related to horizontal concerns. Similarly, the prohibition decision in *Uniphar/NaviCorp* related to horizontal anti-competitive effects (see **Chapter 8**).

938 The EU Commission applied remedies in two cases involving TV programme distributors and owners of popular TV channels whereby the parties committed to license the TV channels on FRAND terms. The Commission was concerned about the potential for input foreclosure due to the parties refusing to supply the TV channels or increasing the price for supplying them to competitors in the downstream TV distribution market post-merger (Vande Walle, 2023. EU Commission Case Nos. COMP/M.7194 – *Liberty Global/Corelio/*

The CCPC concluded in *Enva/Rilta* that the merged entity as the sole supplier in the markets for the treatment of hazardous oily tank and interceptor waste and hazardous waste lubricant oil would have the ability and incentive to engage in partial input foreclosure by raising its charges for treatment services to rival providers in the markets for the collection of such waste thus raising their costs. The CCPC stated that processing costs represented a significant proportion of downstream operators' costs while there were no alternative inputs. It further argued that other waste operators would likely have to pass on any increase in waste processing charges so that a partial input foreclosure strategy would result in higher prices for customers.[939]

LN-Gaiety/MCD Productions was primarily a vertical merger, although there was some horizontal overlap between the parties as both organised music festivals. The purchaser was described by the CCPC as *"a global live music entertainment company"* (¶1.5). Its main businesses in Ireland involved the provision of outsourced primary ticketing services for live events through its wholly-owned subsidiary Ticketmaster and the operation of live event venues.[940] The target was engaged primarily in the promotion of live music events within the island of Ireland. The CCPC concluded that the transaction was likely to result in input foreclosure as the merging parties would have the ability and the incentive to refuse (or threaten to refuse) to host live music events in venues or offer less favourable terms for events in venues which did not use Ticketmaster for the provision of primary ticketing services.[941] The CCPC concluded that the transaction was unlikely to result in customer foreclosure by denying other primary ticketing services providers access to MCD because MCD already used Ticketmaster's services and was unlikely to switch to an alternative

---

W&W/De Vijver Media, 24.2.2015 and COMP/M.9064 – *Telia/Bonnier Broadcasting*, 12.11.2019). See earlier discussion of US *Time-Warner/Turner* case.

939 As noted in **Chapter 8**, the transaction was cleared subject to remedies which are considered in **Chapter 11**.

940 Primary ticketing services refers to the sale of tickets for live events whereas secondary ticketing services involve the resale of tickets to such events. The purchaser owned the 3Arena and managed three other theatre venues in Dublin.

941 The CCPC cleared the transaction subject to remedies which it said would address such concerns. The remedies are similar in many ways to those which are widely considered to have been inadequate in the US *Ticketmaster/Live Nation* case (see **Chapter 11**). The CA had previously found that Ticketmaster was not dominant in the market for outsourced ticketing services, despite having a monopoly (CA E/06/001, *Alleged excessive booking fees by TicketMaster Ireland and its exclusive contractual relationships with MCD Promotions Limited and Aiken Promotions Limited*, 26.9.2005). Gorecki (2006) argues that this decision was correct.

provider. Nevertheless, the CCPC had concerns that the transaction would strengthen the links between Ticketmaster and MCD. The transaction was cleared subject to remedies which the CCPC stated addressed these concerns. The CCPC found that, while the parties would have the ability to foreclose rival music event promoters by denying them access to Ticketmaster's ticketing services, they would have no incentive to do so as this would reduce Ticketmaster's profits. Similarly, it found that the parties would have the ability but not the incentive to deny rival music promotes access to live music venues.

There was a significant vertical overlap between the parties in *Irving/ Tedcastles.* The purchaser operated the State's only oil refinery located at Whitegate in County Cork and supplied refined fuel products to the target from the refinery for both its wholesale and retail businesses. The target was engaged in the wholesale and retail distribution of refined fuel products but also imported such products through its terminal in Dublin Port. The CCPC argued that, although Irving would account for [35-45]%, [40-50]%, [30-40]% and [25-35]% share in the wholesale supply of petrol, diesel, gasoil 10ppm and kerosene respectively, it would not have the capability to engage in input foreclosure in respect of the supply of refined fuels as there were three alternative suppliers that customers could obtain supplies from. Arguably Irving's shares in some markets were sufficiently high to raise concerns of possible input foreclosure.[942] Similar issues arose in *Brookfield (Greenenergy)/Amber Oil* as the purchaser had a market share of [30-40]% in the market for petrol in the Munster region where it faced two competitors. The CCPC nevertheless concluded that input foreclosure was unlikely.

The CCPC raised concerns that the acquirer's very strong position in the provision of the service of channelling national advertising to local/regional and digital newspaper titles in the State combined with its ownership of local/regional newspapers and websites would give it the ability and the incentive to foreclose its local/regional newspaper competitors in *Formpress/Midland Tribune*. The CCPC stated that it could:

i. Potentially direct national advertising allocated to local/regional newspapers and digital newspaper titles to its own group titles to the detriment of competing titles; and
ii. Access confidential information from Formpress' competitors and the common ownership of Formpress and Mediaforce could lead to

942 The CCPC reasonably ruled out customer foreclosure as Tedcastles accounted for only 15% of the retail market.

the potential for the exchange of competitively sensitive information of Formpress' competitors if there was an overlap in management or employees or roles/functions between them.

The transaction was cleared subject to remedies which the CCPC stated addressed its concerns (see **Chapter 11**).[943]

The CCPC addressed the issue of foreclosure at some length in *ESB/Coillte (JV)* but ultimately concluded that Coillte would have neither the ability nor the incentive to engage in either partial or total foreclosure following the implementation of the proposed transaction. It raised concerns that information exchange could facilitate potential horizontal coordination (see **Chapter 8**). It suggested that the transaction could also potentially lead to the exchange of commercially sensitive information between Coillte, the JV and ESB regarding third parties seeking access to Coillte-owned land for the purposes of developing and constructing onshore wind farms in the State, resulting in vertical coordinated effects.[944] The merger was subject to remedies which the CCPC said addressed its concerns.

The CCPC concluded in *Uniphar/NaviCorp*[945] that the proposed transaction would not lead to customer foreclosure in the wholesale supply of pharmacy-only human pharmaceutical products (POHPPs), *i.e.,* human pharmaceuticals sold only in pharmacies. Although [60-70]% of all pharmacies in the State would be affiliated to the merged entity, the CCPC stated that customer foreclosure would not occur as [40-50]% of pharmacies were members of buying groups linked to the only other full-line pharmacy wholesaler in the State. In addition, the CCPC found that the merged entity could not engage in input foreclosure, despite its large share of the market for the supply of POHPPs, because it faced a strong rival wholesale supplier whose buying groups did not negotiate wholesale supply terms with Uniphar. The CCPC concluded in *Heineken/Coman's I* that Heineken would not have the ability to foreclose rival wholesalers post-merger because it had insufficient market power despite having a market share of [45-50]% (¶s36 & 38).

---

943 Although there was a vertical overlap between the merging parties in *Celtic News/Westmeath Examiner* (the acquirer provided printing services to the target) this was not addressed in the CA Determination.

944 The CA had also expressed concerns about possible information exchange in *ESB/NIE*.

945 As noted in **Chapter 8**, the proposed transaction was prohibited because it would result in horizontal unilateral effects.

The CCPC concluded in *Synch (JV)* that, following implementation of the Proposed Transaction, the JV and its parents would have the ability and incentive to engage in a total or partial foreclosure strategy in relation to the market for the upstream inputs required to offer MIPS in the State. In its view such foreclosure would be likely to harm consumers in the markets for:

i. The provision of P2P MIPS;

ii. The provision of P2B mobile payments services;

iii. The provision of banking services (including current accounts).

Total or partial foreclosure of potential providers of MIPS would enable the JV parents to protect and maintain their existing high combined share in the provision of banking services (including current accounts). The CCPC view was that it was likely to be very difficult for potential MIPS providers and existing and potential providers of banking services (including current accounts) to compete effectively if they were foreclosed access wholly or partially to the Synch Mobile Payments Service.[946]

Conglomerate Mergers

OECD (2002, p.21) defines a conglomerate merger as one where the parties *"are not actual or potential competitors and the parties do not have an actual or potential customer-supplier relationship"*. Conglomerate mergers involving firms in different industries are generally considered unlikely to pose a competition threat unless at least one of the merging parties has market power in one or more of the markets prior to the merger. Traditionally concerns about conglomerate mergers focused on the potential for the merged firm to use profits in one market to finance predatory pricing in another. It has been suggested that this was a consideration in the EU Commission decision in *ATB/de Havilland*[947] (OECD, 2002). Possible competition concerns in the case of conglomerate mergers focus on:

i. Portfolio effects, *i.e.*, where a merger that may not increase concentration in any one market creates a merged entity with a strong position in several markets;

---

[946] The CCPC noted that the provision of MIPS and banking services (including current accounts) were inextricably linked because users had to have a current account with a regulated payment services provider in order to make a MIP.

[947] Scherer & Ross (1990) noted that challenges to conglomerate mergers based on such theories had fallen into disuse in the US.

ii. Tying or bundling of products, *i.e.*, where the merged entity is able to tie the purchase of one product to the purchase of one or more other products.

CCPCMG2014 suggest that, in the case of conglomerate mergers, coordinated effects may occur across non-substitutable products or services but offers no further explanation of how this might arise beyond stating that factors facilitating coordination in the case of vertical mergers also apply to conglomerate mergers (see above).

Portfolio Effects

Portfolio effects arise where a merger that does not increase concentration in any individual market brings together a strong position in several markets (*e.g.*, a firm with 50% of market A and 0% of market B unites with a firm with 50% of market B and nothing in A) (CAMG2002, ¶6.7). The theory of portfolio effects suggests that market power may be created or enhanced because the merged firm is better able to leverage its products by tying, bundling or other means (*e.g.*, it can use its strength across a range of markets to force buyers to obtain all inputs from it, thereby increasing market share). Conglomerate mergers frequently involve complementary products and may therefore be efficiency-enhancing so that any portfolio effects might well be outweighed by pro-competitive factors.

OECD (2002) described portfolio effects as *"a somewhat vague term for which we could find no generally accepted definition"*. It further argued that portfolio effects did not present new competition concerns but presented traditional issues in new guises. It suggested that, to a considerable degree, the analysis of vertical mergers suspected of having exclusionary effects may be applicable to conglomerate mergers involving portfolio effects.

Portfolio effects theory has been somewhat controversial (Lyons, 2008). The EU Commission concluded in *Guinness/Grand Metropolitan* that post-merger the parties would be able to exercise portfolio power.[948] In *GE/Honeywell* the EU Commission prohibited a proposed acquisition based on a portfolio effects theory that the merged entity might be able to leverage the market power of both companies into the products of the other. As noted in **Chapter 3**, the decision proved highly controversial and was

---

[948] The transaction was ultimately cleared subject to the divestment by the parties of two whisk(e)y brands, the termination of a vodka distribution agreement, the appointment of a third-party distributor for gin in Belgium/Luxembourg and termination of a distribution agreement for *Bacardi* rum in Greece.

heavily criticised (Akbar, 2002 and Motta, 2004). Nalebuff (2004) argues that the evidence did not support the Commission's bundling claim and rejects the view that bundling would have caused rivals to exit the market.[949] The EU Commission decision in *Boeing/Hughes*[950] provides a good illustration of portfolio effects, although the term does not appear in the decision (OECD, 2002). The Commission considered six tying-related potentially adverse effects of the merger but ultimately concluded that these were unlikely to materialise.

EUNHMG2008 contain no explicit reference to portfolio effects but state:

> *"The main concern in the context of conglomerate mergers is that of foreclosure. The combination of products in related markets may confer on the merged entity the ability and incentive to leverage a strong market position from one market to another by means of tying or bundling or other exclusionary practices" (¶93, footnotes omitted).*

They go on to state:

> *"The fact that the merged entity will have a broad range or portfolio of products does not, as such, raise competition concerns"[951] (¶93).*

CAMG2002 argued that portfolio effects theory was subject to several important limitations:

i. It is only applicable to mergers involving complementary goods. If the products are substitutes, the merger should be classified as horizontal. If the products are unrelated (neither substitutes nor complements), it is difficult to see how leverage could occur;
ii. In the case of complements, the merger may be efficiency-enhancing so that any portfolio effects, assuming they exist, could easily be outweighed by pro-competitive factors;
iii. The bringing together of different product lines may result in (or be motivated by) economies of scope for the merging firm, whereby

---

949 Lyons (2008) notes that the General Court was critical of such theories in *Tetra Laval v. Commission* and *General Electric v. Commission*, Case No. T-210/01, ECLI:EU:T:2005:456, 2005 II-05575 while stating that there was evidence of problems much earlier in some of the analysis in *Guinness/Grand Metropolitan*. Akbar (2002) argues that the USDoJ applied a similar argument in *United States v. Microsoft Corporation*, 253 F.3d 34 (D.C. Cir. 2001).

950 EU Commission Case No. COMP/M.1879 – *Boeing/Hughes*, 29.10.2000.

951 Citing Case No. COMP/M.2608 – *INA/FAG*, 18.10.2001, ¶34 in support. This also seems somewhat at odds with CCPCMG2014 ¶5.20(a) (see above).

the total production cost is lowered which would not harm competition;

iv. The theory requires that there is already an element of market power in at least one of the markets.

For these reasons, the CA concluded that *"anti-competitive harm from portfolio effects is extremely unlikely"* (CAMG2002, ¶6.7). It went on to say that, in the exceptional event that portfolio effects were considered, it would need to be clear that prices for consumers would rise within a reasonable time-frame.

The CA concluded in *Sarcon/Barlo:*

> *"There is nothing to indicate that any portfolio effects would occur as a result of the proposed acquisition" (¶6).*

The CA similarly concluded that portfolio effects would not arise in *Diageo/Bushmills* stating that the transaction would not enable Diageo to engage in tying.

CCPCMG2014 are less dismissive of portfolio effects, although their discussion of such effects is somewhat vague.

> *"Portfolio effects,* i.e., *where a merger that may not increase concentration in any one market creates a merged entity with a strong position in several markets" (¶5.20(a)).*

This begs the question of whether the creation of *"a strong position in several markets"* of itself would result in an SLC. In addition, clarity is required as to what constitutes *"a strong position"* and in how many markets the merged entity must have such a position.

Tying/Bundling

CCPCMG2014 state:

> *"The Commission's analysis of unilateral effects, in the context of conglomerate mergers, includes an examination of (i) the strength of competitive constraints and/or consumer behaviour, (ii) the ability of the merged entity to bundle or tie products, (iii) the merged entity's incentive to bundle or tie products, and (iv) the effect on competition, particularly whether bundling or tying would result in an SLC" (¶5.23).*

Tying describes the practice of linking the sale of one or more products to the sale of another. Thus, for example, a firm with market power with respect to product A may supply it only on condition that customers also purchase product B from it. Good A is described as the tying product and good B as the tied product. Bundling refers to a practice where a supplier only sells two or more goods together as a package, usually in fixed proportions.[952] OECD (2002) notes that conglomerate mergers could facilitate tying, bundling or similar conduct. Such behaviour could either increase or reduce welfare. The probability of a reduction in welfare is greater the more the following elements are present:

i. The greater the degree of market power in the tying product or one of the bundled products;
ii. The lower are the efficiencies from such practices;
iii. The greater is the increase in rivals' costs from such practices;
iv. There are a large number of purchasers interested in buying only the tied product or a subset of the bundled products;
v. The more rivals find it unprofitable to match the tying/bundling strategy;
vi. The more certain are prices to rise above pre-merger levels due to foreclosure effects;
vii. The greater the extent to which expected long term price increases above pre-merger levels will be sufficiently large, quickly realised and durable.

CCPCMG2014 state that portfolio effects and tying or bundling do not necessarily result in consumer harm.[953] Consumers may benefit from the bundling of complementary products and from efficiencies arising due to economies of scope resulting from a conglomerate merger (CCPCMG2014, ¶5.22). Competition concerns may arise, however, if the merger leads to a price increase for one or more of the tied products, or if competitors, in order to compete, must expand to also sell the tied or bundled goods. They also note that the cost of establishing the capacity to supply both goods could be a barrier to entry and/or expansion.

The CCPC dismissed the possibility of portfolio effects or tying/bundling arising in *Uniphar/Allcare*[954] without advancing any reasons

---

[952] A variant, referred to as mixed bundling, involves selling the products both separately and as a bundle where the price of the bundle is lower than the combined price of the products sold separately.

[953] Economists frequently cite cars as an example of a bundled product.

[954] The Determination states that the transaction would not lead to *"adverse conglomerate effects resulting in harm to consumers"* (¶15) and this is followed by an analysis of possible foreclosure (see above).

for its conclusions. It considered a possible bundling theory of harm in *CVC/Six Nations* without properly outlining the basis for such a theory. The UKCMA also advanced a bundling theory in relation to this case whereby the transaction could be viewed as a conglomerate merger if broadcast rights for *"non-seasonal"* tournaments, such as the Six Nations and Autumn rugby internationals, and *"seasonal"* competitions, such as the Pro-14 and Rugby Premiership constituted different markets. Both agencies concluded that the merged entity would not have the ability to bundle the broadcast rights for international and club rugby tournaments.

Other Conglomerate Theories of Harm

The EU Commission found that a *"network externalities"* effect in *WorldCom/MCII*[955] would have enabled the merged entity to behave independently of its competitors and customers, and to degrade the quality of rivals' internet-related services.[956] One of the arguments advanced by the EU Commission for blocking the proposed *Tetra Laval/Sidel*[957] merger was that Tetra Laval could leverage its dominant position in the aseptic cartons market into other closely-related markets. The decision was overturned by the EU General Court on the grounds that leveraging was unlikely in this particular case, although the Court accepted that such a theory of harm was plausible.[958]

Conclusions

Economics indicates that vertical and conglomerate mergers are far less likely to harm competition than horizontal mergers. It also indicates that harmful effects are unlikely if the merging parties lack market power in one or more markets. Not surprisingly therefore the CA/CCPC has rarely identified competition harms in vertical and conglomerate merger cases. It remains to be seen whether the EU Commission's increasing focus on non-horizontal mergers will influence the CCPC's approach going forward. EUHMG apply a combination of market share and post-merger HHIs as a screening device for identifying vertical mergers where the merging parties

---

955 EU Commission Case No. COMP/M.1069 – *WorldCom/MCII*, 8.7.1998.

956 Network externalities refer to the fact that the more customers there are in a network, the more attractive the network becomes. See Koboldt (1999) for a critique of the Commission decision in this case.

957 EU Commission Case No. COMP/M.2416 – *Tetra Laval/Sidel*, 30.10.2001.

958 *Tetra Laval v. Commission*. The judgement was subsequently upheld by the CJEU. *Commission v. Tetra Laval*.

are unlikely to have significant market power. The CA/CCPC has not explicitly followed such an approach, although the introduction of SMNP means that vertical mergers where the parties have market shares of less than 25% in any related market are likely to be cleared following a preliminary review. There may be some merit in adopting the EU thresholds for identifying vertical mergers, which fall outside the SMNP but are, nevertheless, unlikely to pose any competition concerns, although having, in effect, two relatively close market share thresholds for defining innocuous mergers may appear somewhat cumbersome.

10: EFFICIENCIES

Introduction

The need to weigh anti-competitive effects against possible efficiency gains was originally mooted by Williamson (1968). Efficiencies may be sufficient to offset the effect of any decline in competition if they result in a decline in marginal cost which outweighs the price increasing effect of a reduction in rivalry (Werden, 1998). In that case, the net effect may be to leave price unchanged or lower than prior to the merger. Hovenkamp (2024) notes that a significant minority of mergers, even in highly concentrated markets, result in lower prices. It is now standard practice for competition agencies to consider whether any anti-competitive effects of a proposed merger are likely to be outweighed by merger-related efficiency gains (Massey & Daly, 2003). Competition is supposed to promote greater efficiency and thus merger policy should favour efficiency-enhancing mergers. Although it is widely accepted that mergers that are efficiency-enhancing should be permitted, many competition agencies have frequently been reluctant to approve mergers purely on the basis of efficiencies. Consequently, parties seeking to justify a merger on efficiency grounds tend to face a high evidentiary burden. As noted in **Chapter 3**, the treatment of efficiencies constitutes a key test of the welfare standard applied by a competition agency (Lyons, 2002).[959]

---

959 A consumer welfare standard asks whether the price-reducing effect of a decline in marginal cost, due to efficiency gains, will at least offset the price-increasing effect of reduced rivalry as a result of the merger. If a merger results in higher prices because efficiencies are insufficient to offset the price-increasing effect of reduced rivalry, a total welfare standard asks whether the gains to producers from higher profits outweigh the loss to consumers from higher prices.

The Evolving Role of Efficiencies in Merger Cases

In the 1960s efficiencies were regarded as a source of unfair competitive advantage in US merger cases (Williamson, 2002). The USFTC in *Foremost Dairies* ruled that the necessary proof of violation of Section 7 *"consists of types of evidence showing that the acquiring firm possesses significant power in some markets* **or** *that its over-all organization gives it a decisive advantage in efficiency over its smaller rivals".*[960] This was described as bad law and bad economics (Turner, 1965, p.1324). Nevertheless, the Supreme Court rejected economic arguments that mergers which resulted in increased efficiencies should be permitted in *FTC v. Proctor & Gamble*[961] on the grounds that they would threaten the survival of less efficient rivals (Ornstein, 1989). Gotts & Goldman (2002) identified eight USFTC decisions in the 1970s which suggested that evidence of efficiencies supported a finding that a merger was illegal. Weir (1993) noted that few firms involved in UK merger cases were able to quantify efficiencies and were thus generally unable to convince the UKMMC that efficiencies would offset any likely anti-competitive effects.

USHMG1968 contained no reference to efficiencies, which were first included in USHMG1984 (Coate & McChesney, 1992).[962] The role of efficiencies was expanded in subsequent versions of the *Horizontal Merger Guidelines* and the revisions in USHMG1997 were only concerned with efficiencies (Coate & Heimart, 2009). These revisions tied efficiencies directly to the competitive effects analysis (Gotts & Goldman, 2002) and contained *"a real sympathy to efficiencies"* (Farrell & Shapiro, 2001).

Coate & Heimart (2009) report that the merging parties advanced efficiency claims in 147 out of 186 USFTC Phase 2 investigations in the decade from April 1997 to March 2007 but the USFTC did not reach any conclusions on efficiencies in the majority of these cases. They state that the USFTC generally tended to reduce the magnitude of claimed efficiencies rather than reject them completely in cases where the parties failed to adequately substantiate their claims.

George & Jacquemin (1992) state that, although early drafts of the ECMR provided for an efficiencies defence, it was not included in the final version,

---

960 In *re Foremost Dairies, Inc.*, 60 F.T.C. 944 1084 (1962), emphasis added.

961 Williamson (2002) notes that Proctor & Gamble's defence argued that the merger would not produce any cost savings.

962 Williamson (2002) states the shift in agency thinking on efficiencies stemmed from a merger involving two local newspapers, although the USDoJ remained cautious about admitting an efficiencies defence, which prevented its inclusion in USHMG1982.

ironically, in light of more recent developments, due to concerns that it would give the Commission too much freedom to approve mergers on industrial policy grounds. Neven *et al.* (1993) found that merger efficiencies were considered a negative factor in early decisions under the ECMR. Korah (2000) argues that this was because the EU Commission regarded efficiencies as likely to strengthen a dominant position. Röller *et al.* (2000) cite policy statements by the Commission stating that there was no legal basis for an efficiencies defence under the ECMR. Similarly, Duso *et al.* (2024) state that, although the EU Commission mentioned efficiency gains in some pre-2004 cases, it rarely took them into account in its analysis, probably due to a belief that there was no legal basis for an efficiencies defence under the ECMR.

Kovacic (2001) notes that some of the anti-competitive effects identified by the EU Commission in *Boeing/McDonnell Douglas* would have been regarded as efficiencies in the US. Gotts & Goldman (2002, p.204) argue that *"efficiencies have been more of a detriment than a benefit to merging entities"* in EU merger decisions. Lyons (2008, p.27) refers to a *"fear"* of claiming efficiencies which became known as *"the efficiencies **offence**"* (emphasis in original). In *Lagardère/Natexis/VUP*[963] efficiencies related to vertical and conglomerate aspects of the merger were viewed *"as highly problematic because they would harm competitors"* (Lyons, 2008, p.36). Motta (2004) points out that the possibility that a merger which generates efficiency gains might reduce welfare by forcing out most or all of the competitors in a market seems unlikely, as such a result only arises under very strong assumptions.

The issue of efficiencies tends to be addressed if a merger raises substantial competition concerns (Farrell & Shapiro, 2001). Most competition agencies, including the CA/CCPC, place the burden of proof on the merging parties to show that claimed efficiencies are likely to be realised. Stelzer (2002) observes that most mergers failed to achieve the efficiencies claimed *ex ante.* USHMG1997 §4 required merging parties to *"substantiate efficiency claims so that the Agency can verify by reasonable means the likelihood and magnitude of each asserted efficiency".*

Prior to approval of the merger, the parties are not in a position to exchange detailed cost and pricing information. The parties individually have information about their own costs, while the CA/CCPC has the power to obtain such information from both parties. Baxt *et al.* (2004) recognised that merging parties may face difficulties estimating efficiency gains. They

963 EU Commission Case No. COMP/M.2978 – *Lagardère/Natexis/VUP*, 7.1.2004.

may be required to define and demonstrate anticipated efficiencies at a very preliminary stage in their due diligence and business planning. The acquirer's estimates of efficiency gains may be based on a significant post-merger rationalisation of the target. It may be reluctant to disclose this information to the target's management because it is reliant on their support and goodwill to complete the acquisition. Banal-Estañol *et al.* (2008) warn that treating efficiency gains as exogenous may lead to competition agencies blocking welfare-enhancing mergers (Type I errors) and approving harmful mergers (Type II errors). They urge caution in accepting efficiency claims, especially if information about costs and gains from investing are difficult to verify. Froeb *et al.* (2003) point out that Bertrand oligopoly models indicate that second order demand properties that cause large price increases in the absence of merger synergies also cause high rates of merger synergies pass-through.

Yarrow (1999) notes that efficiency claims tended to be overstated in many UKMMC merger cases.[964] Merging parties have an incentive to overstate expected savings in merger cases (Massey, 2001). Valentine (2000) reported that documents prepared for the boards of the merging firms in *Staples/Office Depot* showed estimated efficiency savings that were one-fifth of the level that the parties claimed to the USFTC.[965] Baker (2004) states that the appeal court in *Heinz/Beech Nut* was highly sceptical of the merging parties' efficiency claims. The parties' claims of substantial efficiency gains in *AT&T/T-Mobile* were seen as lacking credibility (Besen *et al.*, 2013). An analysis of 75 US electricity mergers between 1994 and 2003 found no evidence of efficiency gains post-merger (Kwoka & Pollitt, 2010). Pittman & Li (2013) urge caution in expecting massive cost reductions from an increase in the size of an already large firm.[966] In contrast, Prince & Simon (2017) report quality improvements linked to efficiency gains in five post-2000 US domestic airline mergers.

The CA in *Statoil/Conoco* asked the merging parties to quantify and produce evidence to support their claim that the transaction would

---

964 Based on this experience, the UKMMC tended to discount such claims more heavily over time (*ibid*).

965 Ashenfelter *et al.* (1998) reported that a historic analysis indicated that Staples passed-on 15% of firm-specific cost savings, *i.e.*, it reduced prices on average by 0.15% in response to a 1% reduction in marginal cost.

966 Chen & Li (2018) caution that competition agencies should not presume that efficiencies will offset the potential anti-competitive effects of a merger based on a model showing that, under certain conditions, efficiencies may result in price increases.

generate significant efficiencies. The parties provided estimates of the expected efficiencies, but no supporting evidence and the CA stated that it could not *"merely accept claims that are not fully substantiated"* (¶6.18).

The Analysis of Efficiencies

The level of cost savings required to offset a potential price increase post-merger can be estimated using the following formula:

$$(m/(1-m)) \times (D/(1-D)) \qquad [10.1]$$

where *m* is the firms' price-marginal cost margin and *D* is the diversion ratio (see **Chapter 8**), *i.e.*, the proportion of sales lost by one of the merging brands in the event of a price increase that would be captured by the other (Werden, 1998).[967]

Farrell & Shapiro (1990) state that transferring production from higher to lower cost plants does not expand joint production possibilities and is not therefore a convincing efficiency. The consideration of possible efficiencies should be limited to those which are merger specific, *i.e.*, they must not be capable of being achieved by alternative less anti-competitive means such as internal expansion.[968] It is not sufficient, however, for competition agencies to claim that there are theoretical alternative ways for merging parties to achieve projected efficiencies. Competition agencies need to demonstrate that alternative ways of achieving efficiencies are realistic in light of the circumstances in which the firms operate. Baxt *et al.* (2004) point out that there may be very good reasons why firms are unable to achieve efficiencies unilaterally. Farrell & Shapiro (2001), while suggesting that claims that efficiencies are merger-specific should be viewed sceptically, nevertheless state *"the inquiry into merger-specificity should be a* ***realistic*** *one, focussing on what* ***will*** *happen with and without a merger"* (emphasis in original). In the US efficiencies are considered non-merger-specific only if the alternatives are *"practical in the business situation faced by the merging parties"*. The competition agencies can only advance alternatives that are realistic not ones that are merely hypothetical (Coate & Heimart, 2009).

Greater weight is generally afforded to variable cost savings rather than reductions in fixed costs, on the grounds that variable cost reductions are

---

967 Goppelsroeder *et al.* (2008) devised a measure, described as the Werden-Froeb Index (WFI), that measures the weighted average marginal cost reduction required to restore pre-merger equilibrium prices and quantities post-merger.

968 This is reflected in CAMG 2002 and CCPCMG2014.

more likely to be passed on to consumers in the form of price cuts.[969] Froeb *et al.* (2003) argued that merger policy in both the EU and US afforded little or no weight to fixed cost reductions as they were not expected to be passed on to consumers but point out that fixed cost savings may influence long-run price formation as all costs are variable in the long-run. In practice the US anti-trust agencies take fixed cost savings into account (see below).[970]

Farrell & Shapiro (2001) suggest that competition agencies should be relatively sceptical of efficiency claims based on simple scale economies. They note that scale economies can be achieved without a merger and that competition will force firms to achieve available scale economies. They also warn that, under a consumer welfare standard, merger-specific simple scale economies are unlikely to be large enough and sufficiently passed on to benefit consumers. An acquisition may, however, enable scale economies to be achieved sooner as organic growth may take time and this should be considered in any assessment of efficiencies.

References to efficiency claims only appear in EU Commission merger decisions post-2004. Fifty pages of the EU Commission prohibition decision in *Hutchinson 3G UK/Telefonica UK*[971] was devoted to a detailed analysis of efficiencies (Duso *et al.*, 2024).

The CA/CCPC's Treatment of Efficiencies

Efficiencies have played an extremely limited role in CA/CCPC merger reviews. Gorecki *et al.* (2007, p.365) stated that efficiencies had not played a *"decisive role"* in the 300-plus mergers notified to the CA up to that point and claimed that *"in the two mergers that were blocked by the Authority no serious attempt was made by the merging parties to document the efficiencies that would accrue"*. A review of the 102 horizontal merger cases that were subject to an extended Phase 1/Phase 2 investigation indicates that efficiencies were only considered in 14 cases. In several other cases the parties referred to possible efficiencies as a rationale for the proposed transaction without providing any details.

The CA Determination in *IBM/Schlumberger* states:

---

969 CAMG2002 ¶5.13 and CCPCMG2014 ¶8.16(a).

970 Rubinovitz (2009) shows that fixed cost savings can increase consumer welfare and argues that fixed cost savings should be given some weight in merger analysis.

971 EU Commission Case No. COMP/M.7612 – *Hutchison 3G UK/Telefonica UK*, 11.5.2016.

> *"The Authority is of the view that this transaction would not lead to any demonstrable efficiencies that would be passed on to consumers and that could ameliorate any negative competitive effects. Nor did the parties put forward arguments about efficiencies" (¶5.1).*

The merging parties in *Grafton/Heiton* submitted an accountant's report which estimated potential efficiencies from the transaction due to head office overhead savings, other overhead savings, and savings on purchasing costs. The parties claimed that *"a significant proportion of such savings will inevitably be passed on in the form of downward pressure on margins and prices"* (¶1.6). The CA did not, however, address the issue of efficiencies in its decision. Having found that the transaction would not result in an SLC, it concluded that the issue of efficiencies was arguably redundant. It might have been useful for the CA to have taken the opportunity to outline its approach to efficiencies in its Determination.

The parties in *Kingspan/Xtratherm* argued that the transaction would generate efficiencies in the UK, but the CA pointed out that this was not relevant as its role was to consider the effect of the transaction on competition in the State (¶5.1).

Submissions to the CA in *eircom/Meteor* argued that eircom might use profits from its fixed-line business to cross-subsidise retail mobile pricing. The CA dismissed such arguments describing efficiencies as a benefit, but the Determination contains no analysis of potential efficiencies.

> *"Lower retail prices for mobile calls are one of the expected benefits of the proposed acquisition. Preventing the post-acquisition entity from realizing efficiencies to provide lower retail prices for mobile calls would eliminate one of the most beneficial outcomes of the transaction and would in no way benefit consumers" (¶44).*

Kerry/Breeo

Kerry/Breeo was the first merger case in which the CA addressed efficiencies.[972] Many of the arguments put forward by the CA for rejecting the parties' efficiency estimates in that case appear inconsistent with both the economics literature and international best practice.

The Determination included a detailed breakdown of how the parties' efficiency estimates were arrived at (¶s9.3-9.16; Table 9.1). Estimated

---

972 *Competition Authority publishes details of decision to block the acquisition of Breeo Foods by Kerry Group*, Press Release, 26 Sep. 2008, cited in Massey (2011).

distribution savings, for example, were based on detailed estimates of the number of delivery vans, distribution depots, and so on required to supply the merged entity's customer base and cost savings that would accrue due to the elimination of overlaps in the parties' distribution networks. There was evidence that Kerry had an established track record of achieving efficiencies in previous acquisitions.

CAMG2002 provided that, in general, efficiencies that reduce marginal costs will be treated more sympathetically than those that reduce fixed costs as marginal cost reductions were more likely to be passed on to consumers while economics theory was less clear on the extent to which lower fixed costs will be passed on. *Kerry/Breeo* adopted a more stringent approach.

> *"It is **only** reductions in marginal cost that will feed through to price reductions, and hence less weight is attached to changes in fixed costs." (¶9.18, emphasis added).*

The distinction between fixed and variable costs is not always clear cut and all costs are variable in the long-run. Baxt *et al.* (2004) point out that firms tend to regard the merger process as a long-run phenomenon in which all costs should be considered variable while competition agencies treat mergers as a short-run phenomenon which gives rise to conflicting views on the ultimate effects of mergers. Studies have found that a high proportion of firms take fixed costs into account in setting prices. Non-linear pricing or long-term contracts may also enable fixed cost reductions to be passed on to consumers (Froeb *et al.*, 2003). A review of USFTC merger cases between 1997 and 2007 found that fixed costs savings were as likely to be accepted as variable cost savings because, even if they did not lead to a reduction in prices in the short-term, they could benefit consumers in the long-run (Coate & Heimart, 2009).[973]

The CA stated that purchasing savings were not a legitimate efficiency gain. Lower purchasing costs may reflect genuine cost savings for suppliers. The merged entity may purchase larger volumes, may require delivery to fewer locations and may reduce suppliers' administrative costs. Thus, a reduction in purchasing costs may represent genuine efficiencies. It is therefore wrong to dismiss purchasing cost savings *per se*. The nature of such cost savings needs to be considered, which the CA failed to do in this case.

---

973 Focarelli & Panetta (2003) report strong evidence that bank mergers generated adverse price effects which are temporary but in the long run efficiency gains dominated market power effects and resulted in price benefits for consumers.

The Determination argued that the efficiencies were not merger-specific but were due to Kerry becoming larger as a result of the acquisition and therefore could have been realised through organic growth. It suggested that Kerry should have sought to win more private label contracts and/or increase its exports. It also claimed that the distribution savings could be achieved by the parties establishing a distribution joint venture. Such arguments overlooked the fact that:

i. The evidence indicated that private label business was commonly shifted at very short notice and was thus highly uncertain so that expanding capacity to supply such products involved considerable risk;

ii. Kerry already exported large amounts of product and would presumably have increased its export sales if it were possible to do so. The CA produced no evidence that there was scope for Kerry to increase exports;

iii. The acquisition stemmed from Breeo's decision to exit the relevant business so the CA's suggestion that the two firms establish a distribution joint venture to achieve distribution efficiencies was clearly a non-runner.[974]

The CA argued *inter alia* that Kerry's estimates of the efficiency savings were biased upwards.[975] It claimed that the production cost savings might be overstated because the price paid by Breeo to its external suppliers may have included a contribution toward the latter's fixed costs, whereas only reductions in variable costs should be considered. As Breeo had outsourced production, its variable cost was the price it paid to its suppliers. Therefore, whether this price included a contribution toward its suppliers' fixed costs was irrelevant. If Kerry's variable costs were lower than the price paid by Breeo to its suppliers, then this represented a variable cost saving to the merged entity.[976]

---

974 In addition, Coate & Heimart (2009) point out that the theoretical possibility that efficiencies could be achieved through a joint venture does not necessarily rule out an efficiency claim, because there may be other transactions costs (such as monitoring) that render the joint venture option inferior to a merger.

975 The Determination stated that documents supplied by Kerry included only *"one short document"* related to the claimed efficiencies but cited no documents supporting the claim the estimated efficiency gains were overstated.

976 Suppose, for example, Breeo paid its suppliers €50 per tonne for cooked ham. If it bought one tonne less, its costs would fall by €50, *i.e.*, the variable cost to Breeo was €50. If Kerry's variable costs were €40 per tonne, then the variable cost saving as a result of the merger was

The CA argued that the estimated distribution savings might not be achieved if some of the parties' (retailer) customers switched to other suppliers. It is difficult to reconcile that claim with the CA conclusion that the merged entity would be able to raise prices for several of its products because there were no alternative brands that customers could substitute for those of the merging parties.

The CA claimed that the estimated efficiency savings, even if achieved, would be relatively insignificant as they only amounted to around 1% of total retail sales in each of the relevant product markets. The issue is whether the merged firm's marginal costs will fall sufficiently to offset any potential price increase. Thus, the correct approach is to estimate the cost savings as a proportion of the merged entity's (variable) costs. There is no basis for the claim that cost savings as a proportion of total retail sales of the relevant products is the relevant measure.

During the appeal hearing against the CA's prohibition decision, the court was told that the CA's Assessment concluded that the parties' estimates of production and distribution efficiencies might be biased upwards because the social benefits or savings would be less than the savings to the merging parties. Social costs and savings are not relevant in the context of a consumer welfare test. The Court was also told that references to social costs and benefits were retained in a draft Determination which was sent to an external economist retained by the CA to advise on the case. In an e-mail sent the day before the CA's final decision, the economist pointed out that the CA's arguments were incorrect and that, when applying a consumer welfare test, the issue was whether prices would rise or fall post-merger and social costs and benefits were not relevant to such calculations. The e-mail stated that transferring production from Breeo's suppliers to Kerry's facilities would yield cost savings *"and that is what would influence Kerry's price"* (Massey, 2010 & 2011).

The CA Determination claimed:

"The Authority is not arguing for a wider industry welfare standard. The assessment in discussing certain of the savings did use perhaps infelicitously the terms 'social gains' and 'social savings'" (¶9.49).

€10 per tonne. The fact that Breeo's suppliers might have had variable costs of €40 and fixed costs of €10 is irrelevant.

The suggestion that the references to social costs and benefits was the result of poor drafting in the Assessment seems questionable.[977]

The CA also submitted at the appeal hearing that the assessment of whether efficiency savings were sufficient to offset a possible price increase was not a quantitative exercise, *i.e.*, it was not a matter of quantifying the likely efficiency savings and establishing if they were sufficient to offset a predicted price increase. CAMG2002 stated that *"[e]fficiencies must be sufficient in magnitude not only to outweigh any increase in price-cost margins but also to offset any higher uncertainties about whether such efficiencies will be realised"* (¶5.15).

Other CA/CCPC Cases

The CA in *Metro/Herald AM* stated that the parties provided little or no data to support claims that estimated efficiencies were merger-specific. A submission by a competitor in *Topaz/Esso* argued that scale efficiencies arising from the merger would harm competition.

> *"this is a significant threat to the conditions of competition and therefore our ability to compete as they [i.e. the merged entity] can access efficiencies of scale to achieve disproportionate competitive advantages that smaller operators ...., cannot compete with" (¶168).*

This point was not addressed in the Determination.

The CCPC in *PandaGreen/Exomex* cited a CCPC report which argued that waste collection services displayed natural monopoly characteristics (CCPC, 2018, September 28).

> *"The household waste collection sector exhibits characteristics of a natural monopoly, including economies of density and scale, high fixed costs and a large cost advantage for a single operator" (¶38).*

The report argued:

> *"However, the ability of the merger review mechanism to address issues in the context of a natural monopoly is limited. There may be significant efficiencies in allowing a single company to operate in areas, but the monopoly effects can only be addressed through a clear policy and regulatory framework. The merger review process is not suitable for this purpose. Indeed, it is likely that the*

---

977 The Court did not address the efficiencies issue as it found that there were sufficient other grounds to overturn the CA decision (*Rye Investments*).

> *continuation of mergers within the industry will only further highlight the need for a regulatory solution" (¶3.51).*

A natural monopoly arises when a single firm can satisfy the entire market demand for a product at a lower total cost than any combination of firms (Newbury, 1999).[978] If waste collection services constitute a natural monopoly, then mergers between waste collection operators are likely to yield significant efficiencies, some of which are likely to be passed on to customers.[979] The CCPC failed to address this point in *PandaGreen/Exomex* and *Thornton's/Carducci.*

The CCPC stated in *PTSB/Ulster Bank* that:

> *"The Commission has not received any submission from the parties on efficiencies which meets the criteria set out in paragraph 8.2 of the* Merger Guidelines*" (¶8.2).*

This wording was repeated *verbatim* in several subsequent decisions.[980] The failure to provide any detail regarding the parties' efficiency claims, along with a thorough explanation of why they were considered inadequate, is highly unsatisfactory. Such information is essential if merger Determinations are to provide useful guidance to merging parties.

In *AIB/Ulster Bank* the CCPC argued that cost savings identified by Ulster Bank were related to a once-off elimination of switching costs for customers. It stated that such unverified cost savings might not satisfy the requirements in CCPCMG2014 but did not elaborate further. In *Uniphar/NaviCorp* the parties claimed that the transaction would produce efficiencies under seven different headings. While the Determination appears to contain a fairly detailed discussion of efficiencies, much of this was redacted, rendering it impossible to assess the parties' claims and the

---

978 See also Baumol *et al.* (1982) and Tirole (1988).

979 A firm's profit maximising price is determined as the point where marginal cost equals marginal revenue, i.e. the cost of producing an additional unit equals the additional revenue generated. If marginal cost declines, the profit maximising level of output increases and price will fall. A monopolist will not pass the entire amount of any cost savings, but it can be shown that even a monopolist will pass on half of any marginal cost savings to customers so the reduction in marginal costs may be sufficient to reduce prices. Whether the CCPC is correct in arguing that waste collection services constitute a natural monopoly is considered in **Chapter 11**.

980 *Thornton's/Carducci* (¶8.2); *Q-Park/Tazbell* (¶9.2); *Berendsen/King's Laundry* (¶4.389); and *Bank of Ireland/KBC* (¶9.2). The CCPC stated in *Aurivo/Arrabawn* that: *"The Commission has not, to date, received any submission from the Parties on efficiencies which meets the criteria set out in paragraph 8.2 of the Commission's Merger Guidelines"* (¶8.2).

CCPC's conclusions. The CCPC stated that none of the claimed efficiencies satisfied all three of the required criteria contained in CCPCMG2014.[981] In *daa/Gannon* the discussion of efficiencies runs to just over three pages, much of which is taken up by quotes from the merging parties, in a 295-page Determination.

Conclusions

Economics recognises that mergers may generate efficiencies and that, in some cases, merger-related efficiencies may be sufficient to offset the price increasing effects of a reduction in competition resulting from the merger. Efficiencies may even lead to price reductions. Consequently, economics suggests that potential efficiency gains need to be considered as part of the assessment of mergers. Historically, competition agencies tended to adopt a sceptical approach to efficiency claims and, in some cases, viewed them negatively.

Efficiencies have played a very limited role in mergers decided by the CA/CCPC. Only a handful of cases involved any detailed consideration of efficiencies. The CA's analysis of efficiencies in *Kerry/Breeo,* the first case involving a detailed efficiencies claim, was seriously flawed. In several other cases the CA/CCPC has simply stated that the parties' efficiency claims did not meet the requirements specified in the *Merger Guidelines,* while providing no details. The CA/CCPC treatment of efficiencies is highly unsatisfactory and needs to be revisited as a matter of urgency.

981 This provides that efficiencies must be (i) merger specific; (ii) verifiable; and (iii) benefit consumers.

11: MERGER REMEDIES

Introduction

The objective of the competition agency is to ensure that a merger does not reduce competition, and this may be achievable through the imposition of remedies. Consequently, few mergers are prohibited outright as competition agencies generally seek modifications of problematic deals[982] (Cosnita-Langlais & Sørgard, 2018). Vande Walle (2021) notes that in the first thirty years of the ECMR, the EU Commission only prohibited 30 mergers while clearing 450 subject to remedies. In the US there was a long-standing expectation that remedies would generally be capable of addressing any competition concerns and it was common for sellers to require a commitment from buyers to do whatever was required to secure merger clearance (Shapiro, J., 2024). In recent years competition agencies in several jurisdictions including the EU and UK have adopted a stricter approach, while the US anti-trust agencies have become openly hostile to merger remedies (Reilly *et al.*, 2023; Shapiro, J., 2024).

The objective of merger remedies is to preserve the pre-merger level of competition with as much certainty as possible (Parker & Balto, 2000). This is reflected in the EU Commission *Remedies Guidelines*:

> *"The commitments have to eliminate the competition concerns entirely and have to be comprehensive and effective from all points of view. Furthermore, commitments must be capable of being implemented effectively within a short period of time as the*

[982] Vande Walle (2021) notes that Germany is an exception in this regard, with a roughly equal split between prohibitions and remedies in merger cases.

> *conditions of competition on the market will not be maintained until the commitments have been fulfilled" (EU Commission, 2008b, ¶19).*

Despite the widespread use of remedies in merger cases, they have received little attention in the competition literature (Vande Walle, 2021). Given their importance, if remedies are ineffective then merger policy is also likely to be largely ineffective.

Merger Remedies

There are two types of merger remedies:

i. Structural, generally involving some divestment of assets by the merging parties; and
ii. Behavioural, which involves certain commitments by the merging parties to operate in a certain way post-merger.

In some cases, a combination of both structural and behavioural remedies may be applied.

Kolasky (2001, p.797) states that the US anti-trust agencies and courts *"have a very strong bias in favour of structural"* remedies and will only accept behavioural remedies *"in the most exceptional circumstances"*. Structural remedies, involving some divestment of assets, are generally considered superior to behavioural remedies for addressing competition concerns in merger cases (Kwoka, 2015). Brandenburger & Janssens (2001) report that the EU Commission tended to favour structural remedies, and this tendency has increased over time (Jean *et al.*, 2019), a view confirmed by EU Competition Commissioner Margrethe Vestager:

> *"[P]arties are well aware of our preference for 'clean slate' remedies, by which I mean stand-alone divestitures" (Vestager, 2022, March 25).*

Studies by the Australian,[983] Canadian[984] and UK[985] competition agencies as well as the International Competition Network (ICN)[986] all reveal a widespread preference for structural remedies, coupled with a general recognition of the problems associated with conduct remedies (Kwoka, 2015). The EU General Court in *Gencor* confirmed that structural remedies are generally preferable to behavioural remedies, although it rejected the

983 ACCC (2008).
984 Canada Competition Bureau (2011).
985 UKCC (2010).
986 ICN (2005).

EU Commission's claim that behavioural remedies were precluded under the ECMR.[987]

Structural *versus* Behavioural Remedies

Behavioural remedies are generally considered less effective than structural remedies (Massey & Daly, 2003). In the US behavioural remedies were found to be far less effective at restraining post-merger price increases than structural remedies (Kwoka, 2015).[988] Behavioural remedies require ongoing policing and monitoring of the merged undertaking by the competition agency. The role of competition authorities is to try and maintain competitive markets, not to engage in ongoing regulatory control of individual businesses. Behavioural remedies may also be quite difficult to enforce.[989] The fundamental problem with behavioural remedies, however, is that they do not alter the incentives for the merged entity to act anti-competitively. Thus, behavioural remedies attempt to prevent merging parties from acting in their own best interests (Kwoka, 2015). Malone & Sidak (2007) question whether behavioural remedies involving price regulation are legal under US law, arguing that the introduction of price regulation is a matter for the legislature while the role of the anti-trust agencies is to enforce competition law. Sidak & Singer (2008) argue that price freeze remedies offered by the parties in the US *XM/Sirius* satellite radio merger may have reduced consumer welfare *inter alia via* non-price changes.

Behavioural remedies encounter similar practical difficulties to utility industry regulation, including:

i. Information asymmetries as the competition agency knows less about the business and market than the merged entity;

---

987 *Gencor v. Commission*, Case T/102/96 [1999] ECR II-753. EU Commission (2008, October 22) states that divestment represents "*the best way to eliminate competition concerns resulting from horizontal overlaps and may also be the best means of resolving problems resulting from vertical or conglomerate concerns*"(¶17).

988 Vande Walle (2024) states that in the early 2010s there was an increased acceptance of bahavioural remedies by the US anti-trust agencies but this proved short lived.

989 Kwoka (2015) and Gastelum (2024) describe difficulties experienced by the US authorities in enforcing behavioural remedies in *Ticketmaster/Live Nation* (see below); *Comcast/NBCU;* and *Google/ITA*. As noted in **Chapter 9**, Suzuki (2009) reported that behavioural remedies proved ineffective in *Time-Warner/Turner.*

ii. Inherently unspecifiable aspects of the transaction, *i.e.*, it is not possible to fully specify the intended protections of the remedy, providing scope for the firm to behave anti-competitively;
iii. The competition agency and the firm have different objectives which means the merged entity will try and circumvent any remedy;
iv. Market dynamics which may render stated restrictions irrelevant and create new opportunities for anti-competitive behaviour.

Chiquita/Fyffes is among the rate examples of horizontal merger cases where the EU Commission accepted purely behavioural remedies.[990] Behavioural remedies are more frequently employed in non-horizontal mergers where structural remedies are difficult to construct (Vande Walle, 2021).

Structural remedies on the other hand do not require ongoing monitoring. Once a structural remedy has been implemented, the merged entity can be left to get on with running its business. This point was clearly articulated by Brennan J. in the US *du Pont* case.

> *"Divestiture has been called the most important of anti-trust remedies. It is simple, relatively easy to administer, and sure. It should be in the forefront of the Court's mind when a violation of §7 [of the* Clayton Act*] has been found."*[991]

Nevertheless, structural remedies may also exhibit shortcomings.

Compte *et al.* (2002) argue that the Commission decision to approve the *Nestlé/Perrier* merger, subject to the parties divesting the *Volvic* brand to *BSN*, actually increased the likelihood of collusion post-merger. Cabral (2003) argues that asset sales may dissuade entrants from opening new plants or retail outlets.

A study of US divestments over a 20-year period by Baer (1999) found that divestments were far more likely to promote successful entry when they involved an ongoing business, or a recognisable business unit as opposed to an untested combination of assets. The USFTC introduced several policy changes on the back of this report, including a requirement for upfront buyers if the divestments involved less than an ongoing business or if there were particular risks of a deterioration in the assets being divested and a reduction

990 EU Commission Case No. COMP/M.7220 – *Chiquita/Fyffes*, 3.10.2014. The parties committed to release the shipping company Maersk from an exclusivity clause and to refrain from agreeing similar exclusivity provisions with other shipping companies or incentivising shipping companies to refuse to provide services for other banana suppliers.

991 *United States v. E.I. du Pont de Nemours & Co.* 366 US 316 (1961) ¶330.

in the default divestment period for *ex post* buyers from a year to six months or less (Reilly *et al.*, 2023). Between 2012 and 2021 43% of all challenged US mergers were resolved with divestments, with the remainder being either litigated or abandoned (*ibid.*). A subsequent review reported that 83% of divestments in merger cases between 2006 and 2012 were successful in terms of restoring pre-merger levels of competition, with a 100% success rate in the case of divestments involving an on-going business (USFTC, 2017). In contrast, a 2005 review of EU merger remedies by the Commission found that 80% of divestments were inadequate as the assets transferred were insufficient to allow the purchaser stand-alone from the former parent. In one-third of these cases, the problem remained unresolved after three to five years. Transfer issues and inadequate preservation of the assets prior to transfer was cited as a problem in two thirds of cases while the lack of a suitable purchaser was identified in 20% of cases. DG competition nevertheless considered that 57% of divestment remedies had been effective (Lyons, 2008).[992] Smith (2004) found that UK supermarket mergers raised retail grocery prices but that, where such mergers were subject to structural remedies, this resulted in price reductions.[993]

Some observers question the effectiveness of remedies in general. Studies report that prohibitions protect competition and deter anti-competitive mergers whereas mild remedies and mutually negotiated agreements perform significantly worse (EU Commission, 2005; Duso *et al.*, 2006). Duso *et al.* (2013) found that the EU Commission placed an increased emphasis on remedies at the expense of prohibitions following the 2004 reform of the ECMR but suggested that remedies had proven largely ineffective and that only prohibitions were effective at preventing competitive harm. Seldeslachts *et al.* (2009) find that prohibitions have a deterrent effect, but remedies do not. Vergé (2010) found that divestments can never compensate for the negative impacts of three to two mergers. Cosnita-Langlais & Sørgard (2018) warn that remedies may encourage rather than deter anti-competitive mergers and be welfare-reducing.

Based on a review of more than 4,200 EU merger decisions between 1990 and 2009, Cloughterty *et al.* (2016) conclude that Phase 1 remedies have a deterrent effect whereas Phase 2 remedies do not. They attribute this to the

---

992 It subsequently introduced a number of refinements to its remedies procedures (OECD, 2009a).

993 Tenn & Yun (2011) report that structural remedies successfully maintained the pre-merger level of competition in *Johnson & Johnson/Pfizer*.

fact that merging parties may be more willing to accept stronger remedies during Phase 1 in order to avoid a lengthy Phase 2 investigation which would delay implementation of the merger. In contrast, at Phase 2, they suggest the Commission's bargaining position is weaker, it has much less scope to delay implementation of the merger and must either accept commitments offered or proceed to a prohibition decision. Lyons (2008) argues that the original tight timelines in the ECMR afforded the EU Commission too little time to consider sensible, effective remedies short of prohibition.[994] During periods when case-loads were heavy, early settlements in complex EU merger cases may have resulted in inadequate remedies (Garrod & Lyons, 2016).[995] Duso *et al.* (2024) report that the proportion of Phase 1 remedies in EU merger cases has increased over time.

The UK Court of Appeal rejected Ryanair's arguments that the objective of a remedy imposed by the UKCMA was to remove the probability of an SLC and that it could only take action to the extent necessary to ensure that an SLC was no longer more likely than not.

> *"What the CMA has to decide on the ordinary civil standard of proof is whether an SLC has or may be expected to result. Once it has reached that conclusion then the action which it has to take must be such as to remedy or prevent the SLC concerned" (¶57).*

Designing Effective Remedies

Parker & Balto (2000) pointed out that designing effective merger remedies had become increasingly complex. Divestments can be complicated by a number of factors, which may lessen the likelihood of success. Merging parties have a clear incentive to offer a divestment package that is too narrow, to propose a weak buyer, and to engage in strategic behaviour to impede the success of the purchaser. Even if they do not positively try to impede the buyer, they normally have little incentive to cooperate with them (*ibid.*). For this reason, upfront buyers are frequently considered important for successful divestment (see below).

The EU Commission rejected remedies offered by the merging parties in *Siemens/Alstom* as inadequate. In the case of very high-speed trains, the parties offered to divest a train that was not capable of running at very high

994 The timelines were extended in 2014.

995 They suggest providing for some degree of budget flexibility that would enable competition agencies to buy-in skilled support at times when there is a very high case load.

speeds or a licence for Siemens' Velaro very high-speed technology, subject to multiple restrictive terms and carve-outs. Neither option would have afforded a buyer the ability and incentive to develop a competing very high-speed train. In respect of signalling equipment, the parties offered to divest a complex mix of assets from Siemens and Alstom, whereby they would have transferred some assets while keeping others. The divested assets did not constitute a stand-alone viable business that a buyer could have used to compete effectively and independently against the merged entity. The purchaser of the divestment package also would have remained dependent on the merged entity for a number of licence and service agreements (Kotzeva *et al.*, 2019).[996]

Structural remedies therefore need to be carefully designed if they are to be successful. Competition agencies generally lack the skills and expertise required to establish what combination of assets is necessary to enable a rival to compete effectively in the relevant market. Divestment of an entire business is far more likely to be successful and to resolve competition concerns.[997] At the very least, such divestments are likely to provide sufficient evidence to enable the competition agency to establish whether the divested business unit has a record of operating effectively and efficiently and competing in the market. In contrast a divestment involving a mixture of assets from each of the merging parties requires more careful review because it is difficult to establish whether such a combination can function effectively as an ongoing business (Parker & Balto, 2000). The EU Commission has tended to be sceptical of such "mix and match" divestments (Vande Walle, 2021). Shapiro (2019) states that remedies should result in a market structure that preserves competition and suggests that divestments that do not make good business sense should be viewed sceptically while little or no weight should be placed on behavioural commitments, *e.g.*, commitments not to increase prices. It is also important that the purchaser of a divested business has the necessary financial resources to operate it successfully (OECD, 2023). If a remedy proves

---

996 Remedies need to be implemented quickly to prevent competitive harm whereas the proposed software licensing arrangements would have taken years to implement (Vande Walle, 2021).

997 In several EU cases, divestments included activities where the merger raised no competition concerns to ensure their viability (Vande Walle, 2021), e.g., *Dow/DuPont* involved the divestment of DuPont's entire global crop protection R&D organisation, although the competition concerns were limited to a number of specific areas. The EU Commission generally requires that divested businesses be profitable.

unsuccessful, it may be difficult for the competition agency to re-open the case and seek an alternative.[998]

Proposals by the parties to divest 63 stores were rejected by the USFTC in *Staples/Office Depot* because the remedy failed to deal with potential competition concerns.[999] Prior to the proposed merger, the parties had been moving into each other's local geographic markets resulting in lower prices. In addition to reducing competition in markets where the merging parties were already present, the proposed merger would have eliminated such potential competition while the divested stores would likely have been acquired by the third office supply superstore operator resulting in a duopoly. Competition between the parties increased following the blocking of the proposed merger.

> *"Both firms are competing aggressively, invading each other's markets and driving prices down to levels not seen before the merger was proposed" (Parker & Balto, 2000, p.11).*

Akbar (2002) claims the remedy proposed by the EU Commission in *GE/Honeywell* undermined the rationale for the merger. McCabe (2002) reports that the EU Commission sought significant divestments which upset the financial logic underpinning the proposed merger objectives in *Reed Elsevier/Wolters Kluwer*.[1000] Divestments of price-setting generation plants, network assets and controlling shareholdings in rival undertakings were found to be effective remedies in EU electricity sector mergers (Federico, 2011).

Behavioural remedies include access remedies, *i.e.*, remedies which require the merging parties to grant access to certain infrastructure or rights. They tend to be used infrequently but are common, for example, in the digital, telecommunications and media sectors and in airline mergers, where slot remedies are common (Vande Walle, 2021). Access remedies seek to address competition concerns by facilitating market entry.[1001] The EU Commission has applied interoperability remedies in several mergers in the digital sector in

---

998 Remedies in EU cases normally include a general review clause, allowing for amendments.

999 Cabral (2003) warns that divestments offered by merging parties may represent a means of "buying-off" would-be entrants and will negatively affect consumer welfare and suggests that Staples' proposed divestments were consistent with this view.

1000 Case No. COMP/M.1040 – *Reed Elsevier/Wolters Kluwer*, 9.3.1998 (withdrawn).

1001 Access remedies proved largely unsuccessful in EU Commission Case No. COMP/M.6992 – *Hutchison 3G UK/Telefónica Ireland*, 28.5.2014. One of the two mobile virtual network operators (MVNOs) that was supposed to enter the market soon exited while the other secured a negligible market share (Vande Walle, 2021). MVNOs do not own a mobile phone network but use another network to provide mobile telecommunications services.

order to address concerns that post-merger the merged entity would degrade interoperability between its products and those of its competitors.[1002] Slot remedies have frequently been applied by the EU Commission in airline merger cases, including *IAG/Aer Lingus*.[1003] Such remedies involve a commitment by the merged entity to make landing/take-off slots available to competitors, enabling them to complete on routes where the merger raises competition concerns.[1004]

The CA/CCPC's Approach to Remedies

> *"Where the CCPC identifies competition concerns, it only approves such mergers where remedies are identified which: (i) are comprehensive and effective; (ii) are capable of being implemented effectively within a short period of time; and (iii) eliminate the competition concerns entirely" (CCPC, M&A Annual Report 2022, p.2, emphasis added).*

Table 11.1 provides details of cases subjected to remedies and the types of remedies applied in CA/CCPC merger cases between 2003 and 2023. Altogether 45 (3.6%) out of the 1,264 mergers notified to the CA/CCPC over the 2003-2023 period were subject to remedies: 37 (81%) were horizontal mergers while four (9%) had horizontal and vertical elements; 10 cases (22%) involved structural remedies, while a further four (9%) involved a combination of structural and behavioural remedies. 21 cases (47%) involved behavioural remedies, while two (4%) involved behavioural remedies combined with a requirement to notify future below the threshold mergers; six more cases (13%) involved a remedy requiring future notification of below the threshold mergers (see **Chapter 3**). A further two cases were cleared on the basis of undertakings in relation to ancillary restraints.[1005]

1002 Examples include EU Commission Case Nos. COMP/M.5984 – *Intel/McAfee*, 26.1.2011 and COMP/M.8124 – *Microsoft/LinkedIn*, 6.12.2016.

1003 EU Commission Case No. COMP/M.7541 – *IAG/Aer Lingus*, 14.7.2015. The Commission rejected a proposal to make slots at London Heathrow available in *Ryanair/Aer Lingus I* as inadequate to address competition concerns, in part because minority shareholders had a right of veto over such slot transfers.

1004 As previously noted, airport slots arguably constitute the main barrier to entry in airline markets. Slot remedies seek to lower such barriers to facilitate entry or expansion by competitors.

1005 *Kingspan/Century Homes; Sean Loughnane/Crinkle*. In contrast, the CCPC in *Direct Card/DCI* stated: *"Following engagement with the Commission, the parties subsequently decided to withdraw their request that the non-compete obligation in the SPA be considered by the Commission as a restriction that is directly related and necessary to the implementation of the Proposed Transaction.*

Table 11.1 Details of CA/CCPC Merger Cases Involving Remedies, 2003-2023

Type of Case	Number of Cases	% of Cases	Type of Remedy	Number of Cases	% of Cases
Horizontal	37	82.0	Structural	10	22.2
Horizontal/ Vertical	4	8.9	Structural/ Behavioural	4	8.9
Horizontal/ Conglomerate	1	2.2	Behavioural	21	46.7
Vertical	3	6.7	Behavioural/Future Notification	2	4.4
			Future Notification	6	13.3
			Ancillary	2	4.4
Total	**45**	**100.0**		**45**	**100.0**

Source: CA/CCPC.

The CA/CCPC preference for behavioural rather than structural remedies is out of step with international best practice and economics thinking. A leading Irish commercial law firm described the CCPC's approach as *"unusual"*, citing a lower intervention rate than the EU Commission combined with a greater willingness to accept behavioural remedies (Kelly *et al.*, 2021). In the UK 75% of merger remedies involved structural remedies while just 25% involved behavioural remedies.

Table 11.2 analyses the pattern of remedies over time and whether the case involved an extended Phase 1 or a full Phase 2 investigation.[1006] It is important to recognise that, in some instances, the number of cases is quite small, given that there were only 45 remedies cases in total. Overall, the proportion of structural remedies was higher for Phase 2 than for Extended Phase 1 investigations. The data also indicate that there has been a significant increase in the proportion of structural remedies since 2019, with some decline in the proportion of behavioural remedy cases and a very marked fall in the proportion of future notification/ancillary restraint type remedies. This is consistent with other evidence indicating a stricter approach since the

Such obligation is therefore not addressed further in this Determination and will not benefit from the protection offered by sections 4(8) and 5(3) of the Act" (¶28).

1006 The table classifies cases into three categories: "structural" combines structural and structural/ behaviour; "behavioural" also includes the two behavioural/future notification cases and "other" refers to the six future notification and the two ancillary restraint remedy cases.

beginning of 2020. The CCPC informed the parties in *Q-Park/Tazbell* that it was unlikely that behavioural remedies would be sufficient to ameliorate the structural effects of the proposed transaction (¶1.45).

Table 11.2: Distribution of Merger Remedies by Type of Remedy, 2003-2023

	2002-2013	2014-2019	2020-2023	2003-2023
Extended Phase 1 Investigations				
Structural	20.0	9.6	33.3	14.8
Behavioural	50.0	66.7	50.0	63.0
Other	30.0	23.8	16.7	22.2
Total	**100.0**	**100.0**	**100.0**	**100.0**
Phase 2 Investigations				
Structural	33.3	53.9	60.0	55.6
Behavioural	33.3	30.8	40.0	33.3
Other	33.3	15.4	0.0	11.1
Total	**100.0**	**100.0**	**100.0**	**100.0**
All Remedy Cases				
Structural	25.1	26.5	45.5	31.1
Behavioural	43.8	52.9	45.5	51.1
Other	31.3	20.6	9.1	17.8
Total	**100.0**	**100.0**	**100.0**	**100.0**

Source CA/CCPC.

Individual Cases

Where merging parties propose remedies, the CA/CCPC will generally market test them, by seeking the views of interested parties including potential purchasers of the assets where a structural remedy is involved as well as customers and competitors.[1007] Competitors, customers and suppliers of the merging parties will frequently be able to spot shortcomings in a remedy that may not be obvious to a competition agency.[1008]

1007 Market testing normally requires the preparation of a non-confidential version of the proposals which third parties may be asked to comment on. However, excessive redactions in the non-confidential version would render it impossible for third parties to properly assess the workability of any remedies proposal, making it impossible for the competition agency to assess their adequacy (Vande Walle, 2021).

1008 In *Deutsche Börse/London Stock Exchange*, the EU Commission's market testing revealed that the business the parties proposed to divest was vitally dependent on the London Stock Exchange's MTS trading platform, which had not been included in the proposed

Table 11.3 provides details in respect of the 45 mergers that were cleared subject to remedies by the CA/CCPC.

Structural Remedies

Several of the structural remedy cases were relatively straightforward. *Valeo/Wardell/Robert Roberts*, for example, raised concerns due to the parties having the two largest brown sauce brands and involved the parties divesting the YR brown sauce brand. *Topaz/Esso* involved the parties divesting the target's 50% interest in a joint venture which owned one of three fuel import terminals at Dublin Port, where the purchaser already owned and operated one of the other terminals.[1009] *Tesco/Joyce's Supermarkets* involved a divestment of an individual supermarket. *SRH/Capital Radio* combined the divestment of a minority shareholding in a rival radio station (due to concerns about information exchange) along with certain behavioural remedies. In *Communicorp/SRH* the CA concluded that two of the merging radio stations were close competitors and that the transaction would give rise to unilateral effects. The transaction was cleared subject to the merged entity divesting one of the stations to an upfront purchaser.[1010]

---

divestment. The Commission concluded that the proposed divestment would not be viable and prohibited the transaction (*ibid.*).

1009 The CCPC rejected a proposed buyer of the parties' JFT shareholding having concluded that it raised similar competition concerns to the original transaction but afforded the parties an opportunity to seek an alternative purchaser (see below) (CA, *Annual Report 2016*, p.54). The remedy also involved the divestment of a small number of retail filling stations.

1010 Normally in divestment cases, the parties may close the transaction subject to a requirement to complete the divestment within a relatively short period of time. In cases involving upfront purchasers, they cannot complete the merger until they have entered into a binding agreement for the sale of the divestment business. This differs from a *"fix-it-first"* approach whereby the divestment sale may be agreed before the merger review process is complete. Upfront and fix-it-first remedies provide safeguards where (a) there are few interested buyers; (b) there are significant obstacles to divestment, *e.g.*, a requirement for regulatory approval; and (c) there is a risk of a potential degradation of the divestment business. The remedy in *Communicorp/SRH* also involved a commitment by the parties not to obtain or exercise a controlling interest in or any substantial interest in or over the affairs of Independent Radio Sales (IRS) and to continue to offer airtime to it on usual commercial terms.

Table 11.3: Merger Remedies in CA/CCPC Cases, 2003-2023

Case No.	*Case Name*	Horizontal/Vertical	Decision Date	Investigation Stage	Type of Conditions
M/06/098	*Premier Foods/RHM*	Horizontal	9.2.2007	Phase 1	Structural
M/14/026	*Valeo/Wardell/Robert Roberts*	Horizontal	17.2.2015	Phase 2	Structural
M/15/020	*Topaz/Esso*	Horizontal	15.10.2015	Phase 2	Structural
M/16/008	*PandaGreen/Greenstar*	Horizontal/ Vertical	16.8.2016	Phase 2	Structural
M/18/063	*Berendsen/King's Laundry*	Horizontal	8.7.2019	Phase 2	Structural
M/21/016	*PandaGreen/Exomex*	Horizontal	30.9.2021	Ext. Phase 1	Structural
M/21/071	*Tesco/Joyce's*	Horizontal	7.6.2022	Phase 2	Structural
M/22/040	*Q-Park/Tazbell*	Horizontal	15.8.2023	Phase 2	Structural
M/22/049	*Uniphar/LXV Remedies (Sam McCauley)*	Horizontal	20.1.2023	Ext. Phase 1	Structural
M/22/067	*Thornton's/Carducci*	Horizontal	13.7.2023	Phase 2	Structural
M/03/033	*SRH/Capital Radio*	Horizontal	23.2.2004	Phase 2	Structural/ Behavioural
M/06/044	*Topaz/Statoil**	Horizontal	9.10.2006	Ext. Phase 1	Structural/ Behavioural
M/07/040	*SRH/Communicorp*	Horizontal	7.12.2007	Phase 2	Structural/ Behavioural
M/18/036	*Enva/Rilta*	Horizontal	20.12.2018	Phase 2	Structural/ Behavioural
M/05/024	*UGC (Chorus)/NTL*	Horizontal	4.11.2005	Phase 2	Behavioural
M/05/025	*SRH/Highland Radio*	Horizontal	12.8.2005	Ext. Phase 1	Behavioural

Case No.	***Case Name***	**Horizontal/Vertical**	**Decision Date**	**Investigation Stage**	**Type of Conditions**
M/05/050	*eircom/Meteor*	Horizontal	18.11.2005	Ext. Phase 1	Behavioural
M/07/022	*Thomas Crosbie Holdings/South East Broadcasting*	Horizontal	5.9.2007	Ext. Phase 1	Behavioural
M/09/013	*Metro/Herald AM*	Horizontal	6.11.2009	Phase 2	Behavioural
M/10/026	*ESB/NIE*	Horizontal/ Vertical	29.10.2010	Ext. Phase 1	Behavioural
M/13/033	*Sappho/Thomas Crosbie Holdings*	Horizontal	10.1.2014	Ext. Phase 1	Behavioural
M/16/040	*Bon Secours/Barrington's Hospital*	Horizontal	21.12.2016	Ext. Phase 1	Behavioural
M/17/012	*Kantar/Newsaccess*	Horizontal	11.7.2017	Ext. Phase 1	Behavioural
M/17/021	*Applegreen/JFT*	Vertical	30.6.2017	Ext. Phase 1	Behavioural
M/18/009	*BWG/4 Aces*	Horizontal	5.5.2018	Ext. Phase 1	Behavioural
M/18/016	*Trinity Mirror/Northern & Shell*	Horizontal	12.9.2018	Phase 2	Behavioural
M/18/031	*Uniphar/Sisk Healthcare*	Horizontal	17.8.2018	Ext. Phase 1	Behavioural
M/18/042	*Oaktree/Alannis/Lioncor*	Horizontal	12.9.2018	Ext. Phase 1	Behavioural
M/18/053	*PandaGreen/Knockharley*	Vertical	6.2.2019	Ext. Phase 1	Behavioural
M/19/010	*Formpress/Midland Tribune*	Vertical	9.10.2019	Ext. Phase 1	Behavioural
M/20/005	*ESB/Coillte*	Horizontal/ Vertical	5.2.2021	Phase 2	Behavioural
M/21/004	*Synch*	Horizontal	16.6.2022	Phase 2	Behavioural
M/21/021	*Bank of Ireland/KBC*	Horizontal	23.5.2022	Phase 2	Behavioural
M/22/047	*BWG/McCarrick*	Horizontal	7.11.2022	Ext. Phase 1	Behavioural
M/23/010	*BWG/Tuffy Wholesale*	Horizontal	3.5.2023	Ext. Phase 1	Behavioural

Case No.	*Case Name*	Horizontal/Vertical	Decision Date	Investigation Stage	Type of Conditions
M/17/027	*Dalata/Clarion/Clayton*	Horizontal	29.8.2017	Ext. Phase 1	Behavioural/ Future Notification
M/18/067	*LN-Gaiety/MCD Productions*	Horizontal/ Vertical	5.7.2019	Phase 2	Behavioural/ Future Notification
M/04/016	*Stena/P&O*	Horizontal	5.4.2004	Phase 1	Future Notification
M/04/051	*Grafton/Heiton*	Horizontal	6.1.2005	Phase 2	Future Notification
M/05/027	*MJ Gleeson/UBH*	Horizontal	23.8.2005	Ext. Phase 1	Future Notification
M/05/028	*Eason/Alphyra*	Horizontal	14.7.2005	Phase 1	Future Notification
M/19/034	*CVC/Celtic Rugby*	Horizontal/ Conglomerate	15.1.2020	Ext. Phase 1	Future Notification
M/21/024	*Orpea/First Care*	Horizontal	6.7.2021	Ext. Phase 1	Future Notification
M/05/009	*Kingspan/Century Homes*	Horizontal	13.4.2005	Phase 1	Ancillary
M/17/036	*Sean Loughnane/Crinkle*	Horizontal	3.10.2017	Ext. Phase 1	Ancillary

Source: CA/CCPC.

*CA missed the deadline for launching of Phase 2 investigation, but parties agreed to abide by commitments offered during Phase 1.

In *Premier Foods/RHM*, the CA concluded that the transaction would likely result in a unilateral price increase in the gravies market. The parties offered two alternative divestment options:

i. Divestment of all Erin brand meal enhancers (including gravies, pour-over sauces, and casserole mixes) but excluding Erin's soup products; or
ii. The entire Erin business.

Although the first option was not limited to products where there was a competition concern, potential buyers expressed the view that, while it could address the competition issues in respect of gravies, the splitting of the brand could lead to conflicts and damage the brand while also preventing a purchaser from expanding the brand beyond meal enhancers. The CA, therefore, decided to accept the second remedy. This involved the divestment of a specific business with a proven history which included the larger of Premier's two gravy brands, although it did not fully restore the pre-merger position as the parties retained Premier's second gravy brand.[1011]

PandaGreen/Greenstar was cleared subject to the divestment of a number of domestic waste collection customers in two Dublin local authority areas: Dún Laoghaire-Rathdown and Fingal counties, where the Target had market shares of [5-10]% and [0-5]% respectively.[1012] The divestment in *Thornton's/Carducci* was much more limited as it was confined to the increment in domestic customer numbers in very localised areas in which the parties overlapped within the relevant local authority areas. Details of the divested customers in this case are provided in **Table 11.4** which also includes estimates of the parties' total domestic waste collection customers in each of the three local authority areas.[1013] The divested customers amounted to 0.1% of all households in Fingal and [0.3-0.5]% of the parties' domestic waste customers in the county. In Dublin City the divested households represented 1.4% of all households and [3-4]% of the merging

[1011] Premier's *Erin* brand had a [10-20]% market share while its *Oxo* brand had a [0-5]% share (Table 3).

[1012] The number of divested customers was approximately equal to the target's pre-merger customer numbers.

[1013] Domestic customer numbers for each of the local authority areas were estimated based on the market share ranges for the parties in the Determination and total number of households excluding those in purpose build apartment blocks (which are considered C&I customers) according to CSO *Census of Population Profile 2 – Housing in Ireland F2063 – Private Dwellings in Permanent Housing Units*. Accessed 5.12.2023.

parties' customers while the corresponding figures for South Dublin were 6.4% of all households and [14-18]% of the parties' total customers.

Table 11.4: Domestic Customer Divestment in *Thornton's/Carducci*

Local Authority Area	Postcode	Overlap Area km²	Customer Increment	Parties' Estimated Customer Numbers	
				Thornton's	Citybin
Dublin City	Dublin 6	5	336		
	Dublin 6W	3	778		
	Dublin 8	0.2	33		
	Dublin 12	4	1,188		
	Total	12.2	2,335	[8,000-16,000]	[48,000-56,000]
Fingal	Dublin 15	1	92	[9,000-14,000]	[9,000-14,000]
South Dublin	Dublin 14	3	754		
	Dublin 16	5	1,724		
	Dublin 24	2	824		
	Lucan K78	4	2,231		
	Total	14	5,533	[26,000-30,000]	[4,000-9,000]
Overall Total		**27.2**	**7,960**	**[43,000-60,000]**	**[61,000-78,000]**

Source: Thornton's/Carducci.

An obvious question arises as to whether the divestments were sufficient to address any competition concerns given the limited number of customers involved. The divestment in South Dublin was probably close to the total increment in customer numbers as a result of the merger in the county as a whole and thus arguably came close to restoring the pre-merger position. However, the remedy appears insufficient in Dublin City and Fingal if the proposed transaction was considered to harm competition across the entirety of each of the local authority areas rather than just in the overlap areas (see **Chapter 8**). This illustrates the need to identify an appropriate theory of harm in order to evaluate whether a remedy will be sufficient.

A second issue is that the divestments did not involve an actual business, but a sub-set of both parties' customers located across three local authority areas raising questions about the ability of a purchaser or purchasers to convert the divested assets into a viable business. In addition, the CCPC has consistently argued that domestic waste collection services are characterised by economies of scope and density which constitute barriers to entry and cited this to support its competitive harm findings in this case. If such economies exist, this raises further doubts about the viability of the divested assets. Accepting that the divestments would be effective in addressing its competition concerns is inconsistent with the CCPC's claims regarding economies of scope and density.

In *PandaGreen/Exomex* the remedy involved a divestment of C&I waste collection customers in a number of towns and townlands throughout County Louth. The Determination provides no information on the number of customers affected, which makes it difficult to reach any conclusions as to whether the divested assets were likely to constitute a viable business. They would not appear to constitute a stand-alone business unit as they involved overlapping customers in specific towns and townlands.

The CCPC concluded in *Enva/Rilta* that the transaction would be likely to result in unilateral effects in several markets and give rise to foreclosure in another market. The remedies included the divestment of one of the merging parties' three facilities for the treatment of hazardous oily tank and interceptor waste and hazardous waste lubricant oil collection services along with certain behavioural commitments. The behavioural commitments included a commitment to accept small quantities of hazardous contaminated soil from third parties subject to volume limits. The CCPC concluded, without giving reasons, that this would address any competition concerns in this market where the parties had a combined market share of [90-95]%. It is not entirely clear, therefore, whether this remedy was sufficient to address any competition problem.

The remedy applied in *Berendsen/King's Laundry* required the merging parties to divest three contracts for the provision of laundry services to healthcare customers. Gorecki (2020) observes that replicating the pre-merger competitive influence of King's Laundry would have required that the divested contracts should approximately equate to its pre-merger market share of [10-20]%. He argues that the combined market share of the divested contract should have been at the upper end of the range or even in the low twenties because the CCPC's counterfactual anticipated that, absent the merger, King's Laundry would have increased its market share. The information on market shares was completely redacted in the Determination so there is no way of judging whether the divestment of the three contracts was sufficient to restore competition to its pre-merger level (*ibid.*).

In *Q-Park/Tazbell* the remedy required the merging parties not to enter into a contract to manage, lease or operate a specific [redacted] car park in Dublin City and to divest the top floor of a car park in Galway city. Much of the detail of the proposals along with the CCPC's analysis of whether the remedy would be effective and could be implemented in a timely manner in respect of the Dublin car park are redacted in §6 of the Determination, rendering any assessment impossible.[1014] The CCPC market tested the proposals in relation to Galway but *"did not consider it necessary to market test the Dublin City Proposal"* (¶6.702) before concluding that they would suffice to address any competition concerns.

In the case of Galway, the total number of spaces in the target car park was redacted for some reason, although it is listed on the Galway County Council website as having 480 spaces.[1015] It is difficult to see how divesting the top floor of the car park comprising 86 parking spaces could have restored competition to its pre-merger level. The CCPC also stated that the Port of Galway Docks car park was the closest geographically to the target car park but argued *"it is unlikely to exert as significant a competitive constraint on Tazbell as Q-Park"* (¶6.181), although it would appear to have had more than 86 spaces.

Behavioural Remedies

A large proportion of behavioural remedies in CA/CCPC cases sought to address concerns about potential exchanges of commercially-sensitive information.

> *"Behavioural commitments accepted by the CCPC and TCA have tended to primarily consist of "ring-fencing" commitments to prevent the flow of competitively sensitive information held by the target about its competitors in the context of post-merger management of the merged firm and/or in a joint venture situation. "Ring-fencing" commitments made up 50% of all behavioural remedies, followed by the obligation to notify the CCPC of future acquisitions, even if the transaction is not notifiable (17%), access remedies (12%) and other behavioural remedies (21%)" (CCPC, M&A Report 2021, ¶3.5).*[1016]

1014 While the CCPC is required to have regard for commercial confidentiality, redacting the reasons for finding remedies sufficient to address any competition concerns is unsatisfactory.

1015 https://www.galwaycity.ie/services/roads-and-transport/roads-and-transport-services/parking-in-galway-city. Visited 28.1.2025.

1016 Note the CCPC report defines future notification requirements as behavioural remedies.

The fact that most of the behavioural remedies have focused on the issues of information exchange and future notification of below the threshold mergers raises some questions about the overall effectiveness of CA/CCPC merger remedies.

BWG/4 Aces, *BWG/McCarrick* and *BWG/Tuffy Wholesale* each involved the acquisition by BWG, a grocery wholesaler/franchisor, of three smaller grocery wholesalers each of which was a shareholder in, and had representation on the board of, a wholesaler buying group. In each case, BWG indicated that the Target would continue to purchase grocery goods for resale *via* the buying group rather than BWG. The CCPC expressed concerns about the potential for the exchange of confidential information in relation to the buying group due to the Targets' membership and board representation. All three cases were cleared subject to the parties disposing of their shareholding in and resigning from the board of the buying group.

The CA stated in *UGC (Chorus)/NTL* that *"the impact of the cross ownership and the cross management on the incentives of the merged entity to compete with BSkyB is the primary concern of the Authority"* (¶121). The CA applied a remedy which essentially sought to ringfence the parties' Irish operations by establishing an Irish holding company. It is not entirely clear how this remedy would address the incentive not to compete.[1017] In contrast, *SRH/Highland Radio* was cleared subject to a remedy involving the disposal of a minority shareholding in Independent Radio Sales (IRS) in order to address concerns that this would facilitate coordination in the sale of radio advertising slots. *Thomas Crosbie Holdings/South East Broadcasting* resulted in the only two radio stations that targeted local advertising in Waterford City and County coming under common control but the CA concluded that *"in order to preserve the competition that currently exists at the margin between the two stations going forward, the management of the two radio stations should be kept separate and there should be a limit to the exchange of certain information"* (¶43). Whether such a remedy is sufficient is questionable.

As previously noted, the CA missed the deadline for launching a Phase 2 investigation in *Topaz/Statoil*. In its 2006 *Annual Report*, the CA stated that it had identified competition concerns in relation to import terminalling services in Galway and four local motor fuel retail markets. The CA stated

---

[1017] Similar ring-fencing arrangements designed to address concerns about potential information exchange were applied in *Metro/Herald AM; ESB/NIE; ESB/Coillte; Thomas Crosbie Holdings/Sappho; Trinity Mirror/Northern & Shell; Uniphar/Sisk Healthcare; Oaktree & Alanis Capital/Lioncor (JV)*; and *Dalata/Clarion Liffey Valley/Clayton Cardiff Lane.*

that the parties had offered remedies in advance of the Phase 1 deadline and subsequently agreed to abide by these despite the passage of the deadline for triggering a Phase 2 investigation. The remedies involved a commitment that:

> *"... within a reasonable period of time after the completion of the acquisition, it would undertake a terminalling and throughput agreement, for a substantial term, at its existing Galway terminal with a major independent oil importer...on terms and conditions that the Competition Authority believes will facilitate competition in wholesale supply and will ultimately benefit consumers in the Connacht region" (p.30).*

The parties also agreed to divest a filling station in West Dublin while in another case, its original concerns were resolved as a Statoil dealer station had subsequently switched brands.[1018] The CA had raised a third concern but details of this were redacted on grounds of commercial confidentiality. The fact that the CA attempted to trigger a Phase 2 investigation, despite the parties having offered these remedies, indicates that, initially at least, it had doubts that they would be sufficient.

eircom/Meteor and *PandaGreen/Knockharley* involved behavioural remedies designed to ensure access to facilities and prevent market foreclosure. The CCPC expressed concerns in *Bon Secours/Barrington's Hospital* that the parties might unilaterally seek to increase the rates that Barrington's Hospital charged to insurers without having undertaken investment in upgrading services which the parties stated they had planned to make.[1019] The CCPC nevertheless accepted a remedy involving a commitment by the parties not to raise fees.

Kantar/News Access constituted a merger to monopoly. The transaction was cleared subject to a remedy which involved a commitment:

i. To sell to a prospective new entrant all of the Target's fixed assets necessary to provide the relevant services;

ii. To offer a specified number of the Target's customers on fixed term contracts the option of being released from the remainder of their contracts in order to facilitate market entry by any purchaser of the fixed assets;

1018 As stated, the CA stated that it had concerns in relation to four local retail markets, but details were only provided for these two cases.

1019 Bon Secours reimbursement rates at its other hospitals, in most instances, were higher than those charged by Barrington's Hospital.

iii. To procure that the Target would not unilaterally amend or vary customers' prices;

iv. Not to enforce any non-compete provisions in respect of current or former staff of the Target, excluding directors and shareholders.

The CCPC market-tested the remedies with potential new entrants and stated:

> *"In essence, the proposals had the **potential** to replace the competition that would have been lost as a result of the Proposed Transaction in the potential market for the provision of print and broadcast media monitoring services" (¶55, emphasis added).*

The purpose of a remedy is to eliminate any competitive harm and as far as possible, restore competition to its pre-merger level. The fact that a remedy has the potential to do this is not sufficient; it must actually do so.[1020]

Applegreen/JFT was a vertical merger involving the acquisition of a 50% shareholding in a fuel import terminal at Dublin Port which the CCPC had required to be sold when approving *Topaz/Esso.* The CCPC concluded that the transaction did not raise any foreclosure concerns. Nevertheless, the transaction was subject to a remedy requiring Applegreen to develop and maintain an aviation fuel supply business in Dublin. There was no suggestion that Applegreen's acquisition of a 50% shareholding in JFT, in itself, raised any competition concerns. Esso, which previously owned the shareholding, had exited the aviation fuel business prior to *Topaz/Esso* and there was no suggestion by the CCPC that its decision was merger-related (see **Chapter 5**). The rationale for requiring Applegreen to enter the jet fuel business is hard to fathom. If the business was profitable, entry would be in Applegreen's interest.[1021] The CCPC expressed concerns that, without the remedy, the objective of maintaining competition in aviation fuel terminalling services, which it claimed was the rationale for the remedy in *Topaz/Esso,* would not be secured. The CCPC also stated that it was

---

1020 In contrast, the EU Commission in *Croatian Cement* rejected a proposal to transfer a five-year lease granting access to a cement terminal because the proposed remedy was not equivalent to the divestment of a stand-alone business but merely provided an opportunity for another undertaking to start a cement business from scratch. The transaction was prohibited (EU Commission Case No. COMP/M.7878 – *HeidelbergCement/Schwenk/Cemex Hungary/Cemex Croatia,* 5.4.2017). The parties unsuccessfully appealed the decision (Case T-380/17 *Heidelberg Cement v. Commission* [2020] EU:T:2020:471).

1021 If it were not profitable and was only operated to comply with CCPC requirements, it is unlikely that the purchaser would compete aggressively in this market.

concerned that the purchaser *"should be committed to making a significant investment in the business and growth of the JFT"* (¶31) although no specific remedy was included.[1022]

The CCPC expressed concerns in *Synch (JV)* that the shareholders would have an incentive to stymie innovation by the joint venture. The CCPC accepted that a remedy in relation to the governance of the joint venture would address this concern. *Bank of Ireland/KBC* involved a novel remedy which essentially involved the purchaser committing to provide loans to, and fund product innovations by, non-bank financial institutions (NBFIs) which competed with the merged entity in mortgage lending. The remedies proved unsuccessful. NBFIs dramatically reduced mortgage lending and raised interest rates within months of the CCPC decision, following increases in wholesale market interest rates, while banks' net interest income soared in 2023 as competition from NBFIs declined (*Irish Times,* 2025, February 11).[1023]

1022 Yarrow (2001) warns of the danger of competition agencies seeking to improve the way a market works which may turn into a prescriptive form of state intervention, resembling regulation or industrial policy rather than competition policy. The *Applegreen/JFT* remedies, which go beyond restoring competition to its pre-merger level, is arguably an example of such an approach. As previously stated, remedies requiring future notification of below the threshold mergers which the CA/CCPC applied in several cases is another possible example of such regulatory overreach.

1023 NBFIs had increased their share of mortgage lending in the years prior to the transaction because they enjoyed a significant competitive advantage due to negative wholesale interest rates in the wake of the financial crash and the Covid-19 pandemic. The remedies provided that Bank of Ireland would purchase bonds issued by NBFIs at commercial interest rates. There was no suggestion that NBFIs would not be able to raise funding but rather that they would no longer enjoy a cost advantage relative to banks in a normal interest rate environment. In contrast, banks mainly fund mortgage lending from cheap consumer deposits and excess deposits held with the Central Bank. The second element of the remedy involved Bank of Ireland establishing a fund for mortgage product innovation by third parties. It was subsequently reported that NBFIs had largely withdrawn from mortgage lending as higher wholesale rates rendered them uncompetitive, while banks' net interest margins increased (ICS Mortgages owner sees net interest slide 75% in 2023 on funding–costs spike, *Irish Times,* 2025, February 11; Finance Ireland's move to stop mortgage lending to have limited market impact – analysts, *Irish Times,* 2025, March 26). In late 2024 credit unions announced plans to introduce mortgage loans (*Irish Times,* 2024, October 21), while Revolut also announced that it would enter the market in Autumn 2025 (*Irish Times,* 2025, April 25). Such entry is beyond the normal two year time limit applied by the CCPC and it remains to be seen whether it will be sufficient to replace KBC, which accounted for 10-15% of new mortgage loans prior to its acquisition by Bank of Ireland. The EU Commission rejected proposed remedies in *ArcelorMittal/Ilva* which involved the seller of the divested business providing loans to the purchaser via so-called vendor loan notes. The Commission approved a remedy

There were several elements to the remedy in *LN-Gaiety/MCD Productions,* including:

i. A requirement to give advance notice of any proposal to acquire sole or joint control of a live music festival or an entity controlling one or more live music festivals in the State;

ii. A commitment by the purchaser not to disclose to MCD confidential information regarding third party promoters' plans for music events at a venue owned, operated or managed by the purchaser;

iii. Not to refuse or threaten to refuse to organise live events at a third-party venue if the venue contracted or considered contracting with, a supplier of Outsourced Primary Ticketing Services other than Ticketmaster;

iv. A commitment that any contract or negotiations in respect of the provision of Outsourced Primary Ticketing Services for live events by Ticketmaster to MCD would be conducted on an arm's length basis.

The remedies, however, appear remarkably similar to those accepted by the USDoJ in *Ticketmaster/Live Nation*[1024] which were widely regarded as seriously deficient. They only addressed competition concerns that could be foreseen at the time and could not address unanticipated new strategies by the merged entity, were difficult to enforce, and were couched in language that was inherently and unavoidably ambiguous (Kwoka, 2015). In May 2024, the USDoJ and 30 states sued Ticketmaster and Live Nation alleging monopolisation of the market for live events, contrary to §2 of the *Sherman Act* and sought the break-up of the merged entity (USDoJ, 2024, May 23).

Other Cases

Gorecki (2023, p.17) notes that in the *Uniphar/NaviCorp* prohibition decision the remedies offered by the merging parties were redacted entirely, thus

---

which did not involve the vendor financing or a performance-related purchase price (Vande Walle, 2021) (EU Commission Case No. COMP/M.8444, *ArcelorMittal/Ilva,* 17.4.2019 (purchaser approval decision).

1024 *United States v. Ticketmaster Ent., Inc.,* No. 1:10-cv-00139-RMC (D.D.C. Jan. 28, 2010). Hurwitz (2009) argued strongly at the time that it was highly unlikely that remedies could address the merger's anti-competitive effects and that it should be prohibited. Gastelum (2024) is highly critical of the USDoJ decision to accept remedies.

rendering it impossible to assess whether they were sufficient to address the competition concerns.[1025]

> *"Such an omission makes it not only difficult for an outside observer to examine the merits of the remedy proposals offered by the parties, but also makes it harder for practitioners advising clients in a merger transaction raising serious competition concerns as to what remedy proposals might and might not be acceptable to the CCPC."*

Gorecki (2023) states that remedies were offered by the parties in some other cases but were dismissed by the CA as unnecessary.[1026] In *DTZ/Sherry Fitzgerald Commercial,*[1027] the CCPC stated that documents provided by the parties included an agreement which, in its view, were not directly related to or necessary for the sale and was potentially in breach of §4 of the *Competition Act*. The Determination records that the parties agreed to remove/amend the relevant arrangements, although no formal remedy was involved. In *INM/CMNL* the CCPC expressed concerns about the potential for information exchange in relation to newspaper printing due to cross-shareholdings but accepted assurances from the parties, which are redacted in the Determination, and cleared the transaction without any remedy. In *NTMA/Cork County Council*[1028] the CCPC expressed concern that:

i. The JV could pass on commercially sensitive information received from third parties to the JV partners; and
ii. Cork CC's interest in the JV could create a conflict of interest in relation to its role as planning authority.

The CCPC concluded that the parties would put safeguards in place to address these concerns, based on their replies to queries, but again did not require a remedy.

1025 He notes that it appears the parties' revised second draft proposals included both structural and behavioural (access) elements. He also claims that the parties had prepared a non-confidential version of these proposals with a view to market testing and suggests that this could have been included in the Determination.

1026 He cites *Coillte/Weyerhaeuser* as an example of one such case.

1027 CCPC M/18/055 – *DTZ/Sherry Fitzgerald Commercial*, 3.8.2018.

1028 CCPC M/19/023 – *NTMA/Cork County Council*, 16.8.2019.

Conclusions

Where mergers are likely to harm competition, it is standard practice for competition agencies to consider whether it may be possible to remedy anti-competitive harms. Experience indicates that devising successful remedies may be exceedingly difficult. Ineffective remedies undermine the overall purpose of merger control. It is therefore important to conduct *ex-post* reviews of remedies and implement lessons from such reviews.

A distinction is made between structural remedies which involve some divestment of assets by the merged entity and behavioural remedies which impose restrictions on the future conduct of the merged entity.

Most competition agencies tend to favour structural remedies because they are clearer whereas behavioural remedies require ongoing monitoring and intervention. However, it is important to recognise that structural remedies may also prove ineffective, not least because merging parties have an obvious incentive to propose remedies that are likely to be ineffective. International experience indicates that divestments of an existing business unit are far more likely to be successful than one involving a mixed combination of assets of the merging parties as, by definition, such a combination has no established record of commercial viability. This is compounded by the fact that competition agencies are not well equipped to judge the viability of an untested combination of assets.

The CA/CCPC approach to merger remedies is very much out of step with most competition agencies. It has displayed a marked preference for behavioural rather than structural remedies and, in some cases where it has applied a structural remedy, it has involved an untested combination of assets. A majority of remedies have focused on concerns about potential information exchanges and requirements to notify future below the notification threshold, reflecting the fact that the CA/CCPC has frequently expressed concerns about potential harms resulting from possible future mergers rather than actual harms. This also may reflect false negatives which may have resulted in harmful mergers being approved without a detailed investigation. The results suggest that the CCPC needs to urgently re-think its approach to merger remedies.

Merging parties should consider possible remedies in advance of notifying transactions. Identifying an effective remedy in advance, should it be required, may avoid the need for a Phase 2 investigation, thus reducing cost and delay. In addition, if parties have not considered possible remedies until they find themselves faced with objections from the CCPC, they risk having to identify a solution at relatively short notice.

12: CONCLUSIONS

Teething Problems

Ireland was ahead of most countries in introducing merger control legislation with the enactment of the *Mergers, Takeovers & Monopolies Control Act, 1978*. The merger control regime established by that legislation, however, was very much a creature of its time. Decisions on whether mergers should be permitted were made by the Minister and, in theory, were based on a loosely-defined public interest test. Lyons *et al.* (2012) observe that historically competition policy *"tended to play a subservient role to industrial policy type considerations, and political rhetoric favouring competition was generally not matched by effective action"*. It is perhaps unsurprising, particularly given the relative paucity of international examples, that the legislation largely followed the then UK model.

The 1978 Act preceded the economics revolution in merger control which began in the early 1980s. It is not possible to assess the extent to which such developments influenced merger review under the 1978 Act. Published information on merger cases prior to 2002 is limited to the scant level of detail provided in the *Annual Reports* of the Minster, and published reports of 10 Phase 2 investigations of mergers referred to the CA by the Minister between 1992 and 2002 out of a total of 3,400 mergers notified between 1978 and 2002.

The *Competition Act, 2002,* represented a radical policy shift, de-politicising merger control by transferring responsibility for merger decisions to an independent agency. Some teething problems were perhaps inevitable given that the CA had only been asked to conduct a handful of Phase 2 merger investigations over the course of the previous decade.[1029] It

[1029] As noted in **Chapter 2**, 13 mergers were referred for a Phase 2 investigation but three of these were withdrawn post-referral so that the CA only conducted 10 Phase 2 investigations between 1992 and 2002.

is also perhaps understandable that the CA should have adopted a cautious initial approach, reflected in its broad interpretation of the obligation to notify mergers which resulted in almost 50% of mergers notified in the first four years involving no competition overlap. As noted, the CA revised its interpretation of the *"carrying on business in the island of Ireland"* provision in the legislation at the end of 2006 and this led to a significant decline in unnecessary notifications. The CA's pursuit of mergers falling below the notification thresholds also suggests, in part, an overly cautious approach.

The CA managed to successfully process a large volume of merger notifications within the statutory time limits, with one notable exception. However, it has not always met the statutory deadline for publishing Determinations, particularly in recent years.[1030] In order to address this it is suggested that, when the CCPC announces that it has taken a decision on a notified merger, in addition to stating that the full Determination will be published within 60 working days, it should also state the due date for publication and the subsequent Determination should include both the date of the decision and of the Determination's publication.

Institutional Weaknesses

Institutional structures and legislative foundations can have an important influence on merger case outcomes. Who the decision-makers are, whether politicians, independent agencies or courts also has an important influence on merger decisions. The decision to transfer responsibility for merger decisions from politicians to an independent agency represented a positive step in Irish merger control. However, the current institutional arrangements still suffer from a number of shortcomings.

For example, the substantive test to be applied can affect decisions about which mergers to investigate as well as the final decision. The Irish legislation applies the SLC test which is in line with international best practice and the CA/CCPC applies a consumer welfare standard in line with the vast majority of competition agencies throughout the world. However, the legislation does not require the CA/CCPC to have reasonable grounds for believing that an SLC could occur in order to launch a Phase 2

[1030] In the course of researching this book, the author identified 18 Determinations that were not available on the CCPC website as of 8 October 2024, 12 of which related to the 2021-2023 period, while the Determination, in *Kilsaran/Kilmurray* did not appear until some time after the publication deadline. At the time of going to press in April 2025, several, but not all, of these had been posted since the author brought this to the CCPC's attention.

investigation. This is not in line with other jurisdictions such as the EU and UK. In the vast majority of decisions to conduct a Phase 2 investigation the CA/CCPC stated that it was unable to conclude that an SLC would not occur. This is an *"abundance of caution"* approach to regulation which may involve a waste of time and resources both for the regulator and the entities subject to regulation.

Identifying an appropriate theory of harm early on is likely to be helpful in contentious cases for both the regulator and the merging parties as it can enable both sides to focus on the key issues (Scheffman & Coleman, 2003). To be clear it is not suggested that the CA/CCPC should have reached a conclusion on competitive harm at the end of Phase 1, rather that it should at least try to identify at an early stage which theory of harm it considers relevant in a particular case. As pointed out in **Chapter 3**, almost 80% of CA/CCPC decisions to launch a Phase 2 investigation occurred more than 50 days after the transaction had been notified. It would not appear unreasonable to expect the CCPC to at least be able to identify the type of concern that it considers requires investigation at that point. The lack of a requirement to have reasonable grounds for believing that an SLC could occur before going to Phase 2 creates the potential for regulatory hold-up. Faced with the prospect of a lengthy Phase 2 investigation, merging parties may offer remedies even in cases where an SLC is unlikely to arise, resulting in false positives.

It seems anomalous that merging parties have a right of appeal, thus providing a check against false positives, while there is no third party right of appeal in the case of false negatives. This is inconsistent with EU, UK and US practice.[1031] Addressing both these issues would require legislative change.

The legislation affords the CCPC considerable leeway in terms of setting its own procedures. The CCPC considers that it is not required to provide any feedback to merging parties in relation to possible competition concerns, prior to issuing an Assessment, which is arguably a relatively late stage in the process. This may make it difficult for the merging parties to either devise effective remedies or indeed mount an effective defence in a timely manner. The CA/CCPC has provided feedback at an earlier stage in many but not all cases. To an economist, at least, such inconsistencies appear to raise questions about procedural fairness.

1031 In the US, individual states may challenge mergers that the federal anti-trust agencies have not challenged.

A further issue arises because the same case team is responsible for the conduct of both Phase 1 and Phase 2 investigations. This is compounded by a lack of effective checks and balances which is arguably out of line with the EU and UK. Such checks and balances include the "devil's advocate" process applied by the EU and UK competition agencies. Andrews (2002) called for the appointment of independent hearing officers from outside the CCPC who were competent to adjudicate on both substantive and procedural issues in merger cases. In the wake of the High Court overturning the CA prohibition in *Kerry/Breeo*, Massey (2010, 2011) suggested that external economists should be retained to play a similar role to that of the EU's CCE in providing an independent economics appraisal in important cases, partly because the CA/CCPC lacked sufficient resources to establish such a unit within the organisation. Merging parties must also be afforded an adequate opportunity to challenge innovative concepts and the factual findings on which they are based both with respect to theories of harm and market definition.

Neven (2007) identified a significant imbalance between the number of professional economists in DG Competition and in economics consultancy firms, a view echoed by Lyons (2008). The CA/CCPC for many years has faced capacity constraints, particularly in relation to staff recruitment and retention.[1032] At the end of 2023 13% of CCPC posts were vacant. Over time it has accumulated responsibility for a wide range of issues beyond its original core functions, many of which are not part of the remit of most other competition/consumer protection agencies.[1033] A single division within the CCPC is responsible for civil enforcement of competition law and mergers whereas previously these roles were performed by two separate divisions. The combined division had 25 staff at the end of 2023, 13.4% of the CCPC's total staff numbers. Average length of staff service was three to five years, the latter figure relating to more senior personnel. The CCPC's difficulties in recruiting and retaining appropriate staff have implications for effective merger control bearing in mind that *"experienced staff are often not readily replaceable"* (*ibid.*, p.52). Depriving competition agencies of the necessary resources to operate effectively is an obvious way to undermine their effectiveness (Lancieri & Valetti, 2024).

1032 The following description is based largely on Government of Ireland (2024).

1033 The CCPC's functions include, for example, the authorisation of Alternative Dispute Resolution entities; Credit intermediaries; and Pawnbrokers.

The Need for Transparency & Accountability

Gorecki (2020) states that it is important for reasons of accountability and transparency that CA/CCPC merger Determinations provide sufficient information to enable readers to assess the basis for the decision, including the reasons for concluding that remedies were sufficient to address any competition concerns. Well-reasoned decisions are an important source of guidance for business and merger practitioners. The CA/CCPC performance in this regard merits a "could do better" at best. Unlike the EU Commission, which applies market definitions from previous cases involving similar products as its starting point when reviewing a merger, CCPCMG2014 state that conclusions in respect of market definition in previous cases cannot be relied upon. In many Determinations, important information necessary to understand the CA/CCPC's conclusions is redacted. Examples include redaction of (i) market shares;[1034] (ii) local catchment areas for filling stations; (iii) the grounds for rejecting efficiency claims; (iv) and details of remedies. As pointed out in **Chapter 11**, the CCPC redacted information on the number of parking spaces in a Galway car park managed by the target in *Q-Park/Tazbell*, although the information is available on a Galway County Council website.[1035] Gorecki notes that *Berendsen/King's Laundry* included market share ranges and the CCPC's HHI estimates for the two relevant markets but data on tender participation, frequency of tender success and diversion ratios for the healthcare market were completely redacted. This is in stark contrast to the comprehensive analysis of bidding in Annex I of the EU Commission decision in *General Electric/Alstom*.[1036]

In addition, the reasoning in many cases is vague and ambiguous. As previously stated, the CA/CCPC has cleared many horizontal mergers on the basis that the increase in market share is "small" and/or because there are sufficient competitors to prevent any anti-competitive behaviour begging the question as to what constitutes small and how many competitors are sufficient. These do not constitute reasoned, well-argued decisions. This approach is also inconsistent with CA/CCPC *Guidelines*

1034 In many cases the CA/CCPC has published market share ranges, which as Gorecki (2020) observes is consistent with EU practice, but, as noted in Chapter 8, it has failed to do so in several cases.

1035 It also redacted details of several competing car parks in Galway City. It is difficult to understand how details regarding the location of a car park which offers parking to the public can be regarded as commercially-sensitive.

1036 Although a certain amount of bidding data was redacted, tender participation and win rates were published albeit with ranges of 10 percentage points.

which state that mergers below certain HHI thresholds are unlikely to raise concern while those above those thresholds require further investigation. Failure to adhere to published *Guidelines* violates what Shapiro, C. (2024, p.158) describes as *"the good-government principle that official guidelines should accurately reflect actual Agency practice"*. Several Determinations in recent years, involving mergers which were cleared subject to remedies at Phase 1, state that, in light of the remedies, there is no need for any further consideration of the alleged competitive harm. Thus, the Determination provides no information as to the nature of the competition concern or explanation of how the remedy addresses this. This lack of transparency is simply not good enough. This approach is also symptomatic of a lack of effective accountability which needs to be addressed.

Market Definition Still Matters

Market definition in merger analysis is a means to an end. It is, nevertheless, extremely important as it provides a context and framework for analysing the likely competitive effects of a merger. It enables identification of market shares and concentration which provides a useful mechanism for identifying harmless mergers. Defining markets also provides important guidance for businesses and may improve deterrence. It also provides a constraint against arbitrary regulatory decisions.

Adopting the narrowest possible market definition may frequently be sufficient to conclude that an SLC will not arise rendering precise market definitions unnecessary. However, this approach cannot be relied upon if (a) it places the parties in separate markets or (b) it indicates a possible SLC. In both these situations it is necessary to define the market correctly. Several CA/CCPC Determinations have defined markets too narrowly, whether implicitly or explicitly giving rise to both false positives and negatives.

The CA/CCPC has repeatedly stated that its conclusions would be unaffected whether markets were defined narrowly or widely. A broad market definition may yield a false negative by including products/areas which are not close substitutes and will not therefore exercise an effective constraint on the merging parties post-merger. Thus, little reliance should be placed on wide market definitions unless there is evidence that they are correct. In some cases, by failing to rule out overly broad market definitions, the CA/CCPC has afforded them an unwarranted degree of validity. It would be better to either define the market correctly or apply the narrowest possible market definition.

Market definition is unnecessary when market power can be measured directly, although data deficiencies preclude this in many cases. Even where it is possible, it is arguably best practice to also define the relevant market. In all cases involving a potential SLC, it is important to define the market correctly to avoid a possible false positive. The CA/CCPC has failed to recognise this in several cases. Failing to define markets also creates a worrying potential for arbitrary market definitions and decisions.

Market Concentration

Market concentration can be useful for distinguishing between mergers which are unlikely to be anti-competitive and those that require closer scrutiny. CA/CCPC *Guidelines* define HHI thresholds as a means of differentiating between innocuous mergers and competitively harmful ones. The CA/CCPC, however, has frequently failed to estimate HHIs and apply these thresholds in practice. In many cases the CA/CCPC concluded that the transaction was unlikely to raise concerns because it would only result in a small increase in market share, when economics indicates that even small increases in market shares may harm competition. In focusing purely on market shares and ignoring market concentration the CA/CCPC frequently failed to identify mergers that, according to their own *Guidelines*, should have been subject to a detailed investigation. It has also argued that there were sufficient competitors in the market to exercise an effective constraint even in cases where the merging parties' extremely high market shares (up to 90% in at least one case) suggest this was unlikely. This also ignores the fact that it may be in non-merging firms' interests to raise their prices, albeit to a lesser extent, in response to a post-merger unilateral price increase by the merging parties. Such cases raise the possibility of false negatives.

CCPCMG2014 provides that an increase in the HHI of less than 150 points is unlikely to raise competition concerns irrespective of the post-merger HHI level. As only the parties' market shares are required to estimate the increase in the HHI due to a merger, this offers a relatively simple means for identifying many harmless mergers. Stating in merger Determinations that a transaction would not result in any SLC because it would result in a HHI increase of less than 150 points would be consistent with CCPCMG2014 and would provide greater clarity than references to small or minimal increases which are vague, subjective and likely to result in Type II errors.

In other cases, the CA/CCPC has raised concerns solely on the basis of market concentration, based in some cases on overly narrow market definitions. This is inconsistent both with economics and the CA/CCPC's *Guidelines* which indicate that high market concentration is a necessary but not sufficient condition for a merger to result in competitive harm. The application of remedies in such cases is an example of potential false positive (Type I) errors. This is compounded by the fact that in some of these cases, as previously noted, the CA/CCPC has indicated that the application of a remedy rendered it unnecessary to consider whether the merger as originally notified would have resulted in an SLC. Therefore, we do not know what the CA/CCPC's concerns were or whether they were even valid.

Three to two mergers might be expected to generally raise competition concerns and at the very least require detailed review. The CA/CCPC has cleared several such cases without remedies, sometimes based on a preliminary investigation, but has prohibited or required remedies in others, although the reasons for the different outcomes are not always clear. In one 2023 case the CCPC raised concerns in a five to four merger which was cleared subject to a divestment remedy that maintained five market competitors, while another case was cleared subject to divestment remedies involving two local markets where the transaction reduced the number of competitors from eight to seven and seven to six. It is too early to judge whether these decisions are a harbinger of a tougher approach to merger control.

It's All in the Theory

In order to establish that a merger is likely to result in an SLC, it is necessary to identify a mechanism by which it will harm competition. Historically coordinated effects, the risk that a merger would facilitate collusion whether tacit or overt, constituted the primary concern in the case of horizontal mergers. Since the early 1990s there has been an increasing focus on unilateral effects, as mergers between competitors may enable the merged entity to unilaterally raise price post-merger. More recently, increasing attention has focused on the risk that mergers will harm innovation and product development: innovation theories of harm.

Where the evidence suggests that a merger may be anti-competitive it is also necessary to consider whether new entry, expansion by existing rivals, countervailing buyer power, and, in the case of unilateral effects, product repositioning by rivals may prevent any competitive harm.

The CCPC has analysed potential theories of harm in a relatively limited number of cases. A substantial proportion of horizontal mergers fell below the level of concentration where competition harms are considered likely to arise and thus did not require a detailed analysis. However, many cases which were above these thresholds were cleared without a detailed analysis resulting in potential false negatives. In most cases which were subject to detailed review, it appears from the published Determinations that the CA/CCPC's analysis of theories of harm was sound. In several cases, however, there is evidence suggesting possible Type I (false positive) or Type II (false negative) errors. In a small number of Determinations, the redaction of information makes it impossible to come to any conclusion.

Economics indicates that vertical and conglomerate mergers are far less likely to harm competition than horizontal mergers and that harmful effects are unlikely unless the merging parties have market power in one or more markets. It is not surprising, therefore, that the CA/CCPC has rarely identified competition harms in vertical and conglomerate merger cases. The main focus of its investigations in such cases have centred around potential input and customer foreclosure. EUNHMG2008 apply a combination of market share and post-merger HHIs as a screening device for identifying vertical mergers where the merging parties are unlikely to have significant market power. The SMNP means that vertical merger where the parties have market shares of less than 25% in any related market are likely to be cleared following a preliminary review.

The "Efficiencies Offence"

Horizontal mergers may generate sufficient efficiencies, in some cases, to offset the price increasing effects of a reduction in rivalry. Consequently, potential efficiency gains need to be considered as part of the assessment of mergers. Historically many competition agencies adopted a sceptical approach to efficiency claims and in some cases viewed them as a negative factor.

Efficiencies have played an extremely limited role in CA/CCPC merger cases. Only a handful of cases involved any detailed consideration of efficiencies. The CA's analysis in *Kerry/Breeo,* the first case involving a detailed efficiencies claim, was seriously flawed. In several other cases the CA/CCPC has simply stated that the parties' efficiency claims did not meet the requirements specified in the *Merger Guidelines,* frequently without providing any details. The CA/CCPC treatment of efficiencies is highly unsatisfactory and needs to be revisited as a matter of urgency.

Fixing it

Where mergers are likely to harm competition, it is standard practice for competition agencies to consider whether the merger can be modified in a way that eliminates the risk of competitive harms. A distinction is made between structural remedies which involve some divestment of assets by the merged entity and behavioural remedies which impose restrictions on the future conduct of the merged entity.

Most competition agencies tend to favour structural remedies because they are cleaner and final whereas behavioural remedies require ongoing monitoring and intervention. The evidence indicates that behavioural remedies are far less effective at preventing competitive harm than structural remedies. Structural remedies may also prove ineffective, not least because merging parties have an obvious incentive to propose weak remedies. International experience indicates that divestments of existing business units are far more likely to be successful than those involving a mixed combination of assets of the merging parties as, by definition, such a combination has no established record of commercial viability. This is compounded by the fact that competition agencies are not well equipped to judge the viability of an untested combination of assets.

The CA/CCPC approach to merger remedies is very much out of step with international best practice. It has displayed a marked preference for behavioural rather than structural remedies and, in some cases where it has applied a structural remedy, this has involved a combination of assets rather than a specific business unit. A majority of remedies have focused on concerns about potential information exchanges and requirements to notify future below the notification threshold, which reflect a concern about potential harms from future mergers rather than actual harms resulting from the case at hand. The lack of divestment remedies may reflect false negatives, *i.e.,* harmful mergers being approved without a detailed investigation. The CCPC needs to urgently re-think its approach to merger remedies.

Merging parties should consider possible remedies in advance of notifying transactions. Identifying an effective remedy in advance, should it be required, may avoid the need for a Phase 2 investigation, thus reducing cost and delay, although it is worth repeating that Phase 2 investigations should only occur where the CCPC has reasonable grounds for believing that an SLC is likely in order to avoid regulatory hold-up and false positives due to unnecessary remedies. If parties have not considered possible remedies until they find themselves faced with objections from the CCPC, they risk having to identify a solution at relatively short notice.

An Assessment

Chapter 1 identified four criteria for assessing the effectiveness of a merger control regime:

i. Whether it leads to correct decisions, preventing anti-competitive mergers while permitting mergers that are not anti-competitive;
ii. Whether it provides an effective deterrent to anti-competitive mergers;
iii. Whether it deals with harmless mergers speedily while also minimising regulatory costs for business;
iv. Whether it delivers positive benefits for consumers.

As stated at the outset, no competition agency or merger control regime will get every decision right. Nevertheless, the objective for both policy-makers and competition agencies should be to minimise errors and the resulting welfare losses, to learn from mistakes, and take steps to reduce the potential for repeating errors. It is also important to acknowledge that it is sometimes possible to reach different conclusions based on the same set of facts (Neven, 2007).

Getting Decisions Right

The results in respect of the first criteria are mixed at best. In the 21-year period since the change in Ireland's merger control regime, of the 1,264 mergers notified to the CA/CCPC 89% were cleared unconditionally following a preliminary, Phase 1, investigation. Only five notified mergers have been prohibited and the CA's Determination in one of these cases was overturned by the High Court on appeal. A further 45 mergers were subject to remedies which indicates that they were originally considered likely to result in an SLC.[1037] Overall the CA/CCPC concluded that only 4% of all mergers notified were likely to result in a SLC. The evidence indicates that the CA/CCPC has adopted a more lenient approach to mergers than the EU and US, although both of these have been criticised for being overly lenient.

[1037] Six of these were cleared on foot of undertakings to notify future mergers, even if they were below the notification thresholds, while two others involved ancillary restraints implying that the mergers themselves raised no competition issues.

The low proportion of prohibition and remedy decisions, by definition, indicates that there have been relatively few false positive (Type 1) errors. Nevertheless, an analysis of individual cases suggests several potential false positives. These include *Kerry/Breeo*, where the CA's prohibition decision was overturned by the High Court on appeal. Several cases were remedied at Phase 1 after the CA/CCPC had raised concerns based solely on market concentration without citing any theory of competitive harm. This is inconsistent with economics and with the CA/CCPC's own *Guidelines* which indicate that high market concentration is a necessary but not sufficient condition for a merger to result in competitive harm. The prospect of a lengthy Phase 2 investigation and the costs involved may encourage firms to settle and accept remedies even though the merger would not have resulted in any SLC. It bears repeating that the application of remedies in such cases constitutes a potential false positive. This is compounded by the CA/CCPC's failure to outline any theory of harm in its subsequent Determination in several of these cases on the grounds that it was no longer necessary.

There is considerable evidence, which, while not conclusive, points to a significant level of Type II false negative errors. The very low number of remedies/prohibitions, almost by definition, raises the possibility that a significant number of anti-competitive mergers may have gone undetected. The evidence indicates that before 2020, many mergers which merited a detailed investigation according to CA/CCPC *Guidelines*, were cleared on the basis of a preliminary Phase 1 investigation. The significant upturn in problem cases identified following the introduction of the SMNP in 2020 is a further indicator that many anti-competitive mergers may previously have gone undetected. Many cases were cleared on the grounds that they only involved a *"small"* increment in market share when economics indicates that this is an insufficient basis for concluding that an SLC would not occur. In fairness, the CA/CCPC are not alone in this regard as EU and US competition agencies have been criticised for similar errors. The CA/CCPC in multiple cases has stated that there were sufficient competitors to prevent any post-merger price increase, although unilateral effects theories indicate that it may be in the interests of non-merging firms to go along with any post-merger price increase by raising their own prices, albeit to a lesser extent than the merging parties. The *Heineken/Beamish & Crawford* decision appears to explicitly acknowledge the likelihood of a post-merger price increase (see **Chapter 8**).

There is evidence of a stricter approach post-2019 as the number of high risk cases cleared on the basis of a preliminary Phase 1 investigation has fallen dramatically. It is probably too early to tell whether this trend will be sustained. It is nevertheless welcome as it reduces the risk of false negatives.

Deterrence

An alternative explanation for the small number of cases found to have raised SLC concerns is that the system proved highly effective in deterring anti-competitive mergers. It is extremely difficult to establish the deterrent effect of merger enforcement. By definition, mergers that are deterred will not be observed. There have been attempts in other jurisdictions to estimate the number of deterred mergers based on surveys.[1038] The low rate of prohibitions (five in 21 years) and remedies, coupled with evidence of a potentially high incidence of false negatives, tends to suggest that merger control in Ireland has had a very limited deterrent effect. Since 2016, the proportion of problem cases subject to detailed investigation has increased sharply which is inconsistent with the merger regime having a strong deterrent effect.[1039] Another way of viewing this is to look at the percentage of horizontal mergers defined as high-competition risk based on CA/CCPC HHI thresholds illustrated in **Table 12.1**. If deterrence is strong then one might expect to observe fewer of these cases.[1040] The table indicates that the proportion of such cases declined post-2011 but has increased dramatically post-2019.

Table 12.1: HHI High Risk Mergers as a Percentage of Notified Horizontal Mergers

2003-2007	2008-2011	2012-2015	2016-2019	2020-2023
20.3	20.3	15.3	16.1	28.0

Source: CA/CCPC.

1038 Results for the US pre-1983 suggest that, for every merger challenged by the US anti-trust agencies, 11-16 other mergers were deterred. A 2007 study for the UK found that, for every blocked merger, at least five others were abandoned or modified. Merger controls were also found to have had a deterrent effect in the Netherlands (Sørgard, 2009).

1039 Alternatively, it may be that the increase in the number of problem cases reflects a stricter approach, but this again indicates the possibility of an overly lenient approach with a higher likelihood of false negative (Type II) errors in earlier years.

1040 Sørgard (2009) reports survey evidence for the Netherlands indicating that firms were less likely to pursue mergers in highly concentrated markets.

Clear, well-reasoned decisions are also important for effective deterrence as they provide clear guidance to businesses and merger practitioners in relation to the type of mergers that are likely to be approved (Lyons, 2008). Firms have a clear incentive to pursue mergers that are likely to be approved. Here again, the CA/CCPC approach has arguably been problematic.

According to CCPCMG2014 conclusions in respect of market definition in previous cases cannot be relied upon, in contrast to the EU Commission which applies market definitions used in previous cases involving similar products, as its starting point. As previously noted, in many cases important information necessary to understand the CA/CCPC's conclusions was redacted in published Determinations. A competition agency's credibility requires a high degree of transparency (Trebilcock & Iacobucci, 2002). In addition, the reasoning in many cases is vague and ambiguous.

Fast-Tracking Innocuous Cases

An effective merger control regime should deal with innocuous cases speedily while minimising the regulatory cost and burden for such transactions. The CA responded relatively quickly in late 2006 by amending its interpretation of the notification requirements to reduce the number of notifications of mergers which had no Irish competition nexus.

Average decision times appear to have increased significantly since 2016, while the proportion of quite lengthy cases also has increased sharply. The introduction of SMNP in 2020 has reduced the regulatory burden and speeded up decisions in the case of harmless mergers: 50% of all cases in 2023 were cleared under SMNP. The average duration of such case is approximately 18 days.

Market definition is critical in SMNP cases as the qualifying criteria require (a) that there be no overlap between the parties or (b) that their market shares are below certain levels. It is therefore essential that markets be defined correctly in such cases in order to avoid potential false negatives. Initially SMNP Determinations provided no details on relevant markets. More recently market definitions have been included, at least in some cases. It is important that all SMNP cases should state the market definitions which form the basis for concluding that a merger satisfies the SMNP criteria. This is important from both a clarity and transparency viewpoint but may also provide a safeguard against false positives, as parties will recognise that, as market definitions will be made public, false market definition claims are likely to be exposed. Such publication would also promote public confidence in the merger control regime. It would also be helpful if the CCPC stated if a merger had been cleared under SMNP when announcing decisions.[1041]

The introduction of the SMNP may represent a win-win by speeding up decisions on innocuous cases, reducing the notification burden in such cases, and enabling the CCPC to concentrate its resources on potentially more problematic cases. Some caution is required given that we only have data for a limited period since the introduction of the SMNP.

Producing Benefits for Consumers

As stated in **Chapter 1**, the ultimate test of the effectiveness of a merger control regime is whether it enhances consumer welfare through lower prices, better quality, greater choice, and more rapid technological progress than would otherwise have been the case (Kwoka, 2015). This depends on whether it has been effective at identifying and preventing or remedying mergers which would have had a negative effect on such variables. Any such evaluation is extremely difficult due to a lack of data. Competition agencies generally do not collect data on post-merger performance or conduct *ex post* reviews of merger cases (*ibid.*). Baker & Shapiro (2008) observe that there is no easy way to evaluate the effectiveness of merger enforcement.

The limited number of prohibitions and merger remedies, by definition, suggest that merger control has had a relatively limited positive impact on consumer welfare. This is further compounded by the fact that the effectiveness of the remedies applied in many cases is also questionable. The results to date suggest that deterrent effects are likely to be limited. Evidence of a potentially high level of false positives indicate a failure to prevent consumer harm in a significant number of cases.

The CCPC has produced its own cost-benefit estimates, based on merger cases over the 2017-2020 period, which claim that merger control had increased consumer welfare by €14m per year on average. The CCPC estimates are highly questionable. The CCPC acknowledges that its estimates do not assess whether its interventions were correct or optimal, implying that a false positive remedy is incorrectly treated as having a beneficial effect on consumer welfare. The CCPC methodology also assumes that remedies were beneficial even if they were ineffective. The estimates also assume that

---

1041 It has been somewhat inconsistent in this regard and there appears to be no reason to wait until the final Determination is subsequently published, potentially 60 working days later, to state whether the case was cleared under the SMNP.

structural commitments such as divestment of assets have the same effect on future prices as behavioural commitments which seems highly questionable.[1042] The international evidence outlined in **Chapter 11** indicates that behavioural remedies were far less effective than structural remedies at preventing harm to consumers. Ten of the 14 remedies (71%) included in the CCPC analysis involved purely behavioural remedies. They included *CVC/Celtic Rugby* where the remedy required the parties to notify any future acquisition of a stake in Six Nations Rugby. This remedy did not prevent any price increase and so yielded no benefits to consumers as the CCPC subsequently concluded that *CVC/Six Nations* raised no competition concerns. Thus, the CCPC estimates of the effect of merger control on consumer welfare are likely to be substantially overstated.

The CCPC estimates also ignore harm to consumers due to false negatives. Arguably anti-competitive mergers which went undetected would have occurred anyway in the absence of merger controls. The idea that the costs resulting from a failure to identify anti-competitive mergers should not be considered when analysing the effectiveness of merger controls seems wrong intuitively. Consumers were effectively denied the benefits that would have accrued had such mergers been detected and prevented or effectively remedied and therefore such welfare losses should be included in any assessment of merger control.

As pointed out in **Chapter 8**, the CA implicitly acknowledged that *Heineken/Beamish & Crawford* would result in a price increase. The CA/CCPC have cleared several mergers in the liquid milk market despite it being highly concentrated. **Figure 12.1** compares trends in the retail price of milk and the prices paid to farmers for raw milk. Over most of the period from 2008 to 2021 the retail price failed to reflect declines in prices paid to farmers.[1043] Total national consumption of liquid milk in 2023 amounted to 572 million litres which means that a potential false negative is likely to impose significant costs on consumers. If such mergers had a negative effect on competition, every cent per litre above the competitive price cost consumers €5.7 million.

[1042] The CCPC acknowledged that it is reasonable to suggest that different types of commitment may be preventing different scales of consumer harm.

[1043] The retail price of milk increased by 54% between 2004 and 2023, while overall food prices increased by just 10.5% over the same period, which tends to rule out increased production and distribution costs as an explanatory factor.

Figure 12.1: Trends in Retail & Producer Liquid Milk Prices

Source: National Milk Agency (2023).

Certainly, a more detailed analysis of merger remedies is required than that applied in CCPC (2022). Baker & Shapiro (2008, p.29) state that:

> *"The most compelling way to evaluate the accuracy of merger enforcement policy would be through merger retrospectives - detailed studies evaluating the actual effects of consummated mergers on market prices, product variety, or innovation. The most revealing mergers to study in depth are those that went forward despite presenting serious anti-trust concerns."*[1044]

There are likely to be many such cases on file in the CA/CCPC archives. Conducting a large number of retrospective mergers studies would provide greater insights into the conditions under which horizontal mergers do, and do not, harm consumers. They would also enable an evaluation of the accuracy of the merger review techniques and identify ways in which merger control might be improved. Such retrospective studies are essential if past errors are to be identified, lessons learned and to enhance the effectiveness of merger policy. Carlton (2009) and Farrell & Shapiro (2010a) argued that what is really required is an *ex post* evaluation of post-merger price increases *versus* predicted increases at the time of the merger.

The CA/CCPC is by no means unique. Various studies have highlighted that many competition agencies have failed to identify a significant proportion of anti-competitive mergers. Shapiro (2019) states that the

1044 See Kwoka (2015) for a comprehensive overview of US merger retrospectives.

evidence from merger retrospectives is that US merger policy over the previous 25 years had been too lax. This does not mean that we should simply give up but rather emphasises the necessity to review historic case outcomes so that we can learn to do it better. Any such retrospective review must be independent of the CCPC. Having them correct their own homework is not acceptable.

CASES

Ireland

Cases

Competition Authority v. O'Regan & Ors. [2007] IESC 22.
Nurendale Limited t/a Panda Waste Services v. Dublin City Council, Dún Laoghaire/Rathdown County Council, Fingal County Council & South Dublin County Council [2009] IEHC 488.
Rye Investments v. Competition Authority [2009] IEHC 140.

CA/CCPC Merger Decisions

CA M/03/001 – *Musgrave/Express Check-out*, 13.3.2003.
CA M/03/004 – *General Electric/Agfa*, 14.4.2003 (referred to EU Commission).
CA M/03/005 – *Ryanair/Buzz*, 4.3.2003.
CA M/03/012 – *Smurfit/Lithographic Universal*, 17.7.2003.
CA M/03/016 – *March UK/GUS Ireland*, 15.7.2003.
CA M/03/021 – *Pritchitts/Lakeland*, 17.7.2003.
CA M/03/029 - *Dawn Meats/Galtee Meats*, 20.11.2003.
CA M/03/033 – *SRH/Capital Radio*, 23.2.2004.
CA M/03/035 – *Stena/P&O I*, (withdrawn) February 2004.
CA M/04/003 – *Radio 2000/Newstalk*, 5.3.2004.
CA M/04/004 – *DaimlerChrysler/Mitsubishi*, 6.2.2004.
CA M/04/006 – *Abbott/TheraSense*, 26.2.2004.
CA M/04/009 – *Pfizer/CSL Animal Health*, 4.3.2004.
CA M/04/011 – *Liberty/Princes Holdings*, 9.2.2004.
CA M/04/015 – *ExxonMobil/BP*, 6.04.2004.
CA M/04/016 – *Stena/P&O II*, 5.4.2004.
CA M/04/019 – *Sarcon/Barlo*, 22.4.2004.
CA M/04/020 – *Uniphar/Whelehan*, 20.7.2004.
CA M/04/028 – *Abbott/Aventis*, 19.5.2004.
CA M/04/030 – *Celtic News/Westmeath Examiner*, 30.6.2004.

CA M/04/032 – *IBM/Schlumberger*, 28.10.2004.
CA M/04/040 – *Jacob/Babtie*, 9.8.2024.
CA M/04/042 – *Wolseley/Brooks Group*, 26.8.2004.
CA M/04/043 – *ABF/Littlewoods/St. James*, 25.7.2004.
CA M/04/048 – *Hachette/Hodder Headline*, 13.9.2004.
CA M/04/051 – *Grafton/Heiton*, 17.2.2005.
CA M/04/058 – *Abbott/Natural Supplements Association*, 1.11.2004.
CA M/04/064 – *Timac/Albatross*, 1.12.2004
CA M/04/065 – *Moët Hennessy/Glenmorangie*, 29.11.2004.
CA M/04/070 – *Rice/Albatross Feeds*, 23.12.2004.
CA M/04/071 – *Kantaka/RBS*, 21.12.2004.
CA M/04/073 – *Nestlé/Wagner*, 10.1.2005.
CA M/04/078 – *UTV/Coderidge*, 21.1.2005.
CA M/05/006 – *Glanbia/Dairygold*, 9.3.2005.
CA M/05/007 – *Wavin/Hepworth Building Products*, 22.3.2005.
CA M/05/009 – *Kingspan/Century Homes*, 13.4.2005.
CA M/05/015 – *Tysan/Balcuik* (withdrawn and re-notified), 5.5.2005.
CA M/05/018 – *Tysan/Balcuik*, 19.5.2005.
CA M/05/021 – *William Hill/Stanley Racing*, 2.6.2005.
CA M/05/022 – *Alpha Publications/Midmedia*, 30.5.2005.
CA M/05/024 – *UGC (Chorus)/NTL*, 4.11.2005.
CA M/05/025 – *SRH/Highland Radio*, 12.8.2005.
CA M/05/027 – *MJ Gleeson/UBH*, 23.8.2005.
CA M/05/028 – *Eason/Alphyra*, 14.7.2005.
CA M/05/033 – *Heinz/HP Foods*, 11.8.2005.
CA M/05/036 – *Emap/SRH*, 28.7.2005.
CA M/05/039 – *Diageo/Bushmills*, 4.8.2005.
CA M/05/050 – *eircom/Meteor*, 18.11.2005.
CA M/05/054 – *Hewlett Packard/Scitex Vision*, 23.9.2005.
CA M/05/061 – *Trader Publishing/Webzone*, 3.11.2005.
CA M/05/065 – *Johnston Press/Leinster*, 2.12.2005.
CA M/05/071 – *Associated Newspapers/Irish Times/Metro/Fortunegreen* (*Fortunegreen JV*), 1.12.2005.
CA M/05/079 – *Radio County Sound/Dooley & Feeney*, 1.3.2006.
CA M/06/009 – *Hachette/Time Warner Book Group*, 4.3.2006.
CA M/06/027 – *Tetra Laval/Carlisle*, 11.8.2006.
CA M/06/039 – *Kingspan/Xtratherm*, 25.10.2006.
CA M/06/044 – *Topaz/Statoil*, 9.10.2006.[a]
CA M/06/051 – *Largo Foods/Tayto*, 4.9.2006.
CA M/06/052 – *Debenham's/Roches Stores*, 6.9.2006.
CA M/06/057 – *Coillte/Weyerhaeuser*, 10.11.2006.[b]
CA M/06/059 – *Irish Times/My Home*, 25.9.2006.[c]
CA M/06/061 – *Irish Times/Gloss*, 22.9.2006.

CA M/06/067 – *Connacht Tribune/Galway Bay FM*, 24.10.2006.
CA M/06/084 – *BT/PlusNet*, 18.12.2006.
CA M/06/087 – *Applied Materials/Brooks Software*, 6.2.2007.
CA M/06/089 – *Doughty Hansen/Setanta*, 5.1.2007.
CA M/06/091 – *Barclays/de Smet* (withdrawn).
CA M/06/093 – *Abbott/KOS* (withdrawn).
CA M/06/098 – *Premier Foods/RHM*, 9.2.2007.
CA M/07/002 – *Eason/Menzies*, 1.2.2007.
CA M/07/005 – *River Newspapers/Olok*, 9.2.2007.
CA M/07/007 – *Bernard McNamara/Conrad International/ECHPL*, 21.2.2007.
CA M/07/009 – *UTC/SFS* (withdrawn).
CA M/07/010 – *Irish Times/Gazette*, 22.03.2007.
CA M/07/012 – *Bord na Móna/AES*, 2.5.2007.
CA M/07/021 – *Thomas Crosbie Holdings/WKW FM*, 17.8.2007.
CA M/07/022 – *Thomas Crosbie Holdings/South East Broadcasting*, 15.9.2007.
CA M/07/027 – *Britvic/C&C*, 13.8.2007.
CA M/07/030 – *Glen Dimplex/Applied Energy*, 25.9.2007.
CA M/07/031 – *Galco/Sperrin*, 2.10.2007.
CA M/07/040 – *SRH/Communicorp*, 7.12.2007.
CA M/07/043 – *One51/Hegarty/A1/Galway Metal*, 6.9.2007.[c]
CA M/07/046 – *Smart Telecom/E-NVI*, 17.9.2007.
CA M/07/054 – *Novasep/Pharmachem*, 9.10.2007.
CA M/07/055 – *Bunzl/DGD*, 17.10.2007.
CA M/07/059 – *Resolution/Friends Provident* (withdrawn).
CA M/07/064 – *Johnston Press/Clonnad*, 19.2.2008.
CA M/07/068 – *Nike/Umbro*, 23.1.2008.
CA M/07/069 – *UTV/FM104*, 17.1.2008.
CA M/08/003 – *Independent/Champion*, 10.3.2008.
CA M/08/007 – *Irish Times/Relevance*, 25.3.2008.
CA M/08/009 – *Kerry/Breeo*, 28.8.2008.[c]
CA M/08/011 – *Heineken/Scottish & Newcastle*, 3.10.2008.[c]
CA M/08/014 – *BWG/Mangan's*, 2.5.2008.
CA M/08/016 – *Premier Group/Imprint*, 19.5.2008.
CA M/08/021 – *TV3/Kish Media*, 18.8.2008.
CA M/08/028 – *Eirgrid/SONI*, 25.9.2008.[c]
CA M/08/030 – *Celsa/BRC/McMahon*, 23.10.2008.
CA M/08/032 – *First Choice/Sunshine Cruises*, 24.10.2008.
CA M/08/036 – *Lloyds TSB/HBOS*, 17.12.2008.
CA M/09/002 – *HMV Ireland/Zavvi*, 23.1.2009.
CA M/09/008 – *Chevron/Texoil*, 23.4.2009.
CA M/09/009 – *European Refreshments/Fresh Trading*, 7.5.2009.
CA M/09/010 – *LL/TPDL/FIL/Freshmills/Drummonds*, 18.6.2009.
CA M/09/013 – *Metro/Herald AM*, 6.11.2009.

CA M/09/015 – *Vodafone Ireland/BT Ireland*, 21.8.2009.
CA M/09/016 – *Tedcastles/Fate Park*, 6.8.2009.
CA M/09/018 – *C&C/Tennents*, 17.9.2009.
CA M/09/024 – *Greenstar/Veolia*, 11.3.2010.
CA M/10/003 – *Club Travel/Budget Travel*, 15.2.2010.
CA M/10/015 – *An Post/PostPoint*, 31.5.2010.
CA M/10/018 – *Moy Park/O'Kane*, 23.6.2010.
CA M/10/020 – *Sky/VMtv*, 29.6.2010.
CA M/10/026 – *ESB/NIE*, 29.10.2010.
CA M/10/029 – *Kerry/Newmarket*, 5.10.2010.
CA M/10/031 – *CapVest/Origin Foods/Maiden*, 18.11.2010.
CA M/10/038 – *Barnett/Origin/Hall*, 21.1.2011.
CA M/10/039 – *Kingspan/CRH Insulation*, 2.12.2010.
CA M/10/040 – *Unilever/Alberto Culver*, 23.2.2011.
CA M/10/041 – *Pilgrim (Oaktree Group)/MHL & MCL*, 3.12.2010.
CA M/10/043 – *Stena/DFDS*, 7.4.2011.
CA M/11/003 – *DSM/Martek*, 11.2.2011. (The Determination incorrectly lists the decision date as 11.2.2010).
CA M/11/004 – *Glanbia/Dawn Dairies & Golden Vale*, 1.4.2011.
CA M/11/005 – *JD Sports/Champion Sports*, 30.3.2011.
CA M/11/018 – *Blackstone/Tangerine*, 24.6.2011.
CA M/11/019 – *Amazon/Book Depository*, 26.7.2011.
CA M/11/021 – *Intersnack/Largo Foods*, 3.8.2011.[c]
CA M/11/022 – *Musgrave/Superquinn*, 28.9.2011.
CA M/12/002 – *Millington/Siteserv*, 21.5.2012.
CA M/12/004 – *Southbank/Travel Channel*, 20.4.2012.
CA M/12/007 – *Nestlé/Pfizer Nutrition*, 15.6.2012.
CA M/12/008 – *SSE/Endessa*, 17.7.2012.
CA M/12/010 – *Pallas/Crossgar*, 23.8.2012.
CA M/12/017 – *United Care/Pharmexx*, 17.11.2012.
CA M/12/018 – *Julius Baer/IMWB Merrill Lynch* (withdrawn).
CA M/12/021 – *Henry Schein/C&M Vetlink*, 29.11.2012.
CA M/12/027 – *Uniphar/CMR*, 30.4.2013.
CA M/12/030 – *C&C/Gleeson*, 27.2.2013.
CA M/12/031 – *Top Snacks/KP Snacks*, 22.4.2013.
CA M/12/032 – *Timac/Grassland*, 17.1.2013.
CA M/12/033 – *DCC/Kent*, 27.2.2024.
CA M/13/001 – *Blackrock/CS ETF*, 9.5.2013.
CA M/13/002 – *Capita/Northgate*, 6.3.2013.
CA M/13/003 – *BT/ESPN*, 25.4.2013.
CA M/13/006 – *Clare FM/Tipp FM*, 10.4.2013.
CA M/13/009 – *European Refreshments/Fresh Trading*, 17.4.2013.
CA M/13/011 – *OIF/Mount Kellett/UBIL/Jurys Inn*, 7.5.2013.

CA M/13/013 – *Kepak/Silvercrest*, 21.05.2013.
CA M/13/018 – *Ladbrokes/Chronicle*, 24.6.2013.
CA M/13/026 – *Kepak/McCarren*, 26.10.2013.
CA M/13/031 – *Permira/Griggs*, 29.11.2013.
CA M/13/033 – *Sappho/Thomas Crosbie Holdings*, 10.1.2014.
CA M/13/036 – *Glanbia/Wexford Creamery*, 30.4.2014.
CA M/14/003 – *Future/Wrapports/Aggrego*, 24.2.2014.
CA M/14/008 – *Fitzwilliam/Wittington Canada/Arnotts*, 27.5.2014.
CA M/14/010 – *Irish Wind/SWS*, 17.4.2014.
CA M/14/011 – *Oasis Dental/Smiles*, 2.5.2014.
CCPC M/14/026 – *Valeo/Wardell/Robert Roberts*, 17.2.2015.
CCPC M/14/035 – *Dalata/White's Hotel*, 9.1.2015.
CCPC M/14/036 – *Dalata/Clayton Hotel (Galway)*, 12.1.2015.
CCPC M/14/037 – *Dalata/Pillo Hotel (Galway)*, 13.1.2015.
CCPC M/14/038 – *Maxol/Tom Chawke*, 22.1.2015.
CCPC M/14/040 – *Dalata/Moran's Hotel/Bewley's*, 29.1.2015.
CCPC M/14/041 – *JDM Automotive/Commons Road Cars*, 22.1.2015.
CCPC M/15/002 – *Atlantic Troy/Charleville Park Hotel*, 20.2.2015.
CCPC M/15/005 – *AIG/Laya Healthcare*, 13.3.2015.
CCPC M/15/007 – *Fuelplus/Valero*, 26.3.2015.
CCPC M/15/009 – *BWG/Londis*,15.6.2015.[c]
CCPC M/15/013 – *Paddy Power/Track*, 31.3.2015.
CCPC M/15/014 – *Irish Property/Ballsbridge Holdco*, 22.4.2015.
CCPC M/15/016 – *PRL/Moran Freight Services*, 11.5.2015.
CCPC M/15/019 – *TOP/Ashbourne Oil*, 15.5.2015.
CCPC M/15/020 – *Topaz/Esso*, 15.10.2015.[c]
CCPC M/15/021 – *Lloydspharmacy Ireland Ltd./Walsh's & Friary Allcare*, 21.5.2015.
CCPC M/15/022 – *Paddy Power/Hacketts*, 4.6.2015.
CCPC M/15/023 – *Glanbia/Cold Chain*, 11.6.2015.
CCPC M/15/024 – *Petrogas/Knockmitten Petroleum*, 30.6.2015.
CCPC M/15/025 – *Lloydspharmacy Ireland Ltd./Dargle Pharmacies*, 30.6.2015.
CCPC M/15/026 – *Baxter Healthcare/Fannin Compounding*, 21.10.2015.
CCPC M/15/027 – *Uniphar/Allcare*, 10.7.2015.
CCPC M/15/028 – *Atlantic Troy/Killeshin Hotel*, 3.7.2015.
CCPC M/15/033 – *Paddy Power/Mulholland*, 6.8.2015.
CCPC M/15/035 – *Tetrarch/Dawson Hotel*, 21.8.2015.
CCPC M/15/036 – *Fitzwilliam/Wittington Canada/Arnotts II*, 21.8.2015.
CCPC M/15/039 – *Liberty Global/TV3*, 2.10.2012.
CCPC M/15/044 – *Thornmont/Hilton Kilmainham*, 17.9.2015.
CCPC M/15/045 – *Pat the Baker/Irish Pride*, 18.11.2015.
CCPC M/15/054 – *Sports Direct/Heatons*, 13.11.2015
CCPC M/15/058 – *Fane Valley/Lakeland Dairies*, 27.11.2015.
CCPC M/15/059 – *Paddy Power/Betfair*, 15.1.2016.

CCPC M/15/061 – *East Cork Oil/Tara Oil*, 14.12.2015.
CCPC M/15/062 – *Elvery's/Mahers*, 1.12.2015.
CCPC M/15/065 – *Green Reit/Central Park*, 23.12.2015.
CCPC M/15/069 – *ITV/UTV*, 12.1.2016.
CCPC M/15/070 – *Starwood/Elm Park*, 18.1.2016.
CCPC M/15/071 – *JDM Automotive/Karmann Auto*, 22.1.2016.
CCPC M/15/076 – *Uniphar/Lindchem*, 29.1.2016.
CCPC M/15/077 – *Uniphar/Murrays Medical Equipment Ltd.*, 23.3.2016.
CCPC M/16/002 – *Dunnes/Whelan's Tipperary*, 26.2.2016.
CCPC M/16/004 – *DekaBank/Whitewater*, 3.3.2016.
CCPC M/16/005 – *Dalata/Clarion Sligo*, 19.2.2016.
CCPC M/16/006 – *Dalata/Cavenford/Vizmol*, 8.3.2016.
CCPC M/16/007 – *Ladbrokes/Gala Coral*, 10.3.2016.
CCPC M/16/008 – *PandaGreen/Greenstar*, 16.8.2016.[c]
CCPC M/16/009 – *Tedcastles/Sirio*, 23.3.2016.
CCPC M/16/010 – *Halstonville/Diminuto*, 30.3.2016.
CCPC M/16/011 – *Heineken/Coman's I*, 5.4.2016.
CCPC M/16/012 – *HPC/St. Gobain*, 11.4.2016.
CCPC M/16/014 – *Frank Keane/MSL*, 25.4.2016.
CCPC M/16/015 – *Uniphar/Riverchem*, 26.4.2016.
CCPC M/16/017 – *Molson Coors/Miller*, 13.5.2016.
CCPC M/16/018 – *Amber/Grove Turkeys t/a Grove Farm*, 23.5.2016.
CCPC M/16/021 – *Maxol/Topaz Bull*, 19.5.2016.
CCPC M/16/027 – *Maxol/Topaz Ballindine*, 8.7.2016.
CCPC M/16/028 – *Standard Life/Block B Elm Park*, 14.7.2016.
CCPC M/16/032 – *DCU/St. Patrick's College Drumcondra et al.*, 9.8.2016.
CCPC M/16/033 – *NewsCorp/Wireless Communications*, 2.8.2016.
CCPC M/16/037 – *mytaxi/Hailo*, 2.9.2016.
CCPC M/16/038 – *Liberty Global/UTV Ireland*, 7.9.2016.
CCPC M/16/040 – *Bon Secours/Barrington's Hospital*, 21.12.2016.
CCPC M/16/041 – *Marino Point/Port of Cork* (withdrawn).
CCPC M/16/043 – *Petrogas/MKMH*, 4.10.2016.
CCPC M/16/044 – *INM/CMNL*, 10.11.2016.
CCPC M/16/046 – *DekaBank/DoubleTree Hilton Dublin*, 2.11.2016.
CCPC M/16/047 – *Dalata/DoubleTree Hilton*, 2.11.2016.
CCPC M/16/055 – *UPMC & Bon Secours/Druid Stone JV*, 9.12.2016.
CCPC M/16/060 – *Kepak/John Kelly Meats*, 21.12.2016.
CCPC M/16/062 – *Counterpoint/East Coast/Knockton*, 31.1.2017.
CCPC M/16/066 – *Kepcar JV (Kepak & Oliver Carty)/Green Farm Foods*, 2.2.2017.
CCPC M/17/002 – *Silvereed/Tombolo*, 16.2.2017.[c]
CCPC M/17/003 – *Boyle Sports/Bambury I*, 10.2.2017.
CCPC M/17/004 – *Primeline/Johnson Bros*, 16.2.2017.
CCPC M/17/005 – *VHI/Swiftcare*, 10.5.2017.[c]

CCPC M/17/006 – *Topaz/Casey's of Bantry*, 1.3.2017.
CCPC M/17/007 – *Petrogas/Excol*, 16.3.2017.
CCPC M/17/009 – *Irish Post/Irish TV*, 8.3.2017.
CCPC M/17/011 – *Maxol/Melia's Harold's Cross*, 27.3.2017.
CCPC M/17/012 – *Kantar Media/Newsaccess*, 11.7.2017.
CCPC M/17/015 – *Avanacar/Citröen*, 5.5.2017.
CCPC M/17/016 – *Petrogas/Westmeath Motors*, 28.4.2017.
CCPC M/17/017 – *Landmark/BenchWarmers*, 2.5.2017.
CCPC M/17/019 – *Petrogas/PR Reilly*, 9.5.2017.
CCPC M/17/020 – *Maxol/Great Gas*, 10.5.2017.
CCPC M/17/021 – *Applegreen/JFT*, 30.6.2017.
CCPC M/17/024 – *UPS/Eirpost*, 14.6.2017.
CCPC M/17/027 – *Dalata/Clarion/Clayton*, 29.8.2017.
CCPC M/17/028 – *PRL/Custodian*, 29.6.2017.
CCPC M/17/030 – *Carlyle/Sam McAuley Chemists*, 3.7.2017.
CCPC M/17/035 – *Dawn Meats/Dunbia*, 29.9.2017.
CCPC M/17/036 – Sean *Loughnane/Crinkle*, 3.10.2017.[c]
CCPC M/17/037 – *Tesco Ireland/Tesco Mobile*, 26.7.2017.
CCPC M/17/038 – *Lisavaird/JDS*, 1.8.2017.
CCPC M/17/039 – *TOP/KEC*, 24.7.2017.
CCPC M/17/040 – *INM/Caltray*, 11.10.2017.
CCPC M/17/042 – *Direct Card/DCI*, 29.8.2017.
CCPC M/17/044 – *Kennedy Wilson Holdings/Kennedy Wilson Real Estate Europe*, 8.9.2017.
CCPC M/17/045 – *IIF/GMC*, 12.9.2017.
CCPC M/17/046 – *Hammerson/Teba*, 14.9.2017.
CCPC M/17/049 – *Vermillion/SEPIL*, 21.9.2017.
CCPC M/17/050 – *Joyce's/Nestor's*, 5.10.2017.
CCPC M/17/051 – *ABP/Good Herdsmen*, 13.10.2017.
CCPC M/17/052 – *Cedarglade (Musgrave)/Ballybrit Service Station*, 11.10.2017.
CCPC M/17/053 – *TOP/H2 Blakes*, 28.9.2017.
CCPC M/17/055 – *Siris Capital/Synchronoss* (withdrawn).
CCPC M/17/056 – *Bay/Radio Nova*, 22.1.2018.
CCPC M/17/058 – *Musgrave/Whelan Centra*, 7.12.2017.
CCPC M/17/061 – *Boyle Sport/Bambury II*, 13.12.2017.
CCPC M/17/062 – *DekaBank/Gibson*, 15.12.2017.
CCPC M/17/063 – *Arrow/Commtech*, 19.12.2017.
CCPC M/17/064 – *Tetrarch/Citywest*, 30.1.2018.
CCPC M/17/067 – *Musgrave/La Rousse*, 19.1.2018.
CCPC M/17/068 – *Irish Times/Irish Examiner*, 20.4.2018.
CCPC M/17/069 – *Accenture/Rothco*, 25.1.2018.
CCPC M/17/072 – *Irish Holdings/Galway Leisure Investments*, 2.2.2018.
CCPC M/18/001 – *CMNL/North Dublin Publications*, 8.2.2018.

CCPC M/18/002 – *Aviva/Friends First*, 20.2.2018.
CCPC M/18/004 – *Maxol/Brennan's*, 9.2.2018.
CCPC M/18/005 – *Thornton's/A Plus*, 2.3.2018.
CCPC M/18/006 – *Valero/Riverside Service Station*, 14.2.2018.
CCPC M/18/007 – *BoyleSports/JP Bookmakers*, 19.2.2018.
CCPC M/18/009 – *BWG/4 Aces*, 5.5.2018.
CCPC M/18/010 – *SCIF/McWilliam Park Hotel*, 7.3.2018.
CCPC M/18/012 – *North Cork Co-op/Feales Bridge & Hedleys Bridge*, 16.3.2018.
CCPC M/18/016 – *Trinity Mirror/Northern & Shell*, 12.9.2018.
CCPC M/18/018 – *SHS/3V*, 15.3.2018.
CCPC/M/18/019 – *JDM Automotive/Motorpark*, 22.3.2018.
CCPC M/18/020 – *Armalou Spirit Ford – Lillis O'Donnell*, 22.3.2018.
CCPC M/18/022 – *Carlyle/Fermoy Medical Hall*, 27.3.2018.
CCPC M/18/023 – *Petrogas/Carranstown*, 29.3.2018.
CCPC M/18/024 – *Lloyds Pharmacy Ireland Ltd./McSweeney Group*, 28.3.2018.
CCPC M/18/029 – *Givaudan/Naturex*, 24.5.2018.
CCPC M/18/031 – *Uniphar/Sisk Healthcare*, 17.8.2018.
CCPC M/18/034 – *Big Bus Tours/Irish City Tours*, 7.6.2018.
CCPC M/18/036 – *Enva/Rilta*, 20.12.2018.
CCPC M/18/037 – *SCIF/Connemara Coast Hotel*, 12.6.2018.
CCPC M/18/038 – *Star Group/Sky Betting*, 18.6.2018.
CCPC M/18/042 – *Oaktree/Alannis/Lioncor*, 12.9.2018.
CCPC M/18/048 – *Atlantic Troy/Athlone Springs*, 10.7.2018.
CCPC M/18/050 – *BWG/Keating's Londis*, 11.7.2018.
CCPC M/18/052 – *Sam McAuley (Carlyle)/Nolan's*, 14.8.2018.
CCPC M/18/053 – *PandaGreen/Knockharley*, 6.2.2019.[c]
CCPC M/18/054 – *Cedarglade (Musgrave)/Fortunestown Supermarket*, 1.8.2018.
CCPC M/18/055 – *DTZ/Sherry Fitzgerald Commercial*, 3.8.2018.
CCPC M/18/056 – *TOP/Garrycastle (Spar) Athlone*, 20.8.2018.
CCPC M/18/063 – *Berendsen/King's Laundry*, 8.7.2019.[c]
CCPC M/18/067 – *LN-Gaiety/MCD Productions*, 5.7.2019.
CCPC M/18/071 – *House of Fraser (Dundrum)/Sports Direct*, 2.10.2018.
CCPC M/18/072 – *Petrogas/Glenview Motors*, 2.10.2018.
CCPC M/18/073 – *Alavina/J. Donohoe Motors*, 12.10.2018.
CCPC M/18/074 – *Quarry Park Motors/Linden Copse*, 12.10.2018.
CCPC M/18/075 – *Irving/Tedcastles*, 7.1.2019.
CCPC M/18/078 – *Tetrarch/Seed Portfolio Hotels*, 22.10.2018.
CCPC M/18/079 – *Musgrave/Donnybrook Fair*, 1.11.2018.
CCPC M/18/080 – *JDM Automotive/TKF Autos*, 9.11.2018.
CCPC M/18/082 – *Goldreed/Greene Farm*, 21.1.2019.[c]
CCPC M/18/083 – *Carechoice/TMNH Holdings*, 27.11.2018.
CCPC M/18/085 – *Uniphar/Bradley's Pharmacy Group*, 16.11.2018.
CCPC M/18/086 – *Brightstone/Fitzpatrick Motors*, 7.12.2018.

CCPC M/18/089 – *Lakeland/LacPatrick*, 5.3.2019.[c]
CCPC M/18/092 – *Formpress/River Media*, 28.12.2018.
CCPC M/18/097 – *Uniphar/Inischem*, 1.2.2019.
CCPC M/19/002 – *Kerry FM/Clare Radio*, 5.3.2019.
CCPC M/19/006 – *Wicklow Hotel Partnership/Powerscourt Hotel Resort & Spa*, 3.5.2019.
CCPC M/19/010 – *Formpress/Midland Tribune*, 9.10.2019.
CCPC M/19/012 – *Apcoa Parking/NCPS*, 27.6.2019.
CCPC M/19/018 – *Connolly Motor/Hyundai Galway*, 8.8.2019.
CCPC M/19/019 – *Lloyds Pharmacy/Median BOFH*, 13.8.2019.
CCPC M/19/020 – *Fane Valley/Smyths*, 14.8.2019.
CCPC M/19/021 – *Gowan Group/Opel*, 20.8.2019.
CCPC M/19/022 – *Dunnes Stores/JC Savage*, 30.7.2019.
CCPC M/19/023 – *NTMA/Cork County Council*, 16.8.2019.
CCPC M/19/025 – *EP UK Investments/Tynagh Energy*, 30.9.2019.
CCPC M/19/031 – *Windsor Motors/Holcroft*, 21.11.2019.
CCPC M/19/032 – *Boyle Sport/Bruce Betting*, 14.2.2020.
CCPC M/19/034 – *CVC/Celtic Rugby*, 15.1.2020.
CCPC M/19/037 – *Connolly Motors/Volkswagen Letterkenny*, 18.12.2019.
CCPC M/19/039 – *BWG/Heaney Meats*, 10.1.2020.
CCPC M/19/040 – *DMG/JPIMedia*, 20.3.2020.
CCPC M/19/042 – *Portlon (Parma)/Galway Clinic*, 20.4.2020.
CCPC M/19/044 – *Timac/Grassland*, 27.5.2020.
CCPC M/20/001 – *Flutter/Stars*, 20.4.2020.
CCPC M/20/003 – *Link Group/Pepper* (withdrawn).
CCPC M/20/005 – *ESB/Coillte*, 5.2.2021.
CCPC M/20/009 – *Portlon (Parma)/Hermitage*, 29.7.2020.
CCPC M/20/010 – *Portlon (Parma)/Blackrock*, 29.7.2020.
CCPC M/20/012 – *Eason/Dubray*, 10.9.2020.[c]
CCPC M/20/015 – *Portloon/Blackrock(Tullycorbett/Xroon)*, 29.7.2020.
CCPC M/20/017 – *CapVest/M&M Walshe*, 19.6.2020.
CCPC M/20/020 – *Arthopoda (Orpea)/Brindley Healthcare*, 6.8.2020.
CCPC M/20/021 – *Reach/ISL*, 28.8.2020.
CCPC M/20/023 – *United Molasses/Premier Molasses & Kruden*, 25.11.2020.
CCPC M/20/027 – *Uniphar/Hickey's*, 19.11.2020.[c]
CCPC M/20/028 – *Applied Materials/Kokusai Electric*, 9.10.2020.
CCPC M/20/029 – *Brookfield (Greenenergy)/Amber Oil*, 26.1.2021.
CCPC M/20/031 – *Caldic/Brand-Nu and B&L*, 23.11.2020.
CCPC M/20/036 – *UPMC/Aut Even*, 14.1.2021.
CCPC M/20/038 – *DCC/Campus Oil*, 2.2.2021.
CCPC M/20/040 – *Chadwicks/Haylen*, 4.2.2021.
CCPC M/20/041 – *CapVest/CCIF Core*, 5.2.2021.
CCPC M/21/004 – *AIB, BoI, PTSB Synch Payments JV (Synch)*, 16.6.2022.[d]

CCPC M/21/008 – *DMG/New Scientist*, 12.4.2021.
CCPC M/21/009 – *Citylink/GoBus*, 20.8.2021.
CCPC M/21/011 – *Easycash/Bank of Ireland ATMs*, 16.8.2021.
CCPC M/21/012 – *AIB/Goodbody*, 24.6.2021.
CCPC M/21/016 – *PandaGreen/Exomex*, 30.9.2021.[c]
CCPC M/21/021 – *Bank of Ireland/KBC*, 23.5.2022.[d]
CCPC M/21/024 – *Orpea/First Care*, 6.7.2021.
CCPC M/21/026 – *CVC/Six Nations*, 24.6.2021.
CCPC M/21/031 – *Glennon Bros/Balcas*, 11.10.2021.
CCPC M/21/033 – *Xtratherm/Ballytherm*, 13.8.2021.[c]
CCPC M/21/034 – *Arachas/Hooper Dolan*, 23.8.2021.
CCPC M/21/037 – *Bon Secours/Alliance Medical/Barrington's Hospital JV*, 26.8.2021.
CCPC M/21/040 – *AIB/Ulster Bank*, 28.4.2022.
CCPC M/21/041 – *Pilgrim's Pride/Kerry Foods*, 10.9.2021.
CCPC M/21/043 – *Colas/SIAC*, 9.9.2021.
CCPC M/21/045 – *ILHAWK/Ark Life*, 24.9.2021.
CCPC M/21/046 – *Bank of Ireland/Davy*, 6.12.2021.
CCPC M/21/052 – *DMG/Nalac*, 18.6.2023.
CCPC M/21/054 – *Zeus Packaging/Limerick Packaging*, 16.12.2021.
CCPC M/21/057 – *JDM Automotive/CAB Motor Company*, 19.11.2021.
CCPC M/21/066 – *BoyleSports/Tully Bookmakers*, 22.12.2021.
CCPC M/21/067 – *Sicon/Sensori*, 7.1.2022.
CCPC M/21/068 – *Heineken/Coman's II*, 16.3.2022.
CCPC M/21/071 – *Tesco/Joyce's*, 7.6.2022.
CCPC M/21/076 – *PTSB/Ulster Bank*, 21.7.2022.
CCPC M/21/079 – *Uniphar/NaviCorp*, 15.12.2022.
CCPC M/21/080 – *Grafton (Chadwicks)/Sitetech*, 2.2.2022.
CCPC M/21/XX – *Facebook/Kustomer* (referred to EU Commission).[e]
CCPC M/22/007 – *Assa Abloy/Arran Isle*, 9.6.2022.
CCPC M/22/015 – *East Cork Oil/Misty Lane* (withdrawn).
CCPC M/22/016 – *Keary Motors/Renault Retail Group*, 13.5.2022.
CCPC M/22/017 – *Linnaeus Veterinary/Blackhall* (withdrawn and re-notified).
CCPC M/22/022 – *Wolseley Group/Cooperstorm*, 27.5.2022.
CCPC M/22/025 – *The Agricultural Trust/Irish Garden* (withdrawn).
CCPC M/22/027 – *Ferrero International/Fulfil*, 9.6.2022.
CCPC M/22/032 – *Cathexis/Jones Engineering*, 30.8.2022.
CCPC M/22/033 – *MM/ESNT/Essentra*, 5.9.2022.
CCPC M/22/037 – *Thornton's Recycling/Carducci Holdings* (withdrawn and re-notified).
CCPC M/22/040 – *Q-Park/Tazbell*, 15.8.2023.
CCPC M/22/044 – *AIB/Ulster Bank (Trackers).*
CCPC M/22/047 – *BWG/McCarrick*, 7.11.2022.
CCPC M/22/048 – *Frank Keane/Doran Motors*, 20.10.2022.

CCPC M/22/049 – *Uniphar/LXV Remedies (Sam McCauley)*, 20.1.2023.
CCPC M/22/052 – *Linnaeus Veterinary/Blackhall*, 23.9.2022.
CCPC M/22/054 – *Kavanagh Retailing/Clarke's Barna*, 18.10.2022.
CCPC M/22/059 – *Bauer Media/Siteridge (Red FM)*, 22.12.2022.
CCPC M/22/062 – *Associated Hardware/National Hardware*, 18.5.2023.
CCPC M/22/063 – *Windsor Motors/Green Cars* (withdrawn).
CCPC M/22/065 – *Musgrave/Caulfield*, 24.3.2023.
CCPC M/22/067 – *Thornton's Recycling/Carducci Holdings (City Bin)*, 13.7.2023.
CCPC M/23/001 – *DFDS/McBurney Transport*, 27.2.2023.
CCPC M/23/004 – *John Laing/CCD Group*, 28.4.2023.
CCPC M/23/005 – *John Laing/Towercomm*, 31.5.2023.
CCPC M/23/006 – *Dawn Meats/Kildare Chilling*, 20.9.2023.
CCPC M/23/008 – *Aurivo/Arrabawn Co-Op*, 15.9.2023
CCPC M/23/010 – *BWG/Tuffy Wholesale*, 3.5.2023.
CCPC M/23/011 – *daa/Gannon*, 21.3.2024.
CCPC M/23/012 – *Egis Ingenerie/JB Barry & BeMRA Engineering*, 3.5.2023.
CCPC M/23/016 – *Belbyford/Imperial Hotel (Cork)*, 30.5.2023.
CCPC M/23/017 – *MMM/John Morrison Motors*, 2.6.2023.
CCPC M/23/018 – *Maxol/Kinsella's Fuel Services*, 8.6.2023.
CCPC M/23/022 – *VPO/Lumcloon*, 9.6.2023.
CCPC M/23/027 – *European Bakery Group/Panelto Foods*, 15.8.2023.
CCPC M/23/035 – *Bright Motor City/Gowan Group*, 30.8.2023.
CCPC M/23/036 – *Musgrave/Doyle's Veg Prep*, 12.9.2023.
CCPC M/23/037 – *KTC Edibles/Trilby Trading*, 13.9.2023.
CCPC M/23/038 – *Mediahuis/Euractiv*, 19.9.2023.
CCPC M/23/041 – *Nissan Ireland/Renault Ireland*, 28.9.2023.[c]
CCPC M/23/045 – *Proximus Opal/Route Mobile*, 27.10.2023.
CCPC M/23/049 – *AXA/Laya Healthcare*, 3.10.2024.
CCPC M/23/051 – *Chadwicks/Rooney's Homevalue*, 23.10.2023.
CCPC M/23/052 – *NPP Packaging/Wraptite*, 15.11.2023.
CCPC M/23/059 – *IFX/Blackhall Facilities Management*, 21.12.2023.
CCPC M/23/060 – *Kilsaran/Kilmurray*, 26.7.2024.
CCPC M/23/065 – *Phey Topco/Trasmore*, 11.4.2024.
CCPC M/23/068 – *McMullan Bros/Naas Fuels*, 12.7.2024.
CCPC M/24/019 – *Dunnes Stores/BV Trading*, 12.5.2024.

a *The CA missed the deadline for instigating a Phase 2 investigation in this case.*
b *The author prepared a submission to the CA on behalf of a third party opposing the merger.*
c *The author advised the parties in these cases.*
d *The author advised the CA/CCPC in these cases.*
e *This case had no case number and the date of the referral decision has not been published.*

CIFSA 11/001 – *AIB/EBS*, 27.6.2011.

CA Decisions under Competition Act, 1991 (as amended)

CA Decision No. 285 – *Cooley/Irish Distillers*, 25.2.1994.
CA Decision No. 512 – *Guinness Ireland Group/United Beverages Holdings*, 17.6.1998.

CA Enforcement Decisions

CA E/03/003 – *Agreements between Independent Newspapers (Ireland) Limited and newspaper retailers allegedly fixing the retail price of Independent newspaper titles*, 10.11.2003; and CA E/03/004 – *Agreements between The Irish Times Limited and newspaper retailers allegedly fixing the retail price of* The Irish Times *newspaper*, 24.7.2003.
CA E/05/002 – *Alleged excessive pricing by Greenstar Recycling Holdings Limited in the provision of household waste collection services in northeast Wicklow*, 30.8.2005.
CA E/06/001 – *Alleged excessive booking fees by Ticketmaster Ireland and its exclusive contractual relationships with MCD Promotions Limited and Aiken Promotions Limited*, 26.9.2005.

Ministerial Merger Decisions under the Mergers, Takeovers & Monopolies (Control) Act, 1978 (as amended)

Proposed Merger or Take-Over Conditional Order, 1981 (S.I. 331/1981). Smurfit Investments (Ireland) Ltd/Bedstone Ltd. (*Smurfit/Bedstone).*
Proposed Merger or Take-Over Conditional Order, 1984 (S. I. 217/1984). Governor and Company of the Bank of Ireland/Irish Civil Service Building Society (*Bank of Ireland/Irish Civil Service Building Society*).
Proposed Merger or Take-Over Prohibition Order, 1988 (S.I. 301/1988). GC&C/Irish Distillers (*GC&C/Irish Distillers*).
Proposed Merger or Take-Over Conditional Order, 1988 (S.I. 302/1988). Pernod Ricard/Irish Distillers (*Pernod Ricard/Irish Distillers).*
Proposed Merger or Take-Over Conditional (No. 2) Order, 1990 (S.I. 94/1990). DJS Meats Ltd/Anglo Irish Beef Processors (*Master Meats).*
Proposed Merger or Take-Over Prohibition Order, 1990 (S.I. 42/1990). British Steel plc/C. Walker and Sons (Holdings) Ltd (*Walker Steel).*
Proposed Merger or Take-Over Prohibition Order, 1996. (S.I. 45/1996). Statoil Ireland Ltd/Conoco Ireland Ltd. (*Statoil/Conoco I*).
Proposed Merger or Take-Over Prohibition (Amendment) Order, 1996. (S.I. 214/1996). Statoil Ireland Ltd/Conoco Ireland Ltd. (*Statoil/Conoco II*).
IAWS/R&H Hall.[a]
Telecom Éireann/Cablelink.[a]
Valentia/eircom.[a]

[a] *The parties in these cases furnished undertakings to the Minister but no Orders were made.*

CA Merger Reports (Phase 2 Investigations) under the Competition Act, 1991[1045]

CA, (1991), *Report of investigation of the proposal whereby Independent Newspapers plc would increase its shareholding in the Tribune Group from 29.99% to a possible 53.09%* (*Independent Newspapers/Tribune*), Dublin: Stationery Office Pl 8795.[a]

CA, (1996), *Report of investigation of the proposal whereby Statoil Ireland Limited would acquire the entire issued share capital of Conoco Ireland Limited* (*Statoil/Conoco*), Dublin: Stationery Office, Pn 2405.[a]

CA, (1996), *Report of investigation of the proposal whereby Unilever Ireland Limited would acquire the entire issued share capital of Lyons Irish Enterprises Ltd.* (*Unilever/Lyons Tea*), Dublin: Stationery Office Pn 3012.[a]

CA, (1997), *Report of investigation of the proposal whereby Blockbuster Entertainment (Ireland) Limited would acquire the entire issued share capital of Ardnasillagh Limited (trading within the State as Xtra-Vision Limited)* (*Blockbuster/Xtra-Vision*), Dublin, Stationery Office Pn 3644.

CA, (1998), *Report of investigation of the proposal whereby Coillte Teoranta would acquire the majority of the issued share capital of Balcas Limited* (*Coillte/Balcas*), Dublin; Stationery Office, Pn 5168.[a]

CA, (1998), *Report of investigation of the proposal whereby Ladbrokes (Ireland) Limited would acquire the whole of the issued share capital of Coral Leisure (Ireland) Limited* (*Ladbrokes/Coral*), Dublin: Stationery Office, Pn 5795.

CA, (2000), *Report of investigation of the proposal whereby (i) Princes Holdings Limited would acquire the entire issued share capital of Suir Nore Relays Limited and Liberty Media AL Inc. would acquire the entire issued share capital of Aringour Limited* (*Princes Holdings/Suir Nore Relays*), Dublin: Stationery Office, Pn 7962.

CA, (2002a), *Report of investigation of the proposal whereby GEHE Ireland Limited would acquire the entire issued share capital of Babbingore Limited, Goviltown Limited, Pharmacy, O'Riada Holdings Limited and Kilmaloon Limited, together with its two subsidiaries Ballygall Pharmacy Limited and John Smith & Son Limited* (*GEHE/Unicare*), Dublin: Stationery Office Pn 11320.

CA, (2002b), *Report of investigation of the proposal whereby Solgun Limited, a wholly-owned subsidiary of STA Travel (Holdings) PTE Limited, would acquire approximately 88% of the entire Issued Share Capital of USIT World plc* (*STA Travel/USIT*), Dublin: Stationery Office Pn 11661.

CA, *Report of investigation of the proposal whereby Maxol Energy Limited would acquire the entire issued share capital of Busselle Limited* (*Maxol/Estuary*), Dublin: Stationery Office Pn 12200.

a *Cases in which the author participated as a member of the Competition Authority.*

1045 Three cases were withdrawn following referral to the CA (*Ractrayle/Princes Holdings/Suir Nore Relays, GIG/UBH* and a third case in which the identity of the parties was not disclosed) and no investigation was carried out.

EU

Cases

Aer Lingus v. Commission, Case T-411/07, ECLI:EU:T:2010:281, 2010 II-03691.
Airtours v. Commission, Case T-342/99, (2002) ECR II 2585.
BaByliss SA v. Commission, Case T-114/02 [2003] ECR II-1279 [2003] ECR II-1279
BAT & Reynolds v. Commission, Cases 142 and 156/84, [1987] ECR 4487.
Bertelsmann AG & Sony Corporation of America v. Independent Music Publishers & Labels Association (Impala), Case T-464/04, 2006 II 02289.
Cisco Systems Inc & Messagenet SpA v. Commission, Case T-79/12, [2013] ECR I-000.
CK Telecoms UK Investments v. Commission, Case No. T399/16, 2020 217.
Commission v. CK Telecoms UK Investments, Case C-376/20, ECLI:EU:C:2023:561.
easyJet v. Commission, Case T-177/04, [2006] ECR II-1931.
Europemballage & Continental Can v. Commission, Case 6/72, [1973] ECR 215.
France v. Commission, Cases C-68/94 and C-30/95, 1998 I-01365.
Gencor v. Commission, Case T/102/96 [1999] ECR II-753.
General Electric v. Commission, Case No. T-210/01. ECLI:EU:T:2005:456, 2005 II-5575.
Heidelberg Cement v. Commission, Case No. T-380/17. ECLI: EU:T:2020:471.
Illumina & Grail v. Commission, Case T-227/21, 2022:447.
Illumina v. Commission, joined cases C-611/22 P and C-625/22 P ECLI:EU:C:2024:677.
Kali und Salz AG and *Kali-Chemie AG v. Commission*, Cases 19 and 20/74 of the European Communities, ECLI:EU:C:1975:58.
Ryanair v. Commission, Case T-342/07, 2010 II-03457.
Schneider Electric v. Commission, Case T-77/02, 2002 II-04201.
Tetra Laval v. Commission, Case T-5/02, 25.10.2002.

EU Commission Merger Decisions

Case No. COMP/M.053 – *Aerospatiale-Alenia/de Havilland*, 2.10.1991.
Case No. COMP/M.110 – *ABC/Generale Des Eaux/Canal+/W.H. Smith TV*, 10.9.1991.
Case No. COMP/M.113 – *Courtaulds/SNIA*, 19.12.1991.
Case No. COMP/M.165 – *Alcatel/AEGKabel*, 18.12.1991.
Case No. COMP/M.166 – *Tommas/Sarrio*, 24.2.1992.
Case No. COMP/M.190 – *Nestlé/Perrier*, 22.7.1992.
Case No. COMP/M.197 – *Solvay-Laporte/Interox*, 30.4.1992.
Case No. COMP/M.423 – *Newspaper Publishing*, 14.3.1994
Case No. COMP/M.784 – *Kesko/Tuko*, 19.2.1987.
Case No. COMP/M.779 – *Bertelsmann/CLT*, 7.10.1996.
Case No. COMP/M.833 – *Coca-Cola/Carlsberg*, 11.9.1997.
Case No. COMP/M.877 – *Boeing/McDonnell Douglas*, 30.7.1997.
Case No. COMP/M.914 – *Tesco/ABF*, 5.5.1997.
Case No. COMP/M.938 – *Guinness/Grand Metropolitan*, 15.10.1997.
Case No. COMP/M.1040 – *Reed Elsevier/Wolters Kluwer*, 9.3.1998 (withdrawn).
Case No. COMP/M.1069 – *WorldCom/MCII*, 8.7.1998.

Case No. COMP/M.1080 – *Thyssen/Krupp*, 2.6.1998
Case No. COMP/M.1082 – *Allianze/AGF*, 8.5.1998
Case No. COMP/M/1225 – *Enso/Stora*, 25.11.1998.
Case No. COMP/M.1383 – *Exxon/Mobil*, 29.9.1999.
Case No. COMP/M.1455 – *Gruner+Jahr/Financial Times/JV*, 20.4.1999.
Case No. COMP/M.1524 – *Airtours/First Choice*, 22.9.1999.
Case No. COMP/M.1578 – *Sanitec/Sphinx*, 1.12.1999.
Case No. COMP/M.1630 - *Air Liquide/BOC*, 18.1.2000.
Case No. COMP/M.1672 – *Volvo/Scania*, 15.3.2000.
Case No. COMP/M.1712 – *Generali/INA*, 12.1.2000
Case No. COMP/M.1802 – *Unilever/Amora-Maille*, 8.3.2000.
Case No. COMP/M.1853 - *EDF/EnBW*, 14.9.2006.
Case No. COMP/M.1879 – *Boeing/Hughes*, 29.10.2000.
Case No. COMP/M.1980 – *Volvo/Renault*, 1.9.2000
Case No. COMP/M.1990 – *Unilever/Best Foods*, 28.9.2000.
Case No. COMP/M.2220 – *GE/Honeywell*, 3.7.2001.
Case No. COMP/M.2268 – *Pernod Ricard/Diageo/Seagram*, 9.5.2001.
Case No. COMP/M.2276 – *Coca-Cola/Nestlé/JV*, 27.9.2001.
Case No. COMP/M.2314 – *BASF/Pantochim/Eurodiol*, 11.7.2001.
Case No. COMP/M.2380 – *Skandinaviska Enskilda Banken/FoeningsSparbanken* (withdrawn 19.9.2001).
Case No. COMP/M.2416 – *Tetra Laval/Sidel*, 30.10.2001.
Case No. COMP/M.2498 – *UPM-Kymmene/Haindl*, 21.11.2001.
Case No. COMP/M.2504 – *Cadbury Schweppes/Pernod Ricard*, 29.10.2001.
Case No. COMP/M.2567 – *Nordbanker/Postgirot*, 8.11.2001.
Case No. COMP/M.2608 – *INA/FAG*, 18.10.2001.
Case No. COMP/M.2978 – *Lagardère/Natexis/VUP*, 7.1.2004.
Case No. COMP/M.3083 – *GE/Instrumentarium*, 2.9.2003.
Case No. COMP/M.3216 – *Oracle/PeopleSoft*, 26.10.2024.
Case No. COMP/M.3291 – *Preem/Skandinaviska Raffinaderi*, 1.12.2003.
Case No. COMP/M.3333 – *Sony/BMG*, 3.10.2007.
Case No. COMP/M.3420 – *GIMD/Socpresse*, 16.6.2004.
Case No. COMP/M.3516 – *Repsol YPF/Shell Portugal*, 13.9.2004.
Case No. COMP/M.3752 – *Verizon/MCI*, 7.10.2005.
Case No. COMP/M.3894 – *Unicredito/HVB*, 18.10.2005.
Case No. COMP/M.4257 – *Smithfield/Oaktree/Sara Lee Foods Europe*, 28.7.2006.
Case No. COMP/M.4348 – *PKN/Mazeikiu*, 7.11.2006.
Case No. COMP/M.4439 – *Ryanair/Aer Lingus I*, 27.6.2007.
Case No. COMP/M.4532 – *Lukoil/Conoco Phillips*, 21.2.2007.
Case No. COMP/M.4576 – *AVR/Van Gansewinkel*, 3.4.2007
Case No. COMP/M.4600 – *Tui/First Choice*, 4.6.2007.
Case No. COMP/M.4611 – *Egmont/Bonnier (Books)*, 15.10.2007.
Case No. COMP/M.4844 – *Fortis/ABN Amro*, 3.10.2007.

Case No. COMP/M.4701 – *Generali/PPF Insurance Business*, 3.12.2007.
Case No. COMP/M.4731 – *Google/DoubleClick*, 11.3.2008.
Case No. COMP/M.4919 – *Statoil Hydro/Conoco Phillips*, 21.10.2008.
Case No. COMP/M.4999 – Commission Decision relating to the partial referral of Case No. COMP/M.4999 *Heineken/Scottish & Newcastle* to the competent authorities of Ireland pursuant to Article 9 Regulation (EC) 139/2004, 3.4.2008.
Case No. COMP/M.5046 – *Friesland Foods/Campina*, 17.12.2008.
Case No. COMP/M.5075 – *Vienna Insurance Group/EBV*, 17.6.2008.
Case No. COMP/M.5440 – *Lufthansa/Austrian Airlines*, 28.8.2009.
Case No. COMP/M.5467 – *RWE/Essent*, 23.6.2009.
Case No. COMP/M.5826 – *Anglo Irish Bank/RBS/Arnotts*, 9.8.2010.
Case No. COMP/M.5984 - *Intel/McAfee*, 26.1.2011.
Case No. COMP/M.6166 - *Deutsche Börse/NYSE*, 1.2.2012.
Case No. COMP/M.6360 – *Nynas/Shell/Harburg Refinery*, 2.9.2013.
Case No. COMP/M.6663 – *Ryanair/Aer Lingus III*, 27.2.2013.
Case No. COMP/M.6883 – *Canada Life/Irish Life*, 31.5.2013.
Case No. COMP/M.6924 – *Refresco/Pride Foods*, 4.10.2013.
Case No. COMP/M.6992 – *Hutchison 3G UK/Telefónica Ireland*, 28.5.2014.
Case No. COMP/M.7194 – *Liberty Global/Corelio/W&W/De Vijver Media*, 24.2.2015.
Case No. COMP/M.7220 – *Chiquita/Fyffes*, 3.10.2014.
Case No. COMP/M.7278 – *General Electric/Alstom (Thermal-Renewable Power Grid Business)*, 8.9.2015.
Case No. COMP/M.7541 – *IAG/Aer Lingus*, 14.7.2015.
Case No. COMP/M.7612 – *Hutchison 3G UK/Telefonica UK*, 11.5.2016.
Case No. COMP/M.7878 – *HeidelbergCement/Schwenk/Cemex Hungary/Cemex Croatia*, 5.4.2017.
Case No. COMP/M.7930 – *ABP/Fane Valley/Slaney Foods*, 7.10.2016.[c]
Case No. COMP/M.7932 – *Dow/Dupont*, 27.3 2017.
Case No. COMP/M.7995 – *Deutsche Börse/London Stock Exchange Group*, 29.3.2017.
Case No. COMP/M.8084 – *Bayer/Monsanto*, 29.5.2018.
Case No. COMP/M.8124 – *Microsoft/LinkedIn*, 6.12.2016.
Case No. COMP/M.8222 – *Knorr-Bremse/Haldex* (withdrawn 4.10.2017).
Case No. COMP/M.8229 – *Hammerson/Irish Life/ILAC Shopping Centre*, 14.12.2016.
Case No. COMP/M.8444 – *ArcelorMittal/Ilva*, 7.5.2018.
Case No. COMP/M.8444 – *ArcelorMittal/Ilva*, 17.4.2019 (purchaser approval decision).
Case No. COMP/M.8633 – *Lufthansa/Certain Air Berlin Assets*, 21.12.2017.
Case No. COMP/M.8677 – *Siemens/Alstom*, 6.2.2019.
Case No. COMP/M.8869 – *Ryanair/Laudamotion*, 12.7.2018.
Case No. COMP/M.9056 – *Generali CEE/AS*, 10.12.2018.
Case No. COMP/M.9064 – *Telia/Bonnier Broadcasting*, 12.11.2019.
Case No. COMP/M.9070 – *Eurocar/Vicentini*, 10.9.2018.
Case No. COMP/M.9294 – *BMS/Celgene*, 29.7.2019.

Case No. COMP/M.9820 – *Danfoss/Eaton Hydraulics*, 18.3.2021.
Case No. COMP/M.9969 – *Veolia/Suez*, 14.12.2021.
Case No. COMP/M.10646 – *Microsoft/Activision Blizzard*, 15.5.2023.
Case No. COMP/M.10615 – *Booking/Etraveli*, 25.9.2023.

c *The author advised the parties in this case.*

EU Commission Article 101/102 Decisions

Case 89/93 – *Italian Flat Glass*, 7.12.1988, OJ 1989 L33/44., 4.2.1989.
Case 92/213 – *British Midland v. Aer Lingus*, 26.2.1992, OJ [1993] L96/34, 10.4.1992.
Case 93/252 – *Warner-Lambert/Gillette*, OJ 1993 L116/21, 12.5.1993.
Case 2-37.398 – *Joint selling of the commercial rights of the UEFA Champions League*, 23.7.2003, 2003 OJ L271/25, 8.11.2003.
Case C.2-38.173 – *Joint selling of the media rights to the FA Premier League*, 22.3.2006, 2004 OJ C115/02, 30.4.2004.

EU Commission State Aid Decisions

Fortis Bank, Case No. SA NN 42/2008; NN 46/2008 and NN 53/A/2008, *Restructuring aid to Fortis Bank and Fortis Bank Luxembourg*, C(2008) 8085, 3.12.2008. Available at: https://ec.europa.eu/competition/state_aid/cases/227768/227768_1027866_42_1.pdf#%5B%7B%22num%22%3A985%2C%22gen%22%3A0%7D%2C%7B%22name%22%3A%22XYZ%22%7D%2C20%2C428%2Cnull%5D. Visited 8.11.2022.
Lloyds Bank, Case No. SA N 428/2009 – *Restructuring of Lloyds Banking Group*, C (2009) 9087 final, 18.11.2009. Available at: https://ec.europa.eu/competition/state aid/cases/232373/232373_1069315_136_2.pdf. Visited 8.11.2022.

UK

Court of Appeal

Case No. C3/2014/1376 *Ryanair v. Competition & Markets Authority and Aer Lingus*, [2015] EWCA Civ 83, 12.2.2015.

Competition & Markets Authority

Case No. ME/4694/10 – *Ryanair/Aer Lingus* (Possible Material Change of Circumstances), 11.6.2015.
Case No. ME/6466/14 – *Asda/Co-Op*, 22.12.2014.
Case No. ME/6471/14 – *Motor Fuel/Murco*, 16.2.2015.
Case No. ME/6514/15 – *Linergy/Ulster Farm By-Products II*, Phase 1, 17.7.2015; Phase 2, 6.1.2016.
Case No. ME/6556/15 – *Ladbrokes/Coral*, 11.1.2016.
Case No. ME/6558/15 – *Celesio/Sainsbury's (Pharmacy Business)*, 29.7.2016.

Case No. ME/6597/16 – *Hammerson/Grand Central Shopping Centre*, 28.7.2016.
Case No. ME/6685-17 – *Steven Eagell/Lancaster Motor Company*, 24.7.2017.
Case No. ME/6705/17 – *Refresco/Cott*, 3.1.2018.
Case No. ME/6752/18 – *Sainsbury's/Asda*, 25.4.2019.
Case No. ME/6779/18 – *Lakeland/LacPatrick*, 5.3.2019
Case No. ME/6806/19 – *Sabre/Farelogix*, 9.4.2020.
Case No. ME/6831/19 – *Roche/Spark*, 16.12.2019.
Case No. ME/6930/21 – *CVC/Six Nations Rugby*, 14.7.2021.
Case No. ME/6939/21 – *Glennon Bros/Balcas*, 9.9.2021.
Case No. ME/6983/22 – *Microsoft/Activision Blizzard I*, 26.4.2023.
Case No. ME/7068/23 – *Microsoft/Activision Blizzard II (ex. EEA Cloud Streaming Rights)*, 13.10.2023.

Competition Appeals Tribunal

Case No. 1239/4/12/15, *Ryanair v. Competition & Markets Authority and Aer Lingus* [2015] CAT 14, 15.7.2015.
Case No. 1345/4/12/20, *Sabre Corporation v. Competition & Markets Authority*, [2021] CAT 11, 21.5.2020.

Competition Commission

CHC Helicopter Corporation and Helicopter Services Group ASA: A Report on the Merger Situation (Cm 4556), 19 January 2000 (*CHC/HSG*).
NTL Incorporated and Cable & Wireless Communications Plc: A Report on the Proposed Acquisition, 22.3.2000 (*NTL/Cable & Wireless*).
Safeway plc and Asda Group Limited (owned by Wal-Mart Stores Inc.); Wm. Morrison Supermarkets plc; J Sainsbury plc; and Tesco plc (Groceries): A Report on the Mergers in Contemplation, 26.9.2003 (*Safeway*).
Case No. ME/1237/03 – *Stena/P&O*, 5.2.2004.
Case No. ME/1456/04 – *A Report on the Acquisition by Somerfield plc of 115 Stores from Wm. Morrison Supermarkets plc* (*Somerfield/Morrison*), 23.3.2005.
Case No. ME/1593/05 – *A report on the acquisition by British Salt Limited of New Cheshire Salt Works Limited* (*British Salt/New Cheshire Salt Works*), 8.11.2005.
Case No. ME/1618/04 – *Archant/Independent News & Media*, 22.9.2004.
Case No. ME/1974/05 – *HMV/Ottakar's*, 12.5.2006.
Case No. ME/3986/08 – *Sports Direct/JJB*, 16.3.2010.
Case No. ME/4694/10 – *Ryanair/Aer Lingus*, 28.8.2013.
Case No. ME/4790/10 – *Stena/DFDS*, 29.6.2011.
Case No. ME/5801/12 – *A.G. Barr/Britvic*, 9.7.2013.
Case No. ME/6132/13 – *Tradebe Environmental Services/Sitka*, 28.3.2014.

Monopolies & Mergers Commission

Grand Metropolitan plc and William Hill Organisation Limited: A Report on the Merger Situation, August 1989 (Grand Metropolitan/William Hill).
Kingfisher plc and Dixons Group plc: A Report on the Proposed Merger, May 1990 (*Kingfisher/Dixons*).
Wessex Water Plc and South West Water Plc: a Report on the Proposed Merger, January 1996 (*Wessex Water/South West Water*).
Severn Trent Plc and South West Water Plc: A Report on the Proposed Merger, 27.9.1996 (*Severn Trent/South West Water*).
Bass PLC, Carlsberg A/S and Carlsberg-Tetley PLC: A Report on the Merger Situation, 27.6.1997 (*Bass/Carlsberg-Tetley*).

Office of Fair Trading

ME/1219/04 – *Hachette/Hodder Headline,* 15.9.2004.
ME/1237/03 – *Stena/P&O,* 22.8.2003.
ME/1586/05 – *Future/Highbury House,* 14.4.2005.
ME/1680/05 – *Mean Fiddler/Clear Channel,* 17.6.2005.
ME/1955/05 – *Cott Beverages/Macaw,* 12.12.2005.
ME/2415/06 – *Tetra Laval/Carlisle,* 20.7.2006.
ME/3862/08 – *Lloyds/HBOS,* 24.10.2008.
ME/3986/08 – *Sports Direct/JJB,* 1.5.2009.
ME/4036/09 – *HMV/Zavvi,* 28.4.2009.
ME/4091/09 – *Coca-Cola/Fresh Trading,* 11.6.2009
ME/4570/10 – *Carpetright/Allied Carpets,* 13.9.2010.
ME/4694/10 – *Ryanair/Aer Lingus,* 15.6.2012.
ME/4790/10 – *Stena/DFDS,* 8.2.2011.
ME/4807/10 – *Kingspan/CRH Insulation,* 13.4.2011.
ME/5139/11 – *Rontec/Total UK.*
ME/5294/11 – *Linergy/Ulster Farm By-Products I,* 15.3.2012.

Non-merger cases
CA98/06/2003, *Price-fixing of Replica Football Kit,* 1.8.2003.

US

Cases

Allen-Myland, Inc. v. IBM Corporation, 33 F.3d 194, 209 (3rd Cir. 1994).
Ball Memorial Hospital Inc. v. Mutual Hospital Ins., 784 F.2d 1325, 1336, (7th Cir., 1986).
Brown Shoe Co. v. United States, 370 US 294 (1962).
California v. American Stores Co., 495 U.S. 271 (1990).
Eastman Kodak Co. v. Image Technical Services Inc., 540 US 451 (1992).

Federal Trade Commission v. Arch Coal, 329 F. Supp. 2d 109 (DDC) 2004.
Federal Trade Commission v. Coca-Cola, 641 F. Supp. 1128, 1133 (1986).
Federal Trade Commission v. Eastman Kodak Co., 274 U.S. 619 (1927).
Federal Trade Commission v. H.J. Heinz Co., 246 F.3d 708 (D.C. Cir. 2001).
Federal Trade Commission v. Procter & Gamble Co., 386 US 568 (1967).
Federal Trade Commission v. Staples, Inc., 970 F. Supp. 1066 (DDC) 1997.
Federal Trade Commission v. Steris Corp., 133 F. Supp. 3d 962 (N.D. Ohio, 2015).
Federal Trade Commission v. Whole Foods Market, Inc., 548 F.3d 1028 (D.C. Cir. 2008).
International Shoe Co. v. Federal Trade Commission, 280 US 291 (1930).
State of New York v. Kraft General Foods, Inc., Nabisco Cereals Inc. et. al., 862, F. Supp. 1030, (S.D.N.Y., 1993).
State of New York et al. v. Deutsche Telecom AG et al., 439 F. Supp 3d 179 (SDNY 2020).
Times-Picayune Publishing Co. v. United States, 345 US 594 (1952).
United States v. Aluminium Company of America, 377 US 271 (1964).
United States v. Baker Hughes, Inc., 908 F 2d 981, 992 (DC Cir. 1990).
United States v. E.C. Knight Co., 156 U.S. 1 (1895).
United States v. E.I. du Pont de Nemours & Co., 353 US 586 (1957) (the *Cellophane* case).
United States v. E.I. du Pont de Nemours & Co., 366 US 316 (1961).
United States v. H&R Block, Inc., 833 F. Supp. 2d 36 (D.D.C.2011).
United States v. Interstate Bakeries Corp. and Continental Baking Co. (N.D. Ill, 1995).
United States v. LTV Corp., 1984-2 Trade Cases (CCH) 66,133 (D.D.C.).
United States v. Microsoft Corporation, 253 F.3d 34 (D.C. Cir. 2001).
United States v. Northern Securities Co. et al., 193 US 197 (1904).
United States v. Oracle, 331 F. Supp. 2d. 1098 (N.D. Cal. 2004).
United States v. Pabst Brewing Co., 384 US 546 (1966).
United States v. Philadelphia National Bank, 374 US 321 (1963).
United States v. Ticketmaster Ent., Inc., No. 1:10-cv-00139-RMC (D.D.C., 2010).
United States v. Von's Grocery Company et al., 384 US 270 (1966).

Federal Trade Commission Cases

General Foods Corp., 3 Trade Reg. Rep. (CCH), 142 (1984).
In re Foremost Dairies, Inc., 60 F.T.C. 944 1084 (1962).
In the matter of Time-Warner/Turner, File Number 9610004.

Regulatory Decisions

Federal Communications Commission, *Bell Atlantic/NYNEX*, 12 FCC Rcd 19,985 (August 14,1997)
Federal Reserve System, *In re First Union Corp., Order Approving the Merger of Bank Holding Companies* (April 13, 1998).

Other Countries

Australia

ATPC – *Westpac/Challenge: Background to TPC Decision* (TPC, Canberra, 1995, September)

ACCC – *Westpac Banking Corporation/Bank of Melbourne Limited: Background to Decision on Merger Proposal* (ACCC, Canberra, 25.7.1997).

LEGISLATION

Ireland

Acts of the Oireachtas

Building Societies Act, 1989.
Competition Act, 1991.
Competition Act, 2002.
Competition & Consumer Protection Act, 2014.
Competition (Amendment) Act, 2022.
Credit Institutions (Financial Support) Act, 2008 (CIFSA, 2008).
Freedom of Information Act, 2014.
Mergers, Takeovers & Monopolies (Control) Act, 1978.
Restrictive Practices (Amendment) Act, 1987.

Statutory Instruments

S.I. No. 17/1979. *Mergers, Take-Overs and Monopolies (Newspapers) Order, 1979.*
S.I. No. 230/1985. *Mergers, Take-Overs and Monopolies (Control) Act, 1978 (Section 2) Order, 1985.*
S.I. No. 135/1993. *Mergers, Take-Overs and Monopolies (Control) Act, 1978 (Section 2) Order, 1993.*
S.I. No. 622/2002, *Competition Act, 2002, §18(5), Order 2002.*
S.I. No. 122/2007, *Competition Act, 2002, §s18(5) & (6), Order 2007.*

European Union

European Coal & Steel Community Treaty (ECSCT), 1951.
Treaty of Rome, 1957.
Treaty for the Functioning of the European Union (TFEU), 2009.
Regulation (EEC) No. 4064/89 of 21 December 1989 on the control of concentrations between undertakings. OJ 1989, L395/1 (ECMR).

Regulation (EC) No. 1310/97 of 30 June 1997 amending *Regulation (EEC) No. 4064/89* on the control of concentrations between undertakings.

Regulation (EC) No. 139/2004 of 20 January 2004 on the control of concentrations between undertakings. OJ 2004 L 24/1.

Other Countries

Australia

Trade Practices Act, 1974.

Canada

Combines Investigation Act, 1910.
Competition Act, 1986.

New Zealand

Commerce Act, 1986.

United Kingdom

Enterprise Act, 2002.
Monopolies & Mergers Act, 1965.

United States

Cellar-Kefauver Act, 1950.
Clayton Act, 1914.
Federal Trade Commission Act, 1914.
Hart-Scott-Rodino Act, 1976.
Sherman Act, 1890.
Telecommunications Act, 1996.

France

La loi no.77-806 du 19 juillet 1977 sur le contrôle de la concentration économique, la répression des ententes illicites et des abus de position dominante (Law No. 77-806 of 19 July 1977 on the control of economic concentration, the repression of illicit agreements and abuses of dominant position.

Germany

Gesetz gegen Wettbewerbsbeschränkungen (Law against Restraints on Competition),1957.
Gesetz gegen Wettbewerbsbeschränkungen (Law against Restraints on Competition),1973.

BIBLIOGRAPHY

ACCC, see Australian Competition & Consumer Commission.

Adams, W. & J.W. Brock, (1994). Revitalizing a Structural Antitrust Policy. *Antitrust Bulletin,* 39(1): 235-271.

Adelman, M.A., (1959). Economic Aspects of the Bethlehem Opinion. *Virginia Law Review*, 45(5): 684-696.

Affeldt, P., T. Duso & F. Szucs, (2019). *25 Years of European Merger Control. Deutsches Institute für Wirtschaftsforschung,* Discussion Paper 1797.

Affeldt, P., T. Duso, K. Gugler & J. Piechuka, (2021). *Market Concentration in Europe: Lessons from Antitrust Markets. Deutsches Institute für Wirtschaftsforschung*, Discussion Paper 1930.

Aghion, P. & P. Bolton, (1987). Contracts as a Barrier to Entry. *American Economic Review,* 77(3): 388-401.

Aguzzoni, L., E. Argentesi, L. Ciari, T. Duso & M. Tognoni, (2016). *Ex Post* Evaluation in the UK Retail Market for Books. *Journal of Industrial Economics*, 64(1): 170-200.

Ahdar, R., (2020). *The Evolution of Competition Law in New Zealand.* Oxford: Oxford University Press.

Aigner, G., O. Budzinski & A. Christiansen, (2016). The Analysis of Coordinated Effects in European Merger Control: Where Do We Stand after Sony/BMG and Impala? *European Competition Journal*, 2(2): 119-140.

Akbar, Y., (2002). Grabbing Victory from the Jaws of Defeat: Can the *GE/Honeywell* Merger Facilitate International Policy Co-operation. *World Competition*, 25(4): 403-422.

Albæk, S., P. Møllegaard & P.B. Overgaard, (2010). Transparency and Coordinated Effects in European Merger Control. *Journal of Competition Law & Economics*, 6(4): 839-851.

Allain, M-L., C. Chambolle, S. Turolla & S.B. Villas-Boas, (2017). Retail Mergers and Food Prices: Evidence from France. *Journal of Industrial Economics,* 65(3): 469-509.

Amel, D.F. & T.H. Hannan, (2000). Defining Banking Markets According to Principles Recommended in the *Merger Guidelines. Antitrust Bulletin,* 45(3): 615-639.

Amelio, A., T. Buettner, C. Hariton, G. Koltay, P. Papandropoulous, G. Sapi, T. Valetti & H. Zenger, (2018). Recent Developments at DG Competition: 2017/18. *Review of Industrial Organization,* 53(4): 653-679

Andrews, P., (2002). Strong Independent Hearing Officers Needed for New Irish Mergers Regime. *Competition*, 11(5): 128-130.

Anthony, S.F., (2000, March 9). *Vertical Issues: The Federal View*. Address to the American Law Institute-American Bar Association, *mimeo.* Available at https://www.ftc.gov/news-events/news/speeches/vertical-issues-federal-view. Accessed 23.4.2024.

Areeda, P.E. & D.F. Turner, (1978). *Antitrust Law.* Boston: Little, Brown.

Areeda, P.E. & H. Hovenkamp, (2021). *Antitrust Law: An Analysis of Antitrust Principles and Their Application,* 5th ed. New York: Wolters Kluwer.

Areeda, P.E. & L. Kaplow, (1988). *Antitrust Analysis,* 4th ed. Boston, MA: Little, Brown.

Armentano, D.T., (1986, July 27). Drawing the Line on Mergers: An Action Bordering on the Incoherent. *New York Times,* §3 p.2. Available at: https://www.nytimes.com/1986/07/27/business/drawing-the-line-on-mergers-an-action-bordering-on-the-incoherent.html. Accessed 23.4.2024.

Armstrong, M., S. Cowan & J.S. Vickers, (1994). *Regulatory Reform: Economic Analysis and the British Experience.* Cambridge, MA: MIT Press.

Ashenfelter, O., D. Ashmore, J.B. Baker & S. McKernan, (1998). *Identifying the Firm-Specific Cost Pass-through Rate. US Federal Trade Commission,* Working Paper 217. Available at https://www.ftc.gov/sites/default/files/documents/reports/identifying-firm-specific-cost-pass-through-rate/wp217.pdf. Accessed 1.7.2023.

Ashenfelter, O.C., D. Hosken & M. Weinberg, (2013). The Price Effects of a Large Merger of Manufacturers: A Case Study of *Maytag-Whirlpool. American Economic Journal: Economic Policy,* 5(1): 239-261.

Ashenfelter, O.C., D. Hosken & M. Weinberg, (2014). Did Robert Bork Understate the Competitive Impact of Mergers? Evidence from Consummated Mergers. *Journal of Law & Economics,* 57(S3): S67-S100.

Australian Competition & Consumer Commission (ACCC), (2008). *Merger Guidelines.* Available at: http://www.accc.gov.au/system/files/Merger%20guidelines.pdf.

Averitt, N.W. & R. H. Lande, (2007). Using the Consumer Choice Approach to Antitrust Law. *Antitrust Law Journal,* 74(1): 175-264.

Bachis, E. & C. Piga, (2006, March). *Do Prices Grow More in Euro-land? Evidence from the Airline Industry.* Available at: SSRN: https://ssrn.com/abstract=905534.

Baer, W.J., (1997). Reflections on Twenty Years of Merger Enforcement under the *Hart-Scott-Rodino Act. Antitrust Law Journal* 65(3): 825–863.

Baer, W.J., (1999). *A Study of the Commission's Divestiture Process.* Bureau of Competition Staff Paper. Washington, D.C.: USFTC.

Bailey, E. & W.J. Baumol, (1984). Deregulation and the Theory of Contestable Markets. *Yale Journal of Regulation,* 1(2): 111-137.

Baker, J.B. & C. Shapiro, (2008). Reinvigorating Horizontal Merger Enforcement that has Declined as a Result of Conservative Chicago Analysis. In R. Pitofsky, ed., *Where the Chicago School Overshot the Mark,* pp.235-291. Oxford: Oxford University Press.

Baker, J.B. & T.F. Bresnahan, (1988). Estimating the Elasticity of Demand Facing a Single Firm. *International Journal of Industrial Organization,* 6(3): 283-300.

Baker, J.B., (1997). Unilateral Competitive Effects Theories in Merger Cases. *Antitrust,* 11 (Spring): 21-26.

Baker, J.B., (1999). Econometric Analysis in *FTC v. Staples. Journal of Public Policy & Marketing,* 18(1): 11-21.

Baker, J.B., (2003). The Case for Antitrust Enforcement. *Journal of Economic Perspectives,* 17(4): 27-50.

Baker, J.B., (2004). Efficiencies and High Concentration: Heinz Proposes to Acquire Beech-Nut (2001). Case 6 in J.E. Kwoka, Jr. & L.J. White, eds., *The Antitrust Revolution Economics, Competition & Policy,* 4th ed., pp.150-169. Oxford: Oxford University Press.

Baker, J.B., (2021). Protecting and Fostering Online Platform Competition: The Role of Antitrust Law. *Journal of Competition Law & Economics,* 17(2): 493-501.

Banal-Estañol, A., I. Macho-Stadler & J. Seldeslachts, (2008). Endogenous Mergers and Endogenous Efficiency Gains: The Efficiency Defence Revisited. *International Journal of Industrial Organization*, 26(1): 69-91.

Barrett, S.D., (2004). Bus Competition in Ireland – The Case for Market Forces. *Quarterly Economic Commentary*, (Autumn), pp.69-88.

Baltzopoulos, A., L. Karlinger, D. Magos, P. Régibeau & J. Vareda, (2021). Recent Developments at DG Competition: 2020/2021. *Review of Industrial Organization*, 59(4): 567–598.

Baumol, W.J. & R.D. Willig, (1986). Contestability: Developments Since the Book. Chapter 1 in D.J. Morris, P.J.N. Sinclair, M.D.E. Slater & J.S. Vickers, eds., *Strategic Behaviour & Industrial Competition*. pp.9-36. Oxford: Clarendon Press.

Baumol, W.J., J.C. Pazar & R.D. Willig, (1982). *Contestable Markets and the Theory of Industry Structure*. San Diego: San Diego University Press.

Bavasso, A. & A. Lindsay, (2007). Causation in Merger Control. *Journal of Competition Law & Economics*, 3(2): 181-203.

Baxt, B., M. Randall & A. North, (2004, April). *International Competition Network Merger Guidelines Project*. Chapter 6. Available at: https://www.internationalcompetitionnetwork.org/wp-content/uploads/2018/05/MWG_MergerGuidelinesReport.pdf.

Beesley, M.E., (1990). Collusion, Predation and Merger in the UK Bus Industry, *Journal of Transport Economics & Policy*. 24(3): 295-310.

Belke, R. & D. Braun, (1979). German Merger Control: A European Approach to Anticompetitive Takeovers. *Northwestern Journal of International Law & Business*, 1(2): 371-449.

Bellamy, Sir C., (2000). Ten Years of Merger Control. Address before the EC Merger Control 10th Anniversary Conference in International Bar Association, *EC Merger Control Ten Years On*.

Benson, R.L., (1980). Spatial Competition: Implications for Market Area Delineation in Antimerger Cases. *Antitrust Bulletin*, 25(4): 729-49.

Bergman, M.A., M. Jakobsson & C. Razo, (2005). An Econometric Analysis of the European Commission's Merger Decisions. *International Journal of Industrial Organization*, 23 (9-10): 717-737.

Bergman, M.A., M.B. Coate, A.T.V. Mai & S. Ulrick, (2019). Does Merger Policy Converge After the 2004 European Union Reform. *Journal of Competition Law & Economics*, 15(1): 664-689.

Berry, S., M. Gaynor & F.S. Morton, (2019). Do Increasing Mark-ups Matter? Lessons from Empirical Industrial Organization. *Journal of Economic Perspectives*, 33(3): 44-68.

Besen, S.M., E.J. Murdoch, D.P. O'Brien, S.C. Salop & J.R. Woodbury, (1999). Vertical and Horizontal Ownership in Cable TV: Time Warner-Turner 1996. Case 19 in J.E. Kwoka, Jr. & L.J. White, eds., *The Antitrust Revolution Economics, Competition & Policy*, 3rd ed., pp. 452-475. Oxford: Oxford University Press.

Besen, S.M., S.D. Kletter, S.X. Moresi, S.C. Salop & J.R. Woodbury, (2013). An Economic Analysis of the *AT&T/T-Mobile* USA Wireless Merger. *Journal of Competition Law & Economics*, 9(1): 1-22.

BKA, see *Bundeskartellamt*.

Bon, J., S.S Fung, A. Reilly, T. Ridout, R. Ryan & M. Walker, (2021). Recent Developments at the CMA. *Review of Industrial Organization*, 59(4): 665-692.

Bonanno, A. & R. Lopez, (2005). Private Label Expansion and Supermarket Milk Prices. *Journal of Agricultural & Food Industrial Organization*, 3(1): 1-18.

Bontemps, C., V. Orozco, V. Requillart & A. Trevisiol, (2005). Price Effects of Private Label Development. *Journal of Agricultural & Food Industrial Organization*, 3(1): 19-37.

Borenstein, S., (1990). Airline Mergers, Airport Dominance, and Market Power. *American Economic Review*, 80(2): 400-404.

Borenstein, S., J. Bushnell & C. Knittel, (1999). Market Power in Electricity Markets: Beyond Concentration Measures. *Energy Journal*, 20(4): 65-88.

Botteman, Y., (2006). Mergers, Standards of Proof and Expert Economic Evidence. *Journal of Competition Law & Economics*, 2(1): 71-100.

Bouckaert, J. & P.M. Kort, (2014). Merger Incentives and the Failing Firm Defense. *Journal of Industrial Economics*, 62(3): 436-466.

Brandenburger, R. & T. Janssens, (2001). European Merger Control: Do the Checks and Balances Need to be Re-set? in B. Hawk, ed., *International Antitrust Law & Policy*, pp.135-182, New York: Juris Publications.

Brenner, S., (1999). Potential Competition in Local Telephone Service: *Bell Atlantic/NYNEX* (1997). Case 4 in J.E. Kwoka, Jr. & L.J. White, eds., *The Antitrust Revolution Economics, Competition & Policy*, 3rd ed., pp.116-142. Oxford: Oxford University Press.

Bromfield, J. & M. Olczak, (2018). The Role of the Maverick Firm Concept in European Commission Merger Decisions. *Journal of Competition Law & Economics*, 14(2):179-192.

Brot, Z., Z. Cooper, S.V. Craig & L. Klarnet, (2024). Is There Too Little Enforcement in the US Hospital Sector? *American Economic Review: Insights*, 6(4): 526-542.

Budzinski, O. & A. Stöhr, (2019). *Die Ministererlaubnis als Element der Deutschen Wettbewerbsordnung: Eine Theoretische und Empirische Analyse*. *ORDO*, 69: 216-258.

Budzinski, O. & A. Stöhr, (2021). Public Interest Considerations in European Merger Control Regimes, in D. Bosco & M. Gal, eds., *Challenges to Assumptions in Competition Law*, pp.184-205. Cheltenham: Edward Elgar.

Budzinski, O. & I. Ruhmer, (2010). Merger Simulation in Competition Policy: A Survey. *Journal of Competition Law & Economics*, 6(2): 277-319.

Budzinski, O., (2010). An Institutional Analysis of the Enforcement Problems in Merger Control. *European Competition Journal*, 6(2): 445-474.

Buehler, B., D. Coublucq, C. Harition, G. Langus & T. Valetti, (2017). Recent Developments at DG Competition: 2016/17. *Review of Industrial Organization*, 51(4): 397-422.

Buettner, T., D. Coublucq, R. Kotzeva, L. Sauri-Romero & P. Régibeau, (2022). Recent Developments at DG Competition: 2021/22. *Review of Industrial Organization*, 61(4): 449-487.

Bulow, J. & C. Shapiro (2004). The *BP Amoco/Arco* Merger: Alaskan Crude Oil (2000). Case 5 in J.E. Kwoka, Jr. & L.J. White, eds., *The Antitrust Revolution Economics, Competition & Policy*, 4th ed., pp.128-149, Oxford: Oxford University Press.

Bundeskartellamt (BKA), (2001). *Prohibition Criteria in Merger Control – Dominant Position versus Substantial Lessening of Competition?* Discussion Paper, Bonn: BKA.

CA, see Competition Authority.

Cabral, L.M.B., (2003). Horizontal Mergers with Free Entry – Why Cost Efficiencies May Be a Weak Defense and Asset Based Sales a Poor Remedy. *International Journal of Industrial Organization*, 21(5): 607-623.

Caccinelli, C. & J. Toledano, (2018). Assessing Anticompetitive Practices in Two-Sided Markets. *Journal of Competition Law & Economics*, 14(2): 192-234.

Canada Competition Bureau, (2011). *Merger Remedies Study*. Getineau, Quebec.

Caplin, A.S. & Nalebuff, B.J., (1986). Multi-Dimensional Product Differentiation and Price Competition, in D.J. Morris, P.J.N. Sinclair, M.D.E. Slater & J.S. Vickers, eds. *Strategic Behaviour & Industrial Competition*, pp.129-145, Oxford: Oxford University Press.

Carlton, D.W. & Perloff, J.M., (2000). *Modern Industrial Organisation*, 3rd ed. London: Scott Foresman/Little, Brown.

Carlton, D.W., (2004). Why Barriers to Entry Are Barriers to Understanding. *American Economic Review Papers & Proceedings*, 94(2): 466-470.

Carlton, D.W., (2007). Does Antitrust Need to be Modernized? *Journal of Economic Perspectives*, 21(3): 155-176.

Carlton, D.W., (2009, July). Measuring the Effectiveness of US Merger Policy. *The Economist's Voice*, 6(7): 1-4.

Carlton, D.W., (2010). Revising the Horizontal Merger Guidelines. *Journal of Competition Law & Economics*, 6(3): 619-652.

Cave, M. & R. Crandall, (2001). Sports Rights & the Broadcast Industry. *Economic Journal*, 111, F4–F26.

CCPC, see Competition & Consumer Protection Commission.

Chen, Z. & G. Li, (2018). Do Merger Efficiencies Always Mitigate Price Increases? *Journal of Industrial Economics*, 66(1): 95-125.

Chipty, T., (2001). Vertical Integration, Market Foreclosure, and Consumer Welfare in the Cable Television Industry. *American Economic Review*, 91(3): 428-453.

Chisholm, S. & T. Heideman, (2017). The Decision to Investigate Mergers in the United Kingdom's Voluntary Regime. *Journal of Competition Law & Economics*, 13(3): 637-665.

Clay, K., R. Krishnan, E. Wolff & D. Fernandes, (2002). Retail Strategies on the Web: Price and Non-price Competition in the Online Book Industry. *Journal of Industrial Economics*, 50(3): 351-67.

Clougherty, J., T. Duso & J. Seldeslachts, (2016, April 9). Deterrence in EU Merger Policy. Available at: https://voxeu.org/article/deterrence-eu-merger-policy. Accessed 15.6.2022.

CMRG, see Competition & Mergers Review Group.

Coate, M.B. & A.J. Heimart, (2009). *Merger Efficiencies at the Federal Trade Commission 1997-2007.* Washington, D.C.: Federal Trade Commission.

Coate, M.B. & F.S. McChesney, (1992). Empirical Evidence on FTC Enforcement of the *Merger Guidelines*. *Economic Inquiry*, 30(2): 277-293.

Coate, M.B. & J.H. Fischer, (2008). A Practical Guide to the Hypothetical Monopolist Test for Market Definition. *Journal of Competition Law & Economics*, 4(4): 1031-1063.

Coate, M.B., (2006). Economic Models and the *Merger Guidelines*: A Case Study. *Review of Law & Economics*, 2(1): 53-84.

Coate, M.B., (2008). Theory Meets Practice: Barriers to Entry in Merger Analysis. *Review of Law & Economics*, 4(1): 183-212.

Coate, M.B., (2011). Benchmarking the Upward Pricing Pressure Model with Federal Trade Commission Evidence. *Journal of Competition Law & Economics*, 7(4): 825-846.

Coate, M.B., R.S. Higgins & F.S. McChesney, (1990). Bureaucracy and Politics in FTC Merger Enforcement. *Journal of Law & Economics*, 33(2): 463-482.

Coe, P.J. & D. Krause, (2008). An Analysis of Price-Based Tests of Antitrust Market Definition. *Journal of Competition Law & Economics*, 4(4): 983-1007.

Coleman, M.T., D.W. Meyer & D.T. Scheffman, (2003). Economic Analyses of Mergers at the FTC: The Cruise Ships Mergers Investigation. *Review of Industrial Organization*, 23(2): 121-155.

Collard-Wexler, A., (2014). Mergers and Sunk Costs: An Application to the Ready-Mix Concrete Industry. *American Economic Journal of Microeconomics*, 6(4): 407-447.

Compecon, (2002, September 24). *Analysing Mergers: Submission to the Competition Authority.* Dublin: Compecon.

Competition & Consumer Protection Commission (CCPC) (2021, December). *Mergers & Acquisitions Procedures.* Dublin: CCPC.

Competition & Consumer Protection Commission (CCPC), (2014, October 31). *Guidelines for Merger Analysis* (CCPCMG2014). Dublin: CCPC.

Competition & Consumer Protection Commission (CCPC), (2018, September 28). *The Operation of the Household Waste Collection Market.* Dublin: CCPC.

Competition & Consumer Protection Commission (CCPC), (2020, July). *Simplified Merger Notification Procedure Guidelines.* Available at: https://www.ccpc.ie/business/wp-content/uploads/sites/3/2020/05/Simplified-Merger-Notification-Procedure-Guidelines.pdf. Accessed 27.10.2022.

Competition & Consumer Protection Commission (CCPC), (2020, May 7). *Simplified Merger Notification Procedure Regime to commence on 1 July 2020.* Available at: https://www.ccpc.ie/business/simplified-merger-notification-procedure-regime-to-commence-on-1-july-2020/. Accessed 27.10.2022.

Competition & Consumer Protection Commission (CCPC), (2022, November). *Analysis of the Irish Retail Motor Fuel Market.* Available at: https://www.ccpc.ie/business/wp-content/uploads/sites/3/2022/11/Analysis-of-the-Irish-Retail-Motor-Fuel-Market.pdf. Accessed 22.1.2025.

Competition & Consumer Protection Commission (CCPC), (various years). *Annual Report.* Dublin: CCPC.

Competition & Consumer Protection Commission (CCPC), (various years). *Mergers & Acquisitions Report* (CCPC M&A Reports). Dublin: CCPC.

Competition & Markets Authority (UK) (UKCMA), (2017, April 10). *Retail Mergers Commentary.* Available at: https://assets.publishing.service.gov.uk/media/5a81e8e840f0b62302699d23/retail-mergers-commentary.pdf. Accessed 30.3.2022.

Competition & Markets Authority (UK) (UKCMA), (2021, March 18). *Merger Assessment Guidelines,* CMA 129. Available at: https://assets.publishing.service.gov.uk/government/uploads/system/uploads/attachment_data/file/1051823/MAGs_for_publication_2021_--_.pdf . Accessed 14.11.2022.

Competition & Markets Authority (UK) (UKCMA). *CMA's Jurisdiction and Procedure (as amended on 4.1.2022).* London: UKCMA.

Competition & Mergers Review Group (CMRG), (2000). *The Final Report of the Competition & Mergers Review Group*. Dublin: Stationery Office.

Competition Authority (CA), (2013, September 13). *Draft Merger Guidelines for Consultation* (CAMG2013). Dublin: CA.

Competition Authority (CA), (1995, March 30). *Interim Report of Study on the Newspaper Industry.* Dublin: Stationery Office.

Competition Authority (CA), (2002, December 16). *Notice in Respect of Guidelines for Merger Analysis* (CAMG2002). Decision N/02/004, Dublin: CA.

Competition Authority (CA), (2003, February 18). *Notice in Respect of Certain Terms Used in the Competition Act, 2002 (as amended 18 February 2003).* Dublin: CA.

Competition Authority (CA), (2003, September 30). *Notice in Respect of the Review of Non-Notifiable Mergers & Acquisitions,* N/03/001. Dublin: CA.

Competition Authority (CA), (2004, January 26). *Investigation into a Proposed Agreement/Arrangement in Principle whereby Monaghan Middlebrook Mushrooms Limited would Acquire 100% Shareholding in Carbury Mushrooms Limited,* E/04/001. Dublin: CA.

Competition Authority (CA), (2008). *Grocery Retailing and Wholesaling in Ireland: 2001 to 2006. Grocery Monitor*: Report No.1. Dublin: CA.

Competition Authority (CA), (2010, December 3). *Consultation on Competition Authority Guidelines for Merger Analysis.* Dublin: CA.

Competition Authority (CA), (2013, December 20). *Notice in Respect of Guidelines for Merger Analysis,* Decision N/13/001. Dublin: CA.

Competition Authority (CA), (various years). *Annual Report*. Dublin: CA.

Competition Commission (UK) (UKCC), (2003). *Merger References: Competition Commission Guidelines*. London: UKCC.

Competition Commission (UK) (UKCC), (2008, April 30). *The Supply of Groceries in the UK Market Investigation.* Available at: https://webarchive.nationalarchives.gov.uk/ukgwa/20140402194746/; http://www.competition-commission.org.uk/our-work/directory-of-all-inquiries/groceries-market-investigation-and-remittal/final-report-and-appendices-glossary-inquiry. Accessed 30.3.2025.

Competition Commission (UK) (UKCC), (2010). *Understanding Past Merger Remedies: Report on Case Study Research*. London: UKCC.

Competition Commission (UK) (UKCC)/Office of Fair Trading (UK) (UKOFT), (2011, March). *Commentary on Retail Mergers*. London: UKCC/UKOFT.

Compte, O., F. Jenny & P. Rey, (2002). Capacity Constraints, Mergers and Collusion, *European Economic Review*, 46(1): 1-30.

Cooper, M.N., (2001, March 21). *Mergers Between Major Airlines: The Anti-competition and Anti-consumer Effects of the Creation of a Private Cartel*. Statement to Subcommittee on Commerce, Trade & Consumer Protection Committee on Energy & Commerce, United States House of Representatives.

Cosnita-Langlais, A. & L. Sørgard, (2018). Enforcement and Deterrence in Merger Control: The Case of Merger Remedies. *Review of Law & Economics*, 14(3).

Cournot, A.A., (1838). *Recherches sur les Principes Mathematiques de la Theorie des Richesse.* Translated by N.T. Bacon, (1927). New York: Macmillan.

Cowan, S., (1998), The Water Industry. In D. Helm & T. Jenkinson, eds., *Competition in Regulated Industries*. Oxford: Oxford University Press.

Crandall, R.W. & C. Winston, (2003). Does Antitrust Policy Improve Consumer Welfare? Assessing the Evidence. *Journal of Economic Perspectives*, 17(4): 3-26.

Crowe, (2023, December). *Dublin Hotel Pricing: A Comparative Review*, Failte Ireland. Available at: https://www.failteireland.ie/FailteIreland/media/WebsiteStructure/Documents/Publications/dublin-hotel-pricing-report.pdf?ext=.pdf. Accessed 2.9.2024.

Cruickshank, D., (2005). *Competition in UK Banking: A Report to the Chancellor of the Exchequer.* Available at: https://webarchive.nationalarchives.gov.uk/ukgwa/20050301221631/http:/www.hm-treasury.gov.uk/documents/financial_services/banking/bankreview/fin_bank_reviewfinal.cfm. Accessed 26.9.2023.

Cunningham, C., F. Ederer & S. Ma, (2021). Killer Acquisitions. *Journal of Political Economy*, 129(3): 649-702.

Dáil Debates, (various years). Available at: https://www.oireachtas.ie/en/debates/find/?debateType=dail.

Dalkir, S. & F.R. Warren-Boulton, (1999). Prices, Market Definition, and the Effects of Merger: *Staples/Office Depot* (1997). Case 6 in J.E. Kwoka, Jr. & L.J. White, eds., *The Antitrust Revolution Economics, Competition & Policy*, pp.143-164, Oxford: Oxford University Press.

Davies, S. & A. Majumdar, (2002). *The Development of Targets for Consumer Savings Arising from Competition Policy*, Working Paper No. 4. London: Office of Fair Trading.

Davies, S., M. Olczak & H. Coles, (2011). Tacit Collusion, Firm Asymmetries and Numbers: Evidence from EC Merger Cases. *International Journal of Industrial Organization*, 29(2): 221-231.

Davis, P. & E. Garcés, (2010). *Quantitative Techniques for Competition & Antitrust Analysis.* Princeton, N.J.: Princeton University Press.

De Loecker, J., J. Eeckhout & G. Unger, (2020). The Rise of Market Power and the Macroeconomic Implications. *Quarterly Journal of Economics*, 135(2): 561-644.

Deloitte, (2007). *Deterrence Effect of Competition Enforcement by the OFT*. A report prepared by Deloitte on behalf of OFT, London: UKOFT.

Deneckere, R. & C. Davidson, (1985). Incentives to Form Coalitions with Bertrand Competition. *Rand Journal of Economics*, 16(4): 473-486.

Department for Business, Innovation & Skills (UK) (UKDBIS), (2011). *A Competition Regime for Growth: A Consultation on Options for Reform*. Available at:

https://assets.publishing.service.gov.uk/government/uploads/system/uploads/attachment_data/file/31411/11-657-competition-regime-for-growth-consultation.pdf. Accessed 27.10.2021.
Dertouzos, J.N. & W.B. Trautman, (1990). Economic Effects of Media Concentration: Estimates from a Model of the Newspaper Firm. *Journal of Industrial Economics*, 39(1): 1-14.
DG Competition, (2011, November 17). *Best Practices for the Submission of Economic Evidence & Data Collection in Cases Concerning the Application of Articles 101 & 102, TFEU & in Merger Cases*. Staff Working Paper. Available at: https://eur-lex.europa.eu/legal-content/en/ALL/?uri=CELEX%3A52011SC1216. Accessed 15.6.2022.
Dixit, A., (1980). The Role of Investment in Entry-Deterrence. *Economic Journal*, 90: 95-106.
Dobson, P.W. & M. Waterson, (1996). *Vertical Restraints & Competition Policy*, Office of Fair Trading Research Paper 12. London: UKOFT.
Dobson, P.W. & R. Inderst, (2008). The Waterbed Effect: Where Buying and Selling Come Together. *Wisconsin Law Review*, 2008(2): 331-357.
DotEcon, (2010). *Minority Interests in Competitors.* Office of Fair Trading 1218. London: UKOFT.
Duso, T., K. Gugler & B. Yortuglu, (2006). *How Effective is European Merger Control?* WZB Discussion Paper SP II, 2006-12. Berlin: WZB.
Duso, T., K. Gugler & F. Szucs, (2013). An Empirical Assessment of the 2004 EU Merger Policy Reform. *Economic Journal*, 123: F596-F619.
Duso, T., L. Bernhardt & J. Piechucka, (2024). The Evolution of 'Theories of Harm' in EU Merger Control. *Oxford Review of Economic Policy*, 40(4): 729–762.
Eckbo, B.E. & P. Wier, (1985). Antimerger Policy under the *Hart-Scott-Rodino Act*: A Re-examination of the Market Power Hypothesis. *Journal of Law & Economics*, 28(1): 119-149.
Eckbo, B.E., (1992). Mergers and the Value of Antitrust Deterrence. *Journal of Finance*, 47(3): 1005-1029.
Ederer, F. & B. Pellegrino, (2023). The Great Start-Up Sellout and the Rise of Oligopoly. *American Economic Association Papers & Proceedings*, 113: 274-278.
Elzinga, K. & T. Hogarty, (1973). The Problem of Geographic Market Definition in Antimerger Suits. *Antitrust Bulletin*, 18(1): 45-81.
Elzinga, K. & T. Hogarty, (1978). The Problem of Geographic Market Delineation Revisited. *Antitrust Bulletin*, 23(1): 1-18.
Elzinga, K., (1981). Defining Geographic Market Boundaries. *Antitrust Bulletin*, 26(4): 739-752.
Epstein, R.J. & D.L. Rubinfeld, (2002). Margin Simulation: A Simplified Approach with New Applications. *Antitrust Law Journal*, 69(3): 883-919.
Epstein, R.J. & D.L. Rubinfeld, (2004). Margin Simulation with Brand-Level Margin Data: Extending PCAIDS with Nests. *BE Journal Advances in Economic Analysis & Policy*, 4(1). Available at: http://www.bepress.com/bejeap/advances/vol4/iss1/art2. Accessed 30.5.2023.
EU Commission, (1986, September 3). *Notice on Agreements of Minor Importance Which Do Not Fall Under Article 85(1) of the Treaty Establishing the European Economic Community*, OJ C231.
EU Commission, (1997, December 9). *Notice on Market Definition* (1997MDN). OJ C372.
EU Commission, (1998). *Green Paper on the Review of Council Regulation (EEC) No. 4064/89*. Brussels: EU Commission.
EU Commission, (2002, December 11). *Proposal for a Council Regulation Regarding the Control of Mergers by Undertakings*. 2003 OJ C 20/4.
EU Commission, (2004, February 5). *Guidelines on the Assessment of Horizontal Mergers under the Council Regulation on the Control of Concentrations between Undertakings* (EUHMG). OJ/C 31/5.
EU Commission, (2005). *Merger Remedies Study*. Brussels: EU Commission.
EU Commission, (2008, October 18). *Guidelines on the Assessment of Non-horizontal Mergers under the Council Regulation on the Control of Concentrations between Undertakings* (EUNHMG2008) OJ/C 265/07.

EU Commission, (2008, October 22). *Commission Notice on Remedies Acceptable Under Council Regulation (EC) No. 139/2004 and Under Commission Regulation (EC) No. 802/2004* (EU Remedies Notice). OJ/C 267/1.

EU Commission, (2014, May 7). *Decision on State Aid implemented by Ireland for the Restructuring of Allied Irish Banks plc & EBS Building Society*. Available at: https://ec.europa.eu/competition/state_aid/cases/233873/233873_1581273_451_2.pdf. Accessed 4.11.2022.

EU Commission, (2021). *Support Study Accompanying the Evaluation of the Commission Notice on the Definition of Relevant Market for the Purposes of Community Competition Law Final Report*. Available at: https://competition-policy.ec.europa.eu/system/files/2021-06/kd0221712enn_market_definition_notice_2021_1.pdf. Accessed 1.3.2025.

EU Commission, (2024, February 22). *Commission Notice on the Definition of the Relevant Market for the Purposes of Union Competition Law* (C/2024/1645) (2024MDN). Available at: https://eur-lex.europa.eu/legal-content/EN/TXT/PDF/?uri=OJ:C_202401645. Accessed 1.10.2024.

Evans, D.S. & M.D. Noel, (2008). The Analysis of Mergers that Involve Multisided Platform Analysis. *Journal of Competition Law & Economics*, 4(3): 663-695.

Evans, L., N. Quigley, F. Mathewson & P. Hughes, (1999). *Thresholds for the Scrutiny of Mergers and the Problem of Joint Dominance*. Report prepared for the New Zealand Treasury. Victoria University of Wellington, New Zealand Institute for the Study of Competition & Regulation Working Paper Series No.3926.

Ezrielev, J. & J.J. Simons, (2011). The 2010 *Merger Guidelines*, Critical Loss and Linear Demand. *Journal of Competition Law & Economics*, 7(3): 497-522.

Fair Trade Commission (FTC), (1990). *Study of Competition Law*. Dublin: Stationery Office, Pl 7080.

Fair Trade Commission (FTC), (various years). *Annual Reports*. Dublin: Stationery Office.

Fan, Y., (2013). Ownership Consolidation and Product Characteristics: A Study of the US Daily Newspaper Industry. *American Economic Review*, 103(5): 1598-1628.

Farrell, J. & C. Shapiro, (1990). Horizontal Mergers: An Equilibrium Analysis. *American Economic Review*, 80(1): 107-126.

Farrell, J. & C. Shapiro, (2001). Scale Economies and Synergies in Horizontal Merger Analysis. *Antitrust Law Journal*, 68(3): 685-710.

Farrell, J. & C. Shapiro, (2010a). Antitrust Evaluation of Horizontal Mergers: An Economic Alternative to Market Definition. *BE Journal of Theoretical Economics*, 10(1), Article 9. Available at: http://www.bepress.com/bejte/vol10/iss1/art9. Accessed 1.12.2024.

Farrell, J. & C. Shapiro, (2010b). Upward Pricing Pressure and Critical Loss Analysis: Response. *CPI Antitrust Journal*, (December). Available at https://faculty.haas.berkeley.edu/shapiro/uppcritical.pdf. Accessed 2.12.2024.

Farrington, R., N. Brumfield, G. Paul & H. Ying, (2015). *Below-threshold Transactions: Enforcement & Exposure*. Technical Report. Washington, D.C.: USFTC.

Farronato, C. & A. Fradkin, (2022). The Welfare Effects of Peer Entry: The Case of Airbnb and the Accommodation Industry. *American Economic Review*, 112(6): 1782-1817.

Federico, G., (2011). The Economic Analysis of Energy Mergers in Europe and Spain. *Journal of Competition Law & Economics*, 7(3): 603-629.

Filistrucchi, L., D. Geradin, E. van Damme & P. Affeldt, (2014). Market Definition in Two-Sided Markets: Theory and Practice. *Journal of Competition Law & Economics*, 10(2): 293-339.

Filistrucchi, L., T.J. Klein & T.O. Michielsen, (2012). Assessing Unilateral Merger Effects in a Two-Sided Market: An Application to the Dutch Daily Newspaper Market. *Journal of Competition Law & Economics*, 8(2): 297-329.

Focarelli, D. & F. Panetta, F., (2003). Are Mergers Beneficial to Consumers? Evidence from the Market for Bank Deposits. *American Economic Review*, 93(4): 1152-1172.

Fox, E.M., (2003). We Protect Competition, You Protect Competitors. *World Competition*, 26(2): 149-165.

Frank, M.W., (2008). Media Substitution in Advertising: A Spirited Case Study. *International Journal of Industrial Organization*, 26(1): 308-326.

Franks, J. & Harris, R., (1986). The Role of Mergers and Monopolies Commission in Merger Policy: Costs and Alternatives. *Oxford Review of Economic Policy*, 2(4): 58-78.

Froeb, L., S. Tschantz & G.J. Werden, (2005). Pass-through Rates and the Price Effects of Mergers. *International Journal of Industrial Organization*, 23(9-10): 703-715.

FTC, see Fair Trade Commission.

Furman, J., (2019). *Unlocking Digital Competition*, Report of the Digital Competition Expert Panel. Available at: https://assets.publishing.service.gov.uk/government/uploads/system/uploads/attachment_data/file/785547/unlocking_digital_competition_furman_review_web.pdf. Accessed 10.7.2021.

Gandhi, A., L. Froeb, S. Tschantz & G.J. Werden, (2008). Post-Merger Product Repositioning. *Journal of Industrial Economics*, 56(1): 49-67.

Garrod, L. & B. Lyons, (2016). Early Settlement in European Merger Control. *Journal of Industrial Economics*, 64(1): 27-63.

Garside, L., P.A. Grout & A. Zalewska, (2013). Does Experience Make You Tougher? Evidence from Competition Law, *Economic Journal*, 123: 474-491.

Gastelum, S.E., (2024). The *Ticketmaster/Live Nation* Merger: Why They Should Never Ever Have Been Together. *Boston College Law Review*, 65: 205-239.

Gavil, A.I., (2005). Competition Policy, Economics, and Economists: Are We Expecting Too Much? Chapter 24 in B. Hawk, ed., *International Antitrust Law & Policy*, pp.575-600. New York: Juris Publications.

Gaynor, M.S., S.A. Kleiner & W.B. Vogt, (2013). A Structural Approach to Market Definition with an Application to the Hospital Industry. *Journal of Industrial Economics*, 61(2): 243-289.

George, K. & A. Jacquemin, (1992). Dominant Firms and Mergers. *Economic Journal*, 102: 148-157.

George, L.M. & J. Waldfogel, (2006). The *New York Times* and the Market for Local Newspapers. *American Economic Review*, 96(1): 435-448.

Geroski, P. & A. Jacquemin, (1985). Industrial Change, Barriers to Entry and European Industrial Policy. *Economic Policy*, 1(1): 169-205.

Geroski, P.A., (1994). Entry and Market Share Mobility. In J. Cable, ed., *Current Issues in Industrial Economics*, pp.134-159. Basingstoke: Macmillan Press,.

Gil, R., (2015). Does Vertical Integration Decrease Prices? Evidence from the Paramount Antitrust Case of 1948. *American Economic Journal: Economic Policy*, 7(2): 162-191.

Gilbert, R.J. & A.D. Melamed, (2024). Potential Competition and the 2023 *Merger Guidelines*. *Review of Industrial Organization*, 65(1): 269-302.

Gilbert, R.J. & M.L. Katz, (2001). An Economist's Guide to *US v. Microsoft*. *Journal of Economic Perspectives*, 15(2): 25-44.

Ginsberg, D.H., (2010). Originalism and Economic Analysis: Two Case Studies of Consistency and Coherence in Supreme Court Decision-making. *Harvard Journal of Law & Public Policy*, 33: 217-238.

Glasner, D. & S.P. Sullivan, (2020). The Logic of Market Definition. *Antitrust Law Journal*, 83(2): 293-345.

Goldmanis, M., A. Hortacsu, C. Syverson & O. Emre, (2010). E-commerce and the Market Structure of Retail Industries. *Economic Journal*, 120: 651-683.

Goppelsroeder, M., Schinkel, M-P. & Tuinstra, J., (2008). Quantifying the Scope for Efficiency Defense in Merger Control: The Werden-Froeb Index. *Journal of Industrial Economics*, 56(4): 778-808.

Gorecki, P.K., (2006). Form *versus* Effects-Based Approaches to the Abuse of a Dominant Position: The Case of Ticketmaster Ireland. *Journal of Competition Law & Economics*, 2(3): 233-248.
Gorecki, P.K., (2009). The *Kerry/Breeo* Merger: Two Views on Countervailing Buyer Power – The Competition Authority and the Courts. *European Competition Journal*, 5(2): 585-612.
Gorecki, P.K., (2011). Too Many Unnecessary Notifications in Ireland. *Journal of Competition Law & Economics*, 7(3): 651-701.
Gorecki, P.K., (2012). Competition Policy in Ireland's Recession. *Economic & Social Review*, 43(4): 597-629.
Gorecki, P.K., (2014). The Quality of Analysis of Irish Merger Decisions. *Journal of Competition Law & Economics*, 10(2): 375-397.
Gorecki, P.K., (2020). *The Berendsen (Elis)/King's Laundry Merger: Three Into Two Won't Go*. Dublin: Department of Economics, Trinity College Dublin. Available at: https://mpra.ub.uni-muenchen.de/100477/. Accessed 14.7.2020.
Gorecki, P.K., (2023). *Merger Control in Ireland after the Uniphar/NaviCorp Decision: State of Play Meetings & Market Testing Remedies*, MRPA Discussion Paper, 118/88.
Gorecki, P.K., C. Keating & B. O'Connor, (2007). The Role of Economic Evidence in Merger Control in Ireland: Current and Future Practices. *European Competition Journal*, 3(2): 345-372.
Gotts, I.K. & C.S. Goldman, (2002). The Role of Efficiencies in M&A Global Antitrust Review: Still in Flux? In B. Hawk, ed., *International Antitrust Law & Policy*, pp.201-300. New York: Juris Publications.
Government of Ireland, (2024). *Periodic Critical Review: Competition & Consumer Protection Commission*. Available at: https://enterprise.gov.ie/en/publications/publication-files/periodic-critical-review-ccpc-2024.pdf. Accessed 13.1.2025.
Granger, C., (1969). Investigating Causal Relations by Econometric Models and Cross-Spectral Methods. *Econometrica*, 37(3): 424-438.
Granitz, E. & B. Klein, (1996). Monopolization by "Raising Rivals' Costs": The Standard Oil Case. *Journal of Law & Economics*, 39(1): 1-47
Green, C., (1993). Merger Law, Policy, and Enforcement Guidelines in Canada. *Review of Industrial Organization*, 8(2): 191-201.
Gugler, K., D.C. Mueller, B.B. Yurtoglu & C. Zulehner, (2003). The Effects of Mergers: An International Comparison. *International Journal of Industrial Organization*, 21(5): 655-672.
Gürkaynak, G. & E. Kalkan, (2017). Testing Justification for Segment-based Relevant Product Market Definition in Merger Control: Evidence from Turkey. *Journal of Competition Law & Economics*, 13(2): 328-345.
Harris, B.C. & J.J. Simons, (1989). Focusing Market Definition: How Much Substitution is Necessary? *Journal of Research in Law & Economics*, 12: 207-226.
Hausman, J.A. & G.K. Leonard, (2005). Using Merger Simulation Models: Testing the Underlying Assumptions. *International Journal of Industrial Organization*, 23(9-10): 693-698.
Hawk, B., (2020). *Antitrust & Competition Laws*, New York: Juris Publications.
Haydock, J., & T. Smith, (2019). No Magic Dust: The Relationship Between the National and Local Assessments in *Sainsbury's/Asda*. *Journal of Competition Law & Economics*, 15(4): 538-558.
Heavner, D.L., (2004). Vertical Enclosure: Vertical Integration and the Reluctance to Purchase from a Competitor. *Journal of Industrial Economics*, 52(2): 179-199.
Heimler, A., (2008). Was the Change in Test for Merger Control in Europe Justified? An Assessment (Four Years After the Introduction of SIEC). *European Competition Journal*, 4(1): 85-94.
Henneberry, E., (2004, September 29). *Merger Lessons & Possible Modifications*, Address to Competition Press Conference at the Radisson Hotel, Dublin.
Higgins, R.S., (1997). Diagonal Merger. *Review of Industrial Organization*, 12(4): 607-623.

Hilke, J.C. & P.B. Nelson, (1989). Non-price Predation and Attempted Monopolization: The *Coffee (General Foods)* Case. In J.E. Kwoka & L.J. White, eds., *The Antitrust Revolution*, Glenview: Scott, Foresman & Co.
Hoehn, T. & D. Lancefield, (2003). Broadcasting and Sport. *Oxford Review of Economic Policy*, 19: 552-568.
Horner, N., (2006). Unilateral Effects and the EC *Merger Regulation*: How the Commission Had Its Cake and Ate It Too. *Hanse Law Review*, 2(1): 23-43.
Horowitz, I., (1981). Market Definition in Antitrust Analysis: A Regression-based Approach. *Southern Economics Journal*, 48(1): 1-16.
Hosken, D., D. O'Brien, D. Scheffman & M. Vita, (2002). *Demand System Estimation and Its Application to Horizontal Merger Analysis*. US Federal Trade Commission, WP246, Washington: USFTC.
Houde, J-F., (2012). Spatial Differentiation and Vertical Mergers in Retail Markets for Gasoline. *American Economic Review*, 102(5): 2147-2182.
Hovenkamp, H., (2011). Harm to Competition Under the 2010 *Merger Guidelines*. *Review of Industrial Organization*, 39(1-2): 3-18.
Hovenkamp, H., (2022). Digital Cluster Markets. *Columbia Business Law Review*, 2022(1): 246-278.
Hovenkamp, H., (2024). *Merger Guidelines*: Law, Fact and Method. *Review of Industrial Organization*, 65(1): 39-77.
Hovenkamp, H.J. & C. Shapiro, (2018). Horizontal Mergers, Market Structure, and Burdens of Proof. *Yale Law Journal*, 127(7): 1996-2025.
Howe, M., (1995). *The "Fix-it-First" Approach to Merger Control*, mimeo.
Hurley, S., (2011). The Use of Surveys in Merger and Competition Analysis. *Journal of Competition Law & Economics*, 7(1): 45-68.
Hurwitz, J.D., (2009). *Commentary: Ticketmaster/Live Nation*. American Antitrust Institute White Paper. Available at: https://www.anti-trustinstitute.org/wp-content/uploads/2018/08/TICKETMASTER-Revised.4.28.09_043020092221.pdf. Accessed 31.3.2025.
ICN, see International Competition Network.
ICPAC, (2000). *International Competition Policy Advisory Committee to the Attorney General and Assistant Attorney General, United States Department of Justice, Final Report*. Washington D.C.: Department of Justice.
Innes, R., (2006). Entry Deterrence by Non-Horizontal Merger. *Journal of Industrial Economics*, 54(3): 369-395.
International Competition Network (ICN), (2005). *Report of Merger Remedies Review Project*. Bonn: ICN.
Irish Times, (2025, February 11). *ICS Mortgages owner sees net interest slide 75% in 2023 on funding–costs spike*. Available at: https://www.irishtimes.com/business/2025/02/11/ics-mortgages-owner-sees-net-interest-slide-75-in-2023-on-fundingcosts-spike/. Accessed 11.2.2025.
Irish Times, (2025, March 26). Finance Ireland's move to stop mortgage lending to have limited market impact – analysts. Available at: https://www.irishtimes.com/business/2025/03/26/finance-irelands-move-to-stop-mortgage-lending-to-have-limited-market-impact-analysts/. Accessed 26.3.2025.
Ivaldi, M. & F. Verboven, (2005). Quantifying the Effects from Horizontal Mergers in European Competition Policy. *International Journal of Industrial Organization*, 23(9-10): 669-691.
Jean, S., A. Perrot & T. Philippon, (2019). Competition and Trade: Which Policies for Europe? *Notes du Conseil d'Analyse Economique*, 2019/3 (No.51): 1-12.
Jenny, F., (2001). Collective Dominance and the EC Merger Regulation. In B. Hawk, ed., *International Antitrust Law & Policy 2001*, pp.361-373. New York: Juris Publications.

Jeziorski, P., (2014). Effects of Mergers in Two-Sided Markets: The US Radio Industry. *American Economic Journal: Microeconomics*, 6(4): 35-73.

Johnson, R.L., A.S. Joskow & G.J. Werden, (1989). *The Effects of Mergers on Economic Performance: Two Case Studies from the Airline Industry*. Washington D.C.: United States Department of Justice, Antitrust Division.

Kahn, A.E., (1988). *The Economics of Regulation Principles and Institutions*. Cambridge, MA, MIT Press.

Kalintiri, A., (2014). The Standard of Proof in Phase 1 Merger Proceedings: The Lesson from the *Microsoft/Skype* Appeal. *European Competition Law Review*, 35(6): 279-281.

Kamerschen, D.R. & J. Kohler, (1993). Residual Demand Analysis of the Ready-to-Eat Breakfast Cereal Market. *Antitrust Bulletin*, 38(4): 903-942.

Kamphorst, J.J.A. & V. Pruzhansky, (2012). Vertical Theory of Harm in a Horizontal Merger: The *Friesland Foods/Campina* Case. *Journal of Competition Law & Economics*, 8(2): 417-424.

Karlinger, L., D. Magos, P. Regibeau & H. Zenger, (2020). Recent Developments at DG Competition: 2019/20. *Review of Industrial Organization*, 57(4): 783-814.

Kaserman, D.L. & H. Zeisel, (1996). Market Definition: Implementing the Department of Justice *Merger Guidelines*. *Antitrust Bulletin*, 41(3): 665-90.

Katz, M.L. & C. Shapiro, (2003). Critical Loss: Let's Tell the Whole Story. *Antitrust*, (Spring), 49-56.

Kauper, T.E., (1996). The Problem of Market Definition Under EC Competition Law. In B. Hawk, ed., *International Antitrust Law & Policy*, pp.239-305. New York: Juris Publications.

Kauper, T.E., (2001). The Legacy of *LTV/Republic Steel*. *Antitrust Law Journal*, 68(3): 753-769.

Kauper, T.E., (2008). Influence of Conservative Economic Analysis on the Development of the Law of Antitrust. In R. Pitofsky, ed., *How the Chicago School Overshot the Mark. The Effect of Conservative Economic Analysis on US Antitrust Policy*, pp.40-50. Oxford: Oxford University Press.

Kaysen, C. & D. F. Turner, (1959). *Antitrust Policy*. Cambridge, M.A.: Harvard University Press.

Kelly, H., K. McKenna & C. Watson, (2021, January 14). *Irish Merger Control Update: Key Findings from the CCPC's M&A Report 2020*. Available at: https://www.matheson.com/insights/detail/irish-merger-control-update-key-findings-from-the-ccpcs-ma-report-2020. Accessed 14.6.2022.

Khan, L.M., (2017). Amazon's Antitrust Paradox. *Yale Law Journal*, 126(3): 710-805.

Khan, L.M., (2019). The Separation of Platforms and Commerce. *Columbia Law Review*, 119(4): 973-1098.

Kim, E.H. & V. Singal, (1993). Mergers and Market Power: Evidence from the Airline Industry. *American Economic Review*, 83(3): 549-569.

Kimmel, S., (1987). *Price Correlation and Market Definition*. Economic Analysis Group Discussion Paper, EAG87-8. Washington, D.C.: United States Department of Justice, Antitrust Division.

Klemperer, P., (2007). Bidding Markets. *Journal of Competition Law & Economics*, 3(1): 1-48.

Koboldt, C., (1999). A Backbone to Pick: The European Commission and *MCI/Worldcom*. *London Economics, Competition & Regulation Bulletin*, 10 (January): 1-4.

Kolasky, W.J. & L.B. Greenfield, (2001, July 30). A View to a Kill – The Lost *GE/Honeywell* Deal Reveals a Trans-Atlantic Clash of Essentials. *Legal Times*, 28-29.

Kolasky, W.J., (2001). The FCC's Review of the *Bell Atlantic/NYNEX* and *SBC/Ameritech* Mergers: Regulatory Overreach in the Name of Promoting Competition. *Antitrust Law Journal*, 68(3): 771-803.

Korah, V., (2000). *An Introductory Guide to EC Competition Law & Practice*, 7th ed. Oxford: Hart Publishing.

Kotzeva, R., D. Kovo, S. Lorincz, G. Sapi, L. Sauri & T. Valletti, (2019). Recent Developments at DG Competition: 2018/2019. *Review of Industrial Organization*, 55(4): 551-578.

Kovacic, W.E. & C. Shapiro, (2000). Antitrust Policy: A Century of Economic and Legal Thinking. *Journal of Economic Perspectives*, 14(1): 43-60.

Kovacic, W.E., (2001). Transatlantic Turbulence: The *Boeing/McDonnell Douglas* Merger and International Competition Policy. *Antitrust Law Journal*, 68(3): 805-873.
Krattenmaker, T.G. & S.C. Salop, (1986). Anticompetitive Exclusion: Raising Rivals' Costs to Achieve Power Over Price. *Yale Law Journal*, 96(2): 209-93.
Kroes, N., (2005, September 14). *European Competition Policy – Delivering Better Markets & Better Choice,* mimeo.
Kühn, K.-U. & J. Van Reenen, (2009). Capacity Constraints and Irreversible Investments: Defending Against Collective Dominance in *UPM-Kymmene/Norske Skog/Haindl*. In B. Lyons, ed., *Cases in European Competition Policy: The Economic Analysis,* pp.383-410, Cambridge: Cambridge University Press.
Kwoka, J. & M. Pollitt, (2010). Do Mergers Improve Efficiency? Evidence from Restructuring the US Electric Power Sector. *International Journal of Industrial Organization*, 28(6): 645-656.
Kwoka, J.E. & E. Shumilkina, (2010). The Price Effects of Eliminating Potential Competition; Evidence from an Airline Merger. *SSRN*, 58(4): 767-794.
Kwoka, J.E. & L.J. White, eds., (1999). *The Antitrust Revolution: Economics, Competition & Policy,* 3rd ed. Oxford: Oxford University Press.
Kwoka, J.E. & L.J. White, eds., (2004). *The Antitrust Revolution: Economics, Competition & Policy,* 4th ed. Oxford: Oxford University Press.
Kwoka, J.E., (2003). *The Attack on Antitrust Policy & Consumer Welfare: A Response to Crandall & Winston*, Social Science Research Network, *mimeo.*
Kwoka, J.E., (2015). *Mergers, Merger Control & Remedies*. Cambridge, M.A., MIT Press.
Lamoreaux, N., (2019). The Problem of Bigness: From Standard Oil to Google. *Journal of Economic Perspectives*, 33(3): 94-117.
Lancieri, F.M. & T. Valletti, (2024). Towards an Effective Merger Review Policy: A Defence of Rebuttable Structural Presumptions. *Oxford Review of Economic Policy*, 40(4): 763-775.
Lande, R.H., (1994). Beyond Chicago: Will Activist Antitrust Rise Again? *Antitrust Bulletin*, 39(1): 1-25.
Lande, R.H., (2001). Resurrecting Incipiency: From Von's Grocery to Consumer Choice. *Antitrust Law Journal*, 68(3): 875-898.
Lande, R.H., (2013). A Traditional and Textualist Analysis of the Goals of Antitrust Efficiency Preventing Theft from Consumers and Consumer Choice. *Fordham Law Review*, 81: 2349-2403.
Lerner, A., (1934). The Concept of Monopoly and the Measurement of Market Power. *Review of Economic Studies,* 1(3): 157-75.
Levy, D.T. & J.D. Reitzes, (1992). Anticompetitive Effects of Mergers in Markets with Localized Competition. *Journal of Law, Economics & Organization,* 8(2):427-440.
Levy, N., (1996). *Kimberly-Clark/Scott* and the Power of Brands. *European Competition Law Review*, 17(7): 403-410.
Levy, N., (2003). EU Merger Control from Birth to Adolescence. *World Competition,* 26(2): 195-218.
Levy, N., (2010). The EU's SIEC Test Five Years On: Has it Made a Difference? *European Competition Journal*, 6(1): 211-254.
Levy, N., D.R. Little & H. Mostyn, (2019). European Champions – Why Politics Should Stay Out of European Merger Control. *Concurrences*, 2019(2): 23-30.
London Economics, (1997). *Competition in Retailing*. OFT Research Paper 13. London: UKFTC.
Luco, F. & G. Marshall, (2020). The Competitive Impact of Vertical Integration by Multiproduct Firms. *American Economic Review*, 110(7): 2041-2064.
Lyons, B.R. & M. Zhu, (2013). Compensating Competitors or Restoring Competition? EU Regulation of State Aid for Banks During the Financial Crisis. *Journal of Industry, Competition & Trade*, 13(1): 39-66.

Lyons, B.R., (2002). *Could Politicians Be More Right than Economists? A Theory of Merger Standards.* UEA Centre for Competition & Regulation, WP CCR02-1. Norwich, University of East Anglia.

Lyons, B.R., (2008). An Economic Assessment of EC Merger Control: 1958-2007. In X. Vives, ed., *Competition Policy in the EU: Fifty Years On from the Treaty of Rome*, pp.135-175. Oxford: Oxford University Press.

Lyons, P.M., (2007). *Competition & Merger Law & Practice in Ireland, 1953-2002.* Available at: http://www.tara.tcd.ie/bitstream/handle/2262/11978/Lyons P0507.pdf;jsessionid=21D999A9D9B08BBFD53FFF9CB2D8FCE7?sequence=1.

Lyons, P.M., P. Massey & M. McDowell, (2012). Boston v. Berlin: A Half-Century of Irish Antitrust. In P.S. Mehta, ed., *Evolution of Competition Laws & Their Enforcement: A Political Economy Perspective.* London: Routledge.

Macher, J.T. & J.W. Mayo, (2021). The Evolution of Merger Enforcement Intensity: What Do the Data Show? *Journal of Competition Law & Economics,* 17(3): 708-727.

Malone, F. & J.G. Sidak, (2007). Should Antitrust Consent Decrees Regulate Post-Merger Pricing? *Journal of Competition Law & Economics*, 3(3): 471-490.

Manuszak, M.D. & C.C. Moul, (2008). Prices and Endogenous Market Structure in Office Supply Superstores. *Journal of Industrial Economics*, 56(1): 94-112.

Marshall, A., (1890). *Principles of Economics,* London, Macmillan.

Marshall, G., & T. Pires, (2018). Measuring the Impact of Travel Costs on Grocery Shopping. *Economic Journal,* 128: 2538-2557. doi:10.1111/ecoj.12523.

Marshall, R.C. & L.M. Marx, (2012). *The Economics of Collusion: Cartels & Bidding Rings.* Cambridge, M.A.: MIT Press.

Martin, S., (2002). *Advanced Industrial Economics*, 2nd ed. Oxford: Blackwell.

Massey, P. & D. Daly, (2003). *Competition & Regulation in Ireland: The Law & Economics*. Cork: Oak Tree Press.

Massey, P. & M. McDowell, (2010). Joint Dominance and Tacit Collusion. *European Competition Journal*, 6(2): 427-444.

Massey, P. & M. McDowell, (2021). EU Competition Policy: An Unaffordable Luxury in Times of Crisis? *World Competition*, 44(4): 405-432.

Massey, P., (2000). Market Definition and Market Power in Competition Analysis: Some Practical Issues. *Economic & Social Review,* 31(4): 309-328.

Massey, P., (2001). Merger Control in Ireland. *Irish Banking Review,* (Autumn): 30-42.

Massey, P., (2002). Act Places Economic Analysis at Heart of Merger Assessment. *Competition,* 11(3): 73-75.

Massey, P., (2010). Taking Politics Out of Mergers: A Review of Irish Experience. *Journal of Competition Law & Economics,* 6(4): 853-878.

Massey, P., (2011). A Tale of Two Mergers: Irish Merger Policy After the *Heineken* and *Kerry* Decisions. *World Competition,* 34(1): 113-137.

Mathiesen, L., Ø.A. Nilsen & L. Sørgard, (2012). A Note on Upward Pricing Pressure: The Possibility of False Positives. *Journal of Competition Law & Economics*, 8(4): 881-887.

Matsushima, N., (2009). Vertical Mergers and Product Differentiation. *Journal of Industrial Economics,* 47(4): 812-835.

McAfee, R.P. & M.A. Williams, (1992). Horizontal Mergers and Antitrust Policy. *Journal of Industrial Economics,* 40(2): 181-187.

McAfee, R.P., H.M. Mialon & M.A. Williams, (2004). When Are Sunk Costs Barriers to Entry? Entry Barriers in Economic and Antitrust Analysis. *American Economic Review Papers & Proceedings*: 461-465.

McCabe, M., (2002). Journal Pricing and Mergers: A Portfolio Approach, *American Economic Review*, 92(1): 259-269.
McCarthy, T., (1997). Refining Product Market Definition in the Antitrust Analysis of Bank Mergers. *Duke Law Journal*, 46(4): 865-902.
Meese, A.J. & S.L. Stafford, (2017). Were the 1982 *Merger Guidelines* Old News? *Journal of Competition Law & Economics*, 13(4): 577-608.
Melamed, A.D., (1995). Antitrust: The New Regulation. *Antitrust*, 10(1): 13-15.
Melamed, A.D., (2020). Antitrust Law and Its Critics. *Antitrust Law Journal*, 83(1): 269-291.
Meyer, C. & V. Wang, (2012). A Comprehensive Look at Critical Loss Analysis in a Differentiated Products Market. *Journal of Competition Law & Economics*, 8(4): 863-879.
Miller, N.H., G. Sheu & M.C. Weinberg, (2021). Oligopolistic Price Leadership and Mergers: The United States Beer Industry. *American Economic Review*, 111(10): 3123-3159.
Ministry of Commerce (New Zealand), (1999). *Review of the Competition Thresholds in the Commerce Act, 1986 & Related Issues: A Discussion Document*. Wellington: Ministry of Commerce.
Minster for Industry & Commerce, (various years). *Annual Reports of the Minister for Industry & Commerce in accordance with §15 of the Mergers, Take-Overs & Monopolies Control Act, 1978*. Dublin: Stationery Office.
Moavero Milanesi, E. & A. Winterstein, (2002, February). Minority Shareholdings, Interlocking Directorships and the EC Competition Rules – Recent Commission Practice. *Competition Policy Newsletter*.
Monti, G., (2008). *The New Substantive Test in the EC Merger Regulation – Bridging the Gap Between Economics & Law*, LSE Law, Society & Economy Working Papers, 10/2008. London: LSE.
Monti, M., (2002, November 7). *Merger Control in the European Union: A Radical Reform*. Speech to EU Commission/International Bar Association Conference, mimeo.
Monti, M., (2003). EU Competition Policy After May 2004. Chapter 16, in B. Hawk, ed., *International Antitrust Law & Policy*, pp.403-413, New York: Juris Publications.
Morris, D., (2002). The *Enterprise Act*: Aspects of the New Regime. *Economic Affairs*, 22(4): 15-24.
Morris, J.R. & G.R. Mosteller, (1991). Defining Markets for Merger Analysis. *Antitrust Bulletin*, 36(3): 599-640.
Moss, D.L. & K. Mitchell, (2012). *The Proposed Merger of US Airways and American Airlines: The Rush to Closed Airline Systems*. Washington, D.C.: American Antitrust Institute.
Motta, M., (2004). *Competition Policy: Theory & Practice*. Cambridge, M.A.: Cambridge University Press.
Mulcahy, R., (1998). Authority Fails to Stop Acquisition of Athboy Co-Op by AWG. *Competition*, 8(5): 124-126.
Nalebuff, B., (2004). Bundling: *GE/Honeywell* (2001). Case 16 in J.E. Kwoka, Jr. & L.J. White, eds., *The Antitrust Revolution Economics, Competition & Policy*, 4th ed., pp. 388-412. Oxford: Oxford University Press.
National Transport Authority (NTA), (2024, April 12). *Cessation of Route 706. Public Service Determination.* Available at: https://www.nationaltransport.ie/wp-content/uploads/2024/04/Route-706-PSO-Determination-April-2024.pdf. Accessed 15.1.2025.
Neven, D. & L-H. Röller, (2002). Discrepancies Between Markets & Regulators: An Analysis of the First Ten Years of EU Merger Control. The Pros & Cons of Merger Control. *HEI Working Paper* 10/2002. Geneva: Graduate Institute of International Studies.
Neven, D. & L-H. Röller, (2005, December). Consumer Surplus *vs*. Welfare Standard in a Political Economy Model of Merger Control. *International Journal of Industrial Organization*, 23(9-10): 829-848.
Neven, D., (2006). Competition Economics and Antitrust in Europe. *Economic Policy*, 21(48): 742-791.

Neven, D., (2007). Competition Economics in Europe. In *The 2007 Handbook of Competition Economics*. Available at: https://competition-policy.ec.europa.eu/system/files/2021-09/intro_competition_economics.pdf.

Neven, D., (2010, September 29). *First Impressions on the Revised US & UK Merger Guidelines.* Address to Global Competition Review Conference, Brussels.

Neven, D., R. Nuttall & P. Seabright, (1993). The Merger Decisions of the European Commission. In L. Philips, ed., *Applied Industrial Economics,* pp.413-435, Cambridge: Cambridge University Press.

Nevin, C., (2018). *Irish Retail Bank Profitability 2003-2018*, Central Bank of Ireland Financial Stability Notes, 2018/10. Dublin: Central Bank of Ireland.

New Zealand Commerce Commission (NZCC), (2002). *Mergers & Acquisitions Guidelines,* (NZCC2002). Available at: https://comcom.govt.nz/data/assets/pdf_file/0020/91019/Mergers-and-acquisitions-Guidelines-May-2022.pdf. Accessed 30.10.2024.

Newbury, D.M, (1999). *Privatisation Restructuring & Regulation of Network Utilities.* Cambridge, M.A.: MIT Press.

Nocke, V. & L. White, (2007). Do Vertical Mergers Facilitate Upstream Collusion? *American Economic Review,* 97(4): 1321-1329.

Nocke, V. & M.D. Whinston, (2022). Concentration Thresholds for Horizontal Mergers. *American Economic Review,* 112(6): 1915-1948.

Noonan T.D., M., (2011, March 31). *Statement on Banking Matters in Ireland.* Issued following publication of the results of the stress testing of Ireland's banks. Available at: https://www.socialjustice.ie/system/files/file-uploads/2021-09/2011-03-31-ministerforfinancesstatementonbankingmattersinireland1.pdf. Accessed 4.11.2022.

Normann, H.T., (2011). Vertical Mergers, Foreclosure and Raising Rivals' Costs: Experimental Evidence. *Journal of Industrial Economics,* 59(3): 506-527.

NTA, see National Transport Authority.

O'Malley, D., T.D., (1997, February 24). *Speech to Competition Press Seminar,* mimeo.

OECD, (1999). *Oligopoly*. OECD Policy Roundtables. Paris: OECD.

OECD, (2000). *Mergers in Financial Services*. Paris: OECD.

OECD, (2002). *Portfolio Effects in Conglomerate Mergers*. Paris: OECD.

OECD, (2008). *Minority Shareholdings*. OECD Policy Roundtables. Paris: OECD. Available at: https://www.oecd.org/dataoecd/40/38/41774055.pdf.

OECD, (2009a). *Standard for Merger Review*. OECD Policy Roundtables. Paris: OECD. Available at: https://www.oecd.org/daf/competition/45247537.pdf. Accessed 2.11.2022.

OECD, (2009b). *The Failing Firm Defence*. OECD Policy Roundtables. Paris: OECD. Available at: https://www.oecd.org/daf/competition/45810821.pdf. Accessed 3.11.2022.

Ofcom, (2005). *Premier League Football: Research into Viewing Trends, Stadium Attendances, Fans' Preferences & Behaviour & the Commercial Market. Analysis Advising the Commission of the European Communities relating to a Proceeding under Article 81 of the EC Treaty,* London: Ofcom.

Ofcom, (2007, December 18). *Summary of Quantitative Consumer Research: Annex 14 to Pay-TV Market Investigation Consultation*. London: Ofcom.

Ofcom, (2015). *Review of the Pay-TV Wholesale Must-offer Obligation*. Retrieved from: http://stakeholders.ofcom.org.uk/binaries/consultations/wholesale-must-offer/summary/condoc.pdf.

Office of Fair Trading (UK) (UKOFT), (2003). *Mergers – Substantive Assessment Guidance*. OFT 516. London: UKOFT.

Ordover, J.A. & R.W. Willig, (1983). The 1982 Department of Justice *Merger Guidelines*: An Economic Assessment. *California Law Review,* 71(2): 535-574.

Ornstein, S.I., (1989). Exclusive Dealing and Antitrust. *Antitrust Bulletin,* 34(1), 65-98.

Ottaviani, M. & A.L. Wickelgren, (2011). *Ex Ante* or *Ex Post* Competition Policy? A Progress Report. *International Journal of Industrial Organization*, 29(3): 356-359.

Papaioannou, A., U. Diez, S. Ryan & D. Sjöblom, (2002). Green Paper on the Review of the Merger Regulation. *Competition Policy Newsletter*, 2002(1) (February): 65-68.

Parker, G., G. Petropoulos & M. Van Alstyne, (2021). *Platform Mergers & Antitrust*, Working Paper 01/2021. Brussels: Bruegel. Available at: https://www.bruegel.org/sites/default/files/private/wp_attachments/WP-2021-01.pdf.

Parker, R.G. & D.A. Balto, (2000). *The Evolving Approach to Merger Remedies*. Washington, D.C.: USFTC.

Parkison Hassid, A.J., (2007). An Oracle Without Foresight – Plaintiffs' Arduous Burdens Under *US v Oracle*. *Hastings Law Journal*, 58(4): 891-909.

Persson, L., (2005). The Failing Firm Defense. *Journal of Industrial Economics*, 53(2):175-202.

Philippon, T., (2019). *The Great Reversal. How America Gave Up on Free Markets*. Cambridge, M.A.: Belnap Press.

Philips, L., (1995). *Competition Policy: A Game Theoretic Perspective*. Cambridge: Cambridge University Press.

Pilsbury, S., (2007). The Impala Decision: An Economic Critique. *European Competition* Journal, 3(1): 31-47.

Pinkse, J. & M.E. Slade, (2004). Mergers, Brand Competition, and the Price of a Pint. *European Economic Review*, 48(3): 617-643.

Pittman, R. & Y. Li, (2013). AT&T and T-Mobile: Economies as an Antitrust Defense Applied. *Journal of Competition Law & Economics*, 9(1): 49-63.

Prince, J.F. & D.H. Simon, (2017). The Impact of Mergers on Quality Provision: Evidence from the Airline Industry. *Journal of Industrial Economics*, 65(2): 336-362.

Ratliff, J.D. & D.L. Rubinfeld, (2010). Online Advertising: Defining Relevant Markets. *Journal of Competition Law & Economics*, 6(3): 653-686.

Reilly, M., R. Cunningham & B. Wallace, (2023). Merger Remedy Divestitures: The Agencies Zig and the Courts Zag. *Antitrust*, 37(3): 13-18.

Renckens, A., (2007). Welfare Standards, Substantive Tests, and Efficiency Considerations in Merger Policy: Defining an Efficiency Defense. *Journal of Competition Law & Economics*, 3(2): 149-179.

Restrictive Practices Commission (RPC), (1975). *Report of Studies into Industrial Concentration and Mergers in Ireland*. Dublin: Stationery Office, Prl.5601.

Reynolds, G. & C. Walters, (2008). The Use of Customer Surveys for Market Definition and the Competitive Assessment of Horizontal Mergers, *Journal of Competition Law & Economics*. 4(2): 411-431.

Reynolds, M., S. Macrory & M. Chowdhury, (2011). EU Competition Policy in the Financial Crisis: Extraordinary Measures. *Fordham International Law Journal*, 33(6): 1668-1737.

Riesenkampf, A., (2004). New EC Merger Control Test under Article 2 of the Merger Regulation: The Symposium on European Competition Law. *Northwestern Journal of International Law & Business*, 24(3): 715-727.

Riordan, M., (2008). Competitive Effects of Vertical Integration. In P. Bucirossi, ed., *The Handbook of Antitrust Economics*. Cambridge, M.A.: MIT Press.

Robertson, A., (2002). The Application of European Competition Law to Sports Broadcasting. *World Competition*, 25(4).

Röller, L.-H., J. Stennek & F. Verboven, (2000). *Efficiency Gains from Mergers*. WZB Discussion Paper, No. FS IV 00-09. Berlin: WZB.

Rose, N., & C. Shapiro, C., (2022). What Next for the Horizontal Merger Guidelines? *Antitrust*, 36: 4-13.

Rozanski, G. & D. Rubinfeld, (1997). Mergers and Other Competition Policy Issues. In Banking in OECD/CLP, (1998). *Enhancing the Role of Competition in the Regulation of Banks,* Series Roundtables on Competition Policy, No. 17. Available at: http://www.oecd.daf/clp/roundtables/bank00.htm.

RPC, see Restrictive Practices Commission.

Rubinovitz, R., (2009). The Role of Fixed Cost Savings in Merger Analysis. *Journal of Competition Law & Economics,* 5(2): 233-247.

Rysman, M., (2009). The Economics of Two-Sided Markets. *Journal of Economic Perspectives,* 23(3), 125-143.

Salant, S., Switzer, S. & Reynolds, R., (1983). Losses from Horizontal Merger: The Effects of an Exogenous Change in Industry Structure on Cournot-Nash Equilibrium. *Quarterly Journal of Economics,* 98(2): 185-199.

Salinger, M.A., (1991). Vertical Mergers in Multi-Product Industries and Edgeworth's Paradox of Taxation. *Journal of Industrial Economics,* 34(5): 545-556.

Salinger, M.A., (2024). The 2023 *Merger Guidelines* and The Role of Economics. *Review of Industrial Organization,* 65(1): 243-253.

Salop, S.C. & D.T. Scheffman, (1983). Raising Rivals' Costs. *American Economic Review,* 73(2): 267-271.

Salop, S.C. & D.T. Scheffman, (1987). Cost-raising Strategies. *Journal of Industrial Economics,* 36(1): 19-34.

Salop, S.C., (1991). Comment on Willig, R.D., (1991), Merger Analysis, Industrial Organization Theory, and Merger Guidelines. *Brookings Papers on Economic Activity: Microeconomics 1991,* 313-323.

Salop, S.C., (2000). Analysis of Foreclosure in the EC *Guidelines* on Vertical Restraints. In B. Hawk, ed., *International Antitrust Law & Policy.* New York: Juris Publications.

Salop, S.C., (2013). Merger Settlement and Enforcement Policy for Optimal Deterrence and Maximum Welfare. *Fordham Law Review,* 81: 26-47.

Scheffman, D.T. & M. Coleman, (2003). *Quantitative Analysis of Potential Competitive Effects from a Merger.* Washington D.C.: USFTC.

Scheffman, D.T. & P.T. Spiller, (1987). Geographic Market Definition under the US Department of Justice *Merger Guidelines. Journal of Law & Economics,* 30(1): 123-147.

Scheffman, D.T. & R.S. Higgins, (2003). 20 Years of Raising Rivals' Costs: History Assessment and Future. *George Mason Law Review,* 12(2): 371-387.

Scheffman, D.T. & R.S. Higgins, (2004). Vertical Mergers: Theory and Policy. *George Mason Law Review,* 12(4): 967-977.

Scherer, F.M. & D. Ross, (1990). *Industrial Market Structure & Economic Performance,* 3rd ed. New York: Houghton-Mifflin.

Schmalensee, R., (1987). Horizontal Merger Policy: Problems and Changes. *Journal of Economic Perspectives,* 1(2): 41-54.

Schmalensee, R., (2004). Sunk Costs and Antitrust Barriers to Entry. *American Economic Review Papers & Proceedings*: 471-475.

Schmalensee, R., (2009). Should New *Merger Guidelines* Give UPP Market Definition? *The Antitrust Chronicle,* Release 1. Available at: https://www.competitionpolicyinternational.com/assets/Free/SchmalenseeDEC-91.pdf. Accessed 8.12.2024.

Schrank, W. & Roy, N., (1991). Market Delineation in the Analysis of the United States Groundfish Market. *Antitrust Bulletin,* 36(1): 91-154.

Schuman, L., (1989). *The Effects of FTC Challenges on Rival Firms, 1981-1987: An Analysis of the Use of Stock Returns to Determine the Competitive Effects of Horizontal Mergers.* Washington, D.C.: USFTC.

Schwartz, M., (1986). The Nature and Scope of Contestability Theory. Chapter 2 in D.J. Morris, P.J.N. Sinclair, M.D.E. Slater & J.S. Vickers, eds., *Strategic Behaviour & Industrial Competition,* pp.37-57. Oxford: Clarendon Press.

Scott, A., (2009). *The Evolution of Competition Law and Policy in the United Kingdom*, Law, Society & Economy Working Papers, 9/2009. London: London School of Economics.
Seabright, P., (2002). Ten Years of European Merger Control. Chapter 9 in C. Robinson, ed., *Utility Regulation and Competition Policy*. Cheltenham: Edward Elgar.
Seldeslachts, J., J.A. Clougherty & P.P. Barros, (2009). Settle for Now But Block for Tomorrow: The Deterrence Effects of Merger Policy Tools. *Journal of Law & Economics*, 52(3): 607-634.
Shapiro, C. & H. Shelanski, (2021). Judicial Response to the 2010 *Horizontal Merger Guidelines. Review of Industrial Organization*, 58(1): 51-79.
Shapiro, C., (1996). Mergers with Differentiated Products. *Antitrust*, 10(2): 23-30.
Shapiro, C., (2010). The 2010 *Horizontal Merger Guidelines*: From Hedgehog to Fox in Forty Years. *Antitrust Law Journal, 77*(1): 701-759.
Shapiro, C., (2012). Competition and Innovation: Did the Arrow Hit the Bull's Eye? In J. Lerner & S. Stern, eds., *The Rate and Direction of Inventive Activity Revisited.* National Bureau of Economic Research Conference Report, pp.361-404. Chicago: University of Chicago Press. Available at: https://www.nber.org/books-and-chapters/rate-and-direction-inventive-activity-revisited/competition-and-innovation-did-arrow-hit-bulls-eye. Accessed 18.3.2025.
Shapiro, C., (2019). Protecting Competition in the American Economy: Merger Control, Tech Titans, Labor Markets. *Journal of Economic Perspectives*, 33(3): 69-93.
Shapiro, C., (2024). Evolution of the *Merger Guidelines*: Is This Fox Too Clever by Half? *Review of Industrial Organization*, 65(1): 147-175.
Shapiro, J., (2024). The End of Remedies? *Emory Corporate Governance & Accountability Review*, 11(2): 163-174.
Shepherd, G.B., H.S. Shepherd & W.G. Shepherd, (2000). Sharper Focus: Market Shares in the *Merger Guidelines. Antitrust Bulletin*, 45(4): 835-885.
Sher, S.A., (2004). Closed but Not Forgotten: Government Review of Consummated Mergers under Section 7 of the *Clayton Act. Santa Clara Law Review*, 45(1): 41-98.
Shrieves, R.E., (1978). Geographic Market Areas and Market Structure in the Bituminous Coal Industry. *Antitrust Bulletin*, 23(3): 589-625.
Shy, O., (1995). *Industrial Organization Theory & Applications*. Cambridge, M.A.: MIT Press.
Shy, O., (2001). *The Economics of Network Industries*. Cambridge: Cambridge University Press.
Sidak, J.G. & H.J. Singer, (2008). Evaluating Market Power with Two-sided Demand and Preemptive Offers to Dissipate Monopoly Rent: Lessons for High-Technology Industries from the Antitrust Division's Approval of the XM-Sirius Satellite Radio Merger. *Journal of Competition Law & Economics*, 4(3): 697-751.
Simons, J.J. & M.A. Williams, (1993). The Renaissance of Market Definition. *Antitrust Bulletin*, 38(4): 799-857.
Simons, J.J. & M.B. Coate, (2010). Upward Pressure on Price Analysis: Issues and Implications for Merger Policy. *European Competition Journal*, 6(2): 377-396.
Simons, J.J. & M.B. Coate, (2014). *United States v. H&R Block*: An Illustration of the DoJ's New but Controversial Approach to Market Definition. *Journal of Competition Law & Economics*, 10(3): 543-580.
Simpson, J. & D. Hosken, (1998). *Are Retailing Mergers Anticompetitive? An Event Study Analysis.* United States Federal Trade Commission Working Paper 216. Washington D.C.: USFTC.
Sims, C.A., (1972). Money, Income, and Causality. *American Economic Review*, 62(4): 540-552.
Slade, M.E., (1986). Exogeneity Tests of Market Boundaries Applied to Petroleum Products. *Journal of Industrial Economics*, 34(3): 291-303.
Slade, M.E., (1987). Interfirm Rivalry in a Repeated Game: An Empirical Test of Tacit Collusion. *Journal of Industrial Economics*, 35(4): 499-516.

Slade, M.E., (2004). Market Power and Joint Dominance in the UK Brewing Industry. *Journal of Industrial Economics*, 52(1): 133-163.

Smith, H., (2004). Supermarket Choice and Supermarket Competition in Market Equilibrium. *Review of Economic Studies*, 71: 235-263.

Sørgard, L., (2009). Optimal Merger Policy: Enforcement vs. Deterrence. *Journal of Industrial Economics*, 57(3): 438-456.

Stefanadis, C., (1997). Downstream Vertical Foreclosure and Upstream Innovation. *Journal of Industrial Economics*, 45(4): 445-456.

Stelzer, I.M., (2002). Innovation, Price Competition and the "Tilt" of Competition Policy. *Economic Affairs*, 22(4): 25-31.

Stephan, A., (2011). Did *Lloyds/HBOS* Mark the Failure of an Enduring Economics-based System of Merger Regulation? *Northern Ireland Legal Quarterly*, 62(4): 539-552.

Stigler, G.J. & R.A. Sherwin, (1985). The Extent of the Market. *Journal of Law & Economics*, 28(3): 555-585.

Stigler, G.J., (1968). *The Organization of Industry*. Homewood, I.L.: Richard D. Irwin.

Stigler, G.J., (1982). The Economists and the Problem of Monopoly. *American Economic Review*, 72 (May).

Stöhr, A. & Budzinski, O., (2019). *Gemeinwohl durch Marktmacht? Eine Ex-Post-Analyse der Ministererlaubnis-Fälle. Wirtschaft und Wettbewerb*, 10: 508-515.

Stöhr, A., (2024). Price Effects of Horizontal Mergers: A Retrospective on Retrospectives. *Journal of Competition Law & Economics*, 20(1-2): 155-179.

Stöhr, A., V. Noskova, P. Kunz-Kaltenhäuser, S. Gaenssle & O. Budzinski, (2020). Happily Ever After? Vertical and Horizontal Mergers in the US Media Industry. *World Competition*, 43(1): 139-161.

Strand, N., (2006). A Simple Critical Loss Test for the Geographical Market. *Journal of Competition Law & Economics*, 2(4): 697-707.

Stucke, M.E., (2023). The Good, the Bad, and the Ugly of US Antitrust. *Journal of Antitrust Enforcement*, 1-10.

Sutton, J., (1991). *Sunk Costs & Market Structure: Price Competition, Advertising & the Evolution of Concentration*. Cambridge, M.A.: MIT Press.

Suzuki, A., (2009). Market Foreclosure and Vertical Merger: A Case Study of the Vertical Merger Between Turner Broadcasting and Time Warner. *International Journal of Industrial Organization*, 27(4): 532-543.

Tenn, S. & J.M. Yun, (2011). The Success of Divestitures in Merger Enforcement: Evidence from the *J&J/Pfizer* Transaction. *International Journal of Industrial Organization*, 29(2): 273-282.

Tenn, S., L. Froeb & S. Tschantz, (2010). Mergers When Firms Compete by Choosing Both Price and Promotion. *International Journal of Industrial Organization*, 28(6): 695-707.

The Guardian, (2023, May 16). UK watchdog denies it blocked Microsoft deal on orders of US regulator. Available at https://www.theguardian.com/business/2023/may/16/uk-watchdog-microsoft-us-regulator-competition-markets-authority-activision-blizzard. Accessed 10.10.2023.

Thomas, S., (2017). The Known Unknown: In Search of a Legal Structure of the Significance Criterion for the SIEC Test. *Journal of Competition Law & Economics*, 13(2): 191-224.

Thompson, R.S., (1984). Structure and Conduct in Local Advertising Markets: The Case of Irish Provincial Newspapers. *Journal of Industrial Economics*, 33(2), 241-249.

Tirole, J., (1988). *The Theory of Industrial Organisation*. Cambridge, MA: MIT Press.

Trebilcock, M. & E.M. Iacobucci, (2002). Designing Competition Law Institutions. *World Competition*, 25(3): 361-394.

Turner, D.F., (1965). Conglomerate Mergers and Section 7 of the *Clayton Act*. *Harvard Law Review*, 78 (May): 1313-95.

Turner, D.F., (1980). The Role of the "Market Concept" in Antitrust Law. *Antitrust Law Journal*, 49(3): 1145-1154.

UKCC, see Competition Commission (UK).

UKCMA, see Competition & Markets Authority (UK).

UKDBIS, see Department for Business, Innovation & Skills (UK).

UKOFT, see Office of Fair Trading (UK).

United States Department of Justice (USDoJ), (1968). *Merger Guidelines*. Washington D.C.: USDoJ. Available at: https://www.justice.gov/archives/atr/1968-merger-guidelines. Accessed 7.12.2022.

United States Department of Justice (USDoJ), (1982). *Merger Guidelines*. Washington D.C.: USDoJ. Available at https://www.justice.gov/archives/atr/1982-merger-guidelines. Accessed 7.12.2002.

United States Department of Justice (USDoJ), (1984). *Merger Guidelines*. Washington D.C.: USDoJ. Available at: https://www.justice.gov/archives/atr/1984-merger-guidelines. Accessed 7.12.2022.

United States Department of Justice (USDoJ), (1998, April 10). Justice Department Approves *First Union/Corestates* Merger After Parties Agree to $1.1 Billion Divestiture in Pennsylvania. Available at: https://www.justice.gov/archive/atr/public/press_releases/1998/1630.htm. Accessed 12.10.2023.

United States Department of Justice (USDoJ), (2024, May 23). Justice Department Sues Live Nation-Ticketmaster for Monopolizing Markets Across the Live Concert Industry. Available at: https://www.justice.gov/archives/opa/pr/justice-department-sues-live-nation-ticketmaster-monopolizing-markets-across-live-concert. Accessed 31.3.2025.

United States Department of Justice (USDoJ)/United States Federal Trade Commission (USFTC), (1992). *Horizontal Merger Guidelines*. Washington, D.C.: USDoJ.

United States Department of Justice (USDoJ)/United States Federal Trade Commission (USFTC), (1997). *Merger Guidelines*. Washington D.C.: USDoJ. Available at: https://www.justice.gov/archives/atr/1997-merger-guidelines. Accessed 7.12.2022.

United States Department of Justice (USDoJ)/United States Federal Trade Commission (USFTC), (2010). *Horizontal Merger Guidelines* (USHMG1992). Washington D.C.: USDoJ. Available at: https://www.justice.gov/atr/horizontal-merger-guidelines-08192010. Accessed 7.12.2022.

United States Department of Justice (USDoJ)/United States Federal Trade Commission (USFTC), (2023). *Horizontal Merger Guidelines* (USHMG2010). Washington D.C.: USDoJ. Available at: https://www.justice.gov/atr/2023-merger-guidelines. Accessed 15.12.2024.

United States Federal Trade Commission (USFTC), (2017). *The FTC's Merger Remedies 2006-2012: A Report of the Bureaus of Competition & Economics.* Washington D.C.: USFTC. Available at: https://www.ftc.gov/reports/ftcs-merger-remedies-2006-2012-report-bureaus-competition-economics. Accessed 10.11.2024.

United States White House, (2021, July 9). *Fact Sheet: Executive Order on Promoting Competition in the American Economy.* Available at: https://www.whitehouse.gov/briefing-room/statements-releases/2021/07/09/fact-sheet-executive-order-on-promoting-competition-in-the-american-economy/.

Urban, G., T. Carter, S. Gaskin & Z. Mucha, (1984). Market Share Rewards to Pioneering Brands. *Management Science*, 32: 645-659.

USDoJ, see United States Department of Justice.

USFTC, see United States Federal Trade Commission.

Valentine, D., (2000). Retailer Buyer Power, Abusive Behaviour and Mergers and Acquisitions. Chapter 28, in B. Hawk, ed. *International Antitrust Law & Policy*, pp.513-543. New York: Juris Publications.

Valero, J., (2019, January 9). 19 Countries call for new Antitrust rules to create "European Champions". Available at: https://www.euractiv.com/section/economy-jobs/news/19-eu-countries-call-for-new-anti-trust-rules-to-create-european-champions/. Accessed 7.10.2021.

Valetti, T. & H. Zenger, (2019). Increasing Market Power and Merger Control. *Competition Policy Debate,* 5(1): 26-35.

Valetti, T. & H. Zenger, (2021). Mergers with Differentiated Products: Where Do We Stand? *Review of Industrial Organization,* 58(1): 179-212.

Vande Walle, S., (2021, May 12). *Remedies in EU Merger Control: An Essential Guide.* Working Paper. Available at: https://ssrn.com/abstract=3782333. Accessed 31.1.2025.

Venit, J., (1998). Two Steps Forward and No Steps Back: Economic Analysis and Oligopolistic Dominance After Kali & Salz. *Common Market Law Review,* 35(5): 1101-1134.

Vergé, T., (2010). Horizontal Mergers: Structural Remedies and Consumer Welfare in a Cournot Oligopoly with Assets. *Journal of Industrial Economics,* 58(4): 723-741.

Vestager, M., (2022, March 25). *Competition Policy: Where We Stand and Where We're Going.* Keynote Speech at the Global Competition Law Centre Annual Conference. Available at: https://ec.europa.eu/commission/presscorner/detail/en/SPEECH_22_2079.

Vickers, J., (2006). Market Power in Competition Cases. *European Competition Journal,* 3(1): 12-13.

Vickers, J., (2008, December 15). The Financial Crisis and Competition Policy: Some Economics. *Global Competition Policy.* Available at: https://www.competitionpolicyinternational.com/the-financial-crisis-and-competition-policy-some-economics/.

Voelcker, S., (2004). Mind the Gap: Unilateral Effects Analysis Arrives in EC Merger Control. *European Competition Law Review,* 25(7).

Weinberg, M., (2008). The Price Effects of Horizontal Mergers. *Journal of Competition Law & Economics,* 4(2): 433-447.

Weir, C., (1993). The Implementation of Merger Policy in the UK. *Antitrust Bulletin,* 38(4): 943-967.

Weiss, L., (1989). *Concentration & Price.* Cambridge, M.A.: MIT Press.

Weitbrecht, A., (2008). From Freiburg to Chicago and Beyond: The First 50 Years of European Competition Law. *European Competition Law Review,* 2008(2): 81-89.

Werden, G.J. & L.M. Froeb, (1998). The Entry-Inducing Effects of Horizontal Mergers: An Exploratory Analysis. *Journal of Industrial Economics,* 46(4): 525-543.

Werden, G.J., (1981). The Use and Misuse of Shipments Data in Defining Geographic Markets. *Antitrust Bulletin,* 26(4): 719-737.

Werden, G.J., (1991). Using the Herfindahl-Hirschman Index. Horizontal Mergers: Comment. *American Economic Review,* 81(4): 1002-1006.

Werden, G.J., (1992). Four Suggestions on Market Delineation. *Antitrust Bulletin,* 37(1): 107-121.

Werden, G.J., (1998). Demand Elasticities in Antitrust Analysis. *Antitrust Law Journal,* 66(2): 363-414.

Werden, G.J., (2000). Expert Report in *United States v. Interstate Bakeries Corp. & Continental Baking Co., Economics of Business,* 7(2): 139-148.

Werden, G.J., (2003a). *The Effect of Antitrust Policy on Consumer Welfare: What Crandall & Winston Overlook.* United States Department of Justice, Antitrust Division Economic Analysis Group Discussion Paper EAG 03-2. Washington, D.C.: USDoJ.

Werden, G.J., (2003b). The 1982 *Merger Guidelines* and the Ascent of the Hypothetical Monopolist Paradigm. *Antitrust Law Journal,* 71(1): 253-275.

Werden, G.J., (2008). Unilateral Competitive Effects and the Test for Merger Control. *European Competition Journal,* 4(1): 95-101.

Werden, G.J., (2009). Next Steps in the Evolution of Antitrust Law: What to Expect from the Roberts Court. *Journal of Competition Law & Economics,* 5(1).

Whish, R., (2003). *Competition Law,* 5th ed. London: LexisNexis.

White, L.J., (1989). Application of the *Merger Guidelines*: The Proposed Merger of Coca-Cola and Dr. Pepper. Case 3 in J.E. Kwoka & L.J. White, eds., *The Antitrust Revolution*, pp.76-95, Glenview: Scott, Foresman & Co.

Wiedenfeld, K., (1927). *Cartels & Combines.* Geneva: League of Nations.

Williamson, O.E., (1968). Economies as an Antitrust Defence: The Welfare Trade-offs. *American Economic Review*, 58(1):18-36.

Williamson, O.E., (2002). *The Merger Guidelines of the US Department of Justice in Perspective.* United States Department of Justice, mimeo. Available at: https://www.justice.gov/archives/atr/merger-guidelines-us-department-justice-perspective. Accessed 16.9.2021.

Willig, R.D., (1991). Merger Analysis, Industrial Organization Theory, and *Merger Guidelines*. *Brookings Papers on Economic Activity: Microeconomics 1991,* 281-312.

Wilson, C.S. & K. Klovers, (2021). Same Rule, Different Result: How the Narrowing of Product Markets has Altered Substantive Antitrust Rules. *Antitrust Law Journal*, 84(1): 55-93.

Winston, C., (2021). Back to the Good – or Were they the Bad – Old Days of Antitrust: A Review Essay of Jonathan B. Baker's "The Antitrust Paradigm: Restoring a Competitive Economy". *Journal of Economic Literature,* 59(1): 265-284.

Wollmann, T.G., (2019). Stealth Consolidation: Evidence from an Amendment to the *Hart-Scott-Rodino Act*. *American Economic Review Insights,* 1(1): 77-94.

Wollmann, T.G., (2023). "Terms of the Deal Were Not Announced": Accounting for Mergers with Unpublicized Values. *American Economic Association Papers & Proceedings,* 113: 284-287.

Wright, J.D. & D.H. Ginsberg, (2013). The Goals of Antitrust: Welfare Trumps Choice. *Fordham Law Review*, 81(5): 2405-2423.

Wu, D.-M., (1983). Tests of Causality, Predeterminedness and Exogeneity. *International Economic Review,* 24(3): 547-558.

Yang, Q.G. & M. Pickford, (2016). Modelling the Duration of Merger Reviews in New Zealand. *Journal of Competition Law & Economics,* 12(1): 31-68.

Yang, Y., M.N. Garcia, G. Viglia & J.L. Nicolau, (2021). Competitors or Complements: A Meta-analysis of the Effect of Airbnb on Hotel Performance. *Journal of Travel Research,* 61(7): 1508-1527.

Yarrow, G., (1999). MMC: Retrospect and Prospect. In M.E. Beesley, ed., *Regulating Utilities: A New Era?*, pp.21-41. London: Institute of Economic Affairs.

Yarrow, G., (2001). *Competition Act* Assessments and Economic Efficiency. Chapter 3 in C. Robinson, ed., *Regulating Utilities: New Issues, New Solutions,* pp.56-72. London: Institute of Economic Affairs.

Yarrow, G., (2002). Competition Policy: Its Purposes and Scope. *Economic Affairs*, 22(4): 2-4.

Ziss, S., (1996). Contracts as a Barrier to Entry. *American Economic Review*, 86(3): 672-674.

ABOUT THE AUTHOR

Patrick Massey is a graduate of Trinity College Dublin and has worked as a professional economist for 40 years.

He is a director of Compecon – Competition Economics, a consulting firm specialising in the economic analysis of competition and mergers, which he established in 2001. He has advised parties and the Competition Authority/Competition & Consumer Protection Commission in numerous merger cases and also has advised parties in a number of EU and UK mergers. Prior to establishing Compecon, Patrick was a member of the Competition Authority for 12 years.

Patrick previously co-authored *Competition & Regulation in Ireland: The Law & Economics* (Oak Tree Press, 2003 – with Daragh Daly) and *Competition Law & Policy in Ireland* (Oak Tree Press, 1996 – with Paula O'Hare), as well as *New Zealand: Market Liberalization in a Developed Economy* (St. Martin's Press, 1995), having spent two years working for the New Zealand Treasury. He also worked for DKM Economic Consultants.

He has published numerous papers in peer-reviewed journals and contributed chapters to several books on competition policy. He has lectured on the economics of competition and regulation at both Trinity College Dublin and NUI Maynooth. Patrick is thus able to bring an extensive level of knowledge and expertise to the subject. He has also written extensively on the economics of sports.

INDEX

www.ingramcontent.com/pod-product-compliance
Ingram Content Group UK Ltd.
Pitfield, Milton Keynes, MK11 3LW, UK
UKHW020225290926
15470UKWH00001B/375